In memory

of

SALLY JACOBSEN

Contents

THE ASSOCIATED PRESS
STYLEBOOK
2018
and Briefing on Media Law

Edited by
Paula Froke
Anna Jo Bratton
Oskar Garcia
Jeff McMillan
David Minthorn
Jerry Schwartz

apstylebook.com

Contributors

Shelley Acoca
Eric Carvin
Jon Fahey
David Hamilton
Josh Hoffner
Carla Johnson
Greg Keller
Stephanie Nano

Raphael Satter
Michael Sirolly
David Scott
Emily Swanson
Lindsey Tanner
Troy Thibodeaux
Rachel Zoll

BASIC BOOKS

New York

Basic Books
Hachette Book Group
1290 Avenue of the Americas, New York, NY 10104
www.basicbooks.com

Printed in the United States of America

First Edition by The Associated Press, August 1977
53rd Edition: June 2018

Published by Basic Books, an imprint of Perseus Books, LLC, a subsidiary of Hachette Book Group, Inc. The Basic Books name and logo is a trademark of the Hachette Book Group.

The publisher is not responsible for websites (or their content) that are not owned by the publisher.

Design and content management by Stylebooks.com

Product management by Colleen Newvine

Library of Congress Control Number: 2018940585
ISBNs: 978-1-5416-7238-3 (trade paperback)

LSC-C

10 9 8 7 6 5 4 3 2 1

Foreword

The first Associated Press Stylebook was 60 pages, bound together with staples, a basic guide for newswriting. It has evolved into a comprehensive reference manual that fills more than 600 pages and and is published across an array of digital platforms, encompassing the collective wisdom of the AP staff and Stylebook readers. Despite drastic changes in the media landscape, one constant remains: The AP Stylebook is a definitive resource for writers.

Today's Stylebook still outlines basic rules on grammar, punctuation, usage and journalistic style, but it also reflects changes in common language, offers guidance on media law, explains AP's news values and principles, and helps to navigate the ever-changing world of social media.

A team of top AP editors meets throughout the year to make updates and improvements, many of which appear immediately in Stylebook Online. Contributions come from the AP staff, AP's member news organizations and subscribers, journalism teachers and students, specialists in a host of fields, and everyday readers. Indeed, some of the most-talked-about changes have come at the suggestion of @APStylebook's Twitter followers.

Every update is deeply rooted in respect for language and commitment to the original goal: to be clear, fair and concise around the globe, no matter what the news is or where it happens.

Whether you access it in print or online, The Associated Press Stylebook remains an essential tool in newsrooms, classrooms and boardrooms alike, the perfect resource for journalists and anyone who cares about good writing.

GARY PRUITT
President and Chief Executive Officer

About the AP

Since 1846, The Associated Press has been on the scene wherever news is breaking. AP is a not-for-profit newsgathering cooperative whose content — across subjects, formats and continents — is seen by half of the world's population every day. Our unmatched expertise in global newsgathering, distribution and service makes AP the most trusted, definitive source for news.

The AP's mission is to get it first but first get it right, and to be the first choice for news, by providing the fastest, most accurate reporting from every corner of the globe across all media types and platforms.

Headquartered in New York, AP delivers coverage of news, sports, business, weather, entertainment, politics, lifestyles and technology in text, audio, video, graphics, photos and interactives. AP is also a leader in developing and marketing innovative newsroom technology and newsgathering services.

AP does what it takes to get the story, even in the world's most dangerous and challenging places. Our global network of journalists work in 254 locations in 101 countries worldwide. Journalists staff every statehouse in the United States, providing unrivaled access to more sources of information and newsmakers.

The extensive network that is the AP grew from a single notion more than a century and a half ago: Cooperation can help authoritative news reach readers faster.

In late 1846, hostilities began in what would become the Mexican War. American newspapers, most based in the Northeast at the time, faced huge obstacles in reporting the conflict.

War reports for the New York Sun were sent from Mexico to Mobile, Alabama, by boat, rushed by special pony express to Montgomery and then 700 miles by U.S. Mail stagecoach to the southern terminus of the newly invented telegraph near Richmond, Virginia. That express gave the Sun an edge of 24 hours or more on papers using regular mail.

But Moses Yale Beach, the Sun's publisher, relinquished that advantage by inviting other New York publishers to join a cooperative venture that would avoid duplication of effort by sending one so-called agent, or newsgatherer, to act for the many. Five newspapers signed on: the Sun, the Journal of Commerce, the Courier and Enquirer, the Herald and the Express. It was the beginning of the AP.

AP assumed its modern legal form in 1900 when it incorporated as a not-for-profit cooperative under the Membership Corporation Law of New York state. Today, the AP membership elects the board of directors, the cooperative's governing body.

AP staffers are governed by a comprehensive ethics statement, available for viewing at https://www.ap.org/about/our-story/news-values

More than 170 years since its inception, AP remains the undisputed source for news, delivering fast, unbiased news globally to all media platforms and formats.

What's new

This edition of the Stylebook contains about 200 new and modified entries.

We expanded and updated our *polls and surveys* guidance in a new chapter, and we added an entry with guidance on the terms *act, amendment, bill, law, measure, ordinance, resolution, rule* and *statute*.

A new entry on *sexual harassment* and *sexual misconduct* notes the need to be as specific as possible in describing the kinds of behavior being alleged or admitted. If a shorter term is needed, for example in a headline, AP uses the term *sexual misconduct*.

We added a *survivor, victim* entry, which says to use those terms with care because they can be imprecise and politically and legally fraught. In the *immigration* entry, we expanded our guidance on the term *"Dreamer"* and added guidance on the term *"chain migration."*

We say the terms *biracial* or *multiracial* are acceptable, when relevant, but try to be specific about a person's background when it's pertinent. Avoid *mixed-race* unless the story subject prefers that term. A new *boy, girl* entry notes the need for racial sensitivity about the word *boy*.

Another new entry discusses the terms *fetus* and *unborn baby*.

A new *marijuana, medical marijuana* entry adds more terminology and usage details. We updated some guidance in the *gender* entry and the *LGBT, LGBTQ* entry.

We say to avoid the term *Eskimo* except when paired with a group's ethnic name in Alaska: a *Cu'pik Eskimo*, for example. The term *Inuit* is used in Canada, Greenland and by some groups in northern Alaska. We note that the term *Aborigine*, referring to aboriginal people in Australia, is considered offensive by some and should be avoided.

In the *political parties and philosophies* entry, we say to avoid the term *progressive* as a political descriptor except in quotes or the names of organizations or political parties.

How do you quote *emoji*? Find the answer in a new section of our *quotations in the news* entry. And: We now use *emoji* for the plural.

Other new entries include: *lists, bulleted lists; BASE jumping; LEED; chronic traumatic encephalopathy; HIPPA; coworking; gig economy; timeshare; storm names; fire names; U.S. territories; St. Barts, St. Martin; Western Wall; Gulf Cooperation Council*.

We dropped our rule that two objects must be in motion before they can *collide*. Other changes: no hyphen in *3D*; no hyphen in *breastfeed, breastfeeding, breastfed*; one word for *homepage* and *smartwatch*; and *Walmart* in all uses in line with the company's change. We now say it's OK to start a sentence with a numeral-and-letter combination: *3D movies are drawing more fans*. Also: *AR* is acceptable on second reference for *augmented reality*. The *hurricane* entry has more guidance.

In the food chapter, *naan* is now our spelling for the Indian flatbread, and we revised our guidance on *chile/chili*. New on the menu: *ahi, amaro, chorizo, churros, dressing/stuffing, matcha, soba, turducken, udon* and more.

Key to Stylebook entries

This updated and revised version of The Associated Press Stylebook has been organized like a dictionary. Need the acronym for a government agency? Look under the agency's name. Should you capitalize a word? Check the word itself or the capitalization entry. What's the format for baseball boxes? See baseball.

Following is a key to the entries:

airport Capitalize as part of a proper name: *LaGuardia Airport, O'Hare International Airport.*

The first name of an individual and the word *international* may be deleted from a formal airport name while the remainder is capitalized: *John F. Kennedy International Airport, Kennedy International Airport* or *Kennedy Airport.* Use whichever is appropriate in the context.

Do not make up names, however. There is no *Boston Airport,* for example. The *Boston airport* (lowercase *airport*) would be acceptable if for some reason the proper name, *Logan International Airport,* were not used.

Entry words, in alphabetical order, are in **boldface**. They represent the accepted word forms unless otherwise indicated.

Text explains usage.

Examples of correct and incorrect usage are in italics. AP doesn't use italics in news stories.

airstrike

airtight

Many entries simply give the correct spelling, hyphenation and/or capitalization.

air traffic controller No hyphen.

airways The system of routes that the federal government has established for airplane traffic.

See the **airline, airlines** entry for its use in carriers' names.

Related topics are in **boldface**.

aka Abbreviation for *also known as.*

Abbreviate indicates the correct abbreviation of a word.

Alabama Abbreviate *Ala.* in datelines only; spell out in stories. Postal code: *AL*
See **state names**.

Other abbreviations used in the Stylebook:

n.: noun	**adj.:** adjective
v.: verb	**adv.:** adverb

a

a- The rules of **prefixes** apply, but in general, no hyphen. Some examples: *achromatic* *atonal*

AAA Formerly the American Automobile Association.
Headquarters is in Heathrow, Florida.

a, an Use the article *a* before consonant sounds: *a historic event, a one-year term* (sounds as if it begins with a *w*), *a united stand* (sounds like *you*).
Use the article *an* before vowel sounds: *an energy crisis, an honorable man* (the *h* is silent), *an homage* (the *h* is silent), *an NBA record* (sounds like it begins with the letter *e*), *an 1890s celebration.*

AARP Use only the initials for the organization formerly known as the American Association of Retired Persons.

abaya Robe-like outer garment worn by Muslim women.

abbreviations and acronyms A few universally recognized abbreviations are required in some circumstances. Some others are acceptable depending on the context. But in general, avoid alphabet soup. Do not use abbreviations or acronyms that the reader would not quickly recognize.
Abbreviations and most acronyms should be avoided in headlines.
Guidance on how to use a particular abbreviation or acronym is provided in entries alphabetized according to the sequence of letters in the word or phrase.
An *acronym* is a word formed from the first letter or letters of a series of words: *laser* (light amplification by stimulated emission of radiation). An *abbreviation* is not an *acronym*.
Some general principles:
BEFORE A NAME: Abbreviate titles when used before a full name: *Dr., Gov., Lt. Gov., Mr., Mrs., Rep., the Rev., Sen.* and certain military designations listed in the **military titles** entry.
For guidelines on how to use titles, see **courtesy titles; legislative titles; military titles; religious titles;** and the entries for the most commonly used titles.
AFTER A NAME: Abbreviate *junior* or *senior* after an individual's name. Abbreviate *company, corporation, incorporated* and *limited* when used after the name of a corporate entity. See entries under these words and **company names**.
In some cases, an academic degree may be abbreviated after an individual's name. See **academic degrees**.
WITH DATES OR NUMERALS: Use the abbreviations *A.D., B.C., a.m., p.m., No.,* and abbreviate certain months (Jan., Feb., Aug., Sept., Oct., Nov., Dec.) when used with the day of the month.
Right: *In 450 B.C.; at 9:30 a.m.; in room No. 6; on Sept. 16.*
Wrong: *Early this a.m. he asked*

a

for the No. of your room. The abbreviations are correct only with figures.

Right: *Early this morning he asked for the number of your room.*

See **months** and individual entries for these other terms:

IN NUMBERED ADDRESSES: Abbreviate *avenue, boulevard* and *street* in numbered addresses: *He lives on Pennsylvania Avenue. He lives at 1600 Pennsylvania Ave.*

See **addresses**.

STATES: The names of certain states and the *United States* are abbreviated with periods in some circumstances.

See **state names**; **datelines**; and individual entries.

AVOID AWKWARD CONSTRUCTIONS: Do not follow an organization's full name with an abbreviation or acronym in parentheses or set off by dashes. If an abbreviation or acronym would not be clear on second reference without this arrangement, do not use it.

Names not commonly before the public should not be reduced to acronyms solely to save a few words.

SPECIAL CASES: Many abbreviations are desirable in tabulations and certain types of technical writing. See individual entries.

CAPS, PERIODS: Use capital letters and periods according to the listings in this book. For words not in this book, use the first-listed abbreviation in Webster's New World College Dictionary. Generally, omit periods in acronyms unless the result would spell an unrelated word. But use periods in most two-letter abbreviations: *U.S., U.N., U.K., B.A., B.C.* (*AP*, a trademark, is an exception. Also, no periods in *GI, ID* and *EU*, among others.) In headlines, do not use periods in abbreviations,

unless required for clarity.

Use all caps, but no periods, in longer abbreviations when the individual letters are pronounced: *ABC, CIA, FBI.*

Use only an initial cap and then lowercase for abbreviations and acronyms of more than five letters, unless listed otherwise in this Stylebook or Webster's New World College Dictionary.

ABC Acceptable in all references for *American Broadcasting Cos.* (the plural is part of the corporate name). Owned by The Walt Disney Co.

ABCs

able-bodied

ABM, ABMs Acceptable in all references for *anti-ballistic missile(s),* but the term should be defined in the story. (The hyphen is an exception to Webster's New World College Dictionary.)

Avoid the redundant phrase *ABM missiles.*

Aborigine An outdated term referring to aboriginal people in Australia. It is considered offensive by some and should be avoided.

abortion Use the modifiers *anti-abortion* or *abortion-rights*; don't use *pro-life, pro-choice* or *pro-abortion* unless they are in quotes or proper names. Avoid *abortionist*, which connotes a person who performs clandestine abortions.

aboveboard

absent-minded

Abu Sayyaf Muslim separatist group

based in the southern islands of the Philippines. The name is Arabic for *father of the bearer of the sword.*

academic degrees If mention of degrees is necessary to establish someone's credentials, the preferred form is to avoid an abbreviation and use instead a phrase such as: *John Jones, who has a doctorate in psychology.*

Use an apostrophe in *bachelor's degree, a master's,* etc., but there is no possessive in *Bachelor of Arts* or *Master of Science.*

Also: an *associate degree* (no possessive).

Use such abbreviations as *B.A., M.A., LL.D.* and *Ph.D.* only when the need to identify many individuals by degree on first reference would make the preferred form cumbersome. Use these abbreviations only after a full name — never after just a last name.

When used after a name, an academic abbreviation is set off by commas: *John Snow, Ph.D., spoke.*

Do not precede a name with a courtesy title for an academic degree and follow it with the abbreviation for the degree in the same reference.

See **doctor, Master of Arts, Master of Science, Master of Business Administration**.

academic departments Use lowercase except for words that are proper nouns or adjectives: *the department of history, the history department, the department of English, the English department,* or when *department* is part of the official and formal name: *University of Connecticut Department of Economics.*

academic titles Capitalize and spell out formal titles such as *chancellor, chairman,* etc., when they precede a

name. Lowercase elsewhere.

Lowercase modifiers such as *department* in *department Chairman Jerome Wiesner.*

See **doctor** and **titles**.

academy See **military academies**.

Academy Awards Presented annually by the Academy of Motion Picture Arts and Sciences. Also known as the *Oscars.* (Both *Academy Awards* and *Oscars* are trademarks.)

Lowercase *the academy* and *the awards* whenever they stand alone.

accent marks Do not use any diacritical or accent marks because they cause garble for some users.

accept, except *Accept* means to receive.

Except means to exclude.

accident, crash Generally acceptable for automobile and other collisions and wrecks. However, when negligence is claimed or proven, avoid *accident,* which can be read by some as a term exonerating the person responsible. In such cases, use *crash, collision* or other terms.

accommodate

accounts payable Current liabilities or debts of a business which must be paid within one year.

accounts receivable Amounts due to a company for merchandise or services sold on credit. These are short-term assets.

accused A person is *accused of,* not *with,* a crime.

To avoid any suggestion that an individual is being judged before

a

a trial, do not use a phrase such as *accused slayer John Jones;* use *John Jones, accused of the slaying.*

For guidelines on related words, see **allege**; **arrest**; and **indict**.

Ace A trademark for a brand of elastic bandage. *Elastic bandage* is preferred in all references.

Achilles tendon No apostrophe for the tendon connecting the back of the heel to the calf muscles. But it's *Achilles' heel*, with an apostrophe, for a vulnerable spot.

acknowledgment

acquisition The process of buying or acquiring some asset. The term can refer to the purchase of a block of stock or, more often, to the acquisition of an entire company.

acre Equal to 43,560 square feet or 4,840 square yards. The metric equivalent is 0.4 (two-fifths) of a hectare or 4,047 square meters.

One square mile is 640 acres.

To convert to hectares, multiply by 0.4 (5 acres x 0.4 equals 2 hectares).

Use square miles to describe the size of wildfires.

See **wildfires** and **hectare**.

acronyms See **abbreviations and acronyms**.

act Capitalize when part of the name for pending or implemented legislation: *the Taft-Hartley Act.*

ACT Use only the initials in referring to the previously designated *American College Testing.*

act, amendment, bill, law, measure, **ordinance, resolution, rule, statute** The word *act* is sometimes included in a formal name for pending or implemented legislation. Capitalize when part of the name: *the Taft-Hartley Act.*

An *amendment* is a change or proposed change to a bill or law. Amendments are usually *passed* or *enacted.*

A *bill* is a draft proposal presented to a lawmaking body, such as a legislature, that requires debate, voting and final approval before it can become a *law.* Bills usually *pass* or *fail,* or are *approved* or *signed.* Do not capitalize when part of references to specific legislation: *the Kennedy bill.* Use conditional language for bills throughout the legislative process: *The bill would prohibit such activity; the bill seeks to legalize the drug.*

A *law* is a bill that has been approved by a lawmaking body, usually at the state or federal level, and that sometimes requires the signature of an executive such as a governor or president. Laws are usually *enacted* and don't necessarily *take effect* at the time they are enacted.

An *ordinance* is the municipal equivalent of a *law.* Ordinances are *enacted.* Before they become *ordinances,* they should usually be called *proposals* or *proposed ordinances.* Though terminology varies from place to place, it's usually best to avoid referring to such proposals as *bills,* to avoid confusion with higher levels of government.

A *resolution* is a sentiment or recommendation of a lawmaking body, often described as *binding* or *nonbinding* depending on whether it has the force of law. Resolutions are *adopted* or *fail*.

A *rule* is an authoritative regulation that can be *enacted*, *created* or *ordered* at various levels of government.

A *statute* is a written and enacted *law* or *ordinance*.

Any of the above terms can also be described generically as *measures*, provided no confusion would result.

acting Always lowercase, but capitalize any formal title that may follow before a name: *acting Mayor Peter Barry*.

See **titles**.

act numbers Use Arabic figures and capitalize *act*: *Act 1*; *Act 2, Scene 2*. But: *the first act, the second act*. See **numerals**.

actor (man) **actress** (woman) It is acceptable to use *actor* for a woman if she prefers it.

A.D. Acceptable in all references for *anno Domini*: in the year of the Lord.

Because the full phrase would read *in the year of the Lord 96*, the abbreviation *A.D.* goes before the figure for the year: *A.D. 96*.

Do not write: *The fourth century A.D. The fourth century* is sufficient. If *A.D.* is not specified with a year, the year is presumed to be A.D.

See **B.C.**

addiction Addiction to alcohol and other drugs is considered a disease that affects a person's brain and behavior. It can cause changes in brain circuits and chemistry that lead to inability to control use, despite resulting harmful behavior including damage to health and relationships. Genetics, mental illness and other risk factors make certain people susceptible to addiction.

Addiction is the preferred term for the disease. The term *substance use disorder* is preferred by some clinicians and is acceptable in some uses, such as in quotations or scientific contexts. *Alcoholism* is acceptable for an addiction to alcohol.

Avoid words like *abuse* or *problem* in favor of the word *use* with an appropriate modifier such as *risky*, *unhealthy*, *excessive* or *heavy*. *Misuse* is also acceptable. Don't assume all people who engage in risky use of drugs or alcohol have an addiction.

Avoid words like *alcoholic*, *addict, user, abuser, junkie, drunk* or *crackhead* unless they are in quotations or names of organizations, such as Alcoholics Anonymous. Many researchers and organizations, including the Office of National Drug Control Policy and the International Society of Addiction Journal Editors, agree that stigmatizing or punitive-sounding language can be inaccurate by emphasizing the person, not the disease; can be a barrier to seeking treatment; and can prejudice even clinicians. Instead, choose phrasing like *he was addicted, people with heroin addiction* or *he used drugs*.

Examples: *Keene had trouble keeping his job because of alcoholism*, not *Keene had trouble keeping his job because he was an alcoholic. Yang joined other people with heroin addictions at the conference*, not *Yang joined other heroin addicts at the conference*.

Avoid describing *sobriety* as *clean* unless in quotations, since it implies a previous state of dirtiness instead of disease.

As of early 2018, leading clinicians

a

said disorders with tobacco and gambling can also meet the criteria for addiction. Other compulsive behaviors such as eating, video gaming, sex and shopping did not meet the clinical criteria for addiction.

Do not use the terms *addiction* and *dependence* interchangeably. *Addiction* usually refers to a disease or disorder; *dependence* may not involve one, such as some babies born to mothers who use drugs or cancer patients who take prescribed painkillers.

The term *misuse* can be helpful in cases of legally prescribed medications, such as if a person with a painkiller prescription purposely takes too many to get high, or excessively uses medical marijuana. Such actions do not necessarily entail an addiction but can progress into one.

Note the subtle difference between *prescribed* and *prescription* drugs. *Prescribe* usually is used to describe specific drugs a doctor has authorized for a patient; *prescription* refers to classes of drugs meant for that purpose. *The cancer patient took prescribed painkillers. Health officials observed wide misuse of prescription painkillers.*

See **alcoholic**; **drugs**; **naloxone**; **opiate, opioid**.

addresses Use the abbreviations *Ave.*, *Blvd.* and *St.* only with a numbered address: *1600 Pennsylvania Ave.* Spell them out and capitalize when part of a formal street name without a number: *Pennsylvania Avenue.* Lowercase and spell out when used alone or with more than one street name: *Massachusetts and Pennsylvania avenues.*

All similar words (*alley, drive,*

road, terrace, etc.) always are spelled out. Capitalize them when part of a formal name without a number; lowercase when used alone or with two or more names.

Always use figures for an address number: *9 Morningside Circle.*

Spell out and capitalize *First* through *Ninth* when used as street names; use figures for *10th* and above: *7 Fifth Ave., 100 21st St.*

Abbreviate compass points used to indicate directional ends of a street or quadrants of a city in a numbered address: *222 E. 42nd St., 562 W. 43rd St., 600 K St. NW.* Do not abbreviate if the number is omitted: *East 42nd Street, West 43rd Street, K Street Northwest.* No periods in quadrant abbreviations — NW, SE — unless customary locally.

See **highway designations**.

Use periods in the abbreviation *P.O.* for P.O. Box numbers.

See **numerals**.

adjectives The abbreviation *adj.* is used in this book to identify the spelling of the adjectival forms of words that frequently are misspelled.

The **comma** entry provides guidance on punctuating a series of adjectives.

The **hyphen** entry provides guidance on handling compound modifiers used before a noun.

adjustable-rate mortgage A mortgage that has a fixed interest rate for a short period of time and then resets, usually yearly, over the life of the loan, based on an index tied to changes in market interest rates. *ARM* should be used only in direct quotes.

ad-lib

administration Lowercase: *the administration, the president's administration, the governor's administration, the Trump administration.*

See **government, junta, regime, administration** for distinctions that apply in using these terms.

administrative law judge This is the federal title for the position formerly known as *hearing examiner.* Capitalize it when used as a formal title before a name.

To avoid the long title, seek a construction that sets the title off by commas: *The administrative law judge, John Williams, disagreed.*

administrator Never abbreviate. Capitalize when used as a formal title before a name.

See **titles.**

admiral See **military titles.**

admissible

admit, admitted These words may in some contexts give the erroneous connotation of wrongdoing.

People who say they are recovering from alcoholism, for example, are not *admitting* it. *Said* is usually sufficient.

ad nauseam

adopt, approve, enact, pass See **act, amendment, bill, law, measure, ordinance, resolution, rule, statute** entry.

adoption The adoptive status of children or their parents should be mentioned only when its relevance is made clear in the story. If relevant, use the term *biological parents* to refer to the birth mother and father. Preferred phrasing: *A child is placed for adoption*, rather than *given up for adoption*.

Adrenalin A trademark for the synthetic or chemically extracted forms of epinephrine, a substance produced by the adrenal glands.

The nonproprietary terms are *epinephrine hydrochloride* or *adrenaline.*

adult A person who has reached 18. See **privacy.**

Advance Publications Inc. Privately held company whose holdings include Conde Nast Publications and newspapers in more than 25 U.S. cities. Headquarters is in New York.

adverbs The abbreviation *adv.* is used in this book to identify the spelling of adverbial forms of words frequently misspelled.

See the **hyphen** entry in the **Punctuation** chapter for guidelines on when an adverb should be followed by a hyphen in constructing a compound modifier.

adverse, averse *Adverse* means unfavorable: *He predicted adverse weather.*

Averse means reluctant, opposed: *She is averse to change.*

adviser Not *advisor.*

advisory

Aer Lingus Headquarters of this airline is in Dublin, Ireland.

Aeroflot Headquarters of this airline is in Moscow.

a

Aeromexico Headquarters of this airline is in Mexico City.

aesthetic

affect, effect *Affect*, as a verb, means to influence: *The game will affect the standings.*

Affect, as a noun, is best avoided. It occasionally is used in psychology to describe an emotion, but there is no need for it in everyday language.

Effect, as a verb, means to cause: *He will effect many changes in the company.*

Effect, as a noun, means result: *The effect was overwhelming. He miscalculated the effect of his actions. It was a law of little effect.*

Affordable Care Act Shorthand for the formal title of the health care overhaul that former President Barack Obama signed into law in 2010. Its full name is Patient Protection and Affordable Care Act. Use *former President Barack Obama's health care law* or the *health care law* on first reference. *"Obamacare"* in quotation marks is acceptable on second reference. *Affordable Care Act* can be used on subsequent references when necessary to refer to the law, but should be used sparingly. Polling indicates that not all Americans know the law by its formal name.

Afghan The term for the people and culture of Afghanistan. *Afghani* is the *Afghan* unit of currency.

AFL-CIO Acceptable in all references for the *American Federation of Labor and Congress of Industrial Organizations*. Headquarters is in Washington.

A-frame

African-American Acceptable for an American black person of African descent. Also acceptable is *black*. The terms are not necessarily interchangeable. People from Caribbean nations, for example, generally refer to themselves as *Caribbean-American*. Follow a person's preference. See **nationalities and races** and **race**.

African Union The African Union, established in 2002 to succeed the Organization of African Unity, has the following 55 members:

Algeria, Angola, Benin, Botswana, Burkina Faso, Burundi, Cameroon, Cape Verde, Central African Republic, Chad, Comoros, Congo, Djibouti, Egypt, Equatorial Guinea, Eritrea, Ethiopia, Gabon, Gambia, Ghana, Guinea-Bissau, Guinea, Ivory Coast, Kenya, Lesotho, Liberia, Libya, Madagascar, Malawi, Mali, Mauritania, Mauritius, Morocco, Mozambique, Namibia, Niger, Nigeria, Republic of Congo, Rwanda, Sao Tome and Principe, Senegal, Seychelles, Sierra Leone, Somalia, South Africa, South Sudan, Sudan, Swaziland, Tanzania, Togo, Tunisia, Uganda, Western Sahara, Zambia, Zimbabwe. There are two Congos: *the Republic of Congo* and *the Democratic Republic of Congo*. The latter is *the Congo* in AP style.

after- No hyphen after this prefix when it is used to form a noun:
aftereffect   afterthought
Follow *after* with a hyphen when it is used to form compound modifiers:
after-dinner drink
after-theater snack

after-party

afterward Not *afterwards*.

Agence France-Presse A global news agency with headquarters in Paris. *AFP* acceptable on second reference.

agent Lowercase unless it is a formal title used before a name.
    In the FBI, the formal title is *special agent*. In most cases, make it *agent William Smith* or *FBI agent William Smith*.
    See **titles**.

ages Use when deemed relevant to the situation. If someone is quoted as saying, *I'm too old to get another job*, the age is relevant. Generally, use ages for profiles, obituaries, significant career milestones and achievements unusual for the age. Use ages for people commenting or providing information only if their age is relevant to their comments (e.g., a teenager's comment on video games aimed at that age group). Appropriate background, such as a *parent of two young children* or a *World War II veteran*, may suffice instead of the actual age.
    Always use figures. *The girl is 15 years old; the law is 8 years old; the 101-year-old house.* When the context does not require *years* or *years old*, the figure is presumed to be *years*.
    Use hyphens for ages expressed as adjectives before a noun or as substitutes for a noun.
    Examples: *A 5-year-old boy*, but *the boy is 5 years old. The boy, 7, has a sister, 10. The woman, 26, has a daughter 2 months old. The race is for 3-year-olds. The woman is in her 30s* (no apostrophe).
    See also **boy**, **girl**; **infant**; **youth**; **numerals** and **elderly**.
    See **comma** in punctuation guidelines.

aggregator A website or feed that amasses content from other sources and assembles it in a form digestible to its users.

agnostic, atheist An *agnostic* is a person who believes it is impossible to know whether there is a God.
    An *atheist* is a person who believes there is no God.

A.H. Belo Corp. Owner of The Dallas Morning News and the Denton Record-Chronicle in Texas. Headquarters is in Dallas.

aid, aide *Aid* is assistance.
    An *aide* is a person who serves as an assistant.

aide-de-camp, aides-de-camp A military officer who serves as assistant and confidential secretary to a superior.

AIDS Acceptable in all references for *acquired immune deficiency syndrome*, sometimes called *acquired immunodeficiency syndrome*.
    AIDS is a disease that weakens the immune system, gradually destroying the body's ability to fight infections and certain cancers. It is caused by *human immunodeficiency virus*, or *HIV*. (*HIV virus* is redundant.)
    HIV is spread most often through sexual contact; contaminated needles or syringes shared by drug abusers; infected blood or blood products; and from infected women to their babies at birth or through breast-feeding.
    Several types of tests are available for *HIV*. One is a blood test that looks for antibodies the body has made to defend against *HIV*. Other tests look for parts of the virus

a

itself in blood. Use the *HIV/AIDS* construction with care. People can be infected with the virus and not have *AIDS*; they do not have *AIDS* until they develop serious symptoms. Many remain infected but apparently healthy for years.

ain't A dialectical or nonstandard contraction. Use it only in quoted matter or special contexts.

air bag Two words.

air base Two words. Follow the practice of the U.S. Air Force, which uses *air force base* as part of the proper name for its bases in the United States and *air base* for its installations abroad. Some bases have become joint bases with other services.

On second reference: *the Air Force base, the air base,* or *the base.*

Do not abbreviate, even in datelines:

LACKLAND AIR FORCE BASE, Texas (AP) —

JOINT BASE ANDREWS, Md. (AP) —

Airbnb See **vacation rental websites**.

Air Canada Headquarters of this airline is in Saint-Laurent, Canada.

Air China Headquarters of this airline is in Beijing.

air-condition, air-conditioned (v. and adj.) The nouns are: *air conditioner, air conditioning.*

aircraft names Use a hyphen when changing from letters to figures; no hyphen when adding a letter after figures.

Some examples of aircraft: *B-1,*

C-5A, FH-227, F-15 Eagle, F-16 Falcon, MiG-29, Tu-154, Il-96, Boeing 737-800, 747, 747B. Airbus A380, A380F (no hyphen) is an exception.

This hyphenation principle is the one used most frequently by manufacturers and users. Apply it in all cases for consistency. For other elements of a name, use the form adopted by the manufacturer or user. If in doubt, consult IHS Jane's All the World's Aircraft.

NO QUOTES: Do not use quotation marks for aircraft with names: *Air Force One, the Spirit of St. Louis.*

AVOID PROMOTIONAL NAMES: *Boeing 787,* not *Dreamliner.*

PLURALS: *747s.* But: *747B's.* (As noted in plurals, the apostrophe is used in forming the plural of a single letter.)

SEQUENCE: Use Arabic figures to establish the sequence of aircraft, spacecraft and missiles: *Apollo 10.* Do not use hyphens.

See **numerals**.

aircraft terms Use *engine,* not *motor,* for the units that propel aircraft: a *twin-engine* plane (not *twin engined*).

Use *jet plane* or *jetliner* to describe only those aircraft driven solely by jet engines. Use *turboprop* to describe an aircraft on which the jet engine is geared to a propeller. Turboprops sometimes are called *propjets.*

See **engine, motor**.

airfare One word.

air force Capitalize when referring to U.S. forces: *the U.S. Air Force, the Air Force, Air Force regulations.* Do not use the abbreviation *USAF.*

Congress established the Army Air Forces (note the *s*) in 1941. Prior to that, the air arm was known as the U.S. Army Air Corps. The U.S. Air Force (no *s*) was created as a separate service in 1947.

Use lowercase for the forces of other nations: *the Israeli air force*.

This approach has been adopted for consistency, because many foreign nations do not use *air force* as the proper name.

See **military academies** and **military titles**.

air force base See **air base**.

Air Force One The Air Force applies this name to any of its aircraft the president of the United States may be using.

In ordinary usage, however, *Air Force One* is the name of the Air Force plane normally reserved for the president's use.

Air France Corporate name is *Air France-KLM*. Headquarters of this airline is in Roissy, France.

Air India Headquarters of this airline is in Mumbai, India.

airline, airlines Capitalize *airlines*, *air lines* and *airways* when used as part of a proper airline name.

Companies that use *Airlines* in the title include American, Hawaiian, Japan, Southwest and United.

Companies that use *Airways* include British, JetBlue and Qantas.

Delta uses *Air Lines*.

Companies that use none of these include Aer Lingus, Aeromexico, Air Canada, Air France, Air India, Alitalia, Emirates, Iberia and Virgin America. Alaska Air Group acquired Virgin America in December 2016. Virgin America and Alaska Airlines are expected to become one airline under the name Alaska Airlines by mid-2019.

On second reference, use just the proper name (*Delta*), an abbreviation if applicable, or *the airline*. Acceptable abbreviations are *ANA* for *All Nippon Airways*, *BA* for *British Airways* and *JAL* for *Japan Airlines*. Use airlines when referring to more than one line.

Do not use *air line*, *air lines* or *airways* in generic references to an airline.

airman See **military titles**.

Air National Guard

airport Capitalize as part of a proper name: *LaGuardia Airport*, *O'Hare International Airport*.

The first name of an individual and the word *international* may be deleted from a formal airport name while the remainder is capitalized: *John F. Kennedy International Airport*, *Kennedy International Airport*, or *Kennedy Airport*. Use whichever is appropriate in the context.

Do not make up names, however. There is no *Boston Airport*, for example. The *Boston airport* (lowercase *airport*) would be acceptable if for some reason the proper name, *Logan International Airport*, were not used.

airsoft gun A gun that commonly shoots plastic spheres, typically propelled by compressed air or springs. *Pellet gun* is acceptable on first reference.

airstrike

airtight

air traffic controller No hyphen.

a

airways The system of routes that the federal government has established for airplane traffic.

See the **airline, airlines** entry for its use in carriers' names.

aka Abbreviation for *also known as.*

Alabama Abbreviate *Ala.* in datelines only; spell out in stories. Postal code: *AL*

See **state names**.

Al-Aqsa Mosque The mosque completed in the eighth century atop the Haram al-Sharif, or *Noble Sanctuary*, in the Old City of Jerusalem; Arabs also use *Al-Aqsa* to refer to the whole area, which houses the Dome of the Rock shrine, too. To Jews the area is known as the *Temple Mount*, the site of the ancient Jewish temples.

alarms Avoid referring to a fire in terms of the number of "alarms," which may mean little to a distant reader. Depending on the city or town, a two-alarm fire could involve widely varying numbers of firefighters. Instead, specify the number of firefighters or quantity of equipment.

Alaska Do not abbreviate in datelines or stories. Largest land area of the 50 states. Postal code: *AK*
See **state names**.

Alaska Air Group Inc. Headquarters is in Seattle. A merger of its subsidiary Alaska Airlines and Virgin America is planned to be completed by mid-2019.

Alaska Native See **Indians**.

Alaska Standard Time The time zone used in all of Alaska, except the western Aleutian Islands and St. Lawrence Island, which are on *Hawaii-Aleutian Standard Time*.

There is also an *Alaska Daylight Time*.
See **time zones**.

Alberta A province of western Canada. Do not abbreviate.
See **datelines**.

albino, albinos

alcoholic As an adjective, use it to describe beverages. For people, say *people* or *person with alcoholism*, or *person recovering from alcoholism*. Many people with the disease refer to themselves as *alcoholics*, but leading authorities on addiction say such language can be self-punitive and stigmatizing. Avoid describing people as *drunks*, though the word can be used as an adjective to describe someone who is temporarily intoxicated by alcohol. See **addiction**.

Alcoholics Anonymous *AA* is acceptable on second reference.

alderman Do not abbreviate. See **legislative titles**.

alert See **weather terms**.

Alibaba Group Holding Ltd. An e-commerce and online services provider. Headquarters is in Hangzhou, China.

A-list

Alitalia Airlines Headquarters of this airline is in Rome.

Al-Jazeera Pan-Arab satellite

a

television news network based in
Doha, Qatar.

all- Use a hyphen:
all-around (*not all-round*)   *all-out*
all-clear   *all-star*
See **all right** and the **all time, all-time** entries.

Allah The Arabic word for God. The
word *God* should be used, unless
the Arabic name is used in a quote
written or spoken in English.

Allahu akbar The Arabic phrase for
God is great.

allege The word must be used with
great care.
Some guidelines:
— Avoid any suggestion that the
writer is making an allegation.
— Specify the source of an
allegation. In a criminal case, it
should be an arrest record, an
indictment or the statement of
a public official connected with
the case.
— Use *alleged bribe* or similar phrase
when necessary to make it clear
that an unproved action is not
being treated as fact. Be sure
that the source of the charge is
specified elsewhere in the story.
— Avoid, where possible, *alleged
victim.* It is too easily construed
as skepticism of a victim's
account.
— Avoid redundant uses of *alleged.*
It is proper to say: *The district
attorney alleged that she took a
bribe.* Or: *The district attorney
accused her of taking a bribe.* But
not: *The district attorney accused
her of allegedly taking a bribe.*
— Do not use *alleged* to describe
an event that is known to have
occurred, when the dispute is

over who participated in it. Do
not say: *He attended the alleged
meeting* when what you mean is:
He allegedly attended the meeting.
— Do not use *alleged* as a routine
qualifier. Instead, use a word such
as *apparent, ostensible* or *reputed.*
For guidelines on related words,
see **accused**; **arrest**; and **indict**.

Allegheny Mountains Or simply: *the
Alleghenies.*

Allegiant Air Airline is owned by
Allegiant Travel Co. Headquarters is
in Las Vegas.

alley Do not abbreviate. See **addresses**.

allies, allied Capitalize *allies* or
allied only when referring to the
combination of the United States
and its Allies during World War I
or World War II: *The Allies defeated
Germany. He was in the Allied invasion
of France.*

All Nippon Airways Headquarters of
this airline is in Tokyo.

all right Never *alright.* Hyphenate only
if used colloquially as a compound
modifier: *He is an all-right guy.*

all-terrain vehicle *ATV* is acceptable
on second reference.

all time, all-time An *all-time high,* but
the greatest runner of all time.
Avoid the redundant phrase *all-time record.*

allude, refer To *allude* to something
is to speak of it without specifically
mentioning it.
To *refer* is to mention it directly.

allusion, illusion *Allusion* means an

a

indirect reference: *The allusion was to his opponent's war record.*

Illusion means an unreal or false impression: *The scenic director created the illusion of choppy seas.*

alma mater

Alphabet Inc. See **Google.**

al-Qaida Muslim militant group founded by Osama bin Laden that carried out the attacks in the United States on Sept. 11, 2001. Bin Laden was killed by U.S. forces in Pakistan in May 2011. Al-Qaida's current leader is Ayman al-Zawahri.

Affiliated groups include:
al-Qaida in the Arabian Peninsula, operating in Yemen and Saudi Arabia.

Nusra Front, operating in Syria.
al-Qaida in the Islamic Maghreb, operating in the Sahel region, a region along the Sahara Desert stretching across North Africa.

Khorasan group, an al-Qaida cell that the United States says operated in Syria to plot attacks on the U.S.

Al-Quds The Arabic name for Jerusalem; it means *the holy.*

al-Shabab The preferred spelling for the Somali militant group.

also-ran (n.)

altar, alter An *altar* is a tablelike platform used in a religious service. *To alter* is to change.

Altria Group Inc. Headquarters is in Richmond, Virginia.

"alt-right" A political grouping or tendency mixing racism, white nationalism and populism; a name currently embraced by some white supremacists and white nationalists to refer to themselves and their ideology, which emphasizes preserving and protecting the white race in the United States.

In AP stories discussing what the movement says about itself, the term *"alt-right"* (quotation marks, hyphen and lowercase) may be used in quotes or modified as in *the self-described "alt-right"* or *so-called alt-right.* Avoid using the term generically and without definition, however, because it is not well-known and the term may exist primarily as a public relations device to make its supporters' actual beliefs less clear and more acceptable to a broader audience.

Depending on the specifics of the situation, such beliefs might be termed *racist, white supremacist* or *neo-Nazi*; be sure to describe the specifics. Whenever *"alt-right"* is used in a story, include a definition: *an offshoot of conservatism mixing racism, white nationalism and populism,* or, more simply, *a white nationalist movement.*

When writing on extreme groups, be precise and provide evidence to support the characterization. Report their actions, associations, history and positions to reveal their actual beliefs and philosophy, as well as how others see them.

Some related definitions:
racism The broad term for asserting racial or ethnic discrimination or superiority based solely on race, ethnic or religious origins; it can be by any group against any other group.

white nationalism A subset of racist beliefs that calls for a separate territory and/or enhanced legal rights and protections for white people. Critics accuse white nationalists of being white supremacists in disguise.

white separatism A term sometimes used as a synonym for *white nationalism* but differs in that it advocates a form of segregation in which races would live apart but in the same general geographic area.

white supremacy The racist belief that whites are superior to justify political, economic and social suppression of nonwhite people and other minority groups.

neo-Nazism Combines racist and white supremacist beliefs with admiration for an authoritarian, totalitarian style of government such as the German Third Reich to enforce its beliefs..

alumnus, alumni, alumna, alumnae

Use *alumnus* (*alumni* in the plural) when referring to a man who has attended a school.

Use *alumna* (*alumnae* in the plural) for similar references to a woman.

Use *alumni* when referring to a group of men and women.

Alzheimer's disease A progressive, irreversible neurological disorder and the most common form of dementia. Most victims are older than 65, but Alzheimer's can strike in the 40s or 50s.

Symptoms include gradual memory loss, impairment of judgment, disorientation, personality change, difficulty in learning and loss of language skills.

No cure is known.

AM Acceptable in all references to the *amplitude modulation* system of radio transmission.

ambassador Capitalize as a formal title before a name.
See **titles**.

Amber Alert A procedure for rapidly publicizing the disappearance of a child.

amendments to the Constitution

Use *First Amendment, 10th Amendment*, etc.

Colloquial references to the Fifth Amendment's protection against self-incrimination are best avoided, but where appropriate: *He took the Fifth seven times.*

American An acceptable description for a citizen of the United States.

American Airlines Headquarters is in Fort Worth, Texas. Parent company is American Airlines Group Inc. The company is the result of the 2013 merger of AMR Corp. and US Airways Group.

American Baptist Association See **Baptist churches** in **Religion** chapter.

American Baptist Churches in the U.S.A. See **Baptist churches** in **Religion** chapter.

American Bar Association *ABA* is acceptable on second reference. Also: *the bar association, the association.*

Headquarters is in Chicago.

American Broadcasting Cos. See **ABC**.

American Civil Liberties Union *ACLU* is acceptable on second reference.

Headquarters is in New York.

a

a

American depositary receipt A negotiable certificate representing a foreign company's equity or debt. *ADR* is acceptable on second reference.

American depositary share A security issued by a foreign company representing an ownership interest in that company. It can represent a fixed number of securities on deposit, or a fraction of them. *ADS* is acceptable on second reference.

American Express Co. Headquarters is in New York.

American Federation of Government Employees Use this full name on first reference to prevent confusion with other unions that represent government workers. *AFGE* is acceptable on second reference.
Headquarters is in Washington.

American Federation of Labor and Congress of Industrial Organizations *AFL-CIO* is acceptable in all references.
Headquarters is in Washington.

American Federation of State, County and Municipal Employees *AFSCME* is acceptable on second reference.
Headquarters is in Washington.

American Federation of Teachers *AFT* is acceptable on second reference.
Headquarters is in Washington.

American Hospital Association *AHA* is acceptable on second reference. Also: *the hospital association, the association*.
Headquarters is in Chicago.

American International Group Inc. *AIG* is acceptable on second reference. Headquarters is in New York.

Americanisms Words and phrases that have become part of the English language as spoken in the United States are listed with a star in Webster's New World College Dictionary.
Most Americanisms are acceptable in news stories, but let the context be the guide.

American Legion Capitalize also *the Legion* in second reference. Members are *Legionnaires*, just as members of the Lions Club are *Lions*.
Legion and *Legionnaires* are capitalized because they are not being used in their common noun sense. A *legion* (lowercase) is a large group of soldiers or, by derivation, a large number of items: *His friends are legion*. A *legionnaire* (lowercase) is a member of such a legion.
See **fraternal organizations and service clubs**.

American Medical Association *AMA* is acceptable on second reference. Also: *the medical association, the association*.
Headquarters is in Chicago.

American Petroleum Institute *API* is acceptable on second reference.
Headquarters is in Washington.

American Postal Workers Union This union represents clerks and similar employees who work inside post offices.
Use the full name on first reference to prevent confusion with the National Association of Letter Carriers. The shortened form *Postal*

Workers union is acceptable on second reference.

Headquarters is in Washington.

American Press Institute *API* is acceptable on second reference.

Headquarters is in Arlington, Virginia.

American Society for the Prevention of Cruelty to Animals
This organization is limited to the five boroughs of New York City and neighboring Suffolk County in providing animal adoption services, although it has offices elsewhere that offer legal advice and other services to other animal welfare organizations. *ASPCA* is acceptable on second reference.

See **Society for the Prevention of Cruelty to Animals**.

American Society of Composers, Authors and Publishers *ASCAP* is acceptable on second reference.

Headquarters is in New York.

AmeriCorps

amid Not *amidst*.

ammunition See **weapons**.

amnesty See **pardon, parole, probation**.

amok Not *amuck*.

among, between The maxim that *between* introduces two items and *among* introduces more than two covers most questions about how to use these words: *The funds were divided among Ford, Carter and McCarthy. The games between the Yankees, Phillies and Mets have been rollicking ones.*

As with all prepositions, any pronouns that follow these words must be in the objective case: *among us, between him and her, between you and me.*

amount, number Use *amount* for things that cannot be counted individually: *the amount of milk in the refrigerator, the amount of courage it takes to climb Mount Everest.* For things that can be counted individually, use *number*: *The number of soldiers in an army, the number of books in a library.* Similarly, use *less* for things that can't be counted — *less paper, less paint* — and *fewer* for things that can: *fewer days, fewer votes.* However, some expressions are exceptions: *Write the jingle in 25 words or less.*

ampersand (&) Use the ampersand when it is part of a company's formal name or composition title: *House & Garden, Procter & Gamble, Wheeling & Lake Erie Railway.*

The ampersand should not otherwise be used in place of *and*, except for some accepted abbreviations: *B&B, R&B.*

a.m., p.m. Lowercase, with periods. Avoid the redundant *10 a.m. this morning.*

Amsterdam The city in the Netherlands stands alone in datelines.

Amtrak This acronym, drawn from the words *American travel by track*, may be used in all references to the *National Railroad Passenger Corp*. Do not use *AMTRAK*. Headquarters is in Washington.

AMVETS Acceptable in all references

a

for *American Veterans*, the organization formerly known as *American Veterans of World War II, Korea, and Vietnam*.

Headquarters is in Washington.

anchor, anchorman, anchorwoman, co-anchor

anemia, anemic

Android An operating system created by Google that's used in many smartphones and tablets.

Anglo- Always capitalized. No hyphen when the word that follows is in lowercase:

Anglomania   Anglophobe Anglophile

Use a hyphen when the word that follows is capitalized:

Anglo-American   Anglo-Indian Anglo-Catholic   Anglo-Saxon

angry *At* someone or *with* someone.

animals Do not apply a personal pronoun to an animal unless its sex has been established or the animal has a name: *The dog was scared; it barked. Rover was scared; he barked. The cat, which was scared, ran to its basket. Susie the cat, who was scared, ran to her basket. The bull tosses his horns.*

Capitalize the name of a specific animal, and use Roman numerals to show sequence: *Bowser, Whirlaway II*.

For breed names, follow the spelling and capitalization in Webster's New World College Dictionary. For breeds not listed in the dictionary, capitalize words derived from proper nouns; use lowercase elsewhere: *basset hound, Boston terrier*.

animal welfare activist Use instead of *animal rights activist*.

anniversary Avoid terms such as *six-month anniversary* (or other time spans less than a year).

anno Domini See **A.D.**

annual Avoid the term *first annual*.

annual meeting Lowercase in all uses.

anonymous sources Whenever possible, we pursue information on the record. When a source insists on background or off-the-record ground rules, we must adhere to a strict set of guidelines.

Under AP's rules, material from anonymous sources may be used only if:
— The material is information and not opinion or speculation, and is vital to the news report.
— The information is not available except under the conditions of anonymity imposed by the source.
— The source is reliable, and in a position to have accurate information.

Reporters who intend to use material from anonymous sources must get approval from their news managers.

Explain in the story why the source requested anonymity. And, when it's relevant, describe the source's motive for disclosing the information.

The story also must provide attribution that establishes the source's credibility; simply quoting *a source* is not allowed. Be as descriptive as possible about the source of information. If space is limited, use *source* as a last resort. *Official* or a similar word will often suffice, including in headlines. See **source**.

Examples:

Speaking on customary condition of anonymity in line with government rules, the official said the two sides were engaged "in very fierce" battles near the border crossing, and that one woman was wounded by a stray bullet.

Incorrect: Granting anonymity *"on customary condition ... in line with government rules"* is insufficient. Readers need a plausible explanation of such a condition, and why we're accepting it. For instance, *"The rules of the official's job did not allow him to be quoted by name."*

A security official, who requested anonymity because of the sensitivity of the case, said the suspect was monitoring and recording the movements of tourists before his arrest in July.

Incorrect: Explanation: First, we grant anonymity only to those who insist on it, not those who *request* it. Second, granting anonymity because of the *sensitivity of the case* is insufficient explanation. Did the official insist on anonymity because he was not allowed to speak with reporters? Because he was not authorized to release information in advance of a public announcement of details of the case?

Speaking privately, a senior Foreign Ministry official said any further increase in tension could strengthen "warlike" sentiment on both sides and make a resolution of the problem even more difficult.

Incorrect: *Speaking privately* isn't the same thing as insisting on anonymity, so we cannot use the *privately* explanation. Moreover, the official is speculating on something

that might happen. We grant anonymity for factual information, not speculation or opinion.

Sometimes a government or corporation intentionally leaks information, but insists we publish it attributed to an anonymous official. If we cannot convince the government or company to go on the record, it's best to use a formulation that implies that the release of the information was official, even though anonymous. For instance: "... according to the official, who insisted on anonymity because he was not allowed to use his own name in releasing the findings."

For additional guidance, see **Statement of News Values**.

another *Another* is not a synonym for *additional*; it refers to an element that somehow duplicates a previously stated quantity.

Right: *Ten people took the test; another 10 refused.*

Wrong: *Ten people took the test; another 20 refused.*

Right: *Ten people took the test; 20 others refused.*

Antarctic, Antarctica, Antarctic Ocean

ante- The rules in **prefixes** apply, but in general, no hyphen. Some examples:

antebellum   antedate

anthems See **composition titles**. Lowercase the term *national anthem*.

anti- Hyphenate all except the following words, which have specific meanings of their own:

antibiotic   antipasto
antibody   antiperspirant
anticlimax   antiphon

a

antidepressant	*antiphony*
antidote	*antipollution*
antifreeze	*antipsychotic*
antigen	*antiseptic*
antihistamine	*antiserum*
antiknock	*antithesis*
antimatter	*antitoxin*
antimony	*antitrust*
antiparticle*	*antitussive*

*And similar terms in physics such as *antiproton*.

This approach has been adopted in the interests of readability and easily remembered consistency.

It's *anti-lock* in Webster's New World College Dictionary. But note these Stylebook exceptions to Webster's spellings:

anti-abortion	*anti-social*
anti-aircraft	*anti-war*
anti-labor	

See **Antichrist, anti-Christ** in **Religion** chapter.

anticipate, expect *Anticipate* means to expect and prepare for something; *expect* does not include the notion of preparation:

They expect a record crowd. They have anticipated it by adding more seats to the auditorium.

antitrust Any law or policy designed to encourage competition by curtailing monopolistic power and unfair business practices.

anybody, any body, anyone, any one One word for an indefinite reference: *Anyone can do that.*

Two words when the emphasis is on singling out one element of a group: *Any one of them may speak up.*

AOL An online services provider owned by Verizon Communications Inc. subsidiary Oath Inc. Do not use its former name, America Online.

Headquarters is in New York.

AP Acceptable on second reference for *The Associated Press.*

On second reference, *AP* or *the AP* (no capital on *the*) may be used. See **Associated Press**.

API Abbreviation for *application programming interface.* A programming interface that a website or a piece of software uses to allow other websites or software to interact with it. *API* acceptable on second reference.

apostolic delegate, papal nuncio An *apostolic delegate* is a Roman Catholic diplomat chosen by the pope to be his envoy to the church in a nation that does not have formal diplomatic relations with the Vatican.

A *papal nuncio* is the pope's envoy to a nation with which the Vatican has diplomatic relations.

apostrophe (') See entry in **Punctuation** section.

app Short for *application* and acceptable on first reference. A program that runs inside another service. Many cellphones, tablets, operating systems and web browsers allow apps to be downloaded to give the user access to additional functions.

Appalachia In the broadest sense, the word applies to the entire region along the Appalachian Mountains, which extend from Maine into northern Alabama.

In a sense that often suggests economic depression and poverty, the reference is to sections of eastern Tennessee, eastern

Kentucky, southeastern Ohio and the western portion of West Virginia.

The Appalachian Regional Commission, established by federal law in 1965, has a mandate to foster development in 397 counties in 13 states — all of West Virginia and parts of Alabama, Georgia, Kentucky, Maryland, Mississippi, New York, North Carolina, Ohio, Pennsylvania, South Carolina, Tennessee and Virginia.

When the word *Appalachia* is used, specify the extent of the area in question.

Appalachian Mountains Or simply: *the Appalachians*.

appeals court See **U.S. Court of Appeals**.

Apple Inc. Headquarters is in Cupertino, California.

appreciation Increase in value of property, as opposed to *depreciation*.

approve See **act, amendment, bill, law, measure, ordinance, resolution, rule, statute** entry.

April Fools' Day

APTN, AP Radio Do not refer to these units of The Associated Press as if they were separate entities. Say *Alexander Barbosa told the AP [not APTN] in Rio de Janeiro; AP [not APTN] video journalist John Smith contributed to this report.* See **Associated Press, The**.

Arab Spring Wave of pro-democratic protests, revolutions and civil wars that have swept some Arab nations since 2011.

Arabic names In general, use an English spelling that approximates the way a name sounds in Arabic.

If an individual has a preferred spelling in English, use that. If usage has established a particular spelling, use that.

Problems in transliteration of Arabic names often are traceable to pronunciations that vary from region to region. The *g*, for example, is pronounced like the *g* of *go* mainly in Egypt, and the *j* of *joy* in the rest of the Arab world. Thus it is *Gamal* in Egypt and *Jamal* in nations on the peninsula. Follow local practice in deciding which letter to use.

Arabs commonly are known by two names (*Hassan Nasrallah*), or by three (*Mohammed Mahdi Akef*). Follow the individual's preference on first reference. On second reference, use only the final name in the sequence.

The articles *al-* or *el-* may be used or dropped depending on the person's preference or established usage. (*Ayman al-Zawahri, al-Zawahri,* or *Moammar Gadhafi, Gadhafi*). The article *al-* or *el-* should not be capitalized.

The Arabic word for son (*ibn* or *bin*) is sometimes part of a name. On second reference, it is often dropped, using only the final name. In cases of personal preference or common usage, it should be retained. (*Osama bin Laden, bin Laden; Abdul-Aziz bin Baz, bin Baz*).

The word *abu* or *abou*, meaning *father of*, occasionally is used as a last name (*Abdel-Halim Abou Ghazala*). Capitalize and repeat it on second reference: *Abou Ghazala*.

The word *abdul*, meaning "servant of (God)," generally does not stand alone as a name, except sometimes in South Asia and Afghanistan.

It is used in combination with a second name (an Arabic word for an attribute of God). This combination should be hyphenated, unless the individual prefers otherwise, and capitalized (*Adil Abdul-Mahdi, Abdul-Mahdi*). In Egypt and some other countries, *Abdul* is often written *Abdel*, reflecting local pronunciation.

For royalty, the titles *king, emir, sheikh* and *imam* are used, but *prince* usually replaces *emir*. Some Arabs are known only by the title and a given name on first reference (*King Abdullah*). Others are known by a complete name (*Sheikh Mohammed bin Rashid Al Maktoum*). Follow the common usage on first reference. On second reference, drop the title and use only the first name (*Abdullah, Mohammed*). The full names of many Gulf royals include the word *Al*, which in their case should be capitalized without a hyphen since it means *family of*.

The *al* should be capitalized in front of most Muslim and Arab institutions, universities, newspapers and major mosques, as in *Al-Azhar*, the university in Cairo; *Al-Aqsa*, the Jerusalem mosque, the newspaper *Al-Ahram* and the satellite television news network *Al-Jazeera*.

Arabic numerals The numerical figures 0, 1, 2, 3, 4, 5, 6, 7, 8, 9.

In general, use Arabic forms unless denoting the sequence of wars or establishing a personal sequence for people or animals. See **Roman numerals**.

Separate entries list more details and examples. For a full list, see **numerals**.

arbitrage Buying currencies, commercial bills or securities in one market and selling them at the same time in another to make a profit on the price discrepancy.

arbitrate, mediate Both terms are used in reports about labor negotiations, but they should not be interchanged.

One who *arbitrates* hears evidence from all people concerned, then hands down a decision.

One who *mediates* listens to arguments of both parties and tries by the exercise of reason or persuasion to bring them to an agreement.

arch- No hyphen after this prefix unless it precedes a capitalized word:
*archbishop   arch-Republican
archenemy   archrival*

archaeology

arctic Lowercase for adjective meaning *frigid*; capitalize for region around the North Pole. **Arctic Circle, arctic fox, Arctic Ocean**

area codes See **telephone numbers**.

Argentine The preferred term for the people and culture of Argentina.

Arizona Abbreviate *Ariz.* in datelines only; spell out in stories. Postal code: AZ
See **state names**.

Arkansas Abbreviate *Ark.* in datelines only; spell out in stories. Postal code: AR
See **state names**.

army Capitalize when referring to U.S. forces: *the U.S. Army, the Army, Army regulations*. Do not use the abbreviation *USA*.

Use lowercase for the forces of

other nations: *the French army.*

This approach has been adopted for consistency, because many foreign nations do not use *army* as the proper name.

See **military academies** and **military titles**.

arrest To avoid any suggestion that someone is being judged before a trial, do not use a phrase such as *arrested for killing.* Instead, use *arrested on a charge of killing.* If a charge hasn't been filed, *arrested on suspicion of,* or a similar phrase, should be used.

For guidelines on related words, see **accused**; **allege**; and **indict**.

arrive It requires the preposition *at.* Do not omit, as airline dispatchers often do in: *He will arrive LaGuardia.*

artifact

artificial intelligence Software or computer systems that emulate aspects of human cognition. Such systems are not sentient, but can accomplish human-level tasks such as visual perception, understanding and using speech, and learning — though only to a limited extent in many cases. *AI* is acceptable on second reference. See **machine learning**.

artillery See **weapons**.

artworks Lowercase *impressionism, modernism* and other art styles and movements unless used in formal titles of shows or exhibits with quotation marks. Exception: *Bauhaus* is capitalized as the name of a school. *Gothic, Renaissance* and other historical periods are capitalized for art and architecture from those

ages. Titles of paintings are enclosed in quotes: *"Mona Lisa."* Sculptures are capitalized without quotes: *The Thinker, Michelangelo's Pieta.*

See **composition titles**.

as See **like, as**.

ASCII An acronym for *American Standard Code for Information Interchange.* A numeric code used to represent the letters of the Roman alphabet, numbers and punctuation marks. Use of the acronym on first reference is acceptable if it is identified as a code.

Asian-American A person of Asian birth or descent who lives in the U.S. When possible, refer to a person's country of origin. For example: *Filipino-American* or *Indian-American.* Follow the person's preference. See **nationalities and races** and **race**.

Asian, Asiatic Use *Asian* or *Asians* when referring to people.

Some Asians regard *Asiatic* as offensive when applied to people.

Asian subcontinent In popular usage the term applies to Bangladesh, Bhutan, India, Nepal, Pakistan, Sikkim and the island nation of Sri Lanka (formerly Ceylon) at the southeastern tip of India.

For definitions of the terms that apply to other parts of Asia, see **Far East; Middle East**; and **Southeast Asia**.

Asperger's syndrome After Hans Asperger, an Austrian pediatrician. A milder form of autism, once a separate diagnosis but now part of a broader term called "autism spectrum disorder." People with this condition can have high intelligence

a

and narrow, sometimes obsessive interests but lack social skills.

assassin, killer, murderer An *assassin* is one who kills a politically important or prominent person.

A *killer* is anyone who kills with a motive of any kind.

A *murderer* is one who is convicted of murder in a court of law.

Preferred use: *Joe Smith was convicted of second-degree murder.*

See **execute** and the **homicide, murder, manslaughter** entry.

assassination Use the term only if it involves the murder of a politically important or prominent individual by surprise attack.

assassination, date of A prominent person is shot one day and dies the next. Which day was he assassinated? The day he was attacked.

assault, battery *Assault* almost always implies physical contact and sudden, intense violence.

Legally, however, *assault* means simply to threaten violence, as in pointing a pistol at an individual without firing it. *Assault and battery* is the legal term when the victim was touched by the assaulter or something the assaulter put in motion.

assembly Capitalize when part of the proper name for the lower house of a legislature: *the California Assembly.* Retain capitalization if the state name is dropped but the reference is specific:

SACRAMENTO, Calif. (AP) — The state Assembly ...

If a legislature is known as a general assembly: *the Missouri General Assembly, the General*

Assembly, the assembly. Legislature also may be used as the proper name, however. See **legislature**.

Lowercase all plural uses: *the California and New York assemblies.*

assemblyman, assemblywoman Do not abbreviate. See **legislative titles**.

assets Everything a company or an individual owns or is owed.

Assets may be broken down as:

Current assets: cash, investments, money due to a corporation, unused raw materials and inventories of finished but unsold products.

Fixed assets: buildings, machinery and land.

Intangible assets: patents and goodwill.

See **goodwill**.

asset-backed security A financial security backed by loans, leases, credit-card debt, royalties, a company's accounts receivables, etc. *ABS* should not be used in copy.

asset, fixed Plant, land, equipment, long-term investments that cannot be readily liquefied without disturbing the operation of the business.

assistant Do not abbreviate. Capitalize only when part of a formal title before a name: *Assistant Secretary of State Richard Boucher.* Whenever practical, however, an appositional construction should be used: *Richard Boucher, assistant secretary of state.*

See **titles**.

associate Never abbreviate. Apply the same capitalization norms listed under **assistant**.

Associated Press, The The newsgathering cooperative dating from 1846.

Use *The Associated Press* on first reference (the capitalized article is part of the formal name).

On second reference, *AP* or *the AP* (no capital on *the*) may be used.

Do not refer to APTN and AP Radio, units of the AP, as if they were separate entities. Say *Alexander Barbosa told the AP [not APTN] in Rio de Janeiro; AP [not APTN] video journalist John Smith contributed to this report.*

The address is 200 Liberty St., New York, NY 10281. The telephone number is 212-621-1500.

Online: http://www.ap.org

See **AP**.

Association Do not abbreviate. Capitalize as part of a proper name: *American Medical Association.*

assure See **ensure, insure, assure**.

asterisk Do not use the symbol. It rarely translates and in many cases cannot be seen by AP computers or received by newspaper or other computers.

astronaut It is not a formal title. Do not capitalize when used before a name: *astronaut John Glenn.*

AT&T Inc. The full name of the business formerly known as American Telephone & Telegraph Co. Headquarters is in Dallas.

atheist See **agnostic, atheist**.

athlete's foot

Atlanta The city in Georgia stands alone in datelines.

Atlantic Ocean

a

Atlantic Standard Time, Atlantic Daylight Time Used in the Maritime Provinces of Canada and in Puerto Rico.

See **time zones**.

at large Usually two words for an individual representing more than a single district: *councilman at large.*

But it is *ambassador-at-large* for an ambassador assigned to no particular country.

ATM Acceptable in all references for *automated teller machine.*

Do not use the redundant *ATM machine.*

attache It is not a formal title. Always lowercase.

attorney general, attorneys general Never abbreviate. Capitalize only when used as a title before a name: *Attorney General Jeff Sessions.*

See **titles**.

attorney, lawyer In common usage the words are interchangeable.

Technically, however, an *attorney* is someone (usually, but not necessarily, a lawyer) empowered to act for another. Such an individual occasionally is called an *attorney in fact.*

A *lawyer* is a person admitted to practice in a court system. Such an individual occasionally is called an *attorney at law.*

Do not abbreviate. Do not capitalize unless it is an officeholder's title: *defense attorney Perry Mason, attorney Perry Mason, District Attorney Hamilton Burger.*

Power of attorney is a written

statement legally authorizing a person to act for another.

See **lawyer**.

attribution AP news reports must attribute facts not gathered or confirmed on our own, whether the pickup is from a newspaper, website, broadcaster or blog, U.S. or international, AP member or subscriber. AP reports must also credit other organizations when they break a story and AP matches or further develops it. News from a government, agency, organization, company or other recognized group may be attributed to that entity on first reference in the story: *the White House announced.* In a follow-up attribution, specify whether the information came from a spokesman or other named official or in a news release.

augur A transitive verb. Do not follow it with the preposition *for.* Correct: *The tea leaves augur a time of success.*

"Auld Lang Syne" Sung to greet the New Year, poem by Robert Burns set to Scottish music.

autism spectrum disorder An umbrella term for a group of developmental disorders that can involve varying degrees of language and social impairments, and repetitive behaviors. It encompasses mild autism and the more classic form. Acceptable to use the term *autism* in stories. See **Asperger's syndrome**.

author A noun. Do not use it as a verb.

automaker, automakers

automatic See **pistol** and **weapons**.

autonomous vehicles Describes cars or trucks that can monitor the road and drive for an entire trip without the intervention of a human. Also can be called *self-driving.* The term *driverless* should not be used unless there is no human backup driver. In cases where vehicles can perform some driving functions themselves but require human intervention for other tasks, such as changing lanes or driving at low speeds, use *semi-autonomous* or *partially self-driving.* As of mid-2018 there were no *autonomous vehicles* for sale to the public, but many with *semi-autonomous capabilities.*

Autopilot The trade name for the *semi-autonomous driving system* offered in Tesla Inc.'s vehicles. *Autopilot* can maintain a set speed, brake automatically, change lanes and keep a vehicle within its lane. A driver's hands need to touch the wheel at certain intervals or the system will turn off. Some other automakers offer similar systems under different trade names, such as Mercedes-Benz's *Drive Pilot.* *Autopilot, Drive Pilot* and other trade names should be capitalized; the generic use of *autopilot* is lowercase. *Tesla is gathering data when owners engage the Autopilot feature. In today's airliners, the autopilot is on nearly the entire time the plane is in the air.*

Auto Train Rail service that carries passengers and their cars. Owned and operated by Amtrak.

autoworker, autoworkers One word when used generically.

But *United Auto Workers* when referring to the union.

autumn See **seasons**.

avatar A version of yourself that you put forward in an online or video game setting. Sometimes bears a strong resemblance to the user; at other times, it is used to highlight a company or organization's brand, make a political statement or act out fantasies of a wished-for identity.

avenue Abbreviate only with a numbered address. See **addresses**.

average, mean, median, norm
Average refers to the result obtained by dividing a sum by the number of quantities added together: *The average of 7, 9, 17 is 33 divided by 3, or 11.*

Mean, in its sense used in arithmetic and statistics, is an *average* and is determined by adding the series of numbers and dividing the sum by the number of cases: *The mean temperature of five days with temperatures of 67, 62, 68, 69, 64 is 66.*

Median is the middle number of points in a series arranged in order of size: *The median grade in the group of 50, 55, 85, 88, 92 is 85. The average is 74.*

Norm implies a standard of average performance for a given group: *The child was below the norm for his age in reading comprehension.*

average of The phrase takes a plural verb in a construction such as: *An average of 100 new jobs are created daily.*

averse See **adverse, averse**.

Avianca Headquarters of this airline is in Bogota, Colombia.

awards and decorations Capitalize them: *Bronze Star, Medal of Honor,* etc.

See **Nobel Prize** and **Pulitzer Prizes**.

awhile (adv.) **a while** *He plans to stay awhile* (adv.). *He plans to stay for a while* (n.).

AWOL Acceptable in all references for *absent without leave.*

ax Not *axe.*
The verb forms: *ax, axed, axing.*

Axis The alliance of Germany, Italy and Japan during World War II.

Aymara An ethnic group around Lake Titicaca, in Bolivia and Peru, or the language of these people.

a

b

baby boom, baby boomer Reference to those born between 1946 and 1964, a span defined by the U.S. Census Bureau. Hyphenated as an adjective: *baby-boom generation*. See **Generation X, millennials**.

baby bump The rounded abdominal area of a pregnant woman. Avoid using.

baby-sit, baby-sitting, baby-sat, baby sitter

baccalaureate

Bachelor of Arts, Bachelor of Science *A bachelor's degree* or *bachelor's* is acceptable in any reference.

See **academic degrees** for guidelines on when the abbreviations *B.A.* or *B.S.* are acceptable.

backfire In wildfires, this term is for a fire set along the inner edge of a fire line to consume the fuel in the fire's path or change its direction.

backstage Part of the stage or theater behind the proscenium, particularly the wings and dressing rooms. Also can refer to the press area where award winners meet with the news media.

backup (n. and adj.) **back up** (v.)

backward Not backwards.

backyard One word in all uses.

bad, badly *Bad* should not be used as an adverb. It does not lose its status as an adjective, however, in a sentence such as *I feel bad*. Such a statement is the idiomatic equivalent of *I am in bad health*. An alternative, *I feel badly*, could be interpreted as meaning that your sense of touch was bad.

See **good, well**.

Baghdad The city in Iraq stands alone in datelines.

Bagram Airfield The preferred spelling for the U.S. base in Afghanistan.

Bahamas In datelines, give the name of the city or town followed by *Bahamas*:
NASSAU, Bahamas (AP) —
In stories, use *Bahamas, the Bahamas* or *the Bahama Islands* as the construction of a sentence dictates.
Identify a specific island in the text if relevant.

bail *Bail* is money or property that will be forfeited to the court if an accused individual fails to appear for trial. It may be posted as follows:
— The accused may deposit with the court the full amount or its equivalent in collateral such as a deed to property.
— A friend or relative may make such a deposit with the court.
— The accused may pay a professional bail bondsman a percentage of the total figure. The bondsman, in turn,

guarantees the court that it will receive from him the full amount in the event the individual fails to appear for trial.

It is correct in all cases to say that an accused *posted bail* or *posted a bail bond* (the money held by the court is a form of bond). When a distinction is desired, say that the individual *posted his own bail*, that *bail was posted by a friend or relative*, or that *bail was obtained through a bondsman*.

balance of payments, balance of trade The *balance of payments* is the difference between the amount of money that leaves a nation and the amount that enters it during a period of time.

The *balance of payments* is determined by computing the amount of money a nation and its citizens send abroad for all purposes — including goods and services purchased, travel, loans, foreign aid, etc. — and subtracting from it the amount that foreign nations send into the nation for similar purposes.

The *balance of trade* is the difference between the monetary value of the goods a nation imports and the goods it exports.

An example illustrating the difference between the two:

The United States and its citizens might send $10 billion abroad — $5 billion for goods, $3 billion for loans and foreign aid, $1 billion for services and $1 billion for tourism and other purposes.

Other nations might send $9 billion into the United States — $6 billion for U.S. goods, $2 billion for services and $1 billion for tourism and other purposes.

The United States would have a *balance-of-payments* deficit of $1 billion but a *balance-of-trade* surplus

of $1 billion.

balance sheet A listing of assets, liabilities and net worth showing the financial position of a company at the specific time. A bank balance sheet is generally referred to as a statement of condition.

ballclub, ballpark, ballplayer, ballroom

balloon mortgage A mortgage whose amortization schedule will not extinguish the debt by the end of the mortgage term, leaving a large payment (called balloon payment) of the remaining principal balance to be paid at that time.

baloney Foolish or exaggerated talk.
The sausage or luncheon meat is *bologna*.

Baltimore The city in Maryland stands alone in datelines.

Band-Aid A trademark for a type of adhesive bandage.

Bangkok The city in Thailand stands alone in datelines.

Bank of America Corp. Headquarters is in Charlotte, North Carolina.

bankruptcy Federal courts have exclusive jurisdiction over bankruptcy cases and each of the 94 federal judicial districts handles bankruptcy matters. The primary purposes of the federal bankruptcy laws are to give honest debtors a fresh start in life by relieving them of most debts, and to repay creditors in an orderly manner to the extent debtors have property available for payment. Bankruptcies can be voluntary or involuntary.

b

Chapter 7 of the Bankruptcy Code is available to both individual and business debtors. Its purpose is to achieve a fair distribution to creditors of the debtor's available non-exempt property. It provides a fresh financial start for individuals, although not all debt is wiped away; debts for certain taxes, fraudulently incurred credit card debt, family support obligations — including child support and alimony — and most student loans must still be repaid. The bankruptcy law that took effect in October 2005 limits Chapter 7 as an option for many Americans: Those deemed by a "means test" to have at least $100 a month left over after paying certain debts and expenses must file a five-year repayment plan under the more restrictive Chapter 13 instead. When a company files for Chapter 7, it usually leads to liquidation. But a company in Chapter 7 proceedings can continue to operate under the direction of a court trustee until the matter is settled, and if it can settle with creditors in the interim, it may not have to be liquidated.

Chapter 11 of the Bankruptcy Code is available for both business and consumer debtors. Its purpose is to rehabilitate a business as a going concern or reorganize an individual's finances through a court-approved reorganization plan. When referring to such a filing, say the company is seeking Chapter 11 protection. This action frees a company from the threat of creditors' lawsuits while it reorganizes its finances. The debtor's reorganization plan must be accepted by a majority of its creditors. Unless the court rules otherwise, the debtor remains in control of the business and its assets.

Chapter 12 of the Bankruptcy Code is designed to give special debt relief to a family farmer with regular income from farming.

Chapter 13 of the Bankruptcy Code is likely to be required for an increasing percentage of individuals seeking to wipe the slate clean. Those deemed by a "means test" to have at least $100 a month left over after paying certain debts and expenses will have to file a five-year repayment plan under Chapter 13 allowing unsecured creditors to recover part or all of what they are owed.

Chapter 15 was added to the Bankruptcy Code in 2005 and covers U.S. filings that are secondary to bankruptcy cases filed overseas. Courts can authorize trustees to act in a foreign country on behalf of a bankruptcy estate in a Chapter 15 proceeding. It represents the U.S. adoption of a model law on cross-border bankruptcy developed by the United Nations.

barbiturate

barrel A standard barrel in U.S. measure contains 31.5 gallons.

A standard barrel in British and Canadian measure contains 36 imperial gallons.

In international dealings with crude oil, a standard barrel contains 42 U.S. gallons or 35 imperial gallons.

See the **oil** entry for guidelines on computing the volume and weight of petroleum products.

barrel, barreled, barreling

barrister See **lawyer**.

barroom

BASE jumping Acceptable on first reference for the extreme sport, but explain later in the story. *BASE* is an acronym for *building, antenna, span* (such as a bridge) and *earth* (such as a cliff).

basis point One one-hundredth of one percentage point. Changes in interest rates are measured in basis points. If the Federal Reserve's target rate was 2 percent and it was cut by 50 basis points, the new rate would be 1.5 percent.

battalion Capitalize when used with a figure to form a name: *the 3rd Battalion, the 10th Battalion.*

battlefield Also: *battlefront, battleground, battleship.* But *battle station.*

battleground states States where candidates from both major political parties have a reasonable chance for victory in a statewide race or presidential vote.

bay Capitalize as an integral part of a proper name: *Hudson Bay, San Francisco Bay.*
   Capitalize also *San Francisco Bay Area* or *the Bay Area* as the popular name for the nine-county region that has San Francisco as its focal point.

B.C. Acceptable in all references to a calendar year in the period *before Christ.*
   Because the full phrase would be *in the year 43 before Christ*, the abbreviation *B.C.* is placed after the figure for the year: *43 B.C.*
   See **A.D.**

bear market A period of generally declining stock prices over a prolonged period, generally defined as a 20 percent or larger decline in broad stock indexes such as the Standard & Poor's 500.

bearer bond A bond for which the owner's name is not registered on the books of the issuing company. Interest and principal is thus payable to the bondholder.

bearer stock Stock certificates that are not registered in any name. They are negotiable without endorsement and transferable by delivery.

because, since Use *because* to denote a specific cause-effect relationship: *He went because he was told.*
   Since is acceptable in a causal sense when the first event in a sequence led logically to the second but was not its direct cause: *They went to the game, since they had been given the tickets.*

bed-and-breakfast *B&B* is acceptable on second reference.

bedbug

before Christ See **B.C.**

Beijing The city in China stands alone in datelines.

Beirut The city in Lebanon stands alone in datelines.

bellwether

benefit, benefited, benefiting

Ben-Gurion International Airport Located at Lod, Israel, about 10 miles southeast of Tel Aviv. See **airport**.

Berkshire Hathaway Inc.

b

Headquarters is in Omaha, Nebraska.

Berlin The city in Germany stands alone in datelines.

Berlin Wall

Bermuda collar, Bermuda grass, Bermuda shorts

beside, besides *Beside* means at the side of.
Besides means in addition to.

best-seller Hyphenate in all uses.

betting odds Use figures and a hyphen: *The odds were 5-4, he won despite 3-2 odds against him.* See **numerals**.

bettor A person who bets.

between See **among, between**.

bi- The rules in **prefixes** apply, but in general, no hyphen. Some examples:
bifocal   bimonthly
bilateral   bipartisan
bilingual

biannual, biennial *Biannual* means *twice a year* and is a synonym for the word *semiannual.*
Biennial means *every two years.*

Bible Capitalize, without quotation marks, when referring to the Scriptures in the Old Testament or the New Testament. Capitalize also related terms such as the *Gospels, Gospel of St. Mark, the Scriptures, the Holy Scriptures.*
Lowercase *biblical* in all uses.
Lowercase *bible* as a nonreligious term: *My dictionary is my bible.*
Do not abbreviate individual books of the Bible.
Old Testament is a Christian designation; Hebrew Bible or Jewish Bible is the appropriate term for stories dealing with Judaism alone.
The standard names and order of Old Testament books as they appear in Protestant Bibles are: Genesis, Exodus, Leviticus, Numbers, Deuteronomy, Joshua, Judges, Ruth, 1 Samuel, 2 Samuel, 1 Kings, 2 Kings, 1 Chronicles, 2 Chronicles, Ezra, Nehemiah, Esther, Job, Psalms, Proverbs, Ecclesiastes, Song of Solomon, Isaiah, Jeremiah, Lamentations, Ezekiel, Daniel, Hosea, Joel, Amos, Obadiah, Jonah, Micah, Nahum, Habakkuk, Zephaniah, Haggai, Zechariah, Malachi.
Jewish Bibles contain the same 39 books, in different order. Roman Catholic Bibles follow a different order, usually use some different names and include the seven Deuterocanonical books (called the Apocrypha by Protestants): Tobit, Judith, 1 Maccabees, 2 Maccabees, Wisdom, Sirach, Baruch.
The books of the New Testament, in order: Matthew, Mark, Luke, John, Acts, Romans, 1 Corinthians, 2 Corinthians, Galatians, Ephesians, Philippians, Colossians, 1 Thessalonians, 2 Thessalonians, 1 Timothy, 2 Timothy, Titus, Philemon, Hebrews, James, 1 Peter, 2 Peter, 1 John, 2 John, 3 John, Jude, Revelation.
Citation listing the number of chapter and verse(s) use this form: *Matthew 3:16, Luke 21:1-13, 1 Peter 2:1.*

Big Board Acceptable on second reference for the *New York Stock Exchange.*

big brother One's older brother is a *big brother. Big Brother* (capitalized) means under the watchful eye of big government, from George Orwell's "1984."

Capitalize also in reference to members of Big Brothers Big Sisters of America Inc. The organization has headquarters in Philadelphia.

Big Three automakers Do not use that term, or *Detroit Three*, for Detroit automakers General Motors, Ford and Fiat Chrysler.

billion A thousand million.
For forms, see **millions, billions**.

Bill of Rights The first 10 amendments to the Constitution.

bimonthly Means *every other month*. *Semimonthly* means *twice a month*.

Bing A web search engine owned by Microsoft Corp.

bin Laden, Osama Use *bin Laden* on all second and later references except at the start of a sentence. It is the family preference for the last name, which is an exception to the general rule on Arabic names. He founded al-Qaida and was killed by U.S. forces in Pakistan in May 2011.

bioterrorism

biracial, multiracial Acceptable, when clearly relevant, to describe people with more than one racial heritage. Usually more useful when describing large, diverse groups of people than individuals. Avoid *mixed-race*, which can carry negative connotations, unless a story subject prefers the term. Be specific if possible, and then use biracial for people of two heritages or multiracial for those of two or

more on subsequent references if needed. Examples: *She has an African-American father and a white mother* instead of *She is biracial*. But: *The study of biracial people showed a split in support along gender lines.* *Multiracial* can encompass people of any combination of races.

bird flu Preferred term for *avian influenza*, viruses that mostly infect poultry and other birds. Several types are known to infect humans and the deadliest form so far appears to be H5N1. Other strains that have infected people include H7N9, H9N2 and H6N1. The viruses mainly infect people who have direct contact with sick birds but human-to-human transmission occasionally occurs.

birthday Capitalize as part of the name for a holiday: *Washington's Birthday*. Lowercase in other uses.

bit Acceptable in all references as an abbreviation for *binary digit*. Actual data take the form of electrical impulses. These can be thought of as either on or off or 1 and 0. The pulses are bits.

bitcoin A digital currency created and exchanged independent of banks or governments. A maximum of 21 million bitcoins can be created, a limit that probably won't be reached for several more decades if the currency survives. Transactions typically are completed anonymously, making the currency popular among people who want to conceal their financial activity. The currency can be converted into cash when deposited into accounts at prices set in online trading. Lowercase in all uses except at the start of a sentence.

biweekly Means *every other week.* *Semiweekly* means *twice a week.*

bizarre Unusual. A fair is a *bazaar.*

black Acceptable for a person of the black race. *African-American* is acceptable for an American black person of African descent. (Use *Negro* only in names of organizations or in quotations.) Do not use *colored* as a synonym. See **African-American**, **nationalities and races** and **race**.

BlackBerry, BlackBerrys A brand of smartphone manufactured by BlackBerry Ltd.

blackout, brownout A *blackout* is a total power failure over a large area or the concealing of lights that might be visible to enemy raiders.

The term *rolling blackout* is used by electric companies to describe a situation in which electric power to some sections temporarily is cut off on a rotating basis to assure that voltage will meet minimum standards in other sections.

A *brownout* is a small, temporary voltage reduction, usually from 2 percent to 8 percent, implemented to conserve electric power.

blastoff (n. and adj.) **blast off** (v.)

blind See **disabled, handicapped**.

blizzard See **weather terms**.

bloc, block A *bloc* is a coalition of people, groups or nations with the same purpose or goal.

Block has more than a dozen definitions, but a political alliance is not one of them.

blog For blog names, use the name as spelled by the writer, capitalizing the first letter and other main words. Don't enclose the name in quotation marks unless it's an unusual spelling that might otherwise be unclear. An update to a blog is a *blog post* or *blog entry*.

blond, blonde Use *blond* as a noun for males and as an adjective for all applications: She has *blond* hair.

Use *blonde* as a noun for females.

blood alcohol content The concentration of alcohol in blood. It is usually measured as weight per volume. For example, 0.02 percent means 0.02 grams of alcohol per deciliter of an individual's blood. The legal limit for intoxication in most states is 0.08 percent. *The jury found he was driving with a blood alcohol level above Florida's 0.08 percent limit.*

bloodbath One word, an exception to Webster's New World College Dictionary.

Bloomberg LP A privately owned provider of financial news and information. Its Bloomberg News service provides news to newspapers and financial professionals. Bloomberg LP also owns the magazine Bloomberg Businessweek and has television and radio divisions. Headquarters is in New York.

blue chip stock Stock in a company known for its long-established record of making money and paying dividends.

Bluetooth A standard for short-range wireless transmissions, commonly used to establish connections between such devices as cellphones, headsets, car audio systems and smartwatches.

Blu-ray Disc A successor to the DVD, *Blu-ray Disc* is a standard used to deliver high-definition video and other digital content.

board Capitalize only when an integral part of a proper name. See **capitalization**.

board of aldermen See **city council**.

board of directors, board of trustees Always lowercase. See **organizations and institutions**.

board of supervisors See **city council**.

boats, ships A *boat* is a watercraft of any size but generally is used to indicate a small craft. A *ship* is a large, seagoing vessel.

The word *boat* is used, however, in some words that apply to large craft: *ferryboat, PT boat.*

Use *it*, not the pronoun *she*, in references to boats and ships.

Use Arabic or Roman numerals in the names of boats and ships: *the Queen Elizabeth 2* or *QE2; Titan I, Titan II.*

The reference for military ships is IHS Jane's Fighting Ships; for nonmilitary ships, IHS Fairplay Register of Ships.

See **numerals**.

body camera Preferred for cameras mounted on clothing, generally of law enforcers. When the condensed version appears in headlines or in quotes, it is *bodycam*, one word.

body mass index A measurement calculated from weight and height. *BMI* is acceptable on second reference. To calculate: multiply weight in pounds by 703, divide by height in inches, divide again by height in inches.

Boeing Co. Headquarters is in Chicago.

Bogota The city in Colombia carries the country name in datelines.

Boko Haram Muslim militant group in northeast Nigeria.

bona fide

bondholder

bond ratings Standard & Poor's, Moody's Investors Service and Fitch Ratings sell information — mainly to institutional investors — about what they view as the relative risk of various issues of debt. They also charge companies, municipalities and even foreign governments that wish to sell debt and have it rated. The ratings are a fundamental way for investors to form an opinion on whether they are likely to be repaid, and then decide whether the interest rate is high enough to compensate for the risk that they may get back none or only a portion of their investment (in the case of a bankruptcy or some other adverse event). The ratings also effectively set benchmarks for how much interest companies will have to pay to sell bonds, commercial paper, preferred stock and for bank loans they obtain. The higher the grade, the lower the interest rate a borrower must pay.

Standard & Poor's bond ratings, for example, include 10 categories that are referred to as investment-grade, from AAA to BBB-, given to borrowers with the strongest ability to repay. Another six categories, from BB+ to CCC-, are assigned to more speculative securities that are commonly referred to as *junk* or *high-yield debt*. The lowest category, D, is for securities that are in payment default.

A reduction in the rating of a company's debt to non-investment-grade can force some mutual funds and pension funds to sell those bonds because they are prohibited from holding junk debt.

book titles See **composition titles**.

book value The difference between a company's assets and liabilities.

The *book value per share* of common stock is the *book value* divided by the number of common shares outstanding.

Bosnia-Herzegovina The country has been divided into a Bosnian Serb republic and a Muslim-Croat federation since 1995. Both have wide autonomy but share a common presidency, parliament and government. In datelines: *SARAJEVO, Bosnia-Herzegovina*. The people are *Bosnians*.

Bosporus, the Not the Bosporus Strait.

Boston The capital of Massachusetts stands alone in datelines.

Boston terrier

boulevard Abbreviated only with a numbered address: *43 Park Blvd*. See **addresses**.

bowlegged

Boxing Day Post-Christmas holiday

Dec. 26 in British Commonwealth countries. Term came from practice of giving gift boxes to employees and others.

box office (n.) **box-office** (adj.)

boy, girl Generally acceptable to describe males or females younger than 18. While it is always inaccurate to call people under 18 *men* or *women* and people 18 and older *boys* or *girls*, be aware of nuances and unintentional implications. Referring to black males of any age and in any context as *boys*, for instance, can be perceived as demeaning and call to mind historical language used by some to address black men. Be specific about ages if possible, or refer to *black youths*, *child*, *teen* or similar.

boycott, embargo A *boycott* is an organized refusal to buy a particular product or service, or to deal with a particular merchant or group of merchants.

An *embargo* is a legal restriction against trade. It usually prohibits goods from entering or leaving a country. The plural is *embargoes*.

boyfriend, girlfriend

Boy Scouts The full name of the national organization is *Boy Scouts of America*. Headquarters is in Irving, Texas.

Cub Scouting is for boys 7 through 10. Members are *Cub Scouts* or *Cubs*.

Boy Scouting is for boys 11 through 17. Members are *Boy Scouts* or *Scouts*. As a rank or formal leadership title, capped before a full name: *Troop 6 Scoutmaster John Smith*. In other uses, lowercase: *John Smith, scoutmaster of Troop 1*.

Exploring is a separate program

open to boys and girls from high school age through 20. Members are *Explorers*, not *Explorer Scouts*. Members of units that stress nautical programs are *Sea Explorers*.

Venturing, originally part of the *Exploring* division, is for young adults, 14 through 20.

See **Girl Scouts**.

BP PLC Formerly British Petroleum. *BP* is acceptable in all references. Headquarters is in London.

brackets See entry in **Punctuation** chapter.

Brahman, Brahmin *Brahman* applies to the priestly Hindu caste and a breed of cattle.

Brahmin applies to aristocracy in general: *Boston Brahmin*.

See **Hindu, Hinduism** in **Religion** chapter.

brain-dead (adj.) **brain death** Complete absence of brain function based on a series of tests. Used as a legal definition of death. In the U.S., most organ transplants are done after the donor has been declared brain-dead. See **clinically dead, clinical death**.

brand names When they are used, capitalize them.

Brand names normally should be used only if they are essential to a story.

Sometimes, however, the use of a brand name may not be essential but is acceptable because it lends an air of reality to a story: *He fished a Camel from his shirt pocket* may be preferable to the less specific *cigarette*.

When a company sponsors a sports or other event identified only by the company's name,

use the name on first reference: Example: *Buick Open*.

However, when an event is clearly identifiable without the company's name, drop the name on first reference and include the sponsor name elsewhere in the story or at the bottom as an Editor's Note. Example: *FedEx Orange Bowl* would be identified in the story only as *Orange Bowl*.

Also use a separate paragraph to provide the name of a sponsor when the brand name is not part of the formal title.

See **trademark** entry.

brand-new (adj.)

Braunschweig The spelling of the German city. Not *Brunswick*.

break-in (n. and adj.) **break in** (v.)

breakup (n. and adj.) **break up** (v.)

breastfeed, breastfeeding, breastfed

Breathalyzer Trademarked name for a device to test blood-alcohol level.

Brexit Shorthand for *"British exit"* — the United Kingdom's vote in a June 23, 2016, referendum to leave the European Union. No quotation marks. Explain what it means when you use it.

bride, bridegroom, bridesmaid *Bride* is appropriate in wedding stories, but use *wife* or *spouse* in other circumstances.

brigadier See **military titles**.

Britain Acceptable in all references for *Great Britain*, which consists of England, Scotland and Wales.

See **United Kingdom**.

b

British Airways PLC Headquarters of this airline is in Hounslow, England. Owned by Consolidated Airlines Group S.A.

British, Briton(s) The people of Great Britain: the English, the Scottish, the Welsh. *Brits* is slang.

British Broadcasting Corp. *BBC* is acceptable in all references.

British Columbia The Canadian province bounded on the west by the Pacific Ocean. Do not abbreviate. See **datelines**.

British Commonwealth See **Commonwealth, the**.

British thermal unit The amount of heat required to increase the temperature of a pound of water 1 degree Fahrenheit. *Btu* (the same for singular and plural) is acceptable on second reference.

British ton See **ton**.

British Virgin Islands Use with a community name in datelines on stories from these islands. Do not abbreviate.
 Specify an individual island in the text if relevant.
 See **datelines**.

broadcast The past tense also is *broadcast*, not *broadcasted*.

Broadway, off-Broadway, off-off-Broadway When applied to stage productions, these terms refer to distinctions made by union contracts, not to location of a theater.
 Actors' Equity Association and

unions representing craft workers have one set of pay scales for *Broadway* productions (generally those in New York City theaters of 500 or more seats) and a lower scale for smaller theaters, classified as *off-Broadway* houses.
 The term *off-off-Broadway* refers to workshop productions that may use Equity members for a limited time at substandard pay. Other unions maintain a hands-off policy, agreeing with the Equity attitude that actors should have an opportunity to develop their talents in offbeat roles without losing their Equity memberships.

Bronze Age The age characterized by the development of bronze tools and weapons, from 3500 to 1000 B.C. Regarded as coming between the Stone Age and the Iron Age.

Brothers Generally abbreviate as *Bros.* in formal company names: *Warner Bros.*, but follow the spelling preferred by the company.
 For possessives: *Warner Bros.' profits*.

brownout See **blackout, brownout**.

brunette Use *brunette* as a noun for females. Use *brown-haired* for males.

Brussels The city in Belgium stands alone in datelines.

Btu The same in singular and plural. See **British thermal unit**.

Bubble Wrap A registered trademark. Unless the trademark name is important to the story, use *cushioning* or *packaging material*.

Budapest The capital of Hungary. In datelines, follow it with *Hungary*.

Bufferin A trademark for buffered aspirin.

bug, tap A concealed listening device designed to pick up sounds in a room, an automobile, or such is a *bug*.

A *tap* is a device attached to a telephone circuit to pick up conversations on the line.

building Never abbreviate. Capitalize the proper names of buildings, including the word *building* if it is an integral part of the proper name: *the Empire State Building*.

buildup (n. and adj.) **build up** (v.)

bull's-eye

bullet See **weapons**.

bullfight, bullfighter, bullfighting

bullion Unminted precious metals of standards suitable for coining.

bullpen One word, for the place where baseball pitchers warm up, and for a pen that holds cattle.

bull market A period of generally rising stock prices over a prolonged period, generally defined as a 20 percent or larger increase in broad stock indexes such as the Standard & Poor's 500.

bureau Capitalize when part of the formal name for an organization or agency: *the Bureau of Labor Statistics*.
Lowercase when used alone or to designate a corporate subdivision: *the Washington bureau of The Associated Press*.

Bureau of Alcohol, Tobacco, Firearms and Explosives ATF is acceptable in subsequent references to this agency of the Department of Justice. (Note the *Explosives* part of the name.)

burglary, larceny, robbery, theft
Legal definitions of *burglary* vary, but in general a *burglary* involves entering a building (not necessarily by breaking in) and remaining unlawfully with the intention of committing a crime.

Larceny is the legal term for the wrongful taking of property. Its non-legal equivalents are *stealing* or *theft*.

Robbery in the legal sense involves the use of violence or threat in committing larceny. In a wider sense it means to plunder or rifle, and may thus be used even if a person was not present: *His house was robbed while he was away*.

Theft describes a larceny that did not involve threat, violence or plundering.

USAGE NOTE: You *rob* a person, bank, house, etc., but you *steal* the money or the jewels.

Burlington Northern Santa Fe LLC The freight railroad, with headquarters in Fort Worth, Texas, is now owned by Berkshire Hathaway Inc.

burn To copy data, audio or video to optical media (such as a CD, a DVD or a Blu-ray Disc) with a laser.

burqa The all-covering dress worn by some Muslim women. See also other garments such as **niqab**, **hijab**, **chador**.

bus, buses Transportation vehicles. The verb forms: *bus, bused, busing*.
In a restaurant, to clear dishes from a table: *The busboy buses tables*. See **buss, busses**.

b

bushel A unit of dry measure equal to 4 pecks or 32 dry quarts. The metric equivalent is approximately 35.2 liters.

To convert to liters, multiply by 35.2 (5 bushels x 35.2 equals 176 liters).

See **liter**.

business editor Capitalize when used as a formal title before a name. See **titles**.

business names See **company names**.

buss, busses Kisses. The verb forms: *buss, bussed, bussing.*

See **bus, buses**.

by- The rules in **prefixes** apply, but in general, no hyphen. Some examples:

byline	*byproduct*
bypass	*bystreet*

By-election is an exception. See the next entry.

by-election A special election held between regularly scheduled elections. The term most often is associated with special elections to the British House of Commons.

bylaw

bylines Our standard byline consists of *By,* followed by the name, in the byline field, and *Associated Press* as the bytitle. The bytitle can also be a special designation, like *AP Sports Writer.*

Use a byline only if the reporter was in the datelined community to gather the information reported.

Nicknames should not be used unless they specifically are requested by the writer.

In the case of a double byline, at least one of the bylined reporters must have reported in the datelined community. If the other reported from elsewhere, note that location in a tag line at the bottom of the story: *Smith reported from Washington.*

For materials or columns contributed by people like politicians or celebrities — cases in which we want to stress that the writer is not working for AP — use the bytitle *For The Associated Press.*

byte The digital basis for quantifying the amount of storage in computers and mobile devices. A byte consists of binary digits known as bits. The definitions of larger storage amounts depend on whether they are counted under binary or decimal measurements. For instance, a kilobyte translates into 1,024 bytes under the binary method, compared with 1,000 bytes in decimal terms. The disk storage on most devices is determined under the decimal system, which defines a megabyte as 1,000 kilobytes (or 1 million bytes), a gigabyte as 1,000 megabytes (or 1 billion bytes) and a terabyte as 1,000 gigabytes (or 1 trillion bytes). Abbreviate *GB* for *gigabyte*, *KB* for *kilobyte*, *MB* for *megabyte* and *TB* for *terabyte.*

C

cabinet Capitalize references to a specific body of advisers heading executive departments for a president, king, governor, etc.: *The president-elect said he has not made his Cabinet selections.*

See **department** for a listing of all the U.S. Cabinet departments.

cactus, cactuses

cadet See **military academies**.

Cairo The city in Egypt stands alone in datelines.

caliber The form: *.38-caliber pistol.* See **weapons**.

California Abbreviate *Calif.* in datelines only; spell in stories. Postal code: *CA*
See **state names**.

call letters, call sign Use all caps. Use hyphens to separate the type of station from the base call letters: *WBZ-AM, WBZ-FM, WBZ-TV.*

If a station is widely known in the market by a nickname, and we wish to use the nickname because it's more familiar or because of station preference, use the call letters as well: "The report on Fox 59 (WXIN-TV) comes six weeks after ..."

The call letters of amateur radio stations typically mix letters and figures: *K2LRX.*
See **channel**; **radio station**; and **television station**.

call-up (n. and adj.) **call up** (v.)

Cameroon See **geographic names**.

campaign manager Do not treat as a formal title. Always lowercase.
See **titles**.

Canada Montreal, Quebec City and Toronto stand alone in datelines. For all other datelines, use the city name and the name of the province or territory spelled out.

The 10 provinces of Canada are Alberta, British Columbia, Manitoba, New Brunswick, Newfoundland and Labrador (but usually known as just Newfoundland), Nova Scotia, Ontario, Prince Edward Island, Quebec and Saskatchewan.

The three territories are the Yukon, the Northwest Territories, and Nunavut (created April 1, 1999).

The provinces have substantial autonomy from the federal government.

The territories are administered by the federal government, although residents of the territories do elect their own legislators and representatives to Parliament.
See **datelines**.

Canada goose

Canadian Broadcasting Corp. *CBC* is acceptable in all references within contexts such as a television column. Otherwise, do not use *CBC* until second reference.

Canadian Press, The Canada's multimedia news agency. Its Francophone counterpart is

La Presse Canadienne. Do not abbreviate *CP*.

canal Capitalize as an integral part of a proper name: *the Suez Canal*.

Canal Zone Do not abbreviate. No longer used except when referring to the Panama Canal area during the time it was controlled by the United States, exclusively or jointly with Panama, 1904-1999.

cancel, canceled, canceling, cancellation

cannabis See **marijuana, medical marijuana**.

cannon, canon A *cannon* is a weapon; plural is *cannons*. See **weapons**.
A *canon* is a law or rule, particularly of a church, or a musical composition.

cannot

cant The distinctive stock words and phrases used by a particular sect or class.
See **dialect**.

Canuck This reference to a Canadian is sometimes considered derogatory. It should be avoided except when in quoted matter or in terms used in Canada, such as references to the hockey team, the *Vancouver Canucks*.

canvas, canvass *Canvas* is heavy cloth.
Canvass is a noun and a verb denoting a survey.

cape Capitalize as part of a proper name: *Cape Cod, Cape Hatteras*. Lowercase when standing alone. Although local practice may call for capitalizing *the Cape* when the rest of the name is clearly understood, always use the full name on first reference.

Cape Canaveral, Florida Formerly Cape Kennedy. See **John F. Kennedy Space Center**.

capital The city where a seat of government is located. Do not capitalize.
When used in a financial sense, *capital* describes money, equipment or property used in a business by a person or corporation.
See **Capitol**.

capital gain, capital loss The difference between what a *capital* asset cost and the price it brought when sold.

capitalization In general, avoid unnecessary capitals. Use a capital letter only if you can justify it by one of the principles listed here.
Many words and phrases, including special cases, are listed separately in this book. Entries that are capitalized without further comment should be capitalized in all uses.
If there is no relevant listing in this book for a particular word or phrase, consult Webster's New World College Dictionary. Use lowercase if the dictionary lists it as an acceptable form for the sense in which the word is being used.
As used in this book, *capitalize* means to use uppercase for the first letter of a word. If additional capital letters are needed, they are called for by an example or a phrase such as *use all caps*.
Some basic principles:
PROPER NOUNS: Capitalize

nouns that constitute the unique identification for a specific person, place, or thing: *John, Mary, America, Boston, England.*

Some words, such as the examples just given, are always proper nouns. Some common nouns receive proper noun status when they are used as the name of a particular entity: *General Electric, Gulf Oil.*

PROPER NAMES: Capitalize common nouns such as *party, river, street* and *west* when they are an integral part of the full name for a person, place or thing: *Democratic Party, Mississippi River, Fleet Street, West Virginia.*

Lowercase these common nouns when they stand alone in subsequent references: *the party, the river, the street.*

Lowercase the common noun elements of names in plural uses: *the Democratic and Republican parties, Main and State streets, lakes Erie and Ontario.* Exception: plurals of formal titles with full names are capitalized: *Presidents Jimmy Carter and Gerald R. Ford.*

Among entries that provide additional guidelines are:

animals
brand names
building
committee
Congress
datelines
days of the week
directions and
  regions
family names
food
geographic names
governmental
  bodies
heavenly bodies
historical periods
  and events
holidays and holy
  days
legislature
months
monuments
nationalities and
  races
nicknames
organizations and
  institutions
planets
plants
police department
religious
  references
seasons
trademarks
unions

POPULAR NAMES: Some places and events lack officially designated proper names but have popular names that are the effective equivalent: *the Combat Zone* (a section of downtown Boston), *the Main Line* (a group of Philadelphia suburbs), *the South Side* (of Chicago), *the Badlands* (of South Dakota), *the Street* (the financial community in the Wall Street area of New York).

The principle applies also to shortened versions of the proper names of one-of-a-kind events: *the Series* (for the World Series), *the Derby* (for the Kentucky Derby). This practice should not, however, be interpreted as a license to ignore the general practice of lowercasing the common noun elements of a name when they stand alone.

DERIVATIVES: Capitalize words that are derived from a proper noun and still depend on it for their meaning: *American, Christian, Christianity, English, French, Marxism, Shakespearean.*

Lowercase words that are derived from a proper noun but no longer depend on it for their meaning: *french fries, herculean, malapropism, pasteurize, quixotic, venetian blind.*

SENTENCES: Capitalize the first word in a statement that stands as a sentence. See **sentences** and **parentheses**.

In poetry, capital letters are used for the first words of some phrases that would not be capitalized in prose. See **poetry**.

COMPOSITIONS: Capitalize the principal words in the names of books, movies, plays, poems, operas, songs, radio and television programs, works of art, etc. See **composition titles**, **magazine names**

C

C

and **newspaper names**.

TITLES: Capitalize formal titles when used immediately before a name. Lowercase formal titles when used alone or in constructions that set them off from a name by commas.

Use lowercase at all times for terms that are job descriptions rather than formal titles.

See **academic titles**, **courtesy titles**, **legislative titles**, **military titles**, **nobility**, **religious titles** and **titles**.

ABBREVIATIONS: Capital letters apply in some cases. See **abbreviations and acronyms**.

Capitol Capitalize *U.S. Capitol* and *the Capitol* when referring to the building in Washington: *The meeting was held on Capitol Hill in the west wing of the Capitol.*

Follow the same practice when referring to state capitols: *The Virginia Capitol is in Richmond. Thomas Jefferson designed the Capitol of Virginia.*

See **capital**.

captain See **military titles** for military and police usage.

Lowercase and spell out in such uses as *team captain Carl Yastrzemski*.

carat, caret, karat The weight of precious stones, especially diamonds, is expressed in *carats*. A carat is equal to 200 milligrams or about 3 grains.

A *caret* is a writer's and a proofreader's mark.

The proportion of pure gold used with an alloy is expressed in *karats*.

carbine See **weapons**.

cardholder, credit card holder

cardinal numbers See **numerals**.

CARE CARE USA has its headquarters in Atlanta. CARE International is based in Geneva. They refer to themselves simply as *CARE*.

Caribbean See **Western Hemisphere**.

Carioca A term applied to the people and culture of the city of Rio de Janeiro. The term for the state of the same name is *Fluminense*.

carmaker, carmakers

Carnival Capitalize when referring specifically to the revelry in many Roman Catholic countries preceding Lent. Otherwise, a *carnival* is lowercase. See **Mardi Gras**.

car pool (n.) **carpool** (v.)

carry-on

carry-over (n. and adj.)

car wash

cash or collect on delivery The abbreviation *c.o.d.* is preferred in all references. This is an exception to Webster's New World College Dictionary.

caster, castor *Caster* is a roller.

Castor is the spelling for the oil and the bean from which it is derived.

catalog, cataloged, cataloger, cataloging, catalogist

Caterpillar A trademark for a brand of crawler tractor. The formal name of the company is *Caterpillar Inc.* Headquarters is in Peoria, Illinois.

Use lowercase for the wormlike larva of various insects.

Cathay Pacific Airways Ltd.

Headquarters of this airline is in Hong Kong.

Catholic, Catholicism
Use *Roman Catholic Church, Roman Catholic* or *Roman Catholicism* in the first references to those who believe that the pope, as bishop of Rome, has the ultimate authority in administering an earthly organization founded by Jesus Christ.

Most subsequent references may be condensed to *Catholic Church, Catholic* or *Catholicism. Roman Catholic* should continue to be used, however, if the context requires a distinction between Roman Catholics and members of other denominations who often describe themselves as Catholic. They include some high church Episcopalians (who often call themselves *Anglo-Catholics*), members of Eastern Orthodox churches, and members of some national Catholic churches that have broken with Rome. Included in this last category is the Polish National Catholic Church.

Lowercase *catholic* where used in its generic sense of general or universal, meanings derived from a similar word in Greek.

Those who use *Catholic* in a religious sense are indicating their belief that they are members of a universal church that Jesus Christ left on Earth.

See **Roman Catholic Church**.

cats See **animals**.

CAT scan See **CT scan**.

cattle See **animals**.

Caucasian

Caucasus Mountains

cave-in (n. and adj.) **cave in** (v.)

CB On first use, *citizens band radio*.

CBS The formal name is CBS Corp., which was created in December 2005 when Viacom Inc. split into two companies. Owner of *Simon & Schuster* book publishing and the *Showtime* cable network, besides TV and radio properties. Headquarters is in New York.

CD See **compact disc**.

CD-ROM Acronym for *compact disc* acting as *read-only memory*.
CD-ROM disc is redundant.

cease-fire, cease-fires (n. and adj.) The verb form is *cease fire*.

cellophane Formerly a trademark, now a generic term.

cellphone

Celsius Use this term rather than *centigrade* for the temperature scale that is part of the metric system.

The Celsius scale is named for Anders Celsius, a Swedish astronomer who designed it. In it, zero represents the freezing point of water, and 100 degrees is the boiling point at sea level.

To convert to Fahrenheit, multiply a Celsius temperature by 9, divide by 5 and add 32 (25 x 9 equals 225, divided by 5 equals 45, plus 32 equals 77 degrees Fahrenheit).

To convert a temperature difference from Celsius to Fahrenheit, multiply by 9 and divide

C

by 5. A difference of 5 degrees C is a 9-degree F difference.

When giving a Celsius temperature, use these forms: *40 degrees Celsius* or *40 C* (note the space and no period after the capital *C*) if degrees and Celsius are clear from the context.

See **Fahrenheit** and **metric system**.

cement *Cement* is the powder mixed with water and sand or gravel to make *concrete*. The proper term is *concrete* (not *cement*) *pavement*, *blocks*, *driveways*, etc.

censer, censor, censure A *censer* is a container in which incense is burned.

To *censor* is to prohibit or restrict the use of something.

To *censure* is to condemn.

census Capitalize only in specific references to the *U.S. Census Bureau*. Lowercase in other uses: *the census data was released Tuesday*.

Centers for Disease Control and Prevention
Located in Atlanta, the Centers for Disease Control and Prevention is part of the U.S. Department of Health and Human Services and works to control and prevent infectious and chronic diseases and promote good health. The agency also works with state and local health officials to provide specialized services.

On first reference, use *Centers for Disease Control and Prevention*, with a singular verb: *The Centers for Disease Control and Prevention is launching a new initiative*. Precede with *national*, *federal* or *U.S.* if needed for clarity. *CDC* is acceptable on second reference and takes a singular verb.

centi- A prefix denoting one-hundredth of a unit. Move a decimal point two places to the left in converting to the basic unit: *155.6 centimeters equals 1.556 meters*.

centigrade See **Celsius**.

centimeter One-hundredth of a meter.

There are 10 millimeters in a centimeter.

To convert to inches, multiply by 0.4 (5 centimeters x 0.4 equals 2 inches).

See **meter**; **metric system**; and **inch**.

Central America See **Western Hemisphere**.

Central Asia The region includes Kyrgyzstan, Kazakhstan, Turkmenistan, Tajikistan and Uzbekistan.

central bank A bank having responsibility for controlling a country's monetary policy.

Central Intelligence Agency *CIA* is acceptable in all references.

The formal title for the individual who heads the agency is *director of central intelligence*. On first reference: *Director Mike Pompeo of the CIA* or *CIA Director Mike Pompeo*.

Central Standard Time (CST), Central Daylight Time (CDT) See **time zones**.

cents Spell out the word *cents* and lowercase, using numerals for amounts less than a dollar: *5 cents*, *12 cents*. Use the $ sign and decimal system for larger amounts: *$1.01*, *$2.50*. See **numerals**.

century Lowercase (unless part of a proper name). Spell out numbers under 10: *the first century, the 21st century.*

CEO, CFO, COO Leading executives of a company.

CEO is acceptable in all references for *chief executive officer*, who typically has the primary decision-making authority. This role is separate from *chief financial officer* and *chief operating officer*, but an individual may hold more than one of these positions at a time.

Use *chief financial officer* on first reference and *CFO* thereafter. Typically handles major financial responsibilities, such as record-keeping and financial planning.

Use *chief operating officer* on first reference and *COO* thereafter. Often responsible for a company's day-to-day operations.

Spell out other *C-level* or *C-suite* positions, such as *chief administrative officer, chief information officer* or *chief risk officer.*

cesarean section *C-section* is acceptable on second reference.

Ceylon It is now *Sri Lanka*, which should be used in datelines and other references to the nation.

The people may be referred to as *Ceylonese* (n. or adj.) or *Sri Lankans.* The language is *Sinhalese.*

chador A cloak worn by some Muslim women, mainly in Iran, which covers the hair, neck and shoulders but not the face. See also other garments such as **burqa, hijab, niqab.**

chain saw

chairman, chairwoman Capitalize as a formal title before a name: *company Chairman Henry Ford, committee Chairwoman Margaret Chase Smith.*

Do not capitalize as a casual, temporary position: *meeting chairman Robert Jones.*

Use *chairperson, chair* or *co-chair* if preferred by an organization.

Chair is acceptable as a verb: *She chaired the meeting; he chairs the committee.*

See **titles.**

chamber of deputies See **legislative bodies.**

chancellor The translation to English for the first minister in the governments of Germany and Austria. Capitalize when used before a name.

See **premier, prime minister** and **titles.**

changeable

changeover

change-up (n. and adj.) **change up** (v.)

channel Capitalize when used with a figure; lowercase elsewhere: *She turned to Channel 3. No channel will broadcast the game.*

Also: *the English Channel*, but the channel on second reference.

chapters Capitalize *chapter* when used with a numeral in reference to a section of a book or legal code. Always use Arabic figures: *Chapter 1, Chapter 20.*

Lowercase when standing alone. See **numerals.**

character, reputation *Character* refers to moral qualities.

Reputation refers to the way a person is regarded by others.

charge off A loan that no longer is expected to be repaid and is written off as a bad debt.

C

Charleston, Charlestown, Charles Town *Charleston* is the name of the capital of West Virginia and a port city in South Carolina.
  Charlestown is a section of Boston. *Charles Town* is the name of a small city in West Virginia.

chauffeur

chauvinism, chauvinist The words mean unreasoning devotion to one's race, sex, country, etc., with contempt for other races, sexes, countries, etc.

check-in (n. and adj.) **check in** (v.) The act of sharing a location via a mobile device on a social network or app.

checkout (n. and adj.) **check out** (v.)

checkup (n.) **check up** (v.)

Chemical Mace A trademark, usually shortened to *Mace*, for a brand of tear gas that is packaged in an aerosol canister and temporarily stuns its victims.

Chennai Indian city formerly known as Madras.

Chevron Corp. Headquarters is in San Ramon, California.

Chevy Not *Chevie* or *Chevvy*. This nickname for the *Chevrolet* should be used only in automobile features or in quoted matter.

Chicago The city in Illinois stands alone in datelines.

Chicago Board of Trade Commodity trading market where contracts are traded for Treasury bonds, corn, soybeans, wheat, gold, silver, etc. Owned by CME Group Inc. See **CME Group Inc.**

Chicago Board Options Exchange Originally set up by the Chicago Board of Trade, the CBOE is the world's largest options exchange. Not part of CME Group Inc., parent company of the Chicago Board of Trade.

Chicano Sometimes used by Mexican-Americans in the Southwest. Not interchangeable with *Mexican-American*. Use only if a person's preference. See **Hispanic**, **Latino**, **nationalities and races**, and **race**.

chickenpox

chief Capitalize as a formal title before a name: *She spoke to police Chief Michael Codd. He spoke to Chief Michael Codd of the New York police.*
  Lowercase when it is not a formal title: *union chief Walter Reuther.*
  See **titles**.

chief justice Capitalize only as a formal title before a name: *Chief Justice John Roberts.* The officeholder is the chief justice of the United States, not of the Supreme Court. See **judge**.

child care Two words, no hyphen, in all cases.

children See **boy, girl**; **names**; **privacy**.

Chile The nation.

China When used alone, it refers to the nation that includes the mainland, Hong Kong and Macau. Use China in mainland datelines; Hong Kong and Macau stand alone in datelines.

Use *People's Republic of China*, *Communist China* and *mainland China* only in direct quotations or when needed to distinguish the mainland and its government from Taiwan. Use *Red China* only in direct quotes.

For datelines on stories from the island of Taiwan, use the name of a community and *Taiwan*. In the body of a story, use *Taiwan* for references to the government based on the island. Use the formal name of the government, the *Republic of China*, when required for legal precision. See **"One China" policy**.

China Eastern Airlines Corp.
Headquarters is in Shanghai.

China Southern Airlines
Headquarters is in Guangzhou, China.

Chinese names A variety of systems are used for spelling Chinese names. For personal and place names from China, use the official Chinese spelling system known as *Pinyin*: *Senior leader Deng Xiaoping, Beijing*, or *Zhejiang province*.

In personal names, Chinese generally place surnames first and then given names, *Deng Xiaoping*. Second reference should be the family name, *Deng* in this case.

Some Chinese have Westernized their names, putting their given names or the initials for them first or sometimes using both an English name and a Chinese name: *P.Y. Chen, Jack Wang, Frank Hsieh Chang-ting*. In general, follow an individual's preferred spelling.

Normally Chinese women do not take their husbands' surnames.

The Pinyin spelling system eliminates the hyphen or apostrophe previously used in many given names. Use the new spelling for *Mao Zedong* and *Zhou Enlai*, but keep the traditional American spelling for such historical figures as *Sun Yat-sen* and *Chiang Kai-shek*.

If the new Pinyin spelling of a proper noun is so radically different from the traditional American spelling that a reader might be confused, provide the Pinyin spelling followed by the traditional spelling in parentheses. For example, the city of *Fuzhou (Foochow)*. Or use a descriptive sentence: *Fuzhou, long known in the West as Foochow, is the capital of Fujian province, on China's eastern coast.*

Use the traditional American spellings for these place names: *China, Inner Mongolia, Shanghai, Tibet.*

Follow local spellings in stories dealing with Hong Kong and Taiwan.

Capitalize the animal names for years in the Chinese lunar calendar: *Year of the Sheep, Year of the Dog.*

chip In electronics, a sliver of semiconducting material (usually but not always silicon) on which an integrated circuit is fabricated. Chips perform a variety of functions, including processing information (microprocessors) and storing information (memory chips).

chipmaker (n.) **chipmaking** (adj.)

Christmas, Christmas Day Dec. 25. The federal legal holiday is observed on Friday if Dec. 25 falls on a Saturday, on Monday if it falls on a

C

Sunday.

Never abbreviate *Christmas* to *Xmas* or any other form.

Christmastime One word.

Christmas tree Lowercase *tree* and other seasonal terms with *Christmas*: *card, wreath, carol*, etc. Exception: *National Christmas Tree*.

chronic traumatic encephalopathy A degenerative brain disease that researchers have linked to concussions or repeated blows to the head. It is most closely associated with football but also has been diagnosed in some athletes from other contact sports and military combat veterans. It can be identified only posthumously through an examination of the brain. *CTE* is acceptable on second reference, and in headlines if essential.

church Capitalize as part of the formal name of a building, a congregation or a denomination; lowercase in other uses: *St. Mary's Church, the Roman Catholic Church, the Catholic and Episcopal churches, a Roman Catholic church, a church*.

Lowercase in phrases where the church is used in an institutional sense: *She believes in the separation of church and state. The pope said the church opposes abortion.*

See **religious titles** and the entry for the denomination in question in the **Religion** chapter.

CIA *CIA* is acceptable in all references.

The formal title for the individual who heads the agency is *director of central intelligence*. On first reference: *Director Richard Helms of the CIA* or *CIA Director Richard Helms*.

Cincinnati The city in Ohio stands alone in datelines.

Cisco Systems Inc. Headquarters is in San Jose, California.

cities and towns See **datelines** for guidelines on when they should be followed by a state or a country name.

Capitalize official names, including separate political entities such as *East St. Louis, Illinois*, or *West Palm Beach, Florida*.

The preferred form for the section of a city is lowercase: *the west end, northern Los Angeles*. But capitalize widely recognized names for the sections of a city: *South Side* (Chicago), *Lower East Side* (New York).

See **city**.

Citigroup Inc. *Citibank* is its banking unit. Headquarters is in New York.

citizen, resident, subject, national, native A *citizen* is a person who has acquired the full civil rights of a nation either by birth or naturalization. Cities and states in the United States do not confer citizenship. To avoid confusion, use *resident*, not *citizen*, in referring to inhabitants of states and cities.

Citizen is also acceptable for those in the United Kingdom, or other monarchies where the term *subject* is often used.

National is applied to a person residing away from the nation of which he or she is a citizen, or to a person under the protection of a specified nation.

Native is the term denoting that an individual was born in a given location.

city Capitalize *city* if part of a proper name, an integral part of an official name, or a regularly used nickname: *Kansas City, New York City, Windy City, City of Light, Fun City.*

Lowercase elsewhere: *a Texas city; the city government; the city Board of Education;* and all *city of* phrases: *the city of Boston.*

Capitalize when part of a formal title before a name: *City Manager Francis McGrath.* Lowercase when not part of the formal title: *city Health Commissioner Frank Smith.*

See **city council** and **governmental bodies**.

city commission See the next entry.

city council Capitalize when part of a proper name: *the Boston City Council.*

Retain capitalization if the reference is to a specific council but the context does not require the city name:

BOSTON (AP) — *The City Council* ...

Lowercase in other uses: *the council, the Boston and New York city councils, a city council.*

Use the proper name if the body is not known as a city council: *the Miami City Commission, the City Commission, the commission; the Louisville Board of Aldermen, the Board of Aldermen, the board.*

Use *city council* in a generic sense for plural references: *the Boston, Louisville and Miami city councils.*

city editor Capitalize as a formal title before a name. See **titles**.

city hall Capitalize with the name of a city, or without the name of a city if the reference is specific: *Boston City Hall, City Hall.*

Lowercase plural uses: *the Boston and New York city halls.*

Lowercase generic uses, including: *You can't fight city hall.*

citywide

civil cases, criminal cases A *civil case* is one in which an individual, business or agency of government seeks damages or relief from another individual, business or agency of government. Civil actions generally involve a charge that a contract has been breached or that someone has been wronged or injured.

A *criminal case* is one that the state or the federal government brings against an individual charged with committing a crime.

Civil War

claim This verb implies doubt, and its use in stories — *Smith claimed* — can imply the reporter does not believe something. Generally, *said* is a better term. *Claim* is most appropriate when an assertion is open to question and the story presents an alternative point of view: *Pro-government forces claimed they seized the town, but rebels denied it.*

cleanup (n. and adj.) **clean up** (v.)

clear-cut (adj.)

clerical titles See **religious titles**.

Cleveland The city in Ohio stands alone in datelines.

cliches, jargon It is tempting to advise writers to avoid cliches like the plague; they are the bane of our existence. Right there, you can see why they are so difficult to shun: Cliches are the junk food of the literary pantry, much loved by lazy writers. But platitudes and shopworn phrases serve as signals to the reader to move along, there's nothing to see here.

Don't push readers away, or lull them to sleep. Engage them with original, specific phrasing.

Jargon presents other issues. It has its place in specialized worlds whose inhabitants use jargon-speak as shortcuts (and sometimes, as code words for those in the know, or as tools to disguise, euphemize or editorialize). To a doctor, "symptomatology" is a patient's set of symptoms; to a businessperson, "due diligence" is putting the necessary effort into research before making a decision; to a military officer, "collateral damage" is the accidental killing of innocent people. To the rest of us, these words may be befuddling.

William Strunk Jr. and E.B. White put it simply in "The Elements of Style": "Be clear." Jargon is the opposite of clarity. Don't just repeat the words. Translate them, and push for the true meaning when necessary.

Here's what not to do:

COMMUNITIES: Pivoting from her image as cheerleader touting pricey government entitlements, Mayor Begonia Jargonne voiced profound dismay at plunging revenue enhancements as she pushed back against self-professed economists who fault her policies. In taking this proactive stance, the tree-lined community's mayor aims to reach out to disgruntled constituents who have referenced her programs as irresponsible. To be sure, these critics had sanctioned such measures before, but more recently are dwelling on the mayor's

pressure points as a big spender. For her part, Jargonne proclaims that citizens soon will witness a sea change in budgetary matters in her drive to rally past their objections. Far from working under the radar, she vowed to commission a blue-ribbon commission, a game-changer that she said that would leave no leaf unturned at the end of the day in formulating shots in the arm for at-risk populations.

GOVERNMENT: Exercising his bully pulpit, the president touted his executive orders as a dramatic, no-holds-barred way to target a laundry list of problems. But his reform proposals sparked a backlash from legislators who said the president had become the poster boy for executive overreach. The disagreement fueled a constitutional standoff on steroids that prompted both sides to take their grievances to court and poisoned the atmosphere.

In a major policy address, the president took the bull by the horns and reached out to disaffected Americans, kicking off a campaign to win over their hearts and minds with a litany of proposals to reduce red tape and cut pork-barrel spending by thinking outside the box. Casting the proposals as a no-brainer, he said his plan would drill down to put more boots on the ground in ramping up the fight against waste, fraud and abuse.

POLITICS: Taking no vote for granted, the candidate crisscrossed the country to take his campaign to key battleground states, where he issued a campaign manifesto with a 10-point funding plan that he had penned on his own. Still facing an uphill battle after failing to get much traction, he huddled with key advisers to map out a new blueprint that would take his campaign to the next level and broaden his support beyond his traditional lane with conservatives, who consider him a rock star. But the new narrative threatened to tarnish his brand as a truth-teller.

After amassing a huge campaign war chest and zigzagging across the heartland, the candidate pressed the flesh as he sprinted to the finish line. In a time-honored tradition, voters trooped to the polls in droves on what promised to be a long night. The candidate holed up in a hotel with top advisers to await the results, which were up for grabs.

BUSINESS: Buoyed by the ongoing efforts of a cutting-edge staff that doubled-down on achieving deliverables to replenish the conglomerate's coffers, CEO Notso Frank — the company's cheerleader-in-chief — downplayed wide-ranging, continuing warnings that the local economy was about to crash and burn. Joining a chorus of naysayers who have chimed in to shed a little daylight on the equities at risk, he said that after crunching the numbers and drilling down into the problem, he was hesitant to put the cart before the horse but that it appeared the company would weather the storm by the skin of its teeth and was working to avoid a worst-case scenario.

That said, Frank acknowledged that his arsenal holds no Hail Mary moves to yield dividends any time soon. Without saying the P-word by name, he termed it a wake-up call for all bucket owners to grow their bandwidth and broaden their portfolios to avoid worst-case scenarios that could be toxic for the more upscale segments.

POLICE AND COURTS: Police say an intoxicated person of interest suffered a self-inflicted gunshot to his left foot in an officer-involved shooting after being pulled over on suspicion of driving at a high rate of speed on a tree-lined street. Police Chief I.M. Kleeshay said responding officers, who were responding to the scene, said the unnamed suspect got into a physical and verbal altercation with them. A gun fired during the fracas, grazing him in the lower extremity. He was transported to a local hospital for treatment of his glancing toe blow, then remanded to be lodged in the local jail after which he may be bound over for trial. "A slay this wasn't, but we must toe the line on gun crimes," Kleeshay said.

Authorities responded to an active shooter situation after students reported seeing a juvenile male discharging a firearm in a dormitory before fleeing the scene on foot. The dorm was fully engulfed in flames and two students were observed to be deceased. A short time later, law enforcement officers spotted an individual matching the description of the suspect walking down a nearby street and he was apprehended without incident.

click-throughs A way of measuring how many people click a link online to see its destination site. Click-throughs are often used to set advertising rates.

clientele

climate change See **global warming**.

clinically dead, clinical death Avoid these terms and seek explanation if used by a medical professional. There is no standard definition, though generally means the heart

C

and breathing have stopped. It's possible in some cases to resuscitate a person, such as a victim of sudden cardiac arrest. See **brain-dead, brain death**.

Clinton, Hillary Clinton no longer routinely uses the full name Hillary Rodham Clinton.

cloak-and-dagger

Clorox A trademark for a brand of bleach.

closed shop A *closed shop* is an agreement between a union and an employer that requires workers to be members of a union before they may be employed.

A *union shop* requires workers to join a union within a specified period after they are employed.

An *agency shop* requires that the workers who do not want to join the union pay the union a fee instead of union dues.

A *guild shop*, a term often used when the union is The Newspaper Guild, is the same as a *union shop*.

See the **right-to-work** entry for an explanation of how some states prohibit contracts that require workers to join unions.

closely held corporation A corporation in which stock shares and voting control are concentrated in the hands of a small number of investors, but for which some shares are available and traded on the market.

close-up (n. and adj.)

cloture Not *closure*, for the parliamentary procedure for closing debate.

Whenever practical, use a phrase such as closing debate or ending debate instead of the technical term.

cloud Remote servers that can be accessed online for the storage of data and the use of related computing services. Popular services include Dropbox, Google Drive and Apple's iCloud.

CME Group Inc. Parent of the Chicago Board of Trade, the Chicago Mercantile Exchange, the New York Mercantile Exchange and COMEX, which operates the CME Globex electronic trading platform and live trading floors in Chicago and New York. Headquarters is in Chicago.

CNN Acceptable in all references for the *Cable News Network*. Owned by Time Warner Inc.

co- Retain the hyphen when forming nouns, adjectives and verbs that indicate occupation or status:

co-author
co-chairman
co-defendant
co-host
co-owner
co-partner
co-pilot

co-respondent (in a divorce suit)
co-signer
co-sponsor
co-star
co-worker

(Several are exceptions to Webster's New World College Dictionary in the interests of consistency.)

As part of a formal title before a name: co-President Alexa Manola, co-Executive Director Alfredo Hudson. But Smith Electric Co-Op if that is the formal name.

Use no hyphen in other combinations:

coed
coeducation

cooperate
cooperative

coequal
coexist
coexistence
coordinate
coordination
copay

Cooperate, coordinate and related words are exceptions to the rule that a hyphen is used if a prefix ends in a vowel and the word that follows begins with the same vowel.

Co. See **company, companies**.

coast Lowercase when referring to the physical shoreline: *Atlantic coast, Pacific coast, east coast.*

Capitalize when referring to regions of the United States lying along such shorelines: *the Atlantic Coast states, a Gulf Coast city, the West Coast, the East Coast.*

Do not capitalize when referring to smaller regions: *the Virginia coast.*

Capitalize *the Coast* when standing alone only if the reference is to the West Coast.

coastal waters See **weather terms**.

Coast Guard Capitalize when referring to this branch of the U.S. armed forces, a part of the Department of Homeland Security: the *U.S. Coast Guard, the Coast Guard, Coast Guard policy.* Do not use the abbreviation *USCG*, except in quotes.

Use lowercase for similar forces of other nations.

This approach has been adopted for consistency, because many foreign nations do not use *coast guard* as the proper name.

See **military academies**.

Coast Guardsman Capitalize as a proper noun when referring to an individual in a U.S. Coast Guard unit: *He is a Coast Guardsman.*

Lowercase *guardsman* when it

stands alone.

See **military titles**.

coastline

coattails

cocaine See **drugs**.

cocktail Do not use *cocktail* in any reference to a mixture of drugs used in capital punishment; *mixture* or *blend* is acceptable. Medical references such as *HIV drug cocktail* and long-standing phrases such as *Molotov cocktail* are acceptable.

c.o.d. Preferred in all references for *cash on delivery* or *collect on delivery.* This is an exception to Webster's New World College Dictionary.

Cold War Capitalize when referring specifically to the post-World War II rivalry between the United States and the former Soviet Union. Use only in the historic sense.

collateral Stock or other property that a borrower is obliged to turn over to a lender if unable to repay a loan.

See **loan terminology**.

collateralized debt obligations Debt, including bonds or mortgages, that is pooled, sliced up and resold to investors.

collectibles

collective nouns Nouns that denote a unit take singular verbs and pronouns: *class, committee, crowd, family, group, herd, jury, orchestra, team.*

Some usage examples: *The committee is meeting to set its agenda. The jury reached its verdict. A herd of cattle was sold.*

Team names and musical group names that are plural take plural verbs. *The Yankees are in first place. The Jonas Brothers are popular.*

Team or group names with no plural forms also take plural verbs: *The Miami Heat are battling for third place.* Other examples: *Orlando Magic, Oklahoma City Thunder, Utah Jazz, Alabama Crimson Tide.*

Most singular names take singular verbs, including places and university names in sports: *Coldplay is on tour. Boston is favored in the playoffs. Stanford is in the NCAA Tournament.*

Some proper names that are plural in form take a singular verb: *Brooks Brothers is holding a sale.*

PLURAL IN FORM: Some words that are plural in form become collective nouns and take singular verbs when the group or quantity is regarded as a unit.

Right: *A thousand bushels is a good yield.* (A unit.)

Right: *A thousand bushels were created.* (Individual items.)

Right: *The data is sound.* (A unit.)

Right: *The data have been carefully collected.* (Individual items.)

collectors' item

college Capitalize when part of a proper name: *Dartmouth College.*
See **organizations and institutions**.

colloquialisms The word describes the informal use of a language. It is not local or regional in nature, as dialect is.

Webster's New World College Dictionary identifies many words as colloquial with the label *Informal.*

Many colloquial words and phrases characteristic of informal writing and conversation are acceptable in some contexts but out of place in others.

Other colloquial words normally should be avoided because they are pejorative. Webster's New World College Dictionary notes, for example, that *ain't* is informal, a "dialectal or nonstandard usage," although "widely used informally by educated speakers." Many still consider it illiterate and it should not be used in news stories unless needed to illustrate nonstandard speech in writing.
See **dialect**.

colon See entry in **Punctuation** chapter.

colonel See **military titles**.

colonial Capitalize *Colonial* as a proper adjective in all references to the *Colonies*. (See the next entry.)

colonies Capitalize only for the British dependencies that declared their independence in 1776, now known as the United States.

Colorado Abbreviate *Colo.* in datelines only; spell out in stories. Postal code: *CO*
See **state names**.

colorblind

Columbus Day The federal legal holiday is the second Monday in October. Some localities mark it as Indigenous Peoples Day. See **Indigenous Peoples Day**.

coma A state of unconsciousness in which the eyes are closed and the patient can't be aroused as if simply asleep. There is no sign of a sleep-wake cycle, or of any awareness of self or environment. The patient cannot communicate or hear, and shows no emotion. Any movement is purely reflex. This is the first stage after a severe brain injury; the patient may recover partially or completely, die, or progress to a vegetative or minimally conscious state.

See **minimally conscious state** and **vegetative state**.

combat, combated, combating

combustible

Comcast Corp. Nation's largest operator of cable TV and residential internet services. Owns NBCUniversal, which includes the NBC television network and such cable channels as MSNBC, CNBC, Bravo and Syfy, the Universal Pictures movie studio and theme parks. Headquarters is in Philadelphia.

comma See entry in **Punctuation** chapter.

commander See **military titles**.

commander in chief Capitalize only if used as a formal title before a name.
See **titles**.

commercial paper Short-term loans, issued primarily by corporations, to finance their daily needs, such as making payroll. Historically, a lower cost alternative to bank loans.

commissioner Do not abbreviate. Capitalize when used as a formal title.
See **titles**.

commitment

committee Do not abbreviate. Capitalize when part of a formal name: *the House Appropriations Committee*.

Do not capitalize committee in shortened versions of long committee names: *The Senate Banking, Housing and Urban Affairs Committee*, for example, became *the Senate banking committee*.
See **subcommittee**.

commodities futures contract A contract to purchase or sell a specific amount of a given commodity at a specified future date.

commodity The products of mining or agriculture before they have undergone extensive processing.

common stock, preferred stock An ownership interest in a corporation.

If other classes of stock are outstanding, the holders of common stock are the last to receive dividends and the last to receive payments if a corporation is dissolved. The company may raise or lower common stock dividends as its earnings rise or fall.

When preferred stock is outstanding and company earnings are sufficient, a fixed dividend is paid. If a company is liquidated, holders of preferred stock receive payments up to a set amount before any money is distributed to holders of common stock.

commonwealth A group of people united by their common interests.
See **state**.

Commonwealth of Independent States Founded Dec. 8, 1991, the

58

C

organization is made up of 11 of the former republics of the USSR, or Soviet Union. Russia is the largest and richest. Three other former republics — Latvia, Lithuania and Estonia — became independent nations earlier in 1991. (The Soviet Union was formally dissolved in December 1991. Its last leader, Mikhail Gorbachev, resigned on Dec. 25, 1991.)

The republics (with adjective form in parentheses):

Armenia (Armenian); Azerbaijan (Azerbaijani); Belarus (Belarusian); Kazakhstan (Kazakh); Kyrgyzstan (Kyrgyz); Moldova (Moldovan); Russia (Russian); Tajikistan (Tajik); Turkmenistan (Turkmen); Ukraine (no *the*) (Ukrainian); Uzbekistan (Uzbek). Georgia (Georgian) quit CIS in 2008.

DATELINES: MOSCOW stands alone. Follow all other datelines with the name of the state. *ALMATY, Kazakhstan.*

Commonwealth, the Formerly the British Commonwealth. The members of this free association of sovereign states recognize the British sovereign as head of the Commonwealth. Some also recognize the sovereign as head of their state; others do not.

The members are: Antigua and Barbuda, Australia, Bahamas, Bangladesh, Barbados, Belize, Botswana, Brunei, Cameroon, Canada, Cyprus, Dominica, Fiji, Gambia, Ghana, Grenada, Guyana, India, Jamaica, Kenya, Kiribati, Lesotho, Malawi, Malaysia, Maldives, Malta, Mauritius, Mozambique, Namibia, Nauru, New Zealand, Nigeria, Pakistan (suspended after the 1999 military coup; suspension lifted 2004), Papua New Guinea,

St. Kitts and Nevis, St. Lucia, St. Vincent and the Grenadines, Samoa, Seychelles, Sierra Leone, Singapore, Solomon Islands, South Africa, Sri Lanka, Swaziland, Tanzania, Tonga, Trinidad and Tobago, Tuvalu, Uganda, United Kingdom, Vanuatu and Zambia. (Zimbabwe withdrew in 2003.)

Communications Workers of America *CWA* is acceptable on second reference.

Headquarters is in Washington.

communism, communist See **political parties and philosophies**.

commutation A legal term for a change of sentence or punishment to one that is less severe.

See **pardon, parole, probations**.

compact disc *CD* is acceptable in all references.

company, companies Use *Co.* or *Cos.* when a business uses either word at the end of its proper name: *Ford Motor Co., American Broadcasting Cos.*

If *company* or *companies* appears alone in second reference, spell the word out.

The forms for possessives: *Ford Motor Co.'s profits, American Broadcasting Cos.' profits.*

company (military) Capitalize only when part of a name: *Company B.* Do not abbreviate.

company names For a company's formal name, consult the New York Stock Exchange, Nasdaq or filings with the Securities and Exchange Commission.

Do not use a comma before *Inc.* or *Ltd.*, even if it is included in the formal name.

You must include the full company name somewhere in the story. This ensures the story will be among the search results on major websites.

The formal name need not be used on first reference — for example, *Costco* is acceptable for *Costco Wholesale Corp.* — but it should be contained in the body of any story in which the subject matter could affect a company's business. For example, include the corporate name in a story on an earnings report, or in a story on a plane crash that could affect the airline's stock price. However, the corporate name might be irrelevant in a story about a political candidate's appearance at a local retail store.

If "The" is part of the formal company name it should be included. For example: *The Walt Disney Co.*

Generally, follow the spelling preferred by the company, but capitalize the first letter of company names in all uses: e.g., *Adidas*, *Lululemon*. Exceptions include company names such as *eBay*, which have a capital letter elsewhere in the name. However, company names should always be capitalized at the beginning of a sentence. For corporate news, AP may use the legal name from the Securities and Exchange Commission filing rather than a company's preference.

Do not use all-capital-letter names unless the letters are individually pronounced: *BMW*. Others should be uppercase and lowercase. *Ikea*, not *IKEA*; *USA Today*, not *USA TODAY*.

Do not use symbols such as exclamation points, plus signs or asterisks that form contrived spellings that might distract or confuse a reader. Use *Yahoo*, not *Yahoo!*; *Toys R Us*, not *Toys "R" Us*; *E-Trade*, not *E*Trade*.

Use an ampersand only if it is part of the company's formal name, but not otherwise in place of *and*.

Use *the* lowercase unless it is part of the company's formal name.

Here are some major U.S. companies, listed alphabetically with ticker symbols and headquarters:

3M Co. (MMM) St. Paul, Minn.

Abbott Laboratories (ABT) Abbott Park, Ill.

Aetna Inc. (AET) Hartford, Conn.

Alcoa Corp. (AA) New York (One of two companies created in November 2016 when the former Alcoa Inc. was split into Alcoa Corp. and Arconic Inc.)

The Allstate Corp. (ALL) Northbrook, Ill.

Alphabet Inc. (GOOGL) Mountain View, Calif.

Altria Group Inc. (MO) Richmond, Va.

Amazon.com Inc. (AMZN) Seattle

American Express Co. (AXP) New York

American International Group Inc. (AIG) New York

Amgen Inc. (AMGN) Thousand Oaks, Calif.

Anadarko Petroleum Corp. (APC) The Woodlands, Texas

Anthem Inc. (ANTM) Indianapolis (previously WellPoint Inc.)

Apple Inc. (AAPL) Cupertino, Calif.

Arconic Inc. (ARNC) Pittsburgh (One of two companies created in November 2016 when the former Alcoa Inc. was split into Alcoa Corp. and Arconic Inc.)

AT&T Inc. (T) Dallas

Bank of America Corp. (BAC) Charlotte, N.C.

Berkshire Hathaway Inc. (BRK.B)

Omaha, Neb.
Best Buy Co. (BBY) Richfield, Minn.
Biogen Idec Inc. (BIIB) Cambridge, Mass.
Boeing Co. (BA) Chicago
Bristol-Myers Squibb Co. (BMY) New York
Carnival Corp. (CCL) Miami
Caterpillar Inc. (CAT) Peoria, Ill.
CBS Corp. (CBS) New York
Chevron Corp. (CVX) San Ramon, Calif.
Cisco Systems Inc. (CSCO) San Jose, Calif.
Citigroup Inc. (C) New York
The Coca-Cola Co. (KO) Atlanta
Colgate-Palmolive Co. (CL) New York
Comcast Corp. (CMCSA) Philadelphia
ConAgra Foods Inc. (CAG) Omaha, Neb.
ConocoPhillips (COP) Houston
Costco Wholesale Corp. (COST) Issaquah, Wash.
CVS Health Corp. (CVS) Woonsocket, R.I.
Deere & Co. (DE) Moline, Ill.
Delta Air Lines Inc. (DAL) Atlanta
DowDuPont Inc. (DWDP) Midland, Mich. (Formed by merger of Dow Chemical Co. and DuPont Co. in August 2017.)
Duke Energy Corp. (DUK) Charlotte, N.C.
eBay Inc. (EBAY) San Jose, Calif.
Eli Lilly and Co. (LLY) Indianapolis
Exelon Corp. (EXC) Chicago
Express Scripts Holding Co. (ESRX) St. Louis
Exxon Mobil Corp. (XOM) Irving, Texas
Facebook Inc. (FB) Menlo Park, Calif.
FedEx Corp. (FDX) Memphis, Tenn.

Ford Motor Co. (F) Dearborn, Mich.
The Gap Inc. (GPS) San Francisco
General Dynamics Corp. (GD) Falls Church, Va.
General Electric Co. (GE) Boston
General Mills Inc. (GIS) Minneapolis
General Motors Co. (GM) Detroit
The Goldman Sachs Group Inc. (GS) New York
Halliburton Co. (HAL) Houston
HP Inc. (HPQ) Palo Alto, Calif.
The Home Depot Inc. (HD) Atlanta
Honeywell International Inc. (HON) Morris Township, N.J.
Intel Corp. (INTC) Santa Clara, Calif.
International Business Machines Corp. (IBM) Armonk, N.Y.
J.C. Penney Co. (JCP) Plano, Texas
Johnson & Johnson (JNJ) New Brunswick, N.J.
JPMorgan Chase & Co. (JPM) New York
Kellogg Co. (K) Battle Creek, Mich.
Kimberly-Clark Corp. (KMB) Irving, Texas
The Kraft Heinz Co. (KHC) Pittsburgh
The Kroger Co. (KR) Cincinnati, Ohio
Lockheed Martin Corp. (LMT) Bethesda, Md.
Lowe's Cos. (LOW) Mooresville, N.C.
Macy's Inc. (M) corporate offices in New York and Cincinnati
Marathon Oil Corp. (MRO) Houston
Mastercard Inc. (MA) Purchase, N.Y.
McDonald's Corp. (MCD) Oak Brook, Ill.
McKesson Corp. (MCK) San

Francisco
Medtronic Inc. (MDT)
Minneapolis
Merck & Co. (MRK) Kenilworth,
N.J.
MetLife Inc. (MET) New York
Microsoft Corp. (MSFT)
Redmond, Wash.
Mondelez International Inc.
(MDLZ) Deerfield, Ill.
Monsanto Co. (MON) St. Louis
Morgan Stanley (MS) New York
News Corp. (NWSA) New York
Nike Inc. (NKE) Beaverton, Ore.
Norfolk Southern Corp. (NSC)
Norfolk, Va.
Northrop Grumman Corp. (NOC)
Falls Church, Va.
Occidental Petroleum Corp.
(OXY) Houston
Oracle Corp. (ORCL) Redwood
City, Calif.
PepsiCo Inc. (PEP) Purchase, N.Y.
Pfizer Inc. (PFE) New York
Phillips 66 (PSX) Houston
PNC Financial Services Group Inc.
(PNC) Pittsburgh
The Procter & Gamble Co. (PG)
Cincinnati
Prudential Financial Inc. (PRU)
Newark, N.J.
Qualcomm Inc. (QCOM) San
Diego
Raytheon Co. (RTN) Waltham,
Mass.
Schlumberger Ltd. (SLB) Houston
Sears Holdings Corp. (SHLD)
Hoffman Estates, Ill.
Simon Property Group Inc. (SPG)
Indianapolis
Southwest Airlines Co. (LUV)
Dallas
Sprint Corp. (S) Overland Park,
Kan.
Starbucks Corp. (SBUX) Seattle
Staples Inc. (SPLS) Framingham,
Mass.
Target Corp. (TGT) Minneapolis

Texas Instruments Inc. (TXN)
Dallas
Time Warner Inc. (TWX) New
York
Travelers Cos. (TRV) St. Paul,
Minn.
Twitter Inc. (TWTR) San
Francisco
Tyson Foods Inc. (TSN)
Springdale, Ark.
Union Pacific Corp. (UNP)
Omaha, Neb.
United Continental Holdings Inc.
(UAL) Chicago
UnitedHealth Group Inc. (UNH)
Minnetonka, Minn.
United Parcel Service Inc. (UPS)
Atlanta
United States Steel Corp. (X)
Pittsburgh
United Technologies Corp. (UTX)
Hartford, Conn.
U.S. Bancorp (USB) Minneapolis
Verizon Communications Inc.
(VZ) New York
Viacom Inc. (VIA) New York
Visa Inc. (V) Foster City, Calif.
Walgreens Boots Alliance Inc.
(WBA) Deerfield, Ill.
Walmart Inc. (WMT) Bentonville,
Ark.
The Walt Disney Co. (DIS)
Burbank, Calif.
Wells Fargo & Co. (WFC) San
Francisco
Whole Foods Market Inc. (WFM)
Austin, Texas
Xerox Corp. (XRX) Norwalk,
Conn.

Here are some major non-U.S.
companies, listed alphabetically with
headquarters:
Airbus Group, Leiden,
Netherlands
Allianz SE, Munich
America Movil SAB de CV, Mexico
City

Anheuser-Busch InBev SA, Leuven, Belgium
ArcelorMittal, Luxembourg
AstraZeneca PLC, London
Baidu Inc., Beijing
Banco Santander SA, Madrid
Bank of China Ltd., Beijing
Barclays PLC, London
Barrick Gold Corp., Toronto
Bayer AG, Leverkusen, Germany
BHP Billiton Ltd., Melbourne, Australia
BMW Group, Munich
BNP Paribas SA, Paris
BP PLC, London
Carrefour SA, Boulogne-Billancort, France
China Construction Bank Corp., Beijing
China Mobile Ltd., Hong Kong
China Petroleum & Chemical Corp. or Sinopec, Beijing
CNOOC Ltd., Beijing
Credit Suisse Group AG, Zurich
Daimler AG, Stuttgart, Germany
Deutsche Bank AG, Frankfurt, Germany
Deutsche Telekom AG, Bonn, Germany
Diageo PLC, London
Electricite de France SA, Paris
Eni SpA, Rome
E.ON SE, Dusseldorf, Germany
Fiat Automobiles SpA, Turin, Italy
Gazprom OAO, Moscow
GlaxoSmithKline PLC, London
Glencore PLC, Baar, Switzerland
H&M Hennes & Mauritz AB, Stockholm
Honda Motor Co., Tokyo
HSBC Holdings PLC, London
Industrial and Commercial Bank of China Ltd., Beijing
ING Groep NV, Amsterdam
L'Oreal SA, Paris
LVMH Moet Hennessy Louis Vuitton SA, Paris
Mitsubishi UFJ Financial Group Inc., Tokyo
Nestle SA, Vevey, Switzerland
Nintendo Co., Kyoto, Japan
Nippon Telegraph & Telephone Corp., Tokyo
Nissan Motor Co., Yokohama, Japan
Nokia Corp., Espoo, Finland
Novartis AG, Basel, Switzerland
Novo Nordisk A/S, Bagsværd, Denmark
PetroChina Co., Beijing
Petroleo Brasileiro SA, Rio de Janeiro
Ranbaxy Laboratories Ltd., Gurgaon, India
Reliance Industries Ltd., Mumbai, India
Rio Tinto PLC, London
Roche Holding AG, Basel, Switzerland
Royal Dutch Shell PLC, The Hague, Netherlands
SABMiller PLC, London
Samsung Electronics Co., Suwon, South Korea
Sanofi SA, Paris
SAP SE, Walldorf, Germany
Siemens AG, Munich
Societe Generale SA, Paris
Sony Corp., Tokyo
Tata Group, Mumbai, India
Telefonica SA, Madrid
Tesco PLC, Hertfordshire, England
Teva Pharmaceutical Industries Ltd., Petach Tikva, Israel
ThyssenKrupp AG, Essen, Germany
Total SA, Paris
Toyota Motor Corp., Toyota City, Japan
UBS AG, Zurich
Unilever NV, London and Rotterdam, Netherlands
Vale SA, Rio de Janeiro
Vivendi SA, Paris
Vodafone Group PLC, Newbury,

England
   Volkswagen AG, Wolfsburg, Germany

compared to, compared with

Use *compared to* when the intent is to assert, without the need for elaboration, that two or more items are similar: *She compared her work for women's rights to Susan B. Anthony's campaign for women's suffrage.*

Use *compared with* when juxtaposing two or more items to illustrate similarities and/or differences: *His time was 2:11:10, compared with 2:14 for his closest competitor.*

compatible

complacent, complaisant

Complacent means *self-satisfied.* Complaisant means *eager to please.*

complement, compliment

Complement is a noun and a verb denoting completeness or the process of supplementing something: *The ship has a complement of 200 sailors and 20 officers. The tie complements his suit.*

Compliment is a noun or a verb that denotes praise or the expression of courtesy: *The captain complimented the sailors. She was flattered by the compliments on her project.*

complementary, complimentary

The husband and wife have complementary careers.

They received complimentary tickets to the show.

compose, comprise, constitute

Compose means *to create or put together.* It commonly is used in both the active and passive voices: *She composed a song. The United States is composed of 50 states. The zoo is composed of many animals.*

Comprise means *to contain, to include all* or *embrace.* It is best used only in the active voice, followed by a direct object: *The United States comprises 50 states. The jury comprises five men and seven women. The zoo comprises many animals.*

Constitute, in the sense of *form* or *make up,* may be the best word if neither *compose* nor *comprise* seems to fit: *Fifty states constitute the United States. Five men and seven women constitute the jury. A collection of animals can constitute a zoo.*

Use *include* when what follows is only part of the total: *The price includes breakfast. The zoo includes lions and tigers.*

composition titles

Apply the guidelines listed here to book titles, computer and video game titles, movie titles, opera titles, play titles, poem titles, album and song titles, radio and television program titles, and the titles of lectures, speeches and works of art.

The guidelines, followed by a block of examples:

— Capitalize the principal words, including prepositions and conjunctions of four or more letters.
— Capitalize an article — *the, a, an* — or words of fewer than four letters if it is the first or last word in a title.
— Put quotation marks around the names of all such works except the Bible, the Quran and other holy books, and books that are primarily catalogs of reference material. In addition to catalogs, this category includes almanacs, directories, dictionaries, encyclopedias,

C

C

gazetteers, handbooks and similar publications. Do not use quotation marks around such software titles as WordPerfect or Windows.

— Translate a foreign title into English unless a work is generally known by its foreign name. An exception to this is reviews of musical performances. In those instances, generally refer to the work in the language it was sung in, so as to differentiate for the reader. However, musical compositions in Slavic languages are always referred to in their English translations.

EXAMPLES: "The Star-Spangled Banner," "The Rise and Fall of the Third Reich," "Gone With the Wind," "Of Mice and Men," "For Whom the Bell Tolls," "Time After Time," the NBC-TV "Today" program, the "CBS Evening News," "The Mary Tyler Moore Show," "Star Wars," "Game of Thrones." See television program names for further guidelines and examples.

REFERENCE WORKS: IHS Jane's All the World's Aircraft; Encyclopaedia Britannica; Webster's New World Dictionary of the American Language, Second Edition.

Names of most websites and apps are capitalized without quotes: Facebook, Foursquare.

EXCEPTION: "FarmVille" and similar computer game apps are in quotes.

Foreign works: Rousseau's "War," not Rousseau's "La Guerre." But: Leonardo da Vinci's "Mona Lisa." Mozart's "The Marriage of Figaro" if sung in English but "Le Nozze di Figaro" if sung in Italian. Mozart's "The Magic Flute" if sung in English but "Die Zauberfloete" if sung in German. "Die Walkuere" and "Goetterdaemmerung" from

Wagner's "Der Ring des Nibelungen" if sung in German but "The Valkyrie" and "The Twilight of the Gods" from "The Ring of the Nibelung" if sung in English. Janacek's "From the House of the Dead," not Janacek's "Z Mrtveho Domu."

— For other classical music titles, use quotation marks around the composition's nicknames but not compositions identified by its sequence.

EXAMPLES: Dvorak's "New World Symphony." Dvorak's Symphony No. 9.

compound adjectives See **hyphen** entry in **Punctuation** chapter.

comptroller, controller *Comptroller* generally is the accurate word for government financial officers.

The U.S. comptroller of the currency is an appointed official in the Treasury Department who is responsible for the chartering, supervising and liquidation of banks organized under the federal government's National Bank Act.

Controller generally is the proper word for financial officers of businesses and for other positions such as *air traffic controller*.

Capitalize *comptroller* and *controller* when used as the formal titles for financial officers. Use lowercase for *air traffic controller* and similar occupational applications of the word.

See **titles**.

concentration camps For World War II camps in countries occupied by Nazi Germany, do not use phrases like *Polish death camps* or *death camps in Poland* that confuse the location and the perpetrators. Use instead, for example, *death camps in Nazi*

Germany-occupied Poland.

conclave A private or secret meeting. In the Roman Catholic Church it describes the private meeting of cardinals to elect a pope.

concrete See **cement**.

Confederate States of America The formal name of the states that seceded during the Civil War. The shortened form *the Confederacy* is acceptable in all references.

Conference Board, The The capitalized article is part of the formal name of the business organization.

confess, confessed In some contexts the words may be erroneous.
See **admit**.

confidant, confidante (n.) A male friend to whom one confides secrets. The female spelling is *confidante*.

conglomerate A corporation that has diversified its operations, usually by acquiring enterprises in widely varied industries.

Congo Note the two countries in Africa: the Democratic Republic of Congo whose capital is Kinshasa, and the Republic of Congo whose capital is Brazzaville.
In datelines:
KINSHASA, Congo (AP) —
BRAZZAVILLE, Republic of Congo (AP) —
Use Congo when referring to the Democratic Republic of Congo. If referring to the country whose capital is Brazzaville, the full name — *Republic of Congo* — should be used.

Congress Capitalize *U.S. Congress* and *Congress* when referring to the U.S. Senate and House of Representatives. Although *Congress* sometimes is used as a substitute for the House, it properly is reserved for reference to both the Senate and House.
Capitalize *Congress* also if referring to a foreign body that uses the term, or its equivalent in a foreign language, as part of its formal name: *the Argentine Congress, the Congress.*
Lowercase when used as a synonym for *convention* or in second reference to an organization that uses the word as part of its formal name: *the Congress of Racial Equality, the congress.*

congressional Lowercase unless part of a proper name: *congressional salaries, the Congressional Quarterly, the Congressional Record.*

Congressional Directory Use this as the reference source for questions about the federal government that are not covered by this stylebook.

congressional districts Use figures and capitalize district when joined with a figure: *the 1st Congressional District, the 1st District.*
Lowercase *district* whenever it stands alone.
See **numerals**.

Congressional Record A daily publication of the proceedings of Congress including a complete stenographic report of all remarks and debates.

congressman, congresswoman Use only in reference to members of the U.S. House of Representatives.

Rep. and *U.S. Rep.* are the preferred first-reference forms when a formal title is used before the name of a U.S. House member. The words *congressman* or *congresswoman*, in lowercase, may be used in subsequent references that do not use an individual's name, just as *senator* is used in references to members of the Senate.

Congressman and *congresswoman* should appear as capitalized formal titles before a name only in direct quotation.

See **legislative titles**.

Congress of Racial Equality *CORE* is acceptable on second reference. Headquarters is in New York.

Connecticut Abbreviate *Conn.* in datelines only; spell out in stories. Postal code: *CT*

See **state names**.

connote, denote *Connote* means to suggest or imply something beyond the explicit meaning: *To some people, the word "marriage" connotes too much restriction.*

Denote means to be explicit about the meaning: *The word "demolish" denotes destruction.*

ConocoPhillips Headquarters is in Houston.

consensus

conservative See **political parties and philosophies**.

constable Capitalize when used as a formal title before a name.
See **titles**.

constitute See **compose, comprise, constitute**.

constitution Capitalize references to the U.S. Constitution, with or without the *U.S.* modifier: *The president said he supports the Constitution.*

When referring to constitutions of other nations or of states, capitalize only with the name of a nation or a state: *the French Constitution, the Massachusetts Constitution, the nation's constitution, the state constitution, the constitution.*

Lowercase in other uses: *the organization's constitution.*

Lowercase *constitutional* in all uses.

consulate A *consulate* is the residence of a consul in a foreign city. It handles the commercial affairs and personal needs of citizens of the appointing country.

Capitalize with the name of a nation; lowercase without it: *the French Consulate, the U.S. Consulate, the consulate.*

See **embassy** for the distinction between a consulate and an embassy.

consul, consul general, consuls general Capitalize when used as a formal title before a noun.
See **titles**.

consumer credit Loans extended to individuals or small businesses usually on an unsecured basis, and providing for monthly repayment. Also referred to as installment credit or personal loans.

Consumer Financial Protection Bureau Created by Congress under the 2010 financial overhaul to oversee mortgages, payday loans and other consumer borrowing. It aimed to close regulatory gaps exposed by the 2008 financial crisis. *CFPB is* acceptable on second reference.

consumer price index A measurement of changes in the retail prices of a constant marketbasket of goods and services. It is computed by comparing the cost of the marketbasket at a fixed time with its cost at subsequent or prior intervals.

It is issued monthly by the Bureau of Labor Statistics, an agency of the Labor Department. It should not be referred to as a *cost-of-living index*, because it does not include the impact of income taxes and Social Security taxes on the cost of living, nor does it reflect changes in buying patterns that result from inflation. It is, however, the basis for computing cost-of-living raises in many union contracts.

The preferred form for second reference is *the index*. Confine *CPI* to quoted material.

The *chained consumer price index* is a version of the CPI used by the government to account for substitutions consumers typically make in their purchases when prices of certain goods change. Some consider it a more accurate gauge of consumer prices than the conventional CPI. Avoid using the term *chained CPI* in stories.

Consumer Product Safety Commission *CPSC* is acceptable on second reference. Headquarters is in Bethesda, Maryland.

contemptible

continent The seven continents, in order of their land size: Asia, Africa, North America, South America, Europe, Antarctica and Australia.

Capitalize *the Continent* and *Continental* only when used as synonyms for Europe or European. Lowercase in other uses such as: *the continent of Europe, the European continent, the African and Asian continents.*

Continental Divide The ridge along the Rocky Mountains that separates rivers flowing east from those that flow west.

continental shelf, continental slope Lowercase. The *shelf* is the part of a continent that is submerged in relatively shallow sea at gradually increasing depths, generally up to about 600 feet below sea level.

The *continental slope* begins at the point where the descent to the ocean bottom becomes very steep.

continual, continuous *Continual* means a steady repetition, over and over again: *The merger has been the source of continual litigation.*

Continuous means uninterrupted, steady, unbroken: *All she saw ahead of her was a continuous stretch of desert.*

Contra, Contras Uppercase when used to describe former Nicaraguan rebel groups.

contractions Contractions reflect informal speech and writing. Webster's New World College Dictionary includes many entries for contractions: *aren't* for *are not*, for example.

Avoid excessive use of contractions. Contractions listed in the dictionary are acceptable, however, in informal contexts where they reflect the way a phrase commonly appears in speech or writing.

See **colloquialisms** and **quotations in the news**.

contrasted to, contrasted with Use *contrasted to* when the intent is to assert, without the need for elaboration, that two items have opposite characteristics: *He contrasted the appearance of the house today to its ramshackle look last year.*

Use *contrasted with* when juxtaposing two or more items to illustrate similarities and/ or differences: *He contrasted the Republican platform with the Democratic platform.*

control, controlled, controlling

controller See **comptroller, controller**.

controversial An overused word. Most issues that are described as controversial are obviously so, and the word is not necessary.

convention Capitalize as part of the name for a specific national or state political convention: *the Democratic National Convention, the Republican State Convention.*

Lowercase in other uses: *the national convention, the state convention, the convention, the annual convention of the American Medical Association.*

convertible bond See **loan terminology**.

convict (v.) Follow with preposition *of*, not *for*: *He was convicted of murder.*

cookie, cookies A file many websites place on computers to save identifying information.

cooperate, cooperative But *co-op* as a short term of *cooperative*, to distinguish it from *coop*, a cage for animals.

coordinate, coordination

cop Be careful in the use of this colloquial term for *police officer*. It may be used in lighter stories and in casual, informal descriptions, but often is a derogatory term out of place in serious police stories.

Copenhagen The city in Denmark carries the country name in datelines.

copter Acceptable shortening of *helicopter*. But use it only as a noun or adjective. It is not a verb.

copy editor Seldom a formal title. Also: *copy editing, copy edit.* See **titles**.

copyright (n., v. and adj.) *A copyright story.*

Use *copyrighted* only as the past tense of the verb: *He copyrighted the article.*

See **Copyright Infringement** in **Briefing on Media Law** section.

co-respondent In a divorce suit.

Corn Belt The region in the north-central Midwest where much corn and corn-fed livestock are raised. It extends from western Ohio to eastern Nebraska and northeastern Kansas.

Corp. See **corporation**.

corporal See **military titles**.

corporate names See **company names**.

corporation An entity that is treated as a person in the eyes of the law. It is able to own property, incur debts, sue and be sued.

Abbreviate *corporation* as *Corp.* when a company or government agency uses the word at the end of its name: *the Federal Deposit Insurance Corp.*

Spell out *corporation* when it occurs elsewhere in a name: *the Corporation for Public Broadcasting.*

Spell out and lowercase *corporation* whenever it stands alone.

The form for possessives: *Chevron Corp.'s profits.*

corps Capitalize when used with a word or a figure to form a proper name: *the Marine Corps, the Signal Corps, the 9th Corps, the Army Corps of Engineers.*

Capitalize when standing alone only if it is a shortened reference to *U.S. Marine Corps* or *Army Corps of Engineers.*

The possessive form is *corps'* for both singular and plural: *one corps' location, two corps' assignments.*

corral, corralled, corralling

correctional facility, correctional institution See **prison, jail**.

Corsica Use instead of *France* in datelines on stories from communities on this island.

Cortes The Spanish parliament. See **legislative bodies**.

cosmonaut A Russian or Soviet astronaut.

cost of living The amount of money needed to pay taxes and to buy the goods and services deemed necessary to make up a given standard of living, taking into account changes that may occur in tastes and buying patterns.

The term often is treated incorrectly as a synonym for the *U.S. Consumer Price Index*, which does not take taxes into account and measures only price changes, keeping the quantities constant over time.

Hyphenate when used as a compound modifier: *The cost of living went up, but he did not receive a cost-of-living raise.*

See **consumer price index** and **inflation**.

cost-plus

Cotton Belt The region in the South and Southwestern sections of the United States where much cotton is grown.

council, counsel A *council* is a body of people or organizations, often appointed or elected. Capitalize councilor, councilman and councilwoman when used as a formal title before a name; otherwise, lowercase.

Counsel (n. or v.) refers to guidance, sometimes legal in nature and given by a lawyer, or a person or people who provide such guidance. *He sought counsel from former bosses as he considered the job offer. Her counsel advised her not to answer questions. The attorney counseled her client.*

Counselor is often synonymous with *lawyer,* shortened from *counselor at law. The lawyer greeted his fellow counselors before the trial began.* It also is a person who gives advice, such as a school guidance counselor or an investment counselor.

A *special counsel* is an official, often appointed, who fulfills a temporary legal duty. *The Justice Department appointed a special counsel to lead the federal investigation.*

Lowercase counsel and special counsel whether before or after a name.

See **council, councilor, councilman, councilwoman** and **lawyer**.

council, councilor, councilman, councilwoman A deliberative body and those who are members of it. Capitalize councilor, councilman and councilwoman when used as a formal title before a name; otherwise, lowercase. See **council, counsel** and **legislative titles**.

Council of Economic Advisers
A group of advisers who help the U.S. president prepare his annual economic report to Congress and recommend economic measures to him throughout the year.

counter- The rules in **prefixes** apply, but in general, no hyphen. Some examples:

counteract	*counterproposal*
countercharge	*counterspy*
counterfoil	

countryside

county Capitalize when an integral part of a proper name: *Dade County, Nassau County, Suffolk County.*

Capitalize the full names of county governmental units: *the Dade County Commission, the Orange County Department of Social Services, the Suffolk County Legislature.*

Retain capitalization for the name of a county body if the proper noun is not needed in the context; lowercase the word *county* if it is used to distinguish an agency from state or federal counterparts: *the Board of Supervisors, the county Board of Supervisors; the Department of*

Social Services, the county Department of Social Services. Lowercase *the board, the department,* etc. whenever they stand alone.

Capitalize *county* if it is an integral part of a specific body's name even without the proper noun: *the County Commission, the County Legislature.* Lowercase *the commission, the legislature,* etc. when not preceded by the word *county.*

Capitalize as part of a formal title before a name: *County Manager John Smith.* Lowercase when it is not part of the formal title: *county Health Commissioner Frank Jones.*

Avoid *county of* phrases where possible, but when necessary, always lowercase: *the county of Westchester.*

Lowercase plural combinations: *Westchester and Rockland counties.*

Apply the same rules to similar terms such as *parish.*

See **governmental bodies**.

county court In some states, it is not a court but the administrative body of a county. In most cases, the *court* is presided over by a *county judge,* who is not a judge in the traditional sense but the chief administrative officer of the county.

The terms should be explained if they are not clear in the context.

Capitalize all references to a specific *county court,* and capitalize *county judge* when used as a formal title before a name. Do not use *judge* alone before a name except in direct quotations.

EXAMPLES:

SEVIERVILLE, Tenn. (AP) — A reluctant County Court approved a school budget today that calls for a 10 percent tax increase for property owners.

The county had been given an ultimatum by the state: Approve the budget or shut down the schools.

The chief administrative officer, County Judge Ray Reagan, said ...

coup d'etat The word *coup* usually is sufficient.

couple When used in the sense of two people, the word takes plural verbs and pronouns: *The couple were married Saturday and left Sunday on their honeymoon. They will return in two weeks.*

In the sense of a single unit, use a singular verb: *Each couple was asked to give $10.*

couple of The *of* is necessary. Never use *a couple tomatoes* or a similar phrase.

The phrase takes a plural verb in constructions such as: *A couple of tomatoes were stolen.*

coupon See **loan terminology** for its meaning in a financial sense.

course numbers Use Arabic numerals and capitalize the subject when used with a numeral: *History 6, Philosophy 209.* Otherwise, lowercase: *calculus, world history.*

court decisions Use figures and a hyphen: *The Supreme Court ruled 5-4, a 5-4 decision.* The word *to* is not needed, but use hyphens if it appears in quoted matter: *The court ruled 5-to-4, the 5-to-4 decision.*

court districts See **court names**.

courtesy titles In general, do not use courtesy titles except in direct quotations. When it is necessary to distinguish between two people who use the same last name, as in married couples or brothers and sisters, use the first and last name.

courthouse Capitalize with the name of a jurisdiction: *the Cook County Courthouse, the U.S. Courthouse.* Lowercase in other uses: *the county courthouse, the courthouse, the federal courthouse.*

Court House (two words) is used in the proper names of some communities: *Appomattox Court House, Virginia.*

court-martial, court-martialed, courts-martial

court names Capitalize the full proper names of courts at all levels.

Retain capitalization if *U.S.* or a state name is dropped: *the U.S. Supreme Court, the Supreme Court, the state Superior Court, the Superior Court, Superior Court.*

For courts identified by a numeral: *2nd District Court, 8th U.S. Circuit Court of Appeals.*

For additional details on federal courts, see **judicial branch** and separate listings under **U.S.** and the court name.

See **judge** for guidelines on titles before the names of judges.

Court of St. James's Note the *'s.* The formal name for the royal court of the British sovereign. Derived from St. James's Palace, the former scene of royal receptions.

courtroom

cover-up (n. and adj.) **cover up** (v.)

coworking (n., adj.) Sharing workspace and amenities, such as Wi-Fi, a printer, fax machine and the like, when people don't actually work for the same company but instead are self-employed or remote workers. No hyphen for this use. But:

co-worker for a colleague within the same company.

Cox Enterprises Inc. Privately held internet and cable TV provider with headquarters in Atlanta. It also owns newspapers, TV and radio stations and Valpak, the direct-marketing service.

CPR Acceptable in all references for *cardiopulmonary resuscitation.*

crackup (n. and adj.) **crack up** (v.)

credit default swaps A form of insurance that promises payment to investors in mortgage securities and other bonds if borrowers default.

Creutzfeldt-Jakob disease A rare degenerative brain disorder. Another form, *variant Creutzfeldt-Jakob disease*, is related to mad cow disease. The word *"variant"* is needed to distinguish it from the classic *Creutzfeldt-Jakob disease*, which is not related to mad cow disease. See **mad cow disease**.

Crimea A Black Sea peninsula seized from Ukraine by Russia and annexed in March 2014. The international community has refused to recognize the Russian annexation, while tacitly acknowledging that Ukraine has lost control over Crimea for the foreseeable future. The capital is Simferopol. In stories, the dateline should be Crimea, without reference to Ukraine or Russia: *SIMFEROPOL, Crimea.*

criminal cases See **civil cases, criminal cases** and **privacy**.

cripple See **disabled, handicapped**.

crisis, crises

crisscross

criterion, criteria

cross-dresser Use this term instead of *transvestite* for someone who wears clothing associated with a different gender, and only when the subject identifies as such. Not synonymous with *drag performer* or *transgender*. See **drag performer, gender**.

cross-examination (n.) **cross-examine** (v.)

crossfire

crossover (n. and adj.)

cross rate The rate of exchange between two currencies calculated by referring to the rates between each and a third currency.

cross section (n.) **cross-section** (v.)

crosstown

crowdfunding A financing method in which money is raised through soliciting relatively small individual contributions from a large number of people, often via a website.

crowdsourcing The practice of asking people online to help gather information, produce ideas or conduct other tasks.

CSX Corp. Freight railroad, with headquarters in Jacksonville, Florida.

CT scan *Computerized tomography*, a method of making multiple X-ray images of the body or parts of the body and using a computer to construct, from those images, cross-sectional views. (Formerly known as *CAT scan*.)

Cub Scouts See **Boy Scouts**.

cup Equal to 8 fluid ounces. The approximate metric equivalents are 240 milliliters or 0.24 of a liter.

To convert to liters, multiply by 0.24 (14 cups x 0.24 = 3.36 liters, or 3,360 milliliters).

See **liter**.

curate In the context of online publishing, to find, select, package and present hand-picked content to the public.

cure-all

currency conversions Currency conversions are necessary in stories that use foreign currency to make clear for readers how a number translates into dollars. But conversions should be used sparingly and preferably not in the lead unless it's a significant part of a story. A conversion is generally needed only the first time a currency is mentioned. The reader can make the necessary conversions after that.

Do not convert amounts that are not current because exchange rates change over time.

If necessary for clarity in the story, specify that the conversion is at current exchange rates.

EXAMPLES:

AMSTERDAM (AP) — Anheuser-Busch InBev, the world's largest brewer, says its third-quarter profits rose as the takeover of new brands and higher selling prices offset the impact of lower sales volumes.

The company, based in Leuven, *Belgium, said Thursday that net profit was up 31 percent to $2.37 billion (1.73 billion euros), from $1.81 billion in the same period a year earlier.*

The gain largely reflects the company's $20 billion purchase in June of the 50 percent of Mexico's Grupo Modelo it didn't already own.

PARIS (AP) — French cosmetics giant L'Oreal says sales of its Maybelline makeup, Garnier shampoo and other beauty aids helped lift earnings to a new record in 2013.

The company behind Lancome cosmetics and the Body Shop retail chain reported net profit of 2.96 billion euros ($4 billion) last year, up 3.2 percent from 2.87 billion in 2012.

For all other currencies, following the amount, spell out the name of the currency followed in parentheses by the equivalent in U.S. dollars. *Japan approved a 1.8 trillion yen ($18 billion) extra budget to partially finance an economic stimulus package.*

When dealing with a dollar currency of a country other than the United States, use the following abbreviations before the amount on second and subsequent references:

AU$ Australian dollars
CA$ Canadian dollars
SG$ Singapore dollars
NZ$ New Zealand dollars
HK$ Hong Kong dollars
NT$ New Taiwan dollars
ZW$ Zimbabwe dollars

Treasurer Wayne Swan approved a 16 billion Australian dollar ($10.74 billion) deal. Swan said AU$8 billion would be reserved for capital expenditure.

currency depreciation, currency devaluation A nation's money *depreciates* when its value falls in relation to the currency of other nations or in relation to its own prior value.

A nation's money is *devalued* when its value is reduced in relation to the currency of other nations, either deliberately by the government or through market forces.

When a nation devalues its currency, the goods it imports tend to become more expensive. Its exports tend to become less expensive in other nations and thus more competitive.

See **devaluations**.

curtain raiser

Customs See **immigration**.

cutback (n. and adj.) **cut back** (v.)

cutoff (n. and adj.) **cut off** (v.)

The CW U.S. television network jointly owned by CBS Corp. and Time Warner Inc.'s Warner Bros. division. Formed through merger of the WB and UPN networks.

cyberattack A computer operation carried out over a device or network that causes physical damage or significant and wide-ranging disruption.

The term is routinely overused.

A computer intrusion that causes damage — i.e., to machinery at a steel mill — or injury or death is unquestionably a *cyberattack*.

Low-tech trickery aimed at robbing people of their passwords by using spam emails or social engineering is not a *cyberattack*. Avoid using the terms *cyberattack* or *attack* in cases where data has merely been stolen or leaked unless the consequences are catastrophic. Also avoid using where the damage is limited (as in the case when a

single device is affected); virtual (as in the case when only data is destroyed); or short-term (as in the case when a network is temporarily rendered inoperable through denial of service.)

If authorities or others term something a *cyberattack*, push for details and be specific in describing what happened or what is alleged. If it doesn't rise to the level of a cyberattack, avoid using the term, even in direct quotations, unless the quote is essential. Avoid putting a number to cyberattacks unless someone can explain in detail how such a figure was derived. Cyberattacks can be counted in so many different ways that figures are only rarely meaningful.

For help in determining whether to call something a *cyberattack*, consider an action's equivalent in the physical world.
— Defacing of a company's website: The physical world equivalent would be someone spraying graffiti or leaving a taunting message on the headquarters building. Typical language would be *vandalize* or *deface*, not *attack*.
— Electronic theft of government data or an official's email: The physical equivalent might be someone stealing sensitive records from filing cabinets. Typical language would be *theft* or *break-in*, but not *attack*.
— A factory's controls are remotely compromised and rogue commands cause an explosion: The physical equivalent here might involve placing a bomb somewhere. Whether electronic or physical, such acts could properly be termed an *attack*.
— A huge amount of data is stolen — data of such sensitivity that

its theft or release causes panic or dramatic financial losses. This might happen for example with the sudden publication of millions of medical records or credit card numbers: Imagine simultaneous break-ins at scores of hospitals or repeated bank robberies across the country. At a catastrophic scale, thefts or leaks can be described as *cyberattacks*. Other examples of wording:

A *denial of service* can range in severity from a nuisance to a major attack. If disruption is minimal, use wording such as *the website was hit by a denial of service* and explain what that means. However, a *denial of service* that blocks millions of customers and businesses from making payments or receiving money for an extended length of time might be described as a cyberattack.

Someone who breaks into a network and copies data is *breaching a network, committing cyberespionage* or *engaged in electronic theft*.

Someone who remotely wipes a smartphone or trashes a company's webpage is an *online vandal* or *a cybercriminal*. But someone who wipes thousands of computers at critical infrastructure provider could be described as a *cyberattacker* given the severity of the potential damage.

cyber-, cyberspace, cyber Follow the general rule for prefixes and do not use a hyphen: *cyberattack, cyberbullying, cybercafe, cybersecurity*. Exceptions: *Cyber Monday* (n.) and *cyber* (adj.) as a separate modifier: e.g., *cyber shopping, cyber liability insurance*.

Cyber Monday The Monday after Thanksgiving, typically the busiest day of the year for online shopping in the U.S.

cyclone See **weather terms**.

Cyclone A trademark for a brand of chain-link fence.

cynic, skeptic A *skeptic* is a doubter. A *cynic* is a disbeliever.

czar Not *tsar*. It was a formal title only for the ruler of Russia and some other Slavic nations.

Lowercase in all other uses.

Czech Republic, the Use the official country name in all instances. Also: *Czech* as an adjective, and *Czechs* for the people. The current government has said that *Czechia* can be used in English-language communications, and registered it at the United Nations, but that name has yet to catch on in common usage.

d

dad See **family names**.

Daimler AG German luxury automaker. Brands are *Mercedes-Benz, smart* and *Maybach*. Headquarters is in Stuttgart, Germany.

Dallas The city in Texas stands alone in datelines.

dam Capitalize when part of a proper name: *Hoover Dam.*

damage, damages *Damage* is destruction or loss: *Authorities said the storm caused more than $1 billion in damage.*

    Damages are awarded by a court as compensation for injury, loss, etc.: *The woman received $25,000 in damages.*

dame See **nobility**.

damn it Use instead of *dammit*, but like other profanity it should be avoided unless there is a compelling reason.

    See **obscenities, profanities, vulgarities**.

dangling modifiers Avoid modifiers that do not refer clearly and logically to some word in the sentence.

    Dangling: *Taking our seats, the game started.* (*Taking* does not refer to the subject, *game*, nor to any other word in the sentence.)

    Correct: *Taking our seats, we watched the opening of the game.* (*Taking* refers to *we*, the subject of the sentence.)

Dardanelles, the Not *the Dardanelles Strait.*

Dark Ages The period beginning with the fall of Rome in 476 and ending about the 10th century. The term is derived from the idea that this period in Europe was characterized by intellectual stagnation, widespread ignorance and poverty.

dark horse

darknet A part of the internet hosted within an encrypted network and accessible only through specialized anonymity-providing tools, most notably the Tor Browser. Examples of *darknets* include the *Tor network*, *I2P* and *Freenet*. Do not confuse with *deep web*. See **deep web**.

dash See entry in **Punctuation** chapter.

dashcam

data A plural noun, it normally takes plural verbs and pronouns.

    See the **collective nouns** entry, however, for an example of when *data* may take singular verbs and pronouns.

    Use *databank* and *database*, but *data processing* (n. and adj.) and *data center.*

date line Two words for the imaginary line that separates one day from another.

    See the **international date line**

entry.

datelines Datelines on stories should contain a city name, entirely in capital letters, followed in most cases by the name of the state, country or territory where the city is located.

DOMESTIC DATELINES: A list of domestic cities that stand alone in datelines:

ATLANTA	MILWAUKEE
BALTIMORE	MINNEAPOLIS
BOSTON	NEW ORLEANS
CHICAGO	NEW YORK
CINCINNATI	OKLAHOMA CITY
CLEVELAND	PHILADELPHIA
DALLAS	PHOENIX
DENVER	PITTSBURGH
DETROIT	ST. LOUIS
HONOLULU	SALT LAKE CITY
HOUSTON	SAN ANTONIO
INDIANAPOLIS	SAN DIEGO
LAS VEGAS	SAN FRANCISCO
LOS ANGELES	SEATTLE
MIAMI	WASHINGTON

Stories from all other U.S. cities should have both the city and state name in the dateline, including *KANSAS CITY, Mo.*, and *KANSAS CITY, Kan.*

Spell out *Alaska, Hawaii, Idaho, Iowa, Maine, Ohio, Texas* and *Utah*. Abbreviate others as listed in this book under the full name of each state.

Use *Hawaii* on all cities outside Honolulu. Specify the island in the text if needed.

Follow the same practice for communities on islands within the boundaries of other states: *EDGARTOWN, Mass.*, for example, not *EDGARTOWN, Martha's Vineyard*.

Use *BEVERLY HILLS, Calif.* It's an incorporated city and the dateline for the Golden Globes movie awards, sponsored by the Hollywood Foreign Press Association and held at the Beverly Hilton Hotel.

STATE SERVICES: Additional cities in a state or region may stand alone.

U.S. POSSESSIONS: Apply the guidelines listed below in the ISLAND NATIONS AND TERRITORIES section and the OVERSEAS TERRITORIES section.

INTERNATIONAL DATELINES: These international locations stand alone in datelines:

AMSTERDAM	MEXICO CITY
BAGHDAD	MILAN
BANGKOK	MONACO
BEIJING	MONTREAL
BEIRUT	MOSCOW
BERLIN	MUNICH
BRUSSELS	NEW DELHI
CAIRO	PANAMA CITY
DJIBOUTI	PARIS
DUBLIN	PRAGUE
GENEVA	QUEBEC CITY
GIBRALTAR	RIO DE JANEIRO
GUATEMALA CITY	ROME
HAVANA	SAN MARINO
HELSINKI	SAO PAULO
HONG KONG	SHANGHAI
ISLAMABAD	SINGAPORE
ISTANBUL	STOCKHOLM
JERUSALEM	SYDNEY
JOHANNESBURG	TOKYO
KUWAIT CITY	TORONTO
LONDON	VATICAN CITY
LUXEMBOURG	VIENNA
MACAU	ZURICH
MADRID	

In addition, use *UNITED NATIONS* alone, without a *N.Y.* designation, in stories from *U.N.* headquarters.

BALKANS: With the independence of Montenegro from Serbia-Montenegro formalized in 2006, use a Montenegro-only dateline, such as *PODGORICA, Montenegro*. Stories originating in Serbia carry a Serbia-only dateline: *BELGRADE, Serbia*. With the independence of Kosovo in 2008, use Kosovo in the dateline, such as *PRISTINA, Kosovo*.

CANADIAN DATELINES: Datelines on stories from Canadian cities other than Montreal, Quebec City and Toronto should contain the name of the city in capital letters followed by the name of the province. Do not abbreviate any province or territory name.

COMMONWEALTH OF INDEPENDENT STATES: For cities in the former Soviet Union, datelines include city and republic name: *ALMATY, Kazakhstan*.

OTHER NATIONS: Stories from other international cities that do not stand alone in datelines should contain the name of the country or territory (see the next section) spelled out.

SPELLING AND CHOICE OF NAMES: In most cases, the name of the nation in a dateline is the conventionally accepted short form of its official name: *Argentina*, for example, rather than *Republic of Argentina*. (If in doubt, look for an entry in this book. If none is found, follow Webster's New World College Dictionary.)

Note these special cases:
— Instead of *United Kingdom*, use *England, Northern Ireland, Scotland* or *Wales*.
— For divided nations, use the commonly accepted names based on geographic distinctions: *North Korea, South Korea*.
— Use an article only with *El Salvador*. For all others, use just a country name — *Gambia, Netherlands, Philippines*, etc.

See **geographic names** for guidelines on spelling the names of international cities and nations not listed here or in separate entries.

ISLAND NATIONS AND TERRITORIES: When reporting from nations and territories that are made up primarily of islands but commonly are linked under one name, use the city name and the general name in the dateline. Identify an individual island, if needed, in the text:

Examples:
British Virgin Islands
Netherlands Antilles
Indonesia   Philippines

OVERSEAS TERRITORIES: Some overseas territories, colonies and other areas that are not independent nations commonly have accepted separate identities based on their geographic character or special status under treaties. In these cases, use the commonly accepted territory name after a city name in a dateline.

Examples:

Bermuda	*Martinique*
Corsica	*Puerto Rico*
Crimea	*Sardinia*
Faeroe Islands	*Sicily*
Greenland	*Sikkim*
Guadeloupe	*Tibet*
Guam	

WITHIN STORIES: In citing other cities within the body of a story:
— No further information is necessary if a city is in the same state as the datelined city. Make an exception only if confusion would result.
— Follow the city name with further identification in most cases where it is not in the same state or nation as the dateline city. The additional identification may be omitted, however, if no confusion would result. For example, *Boston* stands alone without Massachusetts in a story

datelined *NEW YORK*.

— Provide a state or nation identification for the city if the story has no dateline. However, cities that stand alone in datelines may be used alone in those stories if no confusion would result.

dateline selection A dateline should tell the reader that the AP obtained the basic information for the story in the datelined city.

Do not, for example, use a Washington dateline on a story written primarily from information that a newspaper reported under a Washington dateline. Use the home city of the newspaper instead.

This rule does not preclude the use of a story with a dateline different from the home city of a newspaper if it is from the general area served by the newspaper.

Use an international dateline only if the basic information in a story was obtained by a full- or part-time correspondent physically present in the datelined community.

If a radio broadcast monitored in another city was the source of information, use the dateline of the city where the monitoring took place and mention the fact in the story.

When a story has been assembled from sources in widely separated areas, use no dateline.

dates Always use Arabic figures, without *st, nd, rd* or *th*. See **years** and **months**.

daughter-in-law, daughters-in-law

Daughters of the American Revolution *DAR* is acceptable on second reference.

Headquarters is in Washington.

day care Two words, no hyphen, in all uses.

daylight saving time Not *savings*. No hyphen.

When linking the term with the name of a time zone, use only the word *daylight*: *Eastern Daylight Time, Pacific Daylight Time*, etc.

Lowercase *daylight saving time* in all uses and *daylight time* whenever it stands alone.

A federal law specifies that daylight time applies from 2 a.m. on the second Sunday of March until 2 a.m. on the first Sunday of November in areas that do not specifically exempt themselves.

See **time zones**.

daylong, dayslong

Day One Capitalize and spell out as a chronological device for summarizing multiday events such as Day One, Day Two. Lowercase in casual or conversational references.

days of the week Capitalize them. Do not abbreviate, except when needed in a tabular format: *Sun, Mon, Tue, Wed, Thu, Fri, Sat* (three letters, without periods, to facilitate tabular composition).

See **time element** and **today, tonight**.

daytime

day to day, day-to-day Hyphenate when used as a compound modifier: *They have extended the contract on a day-to-day basis.*

D.C. See **District of Columbia**.

D-Day June 6, 1944, the day the Allies invaded Western Europe in World

d

War II.

DDT Preferred in all references for the insecticide *dichlorodiphenyltrichloroethane*.

dead center

dead end (n.) **dead-end** (adj.)

Dead Sea Scrolls

deaf See **disabled, handicapped**.

deaf-mute Avoid the term. The preferred form is to say that an individual cannot hear or speak. A *mute* person may be deaf or may be able to hear.
   Do not use *deaf and dumb*.

dean Capitalize when used as a formal title before a name: *Dean John Jones, Deans John Jones and Susan Smith.*
   Lowercase in other uses: *John Jones, dean of the college; the dean.*

dean's list Lowercase in all uses: *He is on the dean's list. She is a dean's list student.*

deathbed (n. and adj.)

death, die Don't use euphemisms like *passed on* or *passed away* except in a direct quote.

death row

debt The money a company or individual owes a creditor.

debt service The outlay necessary to meet all interest and principal payments during a given period.

decades Use Arabic figures to indicate decades of history. Use an apostrophe to indicate numerals that are left out; show plural by adding the letter *s*: *the 1890s, the '90s, the Gay '90s, the 1920s, the mid-1930s.*
   See **historical periods and events**.

deci- A prefix denoting one-tenth of a unit. Move the decimal point one place to the left in converting to the basic unit: 15.5 decigrams = 1.55 grams.

decimal units Use a period and numerals to indicate decimal amounts. Decimalization should not exceed two places in textual material unless there are special circumstances.
   For amounts less than 1, use the numeral zero before the decimal point: 0.03.
   See **fractions** and **numerals**.

Declaration of Independence Lowercase *the declaration* whenever it stands alone.

decorations See **awards and decorations**.

deep link A web address that is reached without a visit to a website homepage.

deep-sea (adj.)

Deep South Capitalize both words when referring to the region that consists of Alabama, Georgia, Louisiana, Mississippi and South Carolina.

deep water (n.) **deep-water** (adj.)

deep web The part of the web which is not indexed by search engines because it is hidden behind firewalls, protected by passwords or otherwise restricted. The *deep web* includes webmail services such as Gmail, private forums — including large chunks of Facebook — and online banking sites or other proprietary databases. Researchers estimate that the *deep web* is significantly larger than the part of web easily accessible to internet users via search engines. Do not confuse with *darknet*, which consists of sites available only through specialized *anonymity-protecting tools*. See **darknet**.

default The failure to meet a financial obligation, the failure to make payment either of principal or interest when due or a breach or nonperformance of the terms of a note or mortgage.

defendant

defense Do not use it as a verb.

defense attorney Always lowercase, never abbreviate.
See **attorney** and **titles**.

defense spending *Military spending* usually is the more precise term.

definitely Overused as a vague intensifier. Avoid it.

deflation A decrease in the general price level, which results from a decrease in total spending relative to the supply of available goods on the market. Deflation's immediate effect is to increase purchasing power.

degree-day See **weather terms**.

degrees See **academic degrees**.

dek- (before a vowel), **deka-** (before a consonant) A prefix denoting 10 units of a measure. Move the decimal point one place to the right to convert to the basic unit: 15.6 dekameters = 156 meters.

Delaware Abbreviate *Del.* in datelines only; spell out in stories. Postal code: *DE*
See **state names**.

delegate The formal title for members of the lower houses of legislatures in states including Delaware, Maryland, Virginia and West Virginia. Capitalize only before their names. Abbreviate as a formal title before names, as local usage allows.
Always lowercase in other uses: *convention delegate Richard Henry Lee.*

Delta Air Lines Inc. Headquarters is in Atlanta.

demagogue, demagoguery

democrat, democratic, Democratic Party See the **political parties and philosophies** entry.

Democratic Governors Association No apostrophe.

Democratic National Committee On the second reference: *the national committee, the committee* or *the DNC.*
Similarly: *Democratic State Committee, Democratic County Committee, Democratic City Committee, the state committee, the city committee, the committee.*

demolish, destroy Both mean to do away with something completely. Something cannot be partially *demolished* or *destroyed*. It is redundant to say *totally demolished* or *totally destroyed.*

d

Denali Tallest peak in North America at 20,310 feet. Located in Alaska. Formerly *Mount McKinley*.

denote See **connote, denote**.

Denver The city in Colorado stands alone in datelines.

depart Follow it with a preposition: *He will depart from LaGuardia. She will depart at 11:30 a.m.*

department The following are the U.S. Cabinet departments: *Department of Agriculture* (*USDA* acceptable on second reference); *Department of Commerce*; *Department of Defense* (*DOD* or *Pentagon* acceptable on second reference); *Department of Education*; *Department of Energy* (*DOE* acceptable on second reference); *Department of Health and Human Services* (*HHS* acceptable on second reference); *Department of Homeland Security* (*DHS* acceptable on second reference); *Department of Housing and Urban Development* (*HUD* acceptable on second reference); *Department of the Interior*; *Department of Justice* (*DOJ* acceptable on second reference); *Department of Labor*; *Department of State*; *Department of Transportation* (*DOT* acceptable on second reference); *Department of the Treasury*, and *Department of Veterans Affairs* (*VA* acceptable on second reference).

It is preferable to list the subject first in stories, such as the *Agriculture Department* and *Commerce Department*. Exceptions are *Department of Health and Human Services*, *Department of Homeland Security*, *Department of Housing and Urban Development* and *Department of Veterans Affairs*.

Avoid acronyms when possible.

A phrase such as *the department* is preferable on second reference because it is more readable and avoids alphabet soup.

Lowercase *department* in plural uses, but capitalize the proper name element: *the departments of Labor and Justice*.

A shorthand reference to the proper name element also is capitalized: *Kissinger said, "State and Justice must resolve their differences."* But: *Henry Kissinger, the secretary of state.*

Lowercase *the department* whenever it stands alone.

Do not abbreviate *department* in any usage.

TITLES: In stories with U.S. datelines, do not include U.S. before the titles of Secretary of State or other government officials, except where necessary for clarity. Examples: *Secretary of State John Kerry, Attorney General Eric Holder.*

In stories with international datelines, include U.S. before the titles: *U.S. Secretary of State John Kerry, U.S. Attorney General Eric Holder.* Exceptions: *President Donald Trump, Vice President Mike Pence.*

See **academic departments**.

dependent (n. and adj.)

depreciation The reduction in the value of capital goods due to wear and tear or obsolescence.

Estimated depreciation may be deducted from income each year as one of the costs of doing business.

depression Capitalize *Depression* and *the Great Depression* when referring to the worldwide economic hard times generally regarded as having begun with the stock market collapse of Oct. 28-29, 1929.

Lowercase in other uses: *the depression of the 1970s.*

depths See **dimensions**.

deputy Capitalize as a formal title before a name. See **titles**.

derivative A contract whose value depends on the financial performance of its underlying assets, such as mortgages, stock or traded commodities. Credit default swaps are one form of derivative.

derogatory terms Do not use a derogatory term except in extremely rare circumstances — when it is crucial to the story or the understanding of a news event. Flag the contents in an editor's note.

See **obscenities, profanities, vulgarities**.

-designate Hyphenate: *chairman-designate.* Do not capitalize *designate* if used as part of a formal title before a name: *Attorney General-designate John Smith.*

See **titles**.

destroy See **demolish, destroy**.

detective Do not abbreviate. Capitalize before a name only if it is a formal rank: *police Detective Frank Serpico, private detective Richard Diamond.*

See **titles**.

detente

detention center See **prison, jail**.

Detroit The city in Michigan stands alone in datelines.

Deutsche Lufthansa AG The headquarters of this airline is in Cologne, Germany. *Lufthansa* is acceptable on first reference.

devaluations Occur when a country's government pushes down the value of its currency in relation to another currency. (When market forces, not the government, push a currency down, it is known as depreciation.)

Suppose China devalues its currency, the yuan, against the U.S. dollar. To calculate the devaluation, you'd look at the value of 1 yuan to the U.S. dollar before the devaluation and the value afterward and calculate the percentage difference.

Example: On Day One, 1 yuan is worth 16.1 cents (or $0.161). The next day, the Chinese government devalues the currency and 1 yuan is equal to 15.8 cents ($0.158). That is a 1.9 percent devaluation — the yuan has dropped 1.9 percent against the U.S. dollar.

Currencies are often reported the other way, showing how much $1 is worth in another currency. In the example above, $1 went from being worth 6.21 yuan to being worth 6.32 yuan. To find out what 1 yuan is worth — so you can show the yuan dropping, not the dollar rising — divide 1 by 6.21 and 6.32 respectively.

devil But capitalize *Satan.*

diabetes A disease in which the body doesn't make enough or properly use insulin, a hormone that turns food into energy. There are two main forms: *Type 1 diabetes,* formerly called juvenile diabetes, and *Type 2 diabetes,* the most common kind, formerly called adult-onset diabetes. Include the type when relevant or necessary, for example, when discussing specific treatments.

dialect The form of language peculiar to a region or a group, usually in matters of pronunciation or syntax. Dialect should be avoided, even in quoted matter, unless it is clearly pertinent to a story.

There are some words and phrases in everyone's vocabulary that are typical of a particular region or group. Quoting dialect, unless used carefully, implies substandard or illiterate usage.

When there is a compelling reason to use dialect, words or phrases are spelled phonetically, and apostrophes show missing letters and sounds: *"Din't ya yoosta live at Toidy-Toid Street and Sekun' Amya? Across from da moom pitchers?"*

See **colloquialisms** and **quotes in the news**.

dialogue (n.)

diarrhea

dictionaries For spelling, style and usage questions not covered in this stylebook, consult Webster's New World College Dictionary, Fifth Edition, Houghton Mifflin Harcourt, Boston and New York, 2016.

Use the first spelling listed in Webster's New World College Dictionary unless a specific exception is listed in this book.

If Webster's New World College Dictionary provides different spellings in separate entries (*tee shirt* and *T-shirt*, for example), use the spelling that is followed by a full definition (*T-shirt*).

If Webster's New World College Dictionary provides definitions under two spellings for the same sense of a word, either use is

acceptable.

Webster's New World College Dictionary is also the first reference for geographic names not covered in this stylebook. See **geographic names**.

die-hard (n. and adj.)

Diet The Japanese parliament. See **legislative bodies**.

dietitian

different Takes the preposition *from*, not *than*.

differ from, differ with To *differ from* means to be unlike.

To *differ with* means to disagree.

Digital First Media New York-based media company that owns dailies including The Denver Post, San Jose Mercury News and The Detroit News.

dilemma It means more than *a problem*. It implies a choice between two unattractive alternatives.

dimensions Use figures and spell out *inches, feet, yards*, etc., to indicate depth, height, length and width. Hyphenate adjectival forms before nouns.

EXAMPLES: *He is 5 feet, 6 inches tall, the 5-foot-6-inch man, the 5-foot man, the basketball team signed a 7-footer.*

The car is 17 feet long, 6 feet wide and 5 feet high. The rug is 9 feet by 12 feet, the 9-by-12 rug.

The storm left 5 inches of snow.

The building has 6,000 square feet of floor space.

Use an apostrophe to indicate feet and quote marks to indicate inches (5'6") only in very technical contexts.

Diners Club No apostrophe, in keeping with the practice the company has adopted for its public identity.

directions and regions In general, lowercase *north, south, northeast, northern*, etc., when they indicate compass direction; capitalize these words when they designate regions.

Some examples:

COMPASS DIRECTIONS: *He drove west. The cold front is moving east.*

REGIONS: *A storm system that developed in the Midwest is spreading eastward. It will bring showers to the East Coast by morning and to the entire Northeast by late in the day. Showers and thunderstorms were forecast in the Texas Panhandle. High temperatures will prevail throughout the Western states.*

The North was victorious. The South will rise again. Settlers from the East went to the West in search of new lives. The customs of the East are different from those of the West. The Northeast depends on the Midwest for its food supply.

She has a Southern accent. He is a Northerner. Asian nations are opening doors to Western businessmen. The candidate developed a Southern strategy.

The storm developed in the South Pacific. European leaders met to talk about supplies of oil from Southeast Asia.

WITH NAMES OF NATIONS: Lowercase unless they are part of a proper name or are used to designate a politically divided nation: *northern France, eastern Canada, the western United States.*

But: *Northern Ireland, South Korea.*

WITH STATES AND CITIES: The preferred form is to lowercase directional or area descriptions when referring to a section of a state or city: *western Montana, southern Atlanta.*

But capitalize compass points:
— When part of a proper name: *North Dakota, West Virginia.*
— When used in denoting widely known sections: *Southern California, West Texas, the South Side of Chicago, the Lower East Side of New York.* If in doubt, use lowercase.

IN FORMING PROPER NAMES: When combining with another common noun to form the name for a region or location: *the North Woods, the South Pole, the Far East, the Middle East, the West Coast* (the entire region, not the coastline itself — see **coast**), *the Eastern Shore* (see separate entry), *the Western Hemisphere.*

direct message A private message sent via Twitter to one of your followers, or to another user who has switched on a setting to receive such messages from anyone. *DM* is acceptable on second reference. Can also be used as a verb: *to direct-message* or *DM someone.*

dis- The rules in **prefixes** apply, but in general, no hyphen. Some examples:

dismember	*disservice*
dissemble	*dissuade*

dis, dissing, dissed

disabled, handicapped In general, do not describe an individual as disabled or handicapped unless it is clearly pertinent to a story. If a description must be used, try to be specific. *An ad featuring actor Michael J. Fox swaying noticeably from*

d

*the effects of Parkinson's disease drew
nationwide attention.*

Avoid descriptions that connote
pity, such as *afflicted with* or *suffers
from multiple sclerosis.* Rather, *has
multiple sclerosis.*

Some terms include:

blind Describes a person with
complete loss of sight. For others,
use terms such as *visually impaired* or
person with low vision.

cripple Considered offensive when
used to describe a person who is
disabled.

deaf Describes a person with total
hearing loss. For others, use *partial
hearing loss* or *partially deaf.* Avoid
using *deaf-mute.* Do not use *deaf and
dumb.*

disabled A general term used for
a physical, mental, developmental
or intellectual disability. Do not use
mentally retarded.

handicap It should be avoided in
describing a disability.

mute Describes a person who
cannot speak. Others with speaking
difficulties are *speech impaired.*

wheelchair user People use
wheelchairs for independent
mobility. Do not use *confined to a
wheelchair,* or *wheelchair-bound.* If a
wheelchair is needed, say why.

See **mental illness**.

disc jockey *DJ* is acceptable in all
references.

discount Interest withheld when a
note, draft or bill is purchased.

discount rate The rate of interest
charged by the Federal Reserve on
loans it makes to member banks.
This rate has an influence on the
rates banks then charge their
customers.

discreet, discrete *Discreet* means
prudent, circumspect: "I'm afraid I was
not very discreet," she wrote.

Discrete means *detached, separate:
There are four discrete sounds from a
quadraphonic system.*

diseases Do not capitalize *arthritis,
emphysema, leukemia, pneumonia,* etc.

When a disease is known by the
name of a person or geographical
area identified with it, capitalize only
the proper noun element: *Alzheimer's
disease, Parkinson's disease, Ebola
virus,* etc.

Avoid such expressions as: *He is
battling cancer. She is a stroke victim.*
Use neutral, precise descriptions:
*He has stomach cancer. She is a stroke
patient.*

See **disabled, handicapped**.

disinterested, uninterested
Disinterested means *impartial,* which
is usually the better word to convey
the thought.

Uninterested means that someone
lacks interest.

disk, disc Use *disk* for computer-
related references (*diskette*) and
medical references, such as a *slipped
disk.* Use the *disc* spelling for optical
and laser-based devices (a *Blu-ray
Disc, CD, DVD*) and for *disc brake.*

dispel, dispelled, dispelling

disposable personal income The
income that a person retains after
deductions for income taxes, Social
Security taxes, property taxes and
for other payments such as fines
and penalties to various levels of
government.

Disposall A trademark for a type of
mechanical garbage disposer.

dissociate Not *disassociate*.

distances Always use figures: *He walked 4 miles.* See **numerals**.

district Always spell it out. Use a figure and capitalize *district* when forming a proper name: *the 2nd District.*

district attorney Capitalize when used as a formal title before a name: *District Attorney Hamilton Burger.*
   DA acceptable on second reference.
   See **titles**.

district court See **court names** and **U.S. District Court**.

District of Columbia In datelines Washington doesn't take *D.C.* Generally use *District of Columbia* within a story only for official designations, such as local government names, or to avoid confusion with other localities of that name. *Washington* should be used in most story references to the U.S. capital because of the name recognition globally. Use *Washington, D.C.,* with the added abbreviation only if the city might be confused with the state. Do not use *D.C.* standing alone other than in quotations. On second reference, *the district* is acceptable. Postal code: *DC*. See **state names**, **Washington**.

dive, dived or **dove, diving**

divided nations See **datelines** and entries under the names of these nations.

dividend In a financial sense, the word describes the payment per share that a corporation distributes to its stockholders as their return on the money they have invested in its stock.
   See **profit terminology**.

division See **organizations and institutions**; **military units**; and **political divisions**.

divorce Use the same standards for men and women in deciding whether to mention marital status in a story. Avoid describing a woman as a *divorcee*, or a man as a *divorce*, unless used in an essential quote. When the news isn't about a marital breakup, but marital status is relevant, say in the body of the story that the woman or man is divorced.

Dixie cup A trademark for a paper drinking cup.

Djibouti Stands alone in datelines for the East African country and capital.

DNA Acceptable for all reference to deoxyribonucleic acid, which carries genetic information in the cell.

DNS Abbreviation for the *Domain Name System*, an international network of internet domain servers, names and addresses. Spell out on first reference.

doctor Use *Dr.* in first reference as a formal title before the name of an individual who holds a doctor of dental surgery, doctor of medicine, doctor of optometry, doctor of osteopathic medicine, doctor of podiatric medicine, or doctor of veterinary medicine: *Dr. Jonas Salk.*
   The form *Dr.*, or *Drs.*, in a plural construction, applies to all first-reference uses before a name, including direct quotations.

d

d

If appropriate in the context, *Dr.* also may be used on first reference before the names of individuals who hold other types of doctoral degrees. However, because the public frequently identifies *Dr.* only with physicians, care should be taken to ensure that the individual's specialty is stated in first or second reference. The only exception would be a story in which the context left no doubt that the person was a dentist, psychologist, chemist, historian, etc.

In some instances it also is necessary to specify that an individual identified as *Dr.* is a physician. One frequent case is a story reporting on joint research by physicians, biologists, etc.

Do not use *Dr.* before the names of individuals who hold only honorary doctorates.

Do not continue the use of *Dr.* in subsequent references.

See **academic degrees**; **courtesy titles**; and **religious titles**.

Doctors Without Borders Use the full English name on first reference. *MSF* is acceptable in quotations and second references, noting that it is the abbreviation for the French name of the group, *Medecins sans frontieres.* Do not use *MSF* in headlines.

dog walker Two words.

dogs See **animals**.

dollars Always lowercase. Use figures and the *$* sign in all except casual references or amounts without a figure: *The book cost $4. Dad, please give me a dollar. Dollars are flowing overseas.*

For specified amounts, the word takes a singular verb: *He said*

$500,000 is what they want.

For amounts of more than $1 million, use up to two decimal places. Do not link the numerals and the word by a hyphen: *He is worth $4.35 million. He proposed a $300 billion budget.*

The form for amounts less than $1 million: *$4, $25, $500, $1,000, $650,000.*

See **cents**.

domain names The address used to locate a particular website or reach an email system. In email addresses, it is the portion to the right of the @ sign. It includes a suffix defining the type of entity, such as ".com" (for commerce, the most common suffix); ".net" initially for network service providers, but often used when ".com" is unavailable; ".org" (organizations); ".edu" (educational institutions); ".gov" (U.S. government) and ".mil" (U.S. military). There are also country-code suffixes (such as ".fr" for France, ".us" for the United States), along with many other types of available domain names.

domino, dominoes

"don't ask, don't tell" The law barring gays from serving in the U.S. military if they acknowledged their sexual orientation. The 1993 law was repealed by Congress in 2010, effective in 2011. Gays now may serve openly.

door to door, door-to-door Hyphenate when used as a compound modifier: *He is a door-to-door salesman.*

But: *He went from door to door.*

do's and don'ts

dot-com An informal description of companies that do business mainly on the internet.

double-click

double-faced

doughnut

Dow Jones & Co. The company, a subsidiary of News Corp., publishes The Wall Street Journal and Barron's magazine. It also operates the Dow Jones News Service. Headquarters is in New York.

Dow Jones industrial average The market indicator comprises 30 leading U.S. stocks. The average is calculated and published by S&P Dow Jones Indices LLC, which is jointly owned by S&P Global Inc. and CME Group Inc. The average is maintained by S&P Dow Jones Indices' averages committee, comprising representatives of S&P Dow Jones Indices and The Wall Street Journal. Always use the full name on first reference in stories. On subsequent references, use *the Dow*.

-down Follow Webster's New World College Dictionary. Some examples, all nouns and/or adjectives:

breakdown *rundown*
countdown *sit-down*

All are two words when used as verbs.

down- The rules in **prefixes** apply, but in general, no hyphen. Some examples:

downgrade *downtown*

Down East Use only in reference to Maine.

down payment

downside risk The probability that the price of an investment will fall.

downstage

downstate Lowercase unless part of a proper name: *downstate Illinois*. But: *the Downstate Medical Center*.

Down syndrome Not *Down's*, for the genetic, chromosomal disorder first reported in 1866 by Dr. J. Langdon Down.

Down Under Australia, New Zealand and environs.

dpa *Deutsche Presse-Agentur GmbH* is an international news agency with headquarters in Hamburg, Germany. Lowercase *dpa* is acceptable in all references, though it's *Dpa* to start a sentence.

Dr. See **doctor**.

drag performer, drag queen, drag king Entertainers who dress and act as a different gender. *Drag queens* act as women; *drag kings* act as men. *Male impersonator* or *female impersonator* is also acceptable. Not synonymous with *cross-dresser* or *transgender*, although some *drag performers* are also *transgender*. See **gender**.

drama See **composition titles**.

Dramamine A trademark for a brand of motion sickness remedy.

dreidel Toy spinning top used in games played during Hanukkah.

dressing room

drive See **addresses**.

drive-by (adj.) *A drive-by shooting.*

drive-in (n.)

driver's license(s)

drive-thru (n. and adj.)

drop-down (adj.)

dropout (n.) **drop out** (v.)

drought

drowned, was drowned If a person suffocates in water or other fluid, the proper statement is that the individual *drowned*. To say that someone *was drowned* implies that another person caused the death by holding the victim's head under the water.

Drug Enforcement Administration *DEA* on second reference.

drugmaker

drugs Acceptable as a term for both narcotics and medications. Use *illegal* or *illicit drug*, or *medicine* or *medication*, if needed to distinguish.

The names used for some street drugs can often be misleading, so ensure they are described correctly. Details on some drugs:

bath salts Any of a number of drugs that contain synthetic chemicals related to the natural stimulant cathinone and sometimes marketed as *bath salts*. Ensure that stories explain they are unrelated to actual bathing products.

cocaine The slang term *coke* should appear only in quotations. *Crack* is a refined cocaine in crystalline rock form; mention it separately from *cocaine* only if pertinent to the story.

ecstasy, molly, MDMA All acceptable shorthand for the party drug *methylenedioxymethamphetamine*, though molly refers to a purer form of the drug. Lowercase (other than *MDMA*) unless it's a brand name.

fake pot See **synthetic marijuana** below.

fentanyl An opioid painkiller many times more powerful than heroin, and typically prescribed to treat severe pain. Now frequently appears as an illegal street drug mixed with heroin.

heroin An opioid related to morphine, but more potent and addictive. Authorities attribute recent increases in heroin use largely to crackdowns on prescription opioids like Vicodin and OxyContin, which contain similar chemicals and can produce a similar high.

LSD Acceptable on first reference for the hallucinogenic drug *lysergic acid diethylamide*. Also known as *acid*.

marijuana, medical marijuana *Marijuana* is the dried flower of the cannabis plant, used as a drug for recreational or medical purposes. *Cannabis* is the usual term outside North America; it and *pot* are also acceptable. Slang terms such as *weed*, *reefer*, *ganja* or *420* are acceptable in limited, colloquial cases or in quotations. In the United States, many states have legalized marijuana for medical purposes; others have legalized the drug for recreational use. Possession and distribution of marijuana remains a federal offense. See separate full entry **marijuana, medical marijuana** for more detail.

meth Usually acceptable on first reference for *methamphetamine* unless it could be confused with other drugs, such as *methcathinone* or *methadone*.

PCP Acceptable on first reference for the hallucinogenic drug *phencyclidine*. Also known as angel dust.

synthetic marijuana One of the preferred terms along with various variations including *synthetic cannabis/pot* or *imitation marijuana/ cannabis/pot*) for the recreational drugs marketed under brand names such as Spice and K2. Do not refer to it as *fake pot* or the awkward but accurate term *synthetic cannabinoids*, though the latter is acceptable with explanation in scientific contexts. Do not refer to it as *synthetic THC*, since it often contains other chemicals and could be confused with pharmaceuticals containing that compound. See separate full entry **marijuana, medical marijuana** for more detail.

See **marijuana, medical marijuana**.

drugstore

drunk, drunken *Drunk* is the spelling of the adjective used after a form of the verb *to be*: *He was drunk*.

Drunken is the spelling of the adjective used before nouns: *a drunken driver, drunken driving*.

DUI, driving under the influence; *DWI, driving while intoxicated*; follow official state usage. See **addiction**.

drunkenness

DSL Abbreviation acceptable in all references for *digital subscriber line*, for high-speed access to the internet over a telephone network.

Dublin The city in Ireland stands alone in datelines.

duel A contest between two people. Three people cannot duel.

duffel

DUI, DWI Abbreviations for *driving under the influence* or *driving while intoxicated*. Acceptable in all references. See **drunk, drunken**.

dumping The selling of a product in a foreign market at a price lower than the domestic price. It is usually done by a monopoly when it has such a large output that selling entirely in the domestic market would substantially reduce the price.

dumpster A large metal trash bin.

Dunkirk Use this spelling rather than *Dunkerque*, in keeping with widespread practice.

durable goods Long-lasting goods such as appliances that are bought by consumers.

dust storm See **weather terms**.

Dutch auction A bidding process where the price is lowered until the lowest price at which all securities will sell becomes the set price. Used on Treasury auctions and in risk arbitrage.

DVD Abbreviation for *digital video disc* (or *digital versatile disc*), similar to CD-ROMs, but able to hold more music, video or data.

The abbreviation is acceptable in all references.

DVR Acceptable on second reference for *digital video recorder*. TiVo is the trademark for one type of *DVR*. Do not use *TiVo* to describe the generic

d

DVRs offered by many cable systems.

dwarf The preferred term for people with a medical or genetic condition resulting in short stature. Plural is *dwarfs*.

d

dyed-in-the-wool (adj.)

dyeing, dying *Dyeing* refers to changing colors.
Dying refers to death.

e

each Takes a singular verb.

each other, one another Two people look at *each other*.

More than two look at *one another*.

Either phrase may be used when the number is indefinite: *We help each other. We help one another.*

earmark

earth Generally lowercase; capitalize when used as the proper name of the planet. *She is down-to-earth. How does the pattern apply to Mars, Jupiter, Earth, the sun and the moon? The astronauts returned to Earth. He hopes to move heaven and earth.*

See **planets**.

earthquakes The best source for information on major earthquakes is the National Earthquake Information Center, operated by the U.S. Geological Survey, in Golden, Colorado.

Earthquake magnitudes are measures of earthquake size calculated from ground motion recorded by seismometers. The Richter scale, named for Charles F. Richter, is no longer widely used.

Magnitudes are usually reported simply as *magnitude 6.7* (or *6.7 magnitude*), for example. Do not use hyphens when the magnitude is used as a modifier: *a magnitude 6.7 quake, a 6.7 magnitude quake.*

In the first hours after a quake, earthquake size should be reported as a *preliminary magnitude* at a *preliminary depth*.

The most commonly used measure is the *moment magnitude*, related to the area of the fault on which an earthquake occurs and the amount the ground slips.

The magnitude scale being used should be specified only when necessary, for example, when two earthquake centers report different magnitudes. An example would be when two centers are reporting different magnitudes because they are using different scales. The various scales usually differ only slightly.

With each scale, every increase of one number, say from 5.5 to 6.5, means that the quake's magnitude is 10 times as great. Theoretically, there is no upper limit to the scales.

Some indications of earthquake strength:

Magnitude 2.5 to 3: The smallest generally felt by people.

Magnitude 4: Can cause moderate damage.

Magnitude 5: Can cause considerable damage.

Magnitude 6: Can cause severe damage.

Magnitude 7: A major earthquake, capable of widespread, heavy damage.

Magnitude 8: An earthquake capable of tremendous damage.

Depth is a key factor in determining how damaging an earthquake will be. The closer to the surface an earthquake starts, the more ground shaking and potential damage it will cause, particularly in places without strict building codes. Two different earthquakes of the same magnitude can result in vastly different damage and deaths depending on the depth.

Quakes are divided into three categories: shallow, intermediate and deep. Shallow quakes are at depths of less than 70 km (43 miles) and are the ones that have broader damage. Intermediate quakes are between 70 km and 300 km in depth (43 miles to 186 miles). Deep quakes are deeper than 300 km (186 miles).

The deadliest quake on record occurred in Shaanxi province of China on Jan. 23, 1556. It killed 830,000 people.

Initial earthquake reports from seismic monitoring networks are usually generated automatically and should be confirmed if the reporter did not feel the tremor. Some reports result from system errors and will be deleted after review by a seismologist. A very large earthquake anywhere in the world may cause a seismic network to produce erroneous reports of one or more quakes in its monitoring area.

The USGS' "Did You Feel It" webpages collect unvetted reports from the public. These may be useful in characterizing how widely a quake was felt but singular reports from distant locations should be confirmed.

OTHER TERMS: The word *temblor* (not tremblor) is a synonym for *earthquake*.

The word *epicenter* refers to the point on Earth's surface above the underground center, or focus, of an earthquake.

Earthquake early warning systems do not predict earthquakes. When an earthquake begins they provide warning to distant locations where the shaking has not yet begun.

east, eastern See **directions and regions**.

Easter Christian holy day commemorating the resurrection of Jesus Christ. Christians believe Jesus was raised from the dead three days after his crucifixion.

Western Christian churches and most Orthodox Christian churches follow different calendars and observe Easter on different dates.

Eastern Europe No longer a separate political unit, but can be used in specific references to the region. Use only in historic sense. (Also *Western Europe*.)

Eastern Hemisphere The half of the Earth made up primarily of Africa, Asia, Australia and Europe.

Eastern Orthodox churches The term applies to a group of churches that have roots in the earliest days of Christianity and do not recognize papal authority over their activities.

Churches in this tradition were part of the undivided Christendom that existed until the Great Schism of 1054. At that time, many of the churches in the western half of the old Roman Empire accorded the bishop of Rome supremacy over other bishops. The result was a split between eastern and western churches.

The autonomous churches that constitute Eastern Orthodoxy are organized along mostly national lines. They recognize the patriarch of Constantinople (modern-day Istanbul) as their leader. He convenes councils, but his authority is otherwise that of a "first among equals."

Eastern orthodox churches

include the Greek Orthodox Church and the Russian Orthodox Church.

In the United States, organizational lines are rooted in the national backgrounds of various ethnic groups, such as the Greek Orthodox Archdiocese of America, and the Orthodox Church in America, which includes people of Bulgarian, Romanian, Russian and Syrian descent.

The churches have their own disciplines on matters such as married clergy — a married man may be ordained, but a priest may not marry after ordination.

Some of these churches call the archbishop who leads them a *metropolitan*; others use the term *patriarch*. He normally heads the principal archdiocese within a nation. Working with him are other archbishops, bishops, priests and deacons.

Archbishops and bishops frequently follow a monastic tradition in which they are known only by a first name. When no last name is used, repeat the title before the sole name in subsequent references.

Some forms: *Metropolitan Tikhon, archbishop of Washington and metropolitan of America and Canada.* On second reference: *Metropolitan Tikhon. Archbishop* may be replaced by *the Most Rev.* on first reference. *Bishop* may be replaced by *the Rt. Rev.* on first reference.

Use *the Rev.* before the name of a priest on first reference.

See **religious titles**.

Eastern Seaboard Synonym for *East Coast*.

Eastern Shore A region on the east side of Chesapeake Bay, including parts of Maryland and Virginia.

Eastern Shore is not a synonym for *East Coast*.

Eastern Standard Time (EST), Eastern Daylight Time (EDT) See **time zones**.

easygoing

eBay Inc. The online auctioneer is based in San Jose, California. Lowercase *e* unless it's the start of a sentence.

Ebola A virus that causes a severe and often fatal illness. It is named for a river in the Democratic Republic of Congo in Africa where one of the first outbreaks of the disease occurred in 1976. About two dozen outbreaks have occurred in Africa since then. The one that began in early 2014 was by far the largest. It killed 11,325 people, and was declared over in 2016 by the World Health Organization.

Ebola virus comes from wild animals and then spreads person-to-person through direct contact with an infected person or contaminated materials. Symptoms can include sudden fever, muscle pain, headache, sore throat, vomiting, diarrhea, rash, kidney or liver problems and bleeding. People are not infectious until they develop symptoms, and the incubation period is two to 21 days.

No specific drugs or vaccines are approved to treat Ebola but some experimental ones are being tested. Early supportive care, such as intravenous fluids, can improve survival odds. Usage: *the Ebola virus* or just *Ebola*.

e-book The electronic version of a

book or publication, sold digitally and commonly consumed on a hand-held device called an *e-book reader* or *e-reader*, or on an *e-reader app* on a smartphone, tablet or PC.

E. coli Acceptable in all references for *Escherichia coli O157:H7 bacteria*.

ecology The study of the relationship between organisms and their surroundings. It is not synonymous with *environment*.
Right: *The laboratory is studying the ecology of man and the desert.*
Wrong: *Even so simple an undertaking as maintaining a lawn affects ecology.* (Use *environment* instead.)

ecosystem

ecotourism

ecstasy See **drugs**.

Ecuadorean The term for the people and culture of Ecuador.

editor Capitalize *editor* before a name only when it is an official corporate or organizational title. Do not capitalize as a job description.
See **titles**.

editor-in-chief Use hyphens and capitalize when used as a formal title before a name: *Editor-in-Chief Horace Greeley*. The hyphens, reflecting industry usage, are an exception to Webster's New World College Dictionary.
See **titles**.

eerie

EFE An international news agency with headquarters in Madrid, Spain.

effect See **affect, effect**.

e.g. Meaning *for example*, it is always followed by a comma.

Eglin Air Force Base, Florida

Eid al-Adha Meaning "Feast of Sacrifice," this most important Islamic holiday marks the willingness of the Prophet Ibrahim (Abraham to Christians and Jews) to sacrifice his son. During the holiday, which in most places lasts four days, Muslims slaughter sheep or cattle, distribute part of the meat to the poor and eat the rest. The holiday begins on the 10th day of the Islamic lunar month of Dhul-Hijja, during the annual hajj pilgrimage to Mecca.

Eid al-Fitr A three-day holiday marking the end of Ramadan, Islam's holy month of fasting.

either Use it to mean *one or the other*, not *both*.
Right: *She said to use either door.*
Wrong: *There were lions on either side of the door.*
Right: *There were lions on each side of the door. There were lions on both sides of the door.*

either ... or, neither ... nor The nouns that follow these words do not constitute a compound subject; they are alternate subjects and require a verb that agrees with the nearer subject:
Neither they nor he is going. Neither he nor they are going.

El Al Israel Airlines. An *El Al airliner* is acceptable in any reference. Headquarters in Tel Aviv.

elderly Use this word carefully and

sparingly. Do not refer to a person as *elderly* unless it is clearly relevant to the story. Apply the same principle to terms such as *senior citizen*.

It is appropriate in generic phrases that do not refer to specific individuals: *concern for elderly people, a home for senior citizens*, etc.

If the intent is to show that an individual's faculties have deteriorated, cite a graphic example and give attribution for it. Use age when available and appropriate.

-elect Always hyphenate and lowercase: *President-elect Donald Trump*.

Election Day, election night The first Tuesday after the first Monday in November.

election returns Use figures, with commas every three digits starting at the right and counting left. Use the word *to* (not a hyphen) in separating different totals listed together: *Jimmy Carter outpolled Gerald Ford 40,827,292 to 39,146,157 in 1976.*

Use the word *votes* if there is any possibility that the figures could be confused with a ratio: *Nixon outpolled McGovern 16 votes to 3 votes in Dixville Notch.*

Do not attempt to create adjectival forms such as *the 40,827,292-39,146,157 vote*.

See **vote tabulations**.

Electoral College But *electoral vote(s)*. The process by which the United States selects its president. The "college" consists of 538 electors from the states. Each state gets as many electoral votes as it has members of Congress, and the District of Columbia gets three. To be elected president, the winner

must get at least half the total plus one — or 270 electoral votes. Most states give all their electoral votes to whichever candidate wins that state's popular vote. The electoral system has delivered a split verdict five times, most recently in 2016, with one candidate winning the popular vote and another the presidency.

e

electrocardiogram *EKG* is acceptable on second reference.

eleventh Spell out only in the phrase *the eleventh hour*, meaning at the last moment; otherwise use the numeral.

ellipsis See entry in **Punctuation** chapter.

El Salvador The use of the article in the name of the nation helps to distinguish it from its capital, *San Salvador*.

Use *Salvadoran(s)* in references to citizens of the nation.

email Acceptable in all references for *electronic mail*. Also: *esports*. Use a hyphen with other *e-* terms: *e-book, e-reader, e-commerce*.

embargo See **boycott, embargo**.

embargo times Embargoed copy contains *HFR* (Hold for Release) in the keyword.

embarrass, embarrassing, embarrassed, embarrassment

embassy An *embassy* is the official office of an ambassador in a foreign country and the office that handles the political relations of one nation with another.

A *consulate*, the office of a consul

in a foreign city, handles the commercial affairs and personal needs of citizens of the appointing country.

Capitalize with the name of a nation; lowercase without it: *the French Embassy, the U.S. Embassy, the embassy.*

e

embryo, fetus, unborn baby, unborn child While the terms are essentially interchangeable in many common uses, each has become politicized by the abortion debate even in uses not involving abortion. Anti-abortion advocates say *fetus* devalues a human life; abortion-rights supporters argue *unborn child* or *baby* equate termination of a pregnancy with murder by emphasizing the fetus's humanity.

Write clearly and sensitively, using any of the terms when appropriate:

Fetus, which refers to the stage in human development from the eighth week of pregnancy to birth, is preferred in many cases, including almost all scientific and medical uses: *The virus can be disastrous to a fetus. The lawsuit alleges harm to a fetus that prosecutors claim was viable. The research was conducted on fetal tissue.*

In scientific uses referring to the first seven weeks of human development after conception, use *embryo.*

The context or tone of a story can allow for *unborn baby* or *child* in cases where *fetus* could seem clinical or cold: *Weiss said her love for her unborn baby was the strongest feeling she had ever felt. The expectant mother lost her baby in the seventh month of pregnancy.*

See **abortion.**

emcee, emceed, emceeing A

phrase such as: *He was the master of ceremonies* is preferred.

em dash, en dash, hyphen References in this book to *dashes* denote what some styles call *em dashes, long dashes* or *thick dashes.* Because of news industry specifications for text transmission, AP has never used *en dashes,* also known as *short dashes.*

Some elaboration:

HYPHENS Use *hyphens* as joiners, such as for compound modifiers: *small-business owner.* AP also uses *hyphens* for ranges, such as *Jan. 1-4,* while some other styles use en dashes. There should be no spaces surrounding a hyphen.

EN DASHES AP does not use *en dashes.* Some other styles call for *en dashes* to indicate ranges, such as ranges of dates or times, or with some compound modifiers. An *en dash* is about half the width of an *em dash,* approximating the width of a capital letter *N.*

EM DASHES AP refers to these simply as *dashes* and covers their use in the **dash** entry. They are used to signal abrupt change; as one option to set off a series within a phrase; before attribution to an author or composer in some formats; after datelines; and to start lists. AP style calls for a space on both sides of a *dash* in all uses except the start of sports agate summaries. An *em dash* is approximately the width of a capital letter *M* in the typeface being used.

See **hyphen** and **dash.**

emergency room *ER* is acceptable on second reference.

emeritus This word often is added to formal titles to denote that individuals who have retired retain their rank or title.

When used, place *emeritus* after the formal title, in keeping with the general practice of academic institutions: *Professor Emeritus Samuel Eliot Morison, Dean Emeritus Courtney C. Brown, Publisher Emeritus Barnard L. Colby.*

Or: *Samuel Eliot Morison, professor emeritus of history; Courtney C. Brown, dean emeritus of the faculty of business; Barnard L. Colby, publisher emeritus.*

Use *emerita* for similar references if a woman prefers it.

emigrate, immigrate One who leaves a country *emigrates* from it.

One who comes into a country *immigrates.*

The same principle holds for *emigrant* and *immigrant.*

Emirates The airline's headquarters is in Dubai, United Arab Emirates.

Emmy, Emmys The annual awards by the Academy of Television Arts & Sciences (for prime-time programming; based in Los Angeles) and the National Academy of Television Arts and Sciences (for daytime, news and sports; based in New York).

emoji (s. and pl.) A symbol, such as a cartoon face, hand gesture, animal or other object, that might be used instead of a word or as an illustration in text messages or on social media. See **emoticon**. For guidance on quoting social media posts with emoji, see **quotations in the news**.

emoticon A typographical cartoon or symbol generally used to indicate mood or appearance, as :-) and sometimes looked at sideways. Also known as *smileys.* See **emoji**.

employee

empty-handed

enact See **act, amendment, bill, law, measure, ordinance, resolution, rule, statute** entry.

encyclopedia But follow the spelling of formal names: *Encyclopaedia Britannica.*

end user (n.) **end-user** (adj.) A phrase commonly referred to by technology developers when imagining the audience for software or hardware. *End-user experience.*

enforce But *reinforce.*

engine, motor An *engine* develops its own power, usually through internal combustion or the pressure of air, steam or water passing over vanes attached to a wheel: *an airplane engine, an automobile engine, a jet engine, a missile engine, a steam engine, a turbine engine.*

A *motor* receives power from an outside source: *an electric motor, a hydraulic motor.*

England *LONDON* stands alone in datelines. Use *England* after the names of other English communities in datelines.

See **datelines** and **United Kingdom**.

enroll, enrolled, enrolling

en route Always two words.

ensign See **military titles**.

ensure, insure, assure Use *ensure* to

e

mean *guarantee*: *Steps were taken to ensure accuracy.*

Use *insure* for references to insurance: *The policy insures his life.*

Use *assure* to mean *to make sure or give confidence*: *She assured us the statement was accurate.*

entitled Use it to mean *a right to do or have something*. Do not use it to mean *titled*.

Right: *She was entitled to the promotion.*

Right: *The book was titled "Gone With the Wind."*

enumerations See examples in **dash** and **periods** entries in **Punctuation** chapter.

envelop (v.) Other verb forms: *enveloping, enveloped*. But: *envelope* (n.)

environment See **ecology**.

Environmental Protection Agency *EPA* is acceptable on second reference.

envoy Not a formal title. Lowercase. See **titles**.

epicenter The point on the Earth's surface above the underground center, or focus, of an earthquake. See **earthquakes**.

epidemic, pandemic An *epidemic* is the rapid spreading of disease in a certain population or region; a *pandemic* is an *epidemic* that has spread worldwide. Use sparingly; follow declarations of public health officials.

epoch See **historical periods and events**.

equal An adjective without comparative forms.

When people speak of a *more equal* distribution of wealth, what is meant is *more equitable*.

Equal Employment Opportunity Commission *EEOC* is acceptable on second reference.

equal, equaled, equaling

equally as Do not use the words together; one is sufficient.

Omit the *equally* shown here in parentheses: *She was (equally) as wise as Marilyn.*

Omit the *as* shown here in parentheses: *She and Marilyn were equally (as) wise.*

equal time *Equal time* applies to the Federal Communications Commission regulation that requires a radio or television station to provide a candidate for political office with air time equal to any time that an opponent receives beyond the coverage of news events.

equator Always lowercase.

equitable See **equal**.

equity When used in a financial sense, *equity* means the value of property beyond the amount that is owed on it.

A *stockholder's equity* in a corporation is the value of the shares he holds.

A *homeowner's equity* is the difference between the value of the house and the amount of the unpaid mortgage.

ERA Acceptable in all references to baseball's *earned run average*.

eras See **historical periods and events**.

e-reader Or *e-book reader*. A device used to display electronic books and other digital publications. Other devices have e-reader software that can perform similar functions.

escalator clause A clause in a contract providing for increases or decreases in wages, prices, etc., based on fluctuations in the cost of living, production, expenses, etc.

Eskimo In general, avoid the term *Eskimo* for the native peoples of northern North America except when paired with a group's ethnic name in Alaska: *Inupiat Eskimos*, a *Yup'ik Eskimo community*, a *Cu'pik Eskimo*, etc. Follow the preference of those involved in the story, such as identifying someone simply as *Yup'ik*. The term *Eskimo* was assigned by non-native people and in some cultures, has since taken on offensive connotations. The term *Inuit* is used in Canada, Greenland and by some groups in northern Alaska.

ESOP Acronym for *employee stock ownership plan*. Spell out on first reference.

essential clauses, nonessential clauses These terms are used in this book instead of *restrictive clause* and *nonrestrictive clause* to convey the distinction between the two in a more easily remembered manner.

Both types of clauses provide additional information about a word or phrase in the sentence.

The difference between them is that the *essential clause* cannot be eliminated without changing the meaning of the sentence — it so *restricts* the meaning of the word or phrase that its absence would lead to a substantially different interpretation of what the author meant.

The *nonessential clause*, however, can be eliminated without altering the basic meaning of the sentence — it does not *restrict* the meaning so significantly that its absence would radically alter the author's thought.

PUNCTUATION: An essential clause must not be set off from the rest of a sentence by commas. A nonessential clause must be set off by commas.

The presence or absence of commas provides the reader with critical information about the writer's intended meaning. Note the following examples:

— *Reporters who do not read the Stylebook should not criticize their editors.* (The writer is saying that only one class of reporters, those who do not read the Stylebook, should not criticize their editors. If the *who ... Stylebook* phrase were deleted, the meaning of the sentence would be changed substantially.)

— *Reporters, who do not read the Stylebook, should not criticize their editors.* (The writer is saying that all reporters should not criticize their editors. If the *who ... Stylebook* phrase were deleted, this meaning would not be changed.)

USE OF WHO, WHOM, THAT, WHICH. See separate entries on **that (conjunction); that, which (pronouns); who, whom**.

That is the preferred pronoun to introduce essential clauses that refer to an inanimate object or an animal without a name. *Which* is the only acceptable pronoun to introduce a nonessential clause that refers to an inanimate object or an animal without a name.

The pronoun *which* occasionally may be substituted for *that* in the introduction of an essential clause that refers to an inanimate object or an animal without a name. In general, this use of *which* should appear only when *that* is used as a conjunction to introduce another clause in the same sentence: *He said Monday that the part of the army which suffered severe casualties needs reinforcement.*

See **that (conjunction)** for guidelines on the use of *that* as a conjunction.

essential phrases, nonessential phrases

These terms are used in this book instead of *restrictive phrase* and *nonrestrictive phrase* to convey the distinction between the two in a more easily remembered manner.

The underlying concept is the one that also applies to clauses:

An *essential phrase* is a word or group of words critical to the reader's understanding of what the author had in mind.

A *nonessential phrase* provides more information about something. Although the information may be helpful to the reader's comprehension, the reader would not be misled if the information were not there.

PUNCTUATION: Do not set an essential phrase off from the rest of a sentence by commas:

We saw the award-winning movie "One Flew Over the Cuckoo's Nest." (No comma, because many movies have won awards, and without the name of the movie the reader would not know which movie was meant.)

They ate dinner with their daughter Julie. (Because they have more than one daughter, the inclusion of Julie's name is critical if the reader is to know which daughter is meant.)

Set off nonessential phrases by commas:

We saw the 1975 winner of the Academy Award competition for best picture, "One Flew Over the Cuckoo's Nest." (Only one movie won the award. The name is informative, but even without the name no other movie could be meant.)

They ate dinner with their daughter Julie and her husband, David. (Julie has only one husband. If the phrase read *and her husband David*, it would suggest that she had more than one husband.)

The company chairman, Henry Ford II, spoke. (In the context, only one person could be meant.)

Indian corn, or maize, was harvested. (*Maize* provides the reader with the name of the corn, but its absence would not change the meaning of the sentence.)

DESCRIPTIVE WORDS: Do not confuse punctuation rules for nonessential clauses with the correct punctuation when a nonessential word is used as a descriptive adjective. The distinguishing clue often is the lack of an article or pronoun:

Right: *Julie and husband Jeff went shopping. Julie and her husband, Jeff, went shopping.*

Right: *Company Chairman Henry Ford II made the announcement. The company chairman, Henry Ford II, made the announcement.*

ETF Abbreviation for *exchange-traded fund.* A security that tracks a benchmark much as a mutual fund does, but trades throughout market days like a stock on the exchange. Spell out on first reference.

ethanol Fuel additive distilled from mashed and fermented grain. Gasoline blends are written as a percentage of *ethanol*, e.g., *E85* for *85 percent ethanol and 15 percent gasoline.*

ethnic cleansing Euphemism for a campaign to force a population from a region by expulsions and other violence often including killings and rapes. The term came to prominence in former Yugoslavia during the 1990s to whitewash atrocities of warring ethnic groups, then usage spread to other conflicts. AP does not use the term *ethnic cleansing* on its own. It must be enclosed in quotes, attributed and explained. Don't use the term as a keyword or in headlines.

euro The common currency of 19 of the 28 members of the European Union, known as the *eurozone*: Austria, Belgium, Cyprus, Estonia, Finland, France, Germany, Greece, Ireland, Italy, Latvia, Lithuania, Luxembourg, Malta, Netherlands, Portugal, Slovakia, Slovenia and Spain. Some smaller countries and territories also use the euro, either through agreement with the EU or as a de facto currency.

Plural is *euros*. Write euro amounts in the form *100 euros*. Do not use the "€" sign. See **currency conversions**.

eurodollar A U.S. dollar on deposit in a European bank, including foreign branches of U.S. banks.

European Union *EU* (no periods). The 28-nation European Union, based in Brussels, was created by the Treaty on European Union, which was signed in February 1992 and took effect Nov. 1, 1993. Its executive body is the 28-member European Commission, which runs the EU's day-to-day affairs, drafts European laws and, after their adoption by governments, ensures their enforcement across the bloc. It also represents the EU in international trade negotiations and conducts antitrust investigations. The six founding members are: France, Germany, Italy, Netherlands, Belgium and Luxembourg. Other members are: Austria, Britain, Bulgaria, Croatia, Cyprus, Czech Republic, Denmark, Estonia, Finland, Greece, Hungary, Ireland, Latvia, Lithuania, Malta, Poland, Portugal, Romania, Slovakia, Slovenia, Spain and Sweden. See **Brexit**.

eurozone See **euro**.

Eve Capitalize when used with *New Year's Eve, Christmas Eve.*

events Titles of special events, such as art exhibits and touring displays, are enclosed in quotes with primary words capitalized: *"Mummies: New Secrets From the Tombs" at Chicago's Field Museum.* Names of annually recurring events are capitalized without quotes: *North American International Auto Show in Detroit; Calgary Stampede.* For athletic events, refer to **sports sponsorship** in the Sports section.

every day (adv.) **everyday** (adj.)

every one, everyone Two words when it means each individual item: *Every one of the clues was worthless.*

One word when used as a pronoun meaning all persons: *Everyone wants their life to be happy.* (Don't use *his* with everyone; it presumes maleness. *They/them/their* may be used as singular in such constructions if essential, but rewriting is preferred: *All people want their lives to be happy.*) See **they, them, their**.

ex- Use no hyphen for words that use *ex-* in the sense of *out of*:

excommunicate   expropriate

Hyphenate when using *ex-* in the sense of *former*:

ex-convict   ex-president

Do not capitalize *ex-* when attached to a formal title before a name: *ex-President Richard Nixon.* The prefix modifies the entire term: *ex-New York Gov. Mario Cuomo*; not *New York ex-Gov.*

Usually *former* is better.

exaggerate

except See **accept, except**.

exclamation point See entry in **Punctuation** chapter.

execute, execution To *execute* a person is to kill that person in compliance with a military order or judicial decision.

See **assassin, killer, murderer** and **homicide, murder, manslaughter**.

execution-style Avoid use of this term to describe how people are killed, since it means different things to different people. Be specific as to how the person was killed, if that information is necessary.

executive branch Always lowercase.

executive director Capitalize before a name only if it is a formal corporate or organizational title. See **titles**.

Executive Mansion Capitalize only

in references to the White House.

executor Use for both men and women.

Not a formal title. Always lowercase.

See **titles**.

expel, expelled, expelling

Explorers See **Boy Scouts**.

exponential growth Used when something has grown by increasing amounts. For instance, a population might increase by 5 percent from 1980 to 1990, 10 percent from 1990 to 2000 and 15 percent from 2000 to 2010. Not simply a synonym for a large increase.

Export-Import Bank of the United States *Export-Import Bank* is acceptable in all references; *Ex-Im Bank* is acceptable on second reference.

Headquarters is in Washington.

extol, extolled, extolling

extra- Do not use a hyphen when *extra* means *outside of* unless the prefix is followed by a word beginning with *a* or a capitalized word:

extralegal   extraterrestrial
extramarital   extraterritorial

Follow *extra-* with a hyphen when it is part of a compound modifier describing a condition beyond the usual size, extent or degree:

extra-base hit   extra-large book
extra-dry drink   extra-mild taste

extraordinary loss, extraordinary income See **profit terminology**.

extrasensory perception *ESP* is acceptable on second reference.

extreme unction See **sacraments**.

Exxon Mobil Corp. Headquarters is in Irving, Texas, with exploration, production and chemical operations based in Houston. *Exxon Mobil* is acceptable on second reference.

eye, eyed, eyeing

eye to eye, eye-to-eye Hyphenate when used as a compound modifier: *an eye-to-eye confrontation.*

e

f

Facebook The world's most popular social network with more than 2 billion monthly active users. Based in Menlo Park, California.

face-lift

fact checks, fake news Holding politicians and public figures accountable for their words often requires reporting or research to verify facts that affirm or disprove a statement, or that show a gray area.

Fact-checking also is essential in debunking fabricated stories or parts of stories done as hoaxes, propaganda, jokes or for other reasons, often spread widely on the internet and mistaken as truth by some news consumers.

The term *fake news* may be used in quotes or as shorthand for the modern phenomenon of deliberate falsehoods or fiction masked as news circulating on the internet.

However, do not label as *fake news* specific or individual news items that are disputed. If *fake news* is used in a quote, push for specifics about what is meant. Alternative wording includes *false reports, erroneous reports, unverified reports, questionable reports, disputed reports* or *false reporting*, depending on the context.

In all cases, the goal of fact-checking is to push back on falsehoods, exaggeration and political spin. Be specific in describing what is false and back up those descriptions with facts.

Basic fact-checking should always be part of the main story, including wording noting when an assertion differs with known facts. Often, however, additional reporting is required to explore disputed points or questions more fully. In those cases, a separate fact check piece should be done. Some points:

— Present the assertion that's being checked, and quickly state what's wrong with it or what is correct. Use the exact quote or quotes that are being examined. Follow with the facts, backed by appropriate citations and attribution.

— Stick to checking facts, rather than opinion. A person's personal tastes and preferences might lie outside the mainstream, but as opinions they are not a topic for a fact check.

— Fact checks need not show statements to be clearly correct or clearly incorrect. Words can be true, false, exaggerated, a stretch, a selective use of data, partly or mostly true, etc. Use the most apt description that's supported by what the facts show.

— If a statement can't be confirmed, or can't be immediately confirmed, say so.

Usage notes: *fact check* and *fact-checking* (n.), to *fact-check* (v.)

fact-finding (adj.)

factor A financial organization whose primary business is purchasing the accounts receivable of other firms, at a discount, and taking the risk and responsibilities of making collection.

Faeroe Islands Use in datelines after a community name in stories from this group of Danish islands in the northern Atlantic Ocean between Iceland and the Shetland Islands.

Fahrenheit The temperature scale commonly used in the United States.

The scale is named for Gabriel Daniel Fahrenheit, a German physicist who designed it. In it, the freezing point of water is 32 degrees and the boiling point is 212 degrees.

To convert to Celsius, subtract 32 from Fahrenheit figure, multiply by 5 and divide by 9 (77 - 32 = 45, times 5 = 225, divided by 9 = 25 degrees Celsius.)

To convert a temperature difference from Fahrenheit to Celsius, multiply by 5 and divide by 9. A difference of 18 degrees F is a 10-degree C difference.

In cases that require mention of the scale, use these forms: *86 degrees Fahrenheit* or *86 F* (note the space and no period after the *F*) if degrees and Fahrenheit are clear from the context.

See **Celsius** and **Kelvin scale**.

For guidelines on when Celsius temperatures should be used, see **metric system** entry.

TEMPERATURE CONVERSIONS

Following is a temperature conversion table. Celsius temperatures have been rounded to the nearest whole number.

F	C	F	C	F	C
-26	-32	19	-7	64	18
-24	-31	21	-6	66	19
-22	-30	23	-5	68	20
-20	-29	25	-4	70	21
-18	-28	27	-3	72	22
-17	-27	28	-2	73	23
-15	-26	30	-1	75	24
-13	-25	32	0	77	25
F	C	F	C	F	C
-11	-24	34	1	79	26
-9	-23	36	2	81	27
-8	-22	37	3	82	28
-6	-21	39	4	84	29
-4	-20	41	5	86	30
-2	-19	43	6	88	31
0	-18	45	7	90	32
1	-17	46	8	91	33
3	-16	48	9	93	34
5	-15	50	10	95	35
7	-14	52	11	97	36
9	-13	54	12	99	37
10	-12	55	13	100	38
12	-11	57	14	102	39
14	-10	59	15	104	40
16	-9	61	16	106	41
18	-8	63	17	108	42

fake news See **fact checks, fake news**.

fake pot See **marijuana, medical marijuana**.

fall See **seasons**.

fallout (n.)

family names Capitalize words denoting family relationships only when they substitute for a person's name: *I wrote Mom a letter. I wrote my father a letter.*

Fannie Mae A government-controlled company that helps provide money for the U.S. housing market by buying residential mortgages and packaging pools of those loans for sale to investors. The company, whose name is short for *Federal National Mortgage Association*, was seized by the government in September 2008 and is overseen by the Federal Housing Finance Agency.

FAQ Acceptable in all uses for *frequently asked questions.*

Far East The easternmost portions of the continent of Asia: China, Japan,

f

North and South Korea, Taiwan, Hong Kong and the eastern portions of Russia.

Confine *Far East* to this restricted sense. Use the *Far East and Southeast Asia* when referring to a wider portion of eastern Asia.

See **Asian subcontinent** and **Southeast Asia**.

far-flung (adj.)

farmworker

far-off (adj.)

far-ranging (adj.)

farsighted When used in a medical sense, it means that a person can see objects at a distance but has difficulty seeing materials at close range.

farther, further Farther refers to physical distance: *He walked farther into the woods.*

Further refers to an extension of time or degree: *She will look further into the mystery.*

Far West For the U.S. region, generally west of the Rocky Mountains.

FASB Abbreviation for *Financial Accounting Standards Board*. Spell out on first reference.

fascism, fascist See **political parties and philosophies**.

Fatah A secular Palestinian party and former guerrilla movement founded by Yasser Arafat. Do not use with the prefix *al-*.

father Use *the Rev.* in first reference before the names of Episcopal, Orthodox and Roman Catholic priests. Use *Father* before a name only in direct quotations.

See **religious titles**.

Father's Day The third Sunday in June.

father-in-law, fathers-in-law

Father Time

faze, phase *Faze* means to embarrass or disturb: *The snub did not faze her.*

Phase denotes an aspect or stage: *They will phase in a new system.*

FBI Acceptable in all references for *Federal Bureau of Investigation*.

featherbedding The practice of requiring an employer to hire more workers than needed to handle a job.

features They are not exempt from normal style rules. See **special contexts** for guidelines on some limited exceptions.

federal Use a capital letter for the architectural style and for corporate or governmental bodies that use the word as part of their formal names: *the Federal Trade Commission*. (See separate entries for governmental agencies.)

Lowercase when used as an adjective to distinguish something from state, county, city, town or private entities: *federal assistance, federal court, the federal government, a federal judge.*

Also: *federal court* (but *U.S. District Court* is preferred) and *federal Judge Ann Aldrich* (but *U.S. District Judge Ann Aldrich* is preferred).

Federal Aviation Administration *FAA* is acceptable on second reference.

Federal Bureau of Investigation *FBI* is acceptable in all references. To avoid alphabet soup, however, use *the bureau* in some references.

Federal Communications Commission *FCC* is acceptable on second reference.

federal court Always lowercase.
The preferred form for first reference is to use the proper name of the court. See entries under **U.S.** and the court name.
Do not create nonexistent entities such as *Manhattan Federal Court*. Instead, use *a federal court in Manhattan*.
See **judicial branch**.

Federal Crop Insurance Corp. Do not abbreviate.

Federal Deposit Insurance Corp. The government agency that insures deposits in banks and thrifts. *FDIC* is acceptable on second reference.

Federal Emergency Management Agency *FEMA* is acceptable on second reference.

Federal Energy Regulatory Commission The government agency that regulates interstate natural gas and electricity transactions.
FERC is acceptable on second reference, but *the agency* or *the commission* is preferred.

Federal Farm Credit Board Do not abbreviate.

Federal Farm Credit System The federally chartered cooperative banking system that provides most of the nation's agricultural loans. The system is cooperatively owned by its farm borrowers and is made up of the regional banks that issue operating and mortgage loans through local land bank associations and production credit associations.

federal funds, federal funds rate Money in excess of what the Federal Reserve says a bank must have on hand to back up deposits. The excess can be lent overnight to banks that need more cash on hand to meet their reserve requirements. The interest rate of these loans is the *federal funds rate*. Its target rate is set by the Federal Reserve's policymaking panel, the Federal Open Market Committee. See **Federal Reserve**.

Federal Highway Administration Reserve the *FHA* abbreviation for the *Federal Housing Administration*.

Federal Home Loan Bank Board Do not abbreviate.

Federal Home Loan Mortgage Corp. See **Freddie Mac**.

Federal Housing Administration *FHA* is acceptable on second reference.

federal legal holidays See **holidays and holy days**.

Federal Mediation and Conciliation Service Do not abbreviate. Use *the mediation service* on second reference.

Federal National Mortgage

Association See **Fannie Mae**.

Federal Register This publication, issued every workday, is the legal medium for recording and communicating the rules and regulations established by the executive branch of the federal government.

Individuals or corporations cannot be held legally responsible for compliance with a regulation unless it has been published in the Register.

In addition, executive agencies are required to publish in advance some types of proposed regulations.

Federal Reserve The central bank of the United States. It comprises the Federal Open Market Committee, which sets interest rates; the Federal Reserve Board, the regulatory body made up of Fed governors in Washington; and the Federal Reserve System, which includes the Fed in Washington and 12 regional Fed banks. Use *Federal Reserve* on first reference, *the Fed* on second reference.

Federal Trade Commission *FTC* is acceptable on second reference.

FedEx Use this official brand name for the delivery service company. The formal name of the parent company is FedEx Corp. Headquarters is in Memphis, Tennessee.

feed An online stream of constantly updated material.

felony, misdemeanor A *felony* is a serious crime. A *misdemeanor* is a minor offense against the law.

A fuller definition of what constitutes a felony or misdemeanor depends on the governmental jurisdiction involved.

At the federal level, a *misdemeanor* is a crime that carries a potential penalty of no more than a year in jail. A *felony* is a crime that carries a potential penalty of more than a year in prison. Often, however, a statute gives a judge options such as imposing a fine or probation in addition to or instead of a jail or prison sentence.

A *felon* is a person who has been convicted of a *felony*, regardless of whether the individual actually spends time in confinement or is given probation or a fine instead.

Convicted felon is redundant.

See **prison, jail**.

female Use *female* as an adjective, not *woman*. *She is the first female governor of North Carolina.*

Ferris wheel

ferryboat

fertility rate As calculated by the federal government, it is the number of live births per 1,000 females age 15 through 44 years.

fetus See **embryo, fetus, unborn baby, unborn child**.

fewer, less In general, use *fewer* for individual items, *less* for bulk or quantity.

Wrong: *The trend is toward more machines and less people.* (People in this sense refers to individuals.)

Wrong: *She was fewer than 60 years old.* (Years in this sense refers to a period of time, not individual years.)

Right: *Fewer than 10 applicants called.* (Individuals.)

Right: *I had less than $50 in my*

pocket. (An amount.) But: *I had fewer than 50 $1 bills in my pocket.* (Individual items.)

Fez The preferred spelling for the city in Morocco.

fiance (man) **fiancee** (woman) Generally acceptable to describe anyone who is engaged to be married, regardless of sexual orientation. If a couple requests not to use those terms or if a gender-neutral option is needed, describe couples as *engaged* or *planning to marry* or similar phrasing.

Fiberglas Note the single *s.* A trademark for fiberglass or glass fiber.

field house

figuratively, literally *Figuratively* means *in an analogous sense,* but not in *the exact sense. He bled them white.*
Literally means in an exact sense; do not use it figuratively.
Wrong: *He literally bled them white.* (Unless the blood was drained from their bodies.)

figure The symbol for a number: *the figure 5.*
See **numerals.**

filibuster To *filibuster* is to make long speeches to obstruct the passage of legislation.
A legislator who used such methods also is a *filibuster,* not a *filibusterer.*

Filipinos The people of the Philippines. *Filipina* is acceptable as the feminine form.

film noir

filmgoer

filmmaker

film ratings See **movie ratings.**

financial editor Capitalize only as a formal title before a name.
See **titles.**

financial institutions Here are 10 major U.S.-based financial institutions and their headquarters.
JPMorgan Chase & Co., New York
Bank of America Corp., Charlotte, N.C.
Citigroup Inc., New York
Wells Fargo & Co., San Francisco
Goldman Sachs Group Inc., New York
MetLife Inc., New York
Morgan Stanley, New York
U.S. Bancorp, Minneapolis
American Express Co., New York
Bank of New York Mellon Corp., New York
HSBC North America Holdings Inc., New York
Travelers Cos., New York

Finland A Nordic state, not part of Scandinavia.

firearms See **weapons.**

fire department See the **governmental bodies** entry for the basic rules on capitalization.
See **titles** and **military titles** for guidelines on titles.

firefight

firefighter, fireman The preferred term to describe a person who fights fire is *firefighter.*
One meaning of *fireman* is a person who tends fires in a furnace.

Fireman is also an acceptable synonym for *firefighter*.

fire names Use descriptors to identify a fire. For example: *the deadly fire burning near San Diego.* While local media may choose to use the names of fires given by local agencies, the AP generally does not use those names because they are not widely known to a global audience. On some occasions, when a fire is particularly significant, the AP may use the name of the fire lower in the story. See **storm names** in the **weather terms** entry.

firewall A device or software designed to stop malicious or unauthorized internet traffic from reaching a computer or local data network. Many firewalls also inspect outgoing traffic.

firm A business partnership is correctly referred to as a *firm: He joined a law firm.*
Do not use *firm* in references to an incorporated business entity. Use *the company* or *the corporation* instead.

first aid (n.) **first-aid** (adj.)

first class, first-class Hyphenate as a modifier before a noun. *The restaurant was first class. It was a first-class restaurant.*

first degree, first-degree Hyphenate when used as a compound modifier: *It was murder in the first degree. He was convicted of first-degree murder.*

first family Always lowercase.

firsthand (adj. and adv.)

first lady , first gentleman Not an official title, always lowercase. Usually reserved for families of heads of state, but acceptable at lower levels such as governor or mayor if that is the local custom. Should the individual hold or have held an official title of high office, that title takes precedence: *Former Secretary of State Hillary Clinton ran for president,* not *former first lady Hillary Clinton ran for president.*

first quarter, first-quarter Hyphenate when used as a compound modifier: *He scored in the first quarter. The team took the lead on his first-quarter goal.*

fiscal, monetary *Fiscal* applies to budgetary matters.
Monetary applies to money supply.

fiscal year The 12-month period that a corporation or governmental body uses for bookkeeping purposes.
The federal government's fiscal year starts three months ahead of the calendar year — fiscal 2007, for example, ran from Oct. 1, 2006, to Sept. 30, 2007.

fitful It means restless, not a condition of being fit.

fjord

flack, flak *Flack* is slang for *press agent.* Avoid using in copy.
Flak is a type of anti-aircraft fire, hence figuratively a barrage of criticism.

flagpole, flagship

flail, flay To *flail* is to swing the arms widely.
To *flay* is, literally, to strip off the

skin by whipping. Figuratively, *to flay* means to tongue-lash a person.

flair, flare *Flair* is conspicuous talent or style.

Flare is a verb meaning to blaze with sudden, bright light or to burst out in anger. It is also a noun meaning a flame.

flak See **flack, flak**.

flare-up (n.) **flare up** (v.) See **flair, flare**.

flash flood See **weather terms**.

flash mob A gathering of people performing an action in a public place designated by a text message, email, social media post or other notification.

flaunt, flout *To flaunt* is to make an ostentatious or defiant display: *She flaunted her intelligence.*

To flout is to show contempt for: *He flouts the law.*

fleet Use figures and capitalize *fleet* when forming a proper name: *the 6th Fleet.*

Lowercase *fleet* whenever it stands alone.

Flickr An image-hosting website owned by Verizon Communications Inc. subsidiary Oath Inc.

flier, flyer *Flyer* is the preferred term for a person flying in an aircraft, and for handbills: *He used his frequent flyer miles; they put up flyers announcing the show.* Use *flier* in the phrase *take a flier*, meaning *to take a big risk.*

flip-flop (n. and v.)

float Money that has been committed but not yet credited to an account, like a check that has been written but has not yet cleared.

flood plain

floods, flood stage See **weather terms**.

floodwaters

floor leader Treat it as a job description, lowercased, rather than a formal title: *Republican floor leader John Smith.*

Do not use when a formal title such as *majority leader, minority leader* or *whip* would be the accurate description.

See **legislative titles** and **titles**.

Florida Abbreviate *Fla.* in datelines only; spell out in stories. Postal code: FL

See **state names**.

Florida Keys A chain of small islands extending southwest from the southern tip of mainland Florida.

Cities, or the islands themselves, are followed by *Fla.* in datelines: *KEY WEST, Fla. (AP) —*

flounder, founder A *flounder* is a fish; to *flounder* is to move clumsily or jerkily, to flop about: *The fish floundered on land.*

To founder is to bog down, become disabled or sink: *The ship floundered in the heavy seas for hours, then foundered.*

flout See **flaunt, flout**.

flowers See **plants**.

fluid ounce Equal to 1.8 cubic inches,

2 tablespoons or 6 teaspoons. The metric equivalent is approximately 30 milliliters.

To convert to milliliters, multiply by 30 (3 ounces x 30 equals 90 milliliters).

See **liter**.

flu-like

fluorescent

flush To become red in the face.

flyer See **flier, flyer**.

FM Acceptable in all references for the *frequency modulation* system of radio transmission.

f.o.b. Acceptable on first reference for *free on board*, meaning a seller agrees to put a commodity on a truck, ship, etc., at no charge, but transportation costs must be paid by the buyer.

-fold No hyphen: *twofold, fourfold* and *hundredfold*.

folk singer, folk song

following The word usually is a noun, verb or adjective: *He has a large following. He is following his conscience. The following statement was made.*

Although Webster's New World College Dictionary records its use as a preposition, the preferred word is *after: He spoke after dinner.* Not: *He spoke following dinner.*

follow-up (n. and adj.) Use two words (no hyphen) in verb form.

food Most food names are lowercase: *apples, cheese, peanut butter.*

Capitalize brand names and

trademarks: *Roquefort cheese, Tabasco sauce.*

Most proper nouns or adjectives are capitalized when they occur in a food name: *Boston brown bread, Russian dressing, Swiss cheese, Waldorf salad.*

Lowercase is used, however, when the food does not depend on the proper noun or adjective for its meaning: *french fries.*

If a question arises, check the separate section on **Food Guidelines**. If there is no entry, follow Webster's New World College Dictionary. Use lowercase if the dictionary lists it as an acceptable form for the sense in which the word is used.

The same principles apply to foreign names for foods: *mousse de saumon* (salmon mousse), *pomme de terre* (literally, "apple of the earth" — for potato), *salade Russe* (Russian salad).

Food and Agriculture Organization Not *Agricultural*. FAO is acceptable on second reference to this U.N. agency.

Food and Drug Administration *FDA* is acceptable on second reference.

foodborne (adj.)

foot The basic unit of length in the measuring system used in the United States. Its origin was a calculation that this was the length of the average human foot.

The metric equivalent is exactly 30.48 centimeters, which may be rounded to 30 centimeters for most comparisons.

For most conversions to centimeters, it is adequate to multiply 30 (5 feet x 30 equals 150 centimeters). For more exact figures, multiply by 30.48 (5 feet x 30.48 equals 152.4 centimeters).

To convert to meters, multiply by 0.3 (5 feet x 0.3 equals 1.5 meters).

See **centimeter**; **meter**; and **dimensions**.

foot-and-mouth disease Not *hoof-and-mouth disease*.

forbear, forebear *To forbear* is to avoid or shun.

A *forebear* is an ancestor.

forbid, forbade, forbidding

force majeure A condition permitting a company to depart from the strict terms of a contract because of an event or effect that can't be reasonably controlled.

forcible rape A redundancy that usually should be avoided. It may be used, however, in stories dealing with both rape and statutory rape, which does not necessarily involve the use of force.

Ford Motor Co. Use *Ford* on second reference.

Headquarters is in Dearborn, Michigan.

fore- The rules in **prefixes** apply, but in general, no hyphen. Some examples:

forebrain   *foregoing*
forefather   *foretooth*

There are three nautical exceptions, based on long-standing practice:

fore-topgallant   *fore-topsail*
fore-topmast

forecast Use *forecast* also for the past tense, not *forecasted*.

See **weather terms**.

foreclosure The process by which a lender seizes property from a mortgage holder who has failed to make payments and is in default.

forego, forgo *To forego* means to go before, as in *foregone conclusion*.

To forgo means to abstain from, as in: *He decided to forgo his senior year of eligibility*.

foreign names For foreign place names, use the primary spelling in Webster's New World College Dictionary. If it has no entry, follow the National Geographic Atlas of the World.

For personal names, follow the individual's preference for an English spelling if it can be determined. Otherwise:

— Use the nearest phonetic equivalent in English if one exists: *Alexander Solzhenitsyn*, for example, rather than *Aleksandr*, the spelling that would result from a transliteration of the Russian letters into the English alphabet.

If a name has no close phonetic equivalent in English, express it with an English spelling that approximates the sound in the original language: *Anwar Sadat*.

In general, lowercase particles such as *de, der, la, le*, and *van, von* when part of a given name: *Charles de Gaulle, Baron Manfred von Richthofen*. But follow individual preferences, as in *bin Laden*, or Dutch names such as *Van Gogh* or *Van der Graaf*. Capitalize the particles when the last names start a sentence: *De Gaulle spoke to von Richthofen*.

For additional guidelines, see **Arabic names**; **Chinese names**; **Portuguese names**; **Russian names**; **Spanish names**.

foreign words Some foreign words and abbreviations have been accepted universally into the English language: *bon voyage*; *versus, vs.*; *et cetera, etc.*

Many foreign words and their abbreviations are not understood universally, although they may be used in special applications such as medical or legal terminology. If such a word or phrase is needed in a story, place it in quotation marks and provide an explanation: *"ad astra per aspera," a Latin phrase meaning "to the stars through difficulty."*

foreman, forewoman Seldom a formal title. Never use foreperson.

formal titles See **titles**.

former Always lowercase. But retain capitalization for a formal title used immediately before a name: *former President Bill Clinton*.

Formica A trademark for a brand of laminated plastic.

formula, formulas Use figures in writing formulas. See **metric system**.

forsake, forsook, forsaken

fort Do not abbreviate for cities or for military installations.
In datelines for cities:
FORT LAUDERDALE, Fla. (AP) —
In datelines for military installations:
FORT BRAGG, N.C. (AP) —

fortuneteller, fortunetelling

forward Not *forwards*.

foul, fowl *Foul* means offensive, out of line.

A *fowl* is a bird, especially the larger domestic birds used as food: chickens, ducks, turkeys.

founder See **flounder, founder**.

Founding Fathers Capitalize when referring to the creators of the U.S. Constitution.

Four-H Club *4-H Club* is preferred. Members are *4-H'ers*.

four-star general

Fourth Estate Capitalize when used as a collective name for journalism and journalists.

The description is attributed to Edmund Burke, who is reported to have called the reporters' gallery in Parliament a "Fourth Estate."

The three estates of early English society were the Lords Spiritual (the clergy), the Lords Temporal (the nobility) and the Commons (the bourgeoisie).

Fourth of July, July Fourth Also *Independence Day*. The federal legal holiday is observed on Friday if July 4 falls on a Saturday, on Monday if it falls on a Sunday.

4x4 *Four-wheel drive* is preferred, unless *4x4* is part of the car model's proper name.

401(k) (no space)

Fox U.S. television network owned by Twenty-First Century Fox Inc. See **News Corp.** and **Twenty-First Century Fox Inc.**

fracking Acceptable with brief explanation. The energy industry uses the technique to extract oil and gas from rock by injecting high-pressure mixtures of water, sand or gravel and chemicals. See **hydraulic fracturing**.

fractions Generally spell out amounts less than 1 in stories, using hyphens between the words: *two-thirds, four-fifths, seven-sixteenths,* etc.

Use figures for precise amounts larger than 1, converting to decimals whenever practical.

When using fractional characters, use a forward-slash mark (/): 1/8, 1/4, 5/16, 9/10, etc. For mixed numbers, use 1 1/2, 2 5/8, etc. with a full space between the whole number and the fraction. AP systems may automatically replace some fractions with single-character versions: 1/2 may be replaced by ½. These can be left in the form the system changes them to. (You may also choose to set the options on your system so that these replacements are not made.)

See **numerals** and **percent**.

fragment, fragmentary *Fragment* describes a piece or pieces broken from the whole: *She sang a fragment of the song.*

Fragmentary describes disconnected and incomplete parts: *Early returns were fragmentary.*

frame-up (n.) **frame up** (v.)

Frankfurt The city in Germany carries the name of the country in datelines.

fraternal organizations and service clubs Capitalize the proper names: *American Legion, Lions Club, Independent Order of Odd Fellows, Rotary Club.*

Capitalize also words describing membership: *He is a Legionnaire, a Lion, an Odd Fellow, an Optimist and*

a Rotarian. See **American Legion** for the rationale on *Legionnaire.*

Capitalize the formal titles of officeholders when used before a name.

See **titles**.

Freddie Mac A government-controlled company that helps provide money for the U.S. housing market by buying residential mortgages and packaging pools of those loans for sale to investors. The company, whose name is short for *Federal Home Loan Mortgage Corp.,* was seized by the government in September 2008 and is overseen by the Federal Housing Finance Agency.

free-for-all (n. and adj.)

freelancer (n.) **freelance** (v. and adj.)

freely floating Describes an exchange rate that is allowed to fluctuate in response to supply and demand in the foreign markets.

free on board See **f.o.b.**

Free Syrian Army Armed opposition group in Syria. Active in the Syrian civil war that began in March 2011.

freewheeling

freeze-dry, freeze-dried, freeze-drying

freezing drizzle, freezing rain See **weather terms**.

French Canadian A Canadian whose native language, though not necessarily family origin, is French. In Quebec, the term refers to shared French culture and language among diverse citizens rather than strictly dual heritage. No hyphen.

French Foreign Legion Retain capitalization if shortened to the Foreign Legion.

Lowercase *the legion* and *legionnaires*. Unlike the situation with the American Legion, the French Foreign Legion is a group of active soldiers.

frequent flyer

freshman, freshmen *Freshman* is a singular noun or adjective: *a college freshman, the freshman class. Freshmen* is a plural noun: *The freshmen assembled quietly.*

friend, follow, like Acceptable in a social media context as both nouns and verbs. Actions by which users connect to other users on social networks and engage with their content.

Frigidaire A trademark for a brand of kitchen and laundry appliances.

Frisbee A trademark for a plastic disc thrown as a toy. Use *Frisbee disc* for the trademarked version and *flying disc* for other generic versions.

Frontier Airlines Headquarters is in Denver.

front line (n.) **front-line** (adj.)

frontman

front page (n.) **front-page** (adj.)

front-runner

frost See **weather terms**.

fruits See **food**.

fulfill, fulfilled, fulfilling

full- Hyphenate when used to form compound modifiers:

full-dress	*full-page*
full-fledged	*full-scale*
full-length	

See the listings that follow and Webster's New World College Dictionary for the spelling of other combinations.

full-body scanner

full faith and credit bond See **loan terminology**.

full house Three of a kind and a pair in poker.

full time, full-time Hyphenate when used as a compound modifier: *He works full time. She has a full-time job.*

fulsome It means disgustingly excessive. Do not use it to mean lavish or profuse.

fundraising, fundraiser One word in all cases.

funnel cloud See **weather terms**.

furlough

further See **farther, further**.

fuselage

fusillade

futures *Futures* contracts are agreements to deliver a quantity of goods, generally commodities, at a specified price at a certain time in the future. *Options*, which also are widely traded on the nation's commodities exchanges, give buyers the right but not the obligation to buy or sell something at a certain price within a specified period.

The purpose of the futures exchanges is to transfer the risk of price fluctuations from people who don't want the risk, such as farmers or metals processors, to speculators who are willing to take a gamble on making big profits.

Major U.S. commodities markets are the Chicago Board Options Exchange, Chicago Board of Trade, Chicago Mercantile Exchange, New York Mercantile Exchange, the New York Cotton Exchange, and the Coffee, Sugar and Cocoa Exchange.

F-word See **obscenities, profanities, vulgarities**.

f

g

GAAP The acronym stands for *generally accepted accounting principles*. Spell out on first reference.

gage, gauge A *gage* is a security or a pledge.

A *gauge* is a measuring device.

Gauge is also a term used to designate the size of shotguns. See **weapons**.

gaiety

gale See **weather terms**.

gallon Equal to 128 fluid ounces. The metric equivalent is approximately 3.8 liters. There are 42 gallons in a barrel of oil.

To convert to liters, multiply by 3.8 (3 gallons x 3.8 = 11.4 liters).

See **imperial gallon**; **liter**; and **metric system**.

Gallup Poll Prepared by the Gallup Organization, Princeton, New Jersey.

gambling Preferred term instead of *gaming* for risking money or some other stake on the outcome of an event: *gambling on blackjack at a casino*; *gambling on a chess match*. *Betting* and *wagering* are also acceptable: *betting on a horse race*; *the friends wagered on a footrace*; *a betting pool for the NCAA Tournament*. Avoid using the term *gaming* except in quotations, in proper names or when referring to video games.

game plan

gaming See **gambling**.

gamut, gantlet, gauntlet A *gamut* is a scale of notes or any complete range or extent.

A *gantlet* is a flogging ordeal, literally or figuratively.

A *gauntlet* is a glove. *To throw down the gauntlet* means to issue a challenge. To *take up the gauntlet* means to accept a challenge.

Gannett Co. The largest owner of U.S. newspapers, including USA Today and daily publications such as The Arizona Republic, Detroit Free Press and Milwaukee Journal Sentinel. Split off its broadcasting division into a separate company, Tegna Inc., in 2015. Both companies remain headquartered in McLean, Virginia. Gannett bought Journal Media Group, born from the merger of E.W. Scripps and Journal Communications, in 2016.

garnish (v. and n.) **garnishee** (n.) *Garnish* means to adorn or decorate. The noun *garnish* is a decoration or ornament. In a legal context, *garnish* means to attach property or wages as a result of a legal action. A *garnishee* is an individual whose property was attached, or garnished.

gauge See **gage, gauge**.

gay Used to describe people attracted to the same sex, though *lesbian* is the more common term for women. Preferred over *homosexual* except in clinical contexts or references to sexual activity. Include sexual orientation only when it is pertinent to a story, and avoid references to *sexual preference* or to a *gay* or *alternative lifestyle*. See **LGBT, LGBTQ** and **homophobia**. Sexual orientation is not synonymous with gender. See **gender**.

Gazprom Russia's state-controlled gas monopoly. Corporate name is *OAO Gazprom*. Headquarters is in Moscow.

GED A trademark abbreviation for *General Educational Development* tests, a battery of five exams designed by the American Council on Education to measure high school equivalency. *GED* should be used as an adjective, not as a noun. Those passing the tests earn a *GED diploma* or *certificate*, not a *GED*.

G-8 See **G-7**.

gender Not synonymous with *sex*. *Gender* refers to a person's social identity while *sex* refers to biological characteristics. Not all people fall under one of two categories for *sex* or *gender*, according to leading medical organizations, so avoid references to *both*, *either* or *opposite* sexes or genders as a way to encompass all people. When needed for clarity or in certain stories about scientific studies, alternatives include *men and women*, *boys and girls*, *males and females*.

Language around gender is evolving. Newsrooms and organizations outside AP may need to make decisions, based on necessity and audience, on terms that differ from or are not covered by AP's specific recommendations. For instance, the AP recommends the terms *sex reassignment* or *gender confirmation* for the medical procedures used for gender transition, while some groups use other terms, such as *gender affirmation* or *sex realignment*. The AP allows for *LGBT* and *LGBTQ* to be used on first reference without spelling out the acronyms; some other organizations use *LGBTQIA* and other variations on first reference or without explanation. For guidance on pronouns, see **they, them, their**.

Some frequently used terms and definitions:

cisgender May be used if necessary to refer to people who are not *transgender* in stories about gender, as a means to distinguish people from one another. Use only with explanation. Do not use terms like *normal* to describe people who are not *transgender*. *Cisgender* refers to gender and is not synonymous with *heterosexual*, which refers to sexuality.

gender nonconforming (n.), gender-nonconforming (adj.) Acceptable in broad references as a term for people who do not conform to the traditional view of two genders. *The group is providing scholarships for gender-nonconforming students.* When talking about individuals, be specific about how a person describes or expresses gender identity and behavior. *Roberta identifies as both male and female.* Not synonymous with *transgender*. Use other terms like *bigender* (a term for people who identify as a combination of two genders) only if used by subjects to describe themselves, and only with explanation.

intersex Term for people born with genitalia, chromosomes or reproductive organs that don't

g

fit typical definitions for males or females at birth. *Gonzalez is an intersex person, Zimmerman is intersex.* Do not use the outdated term *hermaphrodite.*

sex reassignment or gender confirmation The treatments, surgeries and other medical procedures used by transgender people to match their sex to their gender. The preferred term over *gender reassignment*; do not use the outdated term *sex change. Sex reassignment* or *gender confirmation* surgery is not necessary for people to transition their gender. *Balducci weighed whether to have sex reassignment surgery during his transition.*

transgender An adjective that describes people whose gender identity does not match the sex or gender they were identified as having at birth. Does not require what are often known as *sex reassignment* or *gender confirmation* procedures. Identify people as *transgender* only if pertinent, and use the name by which they live publicly. Generally, avoid references to a transgender person being *born a boy* or *girl*, since describing someone as *transgender* speaks for itself and doesn't take *intersex* babies into account. *Bernard is a transgender man. Christina is transgender.* The shorthand *trans* is acceptable on second reference and in headlines: *Grammys add first man and first trans woman as trophy handlers.*

Do not use as a noun or refer to someone as a transgender, or use the term *transgendered.* Not synonymous with terms like *cross-dresser* or *drag queen*, which do not have to do with gender identity. See **cross-dresser, drag performer**. Do not use the outdated term *transsexual.*

Do not use a derogatory term such as *tranny* except in extremely rare circumstances — only in a quote when it is crucial to the story or the understanding of a news event. Flag the contents in an editor's note.

Use the name by which a transgender person now lives: *Caitlyn Jenner.* Refer to a previous name only if relevant to the story: *Caitlyn Jenner, who won a 1976 Olympic gold medal in decathlon as Bruce Jenner.* See **name changes, LGBT, LGBTQ**.

transition, gender transition The process by which *transgender people* change the physical characteristics associated with the sex or gender they were identified as having at birth to those matching their own gender identity. May include *sex reassignment* or *gender confirmation* procedures, but not necessarily. *Washington is transitioning while helping his daughter consider universities. Chamberlain's family offered support during her transition.*

general assembly See **legislature** for its treatment as the name of a state's legislative body.

Capitalize when it is the formal name for the ruling or consultative body of an organization: *the General Assembly of the World Council of Churches.*

General Assembly (U.N.) *General Assembly* may be used on the first reference in a story under a United Nations dateline.

Use *U.N. General Assembly* in other first references, *the General Assembly* or *the assembly* in subsequent references.

general court Part of the official proper name for the legislatures in

Massachusetts and New Hampshire. Capitalize specific references with or without the state name: *the Massachusetts General Court, the General Court.*

In keeping with the accepted practice, however, *Legislature* may be used instead and treated as a proper name. See **legislature**.

Lowercase *legislature* in a generic use such as: *The General Court is the legislature in Massachusetts.*

General Dynamics Corp. Headquarters is in Falls Church, Virginia.

General Electric Co. *GE* is acceptable on second reference. Headquarters is in Boston.

general, general of the Air Force, general of the Army See **military titles**.

general manager Capitalize only as a formal title before a name: corporate *General Manager Jim Smith.* Lowercase as a job description for sports teams: *Giants general manager Jerry Reese.*

See **titles**.

General Motors Co. *GM* is acceptable on second reference.

Headquarters is in Detroit.

general obligation bond See **loan terminology**.

General Services Administration *GSA* is acceptable on second reference.

Generation X The generation following the 1946 to 1964 baby-boom generation. *Gen X* is acceptable on second reference;

members of this generation are *Gen Xers.* Definitions vary for the years this generation spans; the time period should be specified when possible. See **baby boom, baby boomer** and **millennials**.

Geneva The city in Switzerland stands alone in datelines.

Geneva Conventions Note the final *s*.

gentile Generally, any person not Jewish; often, specifically a Christian.

gentleman Do not use as a synonym for *man*. See **lady**.

genus, species In scientific or biological names, capitalize the first, or generic, Latin name for the class of plant or animal and lowercase the species that follows: *Homo sapiens, Tyrannosaurus rex.*

In second references, use the abbreviated form: *P. borealis, T. rex.*

geographic names The basic guidelines:

DOMESTIC: Do not use the postal abbreviations for state names. For acceptable abbreviations, see entries in this book under each state's name. See **state names** for rules on when the abbreviations may be used.

Abbreviate *Saint* as *St.* (But abbreviate *Sault Sainte Marie* as *Sault Ste. Marie.*)

FOREIGN: The first source for the spelling of all foreign place names is Webster's New World College Dictionary as follows:

— Use the first-listed spelling if an entry gives more than one.

— If the dictionary provides different spellings in separate entries, use the spelling that is followed by a full description of the location.

If the dictionary does not have an entry, use the first-listed spelling in the National Geographic Atlas of the World.

Online: http://maps.nationalgeographic.com/maps

NEW NAMES: Follow the styles adopted by the United Nations and the U.S. Board on Geographic Names for new cities, new independent nations and nations that change their names.

DATELINES: See the **datelines** entry.

CAPITALIZATION: Capitalize common nouns when they form an integral part of a proper name, but lowercase them when they stand alone: *Pennsylvania Avenue, the avenue; the Philippine Islands, the islands; the Mississippi River, the river.*

Lowercase common nouns that are not a part of a specific name: *the Pacific islands, the Swiss mountains, Zhejiang province.*

For additional guidelines, see **addresses**; **capitalization**; **directions and regions**; and **island**.

geolocation, geotagging The act of adding geographical metadata to pieces of media, social media updates or other digital content. Also, the use of a user's physical location to determine access to certain information. The metadata itself is an item's *geolocation* or *geotag*. A *geotagged* tweet, post, photo or video would contain information about the latitude and longitude of the location where the photo was taken, or possibly the name of the city and/or country, or of a landmark or establishment where the user has chosen to check in.

Georgia Abbreviate *Ga.* in datelines only; spell out in stories. Postal code: *GA*
See **state names**.

German measles Also known as *rubella.*

Germany *East Germany* and *West Germany* were reunited as of Oct. 3, 1990. *BERLIN* stands alone in datelines.

getaway (n.)

get-together (n.)

ghetto, ghettos Do not use indiscriminately as a synonym for the sections of cities inhabited by minorities or the poor. *Ghetto* has a connotation that government decree has forced people to live in a certain area.

In most cases, *section, district, slum area* or *quarter* is the more accurate word.

gibe, jibe *To gibe* means *to taunt or sneer*: *They gibed him about his mistakes.*

Jibe means *to shift direction* or, colloquially, *to agree*: *They jibed their ship across the wind. Their stories didn't jibe.*

Gibraltar, Strait of Not *Straits.* The entrance to the Mediterranean from the Atlantic Ocean. The British colony on the peninsula that juts into the strait stands alone in datelines as *GIBRALTAR.*

GIF Acronym for Graphics Interchange Format, a compression format for images. GIF is acceptable in copy but should be explained in the story. Use lowercase in a file name. For guidance on quoting social media posts with GIFs, see **quotations in the news**.

giga- A prefix denoting 1 billion units of a measure. Move a decimal point nine places to the right, adding zeros if necessary, to convert to the basic unit: 5.5 gigatons = 5,500,000,000 tons.

gigabyte See **byte**.

gig economy Job-to-job employment with little security and few employment rights. Include a brief explanation in the text if used.

GI, GIs Believed to have originated as an abbreviation for *government issue* supplies, it describes military personnel in general, but normally is used for the Army. (No periods is an exception to the general rule for two-letter abbreviations.)

Soldier is preferred unless the story contains the term in quoted matter or involves a subject such as the *GI Bill of Rights*.

Ginnie Mae Commonly used for *Government National Mortgage Association*.

girl See **boy, girl**.

girlfriend, boyfriend

Girl Scouts The full name of the national organization is *Girl Scouts of the United States of America*. Headquarters is in New York. Note that *Girl Scout Cookies* is a trademark name.

Girls 6 through 8 are *Brownie Girl Scouts* or *Brownies*. Girls 9 through 11 are *Junior Girl Scouts* or *Juniors*. Girls 12 through 14 are *Cadette Girl Scouts* or *Cadettes*. Girls 15 through 17 are *Senior Girl Scouts* or *Seniors*.

See **Boy Scouts**.

glamour One of the few *our* endings still used in American writing. But the adjective is *glamorous*.

GlaxoSmithKline PLC Headquarters is in London.

Global Positioning System See **GPS**.

global warming The terms *global warming* and *climate change* can be used interchangeably. *Climate change* is more accurate scientifically to describe the various effects of greenhouse gases on the world because it includes extreme weather, storms and changes in rainfall patterns, ocean acidification and sea level. But *global warming* as a term is more common and understandable to the public.

The world is warming, mainly due to rising levels of carbon dioxide and other greenhouse gases. Most of the increase in temperature comes from man-made sources. These sources include the burning of coal, oil and natural gas, deforestation and livestock raising.

This is based on the vast majority of peer-reviewed studies, science organizations and climate scientists.

Identify the source for specific climate change data, and for any detailed predictions of how climate change will affect the earth.

In a joint publication in 2014, the U.S. National Academy of Sciences and the Royal Society of the United Kingdom stated: "Human activities — especially the burning of fossil fuels since the start of the Industrial Revolution — have increased atmospheric carbon dioxide concentrations by about 40 percent, with more than half the increase occurring since 1970. Since 1900, the global average surface temperature has increased by about 0.8 degrees Celsius (1.4 degrees Fahrenheit). This has been accompanied by warming of the ocean, a rise in sea level, a strong decline in Arctic sea ice, and many other associated climate effects. Much of this warming has occurred in the last four decades."

To describe those who don't accept climate science or dispute that the world is warming from man-made forces, use *climate change doubters* or *those who reject mainstream climate science*. Avoid use of *skeptics* or *deniers*.

globe-trotter, globe-trotting But the proper name of the basketball team is the *Harlem Globetrotters*.

GMT For *Greenwich Mean Time*. Also referred to as *Coordinated Universal Time* or *UTC*. See **time zones** and **meridians**.

gobbledygook

go-between (n.)

godchild, goddaughter Also: *godfather, godliness, godmother, godsend* and *godson*. Always lowercase.

gods and goddesses Capitalize *God* in references to the deity of all monotheistic religions. Capitalize all noun references to the deity: *God the Father, Holy Ghost, Holy Spirit, Allah,* etc. Lowercase personal pronouns: *he, him, thee, thou.*

Lowercase *gods* and *goddesses* in references to the deities of

polytheistic religions.

Lowercase *god, gods* and *goddesses* in references to false gods: *He made money his god.*

See **religious references**.

Godspeed

-goer One word. Examples: *concertgoer, moviegoer, partygoer, theatergoer.*

go-go

Goldman Sachs Group Inc. Headquarters is in New York.

goodbye

Good Conduct Medal Military service medal.

Good Friday The Friday before Easter.

good Samaritan But uppercase when used in a title: *Good Samaritan Hospital.*

good, well *Good* is an adjective that means something is as it should be or is better than average.

When used as an adjective, *well* means suitable, proper, healthy. When used as an adverb, *well* means in a satisfactory manner or skillfully.

Good should not be used as an adverb. It does not lose its status as an adjective in a sentence such as *I feel good*. Such a statement is the idiomatic equivalent of *I am in good health*. An alternative, *I feel well*, could be interpreted as meaning that your sense of touch is good.

See **bad, badly** and **well**.

goodwill One word in all uses.

Google Internet company that runs a search engine and digital advertising network. *Google, Googling* and *Googled* are used informally as a verb for performing an internet search. Google has built several other digital products, including Android software for mobile devices, the Chrome web browser, the Gmail email service and the YouTube video site , which the company bought in 2006. As part of a reorganization completed in October 2015, a new company called Alphabet Inc. became Google's parent company and inherited Google's stock symbol, "GOOGL." Alphabet also owns several former Google-run businesses, including an investment division, a health services startup, smart thermostat maker Nest and the "X" laboratory responsible for making self-driving cars and Internet-beaming balloons. Headquarters for both Google and Alphabet is in Mountain View, California.

Google Hangouts A Google service that allows users to have live, multiperson chats, in text, voice or video.

Google Plus A social network owned by Google in which users form communities and share text updates, videos, photos or other content.

GOP Grand Old Party. *GOP* is acceptable on second reference for *Republican Party*.

Gospel(s), gospel Capitalize when referring to any or all of the first four books of the New Testament: *the Gospel of St. John, the Gospels.*

Lowercase in other references: *She is a famous gospel singer.*

government Always lowercase, never abbreviate: *the federal government, the state government, the U.S. government.*

Government Accountability Office
The *Government Accountability Office* is a nonpartisan congressional agency that audits federal programs. (Formerly the General Accounting Office.)

GAO is acceptable on second reference.

governmental bodies Follow these guidelines:

FULL NAME: Capitalize the full proper names of governmental agencies, departments and offices: *The U.S. Department of State, the Georgia Department of Human Resources, the Boston City Council, the Chicago Fire Department.*

WITHOUT JURISDICTION: Retain capitalization in referring to a specific body if the dateline or context makes the name of the nation, state, county, city, etc. unnecessary: *The Department of State* (in a story from Washington), *the Department of Human Resources* or *the state Department of Human Resources* (in a story from Georgia), *the City Council* (in a story from Boston), *the Fire Department* or *the city Fire Department* (in a story from Chicago).

Lowercase further condensations of the name: *the department, the council,* etc.

For additional guidance see **assembly; city council; committee; Congress; legislature; House of Representatives; Senate; Supreme Court of the United States**; and **supreme courts of the states.**

FLIP-FLOPPED NAMES: Retain capital names for the name of a governmental body if its formal name is flopped to delete the word of: *the State Department, the Human Resources Department.*

GENERIC EQUIVALENTS: If a generic term has become the equivalent of a proper name in popular use, treat it as a proper name: *Walpole State Prison,* for example, even though the proper name is the *Massachusetts Correctional Institute-Walpole.*

For additional examples, see **legislature**; **police department**; and **prison, jail**.

PLURALS, NONSPECIFIC REFERENCES: All words that are capitalized when part of a proper name should be lowercased when they are used in the plural or do not refer to a specific, existing body. Some examples:

All states except Nebraska have a state senate. The town does not have a fire department. The bill requires city councils to provide matching funds. The president will address the lower houses of the New York and New Jersey legislatures.

NON-U.S. BODIES: The same principles apply.

Capitalize the names of the specific governmental agencies and departments, either with the name of the nation or without it if clear in the context: *French Foreign Ministry, the Foreign Ministry.*

Lowercase *the ministry* or a similar term when standing alone.

government, junta, regime, administration A *government* is an established system of political administration: *the U.S. government.*

A *junta* is a group or council that often rules after a coup: *A military junta controls the nation.* A *junta* becomes a government after it establishes a system of political administration.

A *regime* is a form of political system, generally an oppressive or undemocratic one: *an authoritarian regime, a communist regime.* The word regime should be used only in general terms. Do not use in references to a specific country or leader: *the North Korean regime, Assad's regime.*

An *administration* consists of officials who make up the executive branch of a government: *the Reagan administration.*

governor Capitalize and abbreviate as *Gov.* or *Govs.* when used as a formal title before one or more names.

See the next entry and **titles**.

governor general, governors general The formal title for the British sovereign's representatives in Canada and some other countries of the Commonwealth.

Do not abbreviate in any use.

GPA Acceptable in all references for *grade-point average.*

GPS Acceptable in all references to *Global Positioning System.* If a descriptive word is used following, use it in lowercase: *the GPS satellite.*

grade, grader Hyphenate in combining forms: *a fourth-grade student, a 12th-grade student, first-grader, 10th-grader.* But: *She is in the fifth grade.*

graduate (v.) *Graduate* is correctly used in the active voice: *She graduated from the university.*

It is correct, but unnecessary, to use the passive voice: *He was graduated from the university.*

Do not, however, drop *from: John Adams graduated from Harvard.* Not: *John Adams graduated Harvard.*

Graham Holdings Co. Formerly known as The Washington Post Co. Its properties include the online magazine Slate, several television stations and Kaplan, an education, test-preparation, language instruction and professional training business. Headquarters is in Arlington, Virginia.

grain The smallest unit in the system of weights that has been used in the United States. It originally was defined as the weight of 1 grain of wheat.

It takes 437.5 grains to make an ounce. There are 7,000 grains to a pound.

See **ounce (weight)** and **pound**.

gram The basic unit of mass in the metric system. It is equal to approximately one-twenty-eighth of an ounce. To convert to ounces, multiply by .035 (86 grams x .035 equals 3 ounces).

See **metric system**.

Grammy Awards Presented annually by the Recording Academy. Also known as *the Grammys*.

granddad, granddaughter Also: *grandfather, grandmother, grandson, grandma*, etc. See **family names**.

grand jury Always lowercase: *a Los Angeles County grand jury, the grand jury*.

This style has been adopted because, unlike the case with city council and similar governmental units, a jurisdiction frequently has more than one grand jury session.

grant-in-aid, grants-in-aid

gray Not *grey*. But:

greyhound.

great- Hyphenate *great-grandfather, great-great-grandmother*, etc.

Use *great grandfather* only if the intended meaning is that the grandfather was a great man.

Great Britain It consists of England, Scotland and Wales, but not Northern Ireland.

Britain is acceptable in all references.

See **United Kingdom**.

Great Depression See **Depression**.

greater Capitalize when used to define a community and its surrounding region: *Greater Boston*.

Great Lakes The five, from the largest to the smallest: Lake Superior, Lake Huron, Lake Michigan, Lake Erie, Lake Ontario.

Great Plains Capitalize *Great Plains* or *the Plains* when referring to the U.S. prairie lands that extend from North Dakota to Texas and from the Rocky Mountains east to the Mississippi River valley. Use *northern Plains, southwestern Plains*, etc., when referring to a portion of the region.

Great Recession The recession that began in December 2007 and became the longest and deepest since the Great Depression of the 1930s. It occurred after losses on subprime mortgages battered the U.S. housing market. The National Bureau of Economic Research said it officially ended in June 2009, having lasted 18 months.

Green Berets See **special forces**.

gringo A derogatory term for a foreigner, especially an American, in parts of Latin America. Use only in direct quotes when essential to the story. See **nationalities and races**.

grisly, grizzly *Grisly* is horrifying, repugnant.
Grizzly means grayish or is a short form for *grizzly bear*.

gross domestic product The sum of all goods and services produced within a nation's borders. In the U.S., it is calculated quarterly by the Commerce Department.
Lowercase in all uses, but *GDP* is acceptable in later references.

Groundhog Day Feb. 2.

groundskeeper

groundswell

ground zero

group Takes singular verbs and pronouns: *The group is reviewing its position.*

grown-up (n. and adj.)

G-7 Use a hyphen in the abbreviated form for the *Group of Seven*, made up of representatives of the major industrial nations, Britain, Canada, France, Germany, Italy, Japan and the United States. Russia was suspended from the Group of Eight in March 2014. A general description rather than the full name is preferred on first reference: *Leading industrial nations*. See **G-20**.

G-string

G-20 Use a hyphen in the abbreviated form for the *Group of 20*, made up of representatives of industrial and emerging-market nations. A general description rather than the full name is preferred on first reference: *Leading rich and developing nations*. Members are the European Union and the following 19 countries: Argentina, Australia, Brazil, Britain, Canada, China, France, Germany, India, Indonesia, Italy, Japan, Mexico, Russia, Saudi Arabia, South Africa, South Korea, Turkey and the United States.

Guadalupe (Mexico)

Guadeloupe (West Indies)

Guam Use in datelines after the name of a community. See **datelines**.

Guangzhou City in China formerly known as Canton.

guarantee Preferred to *guaranty*, except in proper names.

guard Usually a job description, not a formal title. See **titles**.

guardsman See **National Guard** and **Coast Guardsman**.

Guatemala City Stands alone in datelines.

gubernatorial

guerrilla Unorthodox soldiers and their tactics.

guest Do not use as a verb except in quoted matter.

Guinness World Records The book is published by Guinness World Records Ltd.

Gulf Cooperation Council A regional bloc, based in Riyadh, Saudi Arabia, and representing Bahrain, Kuwait, Oman, Qatar, Saudi Arabia and the United Arab Emirates. Formed in 1981, the council makes economic policies across these Gulf nations and serves as a Sunni-led Arab counterweight to Shiite power Iran. *GCC* is acceptable on second reference.

Gulf, Gulf Coast Capitalize when referring to the region of the United States lying along the Gulf of Mexico. Also: *Mexico's Gulf Coast* or *Gulf Coast of Mexico*.
See **coast**.

Gulf Stream But the racetrack is *Gulfstream Park*.

gunbattle, gunboat, gunfight, gunfire, gunpoint, gunpowder

gung-ho A colloquialism to be used sparingly.

guns See **weapons**.

gyp (n. and v.) Fraud or swindle or to cheat someone. Avoid use. Offensive to Gypsies, also known as Roma.

Gypsy See **Roma, Gypsy**.

gypsy moth

h

habeas corpus A writ ordering a person in custody to be brought before a court. It places the burden of proof on those detaining the person to justify the detention.

When *habeas corpus* is used in a story, define it.

hacker The term is commonly used to describe someone who unlawfully penetrates proprietary computer systems, but it has also evolved to mean anyone who tinkers with technology to explore new uses.

Hades But lowercase *hell*.

Hague, The In datelines:
THE HAGUE, Netherlands (AP) —
In text: *The Hague*.

hajj The pilgrimage to Mecca required once in a lifetime of every Muslim who can afford it and is physically able to make it. Some Muslims make the journey more than once. The hajj occurs once a year during the Islamic lunar month of Dhul-Hijja, the 12th and final month of the Islamic calendar year. The person making the *hajj* is a *hajji*.

half It is not necessary to use the preposition *of*: *half the time* is correct, but *half of the time* is not wrong.

half- Follow Webster's New World College Dictionary. Hyphenate if not listed there.

Some frequently used words without a hyphen:
halfback   *halftone*

halfhearted   *halftrack*

Also: *halftime*, in keeping with widespread practice in sports copy.

Some frequently used combinations that are two words without a hyphen:
half brother   *half size*
half dollar

Some frequently used combinations that include a hyphen:
half-baked   *half-life*
half-blood   *half-moon*
half-cocked   *half-truth*
half-hour

half day (n.) **half-day** (adj.)

half-mast, half-staff On ships and at naval stations ashore, flags are flown at *half-mast*.
Elsewhere ashore, flags are flown at *half-staff*.

hallelujah Lowercase the biblical praise to God, but capitalize in composition titles: Handel's "Hallelujah" chorus.

Halley's comet After Edmund Halley, an English astronomer who predicted the comet's appearance once every 75 years. It was last seen in 1985-86.

Halliburton Co. Headquarters is in Houston.

Halloween

halo, halos

Hamas A Palestinian Islamic political party, which has an armed wing of the same name. The word is an acronym for the Arabic words for *Islamic Resistance Movement*.

Hamburg The city in Germany carries the country name in datelines.

handheld (n.) **hand-held** (adj.)

handicapped See **disabled, handicapped**.

handle A self-selected, public-facing username on a social network. May be used interchangeably with *username*.

handmade

hand-picked

hands-free

hands off, hands-off Hyphenate when used as a compound modifier: *He kept his hands off the matter. He follows a hands-off policy.*

hand to hand, hand-to-hand, hand to mouth, hand-to-mouth Hyphenate when used as compound modifiers: *The cup was passed from hand to hand. They live a hand-to-mouth existence.*

hand-washing

hangar, hanger A *hangar* is a building. A *hanger* is used for clothes.

hang, hanged, hung One *hangs* a picture, a criminal or oneself. For past tense or the passive, use *hanged* when referring to executions or suicides, *hung* for other actions.

hangover

hang-up (n.) **hang up** (v.)

Hannover The spelling of the German city.

Hanukkah The Jewish Festival of Lights, an eight-day commemoration of rededication of the Temple by the Maccabees after their victory over the Syrians. Usually occurs in December but sometimes falls in late November.

happy holidays, merry Christmas, season's greetings, happy birthday, happy new year Lowercase except in exclamations (*Christmas* is always capitalized): *Have a happy new year, wishing you a merry Christmas, sending season's greetings your way.* In exclamations: *Happy holidays! Merry Christmas! Season's greetings! Happy New Year!* (*New Year* is up in this use for the Jan. 1 holiday.) *Happy birthday!* See **New Year's, New Year's Day, New Year's Eve, Happy New Year**.

Haqqani network Militant Islamic group based in Pakistan that seeks to establish Islamic law in Afghanistan.

harass, harassment

harelip Avoid. *Cleft lip* is preferred.

hard line (n.) **hard-liner** (n.) **hard-line** (adj.)

Harper's Magazine Not to be confused with Harper's Bazaar.

Harris Poll Prepared by Harris Interactive of New York.

Hartford Financial Services Group

Inc. Headquarters is in Hartford, Connecticut.

hashish See **marijuana, medical marijuana**.

hashtag A term starting with a number or hash sign (#) in a social network post; it conveys the subject of the post so that it can be easily found by users interested in that subject. For example, the hashtag #UNGA is commonly used for the annual meeting of the U.N. General Assembly. A hashtag needs to be an uninterrupted string of characters, with no spaces. When tweeting or posting, take note that the use of a hashtag associated with a movement or cause could be interpreted as a sign of support. AP journalists should avoid this, unless the hashtag itself is the subject of the post. In stories, write the hashtag as it would appear on a social network: *The #Jan25 hashtag was credited with spreading support for the Egyptian uprising in its early days.*

Havana The city in Cuba stands alone in datelines.

Hawaii Do not abbreviate the state name in datelines or stories. Postal code: *HI*

Hawaiians are members of an ethnic group indigenous to the Hawaiian Islands and are also called *Native Hawaiians*. Use *Hawaii resident* for anyone living in the state.

The state comprises 132 islands about 2,400 miles southwest of San Francisco. Collectively, they are the *Hawaiian Islands.*

The largest island in land area is Hawaii. Honolulu and Pearl Harbor are on Oahu, where more than 80 percent of the state's residents live.

Honolulu stands alone in datelines. Use *Hawaii* after all other cities in datelines, specifying the island in the text, if needed.

See **datelines** and **state names**.

Hawaiian Airlines Headquarters is in Honolulu.

Hawaii Standard Time The time zone used in Hawaii. There is no daylight saving time in Hawaii.

headlines All AP stories need a short headline and a long headline. Only the first word and proper nouns are capitalized. Exception: First word after colon is always uppercase in headlines.

Use numerals for all numbers except in casual uses: "hundreds" instead of "100s." Use single quotes for quotation marks. Exception: use *US, UK* and *UN* (no periods) in all headlines.

Label opinion pieces. Short and long headlines for news analyses must begin with *"Analysis:"* followed by a colon. Likewise, reviews must begin with *"Review:"*

Attribute carefully. Attribution is as important in headlines as in stories.

Use locators when necessary. They should be spelled out whenever possible; limit the use of abbreviations. If an abbreviation is essential because of space constraints, don't use periods for U.S. states abbreviated with two capital letters: NY, NJ, NH, NM, NC, SC, ND, SD and RI. Also DC. Other states retain periods: Ga., Ky., Mont., Conn. Do not use postal abbreviations.

headlong

head-on (adj. and adv.)

headquarters May take a singular or a plural verb.

headscarf, headscarves

health care

hearing examiner See **administrative law judge**.

hearsay

heart attack, heart failure, cardiac arrest A *heart attack* (myocardial infarction) occurs when one or more arteries supplying blood to the heart become blocked. *Heart failure* is a chronic condition that occurs when a weakened heart can no longer effectively pump blood. *Cardiac arrest*, or *sudden cardiac arrest*, occurs when the heart suddenly stops beating. It can be due to a *heart attack*, a heart rhythm problem, or as a result of trauma.

heaven

heavenly bodies Capitalize the proper names of planets, stars, constellations, etc.: *Mars, Arcturus, the Big Dipper, Aries*. See **earth**.

Lowercase *red planet* when referring to Mars.

For comets, capitalize only the proper noun element of the name: *Halley's comet*.

Lowercase *sun* and *moon*, but capitalize them if their Greek or Latin names are used: *Helios, Luna*.

Capitalize nouns and adjectives derived from the proper names of planets: *Martian, Venusian*, but lowercase adjectives derived from other heavenly bodies: *solar, lunar*.

hect- (before a vowel), **hecto-** (before a consonant) A prefix denoting 100 units of a measure. Move a decimal point two places to the right, adding zeros if necessary, to convert to the basic unit: 5.5 hectometers = 550 meters.

hectare A unit of surface measure in the metric system equal to 100 ares or 10,000 square meters.

A hectare is equal to 2.47 acres, 107,639.1 square feet or 11,959.9 square yards.

To convert to acres, multiply by 2.47 (5 hectares x 2.47 = 12.35 acres). See **acre** and **metric system**.

hedge fund Unregulated funds that pool money from wealthy investors and trade in everything from commodities to real estate to complex derivative investments. The private investment funds use sophisticated techniques to try to achieve higher returns than the stock market.

hedging A method of selling for future delivery whereby a dealer protects himself from falling prices between the time he buys a product and the time he resells or processes it. A miller, for example, who buys wheat to convert to flour will sell a similar quantity of wheat he doesn't own at near the price at which he bought his own. He will agree to deliver it at the same time his flour is ready for market. If at that time the price of wheat and therefore flour has fallen, he will lose on the flour but can buy the wheat at a low price and deliver it at a profit. If prices have risen, he will make an extra profit on his flour which he will have to sacrifice to buy the wheat for delivery. But either way he has protected his profit.

h

he, him, his, thee, thou Personal pronouns referring to the deity are lowercase.
See **deity**.

heights See **dimensions**.

heliport

hell But capitalize *Hades*.

Hells Angels

Helsinki The city in Finland stands alone in datelines.

helter-skelter

hemisphere Capitalize *Northern Hemisphere, Western Hemisphere*, etc. Lowercase *hemisphere* in other uses: *the Eastern and Western hemispheres, the hemisphere*.

hemorrhage The word *bleed* can be used instead in most cases.

hemorrhoid

hemp See **marijuana.**

her Do not use this pronoun in reference to nations, ships or storms, except in quoted matter.
Use *it* instead.

here The word is frequently redundant, particularly in the lead of a datelined story. Use only if there is some specific need to stress that the event being reported took place in the community.
If the location must be stressed in the body of the story, repeat the name of the datelined community, both for the reader's convenience and to avoid problems if the story is topped with a different dateline.

Her Majesty Capitalize when it appears in quotations or is appropriate before a name as the long form of a formal title.
For other purposes, use the woman's name or *the queen*.
See **nobility**.

heroes

hertz This term, the same in singular or plural, has been adopted as the international unit of frequency equal to one cycle per second.
In contexts where it would not be understood by most readers, it should be followed by a parenthetical explanation: *15,400 hertz (cycles per second)*.
Do not abbreviate.

Hewlett-Packard Co. Split into two separate companies in 2015. See **HP Inc.** and **Hewlett Packard Enterprise**.

Hewlett Packard Enterprise The former business-computing arm of Hewlett-Packard Co., which split into two companies in 2015 — HP Inc. and Hewlett Packard Enterprise. Hewlett Packard Enterprise primarily sells computer servers, data storage and data analysis products to businesses and government agencies. *HP Enterprise* is acceptable on second reference.

Hezbollah The Lebanese Shiite Muslim political party, which has an armed wing of the same name. The word means *party of God* in Arabic.

hideaway

hideout

high blood pressure Preferred term. Avoid using *hypertension*.

high definition (n.) **high-definition** (adj.) The term refers to moving-image hardware and content that produces at least 720 lines of vertical resolution. *HD* is acceptable on second reference. *HDTV* is acceptable on second reference for a high-definition television set. A U.S. DVD or analog TV broadcast has 480 lines of vertical resolution — neither is HD.

high-five (n.) **high-fived** (v.)

high-rise (n. and adj.)

high-tech

highway designations Use these forms, as appropriate in the context, for highways identified by number: *U.S. Highway 1, U.S. Route 1, U.S. 1, state Route 34, Route 34, Interstate Highway 495, Interstate 495.* On second reference only for *Interstate*: *I–495.*

When a letter is appended to a number, capitalize it but do not use a hyphen: *Route 1A.*

See **addresses** and **numerals**.

highway patrol Capitalize if used in the formal name of a police agency: *the Kansas Highway Patrol, the Highway Patrol.* Lowercase *highway patrolman* in all uses.

See **state police**.

hijab The headscarf worn by some Muslim women. The *h* is pronounced, so it takes the article *a*: *She wore a hijab.* See also other garments such as **niqab, burqa, chador**.

hike Acceptable as a verb for increasing or raising prices sharply.

hillbilly Usually a derogatory term for an Appalachian backwoods or mountain person. Avoid unless in direct quotes or special context.

HIPAA Where possible avoid using the term, which is an acronym for the Health Insurance Portability and Accountability Act of 1996. Instead refer to *privacy laws* or *the federal law restricting release of medical information.* If *HIPAA* is used in a quote, explain it.

hip-hop

Hiroshima On Aug. 6, 1945, this Japanese city and military base were the targets of the first atomic bomb dropped as a weapon. The explosion had the force of 15,000 tons (15 kilotons) of TNT. It destroyed more than 4 square miles and killed 140,000 people, according to an official count taken between August and December 1945. Hiroshima city officials say the toll may exceed 290,000 if including those who died after December 1945 of non-acute injuries or radiation.

Three days later, on Aug. 9, 1945, the U.S. dropped a second atomic bomb, on Nagasaki. The explosion, which had the force of 22,000 tons (22 kilotons) of TNT, destroyed one-third of the city and killed more than 70,000 people by December 1945, according to an official count.

his, her Do not presume maleness in constructing a sentence. Usually it is possible, and always preferable, to reword the sentence to avoid gender: *Reporters try to protect their sources.* If essential, the pronoun *they* may be used as a singular, with a plural verb: *The Obama administration told public schools to grant bathroom access even if*

h

a student's gender identity isn't what's in their record. The official said they are afraid for their safety. Be sure the context makes clear that only one person is involved. See **they, them, their**.

His Majesty Capitalize when it appears in quotations or is appropriate before a name as the long form of a formal title.

For other purposes, use the man's name or *king*.

See **nobility**.

Hispanic A person from — or whose ancestors were from — a Spanish-speaking land or culture. *Latino* and *Latina* are sometimes preferred. Follow the person's preference. Use a more specific identification when possible, such as *Cuban, Puerto Rican* or *Mexican-American*. See **Latino, nationalities and races**, and **race**.

Hispaniola The island shared by the Dominican Republic and Haiti.

See **Western Hemisphere**.

historical periods and events
Capitalize the names of widely recognized epochs in anthropology, archaeology, geology and history: *the Bronze Age, the Dark Ages, the Middle Ages, the Pliocene Epoch.*

Capitalize also widely recognized popular names for the periods and events: *the Atomic Age, the Boston Tea Party, the Civil War, the Exodus* (of the Israelites from Egypt), *the Great Depression, Prohibition.*

Lowercase *century*: *the 18th century*.

Capitalize only the proper nouns or adjectives in general descriptions of a period: *ancient Greece, classical Rome, the Victorian era, the fall of Rome.*

For additional guidance, see separate entries in this book for other epochs, events and historical periods. If this book has no entry, follow the capitalization in Webster's New World College Dictionary, using lowercase if the dictionary lists it as an acceptable form for the sense in which the word is used.

historic, historical A *historic* event is an important occurrence, one that stands out in history.

Any occurrence in the past is a *historical* event.

history Avoid the redundant *past history*.

hit-and-run (n. and adj.) **hit and run** (v.) *The coach told him to hit and run. He scored on a hit-and-run.*

hitchhike, hitchhiker

Hitler, Adolf Not *Adolph*.

HIV See **AIDS**.

hocus-pocus

hodgepodge

Hodgkin lymphoma After Dr. Thomas Hodgkin, the English physician who first described the disease of the lymph nodes. Formerly called *Hodgkin's disease.*

Non-Hodgkin lymphoma, spelled without a possessive, is the more common type and spreads rapidly, especially among older people and those with HIV infections.

ho-hum

holding company A company whose principal assets are the securities it owns in companies that actually provide goods or services.

The usual reason for forming a holding company is to enable one corporation and its directors to control several companies by holding a majority of their stock.

holdup (n. and adj.) **hold up** (v.)

holidays and holy days Capitalize them: *New Year's Eve, New Year's Day, Groundhog Day, Easter, Hanukkah*, etc.

The federal legal holidays are New Year's, Martin Luther King Jr. Day, Washington's Birthday, Memorial Day, Independence Day, Labor Day, Columbus Day, Veterans Day, Thanksgiving and Christmas. See individual entries for the official dates and when they are observed if they fall on a weekend.

The designation of a day as a federal legal holiday means that federal employees receive the day off or are paid overtime if they must work. Other requirements that may apply to holidays generally are left to the states. Many follow the federal lead in designating a holiday, but they are not required to do so.

Hollywood District of the city of Los Angeles where the film industry used to be centered and where film studios and other production facilities, as well as landmark theaters, are still located. It is not a dateline and is most commonly used to describe Southern California's entertainment industry.

Holocaust Capitalize when referring to the mass murder of European Jews and other groups by the Nazi Germans before and during World War II. Lowercase in other references.

Holy Land Capitalize the biblical region.

Holy See The headquarters of the Roman Catholic Church in Vatican City.

Holy Week The week before Easter.

HomeAway See **vacation rental websites**.

homebuilder

homebuyer, homeowner

Home Depot Inc. Headquarters is in Atlanta.

home equity line of credit A line of credit secured by a home. Borrowers can draw on it for a fixed period set by the lender, usually five to 10 years. HELOC is acceptable on second reference.

homefront

homemade

homepage The "front" page of a website.

home schooling (n.) **home-schooler** (n.) **home-school** (v.) **home-schooled** (adj.)

hometown Use a comma to set off an individual's hometown (both the city and, when needed, the state) when it is placed in apposition to a name, whether *of* is used or not: *Tim Johnson, of Vermillion, South Dakota; Mary Richards, Minneapolis.* See **state names** and the **Within Stories** section of **datelines**.

h

h

homicide, murder, manslaughter

Homicide is a legal term for slaying or killing.

Murder is malicious, premeditated homicide. Some states define certain homicides as murder if the killing occurs in the course of armed robbery, rape, etc.

Generally speaking, *manslaughter* is homicide without malice or premeditation.

A *homicide* should not be described as murder unless a person has been convicted of that charge.

Do not say that a victim was *murdered* until someone has been convicted in court. Instead, say that a victim *was killed* or *slain*. Do not write that X was charged with *murdering* Y. Use the formal charge — *murder* — and, if not already in the story, specify the nature of the killing – shooting, stabbing, beating, poisoning, drowning, etc.: *Jones was charged with murder in the shooting of his girlfriend.*

Examples:

An officer pulled over 29-year-old John White, who was arrested and charged with murder, according to Andrew Johnson, the county sheriff's spokesman.

The 66-year-old amateur photographer has pleaded not guilty to four counts of first-degree murder in the slaying of four women.

The killings occurred between 1977 and 1979. Prosecutors say Adams raped, tortured and robbed some of them before killing them.

Cook County Sheriff James Jones says a shooting that left a man and a woman dead appears to be a murder-suicide.

See **execute** and **assassin, killer, murderer**.

homophobia, homophobic

Acceptable in broad references or in quotations to the concept of fear or hatred of gays, lesbians and bisexuals. *The governor denounced homophobia.* In individual cases, be specific about observable actions; avoid descriptions or language that assumes motives. *The leaflets contained an anti-gay slur. The voters opposed same-sex marriage.* See **phobia**, **gay**.

Hong Kong Stands alone in datelines.

Honolulu The city in Hawaii stands alone in datelines. It is on the island of Oahu.

See **Hawaii**.

honorary degrees All references to honorary degrees should specify that the degree was honorary.

Do not use *Dr.* before the name of an individual whose only doctorate is honorary.

hoof-and-mouth disease Use *foot-and-mouth disease*.

hooky

hopefully The traditional meaning is *in a hopeful manner*. Also acceptable is the modern usage: *it's hoped, we hope*.

Correct: *"You're leaving soon?" she asked hopefully.*

Correct: *Hopefully, we'll be home before dark.*

horse meat

horsepower A unit of power. It is not abbreviated. See **watt**.

horse races Capitalize their formal names: *Kentucky Derby, Preakness, Belmont Stakes*, etc.

horses' names Capitalize. See

animals.

hotel Capitalize as part of the proper name for a specific hotel: *the Waldorf-Astoria Hotel*.

Lowercase when standing alone or used in an indefinite reference to one hotel in a chain: *The city has a Sheraton hotel*.

hotline A telephone line for use in an emergency or a crisis, especially between government leaders.

hot spot Two words, for descriptions of the area where computers can connect wirelessly, or for global trouble spots, or areas of intense heat in general.

hourlong, hourslong

household, housing unit In the sense used by the Census Bureau, a *household* is made up of all occupants of a *housing unit*. A *household* may contain more than one family or may be used by one person.

A *housing unit*, as defined by the bureau, is a group of rooms or single room occupied by people who do not live and eat with any other person in the structure. It must have either direct access from the outside or through a common hall, or have a kitchen or cooking equipment for the exclusive use of the occupants.

House of Commons, House of Lords The two houses of the British Parliament.

On second reference: *Commons* or *the Commons, Lords* or *the Lords*.

House of Representatives Capitalize when referring to a specific governmental body: *the U.S. House of Representatives, the Massachusetts House of Representatives*.

Capitalize shortened references that delete the words *of Representatives*: *the U.S. House, the Massachusetts House*.

Retain capitalization if *U.S.* or the name of a state is dropped but the reference is to a specific body.

BOSTON (AP) — The House has adjourned for the year.

Lowercase plural uses: *the Massachusetts and Rhode Island houses*.

Apply the same principle to similar legislative bodies such as *the Virginia House of Delegates*.

See **organizations and institutions** for guidelines on how to handle the term when it is used by a nongovernmental body.

Houston The city in Texas stands alone in datelines.

howitzer See **weapons**.

HP Inc. The former consumer-technology arm of Hewlett-Packard Co., which split into two companies in 2015: HP Inc. and Hewlett Packard Enterprise. HP Inc. is one of the world's biggest sellers of personal computers and printers. HP is acceptable on second reference.

HPV Acceptable on first reference for *human papillomavirus*, which can cause cervical and other types of cancer. *HPV virus* is redundant. Short-term HPV infections are very common, especially in sexually active young people, and usually clear on their own. Infection must persist for several years to pose a cancer risk. The U.S. Centers for Disease Control has recommended HPV vaccines for all boys and girls ages 11 or 12.

HTML For *HyperText Markup Language.* (Lowercase in web addresses.) In stories, describe as *the web programming language known as HTML.*

HTTP For *Hypertext Transfer Protocol.* (Lowercase in web addresses.) In stories, describe as *the start of all web addresses.*

HuffPost A news website that is a brand of Verizon Communications Inc. unit Oath Inc. Do not precede with *the*; do not use its previous name, The Huffington Post. Headquarters is in New York.

human, human being *Human* is preferred, but either is acceptable.

Humane Society of the United States An animal protection agency headquartered in Washington. It operates 10 regional offices across the country, but has no formal affiliation with the many local organizations that use the name *Humane Society.*

Humvee A trademark for a four-wheeled military vehicle, built by AM General and used by U.S. and allied forces. *Hummer* is the sport utility vehicle.

hurricane Capitalize *hurricane* when it is part of the name that weather forecasters assign to a storm: *Hurricane Harvey.*

But use *it* and *its* — not *she, her* or *hers* or *he, him* or *his* — in pronoun references.

Storms lose strength and are downgraded to tropical storm or tropical depression status after being widely known as hurricanes. Depending on the context, it may be more clear to use simply the storm's name on first reference: *Officials released more water Monday from Houston-area reservoirs overwhelmed by Harvey.* Give the storm's current status and history high in the story: *Harvey came ashore Friday night as a major hurricane and has been downgraded to a tropical storm.* Phrasing such as *storm Harvey* or *the remnants of Hurricane Harvey* is also acceptable on first reference, with background later. In broad references to a hurricane and its aftermath: *The damage and economic impact from Hurricane Harvey is substantial* or *the damage and economic impact from Harvey is substantial.*

See **weather terms**.

husband, wife Regardless of sexual orientation, *husband* for a man or *wife* for a woman is acceptable in all references to individuals in any legally recognized marriage. *Spouse* or *partner* may be used if requested or as a gender-neutral option.

hush-hush

hybrid A vehicle that can be powered by more than one energy source, for example, a car with a gasoline engine and an electric motor. See **engine, motor**.

hydraulic fracturing A technique used by the energy industry to extract oil and gas from rock by injecting high-pressure mixtures of water, sand or gravel and chemicals. The short form is *fracking.* Although the industry considers the short form pejorative, AP accepts *fracking* with a brief definition. See **fracking**.

hydro- The rules in **prefixes** apply, but in general, no hyphen. Some

examples:
hydroelectric   hydrophobia

hyper- The rules in **prefixes** apply, but in general, no hyphen. Some examples:
hyperactive   hypercritical

hyperlink A link from one part of a webpage to another page, such as a restaurant homepage with a link to its menu.

hypertension Preferred term is *high blood pressure*.

hypertext A system of linking electronic documents.

hyphen See entry in **Punctuation** chapter.

h

i

Iberia Airlines Headquarters is in Madrid.

IBM Acceptable as first reference for *International Business Machines Corp.* Headquarters is in Armonk, New York.

ICBM, ICBMs Abbreviation for *intercontinental ballistic missile(s).* ICBM is acceptable on second reference. Avoid the redundant *ICBM missiles.*

ice age Lowercase, because it denotes not a single period but any of a series of cold periods marked by glaciation alternating with periods of relative warmth.

Capitalize the proper nouns in the names of individual ice ages, such as the *Wisconsin ice age.*

The most recent series of ice ages happened during the *Pleistocene epoch*, which began about 1.6 million years ago. During that time, glaciers sometimes covered much of North America and northwestern Europe.

The present epoch, the *Holocene* or *Recent*, began about 10,000 years ago, when the continental glaciers had retreated to Antarctica and Greenland.

ice storm See **weather terms**.

ID Acceptable abbreviation for *identification*, including *ID card.* However, spell out verb forms such as *identified.* See **abbreviations and acronyms**.

Idaho Do not abbreviate in datelines or stories. Postal code: *ID* See **state names**.

i.e. Abbreviation for the Latin *id est* or *that is (to say)* and is always followed by a comma.

IED Abbreviation for *improvised explosive device.* IED is acceptable on second reference. *Roadside bomb* is preferable.

IHS Jane's All the World's Aircraft, IHS Jane's Fighting Ships The reference sources for questions about aircraft and military ships not covered in this book.

The reference for nonmilitary ships is IHS Fairplay Register of Ships.

illegal Except in sports and game contexts, use *illegal* only to mean a violation of the law. Be especially careful in labor-management disputes, where one side often calls an action by the other side illegal. Usually it is a charge that a contract or rule, not a law, has been violated.

illegal immigration See **immigration**.

illegitimate Do not refer to the child of unmarried parents as *illegitimate.* If it is pertinent to the story at all, use an expression such as *whose parents were not married.*

Illinois Abbreviate *Ill.* in datelines only; spell out in stories. Postal code: *IL*

See **state names**.

illusion See **allusion, illusion**.

IM Abbreviation for *instant message*; sometimes used as a verb: *IM'ing, IM'd*. Acceptable on second reference for *instant messaging*.

Imax Corp. Headquarters is in Mississauga, Ontario.

imitation marijuana See **marijuana**.

immigrate See **emigrate, immigrate**.

immigration Basic guidelines and definitions for the use of immigration-related terms:

    illegal immigration Entering or residing in a country without authorization in violation of civil or criminal law. Except in direct quotes essential to the story, use *illegal* only to refer to an action, not a person: *illegal immigration*, but not *illegal immigrant*. Acceptable variations include *living in* or *entering a country illegally* or *without legal permission*.

    Do not use the terms *alien, an illegal, illegals* or *undocumented* (except when quoting people or government documents that use these terms).

    Do not describe people as violating immigration laws without attribution.

    Specify wherever possible how someone entered the country illegally and from where. Crossed the border? Overstayed a visa? What nationality?

    DREAM Act, "Dreamers" The DREAM Act — Development, Relief and Education for Alien Minors — is congressional legislation that would allow young immigrants in the country illegally who were brought here as children to remain in the country if they meet certain criteria. The legislation has never been approved by Congress as of March 1, 2018. It is similar to but not the same as the *Deferred Action for Childhood Arrivals* program. Many refer to immigrants who would benefit from either the *DREAM Act* or *DACA* as "Dreamers." The term *"Dreamers"* is acceptable if necessary, but should be used sparingly and in quotation marks in all references. Explain the term soon after use: *They are commonly referred to as "Dreamers," based on never-passed proposals in Congress called the DREAM Act.* For balance, also include wording such as: *Opponents say the law rewards people for breaking the law, encourages illegal immigration and hurts American workers.* Often it is possible in subsequent references to use other terms such as *immigrant, youths* or a person's name instead of *"Dreamer"* or *"Dreamers."*

    Deferred Action for Childhood Arrivals program A program implemented during former President Barack Obama's administration allowing young immigrants living in the country illegally who were brought here as children to remain in the U.S. Many refer to immigrants who would benefit from either the *DREAM Act* or *DACA* as *"Dreamers."* The term *"Dreamers"* is acceptable if necessary, but should be used sparingly and in quotation marks in all references. Explain the term soon after use: *They are commonly referred to as "Dreamers," based on never-passed proposals in Congress called the DREAM Act.* For balance, also include wording such as: *Opponents say the law rewards people for breaking the law, encourages illegal immigration and* *hurts American workers.* Often it is possible in subsequent references to use other terms such as *immigrant, youths* or a person's name instead of *"Dreamer"* or *"Dreamers."* The program does not convey legal status but conveys temporary protection from deportation and permission to legally work, similar to protections offered under DREAM Act proposals.

Use the acronym *DACA* sparingly and only on second reference. Do not describe *DACA* as an executive action; it is an administrative program.

asylum *Asylum-seekers* are people who have left their country of origin and applied for asylum status, typically fleeing persecution and violence in their homeland. *Asylum-seeker* is not interchangeable with *refugee.*

refugee *Refugees* are people forced to leave their home or country to escape war, persecution or natural disaster.

migrant *Migrants* normally are people who move from place to place for temporary work or economic advantage. The term also may be used for those whose reason for leaving is not clear, or to cover people who may also be refugees or asylum-seekers, but other terms are strongly preferred: *people struggling to enter Europe, Cubans seeking new lives in the United States.* NOTE: People moving within the 50 U.S. states, or from a U.S. territory to one of the 50 states, are better referred to as migrants, not immigrants, because they are moving within a single country.

internally displaced person Avoid this jargon. Refer simply to *people who are displaced* within their own countries or otherwise describe their situation. Do not call them refugees if they are within their own country.

U.S. Immigration and Customs Enforcement The investigative arm of the Department of Homeland Security. It incorporates some of the functions of the former Immigration and Naturalization Service and the former Customs service. *ICE* is acceptable on second reference.

Border Patrol Part of *U.S. Customs and Border Protection*, an agency of the Department of Homeland Security. Capitalize *Border Patrol* in all references to the U.S. agency.

Customs Capitalize in *U.S. Immigration and Customs Enforcement* and in *U.S. Customs and Border Protection*, both agencies of the Department of Homeland Security. Lowercase elsewhere: *a customs official, a customs ruling, she went through customs.* Customs and Border Patrol are not interchangeable. Border Patrol agents provide law enforcement at the border; customs agents staff ports of entry at the border and airports.

emigrate, immigrate One who leaves a country *emigrates* from it. One who comes into a country *immigrates*. The same principle holds for *emigrant* and *immigrant*.

"chain migration" A term applied by immigration hardliners to what the U.S. government calls *family-based immigration*, a longstanding program granting preference to people with relatives who already have legal residency or U.S. citizenship. Avoid the term except when used in a quotation, and explain it.

impassable, impassible, impassive

Impassable means that passage is impossible: *The bridge was impassable.*

Impassible and *impassive* describe

lack of sensitivity to pain or suffering. Webster's New World College Dictionary notes, however, that *impassible* suggests an inability to be affected, while *impassive* implies only that no reaction was noticeable: *She was impassive throughout the ordeal.*

impeachment The constitutional process accusing an elected official of a crime in an attempt to remove the official from office. Do not use as a synonym for *conviction* or *removal from office.*

impel, impelled, impelling

imperial gallon The standard British gallon, equal to 277.42 cubic inches or about 1.2 U.S. gallons.
   The metric equivalent is approximately 4.5 liters.
   See **liter.**

imperial quart One-fourth of an imperial gallon.

implausible

imply, infer Writers or speakers *imply* in the words they use.
   A listener or reader *infers* something from the words.

impostor

impromptu It means without preparation or advance thought.

improvised explosive device *IED* is acceptable on second reference. *Roadside bomb* is preferable.

in, into *In* indicates location: *He was in the room.*
   Into indicates motion: *She walked into the room.*

-in Precede with a hyphen:
   break-in   walk-in
   cave-in   write-in

in- No hyphen when it means *not*:
   inaccurate   insufferable
   Other uses without a hyphen:
   inbound   infighting
   indoor   inpatient (n., adj.)
   infield
   A few combinations take a hyphen, however:
   in-depth   in-house
   in-group   in-law
   Follow Webster's New World College Dictionary when in doubt.

"in" When employed to indicate that something is in vogue, use quotation marks only if followed by a noun: *It was the "in" thing to do. Raccoon coats are in again.*

inasmuch as

Inauguration Day Capitalize only when referring to the total collection of events that include inauguration of a U.S. president; lowercase in other uses: *Inauguration Day is Jan. 20. The inauguration day for the change has not been set.*

inbox

Inc. See **incorporated.**

inch Equal to one-twelfth of a foot.
   The metric equivalent is exactly 2.54 centimeters.
   To convert to centimeters, multiply by 2.54 (6 inches x 2.54 equals 15.24 centimeters).
   See **centimeter; foot;** and **dimensions.**

incident A minor event. Anything that causes death, injury, notable damage and the like is not an incident.

include Use *include* to introduce a series when the items that follow are only part of the total: *The price includes breakfast. The zoo includes lions and tigers.*

Use *comprise* when the full list of individual elements is given: *The zoo comprises 100 types of animals, including lions and tigers.*

See **compose, comprise, constitute**.

income See **profit terminology**.

incorporated Abbreviate and capitalize as *Inc.* when used as a part of a corporate name. Do not set off with commas: *Time Warner Inc. announced* ...

See **company names**.

incorporator Do not capitalize when used before a name.
See **titles**.

incredible, incredulous *Incredible* means unbelievable.
Incredulous means skeptical.

incur, incurred, incurring

Independence Day *July Fourth* or *Fourth of July* also are acceptable.
The federal legal holiday is observed on Friday if July 4 falls on a Saturday, on Monday if it falls on a Sunday.

index, indexes

Index of Leading Economic Indicators A composite of 10 economic measurements developed to help forecast shifts in the direction of the U.S. economy.

It is compiled by the Conference Board, a private business-sponsored research group, which took it over from the Commerce Department in 1995.

India Country in South Asia. Use *Indian* to describe its peoples and cultures.

Indiana Abbreviate *Ind.* in datelines only; spell out in stories. Postal code: *IN*
See **state names**.

Indianapolis The city in Indiana stands alone in datelines.

Indian Ocean See **ocean**.

Indians *American Indian* or *Native American* is acceptable for those in the U.S. Follow the person's preference. Where possible, be precise and use the name of the tribe: *He is a Navajo commissioner.* Such words as *wampum, warpath, powwow, teepee, brave, squaw*, etc., can be disparaging and offensive. In Alaska, the indigenous groups include Aleuts, Eskimos and Indians, collectively known as *Alaska Natives.*

First Nation is the preferred term for native tribes in Canada.

Indian is also used to describe the peoples and cultures of the South Asian nation of India.

See **Native American, nationalities and races**, **race** and **tribe, tribal**.

indict Use *indict* only in connection with the legal process of bringing charges against an individual or corporation.

To avoid any suggestion that someone is being judged before a trial, do not use phrases such as *indicted for killing* or *indicted for bribery*. Instead, use *indicted on a charge of killing or indicted on a bribery*

charge.
For guidelines on related words,
see **accused**; **allege**; and **arrest**.

indie Short for *independent film* or
recorded music, meaning that it was
originally made without the support
of a major studio or company.

indigenous A term used to refer
to original inhabitants of a place.
*Aboriginal leaders welcomed a new era
of indigenous relations in Australia.
Bolivia's indigenous peoples represent
some 62 percent of the population.* See
nationalities and races, and **race**.

Indigenous Peoples Day A holiday
celebrating the original inhabitants
of North America, observed instead
of *Columbus Day* in some U.S.
localities. Usually held on the second
Monday of October, coinciding with
the federal Columbus Day holiday.

indiscreet, indiscrete *Indiscreet*
means lacking prudence. Its noun
form is *indiscretion.*
Indiscrete means not separated
into distinct parts. Its noun form is
indiscreteness.

indiscriminate, indiscriminately

individual retirement account *IRA*
is acceptable on second reference.

indispensable

indo- Usually hyphenated and
capitalized:
*Indo-Aryan   Indo-Hittite
Indo-German Indo-Iranian*
But: *Indochina.*

Indonesia Use after the name of a
community in datelines on stories
from this nation.

Specify an individual island, if
needed, in the text.

indoor (adj.) **indoors** (adv.)

infant Applicable to children through
12 months old.

infantile paralysis The preferred
term is *polio.*

inflation A sustained increase in
prices. The result is a decrease in the
purchasing power of money.
There are two basic types of
inflation:
— *Cost-push inflation* occurs when
increases in the price of specific
items, such as oil or food, are big
enough to drive up prices overall.
— *Demand-pull inflation* occurs when
the amount of money available
exceeds the amount of goods and
services available for sale.

infra- The rules in **prefixes** apply,
but in general, no hyphen. Some
examples:
infrared   infrastructure

infrastructure An economy's capital
in the form of roads, railways, water
supplies, educational facilities,
health services, etc., without which
investment in factories can't be fully
productive.

initial public offering *IPO* acceptable
on second reference.

initials Use periods and no space
when an individual uses initials
instead of a first name: *H.L. Mencken.*
Do not give a name with a single
initial (*J. Jones*) unless it is the
individual's preference or a first
name cannot be learned.
See **middle initials**.

injuries They are *suffered*, not *sustained* or *received*.

in-law

innocent, not guilty In court cases, plea situations and trials, *not guilty* is preferable to *innocent*, because it is more precise legally. (However, special care must be taken to prevent omission of the word *not*.) When possible, say a defendant was *acquitted* of criminal charges.

innocuous

innuendo

inoculate

input Do not use as a verb in describing the introduction of data into a computer.

inquire, inquiry Not *enquire, enquiry*.

insignia Same form for singular and plural.

insofar as

in spite of *Despite* means the same thing and is shorter.

Instagram A Facebook-owned social network in which users share photos or short videos with their followers through a mobile app.

Institute for Supply Management Produces monthly reports on manufacturing and service sectors. *ISM* acceptable on second reference.

insure See **ensure, insure, assure**.

Intel Corp. Headquarters is in Santa Clara, California.

inter- The rules in **prefixes** apply, but in general, no hyphen. Some examples:

inter-American *interstate*
interracial

intercontinental ballistic missile See **ICBM, ICBMs**.

Internal Revenue Service *IRS* is acceptable in all references.
Capitalize also *Internal Revenue Service*, but lowercase *the revenue service*.

International Bank for Reconstruction and Development *World Bank* is acceptable in all references. Headquarters is in Washington.

International Brotherhood of Teamsters, Chauffeurs, Warehousemen and Helpers of America *Teamsters* union is acceptable in all references. See **Teamsters union**.

International Court of Justice The principal judicial organ of the United Nations, established at The Hague in 1945.
The court is not open to individuals. It has jurisdiction over all matters specifically provided for either in the U.N. charter or in treaties and conventions in force. It also has jurisdiction over cases referred to it by U.N. members and by nonmembers such as Switzerland that subscribe to the court statute.
The court serves as the successor to the Permanent Court of International Justice of the League of Nations, which also was known as the World Court.
On second reference use *international court* or *world court* in

lowercase. Do not abbreviate.

International Criminal Police Organization *Interpol* is acceptable in all references.

Headquarters is in Lyon, France.

international date line The imaginary line drawn north and south through the Pacific Ocean, largely along the 180th meridian.

By international agreement, when it is 12:01 a.m. Sunday just west of the line, it is 12:01 a.m. Saturday just east of it.

See **time zones**.

International Energy Agency Paris-based energy adviser for developed nations. *IEA* acceptable on second reference.

International Labor Organization

ILO is acceptable on second reference.

Headquarters is in Geneva.

International Monetary Fund *IMF* is acceptable on second reference. Headquarters is in Washington.

A supply of money supported by subscriptions of member nations, for the purpose of stabilizing international exchange and promoting orderly and balanced trade. Member nations may obtain foreign currency needed, making it possible to correct temporary maladjustments in their balance of payments without currency depreciation.

International Space Station

International Telecommunications Satellite Organization *ITSO* is acceptable on first reference, but the body of the story should identify

it as the shortened form of the full name.

(The original name was International Telecommunications Satellite Consortium.)

Headquarters is in Washington.

internet A decentralized, worldwide network of computers and other devices that can communicate with each other.

The web, like email, is a subset of the internet. They are not synonymous and should not be used interchangeably in stories. See **web**.

INTERNET ADDRESSES: In stories, use the name of the website rather than the web address — so it's *Facebook*, not *Facebook.com*. Use ".com" only if it's part of the legal name, as in *Amazon.com Inc.*

When a story prominently mentions a specific website or web service, include the full address, starting with "http://" unless the site contains content considered graphic or otherwise objectionable under AP's standards.

See domain names, as well as separate listings for some commonly used internet, computer and telecommunications terms.

———

Do not mistake the internet for an encyclopedia, and a search engine for a table of contents. The internet is a sprawling information repository. Anything you find should be assessed and vetted with the same care that you use for everything else. Even what may look like an official press release issued by a company can be doctored or fabricated. Be especially leery of press releases posted on sites other than a company or organization's own known website or an established clearinghouse like prnewswire.com, businesswire.com or globenewswire.com.

Be especially careful about websites and social networks that allow anyone to contribute text, photos and other information. The stated name on an account may not actually reflect an individual or group's real identity.

Some points to consider:
— Whom does a webpage belong to? Is the owner's identity verifiable, or is that person pretending to be someone else? You should avoid anonymous pages just as you would avoid a source whose identity you could not verify.
— Is there contact information in case you want to follow up? One way to check who owns a page is through a "Whois" query at a website such as http://www.networksolutions.com/whois/index.jsp. Keep in mind, however, that data is self-reported and could be incorrect.
— The source for the information on the page should be clearly stated. Is it a primary or secondary source? Can it be checked somewhere else?
— Does the website accept user contributions? If so, is there a vetting process? Wikipedia, for instance, allows individuals to contribute to encyclopedia entries regardless of expertise. It may provide a good starting point for research, but you should follow the footnotes for the source material and look for additional sources of information.
— Based on what you know, how accurate does the information seem? If there's something on the site that you know is incorrect, there may be other errors.

— Are there any obvious signs of bias? One possible clue: the type of sites linked to.
— Is the page current? If it hasn't been updated lately, the information may be outdated.
— For social networks, are you sure that the account actually belongs to the individual or group it says it belongs to? Keep in mind that a password to an account could be compromised, and someone may have temporarily taken over a legitimate account. One way to check authenticity is to verify it directly with the individual or group, using contact information independently obtained. A social account can also be considered legitimate if a verifiably authentic website representing the same individual or group links to it.
— Be wary of information in email because the sender's address can be easily forged. Again, it is best to verify information directly with the person you believe is the sender.
— Don't believe everything you see. Software such as Photoshop makes it easy to alter or manufacture photographs or video clips that look real to the untrained eye.
— Use common sense. Just as you wouldn't necessarily trust an anonymous flyer you pick up on the street, be wary of websites and social accounts you stumble across. Do not assume that a site belongs to a particular company or group just because its name is in the web address.

internet radio The broadcasting of audio content over the internet. Some internet radio services, such as Spotify and Pandora, feature social sharing options.

internet service provider *ISP* is acceptable on second reference.

internet TV The display of web content or internet-streamed programming through a television.

Interpol Acceptable in all references for *International Criminal Police Organization.*

intifada An Arabic term for the Palestinian uprising against Israel.

intra- Within, inside. The rules in **prefixes** apply, but in general, no hyphen. Some examples:
    intracity   *intraparty*

intranet A private network inside a company or organization, only for internal use.

in vitro fertilization Creating embryos by mixing eggs and sperm in a lab dish. Do not hyphenate; *IVF* acceptable on second reference. Use *test-tube babies* sparingly.

iOS The operating system used in many Apple mobile devices, including the iPhone and iPad. Use *IOS* when the word starts a sentence or headline.

IOU, IOUs

Iowa Do not abbreviate in datelines or stories. Postal code: *IA*
    See **state names**.

IP address *Internet Protocol address*, a numeric address given to a computer connected to the internet. Most users type in domain names as stand-ins for *IP addresses*, and

domain name servers help with the translation in the background. *IP addresses* can sometimes be used to identify the location of a computer, the company or organization it belongs to, and where it was registered. Avoid the term in most stories. If necessary, *IP address* is acceptable on first reference with explanation, such as: *Hackers targeted the site's IP address, a numeric designation that identifies its location on the internet.* See **domain names**.

iPad A touch-screen tablet sold by Apple Inc. that is much like an iPhone but with a larger screen. Use *IPad* when the word starts a sentence or headline.

iPhone Apple Inc.'s smartphone. Use *IPhone* when the word starts a sentence or headline.

iPod A digital media player sold by Apple Inc. Use *IPod* when the word starts a sentence or headline.

IQ Acceptable in all references for intelligence quotient.

Iran The nation formerly called Persia. It is not an Arab country.
    The official name of the country is the *Islamic Republic of Iran.*
    Uppercase *Islamic Revolution* when referring to the 1979 event.
    The people are *Iranians*, not *Persians* or *Irani.*
    The official language is *Persian*, also known as *Farsi.*

Iran's Revolutionary Guard A paramilitary organization formed in the wake of Iran's 1979 Islamic Revolution to defend its clerically overseen government. The force answers only to Iran's supreme leader, operates independently of the regular military and has vast economic interests across the country. Its branches include the expeditionary Quds — or Jerusalem — Force, the Basij volunteer militia and the country's ballistic missile force. *The Revolutionary Guard* is acceptable on first reference if the context makes Iran clear. *The Guard* is acceptable on second reference.

Iraq The Arab nation coinciding roughly with ancient Mesopotamia.
  Its people are *Iraqis*. The dialect of Arabic is *Iraqi*.

Ireland Acceptable in most references to the independent nation known formally as the Irish Republic.
  Use *Irish Republic* when a distinction must be made between this nation and *Northern Ireland*, a part of the United Kingdom.

Irish Republican Army An outlawed paramilitary group committed to overthrowing Northern Ireland and its links with Britain. Its formal name is Provisional IRA. It was founded in 1969 with the aim of abolishing Northern Ireland as a predominantly British Protestant state. Its members claim direct lineage to the old IRA, which wrested the predominantly Catholic rest of Ireland from British control following a 1919-21 rebellion.
  IRA is acceptable, but *Irish Republican Army* should be spelled out somewhere in the story.
  Sinn Fein (pronounced "shin fane") is a legal political party that is linked with the *IRA*, but not technically a wing of it.

irregardless A double negative. *Regardless* is correct.

IRS Acceptable in all references for *Internal Revenue Service*. Capitalize *Internal Revenue Service*, but lowercase *the revenue service*.

Islam Followers are called Muslims. Their holy book is the Quran, which according to Islamic belief was revealed by Allah (God) to the Prophet Muhammad in the seventh century in Mecca and Medina. The place of worship is a mosque. The weekly holy day is Friday.
  It is the religion of more than 1 billion people in the world, making it the world's second-largest faith, after Christianity. Although Arabic is the language of the Quran and Muslim prayers, not all Arabs are Muslims and not all Muslims are Arabs. Most of the world's Muslims live in a wide belt that stretches halfway around the world: across West Africa and North Africa, through the Arab countries of the Middle East and on to Turkey, Iran, Afghanistan, Pakistan and other Asian countries, parts of the former Soviet Union and western China, to Indonesia and the southern Philippines.
  There are two major divisions in Islam:
— *Sunni* The biggest single sect in Islam, comprising about 85 percent of all Muslims. Nations with Sunni majorities include Egypt, Saudi Arabia and most other Arab nations, as well as non-Arab Turkey and Afghanistan. Most Palestinian Muslims and most West African Muslims are Sunnis.
  The Saudis sometimes are referred to as Wahhabi Muslims. This is a subgroup within the Sunni branch of Islam.
— *Shiite* The second-largest sect. Iran, Iraq, Bahrain and Azerbaijan

all have Shiite majorities. Lebanon and Yemen have large Shiite communities relative to their population.

(The schism between Sunni and Shiite stems from the early days of Islam and arguments over Muhammad's successors as caliph, the spiritual and temporal leader of Muslims during that period. The Shiites wanted the caliphate to descend through Ali, Muhammad's son-in-law. Ali eventually became the fourth caliph, but he was murdered; Ali's son Hussein was massacred with his fighters at Karbala, in what is now Iraq. Shiites considered the later caliphs to be usurpers. The Sunnis no longer have a caliph.)

Titles for the clergy vary from sect to sect and from country to country, but these are the most common:

Grand Mufti — The highest authority in Quranic law and interpretation, a title used mostly by Sunnis.

Sheikh — Used by most clergymen in the same manner that the Rev. is used as a Christian clerical title, especially common among Sunnis. (Not all sheikhs are clergymen. *Sheikh* can also be a secular title of respect or nobility.)

Ayatollah — Used by Shiites, especially in Iran, to denote senior clergymen, such as *Ayatollah Ruhollah Khomeini.*

Hojatoleslam — A rank below ayatollah.

Mullah — Lower-level clergy.

Imam — Used by some sects as a title for the prayer leader at a mosque. Among the Shiites, it usually has a more exalted connotation.

The adjective is *Islamic. Islamist* is an advocate of political Islam, the philosophy that the Quran should rule all aspects of life — religious, political and personal. *Islamic fundamentalist* should not be used as a synonym for *Islamic militant* or *radical.*

Islamabad The city in Pakistan stands alone in datelines.

Islamic State group Islamic militant organization that broke with the al-Qaida network and took control of large parts of Iraq and Syria, where it declared a caliphate, a traditional form of Islamic rule. It is largely made up of Sunni militants from Iraq and Syria but has drawn jihadi fighters from across the Muslim world and Europe. The group is abbreviated as *IS.*

Islamist An advocate or supporter of a political movement that favors reordering government and society in accordance with laws prescribed by Islam. Do not use as a synonym for *Islamic fighters, militants, extremists* or *radicals,* who may or may not be Islamists. Where possible, be specific and use the name of militant affiliations: *al-Qaida-linked, Hezbollah, Taliban,* etc. Those who view the Quran as a political model encompass a wide range of Muslims, from mainstream politicians to militants known as jihadis.

island Capitalize *island* or *islands* as part of a proper name: *Prince Edward Island, the Hawaiian Islands.*

Lowercase *island* and *islands* when they stand alone or when the reference is to the islands in a given area: *the Pacific islands.*

Lowercase all *island of* constructions: *the island of Nantucket.*

U.S. DATELINES: For communities

on islands within the boundaries of the United States, use the community name and the state name:

EDGARTOWN, Mass. (AP) — *Honolulu* stands alone, however.

DATELINES ABROAD: If an island has an identity of its own (*Bermuda, Prince Edward Island, Puerto Rico, Sardinia, Taiwan,* etc.) use the community name and the island name:

HAMILTON, Bermuda (AP) — *Havana, Hong Kong, Macau* and *Singapore* stand alone, however.

If the island is part of a chain, use the community name and the name of the chain:

MANILA, Philippines (AP) — Identify the name of the island in the text if relevant: *Manila is on the island of Luzon.*

For additional guidelines, see **datelines**.

Istanbul The city in Turkey stands alone in datelines.

IT Abbreviation for *information technology*; IT is acceptable on second reference.

italics AP does not italicize words in news stories. Italics are used in Stylebook entries to highlight examples of correct and incorrect usage.

it's, its *It's* is a contraction for *it is* or *it has*: *It's up to you. It's been a long time.*
Its is the possessive form of the neuter pronoun: *The company lost its assets.*

IUD Acceptable on second reference for *intrauterine device.*

IV Acceptable in all references for *intravenous.*

Ivy League Brown University, Columbia University, Cornell University, Dartmouth College, Harvard University, Princeton University, the University of Pennsylvania and Yale University.

j

jack-o'-lantern

Jacuzzi Trademark for a brand of whirlpool products. Generic terms are whirlpool bath or whirlpool spa.

jail Not interchangeable with *prison*. See **prison, jail**.

Japan Airlines Corp. *JAL* is acceptable on second reference. Headquarters is in Tokyo.

Japan Current A warm current flowing from the Philippine Sea east of Taiwan and northeast past Japan.

jargon The special vocabulary and idioms of a particular class or occupational group.
   In general, avoid jargon. When it is appropriate in a special context, include an explanation of any words likely to be unfamiliar to most readers.
   See **cliches, jargon** and **dialect**.

Java A trademark of Oracle Corp. for a computer programming language.

Jaws of Life Trademark name for the tool used to pry open parts of a vehicle to free those trapped inside.

Jaycees Members of the U.S. Junior Chamber of Commerce, affiliated with the worldwide body, Junior Chamber International.
   See **fraternal organizations and service clubs** and **Junior Chamber of Commerce**.

Jay-Z

J.C. Penney Co. Headquarters is in Plano, Texas.

jeep, Jeep Lowercase the military vehicle. Capitalize the civilian vehicle, a brand of FCA US LLC, a unit of Fiat Chrysler Automobiles NV.

Jemaah Islamiyah Southeast Asian Islamic radical group. The words are Arabic for *Islamic congregation*, or *Islamic group*.

jerry-built To be made poorly, or of cheap materials: *flimsy houses were jerry-built on the hillside*. Sometimes confused with *jury-rig*, which means to be set up for temporary or emergency use: *a courtroom jury-rigged in a corner of the factory*.

Jerusalem The city in Israel stands alone in datelines.

Jesus The central figure of Christianity, he also may be called *Jesus Christ* or *Christ*.
   Personal pronouns referring to him are lowercase as is *savior*.

JetBlue Airways Corp. Headquarters is in New York.

jet, jetliner, jet plane See **aircraft terms**.

Jet Ski A registered trademark of Kawasaki for a type of personal watercraft.

jibe See **gibe, jibe**.

Jiddah, Saudi Arabia

jihad Arabic noun used to refer to the Islamic concept of the struggle to do good. In particular situations, that can include holy war, the meaning extremist Muslims commonly use. Use *jihadi* and *jihadis*. Do not use *jihadist*.

job descriptions Always lowercase. See **titles**.

Johannesburg The city in South Africa stands alone in datelines.

John F. Kennedy Space Center

Located in Cape Canaveral, Florida, the National Aeronautics and Space Administration's principal launch site in years past, and in years to come, for manned spacecraft.

Kennedy Space Center is acceptable in all references.

For datelines on launch stories: *CAPE CANAVERAL, Fla. (AP)* — See **Lyndon B. Johnson Space Center**.

Johns Hopkins University No

apostrophes.

Johnson & Johnson Headquarters is in New Brunswick, New Jersey.

Joint Chiefs of Staff Also: *the Joint Chiefs*. But lowercase *the chiefs* or *the chiefs of staff*.

JPEG, JPG Acronyms for *Joint Photographic Experts Group*, a common image format used on the World Wide Web. Acronyms acceptable in all references.

JPMorgan Chase & Co. Formed from the 2000 merger of J.P. Morgan & Co. with Chase Manhattan Corp. and the 2004 merger with Bank One Corp. Acquired Bear Stearns Cos. and Washington Mutual Inc. in 2008. Headquarters is in New York.

Jr. See **junior, senior**.

judge Capitalize before a name when it is the formal title for an individual who presides in a court of law. Do not continue to use the title in second reference.

Do not use *court* as part of the title unless confusion would result without it:

— No *court* in the title: *U.S. District Judge John Bates, District Judge John Bates, federal Judge John Bates, Judge John Bates, U.S. Circuit Judge Priscilla Owen, appellate Judge Priscilla Owen.*

— *Court* needed in the title: *Juvenile Court Judge John Jones, Criminal Court Judge John Jones, Superior Court Judge Robert Harrison, state Supreme Court Judge William Cushing.*

When the formal title *chief judge* is relevant, put the court name after the judge's name: *Chief Judge Royce Lamberth of the U.S. District Court in Washington, D.C.; Chief Judge Karen J. Williams of the 4th U.S. Circuit Court of Appeals.*

Do not pile up long court names before the name of a judge. Make it *Judge John Smith of Allegheny County Common Pleas Court*. Not: *Allegheny County Common Pleas Court Judge John Smith*.

Lowercase *judge* as an occupational designation in phrases such as *contest judge Simon Cowell*.

See **administrative law judge; court names; judicial branch; justice;** and **magistrate**.

j

judge advocate The plural: *judge advocates*. Also: *judge advocate general, judge advocates general*.

Capitalize as a formal title before a name.

See **titles**.

judgment

judicial branch Always lowercase.

The federal court system that exists today as the outgrowth of Article 3 of the Constitution is composed of the Supreme Court of the United States, the U.S. Court of Appeals, U.S. District Courts and the U.S. Customs Court. There are also four district judges for U.S. territories.

U.S. bankruptcy and magistrate judges are fixed-term judges serving in U.S. District Courts. Magistrate judges are generalist judges who preside in cases referred from U.S. district judges. Bankruptcy judges are specialized judges whose authority is restricted to bankruptcy issues.

The U.S. Tax Court and the U.S. Court of Military Appeals for the Armed Forces are not part of the judicial branch as such.

For more detail on all federal courts, see separate entries under the names listed here.

Judicial Conference of the United States This policymaking body for the courts of the judicial branch meets twice a year. Its 27 members are the chief justice of the United States, the chief judges of the 12 regional circuit courts of appeals, the chief judge of the Federal Circuit Court of Appeals, a district judge from each of the regional circuits, and the chief judge of the Court of International Trade.

Day-to-day functions are handled by the Administrative Office of U.S. Courts.

jukebox

jumbo jet Any very large jet plane, including the Airbus A380 and Boeing 747.

jumbo loan A home loan that exceeds $424,100 in much of the country, except in high-cost areas where the limit can go as high as $636,150 for 2017.

Junior Chamber of Commerce A volunteer organization of young men and women involved in civic service and leadership training.

Members are called *Jaycees*.

U.S. headquarters is in Tulsa, Oklahoma; international headquarters in Coral Gables, Florida.

See **Jaycees**.

junior, senior Abbreviate as *Jr.* and *Sr.* and do not precede by a comma: *Martin Luther King Jr.*

The notation *II* or *2nd* may be used if it is the individual's preference. Note, however, that *II* and *2nd* are not necessarily the equivalent of *junior*; they often are used by a grandson or nephew.

Be clear in distinguishing between father and son on second reference if both names appear in a story. *The elder Smith* and *the younger Smith* is one option; *Smith Sr.* and *Smith Jr.* is also acceptable. The possessive form: *Smith Jr.'s career*.

See **names**.

junk bonds Also known as non-investment-grade bonds, these corporate debt securities provide

j

high yields to investors to compensate for their higher-than-normal credit risk. They are typically issued by companies with a lot of debt to repay loans, fund takeovers or buy out stockholders.

junta See **government, junta, regime, administration**.

jury The word takes singular verbs and pronouns: *The jury has been sequestered until it reaches a verdict.*

Include racial and gender breakdown only if relevant.

Do not capitalize: *a U.S. District Court jury, a federal jury, a Massachusetts Superior Court jury, a Los Angeles County grand jury.*

See **grand jury**.

jury-rig To set up something for temporary or emergency use: *a courtroom jury-rigged in a corner of the factory.* Sometimes confused with *jerry-built*, which means to be made poorly, or of cheap materials: *flimsy houses were jerry-built on the hillside.*

justice Capitalize before a name when it is the formal title. It is the formal title for members of the U.S. Supreme Court and for jurists on some state courts. In such cases, do not use *judge* in first or subsequent references.

See **judge; Supreme Court of the United States**; and **titles**.

justice of the peace Capitalize as a formal title before a name. Do not abbreviate.

See **titles**.

justify *Smith justified his actions* means Smith demonstrated that his actions were right. If the actions are still controversial, say *Smith sought to*

justify his actions.

juvenile delinquent Juveniles may be declared delinquents in many states for anti-social behavior or for breaking the law. In some states, laws prohibit publishing or broadcasting the names of juvenile delinquents.

Follow the local law unless there is a compelling reason to the contrary. Consult with regional editors if you believe such an exception is warranted.

See **privacy**.

juveniles See **names, privacy**.

k

K The *K* abbreviation is acceptable in headline and statistical references to kilometers, such as *a 10K race*; in baseball for strikeouts: *pitcher records 12 K's*; and monetary amounts in thousands: *employee earns $80K*.

It is acceptable in stories about athletic events: *She won her first 5K.*

Kabul The city in Afghanistan carries the name of the country in datelines.

kaffiyeh The men's headdress in Arab countries.

Kansas Abbreviate *Kan.* in datelines only; spell out in stories. Postal code: *KS*

See **state names**.

Kansas City Use *KANSAS CITY, Kan.*, or *KANSAS CITY, Mo.*, in datelines to avoid confusion between the two.

Kansas City Southern Freight railroad, with headquarters in Kansas City, Missouri. It is the parent of Kansas City Southern Railway Co. and Kansas City Southern de Mexico SA and it holds a 50 percent stake in Panama Canal Railway Co.

karat See **carat, caret, karat**.

Kardashian West, Kim Use *Kardashian West* on second reference to Kim Kardashian West.

Kathmandu Preferred spelling for the capital of Nepal.

Kelvin scale A scale of temperature based on, but different from, the Celsius scale. It is used primarily in science to record very high and very low temperatures. The Kelvin scale starts at zero and indicates the total absence of heat (absolute zero).

Zero on the Kelvin scale is equal to minus 273.16 degrees Celsius and minus 459.67 degrees Fahrenheit.

The freezing point of water is 273.16 kelvins. The boiling point of water is 373.16 kelvins. (Note temperatures on the Kelvin scale are called *kelvins*, not *degrees*. The symbol, a capital K, stands alone with no degree symbol.)

To convert from Celsius to Kelvin, add 273.16 to the Celsius temperature.

See **Celsius** and **Fahrenheit**.

Kennedy Space Center See **John F. Kennedy Space Center**.

Kentucky Abbreviate *Ky.* in datelines only; spell out in stories. Postal code: *KY*

See **state names**.

keynote address Also: *keynote speech*.

keywords Terms used to define an online search.

KGB Acceptable on first reference, but the story should contain a phrase identifying it as the former Russian secret police and intelligence agency.

The initials stand for the Russian words meaning *Committee for State Security*.

kibbutz An Israeli collective settlement.

The plural is *kibbutzim*.

kidnap, kidnapped, kidnapping, kidnapper

killer See **assassin, killer, murderer**.

kilo- A prefix denoting 1,000 units of a measure. Move a decimal point three places to the right, adding zeros if necessary, to convert to the basic unit: 10.5 kilograms equals 10,500 grams.

kilobyte See **byte**.

kilogram The metric term for 1,000 grams.

A kilogram is equal to approximately 2.2 pounds or 35 ounces.

To convert to pounds, multiply by 2.2 (9 kilograms x 2.2 equals 19.8 pounds).

See **gram**; **metric system**; and **pound**.

kilohertz Equals 1,000 hertz (1,000 cycles per second). Spell out on first reference. Abbreviate *kHz*.

kilometer The metric term for 1,000 meters. Abbreviate *km*.

A kilometer is equal to approximately 3,281 feet, or five-eighths (0.62) of a mile.

To convert to miles, multiply by 0.62 (5 kilometers x 0.62 equals 3.1 miles).

See **meter**; **metric system**; and **miles**.

kilometers per hour The abbreviation *kph* is acceptable in all references.

kiloton, kilotonnage A unit used to measure the power of nuclear explosions. One kiloton has the explosive force of 1,000 tons of TNT.

The atomic bomb dropped Aug. 6, 1945, on Hiroshima, Japan, in the first use of the bomb as a weapon had an explosive force of 20 kilotons.

A *megaton* has the force of a million tons of TNT. A *gigaton* has the force of a billion tons of TNT.

kilowatt-hour The amount of electrical energy consumed when 1,000 watts are used for one hour.

The abbreviation *kWh* is acceptable on second reference. See **watt**.

king, queen Capitalize only when used before the name of royalty: *Queen Elizabeth II, King Felipe VI.* In subsequent references, use only the given name: *Elizabeth, Felipe.*

Lowercase *king* and *queen* when they stand alone: *The queen's birthday is Monday.* Capitalize in plural uses before names: *Kings George and Edward.* Lowercase in phrases such as *strikeout king Nolan Ryan.* See **nobility**.

kindergarten, kindergartners But pre-K, K-12.

Kitty Litter A brand of absorbent material used in cat litter boxes. Use a generic term such as *cat litter*.

Kleenex A trademark for a brand of facial tissue.

Kmart No hyphen, no space, lowercase *m*.

See **Sears Holdings Corp**.

Knesset The Israeli parliament.

k

K-9

knot A knot is 1 nautical mile (6,076.10 feet) per hour. It is redundant to say *knots per hour*.

To convert knots into approximate statute miles per hour, multiply knots by 1.15.

Always use figures: *Winds were at 7 to 9 knots*; *a 10-knot wind*.

See **nautical mile**.

know-how

Kolkata Indian city formerly known as Calcutta.

K-pop A South Korean musical genre often characterized by synthesized music, video art and tightly synchronized dance moves that are often sexually suggestive or comical. In the early 2000s K-pop emerged as one of South Korea's major cultural exports. PSY's 2012 global hit "Gangnam Style" became the first YouTube video to reach 1 billion views.

Koran Use *Quran* in all references except when preferred by an organization or in a specific title or name. See **Quran**.

Korea The Korean Peninsula remains in a technical state of war, divided by the *Demilitarized Zone* into *North Korea*, officially the *Democratic People's Republic of Korea*, and *South Korea*, officially the *Republic of Korea*. On follow-ups, the *North* and the *South* are acceptable. The abbreviations *NKorea* and *SKorea* are used only in headlines. *DMZ* is acceptable on second reference.

Korean Airlines Co. Ltd.

Headquarters of this airline is in Seoul, Korea.

Korean names The style and spelling of names in North Korea and South Korea follow each government's standard policy for transliterations unless the subject has a personal preference.

North Korean names are written as three separate words, each starting with a capital letter: *Kim Jong Un*. Use *Kim* on second reference.

South Korean names are written as two names, with the given name hyphenated and a lowercase letter after the hyphen: *Lee Myung-bak*. Use *Lee* on second reference.

For South Korean place names, use the revised Romanized spellings introduced by the South Korean government in 2000: *Incheon* (formerly Inchon), *Busan* (formerly Pusan).

In both Koreas, the family name comes first.

Korean War But lowercase *Korean conflict*.

kosher Always lowercase.

Kosovo The capital is Pristina.

Kraft Heinz Co., The Headquarters is in Pittsburgh.

Kriss Kringle Not *Kris*. Derived from the German word *Christkindl*, or baby Jesus.

K2 world's second-tallest mountain. No hyphen.

kudos It means credit or praise for an achievement.

The word is singular and takes singular verbs.

Ku Klux Klan A secretive society organized in the South after the Civil War to assert white supremacy, often using violence. The organization splintered, and not all successor groups use the full name. But each may be referred to as *Ku Klux Klan*, and *KKK* may be used on second reference.

Kuomintang The Chinese Nationalist political party. Do not follow with the word *party*. *Tang* means party.

Kuril Islands Use in datelines after a community name in stories from these islands. Name an individual island, if needed, in the text.

Explain in the text that a small portion of the archipelago is claimed by Japan but most are part of Russia.

Kuwait City The capital city of Kuwait stands alone in datelines.

Kyodo News The nonprofit international news agency is based in Tokyo. *Kyodo* is acceptable on second reference.

k

L The name of the Chicago train system. Not *El*.

Labor Day The first Monday in September.

Labrador The mainland portion of the Canadian province of Newfoundland and Labrador.

Use *Newfoundland* in datelines after the name of a community. Specify in the text that it is in Labrador.

lady Do not use as a synonym for *woman*. *Lady* may be used when it is a courtesy title or when a specific reference to fine manners is appropriate without patronizing overtones.

See **nobility**.

lake Capitalize as part of a proper name: *Lake Erie, Canandaigua Lake, the Finger Lakes.*

Lowercase in plural uses: *lakes Erie and Ontario; Canandaigua and Seneca lakes.*

lame duck (n.) **lame-duck** (adj.)

landline

Land Rover No hyphen. A trademark for a brand of all-terrain vehicle. Owned by Tata Motors Ltd. of India.

languages Capitalize the proper names of languages and dialects: *Aramaic, Cajun, English, Gullah, Persian, Serbo-Croatian, Yiddish.*

laptop

larceny See **burglary, larceny, robbery, theft**.

last Avoid the use of *last* as a synonym for *latest* if it might imply finality. *The last time it rained, I forgot my umbrella*, is acceptable. But: *The last announcement was made at noon* may leave the reader wondering whether the announcement was the final announcement, or whether others are to follow.

The word *last* is not necessary to convey the notion of most recent when the name of a month or day is used:

Preferred: *It happened Wednesday. It happened in April.* Correct, but redundant: *It happened last Wednesday.*

But: *It happened last week. It happened last month.*

Las Vegas The city in Nevada stands alone in datelines.

late Do not use it to describe someone's actions while alive.

Wrong: *Only the late senator opposed this bill.* (The senator was not dead at that time.)

latex A resin-based substance used in making elastic materials and paints.

Latin America See **Western Hemisphere**.

Latin American A person who hails from or whose family background is in Mexico, Central America, parts of the West Indies or South America, where Spanish, Portuguese and French are the official languages derived from Latin. The cultures are diverse rather than of a dual heritage, so *Latin American* isn't hyphenated.

Latino Often the preferred term for a person from — or whose ancestors were from — a Spanish-speaking land or culture or from Latin America. *Latina* is the feminine form. Follow the person's preference. Use a more specific identification when possible, such as *Cuban, Puerto Rican, Brazilian* or *Mexican-American*. See **Hispanic**, **nationalities and races**, and **race**.

latitude and longitude *Latitude*, the distance north or south of the equator, is designated by parallels. *Longitude*, the distance east or west of Greenwich, England, is designated by meridians.

Use these forms to express degrees of latitude and longitude: *New York City lies at 40 degrees 45 minutes north latitude and 74 degrees 0 minutes west longitude; New York City lies south of the 41st parallel north and along the 74th meridian west.*

laws Capitalize legislative acts but not bills: *the Taft-Hartley Act, the Kennedy bill.*

lawsuit *Civil lawsuit* is redundant.

lawyer A generic term for all members of the bar.

An *attorney* is someone legally appointed or empowered to act for another, usually, but not always, a lawyer. An *attorney at law* is a lawyer.

A *barrister* is an English lawyer who is specially trained and appears exclusively as a trial lawyer in higher courts. He is retained by a solicitor, not directly by the client. There is no equivalent term in the United States.

Counselor, when used in a legal sense, means a person who conducts a case in court, usually, but not always, a lawyer. A *counselor at law* is a lawyer. *Counsel* frequently is used collectively for a group of counselors.

A *solicitor* in England is a lawyer who performs legal services for the public. A solicitor appears in lower courts but does not have the right to appear in higher courts, which are reserved to barristers.

A *solicitor* in the United States is a lawyer employed by a governmental body. *Solicitor* is generally a job description, but in some agencies it is a formal title.

Solicitor general is the formal title for a chief law officer (where there is no attorney general) or for the chief assistant to the law officer (when there is an attorney general). Capitalize when used before a name.

Do not use *lawyer* as a formal title. See **attorney, lawyer** and **titles**.

lay, lie The action word is *lay*. It takes a direct object. *Laid* is the form for its past tense and its past participle. Its present participle is *laying*.

Lie also has various other meanings, including to recline, to be situated or to exist. It does not take a direct object. Its past tense is *lay*. Its past participle is *lain*. Its present participle is *lying*.

When *lie* means to make an untrue statement, the verb forms are *lie, lied, lying*.

Some examples:
PRESENT OR FUTURE TENSES:
Right: *I will lay the book on the table.*

The prosecutor tried to lay the blame on him.

Wrong: *He lays on the beach all day. I will lay down.*

Right: *He lies on the beach all day. I will lie down. The village lies beyond the hills. The answer lies in the stars.*

IN THE PAST TENSE:

Right: *I laid the book on the table. The prosecutor has laid the blame on him.*

Right: *He lay on the beach all day. He has lain on the beach all day. I lay down. I have lain down. The secret lay in the fermentation process.*

WITH THE PRESENT PARTICIPLE:

Right: *I am laying the book on the table. The prosecutor is laying the blame on him.*

Right: *He is lying on the beach. I am lying down.*

layoff (n.) **lay off** (v.)

Leaning Tower of Pisa

leatherneck Lowercase this nickname for a member of the U.S. Marine Corps. It is derived from the leather lining that was formerly part of the collar on the Marine uniform.

lectern, podium, pulpit, rostrum A speaker stands *behind a lectern, on a podium* or *rostrum,* or *in the pulpit.*

lectures Capitalize and use quotation marks for their formal titles, as described in **composition titles**.

LEED Acronym for *Leadership in Energy and Environmental Design,* the rating system used by the U.S. Green Building Council to measure a building's sustainability and resource-efficiency. *LEED* is acceptable on first reference, but spell out and explain later in the story. Uppercase a LEED rating level: *LEED certified, LEED Gold certified.* Also: *LEED Silver, LEED Platinum,* the highest rating.

left hand (n.) **left-hander** (n.) **left-handed** (adj.)

leftist, ultra-leftist In general, avoid these terms in favor of a more precise description of an individual's political philosophy.

Ultra-leftist suggests an individual who subscribes to a communist view or one holding that liberal or socialist change cannot come within the present form of government.

See **radical** and **rightist, ultra-rightist**.

left wing (n.) **left-winger** (n.) **left-wing** (adj.) Generally try to avoid in describing political leanings.

legal holiday See **holidays and holy days**.

legion, legionnaire See **American Legion** and **French Foreign legion**.

Legionnaires' disease The disease takes its name from an outbreak at the Pennsylvania American Legion convention held at the Bellevue-Stratford Hotel in Philadelphia in July 1976. The bacterium believed to be responsible is found in soil and grows in water, such as air-conditioning ducts, storage tanks and rivers.

legislative bodies In general, capitalize the proper name of a specific legislative body abroad: *the Knesset, the Diet.*

The most frequent names in use are *Congress, National Assembly* and *Parliament.*

GENERIC USES: Lowercase *parliament* or a similar term only when used generically to describe a body for which the formal name is being given: *the Diet, Japan's parliament*.

PLURALS: Lowercase *parliament* and similar terms in plural constructions: *the parliaments of England and France, the English and French parliaments*.

INDIVIDUAL HOUSES: The principle applies also to individual houses of the nation's legislature, just as *Senate* and *House* are capitalized in the United States:

ROME (AP) — New leaders have taken control in the Chamber of Deputies.

Lowercase *assembly* when used as a shortened reference to *national assembly*.

In many countries, *national assembly* is the name of a unicameral legislative body. In some, such as France, it is the name for the lower house of a legislative body known by some other name such as *parliament*.

legislative titles FIRST-REFERENCE

FORM: Use *Rep., Reps., Sen.* and *Sens.* as formal titles before one or more names. Spell out and lowercase *representative* and *senator* in other uses.

Spell out other legislative titles in all uses. Capitalize formal titles such as *assemblyman, assemblywoman, city councilor, delegate,* etc., when they are used before a name. Lowercase in other uses.

Add *U.S.* or *state* before a title only if necessary to avoid confusion: *Former state attorney general Dan Sullivan, a Republican, defeated U.S. Sen. Mark Begich, a Democrat from Alaska, during the 2014 general election.*

In stories with international datelines, include *U.S.* before legislative titles.

FIRST-REFERENCE PRACTICE: The use of a title such as *Rep.* or *Sen.* in first reference is normal in most stories. It is not mandatory, however, provided an individual's title is given later in the story.

Deletion of the title on first reference is frequently appropriate, for example, when an individual has become well known: *Barack Obama declared Americans were ready to "cast aside cynicism" as he looked for a convincing win in the Democratic contest. The Illinois senator was leading in the polls.*

SECOND REFERENCE: Do not use legislative titles before a name on second reference unless they are part of a direct quotation.

CONGRESSMAN, CONGRESSWOMAN: *Rep.* and *U.S. Rep.* are the preferred first-reference forms when a formal title is used before the name of a U.S. House member. The words *congressman* or *congresswoman,* in lowercase, may be used in subsequent references that do not use an individual's name, just as *senator* is used in references to members of the Senate.

Congressman and *congresswoman* should appear as capitalized formal titles before a name only in direct quotation.

ORGANIZATIONAL TITLES: Capitalize titles for formal, organizational offices within a legislative body when they are used before a name: *House Speaker Paul Ryan, Senate Majority Leader Mitch McConnell, House Minority Leader Nancy Pelosi, House Minority Whip Steny Hoyer, President Pro Tem Orrin Hatch, Senate Judiciary Committee Chairman Charles Grassley.*

See **party affiliation** and **titles**.

legislature Capitalize when preceded by the name of a state: *the Kansas Legislature*.

Retain capitalization when the state name is dropped but the reference is specifically to that state's legislature:

TOPEKA, Kan. (AP) — Both houses of the Legislature adjourned today.

Capitalize *legislature* in subsequent specific references and in such constructions as: *the 100th Legislature, the state Legislature*.

If a given context or local practice calls for the use of a formal name such as *Missouri General Assembly*, retain the capital letters if the name of the state can be dropped, but lowercase the word *assembly* if it stands alone. Lowercase *legislature* if a story uses it in a subsequent reference to a body identified as a general assembly.

Lowercase *legislature* when used generically: *No legislature has approved the amendment*.

Use *legislature* in lowercase for all plural references: *The Arkansas and Colorado legislatures are considering the amendment*.

In 49 states the separate bodies are a *senate* and a *house* or *assembly*. The *Nebraska Legislature* is a unicameral body. All members are *senators*.

See **assembly**; **general assembly**; **governmental bodies**; **House of Representatives**; and **Senate**.

lesbian See **gay**.

-less No hyphen before this suffix:
childless *waterless* *tailless*

less See **fewer, less**.

letup (n. and adj.) **let up** (v.)

leverage The use of debt to enhance returns. The expectation is that the cost of the debt will be lower than the earnings generated.

leveraged buyout A corporate acquisition in which the bulk of the purchase price is paid with borrowed money. The debt then is repaid with the acquired company's earnings, money raised by the sale of some of its assets or by the later sale of the entire company.

Levi's A trademark for a brand of jeans.

LGBT, LGBTQ Acceptable in all references for *lesbian, gay, bisexual and transgender*, or *lesbian, gay, bisexual, transgender and questioning and/or queer*. In quotations and the formal names of organizations and events, other forms such as *LGBTQIA* and other variations are also acceptable with the other letters explained. *I* generally stands for *intersex*, and *A* can stand for *asexual* (a person who doesn't experience sexual attraction), *ally* (a person who is not LGBT but who actively supports the LGBT community) or both.

Queer is acceptable for people and organizations that use the term to identify themselves. Do not use it when intended as a slur. Follow guidelines for **obscenities, profanities, vulgarities** as appropriate. See **gay** or **gender**.

liabilities When used in a financial sense, the word means all the claims against a corporation.

They include accounts payable, wages and salaries due but not paid, dividends declared payable, taxes payable, and fixed or long-term obligations such as bonds, debentures and bank loans.

See **assets**.

liaison

liberal, liberalism See **political parties and philosophies**.

Libor The rate that international banks charge for short-term loans to each other. Libor, an acronym for the London Interbank Offered Rate, is calculated every business day.

lie See **lay, lie**.

lie in state Only people who are entitled to a state funeral may formally lie in state. In the United States, this occurs in the rotunda in the Capitol.

Those entitled to a state funeral are a president, a former president, a president-elect or any other person designated by the president.

Members of Congress may lie in state, and a number have done so. The decision is either house's to make, although the formal process normally begins with a request from the president.

Those entitled to an official funeral, but not to lie in state, are the vice president, the chief justice, Cabinet members and other government officials when designated by the president.

lieutenant See **military titles**.

lieutenant governor Capitalize and abbreviate as *Lt. Gov.* or *Lt. Govs.* when used as a formal title before one or more names both inside and outside quotations. Lowercase and

spell out in all other uses.

See **titles**.

life-size

life span

lifestyle

lifetime

liftoff (n. and adj.) **lift off** (v.)

light, lighted, lighting *Lit* is acceptable as the past tense form.

lightning The electrical discharge.

light-year The distance that light travels in one year at the rate of 186,282 miles per second. It works out to about 5.88 trillion miles (5,878,612,800,000 miles).

likable

-like Do not precede this suffix by a hyphen unless the letter l would be tripled or the main element is a proper noun:

bill-like	*Norwalk-like*
businesslike	*shell-like*

An exception is *flu-like*.

like- Follow with a hyphen when used as a prefix meaning similar to:

like-minded	*like-natured*

No hyphen in words that have meanings of their own:

likelihood	*likewise*
likeness	

like, as Use *like* as a preposition to compare nouns and pronouns. It requires an object: *Jim blocks like a pro.*

The conjunction *as* is the correct word to introduce clauses: *Jim blocks the linebacker as he should.*

linage, lineage *Linage* is the number of lines.

Lineage is ancestry or descent.

Lincoln's Birthday Capitalize *birthday* in references to the holiday.

Lincoln was born Feb. 12. His birthday is not a federal legal holiday.

line numbers Use figures and lowercase the word line in naming individual lines of a text: *line 1, line 9.* But: *the first line, the 10th line.* See **numerals**.

LinkedIn A social media site used mainly for professional networking, based in Mountain View, California.

link shortener A tool that allows users to shorten a URL to make it easier to share. Some link shorteners also allow users to track statistics related to clicks on those links, and they may allow "vanity" addresses that carry a brand's name.

liquefied natural gas Natural gas that has been cooled to minus 260 degrees Fahrenheit, making it liquid. The process reduces the volume of the gas, making it easier to transport. *LNG* is acceptable on second reference.

liquefy

liquidation When used in a financial sense, the word means the process of converting stock or other assets into cash.

When a company is liquidated, the cash obtained is first used to pay debts and obligations to holders of bonds and preferred stock. Whatever cash remains is distributed on a per-share basis to the holders of common stock.

liquidity The ease with which assets can be converted to cash without loss in value. The faster it can be sold, the more liquid it is.

lists, bulleted lists AP uses dashes instead of bullets to introduce individual sections of a list; others may choose to use bullets. Put a space between the dash or bullet and the first word of each item in the list. Capitalize the first word following the dash or bullet. Use periods, not semicolons, at the end of each section, whether it is a full sentence or a phrase.

Use parallel construction for each item in a list:

— *Start with the same part of speech for each item (in this example, a verb).*

— *Use the same voice (active or passive) for each item.*

— *Use the same verb tense for each item.*

— *Use the same sentence type (statement, question, exclamation) for each item.*

— *Use just a phrase for each item, if desired.*

Introduce the list with a short phrase or sentence: *Our partners:* or *These are our partners:* or *Our partners are:*

Listserv A trademark for a software program for setting up and maintaining discussion groups through email.

liter The basic unit of volume in the metric system. It is defined as the volume occupied by 1 kilogram of distilled water at 4 degrees Celsius. It works out to a total of 1,000 cubic centimeters (1 cubic decimeter).

It takes 1,000 milliliters to make a liter.

A liter is equal to approximately 34 fluid ounces or 1.06 liquid quarts. A liter equals 0.91 of a dry quart. The metric system makes no distinction between dry volume and liquid volume.

To convert to liquid quarts, multiply by 1.06 (4 liters x 1.06 equals 4.24 liquid quarts).

To convert to dry quarts, multiply by 0.91 (4 liters x 0.91 equals 3.64 dry quarts).

To convert to liquid gallons, multiply by 0.26 (8 liters x 0.26 equals 2.08 gallons).

See **gallon**; **kilogram**; **metric system**; **quart (dry)**; and **quart (liquid)**.

literally See **figuratively, literally**.

literature See **composition titles**.

Little League, Little League Baseball The official name of the worldwide youth baseball and softball organization and its affiliated local leagues.

livable

live blog (n.) **live-blog** (v.) A blog about a particular event with entries added in real time.

livestream, livestreaming One word in all uses.

Lloyds Bank International Ltd. A prominent bank with headquarters in London.

Lloyd's of London A self-regulating market of insurance. Founded in Britain in 1680, it relies on individual investors worldwide, known as Names, along with several hundred companies, to provide the money for underwriting insurance.

loan terminology Note the meanings of these terms in describing loans by governments and corporations:

bond A certificate issued by a corporation or government stating the amount of a loan, the interest to be paid, the time for repayment and the collateral pledged if payment cannot be made. Repayment generally is not due for a long period, usually seven years or more.

collateral Stock or other property that a borrower is obligated to turn over to a lender if unable to repay a loan.

convertible bond A bond carrying the stipulation that it may be exchanged for a specific amount of stock in the company that issued it.

coupon The interest rate stated on a bond and paid to a bondholder, usually semiannually.

debenture A certificate stating the amount of a loan, the interest to be paid and the time for repayment, but not providing collateral. It is backed only by the corporation's reputation and promise to pay.

default A person, corporation or government is in default if it fails to meet the terms for repayment.

full faith and credit bond An alternate term for general obligation bond, often used to contrast such a bond with a moral obligation bond.

general obligation bond A bond that has had the formal approval of either the voters or their legislature. The government's promise to repay the principal and pay the interest is constitutionally guaranteed on the strength of its ability to tax the population.

maturity The date on which a bond, debenture or note must be repaid.

moral obligation bond A government bond that has not had the formal approval of either the voters or their legislature. It is backed only by the government's "moral obligation" to repay the principal and interest on time.

municipal bond A general obligation bond issued by a state, county, city, town, village, possession or territory, or a bond issued by an agency or authority set up by one of these governmental units. In general, interest paid on municipal bonds is exempt from federal income taxes. It also usually is exempt from state and local taxes if held by someone living within the state of issue.

note A certificate issued by a corporation or government stating the amount of a loan, the interest to be paid and the collateral pledged in the event payment cannot be made. The date for repayment is generally more than a year after issue but not more than seven or eight years later. The shorter interval for repayment is the principal difference between a note and a bond.

revenue bond A bond backed only by the revenue of the airport, turnpike or other facility that was built with the money it raised.

Treasury borrowing A *Treasury bill* is a certificate representing a loan to the federal government that matures in three, six or 12 months. A *Treasury note* may mature in one to 10 years or more. A *Treasury bond* matures in more than 10 years. Because Treasurys carry the full backing of the government, they are viewed as the safest investment.

loan (n.) **lend** (v.) The preferred usage.

loath (adj.) **loathe** (v.) Note the difference. She is *loath* to leave. He *loathes* bureaucracy.

local Avoid the irrelevant use of the word.

Irrelevant: *The injured were taken to a local hospital.*

Better: *The injured were taken to a hospital.*

local of a union Always use a figure and capitalize *local* when giving the name of a union subdivision: *Local 123 of the United Auto Workers.*

Lowercase *local* standing alone in plural uses: *The local will vote Tuesday. He spoke to locals 2, 4 and 10.*

See **union names**.

Lockheed Martin Corp. Headquarters is in Bethesda, Maryland.

lodges See **fraternal organizations and service clubs**.

login, logon, logoff (n.) But use as two words in verb form: *I log in to my computer.*

London The city in England stands alone in datelines.

long distance, long-distance (adj.) *We traveled a long distance. She's a long-distance runner.*

longitude See **latitude and longitude**.

longshoreman Capitalize *longshoreman* only if the intended meaning is that the individual is a member of the International Longshore and Warehouse Union or the International Longshoremen's

Association.

See **state names**.

long term, long-term Hyphenate when used as a compound modifier: *We will win in the long term. He has a long-term assignment.*

long time, longtime *They have known each other a long time. They are longtime partners.*

long ton Also known as a *British ton.* Equal to 2,240 pounds. See **ton.**

Los Angeles The city in California stands alone in datelines. *LA* is acceptable on second reference. *Hollywood* is a district of the city of Los Angeles where the film industry used to be centered and where film studios and other production facilities, as well as landmark theaters, are still located. It is not a dateline and is most commonly used to describe Southern California's entertainment industry. *Beverly Hills* is an incorporated city and the dateline for the Golden Globes movie awards.

Lou Gehrig's disease Also called *amyotrophic lateral sclerosis,* or *ALS.* A progressive disease that attacks nerve cells that control muscles throughout the body. It became known as Lou Gehrig's disease after the star baseball player was diagnosed in 1939. Use *Lou Gehrig's disease* on first reference, but include the medical name later. *ALS* is acceptable in headlines and on second reference. Outside of the U.S., it is known as *motor neuron/ neurone disease.*

Louisiana Abbreviate *La.* in datelines only; spell out in stories. Postal code: *LA*

lowercase One word (n., v., adj.) when referring to the absence of capital letters. Originally from printers' practice.

LSD Acceptable in all references for *lysergic acid diethylamide.*

Lt. Gov. See **lieutenant governor.**

Lucite A trademark for an acrylic plastic.

Lunar New Year The most important holiday in several East Asian countries, marking the start of the Chinese lunar calendar. The holiday starts anytime from mid-January to mid-February depending on the year. In China it is marked by a weeklong public holiday and mass travel by Chinese to their hometowns for family reunions. Also celebrated among Chinese communities overseas, especially in Southeast Asia. *Lunar New Year* is preferred over *Chinese New Year* or *Spring Festival,* the name it is known by in China. The holiday is also observed in South Korea, where it is known as *Seollal,* and Vietnam, where it is known as *Tet.*

Luxembourg Stands alone in datelines.

-ly Do not use a hyphen between adverbs ending in *-ly* and adjectives they modify: *an easily remembered rule, a badly damaged island, a fully informed woman.*

See the compound modifiers section of the **hyphen** entry.

Lycra Unless referring to the trademark fiber or fabric, use a generic term such as *spandex* or *elastic* or *stretch fabric.*

Lyme disease

Lyndon B. Johnson Space Center
Located in Houston, the National Aeronautics and Space Administration's principal control and training center for manned spaceflight.

Johnson Space Center is acceptable in all references.

In datelines:
HOUSTON (AP) —

See **John F. Kennedy Space Center**.

m

Macau Stands alone in datelines. Spelling is an exception to Webster's New World College Dictionary.

Mace A trademark, shortened from *Chemical Mace*, for a brand of tear gas that is packaged in an aerosol canister and temporarily stuns its victims.

machine gun (n.) **machine-gun** (v. and adj.) **machine-gunner, machine-gun fire**
See **weapons**.

machine learning A form of *artificial intelligence* in which computers are "trained" to make human-like decisions without being explicitly programmed for them. Examples of machine learning applications include facial recognition, language translation and self-driving cars. See **artificial intelligence**.

Mach number Named for Ernst Mach, an Austrian physicist, the figure represents the ratio of the speed of an object to the speed of sound in the surrounding medium, such as air, through which the object is moving.

A rule of thumb for speed of sound is approximately 750 mph at sea level and approximately 660 mph at 30,000 feet above sea level.

A body traveling at *Mach 1* would be traveling at the speed of sound. *Mach 2* would equal twice the speed of sound.

mad cow disease Acceptable for bovine spongiform encephalopathy, a progressive neurological disease that afflicts cattle. The disorder caused in humans by eating meat from diseased cattle is called *variant Creutzfeldt-Jakob disease*. See **Creutzfeldt-Jakob disease**.

Madrid The city in Spain stands alone in datelines.

Mafia Secret criminal organization operating mainly in the U.S. and Italy and engaged in illegal activities such as gambling, drug-dealing and prostitution. Lowercase as a synonym for organized crime.

magazine names Capitalize the initial letters of the name but do not place it in quotes. Lowercase *magazine* unless it is part of the publication's formal title: Harper's Magazine, Newsweek magazine, Time magazine.

Check the masthead if in doubt.

Magi Wise men who brought gifts to the infant Jesus at Epiphany, celebrated Jan. 6.

magistrate Capitalize when used as a formal title before a name. Use *magistrate judge* when referring to the fixed-term judge who presides in U.S. District Court and handles cases referred by U.S. district judges. See **titles**.

mahjong

mailman *Mail* or *letter carrier* is preferable.

Maine Do not abbreviate *Maine* in datelines or stories. Postal code: *ME* See **state names**.

mainland China See **China**.

major See **military titles**.

majority leader Capitalize when used as a formal title before a name: *Majority Leader John Boehner.* Lowercase elsewhere.
See **legislative titles** and **titles**.

majority, plurality *Majority* means more than half of an amount.
Plurality means more than the next highest number.
COMPUTING MAJORITY: To describe how large a majority is, take the figure that is more than half and subtract everything else from it: If 100,000 votes were cast in an election and one candidate received 60,000 while opponents received 40,000, the winner would have a *majority* of 20,000 votes.
COMPUTING PLURALITY: To describe how large a plurality is, take the highest number and subtract from it the next highest number: If, in the election example above, the second-place finisher had 25,000 votes, the winner's *plurality* would be 35,000 votes.
Suppose, however, that no candidate in this example had a majority. If the first-place finisher had 40,000 votes and the second-place finisher had 30,000, for example, the leader's *plurality* would be 10,000 votes.
USAGE: When *majority* and *plurality* are used alone, they take singular verbs and pronouns: *The majority has*
made its decision.
If a plural word follows an *of* construction, the decision on whether to use a singular or plural verb depends on the sense of the sentence: *A majority of two votes is not adequate to control the committee. The majority of the houses on the block were destroyed.*

-maker Follow Webster's New World College Dictionary. For words not in this book, if the word combination is not listed, use two words for the verb form and hyphenate any noun or adjective forms. Exceptions: *chipmaker, drugmaker, policymaker, coffee maker.*

makeup (n. and adj.) **make up** (v.)

Malaysia Airlines Headquarters of this airline is in Subang, Malaysia.

Maldives Use this official name with a community name in a dateline: *MALE, Maldives.* Refer to the country in the body of the story as *the Maldives: The president won a referendum on the Maldives' future form of government.*

Mallorca Use instead of Spain in datelines on stories from communities on this island.

manageable

manager Capitalize when used as a formal title before a name: *City Manager Dick O'Connell.*
Do not capitalize in job descriptions, including sports teams: *Mets manager Terry Collins.*
See **titles**.

managing editor Capitalize when used as a formal title before a name.

m

See **titles**.

Manitoba A province of central Canada. Do not abbreviate.
See **datelines**.

man-made

man, mankind Either may be used when both men and women are involved and no other term is convenient. In these cases, do not use duplicate phrases such as *a man or a woman* or *mankind and womankind*.

    Frequently the best choice is a substitute such as *humanity*, *a person* or *an individual*.
See **women**.

manslaughter See **homicide, murder, manslaughter**.

mantel, mantle A *mantel* is a shelf. A *mantle* is a cloak.

Maoism (Maoist) The communist philosophy and policies of Mao Zedong. See **political parties and philosophies**.

Marcellus Shale Capitalize major geologic formations.

Mardi Gras Literally *Fat Tuesday*, the term describes a day of merrymaking on the Tuesday before Ash Wednesday, the first day of Lent.

    In New Orleans and many Roman Catholic countries, the Tuesday celebration is preceded by a week or more of parades and parties. See **Carnival**.

margin The practice of purchasing securities in part with borrowed money, using the purchased securities as collateral in anticipation of an advance in the market price. If the advance occurs, the purchaser may be able to repay the loan and make a profit. If the price declines, the stock may have to be sold to settle the loan. The margin is the difference between the amount of the loan and the value of the securities used as collateral.

marijuana, medical marijuana

Marijuana is the dried flower of the cannabis plant, used as a drug for recreational or medical purposes. *Cannabis* is the usual term outside North America; it and *pot* are also acceptable. Some governments and other entities prefer *cannabis* because of arguments that the term *marijuana* was popularized in the United States in the early 20th century to stoke anti-Mexican sentiment. Slang terms such as *weed*, *reefer*, *ganja* or *420* are acceptable in limited, colloquial cases or in quotations.

    In the United States, many states have legalized marijuana for medical purposes; others have legalized the drug for recreational use. Possession and distribution of marijuana remains a federal offense.

    The cannabis plant contains a number of chemical compounds known as *cannabinoids*, a term that is usually awkward in all but scientific contexts; refer to them as *compounds*, *chemicals* or *derivatives* if needed. *THC* is one of them and is acceptable on first reference for *tetrahydrocannabinol*, the plant's main psychoactive component.

    When cannabis is used for medical purposes, it is generally known as *medical marijuana*. The term usually refers to the dried flowers that are smoked, vaporized or incorporated into food known as *edibles*.

Some of the cannabis plant's compounds are found in pharmaceuticals or dietary supplements allowed by the federal government or by states that have not legalized *medical* or *recreational marijuana*, but they still may fall under the umbrella of medical marijuana. Their active ingredients may be isolated naturally or synthesized in labs, and include Marinol, a prescription drug made with *synthetic THC*, and *hemp oil*, approved in many states for medical use and marketed in the U.S. and elsewhere in some over-the-counter products. One popular form of hemp oil is rich in *cannabidiol* and is often shortened to *CBD oil*; both terms are best confined to quotations or product names unless specificity is required.

Some synthetic cannabis compounds are sold or marketed for recreational use, such as Spice and K2, often described as dangerous. They should be referred to as *synthetic* or *imitation marijuana/cannabis/pot*, not *fake pot* or the awkward term *synthetic cannabinoids*, though the latter is acceptable with explanation in scientific contexts. Do not refer to it as *synthetic THC*, since it generally contains other chemicals.

Hashish is a concentrated form of marijuana, and *hashish* or *hash oil* is an extract that can be smoked, vaporized or infused into *edibles*.

Hemp, with some exceptions, such as *hemp oil*, generally refers to the fibers of the plant, used in making rope, clothing, paper and other products.

See **drugs**.

Marines Capitalize when referring to U.S. forces: *the U.S. Marines,* *the Marines, the Marine Corps, Marine regulations*. Do not use the abbreviation *USMC*.

Capitalize *Marine* when referring to an individual in a Marine Corps unit: *He is a Marine.*

Do not describe *Marines* as soldiers, which is generally associated with the Army. Use *troops* if a generic term is needed.

Maritime Provinces The Canadian provinces of Nova Scotia, New Brunswick and Prince Edward Island.

marketbasket, marketplace

mark to market An accounting requirement that securities must be valued at their current price, rather than the purchase price or the price they might fetch later. Also called "fair value."

Marseille Preferred spelling for the French city.

Marshall Islands Named for John Marshall, a British explorer.

In datelines, give the name of a city and *Marshall Islands*. List the name of an individual island in the text.

marshal, marshaled, marshaling, Marshall *Marshal* is the spelling for both the verb and the noun: *Marilyn will marshal her forces. Erwin Rommel was a field marshal.*

Marshall is used in proper names: *George C. Marshall, John Marshall, the Marshall Islands*.

Martin Luther King Jr. Day Federal holiday honoring Martin Luther King Jr., who was born Jan. 15, 1929, is on the third Monday in January. It was

m

first celebrated in 1986.

Marxism (Marxist) The system of thought developed by Karl Marx and Friedrich Engels. See **political parties and philosophies**.

Maryland Abbreviate *Md.* in datelines only; spell out in stories. Postal code: *MD*
See **state names**.

mashup A blending of two or more pieces of content, such as photos or video. For example, a video that combines audio from a song with footage from movies and overlays it with bits of text.

Mason-Dixon Line The boundary line between Pennsylvania and Maryland, generally regarded as separating the North from the South. (Named for 18th-century surveyors Charles Mason and Jeremiah Dixon, the line later was extended to West Virginia.)

Massachusetts Abbreviate *Mass.* in datelines only; spell out in stories. Postal code: *MA*
See **state names**.

Master of Arts, Master of Science, Master of Business Administration Abbreviated *M.A.*, *M.S.* but *MBA*. A *master's degree* or a *master's* is acceptable in any reference.
See **academic degrees**.

matrimony See **sacraments** in Religion Guidelines.

maturity In a financial sense, the date on which a bond, debenture or note must be repaid. See **loan terminology**.

May Day, mayday *May Day* is May 1, often observed as a festive or political holiday.
The compound *mayday* is the international distress signal, from the French *m'aider*, meaning "help me." It is lowercase in *mayday call* and capitalized as an exclamation: "*Mayday!*"

McClatchy Co. U.S. newspaper publisher that owns dailies including the Miami Herald and The Sacramento Bee. Headquarters is in Sacramento, California.

McDonald's Corp. Headquarters is in Oak Brook, Illinois.

M.D. A word such as *physician* or *surgeon* is preferred. The periods in the abbreviation are an exception to Webster's New World College Dictionary.
See **doctor** and **academic titles**.

meager

mean See **average, mean, median, norm**.

mecca Lowercase in the metaphorical sense; capitalize the city in Saudi Arabia.

Medal of Freedom It is now the *Presidential Medal of Freedom*. See entry under that name.

Medal of Honor The nation's highest military honor, awarded by Congress for risk of life in combat beyond the call of duty. Use *Medal of Honor recipient* or a synonym, but not *winner*.
There is no *Congressional Medal of Honor*.

medevac Acceptable abbreviation for *medical evacuation*, especially in referring to aircraft used to transport wounded military personnel.

Medfly Mediterranean fruit fly. The capital *M* is an exception to Webster's New World College Dictionary.

media Generally takes a plural verb, especially when the reference is to individual outlets: *Media are lining up for and against the proposal.* The word is often preceded by "the." Sometimes used with a singular verb when referring to media as a monolithic group: *The media plays a major role in political campaigns.*

median See **average, mean, median, norm**.

mediate See **arbitrate, mediate**.

Medicaid A federal-state program that helps pay for health care for the needy, aged, blind and disabled, and for low-income families with children.

A state determines eligibility and which health services are covered. The federal government reimburses a percentage of the state's expenditures.

medical marijuana See **marijuana, medical marijuana**.

Medicare The federal health care insurance program for people aged 65 and over, and for the disabled. Eligibility is based mainly on eligibility for Social Security.

Medicare helps pay charges for hospitalization, for stays in skilled nursing facilities, for physician's charges and for some associated health costs. There are limitations on the length of stay and type of care.

In Canada, *Medicare* refers to the nation's national health insurance program.

medicine See **drugs, medicine**.

medieval

mega- A prefix denoting 1 million units of a measure. Move the decimal point six places to the right, adding zeros if necessary, to convert to the basic unit: 5.5 megatons = 5,500,000 tons.

megabyte See **byte**.

megahertz A measure of radio frequency or the speed of a computer processor, equal to a million hertz, or cycles per second. Spell out on first reference. Abbreviate *MHz*.

melee

meme A piece of information or visual content that's shared verbally or transmitted widely, often in social media.

memento, mementos

memo, memos

memorandum, memorandums

Memorial Day Formerly May 30. The federal legal holiday is the last Monday in May.

menswear Not *men's wear*.

mental illness Do not describe an individual as mentally ill unless it is clearly pertinent to a story and the diagnosis is properly sourced.

When used, identify the source for the diagnosis. Seek firsthand knowledge; ask how the source knows. Don't rely on hearsay or speculate on a diagnosis. Specify the time frame for the diagnosis and ask about treatment. A person's condition can change over time, so a diagnosis of mental illness might not apply anymore. Avoid anonymous sources. On-the-record sources may be family members, mental health professionals, medical authorities, law enforcement officials or court records. Be sure they have accurate information to make the diagnosis. Provide examples of symptoms.

Mental illness is a general term. Specific conditions are disorders and should be used whenever possible: *He was diagnosed with schizophrenia, according to court documents. She was diagnosed with anorexia, according to her parents. He was treated for depression.*

Some common mental disorders, according to the National Institute of Mental Health (they are lowercase):
— Autism spectrum disorder. Many experts consider autism a developmental disorder, not a mental illness.
— Bipolar disorder (manic-depressive illness)
— Depression
— Obsessive-compulsive disorder (OCD)
— Post-traumatic stress disorder (PTSD)
— Schizophrenia

Here is a link from the NIMH that can be used as a reference:
http://www.nimh.nih.gov/
Do not use derogatory terms,
such as *insane, crazy/crazed, nuts* or *deranged,* unless they are part of a quotation that is essential to the story.

Do not assume that mental illness is a factor in a violent crime, and avoid unsubstantiated statements by witnesses or first responders attributing violence to mental illness.

Studies have shown that the vast majority of people with mental illness are not violent, and experts say most people who are violent are not mentally ill.

Nevertheless, a first responder often is quoted as saying, without direct knowledge, that a crime was committed by a person with a "history of mental illness." If used, such comments must be attributed to law enforcement authorities, medical professionals, family members or others who have knowledge of the history and can authoritatively speak to its relevance. In the absence of definitive information, there should be a disclaimer that a link had yet to be established.

Avoid descriptions that connote pity, such as *afflicted with, suffers from* or *victim of.* Rather, *he has obsessive-compulsive disorder.*

Double-check specific symptoms and diagnoses. Avoid interpreting behavior common to many people as symptoms of mental illness. Sadness, anger, exuberance and the occasional desire to be alone are normal emotions experienced by people who have mental illness as well as those who don't.

When practical, let people with mental disorders talk about their own diagnoses.

Avoid using mental health terms to describe non-health issues.

Don't say that an awards show, for example, was schizophrenic.

Use the term *mental* or *psychiatric hospital*, not *asylum*.

See **disabled, handicapped**; **phobia**; **post-traumatic stress disorder**.

mentally disabled, intellectually disabled, developmentally disabled The preferred terms, not *mentally retarded*. See **disabled, handicapped**.

mention The inclusion of someone's username in a social media post, to notify that user of the post and/or connect readers to the user's profile. Example: *I refer to the @APStylebook as I edit stories.*

Mercedes-Benz Note hyphen in this division of Daimler AG.

merchant marine Lowercase in referring to the ships of a nation used in commerce. Capitalize only in references to the organization the Merchant Marine or the U.S. Merchant Marine Academy. Members are *merchant mariners* or *merchant crewmen*, but not marines.

Merck & Co. Headquarters is in Kenilworth, New Jersey.

merger Few business combinations are truly a merger of equals, so be precise and sparing in the use of the word *merger*. It is not a synonym for acquisition or takeover, which should be the preferred descriptives in most stories. Use the following rules for deciding whether it's a merger or acquisition, and as a guide in concluding who is the acquirer and the company being taken over:
— Is one of the companies' stock being used as the currency? If

the answer is yes, that's usually a good sign that company is the acquirer and it is not a merger.
— What is the message from the exchange ratio in stock transactions? Typically when shareholders of Company A are offered new shares in a combined company at a 1-for-1 ratio, and Company B shares are exchanged at something less or more (i.e., each Company B will be exchanged for 0.47 percent of a share of the new company), it's an indication that Company A's stock is being used as the basis for the transaction. But it also could be a sign that the companies' boards have agreed to a merger that uses a formula to compensate for the differing market value (total number of shares multiplied by the closing stock price the day before the announcement) of the two companies to come up with an exchange ratio for stock in the new company.
— What is the message from the stock movements after the announcement? Shares of companies being acquired typically rise and shares of the acquirer often fall after the announcement. Not always, of course, but that's usually the case because most bidders pay a premium, or an above-market price, for the shares of the company being acquired, and investors often are worried about the amount of debt the acquirer is taking on to complete the transaction.
— Whose cash is being used to fund the cash portion of a transaction? If the announcement says Company A's cash will be used or

m

that its existing lines of credit will be tapped to pay for Company B's shares, that's a strong indication that Company A is the acquirer.

— Which company's executives are filling most of the top management roles? The key distinction usually is who gets the CEO slot. But if one of the two CEOs is named to head the company for a limited period (say two years or less) before his fellow CEO takes over, that's a good sign of a political compromise to paper over the fact that the second CEO's company is going to be in charge long term.

— Which company will end up with the majority of the seats on the new board of directors? This is often a key tie breaker. When Company A and Company B insist it's a merger of equals and other checklist items are inconclusive, if one ends up with 60 percent of the board seats and the other gets 40 percent, that's a good indication of which is going to be in charge. Also, make sure you get not only the short-term makeup of the board of the combined company, but also whether there were any deals cut for some members to retire in short order.

— Where will the company be headquartered? Since CEOs typically do the negotiating and they typically aren't anxious to move, this can be an informative tell.

meridians Use numerals and lowercase to identify the imaginary locater lines that ring the globe from north to south through the poles. They are measured in units of 0 to 180 degrees east and west of the *prime meridian,* which runs through Greenwich, England.

Examples: *33rd meridian* (if location east or west of Greenwich is obvious), *1st meridian west, 100th meridian.*

See **latitude and longitude**.

merry Christmas See **happy holidays, merry Christmas, season's greetings**.

merry-go-round

MERS *Middle East respiratory syndrome.* MERS is acceptable on second reference. MERS is related to SARS but do not describe as SARS-like.

Mesa Air Group Inc. Headquarters of this airline is in Phoenix.

messiah Capitalize in religious uses, such as references to the promised deliverer of the Jews or to Jesus in Christianity. Lowercase when referring to the liberator of a people or country.

metadata Behind-the-scenes data that provide important information about a piece of content. Examples include information about when or where information was created, by whom and in what format. If you refer to metadata in a story, explain what information is being revealed: *Investigators determined that Johnson wrote the document by analyzing its metadata, which indicated that it had been saved on his computer.*

meter The basic unit of length in the metric system.

It is equal to approximately 39.37 inches, which may be rounded off to 39.5 inches in most comparisons.

It takes 100 centimeters to make

a meter.

It takes 1,000 meters to make a kilometer.

To convert to inches, multiply by 39.37 (5 meters x 39.37 = 196.85 inches).

To convert to yards, multiply by 1.1 (5 meters x 1.1 = 5.5 yards).

See **inch**; **metric system**; and **yard**.

metric system The Associated Press typically includes both metric and imperial figures in copy to serve customers throughout the world.

Use the figure widely accepted in the location of the dateline, then the conversion in parentheses after the original figure. Round numbers up or down to avoid decimals unless a greater level of precision is important. For a story out of the U.S.: *He vowed to walk 62 miles (100 kilometers) in a week.* For a story out of France: *He vowed to walk 100 kilometers (62 miles) in a week.*

To avoid the need for long strings of figures, prefixes are added to the metric units to denote fractional

Metric conversion

INTO METRIC			OUT OF METRIC		
multiply	*by this number*	*to get*	*multiply*	*by this number*	*to get*
LENGTH					
inches	2.54	centimeters	millimeters	0.04	inches
feet	0.3	meters	centimeters	0.39	inches
yards	0.91	meters	meters	3.28	feet
miles	1.61	kilometers	kilometers	0.62	miles
AREA					
sq. inches	6.45	sq. centimeters	sq. centimeters	0.16	sq. inches
sq. feet	0.09	sq. meters	sq. meters	0.2	sq. yards
sq. yards	0.84	sq. meters	sq. kilometers	0.39	sq. miles
sq. miles	2.59	sq. kilometers	hectares	2.47	acres
acres	0.39	hectares			
MASS (WEIGHT)					
ounces	28	grams	grams	0.035	ounces
pounds	0.45	kilograms	kilograms	2.2	pounds
short ton	0.91	metric ton	metric ton	1.1	short tons
VOLUME					
teaspoons	5	milliliters	milliliters	0.03	fluid ounces
tablespoons	15	milliliters	liters	2.1	pints
fluid ounces	30	milliliters	liters	1.06	quarts
cups	0.24	liters	liters	0.26	gallons
pints	0.47	liters	cubic meters	35	cubic feet
quarts	0.95	liters	cubic meters	1.3	cubic yards
gallons	3.79	liters			
cubic feet	0.03	cubic meters			
cubic yards	0.76	cubic meters			

m

186

elements or large multiples. The prefixes are: *pico-* (one-trillionth), *nano-* (one-billionth), *micro-* (one-millionth), *milli-* (one-thousandth), *centi-* (one-hundredth), *deci-* (one-tenth), *deka-* (10 units), *hecto-* (100 units), *kilo-* (1,000 units), *mega-* (1 million units), *giga-* (1 billion units), *tera-* (1 trillion units). Entries for each prefix show how to convert a unit preceded by the prefix to the basic unit.

In addition, separate entries for **gram**, **meter**, **liter**, **Celsius** and other frequently used metric units define them and give examples of how to convert them to equivalents in the terminology that has been used in the United States.

Similarly, entries for **pound**, **inch**, **quart**, **Fahrenheit**, etc., contain examples of how to convert these terms to metric forms.

ABBREVIATIONS: The abbreviation mm for millimeter is acceptable in references to film widths (*8 mm film*) and weapons (*a 105 mm cannon*). (Note space between numeral and abbreviation.)

The principal abbreviations, for reference in the event they are used by a source, are: *g* (gram), *kg* (kilogram), *t* (metric ton), *m* (meter), *cm* (centimeter), *km* (kilometer), *mm* (millimeter), *L* (liter, capital L to avoid confusion with the figure 1) and *mL* (milliliter).

metric ton Equal to approximately 2,204.62 pounds. See **ton**.

Metro-Goldwyn-Mayer Inc. *MGM* is acceptable in all references.
Headquarters is in Beverly Hills, California.

Mexico There are 31 states and Mexico City, the capital and an

independent federal district run by a city government. The states are Aguascalientes, Baja California, Baja California Sur, Campeche, Chiapas, Chihuahua, Coahuila, Colima, Durango, Guanajuato, Guerrero, Hidalgo, Jalisco, Mexico, Michoacan, Morelos, Nayarit, Nuevo Leon, Oaxaca, Puebla, Queretaro, Quintana Roo, San Luis Potosi, Sinaloa, Sonora, Tabasco, Tamaulipas, Tlaxcala, Veracruz, Yucatan and Zacatecas.

Mexican states elect their own governor and legislators. Congress is made up of two houses: the lower House of Deputies, with 500 members, and the Senate, with 128 members.

In datelines, use only the city and country.

Mexico City The city in Mexico stands alone in datelines.

Miami The city in Florida stands alone in datelines.

mic (n.) Informal form of *microphone*.

Michigan Abbreviate *Mich.* in datelines only; spell out in stories. Postal code: *MI*
See **state names**.

micro- A prefix denoting one-millionth of a unit.
Move the decimal point six places to the left in converting to the basic unit: 2,999,888.5 microseconds = 2.9998885 seconds.

microsite A tightly focused website typically dedicated to a single topic, product or service.

Microsoft Corp. Headquarters is in Redmond, Washington.

m

mid- No hyphen unless a capitalized word follows: *midair, mid-America, mid-Atlantic, midsemester* and *midterm.*

But use a hyphen when *mid-* precedes a figure: *mid-30s.*

Middle Ages A.D. 476 to approximately A.D. 1450.

Middle Atlantic States As defined by the U.S. Census Bureau, they are New Jersey, New York and Pennsylvania.

Less formal references often consider Delaware part of the group. See **Northeast region**.

middle class (n.) **middle-class** (adj.)

Middle East The term generally applies to southwest Asia west of Pakistan and Afghanistan (Iran, Iraq, Israel, Kuwait, Jordan, Lebanon, Oman, Bahrain, Qatar, Saudi Arabia, Syria, the eastern part of Turkey known also as Asia Minor, United Arab Emirates and Yemen), and northeastern Africa (Egypt and Sudan).

Some consider Libya and other Arabic-speaking countries of the Maghreb to be part of the region.

Popular usage once distinguished between the *Near East* (the westerly nations in the listing) and the *Middle East* (the easterly nations), but the two terms now overlap, with current practice favoring *Middle East* for both areas.

Use *Middle East* unless *Near East* is used by a source in a story.

Mideast is also acceptable, but *Middle East* is preferred.

middle initials Use according to a person's preference.

Include middle initials in stories where they help identify a specific individual. Examples include casualty lists and stories naming the accused in a crime. A middle initial may be dropped if a person does not use one or is publicly known without it: *Mickey Mantle* (not *Mickey C.*), *the Rev. Billy Graham* (not *Billy F.*).

See **names**.

middleman

middle names Use them only with people who are publicly known that way (*James Earl Jones*), or to prevent confusion with people of the same name.

See **middle initials; names**.

midget Considered offensive when used to describe a person of short stature. *Dwarf* is the preferred term for people with that medical or genetic condition. See **dwarf**.

midnight Do not put a 12 in front of it. It is part of the day that is ending, not the one that is beginning.

midshipman See **military academies**.

Midwest region As defined by the U.S. Census Bureau, the region (previously designated the North Central region) is broken into two divisions.

The East North Central states are Indiana, Illinois, Michigan, Ohio and Wisconsin.

The West North Central states are Iowa, Kansas, Minnesota, Missouri, Nebraska, North Dakota and South Dakota.

See **Northeast region; South;** and **West** for the bureau's other regional breakdowns.

MiG The *i* in this designation for a type

m

of Russian fighter jet is lowercase because it is the Russian word for *and*. The initials are from the last names of the designers, Arten Mikoyan and Mikhail Gurevich.

The forms: *MiG-19*, *MiG-21s*.

See **aircraft names**.

migrant See **immigration**.

Milan The city in Italy stands alone in datelines.

mile Also called a statute mile, it equals 5,280 feet.

The metric equivalent is approximately 1.6 kilometers.

To convert to kilometers, multiply by 1.6 (5 miles x 1.6 equals 8 kilometers).

Use figures in all references: *The farm measures 5 miles by 4 miles. The car slowed to 7 mph. The new model gets 4 miles more per gallon. He walked 3 miles.*

See **foot**; **kilometer**; **knot**; **nautical mile** and **numerals**.

miles per gallon The abbreviation *mpg* is acceptable in all references.

miles per hour The abbreviation *mph* is acceptable in all references. No hyphen when used with a figure: *60 mph*.

military academies Capitalize *U.S. Air Force Academy, U.S. Coast Guard Academy, U.S. Merchant Marine Academy, U.S. Military Academy, U.S. Naval Academy*. Retain capitalization if the *U.S.* is dropped: *the Air Force Academy*, etc.

Lowercase *academy* whenever it stands alone.

Cadet is the proper title on first reference for men and women enrolled at the Army, Air Force, Coast Guard and Merchant Marine academies. *Midshipman* is the proper title for men and women enrolled at the Naval Academy.

Use the appropriate title on first reference. On second reference, use only the last name.

military titles Capitalize a military rank when used as a formal title before an individual's name.

See the lists that follow to determine whether the title should be spelled out or abbreviated in regular text.

On first reference, use the appropriate title before the full name of a member of the military.

In subsequent references, do not continue using the title before a name. Use only the last name.

Spell out and lowercase a title when it is substituted for a name: *Gen. John Jones is the top U.S. commander in Afghanistan. The general endorsed the idea.*

In some cases, it may be necessary to explain the significance of a title: *Army Sgt. Maj. John Jones described the attack. Jones, who holds the Army's highest rank for enlistees, said it was unprovoked.*

In addition to the ranks listed on the next page, each service has ratings such as *machinist, radarman, torpedoman*, etc., that are job descriptions. Do not use any of these designations as a title on first reference. If one is used before a name in a subsequent reference, do not capitalize or abbreviate it.

Moreover, each service branch has its own systems of abbreviating officer and enlisted ranks — e.g., COL for colonel in the Army, CMDR for Navy commander — that vary widely from AP style. However, the Department of Defense uses

AP's military titles in news releases because the abbreviations are easily understood.

ABBREVIATIONS: The abbreviations, with the highest ranks listed first:

MILITARY TITLES

Rank	Usage before a name

ARMY

Commissioned Officers

general	Gen.
lieutenant general	Lt. Gen.
major general	Maj. Gen.
brigadier general	Brig. Gen.
colonel	Col.
lieutenant colonel	Lt. Col.
major	Maj.
captain	Capt.
first lieutenant	1st Lt.
second lieutenant	2nd Lt.

Warrant Officers

chief warrant officer five (CW5)	Chief Warrant Officer 5
chief warrant officer four (CW4)	Chief Warrant Officer 4
chief warrant officer three (CW3)	Chief Warrant Officer 3
chief warrant officer two (CW2)	Chief Warrant Officer 2
warrant officer (WO1)	Warrant Officer

Enlisted Personnel

sergeant major of the Army	Sgt. Maj. of the Army
command sergeant major	Command Sgt. Maj.
sergeant major	Sgt. Maj.
first sergeant	1st Sgt.
master sergeant	Master Sgt.
sergeant first class	Sgt. 1st Class
staff sergeant	Staff Sgt.
sergeant	Sgt.
corporal	Cpl.
specialist	Spc.
private first class	Pfc.
private	Pvt.

NAVY, COAST GUARD

Commissioned Officers

admiral	Adm.
vice admiral	Vice Adm.
rear admiral upper half	Rear Adm.
rear admiral lower half	Rear Adm.
captain	Capt.
commander	Cmdr.
lieutenant commander	Lt. Cmdr.
lieutenant	Lt.
lieutenant junior grade	Lt. j.g.
ensign	Ensign

Warrant Officers

chief warrant officer	Chief Warrant Officer

Enlisted Personnel

master chief petty officer of the Navy	Master Chief Petty Officer of the Navy
master chief petty officer	Master Chief Petty Officer
senior chief petty officer	Senior Chief Petty Officer
chief petty officer	Chief Petty Officer
petty officer first class	Petty Officer 1st Class
petty officer second class	Petty Officer 2nd Class
petty officer third class	Petty Officer 3rd Class
seaman	Seaman
seaman apprentice	Seaman Apprentice
seaman recruit	Seaman Recruit

MARINE CORPS

Ranks and abbreviations for commissioned officers are the same as those in the Army. Warrant officer ratings follow the same system used in the Navy. There are no specialist ratings.

Others

sergeant major of the Marine Corps	Sgt. Maj. of the Marine Corps
sergeant major	Sgt. Maj.
master gunnery sergeant	Master Gunnery Sgt.
first sergeant	1st Sgt.
master sergeant	Master Sgt.
gunnery sergeant	Gunnery Sgt.
staff sergeant	Staff Sgt.
sergeant	Sgt.
corporal	Cpl.

m

lance corporal	Lance Cpl.
private first class	Pfc.
private	Pvt.

AIR FORCE

Ranks and abbreviations for commissioned officers are the same as those in the Army.

Enlisted Designations

chief master sergeant of the Air Force	Chief Master Sgt. of the Air Force
chief master sergeant	Chief Master Sgt.
senior master sergeant	Senior Master Sgt.
master sergeant	Master Sgt.
technical sergeant	Tech. Sgt.
staff sergeant	Staff Sgt.
senior airman	Senior Airman
airman first class	Airman 1st Class
airman	Airman
airman basic	Airman

PLURALS: Add *s* to the principal element in the title: *Majs. John Jones and Robert Smith; Maj. Gens. John Jones and Robert Smith; Spcs. John Jones and Robert Smith.*

RETIRED OFFICERS: A military rank may be used in first reference before the name of an officer who has retired if it is relevant to a story. Do not, however, use the military abbreviation *Ret.*

Instead, use *retired* just as *former* would be used before the title of a civilian: *They invited retired Army Gen. John Smith.*

FIREFIGHTERS, POLICE OFFICERS: Use the abbreviations listed here when a military-style title is used before the name of a firefighter or police officer outside a direct quotation. Add *police* or *fire* before the title if needed for clarity: *police Sgt. William Smith, fire Capt. David Jones.*

Spell out titles such as *detective* that are not used in the armed forces.

m

military units Use Arabic figures and capitalize the key words when linked with the figures: *1st Infantry Division* (or *the 1st Division*), *5th Battalion, 395th Field Artillery, 7th Fleet.*

But: *the division, the battalion, the artillery, the fleet.*

See **numerals**.

millennials Members of the generation following Generation X, or two generations after the 1946 to 1964 baby-boom generation. Also known as Generation Y. Definitions vary for the years this generation spans; the time period should be specified when possible. See **baby boom, baby boomers** and **Generation X.**

millennium

milli- A prefix denoting one-thousandth of a unit. Move the decimal three places to the left in converting to the basic unit: 1,567.5 millimeters equals 1.5675 meters.

milligram One-thousandth of a gram.
Equal to approximately one-twenty-eight-thousandth of an ounce.
To convert to ounces, multiply by 0.000035 (140 milligrams x 0.000035 equals 0.0049 ounce).
See **metric system.**

milliliter One-thousandth of a liter.
Equal to approximately one-fifth of a teaspoon.
Thirty milliliters equals 1 fluid ounce.
To convert to teaspoons, multiply by 0.2 (5 milliliters x 0.2 equals 1 teaspoon).
See **liter** and **metric system.**

millimeter One-thousandth of a

meter.

It takes 10 millimeters to make a centimeter.

To convert to inches, multiply by 0.04 (5 millimeters x 0.04 is 0.2 of an inch).

May be abbreviated as *mm* when used with a numeral in first or subsequent references to film or weapons: *35 mm film, 105 mm artillery piece.* (Note space after numeral.)

See **meter**; **metric system**; and **inch**.

millions, billions, trillions Use figures with *million, billion* or *trillion* in all except casual uses: *I'd like to make a billion dollars.* But: *The nation has 1 million citizens. I need $7 billion. The government ran a deficit of more than $1 trillion.*

Do not go beyond two decimal places. *7.51 million people, $256 billion, 7,542,500 people, $2,565,750,000.* Decimals are preferred where practical: *1.5 million.* Not: *1 1/2 million.*

Do not mix *millions* and *billions* in the same figure: *2.6 billion.* Not: *2 billion 600 million.*

Do not drop the word *million* or *billion* in the first figure of a range: *He is worth from $2 million to $4 million.* Not: *$2 to $4 million,* unless you really mean $2.

Note that a hyphen is not used to join the figures and the word *million* or *billion,* even in this type of phrase: *The president submitted a $300 billion budget.*

In headlines, abbreviate only *millions, billions*: *$5M lawsuit, $17.4B trade deficit*

See **numerals**.

Milwaukee The city in Wisconsin stands alone in datelines.

mindset

mini- The rules in **prefixes** apply, but in general, no hyphen. Some examples:
*miniseries   miniskirt
minivan*

minimally conscious state In this condition, the eyes are open, but the patient shows only minimal or intermittent signs of awareness of self and environment and often responds only inconsistently when asked to gesture, move or speak. At times, the patient may be able to reach for objects, indicate yes or no and follow objects with the eyes, but a given patient may not be able to do all these things.

See **coma** and **vegetative state**.

minister It is not a formal title in most religions, with exceptions such as the Nation of Islam, and is not capitalized. Where it is a formal title, it should be capitalized before the name: *Minister John Jones.*

See **religious titles** and the entry for an individual's denomination in the **Religion** chapter.

ministry See **governmental bodies**.

Minneapolis The city in Minnesota stands alone in datelines.

Minnesota Abbreviate *Minn.* in datelines only; spell out in stories. Postal code: *MN*
See **state names**.

minority leader Treat the same as *majority leader.* See that entry and **legislative titles**.

minuscule Not miniscule.

minus sign Use a hyphen, not a dash, but use the word *minus* if there is any danger of confusion.

Use a word, not a minus sign, to indicate temperatures below zero: *minus 10* or *5 below zero.*

mirroring The copying of online content, such as a photo, video or data, so that it simultaneously appears in a second location online or on a storage device. Mirroring is typically done to back up content, to make it easier for users to access or simply to display it in another location.

MIRV, MIRVs Acceptable on first reference for *multiple independently targetable re-entry vehicle(s).*

Explain in the text that a *MIRV* is an intercontinental ballistic missile with several warheads, each of which can be directed to a different target.

misdemeanor See **felony, misdemeanor**.

mishap A minor misfortune. People are not killed in *mishaps.*

missile names Use Arabic figures and capitalize the proper name but not the word *missile*: *Pershing 2 missile.*
See **ABM**; **ICBM**; **MIRV**; and **SAM**.

Mississippi Abbreviate *Miss.* in datelines only; spell out in stories. Postal code: *MS*
See **state names**.

Missouri Abbreviate *Mo.* in datelines only; spell out in stories. Postal code: *MO*
See **state names**.

mistress A woman who has a long-term sexual relationship with, and is financially supported by, a man who is married to someone else. When a relationship is not long-term or does not involve financial support, do not use *mistress*; terms like *companion, friend* or *lover* may apply. Whenever possible, phrasing that acknowledges both people in the relationship is preferred: *"The two were romantically (or sexually) involved."*

mix-up (n. and adj.) **mix up** (v.)

mock-up (n.)

model numbers See **serial numbers**.

modem Acceptable in all references for the acronym formed from *modulator* and *demodulator.*

mom See **family names**.

Monaco After the Vatican, the world's smallest state.

The *Monaco* section stands alone in datelines. The other two sections, *La Condamine* and *Monte Carlo*, are followed by *Monaco*:
MONTE CARLO, Monaco (AP) —

monetary See the **fiscal, monetary** entry.

monetary units See **cents**; **dollars**; and **pounds**.

moneymaker

Montana Abbreviate *Mont.* in datelines only; spell out in stories. Postal code: *MT*
See **state names**.

Montessori method After Maria Montessori, a system of training young children. It emphasizes training of the senses and guidance to encourage self-education.

monthlong, monthslong One word as an adjective.

months Capitalize the names of months in all uses. When a month is used with a specific date, abbreviate only *Jan., Feb., Aug., Sept., Oct., Nov.* and *Dec.* Spell out when using alone, or with a year alone.

When a phrase lists only a month and a year, do not separate the year with commas. When a phrase refers to a month, day and year, set off the year with commas.

EXAMPLES: *January 2016 was a cold month. Jan. 2 was the coldest day of the month. His birthday is May 8. Feb. 14, 2013, was the target date. She testified that it was Friday, Dec. 3, when the crash occurred.*

In tabular material, use these three-letter forms without a period: *Jan, Feb, Mar, Apr, May, Jun, Jul, Aug, Sep, Oct, Nov, Dec.*

See **dates** and **years**.

Montreal The city in Canada stands alone in datelines.

monuments Capitalize the popular names of monuments and similar public attractions: *Lincoln Memorial, Statue of Liberty, Washington Monument, Leaning Tower of Pisa*, etc.

moon Lowercase. See **heavenly bodies**.

mop-up (n. and adj.) **mop up** (v.)

moral obligation bond See **loan terminology**.

more than, over Acceptable in all uses to indicate greater numerical value. *Salaries went up more than $20 a week. Salaries went up over $20 a week.* See **over**.

Morgan Stanley Headquarters is in New York.

Mormon church Acceptable in references to *The Church of Jesus Christ of Latter-day Saints*, but the official name is preferred in first reference in a story dealing primarily with church activities.

See **Church of Jesus Christ of Latter-day Saints, The** in the **Religion** chapter.

mortgage A loan secured by property. The contract between the borrower and the lender gives the lender the right to take possession and resell the property if the borrower defaults. See **adjustable-rate mortgage** and **balloon mortgage**.

mortgage-backed security A bond backed by home or commercial mortgage payments. These provide income from payments of the underlying mortgages.

Moscow The city in Russia stands alone in datelines.

mosquito, mosquitoes

Mother's Day The second Sunday in May.

mother-in-law, mothers-in-law

Mother Nature

motor See the **engine, motor** entry.

mount Spell out in all uses, including the names of communities and of mountains: *Mount Clemens, Michigan; Mount Everest.*

mountains Capitalize as part of a proper name: *Appalachian Mountains, Ozark Mountains, Rocky Mountains.*
Or simply: *the Appalachians, the Ozarks, the Rockies.*

Mountain Standard Time (MST), Mountain Daylight Time (MDT) See **time zones.**

Mountain States As defined by the U.S. Census Bureau, the eight are Arizona, Colorado, Idaho, Montana, Nevada, New Mexico, Utah and Wyoming.

mouse, mice Use *mice* as the plural form of hand-held computer-input devices.

moviegoer

movie ratings The ratings used by the Motion Picture Association of America are:
G — General audiences. All ages admitted.
PG — Parental guidance suggested. Some material may not be suitable for children.
PG-13 — Special *parental guidance* strongly suggested for children under 13. Some material may be inappropriate for young children.
R — Restricted. Under 17 requires accompanying parent or adult guardian.
NC-17 — No one under 17 admitted.
When the ratings are used in news stories or reviews, use these forms as appropriate: *the movie has an R rating, an R-rated movie, the movie is R-rated.*

movie titles See **composition titles.**

MPEG-2 An international standard for digital video compression and decompression. *MPEG* is an acronym for *Moving Picture Experts Group.*

mpg Acceptable in all references for *miles per gallon.*

mph Acceptable in all references for *miles per hour* or *miles an hour.*

MP3 A popular audio compression format.

MRI Magnetic resonance imaging, a noninvasive diagnostic procedure used to render images of the inside of an object. It is primarily used in medical imaging to demonstrate pathological or other physiological alterations of living tissues. *MRI* is acceptable on first reference and in all uses.

MRSA Abbreviation for *methicillin-resistant Staphylococcus aureus. MRSA* is acceptable on first reference but include full name in story.

Muhammad The chief prophet and central figure of the Islamic religion, *the Prophet Muhammad.* Use other spellings only if preferred by a specific person for his own name or in a title or the name of an organization.

mujahedeen Lowercase when using the Arabic for *holy warriors;* uppercase if it is part of the name of a group. The Iranian opposition group is *Mujahedeen-e-Khalq.* The singular for *holy warrior* is *mujahed.*

mullah An Islamic leader or teacher, often a general title of respect for a learned man.

multi- The rules in prefixes apply, but in general, no hyphen. Some

m

examples:

multicolored   multimillion
multilateral   multimillionaire

multiracial See **biracial, multiracial**.

Mumbai India's largest city, formerly known as Bombay.

Munich The city in Germany stands alone in datelines.

municipal bond See **loan terminology**.

murder See **homicide, murder, manslaughter**.

murderer See **assassin, killer, murderer**.

Murphy's law The law is: *If something can go wrong, it will.*

music Capitalize, but do not use quotation marks, on descriptive titles for orchestral works: Bach's Suite No. 1 for Orchestra; Beethoven's Serenade for Flute, Violin and Viola. If the instrumentation is not part of the title but is added for explanatory purposes, the names of the instruments are lowercased: Mozart's Sinfonia Concertante in E flat major (the common title) for violin and viola. If in doubt, lowercase the names of the instruments.

Use quotation marks for nonmusical terms in a title: Beethoven's "Eroica" Symphony. If the work has a special full title, all of it is quoted: "Symphonie Fantastique," "Rhapsody in Blue."

In subsequent references, lowercase *symphony, concerto,* etc.

See **composition titles**.

musket See **weapons**.

Muslim Brotherhood Pan-Arab Islamist political movement.

Muzak A trademark for a type of recorded background music.

Myanmar Use this name for the country (formerly *Burma*). Use *Myanmar's people* or *people of Myanmar* for the inhabitants. Use *Myanmar* for the country's dominant language.

myriad (adj.) Note word is not followed by *of*: *The myriad books in the library.*

m

n

NAACP Acceptable in all references for the *National Association for the Advancement of Colored People*. Define as the nation's oldest civil rights organization. Headquarters is in Baltimore.

naloxone Use the generic *naloxone* for the opioid-overdose antidote often carried by first responders and caretakers of people with heroin addiction, with explanation if necessary. Not synonymous with *Narcan*, which is a brand name for a device that delivers *naloxone*.

name changes In general, use the name by which a person currently lives or is widely known. Include a previous name or names only if relevant to story. See **names**, **pseudonyms**, **nicknames**.

names In general, use only last names on second reference. When it is necessary to distinguish between two people who use the same last name, generally use the first and last name on subsequent references. Generally use the name a person prefers: *Thomas* or *Tom*, depending on preference; Martine McCarthy Chang may prefer *McCarthy Chang* or *Chang* on second reference. If an individual requests it, a public name rather than a real name may be used for a political dissident, or a nom de guerre for a rebel leader, if the person's safety is an issue. In general, call children 15 or younger by their first name on second reference. Use the last name, however, if the seriousness of the story calls for it, as in a murder case, for example. For ages 16 and 17, use judgment, but generally go with the surname unless it's a light story. Use the surname for those 18 and older.

See **Arabic names; Chinese names; Korean names; Russian names; Spanish names**. Also: **anonymous sources; courtesy titles; middle initials; middle names; pseudonyms, nicknames**.

nano- A prefix denoting one-billionth of a unit. Move the decimal point nine places to the left in converting to the basic unit: 2,999,888,777.5 nanoseconds equals 2.9998887775 seconds.

Narcan See **naloxone**.

narrow-minded

Nasdaq composite A major U.S. stock index, often referred to in conjunction with the Dow Jones industrial average and the Standard & Poor's 500 index. The Nasdaq composite is an index of all the stocks listed on the Nasdaq Stock Market. On second reference: *the Nasdaq*.

Nasdaq Stock Market The world's first all-electronic stock market and a direct competitor to the New York Stock Exchange. Parent company is Nasdaq Inc.

national See **citizen, resident, subject, national, native**.

National Aeronautics and Space Administration *NASA* is acceptable in all references.

national anthem Lowercase. But: "The Star-Spangled Banner."

National Broadcasting Co. See **NBC**.

National Education Association *NEA* is acceptable on second reference.
Headquarters is in Washington.

National FFA Organization Formerly the Future Farmers of America. *FFA* is acceptable on second reference.
Headquarters is in Alexandria, Virginia.

National Governors Association Represents the governors of the 50 states and five territories.
Its office is in Washington.

National Guard Capitalize when referring to U.S. or state-level forces, or foreign forces when that is the formal name: *the National Guard, the Guard, the Iowa National Guard, Iowa's National Guard, National Guard troops, the Iraqi National Guard.* On second reference, *the guard.*
When referring to an individual in a National Guard unit, use National Guardsman: *He is a National Guardsman.*
Lowercase *guardsman* when it stands alone.
See **military titles**.

National Hurricane Center See **weather terms**.

National Institutes of Health This agency within the Department of Health and Human Services is the principal biomedical research arm of the federal government. It has 27 institutes and centers, most with headquarters in Bethesda, Maryland. On first reference, use the *National Institutes of Health*, with a singular verb: *The National Institutes of Health is launching a new initiative.* NIH is acceptable on second reference and takes a singular verb.

nationalist Lowercase when referring to a partisan of a country. Capitalize only when referring to alignment with a political party for which this is the proper name.
See **political parties and philosophies**.

Nationalist China See **China**.

nationalities and races Capitalize the proper names of nationalities, peoples, races, tribes, etc.: *Arab, Arabic, African, American, Caucasian, Cherokee, Chinese* (both singular and plural), *Eskimo* (plural *Eskimos*) or *Inuit, French Canadian, Japanese* (singular and plural), *Jew, Jewish, Nordic, Sioux, Swede*, etc.
See **race** for guidelines on when racial identification is pertinent in a story.
Do not use a derogatory term except in extremely rare circumstances — when it is crucial to the story or the understanding of a news event. Flag the contents in an editor's note.

National Labor Relations Board *NLRB* is acceptable on second reference.

National League of Cities Its members include the governments of about 2,000 U.S. cities and 48 state municipal leagues.

It is separate from the U.S. Conference of Mayors, whose membership is limited to mayors of cities with 30,000 or more residents. The office is in Washington.

National Newspaper Association A newspaper association representing community newspapers and their owners, publishers and editors. *NNA* is acceptable on second reference.

Headquarters is at the Missouri School of Journalism, Columbia, Missouri.

National Organization for Women Not *of. NOW* is acceptable on second reference.

Headquarters is in Washington.

National Park Service A bureau of the Interior Department, it manages the National Park System, which includes dozens of national parks as well as monuments, battlefields, historic sites and seashores, and the White House. The National Park Service also helps administer dozens of affiliated sites, the National Register of Historic Places, National Heritage Areas, National Wild and Scenic Rivers, National Historic Landmarks, and National Trails. On second reference, *park service*.

National Rifle Association *NRA* is acceptable on second reference. Headquarters is in Washington.

National Security Agency A U.S. intelligence agency that collects and analyzes signals from foreign and domestic sources for the purpose of intelligence and counterintelligence. It also defends U.S. government signals and codes from intrusion. The NSA is based in Fort Meade,

Maryland. *NSA* is acceptable on second reference.

National Weather Service Use *National Weather Service* on first reference and *weather service* on subsequent references.

See **weather terms**.

nationwide

native See **citizen, resident, subject, national, native**.

Native American Acceptable for those in the U.S. Follow the person's preference. Where possible, be precise and use the name of the tribe: *He is a Navajo commissioner.* Such words or terms as *wampum, warpath, powwow, teepee, brave, squaw*, etc., can be disparaging and offensive.

First Nation is the preferred term for native tribes in Canada.

See **Indians, nationalities and races, race** and **tribe, tribal**.

Nativity scene Only the first word is capitalized.

NATO Acceptable in all references for the *North Atlantic Treaty Organization*.

Naugahyde A trademark for a brand of simulated leather.

nautical mile It equals 1 minute of arc of a great circle of the Earth or 6,076.11549 feet, or 1,852 meters. To convert to approximate statute miles (5,280 feet), multiply the number of nautical miles by 1.15.

See **knot**.

naval, navel Use *naval* in copy pertaining to a navy.

A *navel* is a bellybutton.

A *navel orange* is a seedless orange, so named because it has a small depression, like a navel.

naval station Capitalize only as part of a proper name: *Naval Station Norfolk.*

navy Capitalize when referring to U.S. forces: *the U.S. Navy, the Navy, Navy policy.* Do not use the abbreviation *USN.*

Lowercase when referring to the naval forces of other nations: *the British navy.*

This approach has been adopted for consistency, because many foreign nations do not use *navy* as the proper name.

See **military academies** and **military titles**.

Nazi, Nazism Derived from the German for the National Socialist German Workers' Party, the fascist political party founded in 1919 and abolished in 1945. Under Adolf Hitler, it seized control of Germany in 1933.

See **political parties and philosophies**, **concentration camps** and **Holocaust**.

NBC Acceptable in all references to the National Broadcasting Co. NBC is part of NBCUniversal, which is owned by Comcast Corp.

nearsighted When used in a medical sense, it means an individual can see well at close range but has difficulty seeing objects at a distance.

Nebraska Abbreviate *Neb.* in datelines only; spell out in stories. Postal code: *NE*

See **state names**.

neither ... nor See **either ... or, neither ... nor**.

Nestle Headquarters is in Vevey, Switzerland.

Netherlands In datelines, give the name of the community followed by *Netherlands*:

MAASTRICHT, *Netherlands* (AP) — In stories: *the Netherlands* or *Netherlands* as the construction of a sentence dictates.

Netherlands Antilles In datelines, give the name of the community followed by *Netherlands Antilles*. Do not abbreviate.

Identify an individual island, if needed, in the text.

net income, net profit See **profit terminology**.

net neutrality The idea that everyone with an internet connection should have equal access to video, music, email, photos, social networks, maps and other content, with some exceptions that allow internet service providers to block spam and child pornography. U.S. internet service providers typically oppose net neutrality, arguing it will discourage them from investing in network upgrades. They want the ability to charge Netflix and other content providers to access a fast lane to reach consumers.

Nevada Abbreviate *Nev.* in datelines only; spell out in stories. Postal code: *NV*

See **state names**.

never-ending

New Brunswick One of the three

n

Maritime Provinces of Canada. Do not abbreviate.
See **datelines**.

New Delhi The city in India stands alone in datelines.

New England Connecticut, Maine, Massachusetts, New Hampshire, Rhode Island and Vermont.

Newfoundland This Canadian province, officially renamed Newfoundland and Labrador in 2001, comprises the island of Newfoundland and the mainland section of Labrador. Do not abbreviate.

In datelines, use Newfoundland after the names of all cities and towns. Specify in the text whether the community is on the island or in Labrador.
See **datelines**.

New Hampshire Abbreviate *N.H.* in datelines only; spell out in stories. Postal code: *NH*
See **state names**.

New Jersey Abbreviate *N.J.* in datelines only; spell out in stories. Postal code: *NJ*
See **state names**.

New Mexico Abbreviate *N.M.* in datelines only; spell out in stories. Postal code: *NM*
See **state names**.

New Orleans The city in Louisiana stands alone in datelines.

News Corp. Publishing conglomerate controlled by Rupert Murdoch. The company includes newspapers, book publishing and information services located primarily in the United States, the United Kingdom and Australia that remained after the company split off its entertainment businesses into a separate company called Twenty-First Century Fox Inc. in June 2013. Headquarters is in New York.

News Media Alliance Formerly the Newspaper Association of America. *NMA* is acceptable on second reference; do not call it *the newspaper association*. Headquarters is in Arlington, Virginia.

Newspaper Guild-Communications Workers of America, The
Formerly the American Newspaper Guild, it is a union for newspaper and news service employees, generally those in the news and business departments.

On second reference: *the Guild*. Headquarters is in Washington.

The News Media Guild, formerly the Wire Service Guild, is the local representing employees of The Associated Press.

newspaper names Capitalize *the* in a newspaper's name if that is the way the publication prefers to be known. Do not place name in quotes.

Lowercase *the* before newspaper names if a story mentions several papers, some of which use *the* as part of the name and some of which do not.

It is unnecessary to provide state identification for a newspaper cited in the body of a story if the newspaper is in the same state as the dateline. For example, a story datelined Newport, R.I., would reference the Providence Journal, not the Providence (Rhode Island) Journal.

However, the state should be

included and spelled out in the body of undated stories or stories datelined in other states.

Where location is needed but is not part of the official name, use parentheses: The Huntsville (Alabama) Times.

newsstand

New Testament See **Bible**.

New World The Western Hemisphere.

New Year's, New Year's Day, New Year's Eve, Happy New Year
Capitalize for the days of Dec. 31 and Jan. 1 and in exclamations. For resolutions made on or around Jan. 1, the phrase is *New Year's resolutions*. But lowercase general references to the coming year: *What will the new year bring?* The U.S. federal legal holiday is observed on Friday if Jan. 1 falls on a Saturday, on Monday if it falls on a Sunday. See **happy holidays, merry Christmas, season's greetings, happy birthday, happy new year**.

New York Abbreviate *N.Y.* in datelines only; spell out in stories. Postal code: *NY*
See **state names**.

New York City Use *NEW YORK* in datelines, not the name of an individual community or borough such as *Flushing* or *Queens*.

Identify the borough in the body of the story if pertinent.

New York Stock Exchange *NYSE* is acceptable on second reference. It is owned by Intercontinental Exchange Inc., a publicly traded company that is headquartered in Atlanta and operates other exchanges and clearing houses.

The New York Times Co. Owner of The New York Times and The New York Times International Edition. Headquarters is in New York.

NGO *Nongovernmental organization.* Usually refers to a nonprofit, humanitarian organization. Use *NGO* sparingly and only on second reference.

nicknames See **pseudonyms, nicknames**.

nightclub

nighttime

9/11 For the Sept. 11, 2001, terrorist attacks, *9/11* is acceptable in all references. (Note comma to set off the year when the phrase refers to a month, date and year.)

911 Acceptable in all references for the U.S. emergency call number: *He called 911 to report a crash.* No hyphen in any use: *a 911 call; a 911 call problem.*

niqab The veil worn by the most conservative Muslim women, in which, at most, only the eyes show. See also other garments such as **hijab, burqa, chador**.

nitpicking

nitty-gritty

No. Use as the abbreviation for *number* in conjunction with a figure to indicate position or rank: *No. 1 man, No. 3 choice.*

Do not use in street addresses, with this exception: *No. 10 Downing*

St., the residence of Britain's prime minister.

Do not use in the names of schools: *Public School 19.*

See **numerals**.

Nobel Prize, Nobel Prizes The five established under terms of the will of Alfred Nobel are: Nobel Peace Prize, Nobel Prize in chemistry, Nobel Prize in literature, Nobel Prize in physics, Nobel Prize in physiology or medicine. (Note the capitalization styles.)

The Nobel Memorial Prize in Economic Sciences (officially it is the cumbersome Bank of Sweden Prize in Economic Sciences in Memory of Alfred Nobel) is not a Nobel Prize in the same sense. The Central Bank of Sweden established it in 1968 as a memorial to Alfred Nobel. References to this prize should include the word *Memorial* to help make this distinction. Explain the status of the prize in the story when appropriate.

Nobel Prize award ceremonies are held on Dec. 10, the anniversary of Alfred Nobel's death in 1896. The award ceremony for peace is in Oslo and the other ceremonies are in Stockholm.

Capitalize *prize* in references that do not mention the category: *He is a Nobel Prize winner. She is a Nobel Prize-winning scientist.*

Lowercase *prize* when not linked with the word *Nobel: The peace prize was awarded Monday.*

nobility References to members of the nobility in nations that have a system of rank present special problems because nobles frequently are known by their titles rather than their given or family names. Their titles, in effect, become their names. Generally follow a person's preference, unless the person is widely known in another way.

The guidelines below relate to Britain's nobility. Adapt them as appropriate to members of nobility in other nations.

Orders of rank among British nobility begin with the royal family. The term *royalty* is reserved for the families of living and deceased sovereigns.

Next, in descending order, are dukes, marquesses or marquises, earls, viscounts and barons. There are also life peers who are appointed to the House of Lords and hold their titles only for their lifetimes. On first reference to a life peer, use the person's ordinary name, e.g., *Margaret Thatcher* or *Jeffrey Archer.* Elsewhere, if relevant, explain that the person has been appointed to the House of Lords.

Occasionally the sovereign raises an individual to the nobility and makes the title inheritable by the person's heirs, but the practice is rare. Sovereigns also confer honorary titles, which do not make an individual a member of the nobility. The principal designations are *baronet* and *knight.*

In general, the guidelines in **courtesy titles** and **titles** apply. However, honorary titles and titles of nobility are capitalized when they serve as an alternate name.

Some guidelines and examples:

ROYALTY: Capitalize *king, queen, prince* and *princess* when they are used directly before one or more names; lowercase when they stand alone:

Queen Elizabeth II. *The queen* or *Elizabeth* on second reference. Capitalize a longer form of the sovereign's title when its use is appropriate or in a quote: *Her Majesty Queen Elizabeth*.

Use *Prince* or *Princess* before the names of a sovereign's children: *Princess Anne, Prince Charles*.

In references to the queen's husband first reference should be *Prince Philip* (not *Duke of Edinburgh*, commonly used in Britain). He is *Philip* on second reference.

The male heir to the throne normally is designated *Prince of Wales*, and the title becomes an alternate name. Capitalize when used: *The queen invested her eldest son as Prince of Wales. Prince Charles is now the Prince of Wales. The prince is married. His wife, Camilla, is called the Duchess of Cornwall* (Charles is also the *Duke of Cornwall*, among other titles).

Charles' eldest son is *Prince William*. He is also the *Duke of Cambridge*. Prince William's wife, the former Kate Middleton, is the *Duchess of Cambridge*. Their son is *Prince George* and their daughter is *Princess Charlotte*. A prince or princess is just *William, George* or *Harry* on second reference, as is a princess, whether she is *Charlotte, Beatrice* or *Eugenie*.

DUKE: The full title — *Duke of York*, for example — is an alternate name, capitalized in all uses. Lowercase *duke* when it stands alone.

The wife of a duke is a *duchess: the Duchess of Kent, the duchess*, but never *Duchess Katherine* or *Lady Katherine*.

A duke normally also has a lesser title. It is commonly used for his eldest son if he has one. Use the courtesy titles *Lord* or *Lady* before the first names of a duke or earl's children. On second reference, the children's given name would be used alone.

MARQUESS, MARQUIS, EARL,

VISCOUNT, BARON: The full titles serve as alternate names and should be capitalized. In general, use the name the person goes by. Use *Lady* before the name of a woman married to a man who holds one of these titles, and use *Lady* before the first name of an earl's daughter — *Lady Diana Spencer*, for example. On second reference, *Lady Diana* or *Diana*.

Some examples:

Queen Elizabeth gave her sister's husband, Antony Armstrong-Jones, the title *Earl of Snowdon*. Their son, David, is the *Viscount Linley — Linley* on second reference. They also have a daughter, born Lady Sarah Armstrong-Jones. After her marriage she is now *Lady Sarah Chatto* — on second reference *Lady Sarah* or *Chatto*.

BARONET, KNIGHT: *Sir John Smith* on first reference and *Smith* on second. These are very common titles, and rarely are used in news copy. Do not use both an honorary title and a title of military rank or authority, such as prime minister, before a name.

Honorary titles for celebrities need not be used in every case. *Dame Maggie Smith* is correct, but *Maggie Smith* is preferred when writing about the actress. *Sir Paul McCartney* is correct, but *Paul McCartney* is preferred when writing about the former Beatle.

n

noisome, noisy *Noisome* means *offensive, noxious*.
Noisy means *clamorous*.

Nokia Corp. Headquarters is in Espoo, Finland.

nolo contendere The literal meaning is, "I do not wish to contend." Terms such as *no contest* or *no-contest plea* are acceptable in all references.

When a defendant in a criminal case enters this plea, it means that he is not admitting guilt but is stating that he will offer no defense. The person is then subject to being judged guilty and punished as if he had pleaded guilty or had been convicted. The principal difference is that the defendant retains the option of denying the same charge in another legal proceeding.

no man's land

non- The rules of **prefixes** apply, but in general no hyphen when forming a compound that does not have special meaning and can be understood if *not* is used before the base word. Use a hyphen, however, before proper nouns. Examples of compounds with special meaning include names with proper nouns: *Non-Aligned Movement, non-Euclidean geometry, non-Hodgkin lymphoma.*

nonaligned nations A political rather than economic or geographic term used primarily during the Cold War. Although nonaligned nations do not belong to Western or Eastern military alliances or blocs, they may take positions on international issues. Hyphenate in formal name *Non-Aligned Movement*, a political group representing more than 120 developing nations.

Do not confuse *nonaligned* with *developing nations*, which refers to the economic developing nations of Africa, Asia and Latin America. Avoid use of the term Third World.

noncombat, noncombatant

none It usually means *no single one*. When used in this sense, it always takes singular verbs and pronouns: *None of the seats was in its right place.* Mass nouns — things that can't be counted — also are singular: *None of the coffee was poured.*

Use a plural verb only if the sense is *no two* or *no amount of these things*: *None of the consultants agree on the same approach. None of the taxes have been paid.*

nonprofit

nonrestrictive clauses See **essential clauses, nonessential clauses**.

noon Do not put a 12 in front of it. See **midnight** and **times**.

no one

Norfolk Southern Corp. Freight railroad, with headquarters in Norfolk, Virginia.

norm See **average, mean, median, norm**.

North America See **Western Hemisphere**.

North Atlantic Treaty Organization *NATO* is acceptable in all references.

North Carolina Abbreviate *N.C.* in datelines only; spell out in stories. Postal code: *NC*
See **state names**.

North Dakota Abbreviate *N.D.* in datelines only; spell out in stories. Postal code: *ND*
See **state names**.

Northeast region As defined by the U.S. Census Bureau, the nine-state region is broken into two divisions — the *New England* states and the *Middle Atlantic* states.

Connecticut, Maine, Massachusetts, New Hampshire, Rhode Island and Vermont are the *New England* states.

New Jersey, New York and Pennsylvania are classified as the *Middle Atlantic* states.

See **Midwest region**; **South**; and **West** for the bureau's other regional breakdowns.

Northern Ireland Use *Northern Ireland* after the names of all communities in datelines.

See **datelines** and **United Kingdom**.

north, northern, northeast, northwest See **directions and regions**.

Northrop Grumman Corp. Headquarters is in Falls Church, Virginia.

North Slope The portion of Alaska north of Brooks Range, a string of mountains extending across the northern part of the state.

Northwest Territories A territorial section of Canada. Do not abbreviate. Use in datelines after the names of all cities and towns in the territory.

See **Canada**.

note For use in a financial sense, see **loan terminology**.

notorious, notoriety Some understand these terms to refer simply to fame; others see them as negative terms, implying being well-known because of evil actions. Be sure the context for these words is clear, or use terms like *famous*, *prominent*, *infamous*, *disreputable*, etc.

nouns The abbreviation *n.* is used in this book to identify the spelling of the noun forms of words frequently misspelled.

Novartis AG Headquarters is in Basel, Switzerland.

Nova Scotia One of the three Maritime Provinces of Canada. Do not abbreviate.

See **datelines**.

Novocain A trademark for a drug used as a local anesthetic.

nowadays

NPR Acceptable in all references to National Public Radio. Producer and distributor of noncommercial news, talk and entertainment programming. Headquarters is in Washington, D.C.

Nuclear Non-Proliferation Treaty Global agreement intended to limit the spread of nuclear weapons. It provides civilian nuclear trade in exchange for a pledge from nations not to pursue nuclear weapons and for the United States and other nuclear weapons states to negotiate their nuclear disarmament.

Nuclear Regulatory Commission *NRC* is acceptable on second reference, but *the agency* or *the commission* is preferred.

nuclear terminology In reporting on nuclear energy, include the definitions of appropriate terms, especially those related to radiation.

core The part of a nuclear reactor that contains its fissionable fuel. In a reactor core, atoms of fuel, such as uranium, are split. This releases

n

energy in the form of heat which, in turn, is used to boil water for steam. The steam powers a turbine, and the turbine drives a generator to produce electricity.

fission The splitting of the nucleus of an atom, releasing energy.

gray (Gy) The standard measure of radiation a material has absorbed. It has largely replaced the *rad*. One gray equals 100 rads. This measure does not consider biological effect of the radiation.

meltdown The worst possible nuclear accident in which the reactor core overheats to such a degree that the fuel melts. If the fuel penetrates its protective housing, radioactive materials will be released into the environment.

rad See **gray**.

radiation Invisible particles or waves given off by radioactive material, such as uranium. Radiation can damage or kill body cells, resulting in latent cancers, genetic damage or death.

rem See **sievert**.

roentgen The standard measure of X-ray exposure.

sievert (Sv) The standard measure of radiation absorbed in living tissue, adjusted for different kinds of radiation so that a single sievert of any kind of radiation produces the same biological effect. The sievert has largely replaced the rem. One *Sv* equals 100 rem. A *millisievert* (mSv) is a thousandth of a sievert; a millirem is a thousandth of a rem. On average, a resident of United States receives about 3 mSv, or 300 mrem, every year from natural sources.

uranium A metallic, radioactive element used as fuel in nuclear reactors.

numerals In general, spell out one through nine: *The Yankees finished second. He had nine months to go.*

Use figures for 10 or above and whenever preceding a unit of measure or referring to ages of people, animals, events or things. Also in all tabular matter, and in statistical and sequential forms.

USE FIGURES FOR:

ACADEMIC COURSE NUMBERS: *History 6, Philosophy 209.*

ADDRESSES: *210 Main St.* Spell out numbered streets nine and under: *5 Sixth Ave.; 3012 50th St.; No. 10 Downing St.* Use the abbreviations *Ave., Blvd.* and *St.* only with a numbered address: *1600 Pennsylvania Ave.* Spell them out and capitalize without a number: *Pennsylvania Avenue.*

See **addresses**.

AGES: *a 6-year-old girl; an 8-year-old law; the 7-year-old house.* Use hyphens for ages expressed as adjectives before a noun or as substitutes for a noun. *A 5-year-old boy*, but *the boy is 5 years old. The boy, 5, has a sister, 10. The race is for 3-year-olds. The woman is in her 30s. 30-something*, but *Thirty-something* to start a sentence.

See **ages**.

PLANES, SHIPS AND SPACECRAFT DESIGNATIONS: *B-2 bomber, Queen Elizabeth 2, QE2, Apollo 9, Viking 2.* An exception: *Air Force One,* the president's plane. Use Roman numerals if they are part of the official designation: *Titan I, Titan II.*

See **aircraft names**; **boats, ships**; **spacecraft designations**.

CENTURIES: Use figures for numbers 10 or higher: *21st century.* Spell out for numbers nine and lower: *fifth century.* (Note lowercase.) For proper names, follow the organization's usage: *20th Century*

Fox, Twentieth Century Fund.

COURT DECISIONS: *The Supreme Court ruled 5-4, a 5-4 decision.* The word *to* is not needed, except in quotations: *"The court ruled 5 to 4."*

COURT DISTRICTS: *5th U.S. Circuit Court of Appeals.*

DATES, YEARS AND DECADES: *Feb. 8, 2007, Class of '66, the 1950s.* For the Sept. 11, 2001, terrorist attacks, 9/11 is acceptable in all references. (Note comma to set off the year when the phrase refers to a month, date and year.)

DECIMALS, PERCENTAGES AND FRACTIONS WITH NUMBERS LARGER THAN 1: *7.2 magnitude quake, 3 1/2 laps, 3.7 percent interest, 4 percentage points.* Decimalization should not exceed two places in most text material. Exceptions: blood alcohol content, expressed in three decimals: as in 0.056, and batting averages in baseball, as in .324. For amounts less than 1, precede the decimal with a zero: *The cost of living rose 0.03 percent.* Spell out fractions less than 1, using hyphens between the words: *two-thirds, four-fifths.* In quotations, use figures for fractions: *"He was 2 1/2 laps behind with four to go."*

See **decimal units**; **fractions**; **percent**.

DIMENSIONS, TO INDICATE DEPTH, HEIGHT, LENGTH AND WIDTH: *He is 5 feet 6 inches tall, the 5-foot-6 man* ("inch" is understood), *the 5-foot man, the basketball team signed a 7-footer. The car is 17 feet long, 6 feet wide and 5 feet high. The rug is 9 feet by 12 feet, the 9-by-12 rug. A 9-inch snowfall.* Exception: *two-by-four.* Spell out the noun, which refers to any length of untrimmed lumber approximately 2 inches thick by 4 inches wide.

See **dimensions**.

DISTANCES: *He walked 4 miles. He missed a 3-foot putt.*

GOLF CLUBS: *3-wood, 7-iron, 3-hybrid* (note hyphen).

HIGHWAY DESIGNATIONS: *Interstate 5, U.S. Highway 1, state Route 1A.* (Do not abbreviate *Route.* No hyphen between highway designation and number.)

See **highway designations**.

MATHEMATICAL USAGE: *Multiply by 4, divide by 6. He added 2 and 2 but got 5.*

MILITARY RANKS, USED AS TITLES WITH NAMES, MILITARY TERMS AND WEAPONS: *Petty Officer 2nd Class Alan Markow, Spc. Alice Moreno, 1st Sgt. David Triplett, M16 rifle, 9 mm* (note space) *pistol, 6th Fleet.* In military ranks, spell out the figure when it is used after the name or without a name: *Smith was a second lieutenant. The goal is to make first sergeant.*

See **military units**.

MILLIONS, BILLIONS, TRILLIONS: Use a figure-word combination. *1 million people; $2 billion,* NOT *one million/two billion.* (Also note no hyphen linking numerals and the word *million, billion* or *trillion.*)

See **millions, billions, trillions**; **dollars**.

MONETARY UNITS: *5 cents, $5 bill, 8 euros, 4 pounds.*

See **cents**.

ODDS, PROPORTIONS AND RATIOS: *9-1 long shot; 3 parts cement to 1 part water; a 1-4 chance,* but *one chance in three.*

See **betting odds**; **proportions**; **ratios**.

RANK: *He was my No. 1 choice.* (Note abbreviation for "Number"). *Kentucky was ranked No. 3. The band had five Top 40 hits.*

SCHOOL GRADES: Use figures for grades 10 and above: *10th grade.* Spell out for first through ninth grades: *fourth grade, fifth-grader* (note hyphen).

SEQUENTIAL DESIGNATIONS: *Page 1,*

Page 20A. They were out of sizes 4 and 5; magnitude 6 earthquake; Rooms 3 and 4; Chapter 2; line 1 but first line; Act 3, Scene 4, but *third act, fourth scene; Game 1,* but *best of seven.*

See **act numbers**; **chapters**; **earthquakes**; **line numbers**; **page numbers**; **scene numbers**.

POLITICAL DISTRICTS: *Ward 9, 9th Precinct, 3rd Congressional District.*

See **congressional districts**; **political divisions**.

RECIPES: *2 tablespoons of sugar to 1 cup of milk.*

See **recipes**.

SPEEDS: *7 mph, winds of 5 to 10 mph, winds of 7 to 9 knots.*

SPORTS SCORES, STANDINGS AND STANDARDS: *The Dodgers defeated the Phillies 10-3* (No comma between the team and the score); *in golf, 3 up,* but *a 3-up lead; led 3-2; a 6-1-2 record* (six wins, one loss, two ties); *par 3; 5 handicap, 5-under-par 67* but *he was 5 under par* (or *5 under,* with "par" understood). In narrative, spell out nine and under except for yard lines in football and individual and team statistical performances: *The ball was on the 5-yard line. Seventh hole.* In basketball, *3-point play* and *3-point shot.* In statistical performances, hyphenate as a modifier: *He completed 8 of 12 passes. He made 5 of 6* (shots is understood). *He was 5-for-12 passing. He had a 3-for-5 day. He was 3-for-5. He went 3-for-5* (batting, shooting, etc., is understood).

TEMPERATURES: Use figures, except zero. *It was 8 degrees below zero* or *minus 8. The temperature dropped from 38 to 8 in two hours.*

See **temperatures**.

TIMES: Use figures for time of day except for noon and midnight: *1 p.m., 10:30 a.m., 5 o'clock, 8 hours, 30 minutes, 20 seconds, a winning time of 2:17:3* (2 hours, 17 minutes, 3 seconds). Spell out numbers less than 10 standing alone and in modifiers: *I'll be there in five minutes. He scored with two seconds left. An eight-hour day. The two-minute warning.*

See **times**; **time sequences**.

VOTES: *The bill was defeated by a vote of 6 to 4,* but *by a two-vote margin.*

SPELL OUT:

AT THE START OF A SENTENCE: In general, spell out numbers at the start of a sentence: *Forty years was a long time to wait. Fifteen to 20 cars were involved in the accident.* An exception is years: *1992 was a very good year.* Another exception: Numeral(s) and letter(s) combinations: *401(k) plans are offered. 4K TVs are flying off the shelves. 3D movies are drawing more fans.*

See **years**.

IN INDEFINITE AND CASUAL USES: *Thanks a million. He walked a quarter of a mile. One at a time; a thousand clowns; one day we will know; an eleventh-hour decision; dollar store; a hundred dollars.*

IN FANCIFUL USAGE OR PROPER NAMES: *Chicago Seven, Fab Four, Big Three automakers, Final Four, the Four Tops.*

IN FORMAL LANGUAGE, RHETORICAL QUOTATIONS AND FIGURES OF SPEECH: *"Fourscore and seven years ago ..." Twelve Apostles, Ten Commandments, high-five, Day One.*

IN FRACTIONS LESS THAN ONE THAT ARE NOT USED AS MODIFIERS: *reduced by one-third, he made three-fourths of his shots.*

ROMAN NUMERALS

They may be used for wars and to establish personal sequence for people and animals: *World War I, Native Dancer II, King George V.* Also for certain legislative acts (*Title IX*). Otherwise, use sparingly. Pro football Super Bowls should be identified by the year, rather than the Roman numerals: *1969 Super Bowl,* not *Super Bowl III.*

ORDINALS
Numbers used to indicate order (first, second, 10th, 25th, etc.) are called ordinal numbers. Spell out first through ninth: *fourth grade, first base, the First Amendment, he was first in line.* Use figures starting with 10th.

CARDINAL NUMBERS
Numbers used in counting or showing how many (2, 40, 627, etc.) are called cardinal numbers. The following separate entries provide additional guidance for cardinal numbers:
amendments to the Constitution
channel
court names
decades
election returns
fleet
formula
latitude and longitude
mile
parallels
proportions
serial numbers
telephone numbers
weights

SOME OTHER PUNCTUATION AND USAGE EXAMPLES:
— *3 ounces*
— *4-foot-long*
— *4-foot fence*
— *"The president's speech lasted 28 1/2 minutes,"* she said.
— *DC-10* but *747B*
— *the 1980s, the '80s*

— *the House voted 230-205 (fewer than 1,000 votes)*
— *Jimmy Carter outpolled Gerald Ford 40,827,292 to 39,146,157 (more than 1,000 votes)*
— *Carter outpolled Ford 10 votes to 2 votes in Little Junction (to avoid confusion with ratio)*
— *No. 3 choice,* but *Public School 3*
— *a pay increase of 12-15 percent.* Or: *a pay increase of between 12 and 15 percent*
But: *from $12 million to $14 million*
— *a ratio of 2-to-1, a 2-1 ratio*
— *1 in 4 voters*
— *seven houses 7 miles apart*
— *He walked 4 miles.*
— *minus 10, zero, 60 degrees* (spell out minus)

OTHER USES: For uses not covered by these listings, spell out whole numbers below 10, and use figures for 10 and above: *They had three sons and two daughters. They had a fleet of 10 station wagons and two buses.*

IN A SERIES: Apply the standard guidelines: *They had 10 dogs, six cats and 97 hamsters. They had four four-room houses, 10 three-room houses and 12 10-room houses.*

nuns See **sister.**

Nuremberg Use this spelling for the city in Germany, instead of Nuernberg, in keeping with widespread practice.

N-word Do not use this term or the racial slur it refers to, except in extremely rare circumstances — when it is crucial to the story or the understanding of a news event. Flag the contents in an editor's note. See **obscenities, profanities, vulgarities** and **race.**

nylon Not a trademark.

O

oasis, oases

OB-GYN Acceptable in all references for *obstetrics and gynecology*, a medical specialty.

obscenities, profanities, vulgarities Do not use them in stories unless they are part of direct quotations and there is a compelling reason for them.

Try to find a way to give the reader a sense of what was said without using the specific word or phrase. For example, an *anti-gay* or *sexist slur*.

If a profanity, obscenity or vulgarity must be used, flag the story at the top for editors, being specific about what the issue is:

Eds: Note use of vulgarity "f---" [or "s---"] However, online readers receiving direct feeds of the stories will not see that warning, so consider whether the word in question truly needs to be in the story at all.

When possible, confine the offending language, in quotation marks, to a separate paragraph that can be deleted easily by editors.

In reporting profanity that normally would use the words *damn* or *god*, lowercase *god* and use the following forms: *damn, damn it, goddamn it.*

If the obscenity involved is particularly offensive but the story requires making clear what the word was, replace the letters of the offensive word with hyphens, using only an initial letter: *f---, s---*.

In some stories or scripts, it may be better to replace the offensive word with a generic descriptive in parentheses, e.g., *(vulgarity)* or *(obscenity)*.

When the subject matter of a story may be considered offensive or disturbing, but the story does not contain quoted profanity, obscenities or vulgarities, flag the story at the top:

Eds: Graphic details of the killings could be offensive or disturbing to some readers.

For guidelines on racial or ethnic slurs, see **nationalities and races**.

Occupational Safety and Health Administration *OSHA* is acceptable on second reference.

occupational titles They are always lowercase. See **titles**.

occur, occurred, occurring Also: *occurrence.*

ocean The five, from the largest to the smallest: Pacific Ocean, Atlantic Ocean, Indian Ocean, Antarctic Ocean, Arctic Ocean.

Lowercase *ocean* standing alone or in plural uses: *the ocean, the Atlantic and Pacific oceans.*

oceangoing

odd- Follow with a hyphen:
odd-looking   odd-numbered
See **betting odds**.

oddsmaker

off-Broadway, off-off-Broadway
See **Broadway, off-Broadway, off-off-Broadway**.

offering The issue or sale of a company stock or bond. A company usually will sell financial securities to the public to raise capital.

office Capitalize *office* when it is part of an agency's formal name: *Office of Management and Budget.*
Lowercase all other uses, including phrases such as: *the office of the attorney general, the U.S. attorney's office.*
See **Oval Office**.

officeholder

Office of Thrift Supervision U.S. Treasury Department bureau that regulates the nation's savings and loan industry. *OTS* is acceptable on second reference.

offline No hyphen is an exception to Webster's New World College Dictionary.

off of The *of* is unnecessary: *He fell off the bed.* Not: *He fell off of the bed.*

off-, -off Follow Webster's New World College Dictionary. Hyphenate if not listed there.
Some commonly used combinations with a hyphen:
off-color   off-white
off-peak   send-off

Some combinations without a hyphen:
cutoff   offside
liftoff   offstage
offhand   playoff
offset   standoff
offshore   takeoff

off-site Hyphenated. Also: *on-site*.

Ohio Do not abbreviate in datelines or stories. Postal code: *OH*
See **state names**.

oil In shipping, oil and oil products normally are measured by the ton. For news stories, convert these tonnage figures to gallons.
There are 42 gallons to each barrel of oil. The number of barrels per ton varies, depending on the type of oil product.
To convert tonnage to gallons:
— Determine the type of oil.
— Consult the table on the following page to find out how many barrels per ton for that type of oil.
— Multiply the number of tons by the number of barrels per ton. The result is the number of barrels in the shipment.
— Multiply the number of barrels by 42. The result is the number of gallons.
EXAMPLE: A tanker spills 20,000 metric tons of foreign crude petroleum. The table shows 6.998 barrels of foreign crude petroleum per metric ton. Multiply 6.998 x 20,000 equals 139,960 barrels. Multiply 139,960 x 42 is 5,878,320 gallons.

oil field

OK, OK'd, OK'ing, OKs Do not use *okay*.

Oklahoma Abbreviate *Okla.* in datelines only; spell out in stories. Postal code: *OK*
See **state names**.

Oklahoma City The city in Oklahoma stands alone in datelines.

Old City of Jerusalem The walled part of the city.

Old South The South before the Civil War.

Old Testament See **Bible**.

Old West The American West as it was being settled in the 19th century.

Old World The Eastern Hemisphere: Asia, Europe, Africa. The term also may be an allusion to European culture and customs.

Olympic Airways Headquarters is in Athens, Greece.

Olympics Capitalize all references to the international athletic contests: *the Olympics, the Winter Olympics, the Olympic Games, an Olympic-size pool, an Olympian,* but lowercase *the games* when used alone.

An Olympic-size pool is 50 meters long by 25 meters wide.

on Do not use *on* before a date or day of the week when its absence would not lead to confusion, except at the beginning of a sentence: *The meeting will be held Monday. He will be inaugurated Jan. 20. On Sept. 3, the committee will meet to discuss the issue.*

Use *on* to avoid an awkward juxtaposition of a date and a proper name: *John met Mary on Monday. He told Obama on Thursday that the bill was doomed.*

Use *on* also to avoid any suggestion that a date is the object of a transitive verb: *The House killed on Tuesday a bid to raise taxes. The Senate postponed on Wednesday its consideration of a bill to reduce import duties.*

onboard One word as a modifier: *There was onboard entertainment.* But: *he jumped on board the boat.*

one- Hyphenate when used in writing fractions:
one-half   one-third
Use phrases such as *a half* or *a third* if precision is not intended. See **fractions**.

one another See **each other, one another**.

"One China" policy The U.S. policy under which the U.S. recognizes Beijing as representing China. The U.S. shifted diplomatic recognition to Beijing from Taipei in 1979. Under the policy, the U.S. acknowledges Beijing's view that it has sovereignty over Taiwan, but considers Taiwan's status as unsettled. Taiwan split from the Chinese mainland in 1949 and is self-governing. The policy is distinct from the *"One China" principle*, which is China's view that it has sovereignty over the mainland, Hong Kong, Macau and Taiwan. See **China**, **Taiwan**.

one person, one vote The adjective form: *one-person, one-vote. He supports the principle of one person, one vote. The one-man, one-vote rule.*

Supreme Court rulings all use the phrase *one person, one vote,* not *one man, one vote.*

one-sided

onetime, one-time, one time *He is the onetime (former) heavyweight champion. She is the one-time (once) winner in 2003. He did it one time.*

One World Trade Center Skyscraper opened in 2014 on the site of the twin towers destroyed in the 9/11 attacks. Spell out *One* as used by the Port Authority of New York and New Jersey, which owns both the building and the 16-acre World Trade Center site. Other buildings in the complex are named with numerals 2, 3, etc., as designated by the company that leased them. See **World Trade Center**.

online One word in all cases for the computer connection term.

online petitions Be cautious about quoting the number of signers on such petitions. Some sites make it easy for the person creating the petition or others to run up the number of purported signers by clicking or returning to the page multiple times.

online trading Buying or selling financial securities and/or currencies through a brokerage's internet-based proprietary trading platforms.

onstage

Ontario This Canadian province is the nation's first in total population and second to Quebec in area. Do not abbreviate.
See **datelines**.

OPEC Acceptable in all references for the Organization of the Petroleum Exporting Countries.
Founded in 1960, OPEC has 13 members: Algeria, Angola, Ecuador, Indonesia, Iran, Iraq, Kuwait, Libya, Nigeria, Qatar, Saudi Arabia, United Arab Emirates and Venezuela.
Headquarters is in Vienna, Austria.

operas See **composition titles**.

opiate, opioid *Opiate* refers to drugs derived directly from the poppy plant, such as morphine and codeine.
Opioids are synthetic or partially synthetic manufactured drugs that mimic the properties of opiates. Heroin can be made different ways but is generally considered an opioid, as are more common prescription painkillers such as OxyContin and Vicodin.
When referring to just prescription medications, a general term like *powerful prescription painkillers* can be more accurate. But when referring to the overall class of drugs, *opioid* is the better choice.
The brand name or generic name of a drug can be acceptable, depending on the context and how any given drug is most commonly known. In some cases, it is useful to use both names. *Doctors were urged to limit prescriptions for hydrocodone, an ingredient in painkillers like Vicodin. He was prescribed Tramadol after he complained that over-the-counter pain medications like ibuprofen were not working.* See **addiction**, **drugs**.

opinion polls See **polls and surveys**.

opossum The only North American marsupial. No apostrophe is needed to indicate missing letters in a phrase such as *playing possum*.

option In the financial world, it is a contract that gives an investor the right, but not the obligation, to buy (call) or sell (put) a security or other financial asset at an agreed-upon price (strike price) during a certain period of time or on a specific date (exercise date).

Oracle Corp. Headquarters is in Redwood City, California.

oral, verbal, written Use *oral* to refer
to spoken words: *He gave an oral
promise.*

Use *written* to refer to words
committed to paper: *We had a written
agreement.*

Use *verbal* to compare words with
some other form of communication:
*His tears revealed the sentiments that
his poor verbal skills could not express.*

ordinal numbers See **numerals**.

Oregon Abbreviate *Ore.* in datelines
only; spell out in stories. Postal code:
OR
   See **state names**.

Organization of American States
OAS is acceptable on second
reference. Headquarters is in
Washington.

organizations and institutions
Capitalize the full names of
organizations and institutions:
*the American Medical Association;
First Presbyterian Church; General
Motors Corp.; Harvard University,
Harvard University Medical School;
the Procrastinators Club; the Society of
Professional Journalists.*

Retain capitalization if *Co., Corp.*
or a similar word is deleted from the
full proper name: *General Motors.* See
company, companies; **corporation**;
and **incorporated**.

SUBSIDIARIES: Capitalize the names
of major subdivisions: *the Pontiac
Motor Division of General Motors.*

INTERNAL ELEMENTS: Use
lowercase for internal elements of
an organization when they have
names that are widely used generic
terms: *the board of directors of
General Motors, the board of trustees
of Columbia University, the history
department of Harvard University, the
sports department of the Daily Citizen-
Leader.*

Capitalize internal elements of an
organization when they have names
that are not widely used generic
terms: *the General Assembly of the
World Council of Churches, the House
of Delegates of the American Medical
Association, the House of Bishops and
House of Deputies of the Episcopal
Church.*

FLIP-FLOPPED NAMES: Retain capital
letters when commonly accepted
practice flops a name to delete the
word of: *Harvard School of Dental
Medicine, Harvard Dental School.*

Do not, however, flop formal
names that are known to the public
with the word of: *Massachusetts
Institute of Technology,* for example,
not *Massachusetts Technology Institute.*

ABBREVIATIONS AND ACRONYMS:
Some organizations and institutions
are widely recognized by their
abbreviations: *GOP, NAACP, NATO.*
For guidelines on when such
abbreviations may be used, see the
individual listings and the entries
under **abbreviations and acronyms**
and **second reference**.

Orient, Oriental Do not use when
referring to East Asian nations and
their peoples. *Asian* is the acceptable
term for an inhabitant of those
regions. See **nationalities and races**
and **race**.

original equipment manufacturer A
company that builds components or
systems that are used in production
of another company's systems or
products. *OEM* is acceptable on
second reference.

Oscar, Oscars See **Academy Awards**.

Oslo The city in Norway carries the

country name in datelines.

Ottawa The capital of Canada carries Ontario, the province name, in datelines.

Ouija A trademark for a board used in seances.

ounce (dry) Units of dry volume are not customarily carried to this level. See **pint (dry)**.

ounce (liquid) See **fluid ounce**.

ounce (weight) It is defined as 437.5 grains.

The metric equivalent is approximately 28 grams.

To convert to grams, multiply by 28 (5 ounces x 28 = 140 grams). See **grain** and **gram**.

-out Follow Webster's New World College Dictionary. Hyphenate nouns and adjectives not listed there.

Some frequently used words (all nouns):

cop-out	hideout
fade-out	pullout
fallout	walkout
flameout	washout

Two words for verbs:

fade out	walk out
hide out	wash out
pull out	

out- Follow Webster's New World College Dictionary. Hyphenate if not listed there.

Some frequently used words:

outargue	outpost
outbox	output
outdated	outscore
outfield	outstrip
outfox	outtalk
outpatient (n., adj.)	

outbreak For disease references, reserve for larger numbers of an illness, not a few cases.

Outer Banks The barrier islands along the North Carolina coast.

out of bounds But as a modifier: *out-of-bounds. The ball went out of bounds. He took an out-of-bounds pass.*

out of court, out-of-court *They settled out of court. He accepted an out-of-court settlement.*

out, outing Refers to public knowledge of a person's homosexuality, bisexuality or gender transition. *Brianna McSmith came out as lesbian; Gus Rubenstein came out of the closet; Sam Robinson came out as transgender. Outing* or *outed* is usually used when a person's status is revealed against one's knowledge or will. Do not use terms like *avowed* or *admitted*. See **gay, gender**.

outperform

outsourcing A business practice used by companies to reduce costs by transferring work previously performed in-house to outside suppliers.

outstanding shares Stock held by shareholders of a company.

Oval Office The White House office of the president.

-over Follow Webster's New World College Dictionary. Hyphenate if not listed there.

Some frequently used words (all are nouns, some also are used as adjectives):

carry-over	stopover

holdover   *walkover*
takeover
Use two words when any of these occurs as a verb.
See **suffixes**.

over Acceptable in all uses to indicate greater numerical value. *The crop was valued at over $5 billion.* See **more than, over**.

over- Follow Webster's New World College Dictionary. A hyphen seldom is used. Some frequently used words:
overbuy   *overrate*
overexert   *override*
See the **overall** entry.

overall A single word in adjectival and adverbial use: *Overall, the Democrats succeeded. Overall policy.*
The word for the garment is *overalls*.

over-the-counter stock A stock that isn't listed and traded on an organized exchange. OTC stocks are traditionally those of smaller companies that don't meet the listing requirements of the New York Stock Exchange or Nasdaq Stock Market. *OTC* is acceptable on second reference. See **Pink Sheets**.

owner Not a formal title. Always lowercase: *Dallas Cowboys owner Jerry Jones.*

Oyez Not *oyes.* The cry of court and public officials to command silence. *"Oyez! Oyez!"*

Ozark Mountains Or simply: *the Ozarks.*

p

PAC Acronym for *political action committee*. Raises money and makes contributions to campaigns of political candidates or parties. At the federal level, contribution amounts are limited by law and may not come from corporations or labor unions. Enforcement overseen by the Federal Election Commission. *PAC* acceptable on first reference; spell out in body of story. A *super PAC* is a political action committee that may raise and spend unlimited amounts of money, including from corporations and unions, to campaign independently for candidates for federal office. Its activities must be reported to the FEC, but are not otherwise regulated if not coordinated with the candidate or campaign.

pacemaker Formerly a trademark, now a generic term for a device that electronically helps a person's heart maintain a steady beat.

Pacific Ocean See **ocean.**

Pacific Standard Time (PST), Pacific Daylight Time (PDT) See **time zones.**

page numbers Use figures and capitalize *page* when used with a figure. When a letter is appended to the figure, capitalize it but do not use a hyphen: *Page 1, Page 10, Page 20A.* See **numerals.**

paintings See **composition titles.**

palate, palette, pallet *Palate* is the roof of the mouth.

A *palette* is an artist's paint board.

A *pallet* is a low platform. Also a small bed or pad filled with straw and used directly on the floor.

Palestine Use *Palestine* and *Palestinians* in the context of Palestine's activities in international bodies to which it has been admitted and the actions of the Palestinian Authority: *the Palestinian flag, Palestinian prime minister.* Do not use *Palestine* or *state of Palestine* in other situations, since it is not a fully independent, unified state. For territory, refer specifically to the *West Bank* or *Gaza*, or *the Palestinian territories* in reference to both.

Palestine Liberation Organization Not *Palestinian. PLO* is acceptable in all references.

pan- Prefix meaning "all" takes no hyphen when combined with a common noun:
panchromatic pantheism
Most combinations with *pan-* are proper nouns, however, and both *pan-* and the proper name it is combined with are capitalized:
Pan-African   Pan-Asiatic Pan-American

Panama City The city in Panama stands alone in datelines.

pantsuit

pantyhose

Pap test (or **smear**) After George Papanicolaou, the U.S. anatomist who developed this test for cervical cancer.

paparazzi (plural), **paparazzo** (singular) A photographer, often a freelancer, who takes candid shots, often in an intrusive manner, of celebrities.

parallel, paralleled, paralleling

parallels Use figures and lowercase to identify the imaginary locater lines that ring the globe from east to west. They are measured in units of 0 to 90 degrees north or south of the equator.

Examples: *4th parallel north, 89th parallel south*, or, if location north or south of the equator is obvious: *19th parallel*.

See **latitude and longitude**.

pardon, parole, probation The terms often are confused, but each has a specific meaning. Do not use them interchangeably.

A *pardon* forgives and releases a person from further punishment. It is granted by a chief of state or a governor. By itself, it does not expunge a record of conviction, if one exists, and it does not by itself restore civil rights.

A *general pardon*, usually for political offenses, is called *amnesty*.

Parole is the release of a prisoner before the sentence has expired, on condition of good behavior. It is granted by a parole board, part of the executive branch of government, and can be revoked only by the board.

Probation is the suspension of sentence for a person convicted, but not yet imprisoned, on condition of good behavior. It is imposed and revoked only by a judge.

parentheses See entry in **Punctuation** chapter.

Parent Teacher Association *PTA* is acceptable in all references.

Paris The city in France stands alone in datelines.

parish Capitalize as part of the formal name for a church congregation or a governmental jurisdiction: *St. John's Parish, Jefferson Parish*.

Lowercase standing alone or in plural combinations: *the parish, St. John's and St. Mary's parishes, Jefferson and Plaquemines parishes*.

See **county** for additional guidelines on governmental jurisdictions.

Parkinson's disease After James Parkinson, the English physician who described this degenerative disease of later life.

Parkinson's law After C. Northcote Parkinson, the British economist who came to the satirical conclusion that work expands to fill the time allotted to it.

parliament, Parliament Uppercase when referring to the legislative body in Great Britain or other countries.

parliamentary Lowercase unless part of a proper name.

parole See **pardon, parole, probation**.

partial quotes See **quotation marks** in the **Punctuation** chapter.

particles See **foreign names** entry.

p

part time, part-time Hyphenate when used as a compound modifier: *She works part time. She has a part-time job.*

party See **political parties and philosophies**.

party affiliation A political figure's party affiliation is often relevant, but not always. Include party affiliation if a politician's actions could reasonably be seen as having an effect on policy or debate, or if readers need it for understanding. But reference to party affiliation is not necessary when a story has no link to politics. If in doubt, err on the side of including party affiliation.
— Party affiliation can be used on first reference when it is the most important element to connect with the subject: *Republican Sen. Tim Scott of South Carolina said ...*
— On second reference to add context between the party affiliation and the rest of the story: *Rep. Frank Lucas of Oklahoma, the senior Republican on the House Agriculture Committee, said he supports the amendment.*
— Leave out when the story is clearly not political: *The governor attended the NCAA Tournament basketball game, having graduated from Villanova in 1995. The senator attended her daughter's high school graduation.*
— But use when a political connection exists: *The Democratic governor sat courtside next to the top donor to his campaign. The Republican senator spoke at her daughter's graduation two weeks after voting on the education bill.*
— In stories about party meetings, such as a report on the Republican National Convention,

no specific reference to party affiliation is necessary unless an individual is not a member of the party in question.

SHORT-FORM PUNCTUATION: Set short forms such as *R-S.C.* off from a name by commas: *Sen. Tim Scott, R-S.C., said ...*

Use the abbreviations listed in the entries for each state. (No abbreviations for *Alaska, Hawaii, Idaho, Iowa, Maine, Ohio, Texas* and *Utah.*)

FORM FOR U.S. HOUSE MEMBERS: The normal practice for U.S. House members is to identify them by party and state. In contexts where state affiliation is clear and home city is relevant, such as a state election roundup, identify representatives by party and city: *U.S. Reps. Ander Crenshaw, R-Jacksonville, and Frederica Wilson, D-Miami.* If this option is used, be consistent throughout the story.

FORM FOR STATE LEGISLATORS: Short-form listings showing party and home city are appropriate in state stories. For national stories, the normal practice is to say that the individual is a *Republican* or *Democrat.* Use a short-form listing only if the legislator's home city is relevant.

See **legislative titles**.

pass See **act, amendment, bill, law, measure, ordinance, resolution, rule, statute**.

passenger mile One passenger carried one mile, or its equivalent, such as two passengers carried one-half mile.

passer-by, passers-by

pasteurize

pat-down (n. and adj.)

patrolman, patrolwoman Capitalize before a name only if the word is a formal title. In some cities, the formal title is *police officer*.
See **titles**.

patrol, patrolled, patrolling

payload

PDF Abbreviation for *Portable Document Format*. A file format that allows a document to be shared among several types of computers without losing its formatting. Abbreviation is acceptable in all references.

peacekeeping

peacemaker, peacemaking

peace offering

peacetime

peacock It applies only to the male. The female is a *peahen*. Both are *peafowl*.

peasant Avoid the term, which is often derogatory, in referring to farm laborers (except in quotes or an organization name).

peck A unit of dry measure equal to 8 dry quarts or one-fourth of a bushel. The metric equivalent is approximately 8.8 liters.
To convert to liters, multiply by 8.8 (5 pecks x 8.8 = 44 liters).
See **liter**.

pedal, peddle When riding a bicycle or similar vehicle, you *pedal* it.
When selling something, you may *peddle* it.

peddler

peninsula Capitalize as part of a proper name: *the Florida Peninsula, the Upper Peninsula of Michigan, the Korean Peninsula, the Indochina Peninsula, the Crimean Peninsula.*

penitentiary See **prison, jail**.

Pennsylvania Abbreviate *Pa.* in datelines only; spell out in stories. Postal code: *PA*
See **state names**.

Pennsylvania Dutch The individuals are of German descent. The word *Dutch* is a corruption of *Deutsch*, the German word for "German."

people's Use this possessive form when the word occurs in the formal name of a nation: *the People's Republic of China.*
Use this form also in such phrases as *the people's desire for freedom.*

people, persons Use *person* when speaking of an individual: *One person waited for the bus.*
The word *people* is preferred to *persons* in all plural uses. For example: *Thousands of people attended the fair. What will people say? There were 17 people in the room.*
Persons should be used only when it is in a direct quote or part of a title as in *Bureau of Missing Persons.*
People also is a collective noun that takes a plural verb when used to refer to a single race or nation: *The American people are united.*

PepsiCo Inc. Headquarters is in Purchase, New York.

percent One word. It takes a singular verb when standing alone or when a singular word follows an *of* construction: *The teacher said 60 percent was a failing grade. He said 50 percent of the membership was there.*

It takes a plural verb when a plural word follows an *of* construction: *He said 50 percent of the members were there.*

Use figures for percent and percentages: *1 percent, 2.5 percent* (use decimals, not fractions), *10 percent, 4 percentage points.*

For a range, *12 to 15 percent,* or *between 12 and 15 percent.*

For amounts less than 1 percent, precede the decimal with a zero: *The cost of living rose 0.6 percent.*

See **numerals**.

periods See entry in the **Punctuation** chapter.

perk A shortened form of *perquisite* often used to describe fringe benefits.

permissible

per-share earnings Also earnings per share.

Persian Gulf Use this long-established name for the body of water off the southern coast of Iran.

Some Arab nations call it the *Arabian Gulf.* Use *Arabian Gulf* only in direct quotations and explain in the text that the body of water is more commonly known as the *Persian Gulf.*

-person Acceptable for the formal name of a post or person, or if preferred by an individual: *chairperson* or *spokesperson.*

See **chairman, chairwoman** and **spokesman, spokeswoman, spokesperson**.

personifications Capitalize them: *Grim Reaper, Father Time, Mother Nature, Old Man Winter, Sol,* etc.

persons See **people, persons**.

peshmerga A generic Kurdish term for a fighting group.

Petroleo Brasileiro Headquarters is in Rio de Janeiro.

petty officer See **military titles**.

Pfizer Inc. Headquarters is in New York.

phase See **faze, phase**.

Ph.D., Ph.D.s The preferred form is to say a person *holds a doctorate* and name the individual's area of specialty.

See **academic degrees** and **doctor**.

phenomenon, phenomena

Philadelphia The city in Pennsylvania stands alone in datelines.

Philippines In datelines, give the name of a city or town followed by *Philippines*:

MANILA, *Philippines* (AP) —
In stories: *the Philippines.*

The people are *Filipinos. Filipina* is acceptable as the feminine form. The language is *Filipino,* an offshoot of Tagalog. *Philippine* is the adjective.

phishing A form of internet fraud that aims to steal personal information such as credit card numbers, Social Security numbers, user IDs and passwords.

p

phobia Irrational fear or hatred, sometimes a form of mental illness (*acrophobia*, *claustrophobia*) but also used more generally in political or social contexts: *homophobia*, *Islamophobia*, *xenophobia*. The latter terms are acceptable in broad references or quotations: *She said her prime goals are to fight xenophobia and racism.* In individual cases, be specific about observable actions; avoid descriptions or language that assumes motives.

Phoenix The city in Arizona stands alone in datelines.

Photoshop Trademark for a brand of photo-editing software. Use the generic form if the brand is uncertain, and don't use verbs like *photoshopped* except in direct quotations (in which case use lowercase).

physician assistant No apostrophe in this medical profession title.

picket, pickets, picketed, picket line *Picket* is both the verb and the noun. Do not use *picketer*.

pickup (n. and adj.) **pick up** (v.)

picnic, picnicked, picnicking, picnicker

pico- A prefix denoting one-trillionth of a unit. Move the decimal point 12 places to the left in converting to the basic unit: 2,999,888,777,666.5 picoseconds equals 2.9998887776665 seconds.

pigeonhole (n. and v.)

Pikes Peak No apostrophe. After Zebulon Montgomery Pike, a U.S. general and explorer. The 14,115-foot peak is in the Rockies of central Colorado.

pileup (n. and adj.) **pile up** (v.)

pill Do not capitalize in references to oral contraceptives. Use *birth control pill* on first reference if necessary for clarity.

pilot Not a formal title. Do not capitalize before a name. See **titles**.

pingpong A synonym for *table tennis*. The trademark name is *Ping-Pong*.

Pink Sheets A daily publication compiled by the National Quotation Bureau with bid and ask prices of over-the-counter stocks. See **over-the-counter stock**.

pint (dry) Equal to 33.6 cubic inches, or one-half of a dry quart.
The metric equivalent is approximately 0.55 of a liter.
To convert to liters, multiply by 0.55 (5 dry pints x 0.55 is 2.75 liters). See **liter** and **quart (dry)**.

pint (liquid) Equal to 16 fluid ounces, or two cups.
The approximate metric equivalents are 470 milliliters or 0.47 of a liter.
To convert to liters, multiply by 0.47 (4 pints x 0.47 is 1.88 liters). See **liter**.

Pinterest A social network in which users collect and share images from the web in theme-based collections, also known as *pinboards* or simply *boards*. Images that are shared on Pinterest — or pinned — are sometimes referred to as *pins*.

Pinyin The official Chinese spelling system.
See **Chinese names**.

pipeline

Pittsburgh The city in Pennsylvania stands alone in datelines.

The spelling is *Pittsburg* (no *h*) for communities in California, Illinois, Kansas, New Hampshire, Oklahoma and Texas.

plains See **Great Plains**.

planets Capitalize the proper names of planets: *Jupiter, Mars, Mercury, Neptune, Saturn, Uranus, Venus.* (*Pluto* was redefined as a dwarf planet by the International Astronomical Union in 2006.)

Capitalize *Earth* when used as the proper name of our planet: *The astronauts returned to Earth.*

Capitalize nouns and adjectives derived from the proper names of planets: *Martian, Venusian.* But lowercase adjectives derived from other heavenly bodies: *solar, lunar.*
See **earth** and **heavenly bodies**.

planning Avoid the redundant *future planning.*

plants In general, lowercase the names of plants, but capitalize proper nouns or adjectives that occur in a name.

Some examples: *tree, fir, white fir, Douglas fir; Scotch pine; clover, white clover, white Dutch clover.*

If a botanical name is used, capitalize the first word; lowercase others: *pine tree (Pinus), red cedar (Juniperus virginiana), blue azalea (Callicarpa americana), Kentucky coffee tree (Gymnocladus dioica).*

play titles See **composition titles**.

plead, pleaded, pleading Do not use the colloquial past tense form, *pled.*

Pledge of Allegiance

Plexiglas Note the single *s.* A trademark for plastic glass.

plurality See **majority, plurality**.

plurals Follow these guidelines in forming and using plural words:
MOST WORDS: Add *s: boys, girls, ships, villages.*

WORDS ENDING IN CH, S, SH, SS, X AND Z: Add *es: churches, lenses, parishes, glasses, boxes, buzzes.* (*Monarchs* is an exception.)

WORDS ENDING IN IS: Change *is* to *es: oases, parentheses, theses.*

WORDS ENDING IN Y: If *y* is preceded by a consonant or *qu*, change *y* to *i* and add *es: armies, cities, navies, soliloquies.* (See PROPER NAMES below for an exception.)

Otherwise add *s: donkeys, monkeys.*

WORDS ENDING IN O: If *o* is preceded by a consonant, most plurals require *es: buffaloes, dominoes, echoes, heroes, potatoes.* But there are exceptions: *pianos.* See individual entries in this book for many of these exceptions.

WORDS ENDINGS IN F: In general, change *f* to *v* and add *es: leaves, selves.* (*Roof, roofs* is an exception.)

LATIN ENDINGS: Latin-root words ending in *us* change *us* to *i: alumnus, alumni.* (Words that have taken on English endings by common usage are exceptions: *prospectuses, syllabuses.*)

Most ending in *a* change to *ae: alumna, alumnae* (*formula, formulas* is an exception).

Most ending in *um* add *s: memorandums, referendums, stadiums.*

p

Among those that still use the Latin ending: *addenda, curricula, media.*

Use the plural that Webster's New World College Dictionary lists as most common for a particular sense of word.

FORM CHANGE: *man, men; child, children; foot, feet; mouse, mice;* etc.

Caution: When *s* is used with any of these words it indicates possession and must be preceded by an apostrophe: *men's, children's,* etc.

WORDS THE SAME IN SINGULAR AND PLURAL: *corps, chassis, deer, moose, sheep,* etc.

The sense in a particular sentence is conveyed by the use of a singular or plural verb.

WORDS PLURAL IN FORM, SINGULAR IN MEANING: Some take singular verbs: *measles, mumps, news.*

Others take plural verbs: *grits, scissors.*

COMPOUND WORDS: Those written solid add *s* at the end: *cupfuls, handfuls, tablespoonfuls.*

For those that involve separate words or words linked by a hyphen, make the most significant word plural:

— Significant word first: *adjutants general, aides-de-camp, attorneys general, courts-martial, daughters-in-law, passers-by, postmasters general, presidents-elect, secretaries-general, sergeants major.*

— Significant word in the middle: *assistant attorneys general, deputy chiefs of staff.*

— Significant word last: *assistant attorneys, assistant corporation counsels, deputy sheriffs, lieutenant colonels, major generals.*

WORDS AS WORDS: Do not use *'s: His speech had too many "ifs," "ands" and "buts."*

PROPER NAMES: Most ending in *es* or *s* or *z* add *es: Charleses, Joneses,*

Gonzalezes.

Most ending in *y* add *s* even if preceded by a consonant: *the Duffys, the Kennedys, the two Kansas Citys.* Exceptions include *Alleghenies* and *Rockies.*

For others, add *s: the Carters, the McCoys, the Mondales.*

FIGURES: Add *s: The custom began in the 1920s. The airline has two 727s. Temperatures will be in the low 20s. There were five size 7s.*

(No apostrophes, an exception to Webster's New World College Dictionary guideline under "apostrophe.")

SINGLE LETTERS: Use *'s: Mind your p's and q's. He learned the three R's and brought home a report card with four A's and two B's. The Oakland A's won the pennant.*

MULTIPLE LETTERS: Add *s: She knows her ABCs. I gave him five IOUs. Four VIPs were there.*

PROBLEMS, DOUBTS: Separate entries in this book give plurals for troublesome words and guidance on whether certain words should be used with singular or plural verbs and pronouns. See also **collective nouns** and **possessives**.

For questions not covered by this book, use the plural that Webster's New World College Dictionary lists as most common for a particular sense of a word.

p.m., a.m. Lowercase, with periods. Avoid the redundant 10 *p.m. tonight.*

pocket veto Occurs only when Congress has adjourned. If Congress is in session, a bill that remains on the president's desk for 10 days becomes law without his signature. If Congress adjourns, however, a bill that fails to get his signature within 10 days is vetoed.

Many states have similar procedures, but the precise requirements vary.

podcast A digital audio or video program that can be downloaded or streamed to a computer, smartphone or portable media device. Typically, podcasts allow you to subscribe and get new episodes delivered automatically.

podium See **lectern, podium, pulpit, rostrum**.

poetry See **composition titles** for guidelines on the names of poems.

Capitalize the first word in a line of poetry unless the author deliberately has used lowercase for a special effect. Do not, however, capitalize the first word on indented lines that must be created simply because the writer's line is too long for the available printing width.

poinsettia Note the *ia*.

point Do not abbreviate. Capitalize as part of a proper name: *Point Pleasant*.

point-blank

poison pill In the financial world, any defensive measure to prevent the takeover of a corporation by making its acquisition prohibitively expensive for the party attempting the takeover.

police department In communities where this is the formal name, capitalize *police department* with or without the name of the community: *the Los Angeles Police Department, the Police Department*.

If a police agency has some other formal name such as *Division*

of Police, use that name if it is the way the department is known to the public. If the story uses *police department* as a generic term for such an agency, put *police department* in lowercase.

If a police agency with an unusual formal name is known to the public as a *police department*, treat *police department* as the name, capitalizing it with or without the name of the community. Use the formal name only if there is a special reason in the story.

If the proper name cannot be determined for some reason, such as the need to write about a police agency from a distance, treat *police department* as the proper name, capitalizing it with or without the name of the community.

Lowercase *police department* in plural uses: *the Los Angeles and San Francisco police departments*.

Lowercase *the department* whenever it stands alone.

police titles See **military titles** and **titles**.

policymaker, policymaking

polio The preferred term for *poliomyelitis* and *infantile paralysis*.

Politburo Acceptable in all references for the *Political Bureau of the Communist Party*.

political divisions Use Arabic figures and capitalize the accompanying word when used with the figures: *1st Ward, 10th Ward, 3rd Precinct, 22nd Precinct, the ward, the precinct*. See **numerals**.

political parties and philosophies Capitalize both the name of the party and the word *party* if it is customarily used as part of the organization's proper name: *the Democratic Party, the Republican Party*.

Include the political affiliation of any elected officeholder.

Capitalize *Communist, Conservative, Democrat, Liberal, Republican, Socialist*, etc., when they refer to a specific party or its members. Lowercase these words when they refer to political philosophy (see examples below).

Lowercase the name of a philosophy in noun and adjective forms unless it is the derivative of a proper name: *communism, communist; fascism, fascist*. But: *Marxism, Marxist; Nazism, Nazi*.

EXAMPLES: *John Adams was a Federalist, but a man who subscribed to his philosophy today would be described as a federalist. The liberal Republican senator and his Conservative Party colleague said they believe that democracy and communism are incompatible. The Communist Party member said he is basically a socialist who has reservations about Marxism.*

Generally, a description of specific political views is more informative than a generic label like *liberal* or *conservative*.

Avoid *progressive*, which can imply improvement, as a political descriptor except in quotes or the names of organizations or political parties.

See **convention** and **party affiliation**.

politicking

politics Usually it takes a plural verb: *My politics are my own business.*

As a study or science, it takes a singular verb: *Politics is a demanding profession*.

Ponzi scheme A fraudulent investing technique that promises high rates of return with little risk to investors. In the scheme, money provided by new investors is used to pay seeming high returns to early-stage investors to suggest the enterprise is prosperous. The scheme collapses when required redemptions exceed new investments.

pope Capitalize when used as a formal title before a name; lowercase in all other uses: *Pope Francis spoke to the crowd. At the close of his address, the pope gave his blessing. Pope Emeritus Benedict XVI* or *Benedict XVI, the pope emeritus. Benedict* alone on second reference.

Use *St. John Paul II* and *St. John XXIII* on first reference for the canonized popes. On second reference *John Paul* and *John*. Make clear in the body of a story they were popes.

See **Roman Catholic Church** and **religious titles**.

popular names See **capitalization**.

populism Political philosophy or ideas that promote the rights and power of ordinary people as opposed to political and intellectual elites. Avoid labeling politicians or political parties as *populist*, other than in a quote or paraphrase: *He calls himself a populist.* Using the term in a general context is acceptable: *The panelists discussed the rise of populism in Europe. She appealed to populist fervor.*

pop-up shop Retail store designed to be open for a limited time period.

pore, pour The verb *pore* means to gaze intently or steadily: *She pored over her books.*

The verb *pour* means to flow in a continuous stream: *It poured rain. He poured the coffee.*

Porteno The people and culture of the city of Buenos Aires, Argentina. The term for the province of the same name is *Bonaerense.*

port, starboard Nautical for left and right (when facing the bow, or forward). Port is left. Starboard is right. Change to *left* or *right* unless in direct quotes.

Portuguese names The family names of both the father and mother usually are considered part of a person's full name. In everyday use, customs sometimes vary with individuals and countries.

The normal sequence is given name, mother's family name, father's family name: *Maria Santos Ferreira.*

On second reference, use only the father's family name (*Ferreira*), unless the individual prefers or is widely known by a multiple last name (*Ferreira Castro*).

Some Portuguese use an *e* (for *and*) between the two names: *Joao Canto e Castro.* This would not be split on second reference, but would be *Canto e Castro.*

When a surname is preceded by *da, do, dos,* or *das,* include it in the second reference. *Jorge da Costa,* for example, would be *da Costa* on second reference.

A married woman adds her husband's surname to the end of hers. If *Maria Santos Ferreira* married *Joao Costa da Silva,* her full name would be *Maria Ferreira da Silva.*

Occasionally, a woman may choose not to take her husband's surname for personal reasons or because the mother's family has an aristocratic or famous surname. Use both surnames if the individual's choice is not known.

possessives Follow these guidelines:

PLURAL NOUNS NOT ENDING IN S: Add *'s*: *the alumni's contributions, women's rights.*

PLURAL NOUNS ENDING IN S: Add only an apostrophe: *the churches' needs, the girls' toys, the horses' food, the ships' wake, states' rights, the VIPs' entrance.*

NOUNS PLURAL IN FORM, SINGULAR IN MEANING: Add only an apostrophe: *mathematics' rules, measles' effects.* (But see **INANIMATE OBJECTS** below.)

Apply the same principle when a plural word occurs in the formal name of a singular entity: *General Motors' profits, the United States' wealth.*

NOUNS THE SAME IN SINGULAR AND PLURAL: Treat them the same as plurals, even if the meaning is singular: *one corps' location, the two deer's tracks, the lone moose's antlers.*

SINGULAR NOUNS NOT ENDING IN S: Add *'s*: *the church's needs, the girl's toys, the horse's food, the ship's route, the VIP's seat.*

Some style guides say that singular nouns ending in *s* sounds such as *ce, x,* and *z* may take either the apostrophe alone or *'s.* See **SPECIAL EXPRESSIONS**, but otherwise, for consistency and ease in remembering a rule, always use *'s* if the word does not end in the letter *s*: *Butz's policies, the fox's den, the justice's verdict, Marx's theories, the prince's life, Xerox's profits.*

SINGULAR COMMON NOUNS ENDING IN S: Add *'s*: *the hostess's invitation, the hostess's seat; the witness's answer,*

p

the witness's story. (A change from previous guidance calling for just an apostrophe if the next word begins with *s*.)

SINGULAR PROPER NAMES ENDING IN S: Use only an apostrophe: *Achilles' heel, Agnes' book, Ceres' rites, Descartes' theories, Dickens' novels, Euripides' dramas, Hercules' labors, Jesus' life, Jules' seat, Kansas' schools, Moses' law, Socrates' life, Tennessee Williams' plays, Xerxes' armies.*

SPECIAL EXPRESSIONS: The following exceptions to the general rule for words not ending in *s* apply to words that end in an *s* sound and are followed by a word that begins with *s*: *for appearance' sake, for conscience' sake, for goodness' sake.* Use *'s* otherwise: *the appearance's cost, my conscience's voice.*

PRONOUNS: Personal interrogative and relative pronouns have separate forms for the possessive. None involve an apostrophe: *mine, ours, your, yours, his, hers, its, theirs, whose.*

Caution: If you are using an apostrophe with a pronoun, always double-check to be sure that the meaning calls for a contraction: *you're, it's, there's, who's.*

Follow the rules listed above in forming the possessives of other pronouns: *another's idea, others' plans, someone's guess.*

COMPOUND WORDS: Applying the rules above, add an apostrophe or *'s* to the word closest to the object possessed: *the major general's decision, the major generals' decisions, the attorney general's request, the attorneys general's request.* See the **plurals** entry for guidelines on forming the plurals of these words.

Also: *anyone else's attitude, John Adams Jr.'s father, Benjamin Franklin of Pennsylvania's motion.* Whenever practical, however, recast the phrase to avoid ambiguity: *the motion by Benjamin Franklin of Pennsylvania.*

JOINT POSSESSION, INDIVIDUAL POSSESSION: Use a possessive form after only the last word if ownership is joint: *Fred and Sylvia's apartment, Fred and Sylvia's stocks.*

Use a possessive form after both words if the objects are individually owned: *Fred's and Sylvia's books.*

DESCRIPTIVE PHRASES: Do not add an apostrophe to a word ending in *s* when it is used primarily in a descriptive sense: *citizens band radio, a Cincinnati Reds infielder, a teachers college, a Teamsters request, a writers guide.*

Memory aid: The apostrophe usually is not used if *for* or *by* rather than *of* would be appropriate in the longer form: *a radio band for citizens, a college for teachers, a guide for writers, a request by the Teamsters.*

An *'s* is required, however, when a term involves a plural word that does not end in *s*: *a children's hospital, a people's republic, the Young Men's Christian Association.*

DESCRIPTIVE NAMES: Some governmental, corporate and institutional organizations with a descriptive word in their names use an apostrophe; some do not. Follow the user's practice: *Actors' Equity, Diners Club, Ladies' Home Journal, the National Governors Association.*

QUASI POSSESSIVES: Follow the rules above in composing the possessive form of words that occur in such phrases as *a day's pay, two weeks' vacation, three days' work, your money's worth.*

Frequently, however, a hyphenated form is clearer: *a two-week vacation, a three-day job.*

DOUBLE POSSESSIVE: Two conditions must apply for a double possessive — a phrase such as *a* *friend of John's* — to occur: 1. The word after *of* must refer to an animate object, and 2. The word before *of* must involve only a portion of the animate object's possessions.

Otherwise, do not use the possessive form of the word after *of*: *The friends of John Adams mourned his death.* (All the friends were involved.) *He is a friend of the college.* (Not *college's*, because *college* is inanimate.)

Memory aid: This construction occurs most often, and quite naturally, with the possessive forms of personal pronouns: *He is a friend of mine.*

INANIMATE OBJECTS: There is no blanket rule against creating a possessive form for an inanimate object, particularly if the object is treated in a personified sense. See some of the earlier examples, and note these: *death's call, the wind's murmur.*

In general, however, avoid excessive personalization of inanimate objects, and give preference to an *of* construction when it fits the makeup of the sentence. For example, the earlier references to *mathematics' rules* and *measles' effects* would better be phrased: *the rules of mathematics, the effects of measles.*

post- Follow Webster's New World College Dictionary. Hyphenate if not listed there.

Some words without a hyphen:

postdate	*postnuptial*
postdoctoral	*postoperative*
postelection	*postscript*
postgame	*postwar*
postgraduate	

Some words that use a hyphen:

post-bellum	*post-mortem*
post-convention	

Post-it A trademark for small pieces of paper with an adhesive strip on the back that can be attached to documents.

post office It may be used but it is no longer capitalized because the agency is now the *U.S. Postal Service.*

Use lowercase in referring to an individual office: *I went to the post office.*

post-traumatic stress disorder *PTSD* is acceptable on second reference. See **mental illness**.

pot See **marijuana**.

pothole

pound (monetary) The English pound sign is not used. Convert the figures to dollars in most cases. Use a figure and spell out *pounds* if the actual figure is relevant.

pound (weight) Equal to 16 ounces. The metric equivalent is approximately 454 grams, or 0.45 kilograms.

To convert to kilograms, multiply the number of pounds by 0.45 (20 pounds x 0.45 equals 9 kilograms). See **gram** and **kilogram**.

pour See **pore, pour**.

poverty level An income level judged inadequate to provide a family or individual with the essentials of life. The figure for the United States is adjusted regularly to reflect changes in the Consumer Price Index.

Prague The city in the Czech Republic stands alone in datelines.

pre- The rules in **prefixes** apply. The

following examples of exceptions to first-listed spellings in Webster's New World College Dictionary are based on the general rule that a hyphen is used if a prefix ends in a vowel and the word that follows begins with the same vowel:

pre-election   *pre-establish*
pre-eminent   *pre-exist*
pre-empt

Otherwise, follow Webster's New World College Dictionary, hyphenating if not listed there. Some examples:

prearrange   *prehistoric*
precondition *preignition*
precook   *prejudge*
predate   *premarital*
predecease   *prenatal*
predispose   *prenuptial*
preflight   *pretax*
pregame   *pretest*
preheat   *prewar*

Some hyphenated coinage, not listed in the dictionary:

pre-convention *pre-noon*

precincts See **political divisions**.

preferred stock An ownership in a company that has no voting rights but pays a fixed dividend and has a higher claim on the company's assets and earnings than common stock.

prefixes See separate listings for commonly used prefixes.

Generally do not hyphenate when using a prefix with a word starting with a consonant.

Three rules are constant:
— Except for *cooperate* and *coordinate*, use a hyphen if the prefix ends in a vowel and the word that follows begins with the same vowel.
— Use a hyphen if the word that follows is capitalized.

— Use a hyphen to join doubled prefixes: *sub-subparagraph*.

premiere A first performance.

premier, prime minister These two titles often are used interchangeably in translating to English the title of an individual who is the first minister in a national government that has a council of ministers.

Prime minister is the correct title throughout the Commonwealth, formerly the British Commonwealth. See **Commonwealth** for a list of members.

Prime minister is the best or traditional translation from most other languages. For consistency, use it throughout the rest of the world with these exceptions:
— Use *chancellor* in Austria and Germany.
— Follow the practice of a nation if there is a specific preference that varies from this general practice. For example, use *premier* in China.

Premier is also the correct title for the individuals who lead the provincial governments in Canada and Australia.

See **titles**.

presently Use it to mean *in a little while* or *shortly*, but not to mean *now*.

presidency Always lowercase.

president Capitalize *president* only as a formal title before one or more names: *President Donald Trump, former Presidents Gerald R. Ford and Jimmy Carter.*

Lowercase in all other uses: *The president said Monday he will look into the matter. He is running for president. Lincoln was president during the Civil*

War.

See **titles**.

FULL NAMES: Use the first and family name on first reference to a current or former U.S. president or the president-elect: *former President Barack Obama, President Donald Trump, President-elect Donald Trump.* On subsequent references, use only the last name.

For presidents of other nations and of organizations and institutions, capitalize president as a formal title before a full name: *President Francois Hollande of France, President John Smith of Acme Corp.*

On second reference, use only the last name.

presidential Lowercase unless part of a proper name.

Presidential Medal of Freedom

This is the nation's highest civilian honor. It is given by the president, on the recommendation of the Distinguished Civilian Service Board, for "exceptionally meritorious contribution to the security of the United States or other significant public or private endeavors."

Until 1963 it was known as the Medal of Freedom.

Presidents Day No apostrophe is an exception to Webster's New World College Dictionary. Not adopted by the federal government as the official name of the Washington's Birthday holiday. However, some federal agencies, states and local governments use the term.

presiding officer Always lowercase.

press conference *News conference* is preferred.

press secretary Seldom a formal title. For consistency, always use lowercase, even when used before an individual's name.

See **titles**.

pretax

pretense, pretext A *pretext* is something that is put forward to conceal a truth: *He was discharged for tardiness, but the reason given was only a pretext for general incompetence.*

A *pretense* is a false show, a more overt act intended to conceal personal feelings: *My profuse compliments were all pretense.*

preventive

price-earnings ratio The price of a share of stock divided by earnings per share for a 12-month period. Ratios in AP stock tables reflect earnings for the most recent 12 months.

For example, a stock selling for $60 per share and earning $6 per share would be selling at a price-earnings ratio of 10-to-1. *P/E* is acceptable on second reference.

See **profit terminology**.

priest A vocational description, not a formal title. Do not capitalize.

See **religious titles** and the entries for the **Roman Catholic Church** and **Episcopal Church** in the **Religion** chapter.

prima-facie (adj.)

primary Do not capitalize: *the New Hampshire primary, the Democratic primary, the primary.*

primary day Use lowercase for any of the days set aside for balloting in a

p

primary.

prime meridian See **meridians**.

prime minister See **premier, prime minister**.

prime rate A benchmark rate used by banks to set interest charges on a variety of corporate and consumer loans, including some adjustable home mortgages, revolving credit cards and business loans extended to their most creditworthy customers. Banks almost always raise or lower their rates by a similar amount on the same day Federal Reserve policymakers change their target for overnight loans between banks, known as the *federal funds rate*.

Primero de Mayo May Day, the labor day holiday in Latin America and Spain.

prime time (n.) **prime-time** (adj.)

Prince Edward Island One of the three Maritime Provinces of Canada. Do not abbreviate.
See **datelines**.

prince, princess Capitalize when used as a royal title before a name; lowercase when used alone: *Prince Charles, the prince.*
See **nobility**.

principal, principle *Principal* is a noun and adjective meaning someone or something first in rank, authority, importance or degree: *She is the school principal. He was the principal player in the trade. Money is the principal problem.*
Principle is a noun that means a fundamental truth, law, doctrine or motivating force: *They fought for the principle of self-determination.*
In a business context, *principal* refers to the amount of money that is borrowed in a loan, as distinct from interest that is paid.

prior to *Before* is less stilted for most uses. *Prior to* is appropriate, however, when a notion of requirement is involved: *The fee must be paid prior to the examination.*

prison, jail Do not use the two words interchangeably.
DEFINITIONS: *Prison* is a generic term that may be applied to the maximum security institutions often known as *penitentiaries* and to the medium security facilities often called *correctional institutions* or *reformatories*. All such facilities usually confine people serving sentences for felonies.
A *jail* is normally used to confine people serving sentences for misdemeanors, people awaiting trial or sentencing on either felony or misdemeanor charges, and people confined for civil matters such as failure to pay alimony and other types of contempt of court.
See **felony, misdemeanor**.
The guidelines for capitalization:
PRISONS: Many states have given elaborate formal names to their prisons. They should be capitalized when used, but commonly accepted substitutes should also be capitalized as if they were proper names. For example, use either *Massachusetts Correctional Institution-Walpole* or *Walpole State Prison* for the maximum security institution in Massachusetts.
Do not, however, construct a substitute when the formal name is commonly accepted: It is the *Colorado State Penitentiary*, for

example, not *Colorado State Prison*.

On second reference, any of the following may be used, all in lowercase: *the state prison, the prison, the state penitentiary, the penitentiary*.

Use lowercase for all plural constructions: *the Colorado and Kansas state penitentiaries*.

JAILS: Capitalize *jail* when linked with the name of the jurisdiction: *Los Angeles County Jail*. Lowercase *county jail, city jail* and *jail* when they stand alone.

FEDERAL INSTITUTIONS: Maximum security institutions are known as *penitentiaries*: *the U.S. Penitentiary at Lewisburg* or *Lewisburg Penitentiary* on first reference; *the federal penitentiary* or *the penitentiary* on second reference.

Medium security institutions include the word *federal* as part of their formal names: *the Federal Correctional Institution at Danbury, Connecticut*. On second reference: *the correctional institution, the federal prison, the prison*.

Most federal facilities used to house people awaiting trial or serving sentences of a year or less have the proper name *Federal Detention Center*. The term *Metropolitan Correctional Center* is being adopted for some new installations. On second reference: *the detention center, the correctional center*.

prisoner(s) of war *POW(s)* is acceptable on second reference.

Hyphenate when used as a compound modifier: *a prisoner-of-war trial*.

privacy Special care should be taken with regard to publishing the names of juveniles involved in crimes, or of people who may have been the victims of sexual assault or other abuse.

Generally, we do not identify juveniles (under 18) who are accused of crimes or transmit images that would reveal their identity. However, regional editors or their designates may authorize exceptions to this practice.

Considerations in granting exceptions may include the severity of the alleged crime; whether police have formally released the juvenile's name; and whether the juvenile has been formally charged as an adult. Other considerations might include public safety, such as when the youth is the subject of a manhunt; or widespread publication of the juvenile suspect's name, making the identity de facto public knowledge.

In some situations, state or national laws may determine whether the person's name can be published.

We normally do not identify, in text or through images, juveniles who are witnesses to crimes.

We also do not identify, in text or through images, persons who may have been sexually assaulted (unless they have come forward and voluntarily identified themselves). We should also use discretion in naming victims of other extremely severe abuse.

Sometimes a person may be identified by AP in an abduction or manhunt situation, and it develops later that — because of a sexual assault or other reason — the name should not be used. In such cases we have sometimes refrained from using the identification in future coverage.

private See **military titles**.

privatization The process of

234

transferring a government-owned enterprise to private ownership.

privilege, privileged

pro- Use a hyphen when coining words that denote support for something. Some examples:

pro-labor   *pro-business*
pro-peace   *pro-war*

No hyphen when *pro* is used in other senses: *produce, profile, pronoun, proactive,* etc.

probation See **pardon, parole, probation**.

problem-solving

Procter & Gamble Co. *P&G* is acceptable on second reference. Headquarters is in Cincinnati.

producer price index An index of changes in wholesale prices, produced by the Bureau of Labor Statistics, U.S. Department of Labor, and used as a gauge of inflation. Spell the index name lowercase.

profanity See **obscenities, profanities, vulgarities**.

professor Never abbreviate. Lowercase before a name, but capitalize *Professor Emeritus* as a conferred title before a name: *Professor Emeritus Susan Johnson.* Do not continue in second reference unless part of a quotation.
See **academic titles**, **emeritus** and **titles**.

profit-sharing (n. and adj.) The hyphen for the noun is an exception to Webster's New World College Dictionary.

profit-sharing plan A plan that gives employees a share in the profits of the company. Each employee receives a percentage of those profits based on the company's earnings.

profit-taking (n. and adj.) Avoid this term. It means selling a security after a recent rapid rise in price. It is inaccurate if the seller bought the security at a higher price, watched it fall, then sold it after a recent rise but for less than he bought it. In that case, he would be cutting his losses, not taking his profit.

profit terminology Note the meanings of the following terms in reporting a company's financial status. Always be careful to specify whether the figures given apply to quarterly or annual results.

The terms, listed in the order in which they might occur in analyzing a company's financial condition:

dividend The amount paid per share per year to holders of common stock. Payments generally are made in quarterly installments.

If a company shows no profit during a given period, it may be able to use earnings retained from profitable periods to pay its dividend on schedule.

earnings per share (or **loss per share**, for companies posting a net loss) The figure obtained by dividing the number of outstanding shares of common stock into the amount left after dividends have been paid on any preferred stock.

extraordinary loss, extraordinary income An expense or source of income that does not occur on a regular basis, such as a loss due to a major fire or the revenue from the sale of a subsidiary. Extraordinary items should be identified in any report on the company's financial status to avoid creating the false impression that its overall profit trend has suddenly plunged or soared.

gross profit The difference between the sales price of an item or service and the expenses directly attributed to it, such as the cost of raw materials, labor and overhead linked to the production effort.

income before taxes Gross profits minus companywide expenses not directly attributed to specific products or services. These expenses typically include interest costs, advertising and sales costs, and general administrative overhead.

net income, profit, earnings The amount left after taxes and preferred dividends have been paid.

Some of what remains may be paid in dividends to holders of common stock. The rest may be invested to obtain interest revenue or spent to acquire new buildings or equipment to increase the company's ability to make further profits.

To avoid confusion, do not use the word *income* alone — always specify whether the figure is *income before taxes* or *net income*.

The terms *profit* and *earnings* commonly are interpreted as meaning the amount left after taxes. The terms *net profit* and *net earnings* are acceptable synonyms.

return on investment A percentage figure obtained by dividing the company's assets into its net income.

revenue The amount of money a company took in, including interest earned and receipts from sales, services provided, rents and royalties.

The figure also may include excise taxes and sales taxes collected for the government. If it does, the fact should be noted in any report on revenue. The singular form is preferable in most uses.

sales The money a company received for the goods and services it sold.

In some cases the figure includes receipts from rents and royalties. In others, particularly when rentals and royalties make up a large portion of a company's income, figures for these activities are listed separately.

pro forma In the financial world, it describes a method of calculating a company's sales and earnings as if changes in circumstances existed throughout an entire period covered by a financial report. Pro forma figures are often given for companies that have been involved in a merger or acquisition, gone public or emerged from bankruptcy reorganization. Unlike earnings based on generally accepted accounting principles, pro forma earnings do not comply with any standardized rules or regulations.

Prohibition Capitalize when referring to the period that began when the 18th Amendment to the Constitution prohibited the manufacture, sale or transportation of alcoholic liquors.

The amendment was declared ratified Jan. 29, 1919, and took effect Jan. 16, 1920. It was repealed by the 21st Amendment, which took effect Dec. 5, 1933, the day it was declared ratified.

pronouncers When necessary to use a pronouncer, put it in parentheses immediately following the word or name. The syllable to be stressed should be in caps with an apostrophe: *acetaminophen* (*a-see-tuh-MIHN'-oh-fen*).

p

Here are the basic sounds represented by AP phonetic symbols:

Vowels	Consonants
a — apple, bat	g — got, beg
ah — father, hot	j — gem, job
ahr — part, car	k — cap, keep
aw — law, long	ch — chair
ay — ace, fate	s — see
eh — bed	sh — shut
ehr — merry	y — yes
ee — see, tea	z — zoom
ih — pin, middle	zh — mirage
oh — go, oval	kh — guttural "k"
oo — food, two	
or — for, torn	
ow — cow	
oy — boy	
u — foot, put	
uh — puff	
ur — burden, curl	
y, eye — ice, time	

propeller

proper nouns See **capitalization**.

prophecy (n.) **prophesy** (v.)

proportions Always use figures: *2 parts powder to 6 parts water*.

proposition Do not abbreviate unless in quotations. Capitalize when used with a figure in describing a ballot question: *He is uncommitted on Proposition 15.*

prosecutor Capitalize before a name when it is the formal title. In most cases, however, the formal title is a term such as *attorney general, state's attorney* or *U.S. attorney*. If so, use the formal title on first reference.

Lowercase *prosecutor* if used before a name on a subsequent reference, generally to help the reader distinguish between prosecutor and defense attorney without having to look back to the start of the story.

See **titles**.

prostate gland A gland that surrounds the urethra at the base of the bladder in males. Prostate cancer is among the most common cancers in older men in developed countries. Blood tests to measure *PSA*, or *prostate specific antigen*, are sometimes used for screening but do not indicate the presence of cancer — just the possible need for more definitive tests. *PSA* can be high for reasons other than cancer.

prostitute Avoid terms like *child, underage* or *teenage prostitute*, except in quotations or in referring to criminal charges that may use these terms. The phrasing can suggest that a child is voluntarily trading sex for money. Minors are not able to consent.

protective tariff A duty high enough to assure domestic producers against any effective competition from foreign producers.

protester

prove, proved, proving Use *proven* only as an adjective: *a proven remedy*.

provinces Names of provinces are set off from community names by commas, just as the names of U.S. states are set off from city names: *They went to Halifax, Nova Scotia, on their vacation.*

Do not capitalize *province: They visited the province of Nova Scotia. The earthquake struck Shensi province.*

See **datelines**.

proviso, provisos

provost marshal The plural: *provost marshals*.

proxy An authorization for someone else to vote on behalf of a shareholder at a company's annual shareholder meeting. *Proxy fight* is a strategy used by an acquiring company or investor group in its attempt to gain control of a target company; the acquirer tries to convince other shareholders that the management of the target company should be replaced or a specific corporate action be taken. *Proxy statement* is a document that disclosed important information about issues to be discussed at an annual meeting. It includes the qualifications of management and board directors, serves as a ballot for elections to the board of directors and provides detailed information about executive compensation.

pseudonyms, nicknames A nickname should be used in place of a person's given name in stories only when it is the way the individual prefers to be known: *Jimmy Carter, Bill Clinton, Babe Ruth, Tiger Woods, Magic Johnson.*

When a nickname is inserted into the identification of an individual, use quotation marks: Sen. Henry M. "Scoop" Jackson, Paul "Bear" Bryant.

Capitalize without quotation marks such terms as *Sunshine State, the Old Dominion, Motown, the Magic City, Old Hickory, Old Glory, Galloping Ghost.* See **names**.

PTA Acceptable in all references for *Parent Teacher Association.*

PT boat Acceptable in all references for *patrol torpedo boat,* a small, fast attack vessel used by the U.S. Navy in World War II.

Public Broadcasting Service An association of public television stations organized to buy and distribute programs selected by a vote of the members.

PBS is acceptable on first reference only within contexts such as a television column. Otherwise, do not use *PBS* until second reference.

public schools Use figures and capitalize *public school* when used with a figure: *Public School 3, Public School 10.*

If a school has a commemorative name, capitalize the name: *Benjamin Franklin School.*

publisher Capitalize when used as a formal title before an individual's name: *Publisher Isaiah Thomas of the Massachusetts Spy.*
See **titles**.

Puerto Rico Do not abbreviate. See **datelines** and **U.S. territories**.

Pulitzer Prizes These yearly awards for outstanding work in journalism and the arts were endowed by the late Joseph Pulitzer, publisher of the old New York World, and first given in 1917. They are awarded by the trustees of Columbia University on recommendation of an advisory board.

Capitalize *Pulitzer Prize,* but lowercase the categories: *Pulitzer Prize for public service, Pulitzer Prize for fiction,* etc.

Also: *She is a Pulitzer Prize winner. He is a Pulitzer Prize-winning author.*

pullback (n.) **pull back** (v.)

pullout (n.) **pull out** (v.)

pullup (n.) **pull up** (v.)

pulpit See **lectern, podium, pulpit,**

rostrum.

punctuation The punctuation entries in this book refer to guidelines rather than rules. Guidelines should not be treated casually, however.

See **Punctuation** chapter for separate entries under: **apostrophe; brackets; colon; comma; dash; ellipsis; exclamation point; hyphen; parentheses; periods; question mark; quotation marks;** and **semicolon.**

push-button (n. and adj.)

pushup (n. and adj.) **push up** (v.)

putout (n.) **put out** (v.)

PwC The brand name for the accounting and consulting firm whose legal name is *PricewaterhouseCoopers.* Use *PwC* on first and all references, adding in a lower reference "also known as PricewaterhouseCoopers" or "the brand name for PricewaterhouseCoopers" as appropriate. Headquarters is in London.

pygmy Capitalize only when referring specifically to any of several races of unusually small African or Asian peoples.

p

q

Q&A format Use *Q&A* within the body of a story. See **question mark** in **Punctuation** chapter.

Qantas Airways Ltd. Headquarters of this airline is in Mascot, Australia.

QE2 Acceptable on second reference for the ocean liner Queen Elizabeth 2.

(But use a Roman numeral for the monarch: *Queen Elizabeth II.*)

Q-tips A trademark for a brand of cotton swabs.

quakes See **earthquakes**.

quart (dry) Equal in volume to 67.2 cubic inches. The metric equivalent is approximately 1.1 liters.

To convert to liters, multiply by 1.1 (5 dry quarts x 1.1 is 5.5 liters). See **liter**.

quart (liquid) Equal in volume to 57.75 cubic inches. Also equal to 32 fluid ounces.

The approximate metric equivalents are 950 milliliters or 0.95 of a liter.

To convert to liters, multiply by 0.95 (4 quarts x 0.95 is 3.8 liters). See **liter**.

quasar Acceptable in all references for a *quasi-stellar astronomical object*, often a source of radio waves.

Quebec Use *Quebec City* without the name of the province in datelines.

Do not abbreviate any reference to the province of *Quebec*, Canada's largest in area and second largest in population.

The people are *Quebecois*. See **datelines**.

Quechua An Andean ethnic group in Peru and Bolivia. The language of these people.

queen mother A widowed queen who is mother of the reigning monarch. See **nobility**.

question mark See entry in **Punctuation** chapter.

questionnaire

quick-witted

quiet period Avoid using this term. In the investing world, it is commonly thought to be the period following a company's initial public offering or just before earnings are reported in which it is subject to possible sanctions by the U.S. Securities and Exchange Commission for making public disclosures. But since SEC rules only prohibit disclosures that go beyond what the company has stated in SEC filings, the term *quiet period* is a misnomer.

quotation marks See entry in **Punctuation** chapter.

quotations in the news Never alter quotations even to correct minor grammatical errors or word usage. Casual minor tongue slips may be removed by using ellipses but even that should be done with extreme caution.

Use *sic*, the Latin word meaning *thus* or *so*, to show that quoted material or person's words include a misspelling, incorrect grammar or peculiar usage. Place *(sic)* in the text directly after the problem to show that the passage is precisely reproduced. To call attention to *(sic)* in wire versions of the story, use an editor's note atop the story.

If there is a question about a quote, either don't use it or ask the speaker to clarify.

If a person is unavailable for comment, detail attempts to reach that person. (*Agarwal was out of the country on business; Park did not return phone messages left at the office.*)

Do not use substandard spellings such as *gonna* or *wanna* in attempts to convey regional dialects or informal pronunciations, except to help a desired touch or to convey an emphasis by the speaker.

When quoting spoken words, present them in the format that reflects AP style: *No. 1, St., Gov., $3.* But quotes should not be changed otherwise for reasons of style. If the speaker says *towards*, do not change it to *toward*.

When quoting written words, retain the style used by the writer; do not alter the written words even if they don't match AP style.

Use quotations only if they are the best way to tell the story or convey meaning. Often, paraphrasing is preferable.

FULL VS. PARTIAL QUOTES: In general, avoid fragmentary quotes. If a speaker's words are clear and concise, favor the full quote. If cumbersome language can be paraphrased fairly, use an indirect construction, reserving quotation marks for sensitive or controversial passages that must be identified specifically as coming from the speaker.

CONTEXT: Remember that you can misquote someone by giving a startling remark without its modifying passage or qualifiers. The manner of delivery sometimes is part of the context. Reporting a smile or a deprecatory gesture may be as important as conveying the words themselves.

SOCIAL MEDIA POSTS AND TEXT MESSAGES: Social media posts and text messages often contain *emoji*, *GIFs* or other imagery that need to be conveyed to readers using words. Treat the visual material as context or gestures when important to include, describing by paraphrasing:

Chavis sparked a flurry of responses against the airline after tweeting a GIF of large crowds at the gate, with the message "#missinghoneymoon" and an emoji string of a worried smiley, a ring, an hourglass and an umbrella propped on a beach.

Be aware that some GIFs, emoji or other images may contain hidden meanings and nuances requiring consideration and more than just a simple description of the image posted.

Do not use parentheses to describe an emoji within a direct quote, to avoid confusing readers by making it seem as if the person being quoted wrote out the description in text.

Many story platforms support displaying posts as they actually appear, or hyperlinking to posts on social networks, giving journalists several options to let readers see material for themselves. For example, some production systems may allow you to directly insert emoji into the text of a story. Additionally, most social networks allow for direct embedding of such material, and screen captures may also be acceptable if images are displayed in accordance with your newsroom's visual standards.

OFFENSIVE LANGUAGE: See the **obscenities, profanities, vulgarities** entry.

PUNCTUATION: See the **quotation marks** entry in the **Punctuation** chapter.

PROBLEMATIC QUOTES: See the **(sic)** entry.

Quran The preferred spelling for the Muslim holy book. Use the spelling *Koran* only if preferred by a specific organization or in a specific title or name.

q

race Identification by race or ethnicity is pertinent:
— In biographical and announcement stories that involve significant, groundbreaking or historic events, such as being elected U.S. president, being named to the U.S. Supreme Court or other notable occurrences. *Barack Obama was the first black U.S. president. Sonia Sotomayor is the first Hispanic justice of the U.S. Supreme Court. Jeremy Lin is the first American-born NBA player of Chinese or Taiwanese descent.*
— For suspects sought by the police or missing person cases using police or other credible, detailed descriptions. Such descriptions apply for all races. The racial reference should be removed when the individual is apprehended or found.
— When reporting a demonstration or disturbance involving race or such issues as civil rights or slavery.

In other situations with racial overtones, use news judgment.

Do not use a derogatory term except in extremely rare circumstances — when it is crucial to the story or the understanding of a news event. Flag the contents in an editor's note.

See **obscenities, profanities, vulgarities** and **nationalities and races**.

racket Not *racquet*, for the light bat used in tennis and badminton.

rack, wrack The noun *rack* applies to various types of framework; the verb *rack* means to arrange on a rack, to torture, trouble or torment: *He was placed on the rack. She racked her brain.*

The noun *wrack* means ruin or destruction, as in *wrack and ruin* and *wracked with pain.* Also *nerve-wracking.*

The verb *wrack* has substantially the same meaning as the verb *rack*, the latter being preferred.

radar A lowercase acronym for *radio detection and ranging*. Radar acceptable in all references.

radical In general, avoid this description in favor of a more precise definition of an individual's political views.

When used, it suggests that an individual believes change must be made by tearing up the roots or foundation of the present order.

Although *radical* often is applied to individuals who hold strong socialist or communist views, it also is applied at times to individuals who believe an existing form of government must be replaced by a more authoritarian or militaristic one.

See **leftist, ultra-leftist** and **rightist, ultra-rightist**.

radio Capitalize and use before a name to indicate an official or state-funded broadcast voice: *Radio Free Europe, Radio France International.*

Lowercase and place after the

name when indicating only that the information was obtained from broadcasts in a city. *Mexico City radio*, for example, is the form used in referring to reports that are broadcast on various stations in the Mexican capital.

radio station Use lowercase: *radio station WHEC*.
See **call letters**.

railroads Railroads can be characterized as either freight carriers or passenger railroads. The nationwide U.S. passenger railroad is *Amtrak*.

rainstorm See **weather terms**.

raised, reared Only humans may be *reared*.
All living things, including humans, may be *raised*.

RAM Acronym for *random access memory*, the "working memory" of a computer into which programs can be introduced and then executed. *RAM* is acceptable in all uses.

Ramadan The Muslim holy month, marked by daily fasting from dawn to sunset, ending with the Islamic holiday of Eid al-Fitr. Avoid using *holiday* on second reference.

ranges The form: *$12 million to $14 million*. Not: *$12 to $14 million*. Also: *A pay increase of 12-15 percent*. Or: *A pay increase of between 12 and 15 percent*. For full calendar years, hyphenated *2015-16* is acceptable.

rank and file (n.) **rank-and-file** (adj.)

rape See **privacy**.

rarely It means *seldom*. *Rarely ever* is redundant, but *rarely if ever* often is the appropriate phrase.

ratings agency A company that measures the creditworthiness of companies, municipalities and countries. A ratings agency gauges an entity's ability to repay its debt and assigns a rating based on that assessment. The better the rating, the lower the cost for an entity to borrow money.

ratios Use figures and hyphens: *the ratio was 2-to-1, a ratio of 2-to-1, a 2-1 ratio, 1 in 4 voters*. As illustrated, the word *to* should be omitted when the numbers precede the word *ratio*.
Always use the word *ratio* or a phrase such as *a 2-1 majority* to avoid confusion with actual figures.
See **numerals**.

ravage, ravish *To ravage* is to wreak great destruction or devastation: *Union troops ravaged Atlanta*.
To ravish is to abduct, rape or carry away with emotion: *Soldiers ravished the women*.
Although both words connote an element of violence, they are not interchangeable. Buildings and towns cannot be *ravished*.

re- The rules in **prefixes** apply. The following examples of exceptions to first-listed spellings in Webster's New World College Dictionary are based on the general rule that a hyphen is used if a prefix ends in a vowel and the word that follows begins with the same vowel:

re-elect	re-enlist
re-election	re-enter
re-emerge	re-entry
re-emphasize	re-equip
re-employ	re-establish

r

re-enact   *re-examine*
re-engage

For many other words, the sense is the governing factor:

recover (regain)
re-cover (cover again)
reform (improve)
re-form (form again)
resign (quit)
re-sign (sign again)

Otherwise, follow Webster's New World College Dictionary. Use a hyphen for words not listed there unless the hyphen would distort the sense.

Realtor The term *real estate agent* is preferred. Use *Realtor* only if there is a reason to indicate that the individual is a member of the National Association of Realtors.

reared See **raised, reared**.

rebut, refute *Rebut* means *to argue to the contrary*: *He rebutted his opponent's statement.*

Refute connotes success in argument and almost always implies an editorial judgment. Instead, use *deny, dispute, rebut* or *respond to*.

receivership A legal action in which a court appoints a *receiver* to manage a business while the court tries to resolve problems that could ruin the business, such as insolvency. *Receivership* is often used in federal bankruptcy court proceedings. But it also can be used for nonfinancial troubles such as an ownership dispute.

In bankruptcy proceedings, the court appoints a trustee called a *receiver* who attempts to settle the financial difficulties of the company while under protection from creditors.

recession A falling-off of economic activity that may be a temporary phenomenon or could continue into a depression.

recession-proof

recipes Always use figures. See **fractions** and **numerals**.

Do not use abbreviations. Spell out *teaspoon, tablespoon*, etc.

See the **food** entry for guidelines on when to capitalize the names of foods.

reconnaissance

Reconstruction The process of reorganizing the Southern states after the Civil War.

record Avoid the redundant *new record*.

recur, recurred, recurring Not *reoccur*.

Red Capitalize when used as a political, geographic or military term: *the Red Army*.

red carpet The ceremonial gantlet where guests arriving at award shows strut their finery, greet fans and give media interviews. Red carpets may sometimes be other colors.

Reddit A social network that features message board-style posts, organized into topic-based pages called *subreddits*, where users share and converse about content. Users can vote up or down individual conversation threads and comments, determining which ones are most prominently displayed on the site. *"Ask me anything"* posts give users an opportunity to pose questions to public figures, topic experts and people who have had interesting experiences. *AMA* is acceptable on second reference.

red-haired, redhead, redheaded All are acceptable for a person with red hair.

    Redhead also is used colloquially to describe a type of North American diving duck.

red-handed (adj. and adv.)

red-hot

redneck From the characteristic sunburned neck acquired in the fields by farm laborers. It refers to poor, white rural residents of the South and often is a derogatory term.

re-elect, re-election

refer See **allude, refer**.

referable

reference works Capitalize their proper names.

    Do not use quotation marks around the names of books that are primarily catalogs of reference material. In addition to catalogs, this category includes almanacs, directories, dictionaries, encyclopedias, gazetteers, handbooks, school yearbooks and similar publications.

    EXAMPLES: Congressional Directory, Webster's New World College Dictionary, the AP Stylebook. But: "The Careful Writer" and "The Elements of Style."

    See the **Bibliography** for the principal reference works used in preparing this book.

referendum, referendums

reform The word is not synonymous with *change*. It generally implies faults or shortcomings in the subject at hand. Use care in deciding whether *reform* is the appropriate word or whether a more neutral term is better. Use similar caution with words such as *improvement* or *overhaul*.

reformatory See **prison, jail**.

refugee, migrant, asylum-seeker See **immigration**.

refute See **rebut, refute**.

regifting Passing along an unwanted present to someone else.

regime See **government, junta, regime, administration**.

regions See **directions and regions**.

reign, rein The leather strap for controlling a horse is a *rein*, hence figuratively: *seize the reins, give free rein to*.

    Reign is the period a ruler is on the throne: *The king began his reign*.

religious references The basic guidelines:

    DEITIES: Capitalize the proper names of monotheistic deities: *God, Allah, the Father, the Son, Jesus Christ, the Son of God, the Redeemer, the Holy Spirit*, etc.

    Lowercase pronouns referring to the deity: *he, him, his, thee, thou, who, whose, thy*, etc.

    Lowercase *gods* in referring to the deities of polytheistic religions.

    Capitalize the proper names of pagan and mythological gods and goddesses: *Neptune, Thor, Venus,* etc.

Lowercase such words as *god-awful, goddamn, godlike, godliness, godsend.*

LIFE OF CHRIST: Capitalize the names of major events in the life of Jesus Christ in references that do not use his name: *The doctrines of the Last Supper, the Crucifixion, the Resurrection and the Ascension are central to Christian belief.*

But use lowercase when the words are used with his name: *The ascension of Jesus into heaven took place 40 days after his resurrection from the dead.*

Apply the principle also to events in the life of his mother: *He cited the doctrines of the Immaculate Conception and the Assumption.* But: *She referred to the assumption of Mary into heaven.*

RITES: Capitalize proper names for rites that commemorate the Last Supper or signify a belief in Christ's presence: *the Lord's Supper, Holy Communion, Holy Eucharist.*

Lowercase the names of other sacraments. See **sacraments** in the **Religion** chapter.

Capitalize *Benediction* and *Mass.* But: *a high Mass, a low Mass, a requiem Mass.*

HOLY DAYS: Capitalize the names of holy days. See **holidays and holy days** and separate entries for major Christian, Jewish and Muslim feasts in the **Religion** chapter.

OTHER WORDS: Lowercase *heaven, hell, devil, angel, cherub, an apostle, a priest,* etc.

Capitalize *Hades* and *Satan.*

For additional details, see **Bible**, entries for frequently used religious terms, the entries for major denominations, **religious movements** and **religious titles** and the **Religion** chapter.

religious titles The first reference

to a clergyman or clergywoman normally should include a capitalized title before the individual's name.

In many cases, *the Rev.* is the designation that applies before a name on first reference. Use *the Rev. Dr.* only if the individual has an earned doctoral degree (doctor of divinity degrees frequently are honorary) and reference to the degree is relevant.

On second reference to members of the clergy, use only a last name: *the Rev. Billy Graham* on first reference, *Graham* on second. If known only by a religious name, repeat the title: *Pope John XXIII* on first reference, *John, the pope* or *the pontiff* on second; *Pope Emeritus Benedict XVI* or *Benedict XVI, the pope emeritus. Benedict* alone on second reference. *Metropolitan Herman* on first reference, *Metropolitan Herman* or *the metropolitan* on second.

Detailed guidance on specific titles and descriptive words such as *priest* and *minister* is provided in the entries for major denominations in the **Religion** chapter. In general, however:

CARDINALS, ARCHBISHOPS, BISHOPS: The preferred form for first reference is to use *Cardinal, Archbishop* or *Bishop* before the individual's name: *Cardinal Daniel DiNardo, archbishop of Galveston-Houston.* On second reference: *DiNardo* or *the cardinal.*

Substitute *the Most Rev.* if applicable and appropriate in the context: *He spoke to the Most Rev. Jose Gomez, archbishop of Los Angeles.* On second reference: *Gomez* or *the archbishop.*

Entries for individual denominations tell when *the Most Rev., the Very Rev.,* etc., are applicable. See **Religion** chapter.

MINISTERS AND PRIESTS: Use *the Rev.* before a name on first reference.

Substitute *Monsignor* before the name of a Roman Catholic priest who has received this honor.

Do not routinely use *curate, father, pastor* and similar words before an individual's name. If they appear before a name in a quotation, capitalize them.

RABBIS: Use *Rabbi* before a name on first reference. On second reference, use only the last name.

NUNS: Always use *Sister,* or *Mother* if applicable, before a name: *Sister Agnes Rita* in all references if the nun uses only a religious name; *Sister Mary Ann Walsh* on first reference if she uses a surname. *Walsh* on subsequent references.

OFFICEHOLDERS: The preferred first-reference form for those who hold church office but are not ordained clergy in the usual sense is to use a construction that sets the title apart from the name by commas. Capitalize the formal title of an office, however, if it is used directly before an individual's name.

reluctant, reticent *Reluctant* means *unwilling to act*: *He is reluctant to enter the primary.*

Reticent means *unwilling to speak*: *The candidate's husband is reticent.*

representative, Rep. See **legislative titles** and **party affiliation**.

republic Capitalize *republic* when used as part of a nation's full, formal name: *the Republic of Argentina.* See **datelines**.

Republic Airways Holdings Inc. Headquarters of this airline is in Indianapolis.

Republican Governors Association No apostrophe.

Republican National Committee On second reference: *the national committee, the committee* and *the RNC.*

Similarly: *Republican State Committee, Republican County Committee, Republican City Committee, the state committee, the county committee, the city committee, the committee.*

Republican, Republican Party *GOP* may be used on second reference. See **political parties and philosophies** and **GOP**.

reputation See **character, reputation**.

rescission

Reserve Capitalize when referring to U.S. armed forces, as in *Army Reserve.* Lowercase in reference to members of these backup forces: *reserves,* or *reservists.*

Reserve Officers' Training Corps The *s'* is military practice. *ROTC* is acceptable in all references.

When the service is specified, use *Army ROTC, Navy ROTC* or *Air Force ROTC,* not *AROTC, NROTC* or *AFROTC.*

resident See **citizen, resident, subject, national, native**.

resistible

restaurateur

restrictive clauses See **essential clauses, nonessential clauses**.

restrictive phrases See **essential phrases, nonessential phrases**.

retail sales The sales of retail stores, including merchandise sold and receipts for repairs and similar services.

A business is considered a *retail store* if it is engaged primarily in selling merchandise for personal, household or farm consumption.

retweet The practice, on Twitter, of sharing an existing tweet with your followers. When using the retweet button, users have the option of writing a new tweet and appending the retweeted item — what's known as a *quote tweet*. Spell out *retweet* in all references, though it's commonly called an RT on Twitter.

Reuters See **Thomson Reuters Corp.**

Rev. When this description is used before an individual's name, precede it with the word *the* because, unlike the case with *Mr.* and *Mrs.*, the abbreviation *Rev.* does not stand for a noun.

If an individual also has a secular title such as *Rep.*, use whichever is appropriate to the context.

See **religious titles**.

revaluations Occur when a country's government pushes up the value of its currency in relation to another currency. (When market forces, not the government, push a currency up, it is known as appreciation.)

Suppose China revalues its currency, the yuan, against the U.S. dollar. To calculate the revaluation, you'd look at the value of 1 yuan to the U.S. dollar before the revaluation and the value afterward and calculate the percentage difference.

Example: On Day One, 1 yuan is worth 15.8 cents (or $0.158). The next day, the Chinese government revalues the currency and 1 yuan is equal to 16.1 cents ($0.161). That is a 1.9 percent revaluation — the yuan has risen 1.9 percent against the U.S. dollar.

Currencies are often reported the other way, showing how much $1 is worth in another currency. In the example above, $1 went from being worth 6.32 yuan to being worth only 6.21 yuan. To find out what 1 yuan is worth — so you can show the yuan rising, not the dollar falling — divide 1 by 6.32 and 6.21 respectively.

revenue See **profit terminology**.

revenue bond See **loan terminology**.

reverse auction An auction where the winning bidder is the one willing to take the lowest price. In a reverse auction for subprime mortgage loans, for instance, a bank offering to sell a bundle of bad loans for 50 cents on the dollar would beat a bank offering to sell its loans for 60 cents on the dollar.

Reverse 911 Capitalized trademark for an automated phone alert system.

Use the generic form if the brand is uncertain.

revolution Capitalize when part of a name for a specific historical event: *the American Revolution, the Bolshevik Revolution, the French Revolution.*

The Revolution, capitalized, also may be used as a shorthand reference to the *American Revolution.* Also: *the Revolutionary War.*

Lowercase in other uses: *a revolution, the revolution, the American and French revolutions.*

revolutions per minute The

abbreviation *rpm* is acceptable on first reference in specialized contexts such as an auto column. Otherwise do not use it until second reference.

revolving credit Describes an account on which the payment is any amount less than the total balance, and the remaining balance carried forward is subject to finance charges.

Rh factor Also: *Rh negative, Rh positive.*

Rhode Island Abbreviate *R.I.* in datelines only; spell out in stories. Postal code: *RI*
   See **state names**.

Rhodes scholar Lowercase *scholar* and *scholarship.*

rhythm and blues *R&B* is acceptable on second reference.

RIA Novosti A Russian government news agency, based in Moscow.

Richter scale No longer widely used. See **earthquakes.**

RICO An acronym for *Racketeer Influenced and Corrupt Organizations Act.* Acceptable on second reference, but *anti-racketeering* or *anti-corruption law* is preferred.

ride-hailing, ride-sharing *Ride-hailing services* such as Uber and Lyft let people use smartphone apps to book and pay for a private car service or, in some cases, a taxi. They may also be called *ride-booking services. Ride-sharing* refers to app-based services that let people book a shared shuttle. Zipcar and similar companies are *short-term car rental services.*

rifle See **weapons.**

rifle, riffle To *rifle* is to plunder or steal.
   To *riffle* is to leaf rapidly through a book or pile of papers.

right hand (n.) **right-hander** (n.) **right-handed** (adj.)

rightist, ultra-rightist In general, avoid these terms in favor of more precise descriptions of an individual's political philosophy.
   Ultra-rightist suggests an individual who subscribes to rigid interpretations of a conservative doctrine or to forms of fascism that stress authoritarian, often militaristic, views.
   See **radical** and **leftist, ultra-leftist.**

right of way, rights of way

right-to-work (adj.) A *right-to-work* law prohibits a company and a union from signing a contract that would require the affected workers to be union members.
   See **closed shop** for definitions of various agreements that require union membership.

right wing (n.) **right-winger** (n.) **right-wing** (adj.) Generally try to avoid in describing political leanings.

Rio de Janeiro The city in Brazil stands alone in datelines.

Rio Grande Not *Rio Grande River. Rio* means river in Spanish.

rip-off (n. and adj.) **rip off** (v.)

river Capitalize as part of a proper name: *the Mississippi River.*
   Lowercase in other uses: *the river,*

r

the Mississippi and Missouri rivers.

road Do not abbreviate. See **addresses**.

robbery See **burglary, larceny, robbery, theft**.

Roche Holding AG Headquarters is in Basel, Switzerland.

rock 'n' roll But *Rock and Roll Hall of Fame.*

Rocky Mountains Or simply: *the Rockies.*

roll call (n.) **roll-call** (adj.)

Rollerblade A trademark for a brand of in-line skates.

roller coaster

rollover The selling of new securities to pay off old ones coming due or the refinancing of an existing loan.

Rolls-Royce Note the hyphen in this trademark for a make of automobile.

Rolodex A trademark for a brand of rotary card file.

ROM Acronym for *read-only memory,* computer memory whose contents cannot be modified. *ROM* acceptable in all references.

Roma, Gypsy Capitalize references to the nomadic ethnic group. *Roma* is preferred, because some consider *Gypsy* an offensive term; in the interest of clarity, the word can be explained: *Roma, also known as Gypsies.* Lowercase otherwise: *gypsy cab, gypsy-cab driver, gypsy moth.*

Roman Catholic Church The church teaches that its bishops have been established as the successors of the apostles through generations of ceremonies in which authority was passed down by a laying-on of hands.

Responsibility for teaching the faithful and administering the church rests with the bishops. However, the church holds that the pope has final authority over their actions because he is the bishop of Rome, the office it teaches was held by the Apostle Peter at his death.

The Curia serves as a form of governmental cabinet. Its members, appointed by the pope, handle both administrative and judicial functions.

The pope also chooses members of the College of Cardinals, who serve as his principal counselors. When a new pope must be chosen, they meet in a conclave to select a new pope by majority vote. In practice, cardinals are mostly bishops, but there is no requirement that a cardinal be a bishop.

In the United States, the church's principal organizational units are archdioceses and dioceses. They are headed, respectively, by archbishops and bishops, who have final responsibility for many activities within their jurisdictions and report directly to Rome.

The church counts more than 1 billion members worldwide. In the United States it has more than 66 million members, making it the largest single body of Christians in the nation.

Roman Catholics believe in the Trinity — that there is one God who exists as three divine persons — the Father, the Son and the Holy Spirit. They believe that the Son became man as Jesus Christ.

In addition to the Holy Eucharist,

there are six other sacraments — baptism, confirmation, penance (often called the sacrament of reconciliation), matrimony, holy orders, and the sacrament of the sick (formerly extreme unction).

The clergy below pope are, in descending order, cardinal, archbishop, bishop, monsignor, priest and deacon. In religious orders, some men who are not priests have the title *brother*.

Capitalize *pope* when used as a title before a name: *Pope John XXIII, Pope Francis.* Lowercase in all other uses. See **religious titles**.

The first-reference forms for other titles follow. Use only last names on second reference.

Cardinals: *Cardinal Daniel DiNardo.* The usage *Daniel Cardinal DiNardo,* a practice traceable to the nobility's custom of identifications such as *William, Duke of Norfolk,* is still used in formal documents but otherwise is considered archaic.

Archbishops: *Archbishop Gregory Aymond,* or *the Most Rev. Gregory Aymond, archbishop of New Orleans.*

Bishops: *Bishop Thomas Paprocki,* or *the Most Rev. Thomas Paprocki, bishop of Springfield, Illinois.*

Monsignors: *Monsignor Martin Krebs.* Do not use the abbreviation *Msgr.* Do not use *the Rt. Rev.* or *the Very Rev.* — this distinction between types of monsignors no longer is made.

Priests: *the Rev. James Martin.* See **religious titles**.

Romania

Roman numerals The Roman letters (*I, X,* etc.) were used as numerals until the 10th century.

Use Roman numerals for wars and to establish personal sequence for people and animals: *World War I, Native Dancer II, King George V.* Also for certain legislative acts (*Title IX*).

Pro football Super Bowls should be identified by the year, not the Roman numerals: *1969 Super Bowl,* not *Super Bowl III.*

Use Arabic numerals in all other cases. See **Arabic numerals** and **numerals**.

In Roman numerals, the capital letter *I* equals 1, *V* equals 5, *X* equals 10, *L* equals 50, *C* equals 100, *D* equals 500 and *M* equals 1,000.

Other numbers are formed from these by adding or subtracting as follows:
— The value of a letter following another of the same or greater value is added: *III* equals 3.
— The value of a letter preceding one of greater value is subtracted: *IV* equals 4.

Rome The city in Italy stands alone in datelines.

room numbers Use figures and capitalize *room* when used with a figure: *Room 2, Room 211.*

rooms Capitalize the names of specially designated rooms: *Blue Room, Lincoln Room, Oval Office, Persian Room.*

Rosh Hashana The Jewish new year. Occurs in September or October.

rostrum See **lectern, podium, pulpit, rostrum**.

ROTC See **Reserve Officers' Training Corps**.

roundtable (n. or adj.), **round table** (n.), **Round Table** (n.) The *Knights of the Round Table* will hold a *roundtable discussion* after seating themselves at a *round table*. They likely will refer to their meeting as a *roundtable*.

roundup (n.) **round up** (v.)

route numbers Do not abbreviate *route*. Use figures and capitalize route when used with a figure: *U.S. Route 70, state Route 1A.*
See **highway designations**.

Royal Dutch Shell PLC A 2005 unification of Royal Dutch Petroleum and Shell Transport & Trading Co., with headquarters in The Hague, Netherlands. The company specializes in petroleum and related products. Holdings include Shell Oil Co., a U.S. corporation, with headquarters in Houston.

RSS An abbreviation for *Really Simple Syndication*. A protocol for subscribing to and distributing feeds that notify people of new entries on news sites, blogs, podcasts or other online information sources. Also: *RSS feed. RSS* is acceptable in all references, although the simpler *internet feed* often is sufficient.

RSVP The abbreviation for the French *repondez s'il vous plait*, it means *please reply*.

rubber stamp (n.) **rubber-stamp** (v. and adj.)

rubella Also known as *German measles*.

runner-up, runners-up

running mate

rush hour (n.) **rush-hour** (adj.)

Russia See **Commonwealth of Independent States**.

Russian names When a first name in Russian has a close phonetic equivalent in English, use the equivalent in translating the name: *Alexander Solzhenitsyn* rather than *Aleksandr*, the spelling that would result from a transliteration of the Russian letter into the English alphabet.

When a first name has no close phonetic equivalent in English, express it with an English spelling that approximates the sound in Russian: *Dmitry, Nikita, Sergei*, for example. If an individual has a preference for an English spelling that is different from the one that would result by applying these guidelines, follow the individual's preference. Example: *Foreign Minister Sergey Lavrov.*

For last names, use the English spelling that most closely approximates the pronunciation in Russian. Exception: the *"ev"* ending of names like Gorbachev may be pronounced "yov."

If an individual has a preference for an English spelling that is different from the one that would result by applying these guidelines, follow the individual's preference.

Women's last names often have the feminine ending "*-a.*" But use this ending only if the woman is not married or if she is known under that name (the tennis player *Anna Kournikova*). Otherwise, use the masculine form.

Russian names never end in *off*, except for common mistransliterations such as *Rachmaninoff*. Instead, the transliterations should end in *ov*: *Romanov*. Also, Russian names end

in *"sky,"* rather than *"ski"* typical of
Polish surnames.

Russian Revolution Also: *the
Bolshevik Revolution.*

Rust Belt Areas of the Midwest and
Northeast where factories are old
and closed.

Ryanair Holdings PLC Headquarters
of this airline is in Dublin, Ireland.

r

S

saboteur

Sacagawea

Saddam Use *Saddam* in second reference to Iraq's former leader Saddam Hussein.

safety belt Also: *seat belt*.

Safeway Supermarket chain that has stores under names including Safeway, Vons, Pavilion's, Randall's, Tom Thumb and Carrs. The company was acquired by an investor group led by Cerberus Capital Management in 2014. The combined company has corporate offices in Phoenix, Arizona; Boise, Idaho, and Pleasanton, California.

saint Abbreviate as *St.* in the names of saints, cities and other places: *St. Jude*; *St. Paul, Minnesota*; *St. John's, Newfoundland*; *St. Lawrence Seaway*.
But see the entries for **Saint John** and **Sault Ste. Marie**.

Saint John The spelling for the city in New Brunswick.
To distinguish it from *St. John's, Newfoundland*.

salable

Sallie Mae Commonly used for SLM Corp., a publicly traded financial services company specializing in student loans.

SALT See **Strategic Arms Reduction Treaty (START)**

Salt Lake City The city in Utah stands alone in datelines.

salvo, salvos

same-sex marriage The preferred term over *gay marriage*. In places where it's legal, *same-sex marriage* is no different than other marriages, so the term should be used only when germane and needed to distinguish from marriages between heterosexual couples. *Gertrude Boxer and Savannah Boxer dated for several years before their marriage in 2014. The Boxers petitioned for same-sex marriage before it was legalized in Hawaii in 2013. Sex* is not synonymous with *gender*. See **gender**.

SAM, SAMs Acceptable on second reference for *surface-to-air missile(s)*.

Samsung Electronics Headquarters is in Seoul, South Korea.

Sanaa The capital of Yemen. The double-a reflects the Arabic pronunciation of *San'a*.

San Antonio The city in Texas stands alone in datelines.

sandbag (n. and v.) The verbs: *sandbagged, sandbagging*. And: *sandbagger*.

San Diego The city in California stands alone in datelines.

S&P 500 Use in all references for what was formerly known as the

Standard & Poor's 500 index. It is the market indicator most professional investors use to determine how stocks are performing. It encompasses 500 top companies in leading U.S. industries. Many mutual funds use it as the benchmark they measure their own performance against.

sandstorm See **weather terms**.

San Francisco The city in California stands alone in datelines.

San Marino Use alone in datelines on stories from the Republic of San Marino.

Santa Claus

Sao Paulo The city in Brazil stands alone in datelines.

Sardinia Use instead of Italy in datelines on stories from communities on this island.

SARS Acceptable in all references for *severe acute respiratory syndrome*, but it should be spelled out somewhere in the story.

Saskatchewan A province of Canada north of Montana and North Dakota. Do not abbreviate.
  See **datelines**.

SAT Use only the initials in referring to the previously designated Scholastic Aptitude Test or the Scholastic Assessment Test. Example: *The students scored above average on the SAT.*

Satan But lowercase *devil* and *satanic*.

satellite communications The following are some generally used technical terms dealing with satellite communications.
  uplink The transmission from the ground to the satellite.
  downlink The transmission from the satellite to the ground.
  footprint The area on the ground in which a transmission from a particular satellite can be received.
  earth station Sending or receiving equipment on the ground for a satellite.
  transponder The equipment on a satellite that receives from the ground and sends to the ground. A satellite usually has a number of *transponders*.
  geosynchronous A satellite orbit in which the satellite appears to always be in the same place in reference to the Earth. Most communications satellites are in geosynchronous orbits. Also *geostationary*.

satellites See **spacecraft designations**.

Saturday night special See **weapons**.

Saudi Arabia Use *Saudi* as the adjective in referring to the people or culture of Saudi Arabia. It's *Saudi diplomacy*, not *Saudi Arabian diplomacy*. For the Saudi monarchy, follow the style on British and other monarchies. *Foreign Minister Prince Saud Al-Faisal* would be *Prince Saud* on first reference and *Saud* on second reference.

Saudi Arabian Oil Co. *Saudi Aramco* is acceptable on second reference. Formerly the Arabian American Oil Co.

Sault Ste. Marie, Mich., Sault Ste. Marie, Ontario The abbreviation is *Ste.* instead of *St.* because the full

S

name is *Sault Sainte Marie*.

savings and loan associations
Also called *thrifts* or *savings and loans*. Differ from banks in that they are required by law to have a large proportion of their lending in mortgages and other consumer loans. They are regulated by the Federal Deposit Insurance Corp. and the Treasury Department's Office of the Comptroller of the Currency.

scene numbers Capitalize scene when used with a figure: *Scene 2*; *Act 2, Scene 4*.
But: *the second scene, the third scene.* See **numerals**.

scheme Do not use as a synonym for *a plan* or *a project*.

Schengen Area A group of European countries that have agreed to abolish passport and customs controls among one another. Created by the 1985 Schengen Agreement, it has grown to encompass 26 countries: 22 of the 28 EU member nations plus non-EU nations Norway, Iceland, Switzerland and Liechtenstein. EU members Great Britain and Ireland opted out of the agreement, while four other EU nations — Bulgaria, Croatia, Cyprus and Romania — are candidates to join once all EU member countries give their approval.

school Capitalize when part of a proper name: *Public School 3, Madison Elementary School, Doherty Junior High School, Crocker High School.*

scissors Takes plural verbs and pronouns: *The scissors are on the table. Leave them there.*

Scotch tape A trademark for a brand of transparent tape.

Scotland Use *Scotland* after the names of Scottish communities in datelines. See **datelines** and **United Kingdom**.

Scot, Scots, Scottish A native of Scotland is a *Scot*. The people are the *Scots*, not the *Scotch*.
Somebody or something is *Scottish*.

scraping Copying online data or content, manually or using scraping tools, for use or display elsewhere. Depending on what's being scraped, this can raise intellectual property, security or privacy issues, though there are legitimate uses of the technique.

Screen Actors Guild-American Federation of Television and Radio Artists
SAG-AFTRA is acceptable on second reference.
National offices in Los Angeles and New York.

screen saver

E.W. Scripps Co. Cincinnati-based owner of TV and radio stations. Spun off its newspaper holdings in 2015 after a merger with Journal Communications. Sponsor of the annual National Spelling Bee.

Scripps Networks Interactive Inc.
Owner of HGTV, Food Network, DIY Network and other national television channels. Discovery Communications said in July 2017 that it was buying Scripps Networks. Headquarters is in Knoxville, Tennessee.

Scripture, Scriptures Capitalize

when referring to the religious writings in the Bible.
See **Bible**.

scuba Lowercased acronym for *self-contained underwater breathing apparatus.*

Scud missile

scurrilous

Sea Islands A chain of islands off the coasts of South Carolina, Georgia and Florida.

Islands within the boundaries of South Carolina include Parris Island, Port Royal Island, and St. Helena Island.

Those within Georgia include Cumberland Island (largest in the chain), St. Simons Island and St. Catherines Island (no apostrophes), and Sea Island.

Amelia Island is within the boundaries of Florida.

Several communities have names taken from the island name — Port Royal is a town on Port Royal Island, Sea Island is a resort on Sea Island, and St. Simons Island is a village on St. Simons Island.

In datelines:
PORT ROYAL, S.C. (AP) —
ST. SIMONS ISLAND, Ga. (AP) —

SEAL(s) A special operations force of the Navy. The acronym is for *sea, air, land.*
See **special forces**.

seaman See **military titles**.

search engine optimization Any of a number of methods, both human- and machine-powered, used to improve the prominence of online content in search engines, thus increasing traffic to the content. *SEO* is acceptable on second reference.

Sears Holdings Corp. The company formed when Kmart Holding Corp. bought Sears, Roebuck & Co. in 2005. Headquarters is in Hoffman Estates, Illinois.

seasons Lowercase *spring, summer, fall, winter* and derivatives such as *springtime* unless part of a formal name: *Dartmouth Winter Carnival, Winter Olympics, Summer Olympics.*

seat belt Two words.

Seattle The city in the state of Washington stands alone in datelines.

second guess (n.) The verb form: *second-guess.* Also: *second-guesser.*

second hand (n.) **secondhand** (adj. and adv.)

second-rate (adj.)

second reference When used in this book, the term applies to all subsequent references to an organization or individual within a story.

Acceptable abbreviations and acronyms for organizations frequently in the news are listed under the organization's full name. A few prominent acronyms acceptable on first reference also are listed alphabetically according to the letters of the acronym.

The listing of an acceptable term for second reference does not mean that it always must be used after the first reference. Often a generic word such as *the agency, the commission* or *the company* is more appropriate and less jarring to the reader. At other times, the full name may need to be repeated for clarity.

For additional guidelines that apply to organizations, see **abbreviations and acronyms** and **capitalization**.

For additional guidelines that apply to individuals, see **courtesy titles** and **titles**.

secretary Capitalize before a name only if it is an official corporate or organizational title. Do not abbreviate.
See **titles**.

secretary-general With a hyphen. Capitalize as a formal title before a name: *Secretary-General Ban Ki-moon*.
See **titles**.

secretary of state Capitalize as a formal title before a name.
See **titles**.

secretary-treasurer With a hyphen. Capitalize as a formal title before a name.
See **titles**.

Secret Service A federal agency administered by the Department of Homeland Security.

The *Secret Service Uniformed Division*, which protects the president's residence and offices and the embassies in Washington, formerly was known as the Executive Protective Service.

section Capitalize when used with a figure to identify part of a law or bill: *Section 14B of the Taft-Hartley Act*.

Securities and Exchange Commission *SEC* is acceptable on second reference.

The related legislation is the *Securities Exchange Act* (no *and*).

securitization Bundling together individual assets, such as mortgages, and selling stakes to investors.

Security Council (U.N.) *Security Council* may be used on first reference in stories under a United Nations dateline. Use *U.N. Security Council* in other first references.

Retain capitalization of *Security Council* in all references.

Lowercase *council* whenever it stands alone.

Seeing Eye dog A trademark for a guide dog trained by Seeing Eye Inc. of Morristown, New Jersey. *Guide dog* is preferred in all references.

seesaw

self- Always hyphenate:
self-assured   self-government
self-defense

selfie A self-portrait photo generally taken with a camera-equipped phone or webcam.

sellout (n.) **sell out** (v.)

semi- The rules in **prefixes** apply, but in general, no hyphen.
Some examples:
semifinal   semiofficial
semi-invalid   semitropical
But semi-automatic , semi-autonomous.

semiannual Twice a year, a synonym for *biannual*.
Do not confuse it with *biennial*, which means *every two years*.

semicolon See entry in **Punctuation**

chapter.

semitrailer Or *semitractor-trailer*, but not *semi-tractor trailer*.

Senate Capitalize all specific references to governmental legislative bodies, regardless of whether the name of the state or nation is used: *the U.S. Senate, the Senate, the Virginia Senate, the state Senate, the Senate.*
>   Lowercase plural uses: *the Virginia and North Carolina senates.*
>   See **governmental bodies**.
>   Lowercase references to non-governmental bodies: *the student senate at Yale.*

senatorial Always lowercase.

senator, Sen. See **legislative titles** and **party affiliation**.

send-off (n.) **send off** (v.)

senior See **junior, senior**.

senior citizen Use the term sparingly. See **elderly**.

sentences Capitalize the first word of every sentence, including quoted statements and direct questions:
>   *Patrick Henry said, "I know not what course others may take, but as for me, give me liberty or give me death."*
>   Capitalize the first word of a quoted statement if it constitutes a sentence, even if it was part of a larger sentence in the original: *Patrick Henry said, "Give me liberty or give me death."*
>   In direct questions, even without quotation marks: *The story answers the question, Where does true happiness really lie?*
>   Use a single space between

sentences.
>   See **ellipsis** in **Punctuation** chapter and **poetry**.

Sept. 11 The term for describing the attacks in the United States on Sept. 11, 2001. Use 2001 if needed for clarity. Also acceptable is 9/11. See **9/11**.

Sept. 11 memorial Acceptable in all references to the *National September 11 Memorial & Museum* at *ground zero*. Add location for other memorials with similar names.

sergeant See **military titles**.

sergeant-at-arms

serial numbers Use figures and capital letters in solid form (no hyphens or spaces unless the source indicates they are an integral part of the code): *A1234567.*

server A computer program that responds to requests from remote computers on a network. A web server, for instance, hosts websites and delivers pages to users upon demand. A file server, in another example, stores and delivers documents to users on a network. A server often runs on a specialized computer, though PCs are capable of running such software. The word *server* can also denote the computer on which the server software runs.

serviceable

service clubs See **fraternal organizations and service clubs**.

Service Employees International Union A Washington, D.C.-based labor organization that represents

S

a wide array of service-industry workers in the United States, Puerto Rico and Canada. *SEIU* is acceptable on second reference.

serviceman, servicewoman But *service member*.

sesquicentennial A 150-year period.

setup (n. and adj.) **set up** (v.)

Seven Seas Arabian Sea, Atlantic Ocean, Bay of Bengal, Mediterranean Sea, Persian Gulf, Red Sea, South China Sea.

Seven Wonders of the World The Egyptian pyramids, the hanging gardens of Babylon, the Mausoleum at Halicarnassus, the temple of Artemis at Ephesus, the Colossus of Rhodes, the statue of Zeus by Phidias at Olympia and the Pharos or lighthouse at Alexandria.

sewage Use this term, not *sewerage*, for both the waste matter and the drainage system.

sexual assault See **sexual harassment, sexual misconduct**; **privacy**.

sexual harassment, sexual misconduct These are broad terms that can cover a wide variety of actions or behavior. In stories, be as specific as possible in describing the kinds of behavior that is being alleged or admitted — such as groping, unwanted kissing, disrobing, or verbal or physical abuse or assault.

If a shorter term is needed, for example in a headline, AP uses the generalized description *sexual misconduct*, rather than *sexual harassment*, because it encompasses a broader range of sexual misbehavior and does not run the risk of diminishing some of the alleged acts.

As with all accusations, these allegations should be well-documented and corroborated in some way, including an effort to get comment from the accused individuals or their representatives.

Granting anonymity to accusers should follow AP's strict guidelines on the use of anonymity.

See **anonymous sources**; **privacy**.

sexually transmitted diseases *STDs* is acceptable on second reference.

shah Capitalize when used as a title before a name: *Shah Mohammad Reza Pahlavi of Iran.*

The Shah of Iran commonly is known only by this title, which is, in effect, an alternate name. Capitalize *Shah of Iran* in references to the holder of the title; lowercase subsequent references as *the shah*.

The practice is based on the guidelines in the **nobility** entry.

shake-up (n. and adj.) **shake up** (v.)

shall, will Use *shall* to express determination: *We shall overcome. You and he shall stay.*

Either *shall* or *will* may be used in first-person constructions that do not emphasize determination: *We shall hold a meeting. We will hold a meeting.*

For second- and third-person constructions, use *will* unless determination is stressed: *You will like it. She will not be pleased.*

See **should, would** and **subjunctive mood**.

Shanghai The city in China stands

alone in datelines.

shape-up (n. and adj.) **shape up** (v.)

she Do not use this pronoun in references to ships or nations. Use *it* instead.

Sheetrock A trademark for a brand of gypsum wallboard or plasterboard.

sheikh A title for a religious or tribal leader. Also used as a term of respect. For second references, follow local practices regarding whether *sheikh* should be repeated, and which name or names should be used after the term: *Sheikh Mohammad.*

shell See **weapons**.

sheriff Capitalize when used as a formal title before a name. See **titles**.

ships See **boats, ships**.

shoeshine, shoestring

short An investment term used to describe the position held by individuals who sell stock that they do not yet own by borrowing from their broker in order to deliver to the purchaser.
A person selling short is betting that the price of the stock will fall.

shortchange

short covering The purchase of a security to repay shares of a security borrowed from a broker.

short-lived (adj.) *A short-lived plan. The plan was short-lived.*

short sale In financial markets, a sale

of securities that are not owned by the sellers at the time of sale but which they intend to purchase or borrow in time to make delivery. *Short selling* is a bet that a stock's price will fall. In real estate, a *short sale* is when a bank lets homeowners sell their homes for less than they owe on the mortgage.

short ton Equal to 2,000 pounds. See **ton**.

shot See **weapons**.

shotgun See **weapons**.

should, would Use *should* to express an obligation: *We should help the needy.*
Use *would* to express a customary action: *In the summer we would spend hours by the seashore.*
Use *would* also in constructing a conditional past tense, but be careful:
Wrong: *If Soderholm would not have had an injured foot, Thompson would not have been in the lineup.*
Right: *If Soderholm had not had an injured foot, Thompson would not have been in the lineup.*
See **subjunctive mood**.

shoutout (n.) **shout out** (v.)

showcase, showroom, showtime

showoff (n.) **show off** (v.)

shrapnel Small metal balls from explosive artillery shells or hurled pieces of bombs, hand grenades or similar devices. Use *fragments* to describe particles from objects other than armaments that detonate or disintegrate.

S

shrubs See **plants**.

shutdown (n.) **shut down** (v.)

shut-in

shut-off (n.) **shut off** (v.)

shutout (n.) **shut out** (v.)

(sic) Use the Latin word meaning *thus* or *so* to show that quoted material or person's words include a misspelling, incorrect grammar or peculiar usage. Place (*sic*) in the text directly after the problem to show that the passage is precisely reproduced. Do not insert (*sic*) for quoted material that may be open to challenge, such as a political assertion. Specify that outside the quote in a separate sentence.

To call attention to (*sic*) in wire versions of the story, use an editor's note atop the story. The Eds. note will not appear in the online version.

— — —

Eds. note: [Eds: (sic) in a quote indicates a grammatical error in the original document]
or
Eds. note: [Eds: (sic) indicates the spelling Jorga is correct]

Sicily Use instead of Italy in datelines on stories from communities on this island.

side by side, side-by-side *They walked side by side. The stories received side-by-side display.*

Siemens AG Headquarters is in Munich.

Sierra Nevada, the Not *Sierra Nevada mountains* or *Sierra Nevada mountain range.* (*Sierra* means mountain range.)

sightseeing, sightseer

sign-up (n. and adj.) **sign up** (v.)

Silicon Valley High-tech region encompassing the northern Santa Clara Valley and adjacent areas of Northern California.

Sinai Not *the Sinai.* But: *the Sinai Desert, the Sinai Peninsula.*

Singapore Stands alone in datelines.

Singapore Airlines Headquarters of this airline is in Singapore.

single-handed, single-handedly

sister-in-law, sisters-in-law

sit-down (n. and adj.) **sit down** (v.)

sit-in (n. and adj.) **sit in** (v.)

situp (n.) **sit up** (v.)

sizable

sizes Use figures: *a size 8 dress, size 40 long, 10 1/2B shoes, a 34 1/2 sleeve.*

skeptic See **cynic, skeptic**.

skid row A dilapidated urban area inhabited by a group or groups of homeless, vagrant, derelict or severely impoverished people.

skillful

ski, skis, skier, skied, skiing Also: *ski jump, ski jumping.*

Skype A service, owned by Microsoft Corp., that allows users to communicate by voice, video and instant message over the internet. *Skype* is used informally as a verb for using the service, particularly when communicating on video.

SkyWest Inc. Headquarters of this airline is in St. George, Utah.

slang In general, avoid slang, the highly informal language that is outside of conventional or standard usage.
See **colloquialisms** and **dialect**.

slaying See **homicide, murder, manslaughter**.

sledgehammer

sleet See **weather terms**.

sleight of hand

slideshow

slowdown (n.) **slow down** (v.)

slumlord

slush fund

small-arms fire

smartphone An advanced mobile phone, such as an iPhone or Samsung Galaxy phone, that can be used to check email, browse the web and launch applications. Also: *smartwatch*. But *smart home, smart car*.

smashup (n. and adj.) **smash up** (v.)

Smithsonian Institution Not *Smithsonian Institute*.

smoke bomb, smoke screen

smokejumper One word, lowercase, for the firefighter who gets to fires by aircraft and parachute.

Smokey Or *Smokey Bear*. Not *Smokey the Bear*.
But: *A smoky room*.

smolder Not *smoulder*.

SMS An abbreviation for *Short Message Service*. *Text messaging* is preferred.

snafu Acceptable despite its vulgar origin.

Snapchat A mobile messaging app in which users can capture photos or brief video clips, add text or drawings and share them with friends, who will then be able to see them for a brief period of time defined by the sender. Snapchat "stories" give users the option of publishing content and making it viewable for a full 24 hours, and a Discover section features stories from a handful of media organizations. Use lowercase *snap* for a Snapchat posting. Headquarters in Venice, California.

sneaked Preferred as past tense of *sneak*. Do not use the colloquial *snuck*.

snowdrift, snowfall, snowflake, snowman, snowplow, snowshoe, snowstorm, snowsuit

so called (adv.) **so-called** (adj.) Use sparingly. Do not follow with quotation marks. Example: *He is accused of trading so-called blood diamonds to finance the war.*

socialist, socialism See **political parties and philosophies**.

S

Social Security Capitalize all references to the U.S. system.

The number groups are hyphenated: *123-45-6789*

Lowercase generic uses such as: *Is there a social security program in Sweden?*

Society for the Prevention of Cruelty to Animals *SPCA* is acceptable on second reference.

The *American Society for the Prevention of Cruelty to Animals* is limited to the five boroughs of New York City.

The autonomous chapters in other cities ordinarily precede the organization by the name of the city: On first reference, *the San Francisco Society for the Prevention of Cruelty to Animals*; on second, *the San Francisco SPCA* or *the SPCA* as appropriate in the context.

Society of Professional Journalists (no longer the Society of Professional Journalists, Sigma Delta Chi). On second reference: *SPJ*.

soft-spoken

software titles Capitalize but do not use quotation marks around such titles as WordPerfect or Windows, but use quotation marks for computer games: "Where in the World Is Carmen Sandiego?"

solicitor See **lawyer**.

soliloquy, soliloquies

solvency The ability to pay expenses and debt on time and continue operating. An insolvent company typically has to seek bankruptcy protection from creditors.

Somali A person from Somalia, or an adjective for something linked to Somalia. Do not use *Somalian*.

song titles See **composition titles**.

son-in-law, sons-in-law

SOS The distress signal.

S.O.S (no final period) is a trademark for a brand of soap pad.

sound barrier The speed of sound is no longer a true barrier because aircraft have exceeded it. See **Mach number**.

soundstage

source Avoid the term if possible. Be as specific as possible about the source of information. If space is limited, use *source* as a last resort. *Official* or a similar word will often suffice, including in headlines. See **anonymous sources**.

source code The basic blueprint of a computer program.

South As defined by the U.S. Census Bureau, the 16-state region is broken into three divisions.

The four *East South Central* states are Alabama, Kentucky, Mississippi and Tennessee.

The eight *South Atlantic* states are Delaware, Florida, Georgia, Maryland, North Carolina, South Carolina, Virginia and West Virginia.

The four *West South Central* states are Arkansas, Louisiana, Oklahoma and Texas.

There is no official U.S. Census Bureau definition of Southeast.

See **Midwest region**; **Northeast region**; and **West** for the bureau's other regional breakdowns.

S

South America See **Western Hemisphere**.

South Carolina Abbreviate *S.C.* in datelines only; spell out in stories. Postal code: *SC*
See **state names**.

South Dakota Abbreviate *S.D.* in datelines only; spell out in stories. Postal code: *SD*
See **state names**.

Southeast Asia The nations of the Indochina Peninsula and the islands southeast of it: Cambodia, Indonesia, Laos, Malaysia, Myanmar, Papua New Guinea, the Philippines, Singapore, Thailand and Vietnam.
See **Asian subcontinent** and **Far East**.

south, southern, southeast, southwest See **directions and regions**.

Southwest Airlines Co.
Headquarters of this airline is in Dallas.

Soviet Union See **Commonwealth of Independent States**.

Space Age It began with the launching of Sputnik 1 on Oct. 4, 1957.

space agency See **National Aeronautics and Space Administration**.

space centers See **John F. Kennedy Space Center** and **Lyndon B. Johnson Space Center**.

spacecraft designations Use Arabic figures and capitalize the name: *Gemini 7, Apollo 11, Pioneer 10*. See **numerals**.

spaceship

space shuttle Lowercase *space shuttle*, but capitalize a proper name.
The space shuttle was a reusable winged spaceship capable of carrying people and cargo into Earth orbit. NASA'S shuttles flew from 1981 until 2011, logging 135 missions. Two of the five shuttles were destroyed in flight, Challenger in 1986 and Columbia in 2003.

spacewalk

spam, Spam Use *spam* in all references to unsolicited commercial or bulk email, often advertisements. Use *Spam*, a trademark, to refer to a canned meat product.

Spanish-American War

Spanish names The family names of both the father and mother usually are considered part of a person's full name. In everyday use, customs sometimes vary with individuals and countries.
The normal sequence is given name, father's family name, mother's family name: *Gabriel Garcia Marquez*.
On second reference, use only the father's family name (*Garcia*), unless the individual prefers or is widely known by a multiple last name (*Garcia Marquez*).
Some individuals use a *y* (for *and*) between the two surnames to ensure that both names are used together (including second references): *Gabriel Garcia y Marquez*.
A married woman sometimes uses her father's name, followed by the particle *de* (for *of*) and her husband's name. A woman named *Irma Perez* who married a man named *Anibal Gutierrez* would be known as *Irma*

Perez de Gutierrez.

speaker Capitalize as a formal title before a name. Generally, it is a formal title only for the speaker of a legislative body: *Speaker John Boehner.*
    See **titles**.

special contexts When this term is used in this book, it means that the material described may be used in a regular column devoted to a specialized subject or when a particular literary effect is suitable.
    Special literary effects generally are suitable only in feature copy, but even there they should be used with care. Most feature material should follow the same style norms that apply to regular news copy.

special forces Do not use interchangeably with *special operations forces*. Capitalize when referring specifically to the *U.S. Army Special Forces*, also known as Green Berets. Others, such as Navy SEALs or Army Rangers, should be called *special operations forces*.

species Same in singular and plural. Use singular or plural verbs and pronouns depending on the sense: *The species has been unable to maintain itself. Both species are extinct.*
    See **genus, species**.

speeches Capitalize and use quotation marks for their formal titles, as described in **composition titles**.

speechmaker, speechmaking

speed of sound See **Mach number**.

speeds Use figures. *The car slowed to 7 mph, winds of 5 to 10 mph, winds of 7 to 9 knots, 10-knot wind.*
    Avoid extensively hyphenated constructions such as *5-mile-per-hour winds*.
    See **numerals**.

speedup (n. and adj.) **speed up** (v.)

spelling The basic rule when in doubt is to consult this book followed by, if necessary, a dictionary under conditions described in the **dictionaries** entry.
    Memory aid: Noah Webster developed the following rule of thumb for the frequently vexing question of whether to double a final consonant in forming the present participle and past tense of a verb:
— If the stress in pronunciation is on the first syllable, do not double the consonant: *combat, combating, combated; cancel, canceling, canceled.*
— If the stress in pronunciation is on the second syllable, double the consonant unless confusion would result: *incur, incurred, incurring.* An exception, to avoid confusion with *buss*, is *bus, bused, busing.*
    Avoid spelling simplifications such as *lite*. Exception: *thru* allowed in some compounds: *drive-thru, writethru.*
    British spellings, when they differ from American, are acceptable only in particular cases such as formal or composition titles: *Jane's Defence Weekly, Labour Party, Excel Centre, London Palladium Theatre, Wimbledon's Centre Court.*

spill, spilled, spilling Not *spilt* in the past tense.

spinoff (n.) A distribution that occurs when the company forms a separate company out of a division, a subsidiary or other holdings. The shares of the new company are distributed proportionately to the parent company holders.

Spirit Airlines Headquarters is in Miramar, Florida.

split infinitive See **verbs**.

spokesman, spokeswoman, spokesperson Use *spokesperson* if it is the preference of an individual or an organization.

sports writer This is an exception to Webster's New World College Dictionary.

sport utility vehicle No plural *s* in *sport*; no hyphen.
   SUV is acceptable on first reference.

spot market A market for buying or selling commodities or foreign exchange for immediate delivery and for cash payment.

spot price The price of a commodity available for immediate sale and delivery. The term is also used to refer to foreign exchange transactions.

spouse A gender-neutral alternative in place of *wife* or *husband*. For example: *physicians and their spouses*, not *physicians and their wives*.

spree This term is usually applied to shopping or revelry. Do not use in other circumstances: *killing spree*.

spring See **seasons**.

springtime

sputnik Usually lowercase, but capitalize when followed by a figure as part of a proper name: *Sputnik 1*. It is Russian for *satellite*.

squall See **weather terms**.

square Do not abbreviate. Capitalize when part of a proper name: *Washington Square*.

Sri Lanka Formerly Ceylon. Use *Sri Lanka* in datelines and other references to the nation.
   The people may be called either *Sri Lankans* or *Ceylonese*.
   Before the nation was called Ceylon, it was Serendip, whence comes the word *serendipity*.

SRO Acceptable on second reference for *standing room only*.

SST Acceptable in all references for a *supersonic transport*.

stadium, stadiums Capitalize only when part of a proper name: *Dodger Stadium*.

Stalin, Josef Not *Joseph*.

stall Use care when using *stall* in this sense: when an automobile *stalls*, the engine stops. This may not be true when an airplane *stalls*; it pitches forward or sideways because of a lack of air speed.

stamp, stomp Both are acceptable, but *stamp* is preferred.

stanch, staunch *Stanch* is a verb: *He stanched the flow of blood.*
   Staunch is an adjective: *She is a staunch supporter of equality.*

stand-alone (adj.)

S

Standard & Poor's 500 index See
  S&P 500.

standard-bearer

standard time Capitalize *Eastern
  Standard Time, Pacific Standard Time,*
  etc., but lowercase *standard time*
  when standing alone.
  See **time zones**.

stand-in (n. and adj.) **stand in** (v.)

standoff (n. and adj.) **stand off** (v.)

standout (n. and adj.) **stand out** (v.)

starboard Nautical for *right,* when
  facing the bow, or forward. See **port,
  starboard**.

"The Star-Spangled Banner" But
  lowercase *the national anthem.*

startup One word (n. and adj.) to
  describe a new business venture. An
  exception to Webster's New World
  College Dictionary preference.

"Star Wars" Enclosed in quotes
  in references to the movie series,
  entertainment spinoffs and the
  Strategic Defense Initiative against
  nuclear attack of the 1980s. Also:
  "Star Wars" Day, "Star Wars"
  Canyon.

state Lowercase in all *state of*
  constructions: *the state of Maine, the
  states of Maine and Vermont.*
  Four states — Kentucky,
  Massachusetts, Pennsylvania
  and Virginia — are legally
  commonwealths rather than states.
  The distinction is necessary only
  in formal uses: *The commonwealth
  of Kentucky filed a suit.* For simple
  geographic reference: *Tobacco is*

grown in the state of Kentucky.
  Do not capitalize *state* when
  used simply as an adjective to
  specify a level of jurisdiction:
  *state Rep. William Smith, the state
  Transportation Department, state
  funds.*
  Apply the same principle to
  phrases such as *the city of Chicago, the
  town of Auburn,* etc.
  See also **state names**.

statehouse Capitalize all references
  to a specific statehouse, with or
  without the name of the state: *The
  Vermont Statehouse is in Montpelier.
  The governor will visit the Statehouse
  today.*
  Lowercase plural uses: *the
  Massachusetts and Rhode Island
  statehouses.*

state names Follow these guidelines:
  SPELL OUT: The names of the
  50 U.S. states should be spelled
  out when used in the body of a
  story, whether standing alone or
  in conjunction with a city, town,
  village or military base. No state
  name is necessary if it is the same
  as the dateline. This also applies
  to newspapers cited in a story.
  For example, a story datelined
  Providence, R.I., would reference the
  Providence Journal, not the *Providence
  (Rhode Island) Journal.* See **datelines**.
  EIGHT NOT ABBREVIATED: The names
  of eight states are never abbreviated
  in datelines or text: *Alaska, Hawaii,
  Idaho, Iowa, Maine, Ohio, Texas* and
  Utah.
  Memory aid: Spell out the names
  of the two states that are not part of
  the contiguous United States and of
  the continental states that are five
  letters or fewer.
  IN THE BODY OF STORIES: Except
  for cities that stand alone in

datelines, use the state name in textual material when the city or town is not in the same state as the dateline, or where necessary to avoid confusion: *Springfield, Massachusetts,* or *Springfield, Illinois.* Provide a state identification for the city if the story has no dateline, or if the city is not in the same state as the dateline. However, cities that stand alone in datelines may be used alone in stories that have no dateline if no confusion would result.

ABBREVIATIONS REQUIRED: Use the state abbreviations listed at the end of this section:
— In conjunction with the name of a city, town, village or military base in most datelines. See **datelines** for examples and exceptions for large cities.
— In lists, agate, tabular material, nonpublishable editor's notes and credit lines.
— In short-form listings of party affiliation: *D-Ala., R-Mont.* See **party affiliation** entry for details.

Following are the state abbreviations, which also appear in the entries for each state (postal code abbreviations in parentheses):

Ala. (AL)	Md. (MD)	N.D. (ND)
Ariz. (AZ)	Mass. (MA)	Okla. (OK)
Ark. (AR)	Mich. (MI)	Ore. (OR)
Calif. (CA)	Minn. (MN)	Pa. (PA)
Colo. (CO)	Miss. (MS)	R.I. (RI)
Conn. (CT)	Mo. (MO)	S.C. (SC)
Del. (DE)	Mont. (MT)	S.D. (SD)
Fla. (FL)	Neb. (NE)	Tenn. (TN)
Ga. (GA)	Nev. (NV)	Vt. (VT)
Ill. (IL)	N.H. (NH)	Va. (VA)
Ind. (IN)	N.J. (NJ)	Wash. (WA)
Kan. (KS)	N.M. (NM)	W.Va. (WV)
Ky. (KY)	N.Y. (NY)	Wis. (WI)
La. (LA)	N.C. (NC)	Wyo. (WY)

These are the postal code abbreviations for the eight states that are not abbreviated in datelines or text: AK (Alaska), HI (Hawaii), ID (Idaho), IA (Iowa), ME (Maine), OH (Ohio), TX (Texas), UT (Utah). Also: District of Columbia (DC).

Use the two-letter Postal Service abbreviations only with full addresses, including ZIP code.

PUNCTUATION: Place one comma between the city and the state name, and another comma after the state name, unless ending a sentence or indicating a dateline: *He was traveling from Nashville, Tennessee, to Austin, Texas, en route to his home in Albuquerque, New Mexico. She said Cook County, Illinois, was Mayor Daley's stronghold.*

HEADLINES: Avoid using state abbreviations in headlines whenever possible.

MISCELLANEOUS: Use *New York state* when necessary to distinguish the state from New York City.

Use *state of Washington* or *Washington state* within a story when it's necessary to differentiate the state name from the U.S. capital, Washington. It's written Washington, D.C., with the added abbreviation only if the city might be confused with the state.

State of the Union Capitalize all references to the president's annual address.

Lowercase other uses: *"The state of the union is confused,"* the editor said.

state police Capitalize with a state name if part of the formal description for a police agency: *the New York State Police, the Virginia State Police.*

In most cases, state police standing alone is a shorthand reference for *state policemen* rather than a reference to the agency. For consistency and to avoid hairline distinctions about whether the reference is to the agency or the

officers, lowercase the words *state police* whenever they are not preceded by a state name.
See **highway patrol**.

states' rights

statewide

stationary, stationery To stand still is to be *stationary*.
Writing paper is *stationery*.

statute mile It equals 5,280 feet, or approximately 1.6 kilometers.
To convert to approximate nautical miles, multiply the number of statute miles by .869.
See **kilometer**; **knot**; **mile**; and **nautical mile**.

staunch See **stanch, staunch**.

St. Barts, St. Martin In general, use the English spellings for these Caribbean islands. *St. Martin* is divided by its northern French side, called *Saint-Martin* in French, and its southern Dutch side, called *Sint Maarten* in Dutch. In some uses, if referring specifically to the French half of the island it can be *Saint-Martin*, and if referring specifically to the Dutch side it can be *St. Maarten*. But explain in copy: *The island known as St. Martin in English is divided between French Saint-Martin and Dutch Sint Maarten.* For *St. Barts*, use *Saint Barthelemy* only if needed in quotes, and explain that it is the French name.

stealth When used in connection with military aircraft, ships and vehicles it means the equipment is masked from various types of electronic detection. Stealth equipment can range from radar wave absorbing paint to electronic jamming devices. Like the *cruise missile*, always lowercase, no quotation marks.

stem cell

stepbrother, stepfather Also: *stepsister, stepmother*.

steppingstone

St. John's The city in the Canadian province of Newfoundland and Labrador.
Not to be confused with *Saint John, New Brunswick*.

St. Louis The city in Missouri stands alone in datelines.

stockbroker

Stockholm The city in Sweden stands alone in datelines.

stock index futures Futures contracts valued on the basis of indexes that track the prices of a specific group of stocks. The most widely traded is the future based on the Standard & Poor's 500 stock index. Speculators also trade options on index futures.

stock prices Prices are quoted in dollars and cents. Use active verbs: *Microsoft stock fell 10 cents to $38.01 in afternoon trading.* Avoid rounding individual stock prices in stories. If individual stock prices are rounded, the story should include context. *The stock rose above $100 for the first time.* In headlines, rounding down is acceptable.
When writing about indexes, carry out decimals two places. *The Dow Jones industrial average rose 78.73 points, or 0.5 percent, to close at*

S

16,438.91. However, it is acceptable to round down in shorter stories. *The Dow rose to 16,438.*

stopgap

storm See **weather terms**.

stormwater

storyline

storyteller

straight-laced, strait-laced Use *straight-laced* for someone strict or severe in behavior or moral views.
Reserve *strait-laced* for the notion of confinement, as in a corset.

strait Capitalize as part of a proper name: *Bering Strait, Strait of Gibraltar.*
But: *the Bosporus* and *the Dardanelles.* Neither is followed by *Strait.*

straitjacket

Strategic Arms Reduction Treaty
START is acceptable on first reference to the treaty as long as it is made immediately clear which is being referred to.
Use the *strategic arms treaty* or the *treaties* in some references to avoid alphabet soup.
There are three START treaties:
— START I, signed in 1991.
— START II, signed in 1992. Ratified by U.S. Senate, but never took effect because Senate did not adopt the 1997 protocol and several amendments to Anti-Ballistic Missile treaty demanded by Russian Duma. Shelved by Russia in 2002 after U.S withdrew from ABM treaty.
— New START, signed in 2010.
— Do not confuse with the *Strategic Arms Limitation Treaty* of 1979, known as *SALT.*

street Abbreviate only with a numbered address. See **addresses**.

strikebreaker

strong-arm (v. and adj.)

strong-willed

Styrofoam A trademark for a brand of plastic foam. Use the term *plastic foam* unless referring specifically to the trademarked product. (Note: Cups and other serving items are not made of *Styrofoam* brand plastic foam.)

sub- The rules in **prefixes** apply, but in general, no hyphen. Some examples:
subbasement   submachine gun
subcommittee suborbital
subculture   subtotal
subdivision   subzero

subcommittee Lowercase when used with the name of a legislative body's full committee: *a Ways and Means subcommittee.*
Capitalize when a subcommittee has a proper name of its own: *the Senate Permanent Subcommittee on Investigations.*

subject See **citizen, resident, subject, national, native**.

subjunctive mood Use the subjunctive mood of a verb for contrary-to-fact conditions, and expressions of doubts, wishes or regrets:
If I were a rich man, I wouldn't have to work hard.

S

I doubt that more money would be the answer.

I wish it were possible to take back my words.

Sentences that express a contingency or hypothesis may use either the subjunctive or the indicative mood depending on the context. In general, use the subjunctive if there is little likelihood that a contingency might come true:

If I were to marry a millionaire, I wouldn't have to worry about money.

If the bill passes as expected, it will provide an immediate tax cut.

See **should, would**.

submachine gun See **weapons**.

subpoena, subpoenaed, subpoenaing

subprime A class of borrowers characterized by tarnished credit histories. These borrowers usually entail greater risk for lenders so they are charged a higher interest rate for a loan.

successor

Sudan Use *Sudan* for the East African country whose capital is *Khartoum*. *South Sudan* is the country in the southern region that declared independence July 9, 2011. Its capital is *Juba*.

suffixes See separate listings for commonly used suffixes.

Follow Webster's New World College Dictionary for words not in this book.

If a word combination is not listed in Webster's New World College Dictionary, use two words for the verb form; hyphenate any noun or adjective forms.

suicide Generally, AP does not cover suicides or suicide attempts, unless the person involved is a well-known figure or the circumstances are particularly unusual or publicly disruptive. Suicide stories, when written, should not go into detail on methods used.

Avoid using *committed suicide* except in direct quotations from authorities. Alternate phrases include *killed himself, took her own life* or *died by suicide*. The verb *commit* with *suicide* can imply a criminal act. Laws against suicide have been repealed in the United States and many other places.

Do not refer to an *unsuccessful suicide attempt*. Refer instead to an *attempted suicide*.

Medically assisted suicide is permitted in some states and countries. Advocacy groups call it *death with dignity* or *right-to-die*, but AP doesn't use those phrases on their own. When referring to legislation whose name includes *death with dignity, right-to-die* or similar terms, say the law or proposal allows *the terminally ill to end their own lives*. If the term is in the name of a bill or law, make that clear. *Euthanasia* should not be used to describe *medically assisted suicide* or *physician-assisted suicide*.

suit, suite You may have a *suit* of clothes, a *suit* of cards, or be faced with a *lawsuit*.

There are *suites* of music, rooms and furniture.

summer See **seasons**.

summertime

S

sun Lowercase. See **heavenly bodies**.

sunbathe The verb forms: *sunbathed, sunbathing*. Also: *sunbather*.

Sun Belt Generally those states in the South and West, ranging from Florida and Georgia through the Gulf states into California.

super Avoid the slang tendency to use it in place of *excellent, wonderful*, etc.

super- The rules in **prefixes** apply, but in general, no hyphen. Some frequently used words:
superagency   superhighway
supercarrier   superpower
supercharge   supertanker
As with all prefixes, however, use a hyphen if the word that follows is capitalized: *super-Republican*.

Super Bowl

superconducting super collider

superintendent Do not abbreviate. Capitalize when used as a formal title before a name.
See **titles**.

superior court See **court names**.

supersede

supersonic See **Mach number**.

supersonic transport *SST* is acceptable in all references.

Supreme Court of the United States Capitalize *U.S. Supreme Court* and also *the Supreme Court* when the context makes the *U.S.* designation unnecessary.
The chief justice is properly the *chief justice of the United States*, not *of*

the Supreme Court: *Chief Justice John Roberts*.
The proper title for the eight other members of the court is *associate justice*. When used as a formal title before a name, it should be shortened to justice unless there are special circumstances: *Justice Ruth Bader Ginsburg, Associate Justice Ruth Bader Ginsburg*.
See **judge**.

supreme courts of the states
Capitalize with the state name (*the New Jersey Supreme Court*) and without the state name when the context makes it unnecessary: *the state Supreme Court, the Supreme Court*.
If a court with this name is not a state's highest tribunal, the fact should be noted. In New York, for example, the Supreme Court is a trial court. Appeals are directed to the Appellate Division of the Supreme Court. The state's highest court is the Court of Appeals.

surface-to-air missile(s) *SAM(s)* may be used on second reference. Avoid the redundant *SAM missiles*.

survivor, victim Use these terms with care because they can be imprecise and politically and legally fraught.
Survivor can denote someone who has lived through an injury or disease, but also can apply to someone who endured a threat but escaped injury altogether. Example: *a mass shooting survivor*. Likewise, *victim* can create confusion because it can variously mean someone killed, injured or subjected to mistreatment such as sexual misconduct.
Be specific if there is room for confusion: *The ceremony honored*

people wounded in the mass shooting, not *The ceremony honored victims* and/or *survivors of the mass shooting. The play told the story of those killed in the hurricane,* not *The play told the stories of the hurricane's victims.*

Also be alert to potential biases and assumptions inherent in the word *victim.* A phrase such as *AIDS victim,* for instance, not only makes it unclear whether the subject is alive or dead, but many AIDS patients do not consider themselves victims. Instead, use neutral, precise descriptions: *He has AIDS. She has hepatitis.* In crime stories, avoid *alleged victim* if possible; it is too easily construed as skepticism. In stories in which sexual misconduct or other allegations are leveled, consider calling the person making the allegations an *accuser* instead of a *victim* if shorthand is needed, to avoid implications of guilt on the part of the accused.

Survivor is often used to describe people who have lived through physical or emotional trauma, as in *abuse* or *rape survivor.* It is best to be specific when referring to individuals, especially if the person was never in danger of death. Use of *survivor* gets more latitude when describing groups. *A group of Holocaust survivors met at the memorial.*

See **diseases; homicide, murder, manslaughter; allege; sexual harassment, sexual misconduct**.

SUV See **sport utility vehicle**.

swag Sometimes used to describe the free stuff at gift suites and in gift bags given to presenters and other award-show participants.

swastika

SWAT Acronym for *Special Weapons and Tactics.*

sweatpants, sweatshirt, sweatsuit

swing states States where voters have vacillated between Republican and Democratic candidates in the last three or four presidential elections.

Swiss International Air Lines Switzerland's national carrier. Headquarters in Basel, Switzerland.

Sydney The city in Australia stands alone in datelines.

syllabus, syllabuses

sync Short for synchronization; not *synch.* Also, *syncing.*

synthetic marijuana See **marijuana, medical marijuana**.

t

tablespoon, tablespoonfuls Equal to three teaspoons or one-half a fluid ounce.

The metric equivalent is approximately 15 milliliters.

See **liter** and **recipes**.

table tennis See **pingpong**.

tabular matter Exceptions may be made to the normal rules for abbreviations as necessary to make material fit. But make any abbreviations as clear as possible.

tailspin

tail wind

Taiwan An island off the coast of China that is self-governed by an elected government but also claimed by the People's Republic of China, which has viewed it as sovereign territory since a 1949 split amid civil war. See **China, "One-China" policy**.

take-home pay

takeoff (n. and adj.) **take off** (v.)

takeout (n. and adj.) **take out** (v.)

takeover (n. and adj.) **take over** (v.)

takeup (n. and adj.) **take up** (v.)

Taliban Extremist Islamic movement that ruled Afghanistan until ousted by U.S.-led coalition after the Sept. 11, 2001, attacks. The *Taliban* continue to operate as an insurgent force with adherents in Afghanistan and Pakistan. The name derives from the Arabic word for religious students. The word *Taliban* normally takes a plural verb.

Talmud The collection of writings that constitute the Jewish civil and religious law.

tanks Use Arabic figures, separated from letters by a hyphen: *M-60*. Plural: *M-60s*.

taps Lowercase (without quotation marks) the bugle call for "lights out," also sounded at military funerals.

Target Corp. Headquarters is in Minneapolis.

Taser Trademark for stun gun. Use the generic form if the brand is uncertain. Don't use verbs like *tasered*. Exception: When verb forms appear in direct quotations, use lowercase.

Tass Acceptable on first reference for the Russian government's news agency that is officially *ITAR-Tass*. *ITAR* is an acronym for *Information Telegraph Agency of Russia*.

tattletale

tax-free (adj.)

tea party Movement in the United States that opposes the Washington political establishment and espouses conservative and libertarian

276

philosophy, including reduced government spending, lower taxes and reduction of the national debt and the federal budget deficit. Adherents are *tea partyers*. Formally named groups in the movement are capitalized: *Tea Party Express*.

teachers college No apostrophe.

team Use singular verb and pronoun "it" when referring to the team as a collective unit. However, the team name takes a plural verb: *The Orlando Magic are close to setting a franchise record.*
See **collective nouns**.

teammate

teamster Capitalize *teamster* only if the intended meaning is that the individual is a member of the International Brotherhood of Teamsters, Chauffeurs, Warehousemen and Helpers of America.

Teamsters union Acceptable in all references to the *International Brotherhood of Teamsters*.
See the entry under that name.

tear gas Two words. See also **Chemical Mace**.

teaspoon Equal to one-sixth of a fluid ounce, or one-third of a tablespoon.
The metric equivalent is approximately 5 milliliters.
See **liter**.

teaspoonful, teaspoonfuls Not *teaspoonsful*. See **recipes**.

teen, teenager (n.) **teenage** (adj.) Do not use *teen-aged*.

Teflon A trademark for a type of nonstick coating.

Tegna Inc. See **Gannett Co.**

telecast (n.) **televise** (v.)

telephone numbers Use figures. The form: *212-621-1500*. For international numbers use 011 (from the United States), the country code, the city code and the telephone number: *011-44-20-7535-1515*. Use hyphens, not periods.
The form for toll-free numbers: *800-111-1000*.
If extension numbers are needed, use a comma to separate the main number from the extension: *212-621-1500, ext. 2.*

teleprompter A generic term for an electronic device that rolls a prepared speech or script in front of politicians, award show hosts, presenters and other speakers.

television program titles Follow the guidelines in **composition titles**.
Put quotation marks around *show* only if it is part of the formal name. The word *show* may be dropped when it would be cumbersome, such as in a set of listings.
(Italics are used here only to illustrate examples; do not use italics on the wires.)
In text or listing, treat programs named after the star in any of the following ways: *"The Mary Tyler Moore Show," "Mary Tyler Moore"* or *the Mary Tyler Moore show*. But be consistent in a story or set of listings.
Use quotation marks also for the title of an episode: *"The Clean Room Infiltration," an episode of "The Big Bang Theory."* Also: *"NBC Nightly*

News," the "Today" show, "The Tonight Show."

television sets Most *TV* sets these days are flat-panel models that use liquid-crystal displays, or *LCDs*. These displays function by electronically controlling every pixel, or dot, on the screen. A backlight shines through a layer of liquid crystals; this layer essentially lets through or blocks the light at any given pixel to form the image. Most *LCD* sets are labeled as *LED* sets — a marketing term — and use light-emitting diodes as the backlight.

An older flat-panel technology, *plasma display*, is rarely used these days. The same is true for traditional bulky sets that use cathode-ray tubes.

TV is acceptable on any reference for television set. Other abbreviations in this entry, such as *HD*, *LCD*, *LED*, *4K*, etc., are acceptable on first reference, but should be spelled out and explained if a story dives into technological detail.

Modern televisions offer a sometimes bewildering array of display options. The most common:

RESOLUTION: High-definition television sets typically feature *720p* or *1080p* displays, designations that refer to the number of vertical and horizontal lines in the image. The *1080p* display offers a sharper image; it is also known as *full HD*.

Ultra-high definition, or *UHD*, offers even sharper images by using twice as many horizontal and vertical lines as *full HD*. While *UHD* has twice the resolution of *HD*, it has four times as many pixels. *UHD* is frequently also known as *4K TV*. Although more sets now offer 4K capabilities, programs and movies

are not universally available in 4K.

Television broadcasters are starting to experiment with *8K TV*. It has four times the resolution of *full HD*, and eight times as many pixels.

DVDs are not *full HD*; they display 480 vertical lines. Blu-ray disks offer full HD resolution.

PICTURE QUALITY: A variety of new technologies aim to improve the range and purity of displayed colors and the contrast between the brightest white and the darkest black. A higher contrast produces better-looking images.

So-called *OLED* screens use organic light-emitting diodes to illuminate each pixel. *OLED* sets are not *LCDs*; they have neither backlight nor a liquid-crystal layer. A rival *LCD* technology uses "quantum dots" to reflect light in a way designed to yield more precise colors.

LCDs, including quantum-dot sets, imperfectly filter out light, so they produce a black that is closer to dark gray. *OLED* produces pure blackness, but the displays are more expensive to produce.

Some manufacturers are also developing a feature called high-dynamic range, or *HDR*, for brighter whites, darker blacks and a wider range of colors. *HDR* is an add-on feature for both *OLED* and quantum-dot sets.

television station The call letters alone are frequently adequate, but when this phrase is needed, use lowercase: *television station WTEV*.

telltale

temblor See **earthquakes**.

temperatures Use figures for all

except *zero*. Use a word, not a minus sign, to indicate temperatures below zero.

Right: *The day's low was minus 10.*
Right: *The day's low was 10 below zero.*
Wrong: *The day's low was -10.*
Right: *The temperature rose to zero by noon.*
Right: *The day's high was expected to be 9 or 10.*
Also: *5-degree temperatures, temperatures fell 5 degrees, temperatures in the 30s* (no apostrophe).

Temperatures get *higher* or *lower*, but they don't get *warmer* or *cooler*.
Wrong: *Temperatures are expected to warm up in the area Friday.*
Right: *Temperatures are expected to rise in the area Friday.*
See **Fahrenheit; Celsius; numerals** and **weather terms**.

Temple Mount The walled, elevated area in Jerusalem's Old City that was the site of the ancient Jewish temples. It now houses the centuries-old Dome of the Rock shrine and Al-Aqsa Mosque and is known to Muslims as the *Haram al-Sharif,* or *Noble Sanctuary.* Muslims believe the Prophet Muhammad made his night journey to heaven from the site.

tenfold

Ten Most Wanted Fugitives The FBI's official list.

Tennessee Abbreviate *Tenn.* in datelines only; spell out in stories. Postal code: *TN*
See **state names**.

Tennessee Valley Authority *TVA* is acceptable on second reference.

Headquarters is in Knoxville, Tennessee.

tera- A prefix denoting 1 trillion units of a measure. Move the decimal point 12 places to the right, adding zeros if necessary, to convert to the basic unit: 5.5 teratons = 5,500,000,000,000 tons.

terabyte See **byte**.

terrace Do not abbreviate. See **addresses**.

Texas Do not abbreviate in datelines or stories. Postal code: *TX*
Second in total land area. See **state names**.

Texas Hold 'em The poker game.

text, texting, texted Acceptable in all usages as a verb for *to send a text message.*

texts, transcripts Follow normal style guidelines for capitalization, spelling and abbreviations in handling a text or transcript. Do not use a dateline.
Use quotation marks only for words or phrases that were quoted in the text or by the person who spoke.
Identify a change in speakers by starting a paragraph with the new speaker's name and a colon. Use normal second-reference forms if the speaker has been identified earlier; provide a full name and identification if the individual is being mentioned for the first time.
Use Q: for *question* and A: for *answer* at the start of paragraphs when these notations are adequate to identify a change in speakers.
See **ellipsis** in the **Punctuation** chapter for guidelines on condensing

texts and transcripts.

Thai A native or the language of Thailand.

Siam and *Siamese* are historical only.

Use *siamese* for the cat.

Thai Airways International PLC
Headquarters of this airline is in Bangkok, Thailand.

Thanksgiving, Thanksgiving Day
The fourth Thursday in November.

than, then *Than* is a conjunction used to compare things; *then* is an adverb used to place events in time or things in order. *He wrote a volume that was longer than the AP Stylebook, and then published it.*

that (conjunction) Use the conjunction *that* to introduce a dependent clause if the sentence sounds or looks awkward without it. There are no hard-and-fast rules, but in general:

— *That* usually may be omitted when a dependent clause immediately follows a form of the verb *to say*: *The president said he had signed the bill.*

— *That* should be used when a time element intervenes between the verb and the dependent clause: *The president said Monday that he had signed the bill.*

— *That* usually is necessary after some verbs. They include: *advocate, assert, contend, declare, estimate, make clear, point out, propose* and *state.*

— *That* is required before subordinate clauses beginning with conjunctions such as *after, although, because, before, in addition to, until* and *while*:

Haldeman said that after he learned of Nixon's intention to resign, he sought pardons for all connected with Watergate.

When in doubt, include *that.* Omission can hurt. Inclusion never does.

that, which (pronouns) Use *that* and *which* in referring to inanimate objects and to animals without a name. Use *that* for essential clauses, important to the meaning of a sentence, and without commas: *I remember the day that we met.* Use *which* for nonessential clauses, where the pronoun is less necessary, and use commas: *The team, which finished last a year ago, is in first place.*

(Tip: If you can drop the clause and not lose the meaning of the sentence, use *which*; otherwise, use *that.* A *which* clause is surrounded by commas; no commas are used with *that* clauses.)

See the **essential clauses, nonessential clauses** entry for guidelines on using *that* and *which* to introduce phrases and clauses.

theater Use this spelling unless the proper name is *Theatre*: *Shubert Theatre.*

theatergoer

theft See **burglary, larceny, robbery, theft**.

their, there, they're *Their* is a plural possessive pronoun that, in general, should agree in number with the antecedent. For exceptions, see **they, them, their**.

There is an adverb indicating direction: *We went there for dinner.*

There also is used with the force of a pronoun for impersonal constructions in which the real subject follows the verb: *There is no food on the table.*

They're is a contraction for *they are.*

thermos Formerly a trademark, now a generic term for any vacuum bottle, although one manufacturer still uses the word as a brand name.

Lowercase *thermos* when it is used to mean any vacuum bottle; use *Thermos* when referring to the specific brand.

they, them, their In most cases, a plural pronoun should agree in number with the antecedent: *The children love the books their uncle gave them. They/them/their* is acceptable in limited cases as a singular and/or gender-neutral pronoun, when alternative wording is overly awkward or clumsy. However, rewording usually is possible and always is preferable. Clarity is a top priority; gender-neutral use of a singular *they* is unfamiliar to many readers. We do not use other gender-neutral pronouns such as *xe* or *ze.*

Usage example: A singular *they* might be used when an anonymous source's gender must be shielded and other wording is overly awkward: *The person feared for their own safety and spoke on condition of anonymity.*

Arguments for using *they/them* as a singular sometimes arise with an indefinite pronoun (*anyone, everyone, someone*) or unspecified/unknown gender (*a person, the victim, the winner*). Examples of rewording:

All the class members raised their hands (instead of *everyone raised their hands*).

The foundation gave grants to anyone who lost a job this year

(instead of *anyone who lost their job*).

Police said the victim would be identified after relatives are notified (instead of *after their relatives are notified or after his or her relatives are notified*).

Lottery officials said the winner could claim the prize Tuesday (instead of *their* or *his or her prize*).

In stories about people who identify as neither male nor female or ask not to be referred to as *he/she/him/her*: Use the person's name in place of a pronoun, or otherwise reword the sentence, whenever possible. If *they/them/their* use is essential, explain in the text that the person prefers a gender-neutral pronoun. Be sure that the phrasing does not imply more than one person. Examples of rewording:

Hendricks said the new job is a thrill (instead of *Hendricks said Hendricks is thrilled about the new job* or *Hendricks said they are thrilled about the new job*).

Lowry's partner is Dana Adams, an antiques dealer. They bought a house last year (instead of *Lowry and Lowry's partner bought a house last year* or *Lowry and their partner bought a house last year*).

When *they* is used in the singular, it takes a plural verb: *Taylor said they need a new car.* (Again, be sure it's clear from the context that only one person is involved.)

Do not use *themself.*

Third World Avoid use of this term. *Developing nations* is more appropriate when referring to the economically developing nations of Africa, Asia and Latin America. Do not confuse with *nonaligned*, which is a political term. See **nonaligned nations.**

Thomson Reuters Corp. A news and data provider based in New York. Use Reuters when referring to the news agency.

3D

3M Trademark and name of the company formerly known as Minnesota Mining & Manufacturing. Many of its products are known under the names *3M* and *Scotch*. Headquarters of 3M Co. is in St. Paul, Minnesota.

three R's They are: *reading, 'riting and 'rithmetic.*

throwaway (n. and adj.)

thumbs-up, thumbs-down

thunderstorm See **weather terms**.

Tiananmen Square Large public square in central Beijing. Site of pro-democracy demonstrations in 1989 that ended in bloodshed.

tidbit

tie-in (n. and adj.) **tie in** (v.)

tie, tied, tying

tie-up (n. and adj.) **tie up** (v.)

tilde Do not use the symbol in standard AP wire transmissions. If necessary for internet addresses, write out the word and put it in parentheses.

till Or *until*. But not *'til*.

time element Use the days of the week, not *today* or *tonight*, in news stories.

Use *Monday, Tuesday*, etc., for days of the week within seven days before or after the current date.

Use the month and a figure where appropriate. See **months** for forms and punctuation.

Avoid such redundancies as *last Tuesday* or *next Tuesday*. The past, present or future tense used for the verb usually provides adequate indication of which Tuesday is meant: *He said he finished the job Tuesday. She will return Tuesday.*

Avoid awkward placements of the time element, particularly those that suggest the day of the week is the object of a transitive verb: *The police jailed Tuesday.* Potential remedies include the use of the word *on* (see the **on** entry), rephrasing the sentence, or placing the time element in a different sentence.

See **today, tonight** for further discussion, including usage other than in news stories.

time of day The exact time of day that an event has happened or will happen is not necessary in most stories. Follow these guidelines to determine when it should be included and in what form:

SPECIFY THE TIME:
— Whenever it gives the reader a better picture of the scene: Did the earthquake occur when people were likely to be home asleep or at work? A clock reading for the time in the datelined community is acceptable although *pre-dawn hours* or *rush hour* often is more illustrative.
— Whenever the time is critical to the story: When will the rocket be launched? When will a major political address be broadcast? What is the deadline for meeting a demand?

282

DECIDING ON CLOCK TIME: When giving a clock reading, use the time in the datelined community.

If the story has no dateline, use the clock time in force where the event happened or will take place.

The only exception is a nationwide story or tabular listing that involves television or radio programs. Always use Eastern time, followed by *EDT* or *EST*, and specify whether the program will be broadcast simultaneously nationwide or whether times will vary because of separate transmissions for different time zones. If practical, specify those times in a separate paragraph.

ZONE ABBREVIATIONS: Use *EST*, *CDT*, *PST*, etc., after a clock time only if:
— The story involves travel or other activities, such as the closing hour for polling places or the time of a televised speech, likely to affect people or developments in more than one time zone.
— The item involves television or radio programs. (See above.)
— The item has no dateline.
— The item is an advisory to editors.

CONVERT TO EASTERN TIME? Do not convert clock times from other time zones in the continental United States to Eastern time. If there is high interest in the precise time, add *CDT*, *PST*, etc., to the local reading to help readers determine their equivalent local time.

If the time is critical in a story from outside the continental United States, provide a conversion to Eastern time using this form:
The kidnappers set a 9 a.m. (3 a.m. EDT) deadline.

See **time zones** for additional guidance on forms.

timeout

times Use figures except for *noon* and *midnight*. Use a colon to separate hours from minutes: *11 a.m., 1 p.m., 3:30 p.m., 9-11 a.m., 9 a.m. to 5 p.m.*

Avoid such redundancies as *10 a.m. this morning, 10 p.m. tonight* or *10 p.m. Monday night.* Use *10 a.m.* or *10 p.m. Monday*, etc., as required by the norms in time element.

The construction *4 o'clock* is acceptable, but time listings with *a.m.* or *p.m.* are preferred.

See **midnight**; **noon**; **numerals** and **time zones**.

time sequences Spell out: *50 hours, 23 minutes, 14 seconds.* When using the abbreviated form, as in sports statistics or similar agate use, or subsequent references, the form is: *2:30:21.65* (hours, minutes, seconds, tenths, hundredths).

timeshare (n.) A property with multiple owners who each has rights to use it at certain times of year; typically an apartment or condo-type unit located in a resort or vacation destination.

Time Warner Inc. Media company that owns the Warner Bros. movie and TV studio and pay TV networks including HBO, CNN, TBS and TNT. It spun off its cable arm, then known as Time Warner Cable Inc., in 2009 and spun off its Time Inc. magazine unit, including Time, Sports Illustrated, People and Fortune, into a separate, publicly traded company in 2014. Headquarters is in New York. AT&T bid $85.4 billion to acquire Time Warner in October 2016, a deal that was still pending at time of publication.

time zones Capitalize the full name of the time in force within a particular

International time zones

Irregular time zones are in most cases
30 minutes off normal time zones.

U.S. time zones

Hawaii does not observe daylight saving time.

Difference with GMT

-10

PACIFIC
-8

MOUNTAIN
-7

* Arizona does not observe daylight saving time. Pacific time is used from March until November. Otherwise the state is on Mountain time.

PACIFIC
-8

MOUNTAIN
-7

CENTRAL
-6

CENTRAL
-6

EASTERN
-5

Difference with GMT

EASTERN
-5

zone: *Eastern Standard Time, Eastern Daylight Time, Central Standard Time,* etc. See maps on pages 274 and 275.

Lowercase all but the region in short forms: *the Eastern time zone, Eastern time, Mountain time,* etc.

See **time of day** for guidelines on when to use clock time in a story.

Spell out *time zone* in references not accompanied by a clock reading: *Chicago is in the Central time zone.*

The abbreviations *EST, CDT,* etc., are acceptable on first reference for zones used within the continental United States, Canada and Mexico only if the abbreviation is linked with a clock reading: *noon EST, 9 a.m. PST.* (Do not set off the abbreviations with commas.)

Spell out all references to time zones not used within the contiguous United States: *When it is noon EDT, it is 1 p.m. Atlantic Standard Time and 8 a.m. Alaska Standard Time.*

One exception to the spelled-out form: *Greenwich Mean Time* may be abbreviated as *GMT* on second reference if used with a clock reading. See **GMT**.

tipoff (n. and adj.) **tip off** (v.)

tiptop

titleholder

titles In general, confine capitalization to formal titles used directly before an individual's name.

The basic guidelines:

LOWERCASE: Lowercase and spell out titles when they are not used with an individual's name: *The president issued a statement. The pope gave his blessing.*

Lowercase and spell out titles in constructions that set them off

from a name by commas: *The vice president, Mike Pence, was elected in 2016. Pope Francis, the current pope, was born in Argentina.*

FORMAL TITLES: Capitalize formal titles when they are used immediately before one or more names: *Pope Francis, President Donald Trump, Vice Presidents John Jones and William Smith.*

A formal title generally is one that denotes a scope of authority, professional activity or academic activity: *Sen. Dianne Feinstein, Dr. Benjamin Spock, retired Gen. Colin Powell.*

Other titles serve primarily as occupational descriptions: *astronaut John Glenn, movie star John Wayne, peanut farmer Jimmy Carter.*

A final determination on whether a title is formal or occupational depends on the practice of the governmental or private organization that confers it. If there is doubt about the status of a title and the practice of the organization cannot be determined, use a construction that sets the name or the title off with commas.

ABBREVIATED TITLES: The following formal titles are capitalized and abbreviated as shown when used before a name both inside and outside quotations: *Dr., Gov., Lt. Gov., Rep., Sen.* and certain military ranks listed in **military titles**.

All other formal titles are spelled out in all uses.

GOVERNMENT OFFICIALS: In stories with U.S. datelines, do not include *U.S.* before the titles of Secretary of State or other government officials, except where necessary for clarity.

In stories with international datelines, include *U.S.* before the titles.

ROYAL TITLES: Capitalize *king,*

queen, etc., when used directly before a name. See individual entries and **nobility**.

TITLES OF NOBILITY: Capitalize a full title when it serves as the alternate name for an individual. See **nobility**.

PAST AND FUTURE TITLES: A formal title that an individual formerly held, is about to hold or holds temporarily is capitalized if used before the person's name. But do not capitalize the qualifying word: *former President George W. Bush*, *deposed King Constantine*, *Attorney General-designate Griffin B. Bell*, *acting Mayor Peter Barry*.

LONG TITLES: Separate a long title from a name by a construction that requires a comma: *Charles Robinson, the undersecretary for economic affairs, spoke.* Or: *The undersecretary for economic affairs, Charles Robinson, spoke.*

UNIQUE TITLES: If a title applies only to one person in an organization, insert the word *the* in a construction that uses commas: *John Jones, the deputy vice president, spoke.*

ADDITIONAL GUIDANCE: Many commonly used titles and occupational descriptions are listed separately in this book, together with guidelines on whether and/or when they are capitalized. In these entries, the phrases *before a name* or *immediately before a name* are used to specify that capitalization applies only when a title is not set off from a name by commas.

See **academic titles**; **composition titles**; **legislative titles**; **military titles**; and **religious titles**.

tobacco, tobaccos

Tobago See **Trinidad and Tobago**.

today, tonight Use the day of the week, not *today* or *tonight*, in news stories. In news stories, use *today* or *tonight* only in direct quotations, and in phrases that do not refer to a specific day: *Customs today are different from those of a century ago.*

In other types of writing, *today*, *this morning*, *this afternoon* and *tonight* are acceptable if using the day of the week would be awkward. For example, in an internal note Wednesday to company staff: *Xin Chen took over as vice president for human resources today.* In an external announcement: *Xin Chen took over as vice president for human resources Wednesday.*

See **time element**.

Tokyo The city in Japan stands alone in datelines.

tomorrow Use only in direct quotations and in phrases that do not refer to a specific day: *The world of tomorrow will need additional energy resources.*

Use the day of the week in other cases.

ton There are three types:

A *short ton* is equal to 2,000 pounds.

A *long ton*, also known as a *British ton*, is equal to 2,240 pounds.

A *metric ton* is equal to 1,000 kilograms, or approximately 2,204.62 pounds.

CONVERSION EQUATIONS:

Short to long: Multiply by 0.89 (5 short tons x 0.89 = 4.45 long tons).

Short to metric: Multiply by 0.9 (5 short tons x 0.9 = 4.5 metric tons).

Long to short: Multiply by 1.12 (5 long tons x 1.12 = 5.6 short tons).

Long to metric: Multiply by 1.02 (5 long tons x 1.02 = 5.1 metric tons).

Metric to short: Multiply by 1.1 (5

metric tons x 1.1 = 5.5 short tons).

Metric to long: Multiply by 0.98 (5 metric tons x 0.98 = 4.9 long tons).

See **metric system**.

See **kiloton** for units used to measure the power of nuclear explosions.

See **oil** for formulas to convert the tonnage of oil shipments to gallons.

tonight See **today, tonight** entry.

Tony Awards The most prestigious awards for Broadway shows of the past season, presented by The Broadway League and the American Theatre Wing, both based in New York City. Named after Antoinette Perry, an actress, director, producer and the leader of the American Theatre Wing in World War II. The awards were started in 1947. Plural form: *the Tonys*.

tornado(es) See **weather terms**.

Toronto The city in Canada stands alone in datelines.

Tory, Tories An exception to the normal practice when forming the plural of a proper name ending in *y*.

The words are acceptable on second reference to the Conservative Party in Britain and its members.

Total SA Headquarters of French oil company is in Paris.

total, totaled, totaling The phrase *a total of* often is redundant.

It may be used, however, to avoid a figure at the start of a sentence: *A total of 650 people were killed in holiday traffic accidents.*

touch screen (n.) **touch-screen** (adj.)

toward Not *towards*.

town Apply the capitalization principles in **city**.

town council Apply the capitalization principles in **city council**.

toxic substances, toxins A *toxic substance* is one that is likely to be poisonous, depending on the amount of exposure to it. *Toxins* are poisonous substances that come from plants or animals.

Toyota Motor Corp. Headquarters is in Toyota City, Japan.

Toys R Us

trade-in (n. and adj.) **trade in** (v.)

trademark A trademark is a brand, symbol, word, etc., used by a manufacturer or dealer and protected by law to prevent a competitor from using it: *AstroTurf*, for a type of artificial grass, for example.

In general, use a generic equivalent unless the trademark name is essential to the story.

When a trademark is used, capitalize it.

Many trademarks are listed separately in this book, together with generic equivalents.

The International Trademark Association, located in New York, is a helpful source of information about trademarks. See **brand names**.

trade-off (n. and adj.) **trade off** (v.)

trade show

traffic, trafficked, trafficking

t

trampoline Formerly a trademark, now a generic term.

trans- The rules in **prefixes** apply, but in general, no hyphen. Some examples:

transcontinental transship
transmigrate trans-Siberian
transoceanic

Also: *trans-Atlantic* and *trans-Pacific.* These are exceptions to Webster's New World College Dictionary in keeping with the general rule that a hyphen is needed when a prefix precedes a capitalized word.

transcripts See **texts, transcripts**.

Trans-Dniester A separatist sliver of land in Moldova on the eastern bank of the River Dniester. Trans-Dniester, then a part of the Soviet Union, was joined with Moldova in 1940 when the Soviet Union annexed Moldova from Romania. It fought a separatist war with Moldova in 1992 and has considered itself independent ever since, though no other country recognizes it as such. Most of the population speaks Russian. In stories, the dateline should be Trans-Dniester, without reference to Moldova: *TIRASPOL, Trans-Dniester.*

transfer, transferred, transferring

transgender See **gender**.

Transportation Communications International Union Formerly the Brotherhood of Railway, Airline and Steamship Clerks, Freight Handlers, Express and Station Employees. *TCU* is acceptable on second reference.

Headquarters is in Rockville, Maryland.

transsexual Do not use. See **gender**.

transvestite Use *cross-dresser* instead.

travelogue Not *travelog.*

travel, traveled, traveling, traveler

treasurer Capitalize when used as a formal title immediately before a name. See **titles**.

Caution: The secretary of the U.S. Department of the Treasury is not the same person as the U.S. treasurer.

Treasurys Securities sold by the federal government to investors to fund its operations, cover the interest on U.S. government debt and pay off maturing securities. Because they carry the full backing of the government, Treasurys are viewed as the safest investment.

Treasury bills, Treasury bonds, Treasury notes See **loan terminology**.

trees See **plants**.

trending (v. or adj.) Used to indicate that a particular topic, word, phrase or piece of content is getting a lot of attention on a social network, search engine or website. Do not use without context and explanation, including describing the location of users where the topic is trending. *The Oscars are trending worldwide on Twitter today.*

tribe, tribal Refers to a sovereign political entity, communities sharing a common ancestry, culture or language, and a social group of linked families who may be part of an ethnic group. Identify tribes by the political identity specified by the tribe, nation or community: the *Apache Tribe of Oklahoma*, the *Cherokee Nation*. *Ethnic group* is preferred when referring to ethnicity or ethnic violence. See **Indians** and **nationalities and races**.

trigger-happy

Trinidad and Tobago In datelines on stories from this nation, use a community name followed by either *Trinidad* or *Tobago* — but not both — depending on which island the community is located.

Trojan horse, Trojan War

Tronc Inc. Newspaper publisher formerly known as Tribune Publishing Co. It publishes the Chicago Tribune and other newspapers and digital news sites in various markets. It also operates Spanish-language properties Hoy and El Sentinel. Headquarters is in Chicago.

troop, troops, troupe A *troop*, in its singular form, is a group of people, often military, or animals. *Troops*, in the plural, means several such groups. But when the plural appears with a large number, it is understood to mean individuals: *There were an estimated 150,000 troops in Iraq.* (But not: *Three troops were injured.*) Use *troupe* only for ensembles of actors, dancers, singers, etc.

tropical depression See **weather terms**.

Truman, Harry S. With a period after the initial. Truman once said there

was no need for the period because the S did not stand for a name. Asked in the early 1960s about his preference, he replied, "It makes no difference to me."

AP style has called for the period since that time.

trustee A person to whom another's property or the management of another's property is entrusted.

Do not capitalize if used before a name.

trusty A prison inmate granted special privileges as a trustworthy person.

tryout (n.) **try out** (v.)

TSA Precheck The Transportation Security Administration's expedited screening program that lets approved travelers get through airport security lines faster. *TSA* is acceptable on first reference in this usage, but spell out the agency's full name later. In other uses, *TSA* should be used only on second reference.

tsar Use *czar*.

T-shirt

tsunami See **weather terms**.

tuberculosis *TB* is acceptable on second reference.

Tumblr A social networking website owned by Verizon Communications Inc. subsidiary Oath Inc.

tuneup (n. and adj.) **tune up** (v.)

turboprop See **aircraft terms**.

Turkmen, Turkmens Used to describe the people of Turkmenistan and neighboring regions. *He is Turkmen. They are Turkmens.*

turnpike Capitalize as part of a proper name: *the Pennsylvania Turnpike.* Lowercase *turnpike* when it stands alone.

See **highway designations**.

TV Acceptable as an abbreviated form of *television*, as a noun or adjective.

tweet (n. or v.) A short posting on Twitter.

Twenty-First Century Fox Inc. Entertainment conglomerate controlled by Rupert Murdoch. The company includes the former entertainment businesses of News Corp., such as its movie studio and television networks, which were split off into a separate publicly traded company in June 2013. The company's preference is to use the spelling *21st Century Fox*, but for corporate stories AP uses the legal name reflected in Securities and Exchange Commission filings: Twenty-First Century Fox Inc.

Twentieth Century Fox Film Corp., also known as 20th Century Fox, is the film studio unit of Twenty-First Century Fox. Twentieth Century Fox Film Co. Ltd. operates as a British-based subsidiary of Twenty-First Century Fox Inc.

21-gun salutes True 21-gun salutes are conducted not with rifles but with artillery batteries. In the United States, they are reserved for the arrivals and departures from military installations of the president, president-elect or former presidents, and for their funerals. Visiting foreign heads of state also receive 21-gun salutes. The firing of rifles three times at a military funeral is often incorrectly described as a 21-gun salute. Properly, it should be called a *rifle salute* or *the three volleys*.

20-something

24/7

twin towers The two tallest buildings in the World Trade Center complex destroyed in the 9/11 attack. Also lowercase *north tower* and *south tower*.

Twitter A social network on which users share text, photos, video and links to outside content with their followers, in short tweets. The verb is *to tweet, tweeted*.

two-by-four Spell out the noun, which refers to any length of untrimmed lumber approximately 2 inches thick by 4 inches wide.

typhoons Capitalize typhoon when it is part of the name that weather forecasters assign to a storm: *Typhoon Tilda.*

But use *it* and *its* — not *she, her* or *hers* — in pronoun references.

See **weather terms**.

t

u

U-boat A German submarine. Anything referring to a submarine should be *submarine* unless directly referring to a German vessel of World War I or II vintage.

UFO, UFOs Acceptable in all references for *unidentified flying object(s)*.

ukulele

Ulaanbaatar The preferred spelling for the capital of Mongolia, previously known as *Ulan Bator*.

Ulster Historically, one of the four Irish provinces, covering nine counties. Six of the counties became Northern Ireland, three became part of the Republic of Ireland. Avoid use as a synonym for *Northern Ireland*. See **United Kingdom**.

ultra- The rules in **prefixes** apply, but in general, no hyphen. Some examples:
> *ultramodern   ultrasonic*
> *ultranationalism ultraviolet*

umlaut This diacritical mark (two dots placed over the vowel to change its sound) should not be used in standard AP transmissions. Instead, use two regular letters when needed.

U.N. Use periods in *U.N.*, for consistency with U.S. within texts. In headlines, it's *UN* (no periods). See **United Nations**.

un- The rules in **prefixes** apply, but in general, no hyphen. Some examples:
> *un-American unnecessary*
> *unarmed   unshaven*

Uncle Sam

under- The rules in **prefixes** apply, but in general, no hyphen. Some examples:
> *underdog   undersheriff*
> *underground undersold*

underscore Do not use the symbol in internet addresses; write out the word and put it in parentheses.

undersecretary One word. See **titles**.

underwater In the housing industry, the term for homeowners who owe more on their mortgages than their homes are worth.

underway One word in all uses.

unemployment rate In the United States, this estimate of the number of unemployed residents seeking work is compiled monthly by the Bureau of Labor Statistics, an agency of the Labor Department.

Each month the bureau selects a nationwide cross section of the population and conducts interviews to determine the size of the U.S. workforce. The workforce is defined as the number of people with jobs and the number looking for jobs.

The unemployment rate is expressed as a percentage figure. The essential calculation involves dividing the total workforce into the number of people looking for jobs, followed by adjustments to reflect variable factors such as seasonal trends.

UNESCO Acceptable in all reference for the *United Nations Educational, Scientific and Cultural Organization*.

unfollow To remove an account from the list of accounts that populate one's feed on a social network.

unfriend To remove someone from a list of friends that one is connected to, usually on Facebook.

UNICEF Acceptable in all references for the *United Nations Children's Fund*. The words *International* and *Emergency*, originally part of the name, have been dropped.

unidentified flying object(s) *UFO* and *UFOs* are acceptable in all references.

Uniform Code of Military Justice The laws covering members of the U.S. armed forces.

uninterested See **disinterested, uninterested**.

union Capitalize when used as a proper name of the Northern states during the Civil War: *The Union defeated the Confederacy*.

union names The formal names of unions may be condensed to conventionally accepted short forms that capitalize characteristic words from the full name followed by union in lowercase.

Follow union practice in the use of the word worker in shortened forms: United Auto Workers, United Mine Workers.

When worker is used generically, make autoworkers and steelworkers one word in keeping with widespread practice; use two words for other job descriptions: bakery workers, mine workers.

Some unions frequently in the news:

Amalgamated Transit Union
American Federation of Government Employees
American Federation of Labor and Congress of Industrial Organizations
American Federation of Musicians
American Federation of State, County and Municipal Employees
American Federation of Teachers
American Postal Workers Union
Communications Workers of America
International Association of Machinists and Aerospace Workers
International Brotherhood of Electrical Workers
International Brotherhood of Teamsters
International Longshore and Warehouse Union
International Longshoremen's Association
International Union of Bricklayers and Allied Craftworkers
International Union of Painters and Allied Trades
Laborers' International Union of North America
National Association of Letter Carriers
National Education Association
Newspaper Guild, The
Screen Actors Guild-American Federation of Television and Radio Artists
Service Employees International Union
Sheet Metal Workers International Association

UNITE HERE (no hyphen), a merger of the Union of Needletrades, Industrial and Textile Employees with the Hotel Employees and Restaurant Employees.
  United Auto Workers
  United Brotherhood of Carpenters
  United Electrical, Radio and Machine Workers of America
  United Farm Workers
  United Food and Commercial Workers International Union
  United Mine Workers of America
  United Steelworkers

Union Pacific Corp. Freight railroad, with headquarters in Omaha, Nebraska.

union shop See **closed shop.**

unique It means one of a kind. Do not describe something as *rather unique, most unique* or *very unique.*

United Airlines Headquarters is in Chicago. The parent company is United Continental Holdings Inc.

United Arab Emirates Spell out on first reference in stories and in datelines. *UAE* (no periods) is acceptable on second reference.

United Auto Workers The shortened form of the United Automobile, Aerospace and Agricultural Implement Workers of America is acceptable in all references. Headquarters is in Detroit.

United Farm Workers Headquarters is in Keene, California.

United Kingdom It consists of Great Britain and Northern Ireland.
  Great Britain (or Britain) consists of England, Scotland and Wales.

Ireland is independent of the United Kingdom.
  The abbreviation *U.K.* is acceptable as a noun or adjective. Use *UK* (no periods) in headlines. See **datelines** and **Ireland.**

United Mine Workers of America The shortened forms *United Mine Workers* and *United Mine Workers union* are acceptable in all references.
  UMW and *Mine Workers* are acceptable on second reference.
  Use *mine workers* or *miners,* lowercase, in generic references to workers in the industry.
  Headquarters is in Washington.

United Nations Abbrev: *U.N.* (no space). Use periods in *U.N.,* for consistency with U.S. within texts. In headlines, it's *UN* (no periods).
  In datelines: *UNITED NATIONS (AP) —*
  Use *U.N. General Assembly, U.N. Secretariat* and *U.N. Security Council* in first references not under a United Nations dateline.
  General Assembly, the Secretariat and *Security Council* are acceptable in all references under a United Nations dateline and on second reference under other datelines.
  Lowercase *the assembly* and *the council* when they stand alone. See **UNESCO** and **UNICEF.**

United Press International A privately owned news agency formed in 1958 as a merger of United Press and International News Service.
  Use the full name on first reference. *UPI* is acceptable on second reference.
  Headquarters is in Washington.

United Service Organizations *USO*

293

u

is acceptable in all references.

United States Use periods in the abbreviation, *U.S.* within texts. In headlines, it's *US* (no periods).

United States Conference of Catholic Bishops Formerly the National Conference of Catholic Bishops, it is the national organization of Roman Catholic bishops.

United Steelworkers The shortened form of the United Steel, Paper and Forestry, Rubber, Manufacturing, Energy, Allied Industrial and Service Workers International Union is acceptable in all references. Headquarters is in Pittsburgh, Pennsylvania.

unprecedented It means *having no precedent, unheard of*. Often misused.

-up Follow Webster's New World College Dictionary. Hyphenate if not listed there.

Some frequently used words (all are nouns, some also are used as adjectives):

breakup	*makeup*
call-up	*mix-up*
change-up	*mock-up*
checkup	*pileup*
cleanup	*pushup*
close-up	*roundup*
cover-up	*runners-up*
crackup	*setup*
follow-up	*shake-up*
frame-up	*shape-up*
grown-up	*smashup*
hang-up	*speedup*
holdup	*tie-up*
letup	*walk-up*
lineup	*windup*

Use two words when any of these occurs as a verb.

See **suffixes**.

up- The rules in **prefixes** apply, but in general, no hyphen. Some examples:

upend	*upstate*
upgrade	*uptown*

UPI See **United Press International**.

uppercase One word (n., v., adj.) when referring to the use of capital letters, in keeping with printers' practice.

UPS Inc. Acceptable in all references to *United Parcel Service Inc.* Headquarters is in Atlanta.

upside down (adv.) **upside-down** (adj.) *The car turned upside down. The book is upside-down.*

upstage

upstate Always lowercase: *upstate New York.*

upward Not *upwards.*

URL Acceptable in all references for *Uniform Resource Locator*, an internet address.

U.S. The abbreviation is acceptable as a noun or adjective for *United States.* In headlines, it's *US* (no periods).

USA No periods in the abbreviated form for *United States of America.*

U.S. Agency for International Development *USAID* is acceptable on second reference.

U.S. Air Force See **air force; military academies**; and **military titles**.

US Airways Group Merged in 2013

with American Airlines to form American Airlines Group Inc., based in Fort Worth, Texas. American has phased out the US Airways name, and aircraft fly as American Airlines.

U.S. Army See **army**; **military academies**; and **military titles**.

U.S. Chamber of Commerce On second reference, *the Chamber* is acceptable. For a local chamber of commerce, capitalize the full name: *the Seattle Metropolitan Chamber of Commerce*. But on second reference, *the chamber* is lowercase.

U.S. Coast Guard See **coast guard**; **military academies**; and **military titles**.

U.S. Conference of Mayors The members are the mayors of cities with 30,000 or more residents.

Use *the conference* or *the mayors' conference* on second reference.

There is no organization with the name *National Mayors' Conference*. See **National League of Cities**.

U.S. Court of Appeals The court is divided into 13 circuits as follows:

District of Columbia Circuit.

Federal Circuit.

1st Circuit: Maine, Massachusetts, New Hampshire, Rhode Island, Puerto Rico. Based in Boston.

2nd Circuit: Connecticut, New York, Vermont. Based in New York.

3rd Circuit: Delaware, New Jersey, Pennsylvania, Virgin Islands. Based in Philadelphia.

4th Circuit: Maryland, North Carolina, South Carolina, Virginia, West Virginia. Based in Richmond, Va.

5th Circuit: Louisiana, Mississippi, Texas. Based in New Orleans.

6th Circuit: Kentucky, Michigan, Ohio, Tennessee. Based in Cincinnati.

7th Circuit: Illinois, Indiana, Wisconsin. Based in Chicago.

8th Circuit: Arkansas, Iowa, Minnesota, Missouri, Nebraska, North Dakota, South Dakota. Based in St. Louis.

9th Circuit: Alaska, Arizona, California, Hawaii, Idaho, Montana, Nevada, Oregon, Washington, Guam. Based in San Francisco.

10th Circuit: Colorado, Kansas, New Mexico, Oklahoma, Utah, Wyoming. Based in Denver.

11th Circuit: Alabama, Florida and Georgia. Based in Atlanta.

The courts do not always sit in the cities where they are based. Sessions may be held in other major cities within each region.

REFERENCE FORMS: A phrase such as a *federal appeals court* is acceptable on first reference.

On first reference to the full name, use *U.S. Court of Appeals* or a full name: *8th U.S. Circuit Court of Appeals* or *the U.S. Court of Appeals for the 8th Circuit.*

U.S. Circuit Court of Appeals without a circuit number is a misnomer and should not be used.

In shortened and subsequent references: *the Court of Appeals, the 2nd Circuit, the appeals court, the appellate court(s), the circuit court(s), the court.*

Do not create nonexistent entities such as *the San Francisco Court of Appeals*. Make it *the U.S. Court of Appeals in San Francisco*.

JURISTS: The formal title for the jurists on the court is *judge*: *U.S. Circuit Judge Homer Thornberry* is preferred to *U.S. Appeals Judge Homer Thornberry*, but either is acceptable.

u

See **judge**.

U.S. Court of Appeals for the Armed Forces This court, not part of the judicial branch as such, is a civilian body established by Congress to hear appeals from actions of the Defense Department. It is based in Washington. (Formerly the U.S. Court of Military Appeals.)

U.S. Court of Appeals for the Federal Circuit Commonly known as the CAFC, it replaced U.S. Court of Claims and U.S. Court of Customs and Patent Appeals. It handles lawsuits against the federal government and appeals involving customs, patents and copyright. It is based in Washington.

U.S. Customs and Border Protection An agency of the Department of Homeland Security, it includes the Border Patrol.

U.S. Court of Military Appeals See **U.S. Court of Appeals for the Armed Forces**.

U.S. Customs Court This court, based in New York City, handles disputes over customs duties that arise at any U.S. port of entry.

U.S. District Courts There are 94. In shortened and subsequent references: *the District Court, the District Courts, the court.*

Judge is the formal title for District Court jurists: *U.S. District Judge Frank Johnson.* See **judge**.

user interface The features of a device, program or website that enable control by a user. *UI* is acceptable on second reference. It is a key element of *user experience,*

or *UX*, which is a broader term referring to how people experience a given product or service.

U.S. Immigration and Customs Enforcement See **immigration**.

U.S. Marshals Service No apostrophe.

U.S. Military Academy See **military academies**.

U.S. Navy See **navy**; **military academies**; and **military titles**.

U.S. Postal Service Use *U.S. Postal Service* or *the Postal Service* on first reference. Retain capitalization of *Postal Service* in subsequent references to the agency.

Lowercase *the service* when it stands alone. Lowercase *post office* in generic references to the agency and to an individual office: *I went to the post office.*

USS For *United States Ship, Steamer* or *Steamship,* preceding the name of a vessel: *the USS Iowa.*

In datelines:
ABOARD USS IOWA (AP) —

U.S. Supreme Court See **Supreme Court of the United States**.

U.S. Tax Court This court handles appeals in tax cases.

U.S. territories Do not abbreviate the names of U.S. territories. There are 16 such territories; 11 of them are small islands, reefs or atolls in the Caribbean or the Pacific, without native populations. The others — Puerto Rico, the U.S. Virgin Islands, Guam, the Northern Mariana Islands and American Samoa — are self-governing, unincorporated territories. They send nonvoting representatives to the U.S. Congress.

Residents of Puerto Rico, the U.S. Virgin Islands, Guam and the Northern Marianas are U.S. citizens; American Samoans are considered noncitizen U.S. nationals. Residents of the territories cannot vote in presidential elections, though their delegates participate in national political conventions to choose the nominees.

For datelines, use the community followed by the unabbreviated name of the territory: *SAN JUAN, Puerto Rico.*

Utah Do not abbreviate in datelines or stories. Postal code: *UT*
See **state names**.

U-turn (n. and adj.)

u

V

vacuum

vacation rental websites Sites such as Airbnb, VRBO and HomeAway that connect people offering residences or rooms with others who want to rent them for short-term stays. Other descriptions include *short-term lodging service* or *a website that lists residences or rooms for short-term rental*. Do not call them *home-sharing sites* or *room-sharing sites*.

Valentine's Day Feb. 14. Honors the saint martyred in third-century Rome. Sweethearts mark it by exchanging valentines.

Valium A trademark for a brand of tranquilizer and muscle relaxant. It also may be called *diazepam*.

valley Capitalize as part of a full name: *the Mississippi Valley.*
Lowercase in plural uses: *the Missouri and Mississippi valleys.*

Vaseline A trademark for a brand of petroleum jelly.

Vatican City Stands alone in datelines.

VCR Acceptable in all references to *videocassette recorder.*

V-E Day May 8, 1945, the day the surrender of Germany was announced, officially ending the European phase of World War II.

vegetables See **food.**

vegetative state A condition in which the eyes are open and can move, and the patient has periods of sleep and periods of wakefulness, but remains unconscious, unaware of self or others. The patient can't think, reason, respond, do anything on purpose, chew or swallow. Reaction to a sound or a sight is reflex. Also called *unresponsive wakefulness state.*
See **coma** and **minimally conscious state.**

V-8 The engine.

vendor

verbal See **oral, verbal, written.**

verbs The abbreviation *v.* is used in this book to identify the spelling of the verb forms of words frequently misspelled.
SPLIT FORMS: In general, avoid awkward constructions that split infinitive forms of a verb (*to leave, to help,* etc.) or compound forms (*had left, are found out,* etc.)
Awkward: *She was ordered to immediately leave on an assignment.*
Preferred: *She was ordered to leave immediately on an assignment.*
Awkward: *There stood the wagon that we had early last autumn left by the barn.*
Preferred: *There stood the wagon that we had left by the barn early last autumn.*
Occasionally, however, a split is not awkward and is necessary to convey the meaning:
He wanted to really help his mother.

Those who lie are often found out.
How has your health been?
The budget was tentatively approved.

Verizon Communications Inc.
Headquarters is in New York.

Vermont Abbreviate *Vt.* in datelines
only; spell out in stories. Postal code:
VT
See **state names**.

verses See **poetry** for guidelines on
how to handle verses of poetry
typographically.

versus Spell it out in ordinary
speech and writing: *The proposal to
revamp Medicare versus proposals to
reform Medicare and Medicaid at the
same time* ... In short expressions,
however, the abbreviation *vs.* is
permitted: *The issue of guns vs. butter
has long been with us.*
For court cases, use *v.*: *Marbury v.
Madison.*

Veterans Affairs Formerly Veterans
Administration, it became Cabinet
level in March 1989 with the full title
Department of Veterans Affairs. *VA*
(no periods) is still used on second
reference.

Veterans Day Formerly Armistice
Day, Nov. 11, the anniversary of the
armistice that ended World War I in
1918.
The federal legal holiday, observed
on the fourth Monday in October
during the mid-1970s, reverted to
Nov. 11 in 1978.

Veterans of Foreign Wars *VFW* is
acceptable on second reference.
Headquarters is in Kansas City,
Missouri.

veto, vetoes (n.) The verb forms:
vetoed, vetoing.

Viacom Inc. Media conglomerate
based in New York. Owns *Paramount
Pictures* movie studio and pay TV
channels such as *MTV, Nickelodeon,
Comedy Central* and *BET.*

vice Use two words: *vice admiral, vice
chairman, vice chancellor, vice consul,
vice president, vice principal, vice
regent, vice secretary.*
Several are exceptions to
Webster's New World College
Dictionary. The two-word rule has
been adopted for consistency in
handling the similar terms.

vice president Capitalize or
lowercase following the same rules
that apply to *president.* See **president**
and **titles.**

vice versa

victim See **survivor, victim.**

video game Two words in all uses.

video on demand Spell it out; do not
use *VOD.*

video recording Term for digital
audio and visual recording. Digital
has largely replaced videotaping.

videotape (n. and v.)

Vienna The city in Austria stands
alone in datelines.

Vietnam

Vietnam War

vie, vied, vying

village Apply the capitalization principles in **city**.

Vimeo A video-sharing network owned by IAC, an internet company whose holdings include Match.com and The Daily Beast.

VIP, VIPs Acceptable in all references for *very important person(s)*.

Virgin America Alaska Air Group acquired Virgin America in December 2016. Virgin America and Alaska Airlines are expected to become one airline under the name Alaska Airlines by mid-2019.

Virgin Atlantic Airways Ltd. Headquarters is in Crawley, England.

Virginia Abbreviate *Va.* in datelines only; spell out in stories. Postal code: *VA*

See **state names**.

Virgin Islands Use with a community name in datelines on stories from the U.S. Virgin Islands. Do not abbreviate.

Identify an individual island in the text if relevant.

See **datelines** and **British Virgin Islands**.

virtual private network A service that shields internet users by encrypting their data traffic, preventing others from observing their web browsing and other activities. Organizations use *VPNs* for secure communications over the public internet. Individuals can also use VPN services to mask their location in order to circumvent censorship or geography-based online viewing restrictions. *VPN* is acceptable on second reference.

virtual reality, augmented reality *Virtual reality* is a computer-generated simulation of an interactive, three-dimensional environment. *Virtual reality* experiences typically require the use of headsets, hand-held controllers and other electronic equipment that allow a person to interact with the simulation. A similar concept, *augmented reality*, involves the projection of interactive computer-generated images into a person's real-world surroundings. *VR* and *AR* are acceptable on second reference.

virus, worm A computer *virus* is any malicious, invasive program designed to infect and disrupt computers. A *worm* is a type of virus that spreads on networks such as the internet, copying itself from one computer to another without human intervention.

V-J Day Sept. 2, 1945, the day of formal surrender by Japan to Allied forces in World War II. Some commemorations recognized the date as Aug. 14, 1945, the day fighting with Japan ended and the armistice was declared, but the formal proclamation was not until Sept. 2.

voicemail

Voice of America *VOA* is acceptable on second reference.

VoIP *Voice over Internet Protocol*. A method of transmitting sound as data over the internet, allowing for inexpensive phone conversations. Avoid the term in most stories; if it is necessary, explain it. *VoIP* is acceptable on second reference in such cases.

V

Volkswagen AG Headquarters is in Wolfsburg, Germany.

Volkswagen of America Inc. The name of the U.S. subsidiary of the German company *Volkswagen AG*.

U.S. headquarters is in Herndon, Virginia.

volley, volleys

vote-getter

vote tabulations Always use figures for the totals.

Spell out below 10 in other phrases related to voting: *by a five-vote majority, with three abstentions, four votes short of the necessary two-thirds majority*.

For results that involve fewer than 1,000 votes on each side, use these forms: *The House voted 230-205, a 230-205 vote*.

To make totals that involve more than 1,000 votes on a side easier to read, separate the figures with the word *to* to avoid hyphenated adjectival constructions. See **election returns** for examples.

VRBO See **vacation rental websites**.

vulgarities See **obscenities, profanities, vulgarities**.

V

W

wacky

waitlist (n.) **wait-list** (v.)

wake-up call

Wales Use *Wales* after the names of Welsh communities in datelines. See **datelines** and **United Kingdom**.

walk-up (n. and adj.) **walk up** (v.)

Wall Street When the reference is to the entire complex of financial institutions in the area rather than the actual street itself, *the Street* is an acceptable short form.

Walmart Inc. The world's largest retailer. It changed its legal name from Wal-Mart Stores Inc. in 2018. Headquarters is in Bentonville, Arkansas.

Walt Disney Co., The Family entertainment company that owns TV networks *ESPN* and *ABC*, theme parks and brands such as *Lucasfilm*, *Marvel* and *Pixar*. Headquarters is in Burbank, California.

war Capitalize as part of the name of a specific conflict: *the Afghanistan War, the Iraq War, the Civil War, the Cold War, the Korean War, the Vietnam War, the War of 1812, World War I, World War II, the Gulf War.*

warden Capitalize as a formal title before a name. See **titles**.

wards Use figures. See **political divisions.**

-ward, -wards Virtually none of the words ending with this suffix end with an *s*: *backward, forward, toward, downward, upward, onward, outward, inward, southward, skyward, Earthward, heavenward, homeward.*

warhead

war horse, warhorse Two words for a horse used in battle.
One word for a veteran of many battles: *He is a political warhorse.*

warlike

warlord

warrant officer See **military titles.**

wartime

washed-up (adj.)

Washington Abbreviate *Wash.* in datelines only; spell out in stories. For the U.S. capital, use *WASHINGTON* in datelines and *Washington* within a story. Use *Washington, D.C.*, with the added abbreviation only if the city might be confused with the state. Postal code: WA See **state names.**

The Washington Post The newspaper was sold to Amazon.com Inc. founder Jeff Bezos in October 2013. It's now part of privately held WP Express Publications LLC, a division of Nash Holdings LLC.

Washington's Birthday Capitalize *birthday* in references to the holiday.

The date President George Washington was born is computed as Feb. 22. The federal legal holiday is the third Monday in February.

Some states and some organizations refer to it as *Presidents Day,* but the formal name has not changed.

wastebasket

waterspout See **weather terms**.

watt A unit of power. Do not confuse with *watt-hour,* a unit of energy used to describe electricity consumed or generated over time.

A *watt* is often used to describe the peak or maximum capacity of an electric device, like a light bulb or a power generator. Think of it as a snapshot of a level of electric power at any moment. Common variants include kilowatt, (1,000 watts), megawatt (1 million watts) and gigawatt (1 billion watts). Abbreviations are *W, kW, MW, GW.*

Watt-hours are used to measure power over time. One *watt-hour* is one watt of power over one hour. Most people pay for electricity by the *kilowatt-hour.* Variants are *megawatt-hours* and *gigawatt-hours.* Abbreviations are *Wh, kWh, MWh, GWh.*

Press releases about power plants usually speak of a plant's power in megawatts. However, this is usually just a reference to the plant's peak power. Power plants, particularly those that rely on renewable resources such as sun or wind, don't generate power at peak rates consistently.

The best way to describe a plant's practical ability to generate electricity is to multiply its peak capacity in kilowatts or megawatts by the plant's capacity factor (a percentage that yields the *average* amount of power actually produced by the plant, rather than what it produces just at peak moments).

To determine how many homes can be powered by a plant, multiply the peak power by the capacity factor, then multiply by 8,760 (the number of hours in a year), then divide that by the average consumption of a home over a year in kilowatt hours. In the United States, an average home consumes about 11,000 kwh per year.

Another common unit of power is horsepower. One kilowatt equals 1.34 horsepower.

weapons *Gun* is an acceptable term for any firearm. Note the following definitions and forms in dealing with weapons and ammunition:

anti-aircraft A cannon or other weapon designed for defense against air attack. The form: *a 105 mm anti-aircraft gun.*

artillery A carriage-mounted cannon.

assault rifle, assault weapon Terms for military- or police-style weapons that are shorter than a conventional rifle and technically known as carbines. The precise definitions may vary from one law or jurisdiction to another. Although the terms are often used interchangeably, some make the distinction that *assault rifle* is a military weapon with a selector switch for firing in either fully automatic or semi-automatic mode from a detachable, 10- to 30-round magazine. Comparatively lightweight and easy to aim, this carbine was designed for tactical operations and is used by some law

W

enforcement agencies. The form: *an M16 assault rifle, an AK-47 assault rifle, a Kalashnikov assault rifle*. An *assault weapon* is the civilian version of the military carbine with a similar appearance. This gun is semi-automatic, meaning one shot per trigger pull. Ammunition magazines ranging from 10 to 30 rounds or more allow rapid-fire capability. Other common characteristics include folding stock, muzzle flash suppressor, bayonet mount and pistol grip. Assault weapon sales were largely banned under federal law from 1994 to 2004 to curb gun crimes. The form: *AR-15 carbine with military-style appearance*.

Examples:

Each soldier carried an M16 assault rifle into combat, facing enemy troops armed with AK-47 assault rifles.

Politicians debated sales restrictions on assault weapons, including military-style AR-15 carbines for gun hobbyists.

automatic A firearm that reloads automatically after each shot. The term should not be used to describe the rate of fire. To avoid confusion, specify *fully automatic* or *semi-automatic* rather than simply automatic. Give the type of weapon or model for clarity.

bolt-action rifle A manually operated handle on the barrel opens and closes the breech, ejecting a spent round, loading another and cocking the weapon for triggering. Popular for hunting and target-shooting. Example: *Remington 700*. Some shotguns are bolt-action.

buckshot See **shot**.

bullet The projectile fired by a rifle, pistol or machine gun. Together with metal casing, primer and propellant, it forms a *cartridge*.

caliber A measurement of the diameter of the inside of a gun barrel except for most shotguns. Measurement is in either millimeters or decimal fractions of an inch. The word *caliber* is not used when giving the metric measurement. The forms: *a 9 mm pistol, a .22-caliber rifle*.

cannon A weapon, usually supported on some type of carriage, that fires explosive projectiles. The form: *a 105 mm cannon*. Plural is *cannons*.

carbine A short, lightweight rifle, usually having a barrel length of less than 20 inches. The form: *an M3 carbine*.

cartridge See **bullet**.

clip A device to store multiple rounds of ammunition together as a unit, ready for insertion into the gun. Clips are generally used to load obsolete military rifles. *Clip* is not the correct term for a detachable *magazine* commonly used in modern military rifles, assault rifles, assault weapons, submachine guns and semi-automatic pistols. See **magazine**.

Colt Named for Samuel Colt, it designates a make of weapon or ammunition developed for Colt handguns. The forms: *a Colt .45-caliber revolver, .45 Colt ammunition*.

fully automatic A firearm that fires continuously as long as the trigger is depressed. Examples include *machine guns* and *submachine guns*.

gauge The measure of the size of a shotgun. Gauge is expressed in terms of the number per pound of round lead balls with a diameter equal to the size of the barrel. The bigger the number, the smaller the shotgun.

The forms: *a 12-gauge shotgun, a .410-gauge shotgun*. The .410 actually is a caliber, but commonly is called a gauge. The ball leaving the barrel is 0.41" in diameter.

W

handgun A *pistol* or a *revolver*.

howitzer A cannon shorter than a gun of the same caliber employed to fire projectiles at relatively high angles at a target, such as opposing forces behind a ridge. The form: *a 105 mm howitzer.*

lever-action rifle A handle on the stock ejects and loads cartridges and cocks the rifle for triggering. A firearm often associated with the Old West. Example: *Winchester 94.*

M1, M16 These and similar combinations of a letter and figure(s) designate rifles used by the military. The forms: *an M1 rifle, an M16 rifle.*

machine gun A fully automatic gun that fires as long as the trigger is depressed and bullets are chambered. Such a weapon is generally so large and heavy that it rests on the ground or a mount. A submachine gun is hand-held. The form: *a .50-caliber Browning machine gun.*

magazine The ammunition storage and feeding device within or attached to a firearm. It may be fixed to the firearm or detachable. It is not a *clip.*

Magnum A trademark for a type of high-powered cartridge with a larger case and a larger powder charge than other cartridges of approximately the same caliber. The form: *a .357 Magnum, a .44 Magnum.*

mortar Device used to launch a mortar shell; it is the shell, not the mortar, that is fired.

musket A heavy, large-caliber shoulder firearm fired by means of a matchlock, a wheel lock, a flintlock or a percussion lock. Its ammunition is a musket ball.

pistol A handgun that can be a single shot or a semi-automatic. Differs from a revolver in that the chamber and barrel are one integral part. Its size is measured in calibers. The form: *a .45-caliber pistol.*

revolver A handgun. Differs from a pistol in that cartridges are held in chambers in a cylinder that revolves through the barrel. The form: *a .45-caliber revolver.*

rifle A firearm designed or made to be fired from the shoulder and having a rifled bore. It uses bullets or cartridges for ammunition. Its size is measured in calibers. The form: *a .22-caliber rifle.*

Saturday night special A compact, relatively inexpensive handgun.

semi-automatic A firearm that fires only once for each pull of the trigger. It reloads after each shot. The form: *a semi-automatic rifle, a semi-automatic weapon, a semi-automatic pistol.* The hyphen is an exception to general guidance against hyphenating words formed with *semi-.*

shell The word applies to military or naval ammunition and to shotgun ammunition. For small arms, bullet or round is the common term for ammunition.

shot Small lead or steel pellets fired by shotguns. A shotgun shell usually contains 1 to 2 ounces of shot. Do not use *shot* interchangeably with *buckshot*, which refers only to the largest shot sizes.

shotgun A firearm typically used to fire small spherical pellets called shot. *Shotguns* usually have a smooth bore barrel, but some contain a rifled barrel, which is used to fire a single projectile. Size is measured according to gauge, except for the .410, which is measured according to caliber, meaning the ball leaving the barrel is 0.41" in diameter. The form: *a 12-gauge shotgun, a .410 shotgun.*

submachine gun A lightweight

W

fully automatic gun firing handgun ammunition.

weather-beaten

weatherman The preferred term is *weather forecaster*.

weather terms The following (except for **storm names**) are based on definitions used by the National Weather Service. All temperatures are Fahrenheit. The federal weather glossary is at http://forecast.weather. gov/glossary.php

blizzard Wind speeds of 35 mph or more and considerable falling and/ or blowing of snow with visibility of less than one-quarter mile for three or more hours.

coastal waters The waters within 100 miles of the coast, including bays, harbors and sounds.

cyclone A storm with strong winds rotating about a moving center of low atmospheric pressure.

The word sometimes is used in the United States to mean *tornado* and in the Indian Ocean area to mean *hurricane*.

degree-day A measure of the amount of heating or cooling needed for a building. It is based on the difference between the average daily temperature and 65 degrees. Positive values are cooling degree days and negative values are heating degree days.

derecho A widespread and usually fast-moving straight-line windstorm. It is usually more than hundreds of miles long and more than 100 miles across. Plural: *derechos*.

dew point The temperature to which air must be cooled for dew to form. The higher the *dew point*, the more moisture in the air.

dust devil A small, rapidly rotating wind that is made visible by the dust, dirt or debris it picks up. Also called a *whirlwind*, it develops best on clear, dry, hot afternoons.

dust storm Visibility of one-half mile or less due to dust, wind speeds of 30 mph or more.

El Nino, La Nina El Nino is a naturally occurring worldwide climate phenomenon that starts with unusually warm water in the central and eastern equatorial Pacific and then changes weather worldwide. The term refers to the interaction of that warmth with the atmosphere in the region, shifting currents in the air 5 to 10 miles above sea level. These shifts affect weather for thousands of miles, leading to storm tracks and belts of strong winds. El Nino is the cause of changes in weather, with the weather it brings best referred to as "effects of El Nino." Winter is often milder and wetter in much of the U.S., with heavier winter rains often hitting California from January through March, especially during stronger El Nino periods. El Nino often, but not always, triggers droughts in places like Australia and India. Elsewhere, droughts are quenched and floods may replace them. The Pacific gets more hurricanes; the Atlantic fewer. The world warms, increasing Earth's already rising thermometer from climate change. The effects in the U.S. usually don't go that deep into spring.

The flip side of El Nino is La Nina, which is an occasional but natural cooling of the equatorial Pacific that also changes weather worldwide. There is also a neutral stage with neither unusually warm nor cool water. La Nina's effects are often opposite of El Nino, so there are more hurricanes in the

W

Atlantic and fewer in the Pacific. Parts of Australia and Indonesia get wetter. In the U.S., drier than normal conditions occur in the central Plains in the fall and the Southeast in the winter, while the Pacific Northwest is likely to be wetter than normal.

flash flood A sudden, violent flood. It typically occurs after a heavy rain or the melting of a heavy snow.

flash flood warning Warns that flash flooding is imminent or in progress or is highly likely. Those in the affected area should take necessary precautions immediately.

flash flood watch Alerts the public that conditions are favorable for flash flooding. Those in the affected area are urged to be ready to take additional precautions if a flash flood warning is issued or if flooding is observed.

flood Stories about floods usually tell how high the water is and where it is expected to crest. Such a story should also, for comparison, list flood stage and how high the water is above, or below, flood stage.

Wrong: *The river is expected to crest at 39 feet.*

Right: *The river is expected to crest at 39 feet, 12 feet above flood stage.*

freeze Describes conditions when the temperature at or near the surface is expected to be below 32 degrees during the growing season. Adjectives such as *severe* or *hard* are used if a cold spell exceeding two days is expected. A *hard freeze* is when the temperature drops to 28 degrees in areas that don't normally freeze.

A freeze may or may not be accompanied by the formation of frost. However, use of the term *freeze* usually is restricted for occasions when wind or other conditions prevent frost.

freezing drizzle, freezing rain A drizzle or rain that falls as a liquid but freezes into glaze upon contact with the cold ground or surface structures.

frost Describes the formation of very small ice crystals, which might develop under conditions similar to dew except for the minimum temperatures involved. Phrases such as *frost in low places* or *scattered light frost* are used when appropriate.

funnel cloud A violent, rotating column of air that does not touch the ground, usually a pendant from a cumulonimbus cloud.

gale Sustained winds within the range of 39 to 54 mph (34 to 47 knots).

hail Showery precipitation in the form of irregular pellets or balls of ice more than 5 mm in diameter, falling from a cumulonimbus cloud.

heavy snow It generally means:
a. A fall accumulating to 4 inches or more in depth in 12 hours, or
b. A fall accumulating to 6 inches or more in depth in 24 hours.

high wind Normally indicates that sustained winds of 40 mph or greater are expected to last one hour or longer; or winds of 58 mph regardless of how long they last.

hurricane categories Hurricanes are ranked 1 to 5 according to what is known as the Saffir-Simpson Hurricane Wind Scale.

Category 1 — Hurricane has winds of 74 to 95 mph. Some damage will occur.

Category 2 — Winds from 96 to 110 mph. Extensive damage will occur.

Category 3 — Winds from 111 to 129 mph. Devastating damage will occur.

Category 4 — Winds from 130 to

W

156 mph. Catastrophic damage will occur.

Category 5 — Winds of 157 mph or higher. Catastrophic damage will occur.

Only three *Category 5* storms have hit the United States since record keeping began: the 1935 Labor Day hurricane that hit the Florida Keys and killed 600 people; Hurricane Camille, which devastated the Mississippi coast in 1969, killing 256 and leaving $1.4 billion damage, and Hurricane Andrew, which hit South Florida in 1992, killing 43 and causing $30.5 billion in damage. Hurricane Katrina in 2005 reached Category 5 in open water but hit the coast as a Category 3. Most estimates put the death toll in Katrina at more than 1,800 people, although some estimates are lower depending what deaths are included in the total. The storm caused more than $100 billion in damage; some later estimates peg that number at over $150 billion.

Categories 3, 4 and 5 hurricanes are considered major hurricanes.

hurricane eye The relatively calm area in the center of the storm. In this area winds are light and the sky often is covered only partly by clouds.

hurricane or typhoon A warm-core tropical cyclone in which the minimum sustained surface wind is 74 mph or more.

Hurricanes are spawned east of the international date line. Typhoons develop west of the line. They are known as cyclones in the Indian Ocean and Australia.

When a hurricane or typhoon loses strength (wind speed), usually after landfall, it is reduced to *tropical storm* status.

hurricane season The portion of the year that has a relatively high incidence of hurricanes. In the Atlantic, Caribbean and Gulf of Mexico, this is from June through November. In the eastern Pacific, it is May 15 through Nov. 30. In the central Pacific, it is June 1 through Nov. 30.

hurricane warning An announcement that sustained winds of 74 mph (119 km/hr) or higher are expected somewhere within the specified area in association with a tropical, subtropical or post-tropical cyclone. The warning is issued 36 hours before tropical-storm-force winds are expected to arrive.

hurricane watch An announcement that sustained winds of 74 mph (119 km/hr) or higher are possible within the specified area in association with a tropical, subtropical or post-tropical cyclone. A hurricane watch is issued 48 hours in advance of the expected onset of tropical-storm-force winds.

ice storm warning Reserved for occasions when significant, and possibly damaging, accumulations of ice are expected.

ice storm, freezing drizzle, freezing rain Describes the dangerous freezing of drizzle or rain on objects as it strikes them. *Freezing drizzle* and *freezing rain* are synonyms for *ice storm*. Significant accumulations, which can take down power lines, are usually one-quarter of an inch or greater.

microburst Occurs when a mass of cooled air rushes downward out of a thunderstorm, hits the ground and rushes outward in all directions. Peak winds last less than five minutes and are less 2.5 miles wide. A plane flying through a *microburst* at low altitude, as on final approach or takeoff, would at first experience a strong headwind and increased lift,

W

followed by a strong tail wind and sharply decreased lift.

monsoon Usually refers to a regular season of heavy rain and wind for a particular region, such as in India or Arizona and New Mexico. It is a seasonal warm wind created by temperature difference on land and nearby ocean. It reverses directions with the seasons, so there are dry phases of monsoons, but people don't usually think of the seasonal dry period as a monsoon.

National Hurricane Center The National Weather Service's National Hurricane Center in Miami has overall responsibility for tracking and providing information about tropical depressions, tropical storms and hurricanes in the Atlantic Ocean, Gulf of Mexico, Caribbean Sea and eastern Pacific Ocean.

The service's Central Pacific Hurricane Center in Honolulu is responsible for hurricane information in the Pacific Ocean area north of the equator from 140 degrees west longitude to 180 degrees.

Online: www.nhc.noaa.gov

nearshore waters The waters extended to 5 miles from shore.

nor'easter The term used by the National Weather Service for storms that either exit or move north along the East Coast, producing winds blowing from the northeast.

offshore waters The waters extending to about 250 miles from shore.

polar vortex Usually refers to the gigantic circular upper air weather pattern in the Arctic region, enveloping the North Pole (but it can apply to the South Pole, too). It is a normal pattern that is stronger in the winter and keeps some of the coldest weather bottled up near the North Pole. The jet stream usually pens the polar vortex in and keeps it north. But at times some of the vortex can break off or move south, bringing unusually cold weather south and permitting warmer weather to creep up north.

sandstorm Visibility of one-half mile or less due to sand blown by winds of 30 mph or more.

Santa Ana wind In Southern California, a weather condition in which strong, hot, dry, dust-bearing winds descend to the Pacific Coast from inland desert regions.

severe thunderstorm Describes either of the following:

a. Winds — Thunderstorm-related surface winds sustained or gusts 58 mph or greater.

b. Hail — Surface hail 1 inch in diameter or larger. The word *hail* in a watch implies hail at the surface and aloft unless qualifying phrases such as *hail aloft* are used.

sleet (one form of ice pellet) Describes generally solid grains of ice formed by the freezing of raindrops or the refreezing of largely melted snowflakes before reaching the ground. Sleet, like small hail, usually bounces when hitting a hard surface.

sleet (heavy) Heavy sleet is a fairly rare event in which the ground is covered to a depth of one-half inch or more or a depth of significance to motorists and others.

squall A sudden increase of wind speed by at least 18 mph (16 knots) and rising to 25 mph (22 knots) and lasting for at least one minute.

storm names Major storm names provided by government weather agencies, the European Union or the World Meteorological Organization are acceptable. Do not use names

W

created by private weather agencies or other organizations. See **fire names**.

storm surge An abnormal rise of water above the normal tide, generated by a storm.

storm tide Water level rise due to the combination of storm surge and the astronomical tide.

tidal wave Often used incorrectly as a synonym for *tsunami*. A large wave created by rising tide in a funnel-shaped inlet is called a *tidal bore*. Unusually large waves at sea are sometimes called *rogue waves*.

tornado A violent rotating column of air forming a pendant, usually from a cumulonimbus cloud, and touching the ground. It is often, but not always, visible as a funnel cloud, and usually is accompanied by a loud roaring noise. On a local scale, it is the most destructive of all atmospheric phenomena. Tornadoes can appear from any direction, but in the U.S. most move from southwest to northeast.

Tornado strength is measured by an enhanced F-scale rating from EF0 to EF5, which considers 28 different

Heat index

TEMP. F	RELATIVE HUMIDITY												
	40%	45%	50%	55%	60%	65%	70%	75%	80%	85%	90%	95%	100%
110	136												
108	130	137											
106	124	130	137										
104	119	124	130	137		APPARENT TEMPERATURE							
102	114	119	124	130	137								
100	109	114	118	124	129	136							
98	105	109	113	117	123	128	134						
96	101	104	108	112	116	121	126	132					
94	97	100	102	106	110	114	119	124	129	135			
92	94	96	99	101	105	108	112	116	121	126	131		
90	91	93	95	97	100	103	106	109	113	117	122	127	132
88	88	89	91	93	95	98	100	103	106	110	113	117	121
86	85	87	88	89	91	93	95	97	100	102	105	108	112
84	83	84	85	86	88	89	90	92	94	96	98	100	103
82	81	82	83	84	84	85	86	88	89	90	91	93	95
80	80	80	81	81	82	82	83	84	84	85	86	86	87

Wind chill factor

WIND MPH	AIR TEMPERATURE																	
	40	35	30	25	20	15	10	5	0	-5	-10	-15	-20	-25	-30	-35	-40	-45
	APPARENT TEMPERATURE																	
5	36	31	25	19	13	7	1	-5	-11	-16	-22	-28	-34	-40	-46	-52	-57	-63
10	34	27	21	15	9	3	-4	-10	-16	-22	-28	-35	-41	-47	-53	-59	-66	-72
15	32	25	19	13	6	0	-7	-13	-19	-26	-32	-39	-45	-51	-58	-64	-71	-77
20	30	24	17	11	4	-2	-9	-15	-22	-29	-35	-42	-48	-55	-61	-68	-74	-81
25	29	23	16	9	3	-4	-11	-17	-24	-31	-37	-44	-51	-58	-64	-71	-78	-84
30	28	22	15	8	1	-5	-12	-19	-26	-33	-39	-46	-53	-60	-67	-73	-80	-87
35	28	21	14	7	0	-7	-14	-21	-27	-34	-41	-48	-55	-62	-69	-76	-82	-89
40	27	20	13	6	-1	-8	-15	-22	-29	-36	-43	-50	-57	-64	-71	-78	-84	-91
45	26	19	12	5	-2	-9	-16	-23	-30	-37	-44	-51	-58	-65	-72	-79	-86	-93
50	26	19	12	4	-3	-10	-17	-24	-31	-38	-45	-52	-60	-67	-74	-81	-88	-95
55	25	18	11	4	-3	-11	-18	-25	-32	-39	-46	-54	-61	-68	-75	-82	-89	-97
60	25	17	10	3	-4	-11	-19	-26	-33	-40	-48	-55	-62	-69	-76	-84	-91	-98

FROSTBITE TIME   30 MIN.   10 MIN.   5 MIN.

W

types of damage to structures and trees. It updates the original scale, which estimated wind strength. An EF2 or higher is considered a significant tornado.

Plural is *tornadoes*.

tornado warning A *tornado warning* is issued by a local National Weather Service office to warn the public of an existing tornado.

tornado watch A *tornado watch* alerts the public to the possibility of a tornado in the next several hours.

traveler's advisory Alerts the public that difficult traveling or hazardous road conditions are expected to be widespread.

tropical depression A tropical cyclone in which the maximum sustained surface wind is 38 mph (33 knots) or less.

tropical storm A warm-core tropical cyclone in which the maximum sustained surface winds range from 39 to 73 mph (34 to 63 knots) inclusive.

tsunami (s.), **tsunamis** (pl.) A great sea wave or seismic sea wave caused by an underwater disturbance such as an earthquake, landslide or volcano. It can cause massive death and destruction as was seen in the Indian Ocean *tsunami* in December 2004. It is different from a tidal wave.

typhoon See **hurricane or typhoon** in this listing.

waterspout A tornado over water.

wind chill factor No hyphen.

The *wind chill* is a calculation that describes the combined effect of the wind and cold temperatures on exposed skin. The *wind chill factor* would be minus 4, for example, if the temperature was 15 degrees and the wind was blowing at 25 mph — in other words, a temperature of 4 below zero with no wind.

The higher the wind at a given temperature, the lower the wind chill reading, although wind speeds above 40 mph have little additional cooling effect.

wind shear A sudden shift in wind direction and/or speed.

winter storm warning Notifies the public that a winter storm is producing, or is forecast to produce, heavy snow or significant ice accumulations.

winter storm watch Alerts the public that there is a potential for heavy snow or significant ice accumulations. The watch is usually issued at least 24 to 36 hours in advance.

weather vane

web Short form of *World Wide Web*, it is a service that enables the distribution of image-rich content and information on the internet. The web is not the same as the internet, but is a subset; other applications, such as email, exist on the internet. Also, *website, webcam, webcast, webfeed, webmaster, webpage*. But *web address, web browser*. See **internet**.

web browser Software for viewing and interacting with websites on a computer or mobile device.

website Also, *webcam, webcast, webmaster, webpage, webfeed, the web*.

Webster's New World College Dictionary See **dictionaries**.

weeklong, weekslong One word as an adjective.

weights Use figures: *The baby weighed 9 pounds, 7 ounces. She had a 9-pound, 7-ounce boy.*

W

well Hyphenate as part of a compound modifier: *She is a well-dressed woman. He is well-fed.*

See **hyphen** in the **Punctuation** chapter for guidelines on compound modifiers.

well-being

well-informed

Wells Fargo & Co. Acquired Wachovia Corp. in 2009. Headquarters is in San Francisco.

well-to-do

well-wishers

West, Western, west, western Use *West* to cover the 13-state region as defined by the U.S. Census Bureau and broken into two divisions.

The eight Mountain division states are Arizona, Colorado, Idaho, Montana, Nevada, New Mexico, Utah and Wyoming.

The five Pacific division states are Alaska, California, Hawaii, Oregon and Washington.

Capitalize *Western* for the film or book genre, but lowercase the style of music better known as country.

For directions, *west* and *western*. See **directions and regions**.

Western Hemisphere The continents of North and South America, and the islands near them.

It frequently is subdivided as follows:

Caribbean The islands from the tip of Florida to the continent of South America, plus French Guiana, Guyana and Suriname on the northeastern coast of South America.

Major island elements are Cuba,

Hispaniola (the island shared by the Dominican Republic and Haiti), Jamaica, Puerto Rico, and the West Indies islands.

Central America The narrow strip of land between Mexico and Colombia. Located there are Belize, Costa Rica, El Salvador, Guatemala, Honduras, Nicaragua and Panama.

Latin America The area of the Americas south of the United States where Romance languages (those derived from Latin) are dominant. It applies to most of the region south of the United States except areas with a British heritage: the Bahamas, Barbados, Belize, Grenada, Guyana, Jamaica, Trinidad and Tobago, and various islands in the West Indies. Suriname, the former Dutch Guiana, is an additional exception.

North America Canada, Mexico, the United States and the Danish territory of Greenland. When the term is used in more than its continental sense, it also may include the islands of the Caribbean.

South America Argentina, Bolivia, Brazil, Chile, Colombia, Ecuador, Paraguay, Peru, Uruguay, Venezuela, and in a purely continental sense, French Guiana, Guyana and Suriname. Politically and psychologically, however, the latter three regard themselves as part of the Caribbean.

West Indies An island chain extending in an eastward arc between the southeastern United States and the northern shore of South America, separating the Caribbean Sea from the Atlantic Ocean and including the Bahamas, the Greater Antilles, and the Lesser Antilles.

Major island elements are the nations of Barbados, Grenada, and Trinidad and Tobago, plus smaller

W

islands dependent in various degrees on:
- Britain: British Virgin Islands, Anguilla, and the West Indies Associated States, including Antigua, Dominica, St. Lucia, St. Vincent and St. Christopher-Nevis.
- France: Guadeloupe (composed of islands known as Basse-Terre and Grande-Terre, plus five other islands) and Martinique.
- Netherlands: Netherlands Antilles, composed of Aruba, Bonaire, Curacao, Saba, St. Eustatius and the southern portion of St. Martin Island (the northern half is held by France and is part of Guadeloupe).
- United States: U.S. Virgin Islands, principally St. Croix, St. John and St. Thomas.

Western Wall The last remaining part of the second Biblical temple and the holiest site where Jews can pray. *The Western Wall* is located in Jerusalem's Old City, on the edge of the site known as the *Temple Mount* to Jews and *Haram al-Sharif (the Noble Sanctuary)* to Muslims. Some non-Jews refer to the site as the *Wailing Wall.*

West Indies See **Western Hemisphere**.

West Point Acceptable on second reference to the *U.S. Military Academy.*
    See **military academies**.
    In datelines:
    WEST POINT, N.Y. (AP) —

West Virginia Abbreviate *W.Va.* in datelines only; spell out in stories.
Postal code: *WV*
    See **state names**.

Weyerhaeuser Co. Headquarters is in Federal Way, Washington.

WhatsApp Messaging app owned by Facebook that's popular in much of the world, with more than 1 billion daily active users.

wheat It is measured in bushels domestically, in metric tons for international trade.
    There are 36.7 bushels of wheat in a metric ton.

wheelchair See **disabled, handicapped**.

whereabouts Takes a singular verb: *His whereabouts is a mystery.*

wherever

which See **essential clauses, nonessential clauses; that, which**; and **who, whom**.

whip Capitalize when used as a formal title before a name. See **legislative titles** and **titles**.

whistleblower

white-collar (adj.)

white paper Two words, lowercase, when used to refer to a special report.

whitewash (n., v. and adj.)

WHO The World Health Organization is the specialized health agency of the United Nations and is based in Geneva. It sets internationally accepted guidelines for treating diseases and coordinates responses to disease outbreaks globally. *WHO* is acceptable on second reference and takes a singular verb. Online:

W

www.who.int

wholehearted

wholesale price index A measurement of the changes in the average prices that businesses pay for a selected group of industrial commodities, farm products, processed foods and feed for animals.

Do not capitalize when referring to the U.S. producer price index, issued monthly by the Bureau of Labor Statistics, an agency of the Labor Department.

who's, whose *Who's* is a contraction for *who is*, not a possessive: *Who's there?*

Whose is the possessive: *I do not know whose coat it is.*

who, whom *Who* is the pronoun used for references to human beings and to animals with a name. Write *the person who is in charge*, not *the person that is in charge.*

Who is grammatically the subject (never the object) of a sentence, clause or phrase: *The woman who rented the room left the window open. Who is there?*

Whom is used when someone is the object of a verb or preposition: *The woman to whom the room was rented left the window open. Whom do you wish to see?*

See **essential clauses, nonessential clauses** for guidelines on how to punctuate clauses introduced by *who, whom, that* and *which*. Also see **that, which (pronouns)**.

-wide No hyphen. Some examples:
citywide   nationwide
continentwide statewide
countrywide   worldwide

industrywide

wide- Usually hyphenated. Some examples:
wide-angle   wide-eyed
wide-awake   wide-open
wide-brimmed
Exception: *widespread.*

widget In a technology context, a small module with a specific purpose that appears on a website, desktop or other interface and allows access to content or functions.

widow, widower In obituaries: A man is *survived by his wife*, or *leaves his wife*. A woman is *survived by her husband*, or *leaves her husband*.

In same-sex marriages, a man is *survived by his husband*, or *leaves his husband*. A woman is *survived by her wife*, or *leaves her wife.*

Guard against the redundant *widow (widower) of the late.*

widths See **dimensions**.

Wi-Fi For the wireless networking standards.

wiki Software that allows a group of users to add, delete, edit and share information on a website.

WikiLeaks

Wikipedia An online encyclopedia whose entries are created and edited by its users, regardless of their expertise. May contain useful links but should not be used as a primary source of information. It is operated by the nonprofit Wikimedia Foundation, based in San Francisco.

wildfires Use square miles to describe the size of fires. *The fire has burned*

W

nearly 4 1/2 square miles of hilly brush land. Use acres only when the fire is less than a square mile. When possible, be descriptive: *The fire is the size of Denver.*

wildlife

will See **shall, will** and **subjunctive mood**.

windbreaker

wind chill factor See **weather terms**.

wind-swept

windup (n. and adj.) **wind up** (v.)

wingspan

winter See **seasons**.

wintertime

wiretap, wiretapper (n.) The verb forms: *wiretap, wiretapped, wiretapping.*

Wisconsin Abbreviate *Wis.* in datelines only; spell out in stories. Postal code: *WI*
　　See **state names**.

-wise No hyphen when it means *in the direction of* or *with regard to.* Some examples:
　　clockwise　　otherwise
　　lengthwise　　slantwise
　　Avoid contrived combinations such as *moneywise, religionwise.*
　　The word *penny-wise* is spelled with a hyphen because it is a compound adjective in which *wise* means *smart*, not an application of the suffix *-wise*. The same for *street-wise* in *the street-wise youth* (an exception to Webster's New World

College Dictionary).

WMD Acceptable on second reference for *weapons of mass destruction.*

woman, women Use *female* as an adjective, not *woman. She is the first female governor of North Carolina.*
　　Treatment of the sexes should be evenhanded and free of assumptions and stereotypes. This does not mean that valid and acceptable words such as *mankind* or *humanity* cannot be used. They are proper.
　　See **courtesy titles; divorce; man, mankind;** and **-persons**.

word-of-mouth (n. and adj.)

word processing (adj.)

workbook, workday, workforce, workhorse, workout, workplace, worksheet, workstation, workweek

workers' compensation

working class (n.)　　**working-class** (adj.)

World Bank Acceptable in all references for *International Bank for Reconstruction and Development.*

World Health Organization *WHO* is acceptable on second reference.
　　Headquarters is in Geneva.

World Series Or *the Series* on second reference. A rare exception to the general principles under **capitalization**.

World Trade Center Name of the partially completed complex of buildings that replaced the seven of the same name destroyed on Sept.

W

11, 2001. The complex also includes
the *National September 11 Memorial &
Museum* and the *World Trade Center
Transportation Hub*. The tallest
building is *One World Trade Center*. If
necessary for clarity, refer to the *new
World Trade Center complex*, or to the
old or *destroyed trade center complex*
or *twin towers*, or to *ground zero*. See
One World Trade Center.

World War I, World War II

worldwide

worn-out (adj.)

worthwhile

would See **should, would**.

wrack See **rack, wrack**.

wracked The preferred spelling when
used to say a person is *wracked with
pain*. Also, *nerve-wracking*.

write-down (n. and adj.) **write
down** (v.) An accounting step a
company makes when an asset or
class of assets it holds falls in value.
The decline in value is reflected in
a reduction on the asset side of a
company's balance sheet.

write-in (n. and adj.) **write in** (v.)

wrongdoing

Wyoming Abbreviate *Wyo.* in
datelines only; spell out in stories.
Postal code: WY
See **state names**.

W

xyz

Xerox A trademark for a brand of photocopy machine. Never a verb. Use a generic term, such as *photocopy*.

Headquarters of *Xerox Corp*. is in Norwalk, Connecticut.

Xinhua News Agency The official news agency of the Chinese government is based in Beijing. It was founded in 1931 as the Red China News Agency and adopted its current name in 1937. *Xinhua* is acceptable on second reference.

Xmas Don't use this abbreviation for *Christmas*.

XML For *Extensible Markup Language*, used to sort, search and format information.

X-ray (n., v. and adj.) Use for both the photographic process and the radiation particles themselves.

Yahoo An online services provider owned by Verizon Communications Inc. subsidiary Oath Inc. Do not use the exclamation point in its formal name.

yard Equal to 3 feet.

The metric equivalent is approximately 0.91 meter.

To convert to meters, multiply by 0.91 (5 yards x 0.91 = 4.55 meters).

See **foot**; **meter**; and **distances**.

year-end (n. and adj.)

yearlong, yearslong One word as an adjective.

year-round (adj. and adv.)

years When a phrase refers to a month and day within the current year, do not include the year: *The hearing is scheduled for June 26*. If the reference is to a past or future year, include the year and set it off with commas: *Feb. 14, 2025, is the target date*. Use an *s* without an apostrophe to indicate spans of decades or centuries: *the 1890s, the 1800s*.

Years are an exception to the general rule in numerals that a figure is not used to start a sentence: *2013 was a very good year*.

See **A.D.**; **B.C.**; **century**; **historical periods and events**; **months** and **numerals**.

Yellow Pages Capitalize in describing the business telephone directory.

yesterday Use only in direct quotations and in phrases that do not refer to a specific day: *Yesterday we were young*.

Use the day of the week in other cases.

yesteryear

Yom Kippur The Jewish Day of Atonement. Occurs in September or October.

Young Men's Christian Association The term *the Y* is acceptable in all references to the main organization, which has its headquarters in

Chicago. Use *YMCA* when referring to a specific location: *the YMCA of Greater Louisville.*

Young Women's Christian Association *YWCA* is acceptable in all references.

Headquarters is in New York.

youth Applicable to boys and girls from age 13 until 18th birthday. Use *man* or *woman* for individuals 18 and older. See **names, boy, girl**.

YouTube A video-sharing network owned by Google.

Yukon A territorial section of Canada. Do not abbreviate. Use in datelines after the names of communities in the territory.

See **Canada**.

Yule, Yuletide Old English name for Christmas season. Uppercase is an exception to Webster's New World College Dictionary.

Yum Brands Inc. Owner of the Pizza Hut, KFC and Taco Bell restaurant chains. Do not use the formal exclamation point in the corporate name. Headquarters of Yum Brands is in Louisville, Kentucky.

zero, zeros

zigzag

Zika A virus that can cause severe birth defects if a pregnant woman becomes infected. The birth defects include microcephaly, in which babies are born with abnormally small heads due to underlying brain damage. Most people infected with the Zika virus don't get sick, and those who do usually experience mild symptoms including fever, rash, joint pain and red eyes. A very small proportion of people infected with Zika develop Guillain-Barre, a syndrome that causes temporary muscle weakness and sometimes paralysis.

Zika is primarily spread by a type of tropical mosquito called Aedes aegypti, which can pick up the virus from an infected person's blood. It also can be transmitted by sex. There are no treatments; tests of some experimental vaccines began in humans in the summer of 2016.

The virus is closely related to the dengue and yellow fever viruses. It is named for the Zika forest in Uganda, where it was first identified in a monkey in 1947. Only occasional human cases were described until a 2007 outbreak on the Pacific island of Yap in Micronesia. The link to birth defects didn't become apparent until a large Zika outbreak was reported in Brazil in 2015 and spread rapidly through Latin America and the Caribbean.

Usage: *the Zika virus* or just *Zika.*

ZIP code Use all-caps *ZIP* for *Zone Improvement Plan,* but always lowercase the word *code.*

Run the five digits together without a comma, and do not put a comma between the state name and the ZIP code: *New York, NY 10020.*

zip line

Zurich The city in Switzerland stands alone in datelines.

xyz

Punctuation

Incorrect punctuation can change the meaning of a sentence, the results of which could be far-reaching.

Even if the meaning is not changed, bad punctuation, however inconsequential, can cause the reader to lose track of what is being said and give up reading a sentence.

The basic guideline is to use common sense.

— Punctuation is to make clear the thought being expressed.

— If punctuation does not help make clear what is being said, it should not be there.

"The Elements of Style" by William Strunk Jr. and E.B. White says:

"Clarity, clarity, clarity. When you become hopelessly mired in a sentence, it is best to start fresh; do not try to fight your way through against terrible odds of syntax. Usually what is wrong is that the construction has become too involved at some point; the sentence needs to be broken apart and replaced by two or more shorter sentences."

This applies to punctuation. If a sentence becomes cluttered with commas, semicolons and dashes, start over.

These two paragraphs are full of commas and clauses; all of it equals too much for the reader to grasp:

The Commonwealth Games Federation, in an apparent effort to persuade other nations to ignore the spiraling boycott, ruled Sunday that Budd, a runner who has had a storied past on and off the track, and Cowley, a swimmer who competes for the University of Texas, were ineligible under the Commonwealth Constitution to compete for England in the 10-day event to be held in Edinburgh, Scotland, beginning July 24.

The decision on Budd, who has been the object of a number of demonstrations in the past, and Cowley followed an earlier announcement Sunday by Tanzania that it was joining Nigeria, Kenya, Ghana and Uganda in boycotting the games because of Britain's refusal to support economic sanctions against South Africa's government.

apostrophe (') Follow these guidelines:

POSSESSIVES: See the **possessives** entry in main section.

PLURAL NOUNS NOT ENDING IN S: Add 's: *the alumni's contributions, women's rights.*

PLURAL NOUNS ENDING IN S: Add only an apostrophe: *the churches' needs, the girls' toys, the horses' food, the ships' wake, states' rights, the VIPs' entrance.*

NOUNS PLURAL IN FORM, SINGULAR IN MEANING: Add only an apostrophe: *mathematics' rules, measles' effects.* (But see **INANIMATE OBJECTS** below.)

Apply the same principle when a plural word occurs in the formal name of a singular entity: *General Motors' profits, the United States' wealth.*

NOUNS THE SAME IN SINGULAR AND PLURAL: Treat them the same as plurals, even if the meaning is singular: *one corps' location, the two deer's tracks, the lone moose's antlers.*

SINGULAR NOUNS NOT ENDING IN S: Add 's: *the church's needs, the girl's toys, the horse's food, the ship's route, the VIP's seat.*

Some style guides say that singular nouns ending in s sounds such as *ce, x,* and *z* may take either the apostrophe alone or 's. See **SPECIAL EXPRESSIONS,** but otherwise, for consistency and ease in remembering a rule, always use 's if the word does not end in the letter s: *Butz's policies, the fox's den, the justice's verdict, Marx's theories, the prince's life, Xerox's profits.*

SINGULAR COMMON NOUNS ENDING IN S: Add 's: *the hostess's invitation, the hostess's seat; the witness's answer, the witness's story.* (A change from previous guidance calling for just an apostrophe if the next word begins with s.)

SINGULAR PROPER NAMES ENDING IN S: Use only an apostrophe: *Achilles' heel, Agnes' book, Ceres' rites, Descartes' theories, Dickens' novels, Euripides' dramas, Hercules' labors, Jesus' life, Jules' seat, Kansas' schools, Moses' law, Socrates' life, Tennessee Williams' plays, Xerxes' armies.* (An exception is *St. James's Palace.*)

SPECIAL EXPRESSIONS: The following exceptions to the general rule for words not ending in s apply to words that end in an s sound and are followed by a word that begins with s: *for appearance' sake, for conscience' sake, for goodness' sake.* Use 's otherwise: *the appearance's cost, my conscience's voice.*

PRONOUNS: Personal interrogative and relative pronouns have separate forms for the possessive. None involves an apostrophe: *mine, ours, your, yours, his, hers, its, theirs, whose.*

Caution: If you are using an apostrophe with a pronoun, always double-check to be sure that the meaning calls for a contraction: *you're, it's, there's, who's.*

Follow the rules listed above in forming the possessives of other pronouns: *another's idea, others' plans, someone's guess.*

COMPOUND WORDS: Applying the rules above, add an apostrophe or 's to the word closest to the object possessed: *the major general's decision, the major generals' decisions, the attorney general's request, the attorneys general's request.* See the **plurals** entry for guidelines on forming the plurals of these words.

Also: *anyone else's attitude, John Adams Jr.'s father, Benjamin Franklin of Pennsylvania's motion.* Whenever practical, however, recast the phrase to avoid ambiguity: *the motion by Benjamin Franklin of Pennsylvania.*

JOINT POSSESSION, INDIVIDUAL

POSSESSION: Use a possessive form after only the last word if ownership is joint: *Fred and Sylvia's apartment, Fred and Sylvia's stocks.*

Use a possessive form after both words if the objects are individually owned: *Fred's and Sylvia's books.*

DESCRIPTIVE PHRASES: Do not add an apostrophe to a word ending in *s* when it is used primarily in a descriptive sense: *citizens band radio, a Cincinnati Reds infielder, a teachers college, a Teamsters request, a writers guide.*

Memory aid: The apostrophe usually is not used if *for* or *by* rather than *of* would be appropriate in the longer form: *a radio band for citizens, a college for teachers, a guide for writers, a request by the Teamsters.*

An *'s* is required however, when a term involves a plural word that does not end in *s*: *a children's hospital, a people's republic, the Young Men's Christian Association.*

DESCRIPTIVE NAMES: Some governmental, corporate and institutional organizations with a descriptive word in their names use an apostrophe; some do not. Follow the user's practice: *Actors' Equity, Diners Club, the Ladies' Home Journal, the National Governors Association.*

QUASI POSSESSIVES: Follow the rules above in composing the possessive form of words that occur in such phrases as *a day's pay, two weeks' vacation, three days' work, your money's worth.*

Frequently, however, a hyphenated form is clearer: *a two-week vacation, a three-day job.*

DOUBLE POSSESSIVE: Two conditions must apply for a double possessive — a phrase such as *a friend of John's* — to occur: 1. The word after *of* must refer to an animate object, and 2. The word

before *of* must involve only a portion of the animate object's possessions.

Otherwise, do not use the possessive form of the word after *of*: *The friends of John Adams mourned his death.* (All the friends were involved.) *He is a friend of the college.* (Not *college's*, because *college* is inanimate).

Memory aid: This construction occurs most often, and quite naturally, with the possessive forms of personal pronouns: *He is a friend of mine.*

INANIMATE OBJECTS: There is no blanket rule against creating a possessive form for an inanimate object, particularly if the object is treated in a personified sense. See some of the earlier examples, and note these: *death's call, the wind's murmur.*

In general, however, avoid excessive personalization of inanimate objects, and give preference to an *of* construction when it fits the makeup of the sentence. For example, the earlier references to *mathematics' rules* and *measles' effects* would better be phrased: *the rules of mathematics, the effects of measles.*

OMITTED LETTERS: *I've, it's, don't, rock 'n' roll, 'tis the season to be jolly. He is a ne'er-do-well.* See **contractions** in main section.

OMITTED FIGURES: *The class of '62. The Spirit of '76. The '20s.*

PLURALS OF A SINGLE LETTER: *Mind your p's and q's. He learned the three R's and brought home a report card with four A's and two B's. The Oakland A's won the pennant.*

DO NOT USE: For plurals of numerals or multiple-letter combinations. See **plurals**.

brackets [ ] They cannot be

transmitted over news wires. Use parentheses or recast the material.

See **parentheses**.

colon (:) Capitalize the first word after a colon only if it is a proper noun or the start of a complete sentence: *He promised this: The company will make good all the losses.* But: *There were three considerations: expense, time and feasibility.*

EMPHASIS: The colon often can be effective in giving emphasis: *He had only one hobby: eating.*

LISTS: A frequent use of a colon is at the end of a sentence or phrase to introduce lists, tabulations, texts, etc. See **lists, bulleted lists**.

LISTINGS: Use the colon in such listings as time elapsed (*1:31:07.2*), time of day (*8:31 p.m.*), biblical and legal citations (*2 Kings 2:14; Missouri Code 3:245-260*).

DIALOGUE: Use a colon for dialogue. In coverage of a trial, for example:

Bailey: What were you doing the night of the 19th?

Mason: I refuse to answer that.

Q&A: The colon is used for question-and-answer interviews:

Q: Did you strike him?

A: Indeed I did.

INTRODUCING QUOTATIONS: Use a comma to introduce a direct quotation of one sentence that remains within a paragraph. Use a colon to introduce long quotations within a paragraph and to end all paragraphs that introduce a paragraph of quoted material.

PLACEMENT WITH QUOTATION MARKS: Colons go outside quotation marks unless they are part of the quotation itself.

MISCELLANEOUS: Do not combine a dash and a colon.

comma (,) The following guidelines treat some of the most frequent questions about the use of commas. Additional guidelines on specialized uses are provided in separate entries such as **dates** and **scores**.

As with all punctuation, clarity is the biggest rule. If a comma does not help make clear what is being said, it should not be there. If omitting a comma could lead to confusion or misinterpretation, then use the comma.

For detailed guidance, consult the punctuation section in the back of Webster's New World College Dictionary.

IN A SERIES: Use commas to separate elements in a series, but do not put a comma before the conjunction in most simple series: *The flag is red, white and blue. He would nominate Tom, Dick, Harry or Jeannette.*

Include a final comma in a simple series if omitting it could make the meaning unclear. *The governor convened his most trusted advisers, economist Olivia Schneider and polling expert Carlton Torres.* (If Schneider and Torres are his most trusted advisers, don't use the final comma.) *The governor convened his most trusted advisers, economist Olivia Schneider, and polling expert Carlton Torres.* (If the governor is convening unidentified advisers plus Schneider and Torres, the final comma is needed.)

Put a comma before the concluding conjunction in a series if an integral element of the series requires a conjunction: *I had orange juice, toast, and ham and eggs for breakfast.*

Use a comma also before the concluding conjunction in a complex series of phrases: *The main points to* consider are whether the athletes are skillful enough to compete, whether they have the stamina to endure the training, and whether they have the proper mental attitude.

See **dash** and **semicolon** for cases when elements of a series contain internal commas.

WITH EQUAL ADJECTIVES: Use commas to separate a series of adjectives equal in rank. If the commas could be replaced by the word *and* without changing the sense, the adjectives are equal: *a thoughtful, precise manner; a dark, dangerous street.*

Use no comma when the last adjective before a noun outranks its predecessors because it is an integral element of a noun phrase, which is the equivalent of a single noun: *a cheap fur coat* (the noun phrase is *fur coat*); *the old oaken bucket; a new, blue spring bonnet.*

WITH NONESSENTIAL CLAUSES: A nonessential clause must be set off by commas. An essential clause must not be set off from the rest of a sentence by commas.

See **essential clauses, nonessential clauses** in the main section.

WITH NONESSENTIAL PHRASES: A nonessential phrase must be set off by commas. An essential phrase must not be set off from the rest of a sentence by commas.

See **essential phrases, nonessential phrases** in the main section.

WITH INTRODUCTORY CLAUSES AND PHRASES: A comma is used to separate an introductory clause or phrase from the main clause: *When he had tired of the mad pace of New York, he moved to Dubuque.*

The comma may be omitted after short introductory phrases if no ambiguity would result: *During the night he heard many noises.*

But use the comma if its omission would slow comprehension: *On the street below, the curious gathered.*

WITH CONJUNCTIONS: When a conjunction such as *and, but* or *for* links two clauses that could stand alone as separate sentences, use a comma before the conjunction in most cases: *She was glad she had looked, for a man was approaching the house.*

As a rule of thumb, use a comma if the subject of each clause is expressly stated: *We are visiting Washington, and we also plan a side trip to Williamsburg. We visited Washington, and our senator greeted us personally.* But no comma when the subject of the two clauses is the same and is not repeated in the second: *We are visiting Washington and plan to see the White House.*

The comma may be dropped if two clauses with expressly stated subjects are short. In general, however, favor use of a comma unless a particular literary effect is desired or if it would distort the sense of a sentence.

INTRODUCING DIRECT QUOTES: Use a comma to introduce a complete one-sentence quotation within a paragraph: *Wallace said, "She spent six months in Argentina and came back speaking English with a Spanish accent."* But use a colon to introduce quotations of more than one sentence. See **colon**.

Do not use a comma at the start of an indirect or partial quotation: *He said the victory put him "firmly on the road to a first-ballot nomination."*

BEFORE ATTRIBUTION: Use a comma instead of a period at the end of a quote that is followed by attribution: *"Write clearly and concisely," she said.*

Do not use a comma, however, if the quoted statement ends with a question mark or exclamation point: *"Why should I?" he asked.*

WITH HOMETOWNS AND AGES: Use a comma to set off an individual's hometown when it is placed in apposition to a name (whether *of* is used or not): *Mary Richards, Minneapolis, and Maude Findlay, Tuckahoe, New York, were there.*

If an individual's age is used, set it off by commas: *Maude Findlay, 48, Tuckahoe, New York, was present.*

WITH PARTY AFFILIATION, ACADEMIC DEGREES, RELIGIOUS AFFILIATIONS: See separate entries under each of these terms.

NAMES OF STATES AND NATIONS USED WITH CITY NAMES: *His journey will take him from Dublin, Ireland, to Fargo, North Dakota, and back. The Selma, Alabama, group saw the governor.*

Use parentheses, however, if a state name is inserted within a proper name: *The Huntsville (Alabama) Times.*

WITH YES AND NO: *Yes, I will be there.*

IN DIRECT ADDRESS: *Mother, I will be home late. No, sir, I did not take it.*

SEPARATING SIMILAR WORDS: Use a comma to separate duplicated words that otherwise would be confusing: *What the problem is, is not clear.*

IN LARGE FIGURES: Use a comma for most figures greater than 999. The major exceptions are street addresses (*1234 Main St.*), broadcast frequencies (*1460 kilohertz*), room numbers, serial numbers, telephone numbers, and years (*1876*). See separate entries under these headings.

PLACEMENT WITH QUOTES: Commas always go inside quotation marks.

WITH FULL DATES: When a phrase refers to a month, day and year, set off the year with a comma: *Feb. 14, 2020, is the target date.*

See **semicolon**.

compound adjectives See the **hyphen** entry.

dash (—) Follow these guidelines:

ABRUPT CHANGE: Use dashes to denote an abrupt change in thought in a sentence or an emphatic pause: *Through her long reign, the queen and her family have adapted — usually skillfully — to the changing taste of the time.* But avoid overuse of dashes to set off phrases when commas would suffice.

SERIES WITHIN A PHRASE: When a phrase that otherwise would be set off by commas contains a series of words that must be separated by commas, use dashes to set off the full phrase: *He listed the qualities — intelligence, humor, conservatism, independence — that he liked in an executive.*

ATTRIBUTION: Use a dash before an author's or composer's name at the end of a quotation: *"Who steals my purse steals trash." — Shakespeare.*

IN DATELINES:
NEW YORK (AP) — The city is broke.

IN LISTS: See **lists, bulleted lists**.

WITH SPACES: Put a space on both sides of a dash in all uses except sports agate summaries.

See **em dash, en dash, hyphen**.

ellipsis (…) In general, treat an ellipsis as a three-letter word, constructed with three periods and two spaces, as shown here.

Use an ellipsis to indicate the deletion of one or more words in condensing quotes, texts and documents. Be especially careful to avoid deletions that would distort the meaning.

An ellipsis also may be used to indicate a thought that the speaker or writer does not complete.

Substitute a dash for this purpose, however, if the context uses ellipses to indicate that words actually spoken or written have been deleted.

Brief examples of how to use ellipses are provided after guidelines are given. More extensive examples, drawn from the speech in which President Richard Nixon announced his resignation, are in the sections below marked **CONDENSATION EXAMPLE** and **QUOTATIONS**.

PUNCTUATION GUIDELINES: If the words that precede an ellipsis constitute a grammatically complete sentence, either in the original or in the condensation, place a period at the end of the last word before the ellipsis. Follow it with a regular space and an ellipsis: *I no longer have a strong enough political base. ...*

When the grammatical sense calls for a question mark, exclamation point, comma or colon, the sequence is word, punctuation mark, regular space, ellipsis: *Will you come? ...*

When material is deleted at the end of one paragraph and at the beginning of the one that follows, place an ellipsis in both locations.

CONDENSATION EXAMPLE: Here is an example of how the spacing and punctuation guidelines would be applied in condensing President Richard Nixon's resignation announcement:

Good evening. ...

In all the decisions I have made in my public life, I have always tried to do what was best for the nation. ...

... However, it has become evident to me that I no longer have a strong enough political base in ... Congress.

... As long as there was ... a base, I felt strongly that it was necessary to see the constitutional process through to its conclusion, that to do otherwise would be ... a dangerously destabilizing

precedent for the future.

QUOTATIONS: In writing a story, do not use ellipses at the beginning or end of direct quotes:

"It has become evident to me that I no longer have a strong enough political base," Nixon said.

Not *"... it has become evident to me that I no longer have a strong enough political base ... ," Nixon said.*

SPECIAL EFFECTS: Ellipses also may be used to separate individual items within a paragraph of show business gossip or similar material. Use periods after items that are complete sentences.

exclamation point (!) Follow these guidelines:

EMPHATIC EXPRESSIONS: Use the mark to express a high degree of surprise, incredulity or other strong emotion.

AVOID OVERUSE: Use a comma after mild interjections. End mildly exclamatory sentences with a period.

PLACEMENT WITH QUOTES: Place the mark inside quotation marks when it is part of the quoted material: *"How wonderful!" he exclaimed. "Never!" she shouted.*

Place the mark outside quotation marks when it is not part of the quoted material: *I hated reading Spenser's "Faerie Queene"!*

MISCELLANEOUS: Do not use a comma or a period after the exclamation mark:

Wrong: *"Halt!", the corporal cried.*
Right: *"Halt!" the corporal cried.*

hyphen (-) Hyphens are joiners. Use them to avoid ambiguity or to form a single idea from two or more words.

Use of the hyphen is far from standardized. It is optional in most cases, a matter of taste, judgment and style sense. But the fewer hyphens the better; use them only when not using them causes confusion. (*Small-business owner,* but *health care center.*) See individual entries in this book. If not listed here, use the first listed entry in Webster's New World College Dictionary.

Some guidelines:

AVOID AMBIGUITY: Use a hyphen whenever ambiguity would result if it were omitted: *The president will speak to small-business owners.* Others: *He recovered his health. He re-covered the leaky roof. The story is a re-creation. The park is for recreation.*

COMPOUND MODIFIERS: When a compound modifier — two or more words that express a single concept — precedes a noun, use hyphens to link all the words in the compound except the adverb *very* and all adverbs that end in *-ly*: *a first-quarter touchdown, a bluish-green dress, a full-time job, a well-known man, a better-qualified woman, a know-it-all attitude, a very good time, an easily remembered rule.*

Many combinations that are hyphenated before a noun are not hyphenated when they occur after a noun: *The team scored in the first quarter. The dress, a bluish green, was on sale. She works full time. His attitude suggested that he knew it all.*

But when a modifier that would be hyphenated before a noun occurs instead after a form of the verb *to be,* the hyphen usually must be retained to avoid confusion: *The man is well-known. The woman is quick-witted. The children are soft-spoken. The play is second-rate.*

The principle of using a hyphen to avoid confusion explains why no hyphen is required with *very* and *-ly* words. Readers can expect them to modify the word that follows. But if a combination such as *little-known man* were not hyphenated, the reader could logically be expecting *little* to be followed by a noun, as in *little man.* Instead, the reader encountering *little known* would have to back up mentally and make the compound connection on his own.

TWO-THOUGHT COMPOUNDS: *serio-comic, socio-economic.*

COMPOUND PROPER NOUNS AND ADJECTIVES: Use a hyphen to designate dual heritage: *Italian-American, Mexican-American.*

No hyphen, however, for **French Canadian** or **Latin American**.

PREFIXES AND SUFFIXES: See the **prefixes** and **suffixes** entries, and separate entries for the most frequently used prefixes and suffixes.

AVOID DUPLICATED VOWELS, TRIPLED CONSONANTS: Examples: *anti-intellectual, pre-empt, shell-like.*

WITH NUMERALS: Use a hyphen to separate figures in **odds**, **ratios**, **scores**, some **fractions** and some **vote tabulations**. See examples in entries under these headings.

When large numbers must be spelled out, use a hyphen to connect a word ending in *-y* to another word: *twenty-one, fifty-five,* etc.

SUSPENSIVE HYPHENATION: The form: *He received a 10- to 20-year sentence in prison.*

See **em dash, en dash, hyphen**.

parentheses ( ) In general, use parentheses around logos, as shown in **datelines**, but otherwise be sparing with them.

Parentheses are jarring to the reader. Because they do not appear on some news service printers, there is also the danger that material inside them may be misinterpreted.

The temptation to use parentheses is a clue that a sentence

is becoming contorted. Try to write it another way. If a sentence must contain incidental material, then commas or two dashes are frequently more effective. Use these alternatives whenever possible.

There are occasions, however, when parentheses are the only effective means of inserting necessary background or reference information. When they are necessary, follow these guidelines:

WITHIN QUOTATIONS: If parenthetical information inserted in a direct quotation is at all sensitive, place an editor's note under a dash at the bottom of a story alerting copy desks to what was inserted.

PUNCTUATION: Place a period outside a closing parenthesis if the material inside is not a sentence (*such as this fragment*).

(*An independent parenthetical sentence such as this one takes a period before the closing parenthesis.*)

When a phrase placed in parentheses (*this one is an example*) might normally qualify as a complete sentence but is dependent on the surrounding material, do not capitalize the first word or end with a period.

INSERTIONS IN A PROPER NAME: Use parentheses if a state name or similar information is inserted within a proper name: *The Huntsville (Alabama) Times*. But use commas if no proper name is involved: *The Selma, Alabama, group saw the governor.*

NEVER USED: Do not use parentheses to denote a political figure's party affiliation and jurisdiction. Instead, set them off with commas, as shown under **party affiliation**.

Do not use (*cq*) or similar notation to indicate that an unusual spelling

or term is correct. Include the confirmation in an editor's note at the top of a story.

periods (.) Follow these guidelines:

END OF DECLARATIVE SENTENCE: *The stylebook is finished.*

END OF A MILDLY IMPERATIVE SENTENCE: *Shut the door.*

Use an exclamation point if greater emphasis is desired: *Be careful!*

END OF SOME RHETORICAL QUESTIONS: A period is preferable if a statement is more a suggestion than a question: *Why don't we go.*

END OF AN INDIRECT QUESTION: *He asked what the score was.*

MANY ABBREVIATIONS: For guidelines, see **abbreviations and acronyms**. For the form of frequently used abbreviations, see the entry under the full name, abbreviation, acronym or term.

INITIALS: *John F. Kennedy, T.S. Eliot* (No space between *T.* and *S.*, to prevent them from being placed on two lines in typesetting.)

Abbreviations using only the initials of a name do not take periods: *JFK, LBJ.*

ELLIPSIS: See **ellipsis**.

ENUMERATIONS: After numbers or letters in enumerating elements of a summary: *1. Wash the car. 2. Clean the basement. Or: A. Punctuate properly. B. Write simply.*

PLACEMENT WITH QUOTATION MARKS: Periods always go inside quotation marks. See **quotation marks**.

SPACING: Use a single space after a period at the end of a sentence.

question mark (?) Follow these guidelines:

END OF A DIRECT QUESTION: *Who started the riot?*
Did he ask who started the riot?

(The sentence as a whole is a direct question despite the indirect question at the end.)

You started the riot? (A question in the form of a declarative statement.)

INTERPOLATED QUESTION: *You told me — Did I hear you correctly? — that you started the riot.*

MULTIPLE QUESTIONS: Use a single question mark at the end of the full sentence:

Did you hear him say, "What right have you to ask about the riot?"

Did he plan the riot, employ assistants, and give the signal to begin?

Or, to cause full stops and throw emphasis on each element, break into separate sentences: *Did he plan the riot? Employ assistants? Give the signal to begin?*

CAUTION: Do not use question marks to indicate the end of indirect questions:

He asked who started the riot. To ask why the riot started is unnecessary. I want to know what the cause of the riot was. How foolish it is to ask what caused the riot.

QUESTION-AND-ANSWER FORMAT: Do not use quotation marks. Paragraph each speaker's words:

Q: Where did you keep it?
A: In a little tin box.

PLACEMENT WITH QUOTATION MARKS: Inside or outside, depending on the meaning:

Who wrote "Gone With the Wind"?
He asked, "How long will it take?"

MISCELLANEOUS: The question mark supersedes the comma that normally is used when supplying attribution for a quotation: *"Who is there?" she asked.*

quotation marks (" ") The basic guidelines for open-quote marks (") and close-quote marks ("):

FOR DIRECT QUOTATIONS: To surround the exact words of a speaker or writer when reported in a story:

"I have no intention of staying," he replied.

"I do not object," he said, "to the tenor of the report."

Franklin said, "A penny saved is a penny earned."

A speculator said the practice is "too conservative for inflationary times."

RUNNING QUOTATIONS: If a full paragraph of quoted material is followed by a paragraph that continues the quotation, do not put close-quote marks at the end of the first paragraph. Do, however, put open-quote marks at the start of the second paragraph. Continue in this fashion for any succeeding paragraphs, using close-quote marks only at the end of the quoted material.

If a paragraph does not start with quotation marks but ends with a quotation that is continued in the next paragraph, do not use close-quote marks at the end of the introductory paragraph if the quoted material constitutes a full sentence. Use close-quote marks, however, if the quoted material does not constitute a full sentence. For example:

He said, "I am shocked and horrified by the slaying.

"I am so horrified, in fact, that I will ask for the death penalty."

But: *He said he was "shocked and horrified by the slaying."*

"I am so horrified, in fact, that I will ask for the death penalty," he said.

DIALOGUE OR CONVERSATION: Each person's words, no matter how brief, are placed in a separate paragraph, with quotation marks at the beginning and the end of each person's speech:

"Will you go?"
"Yes."
"When?"
"Thursday."

NOT IN Q-AND-A: Quotation marks are not required in formats that identify questions and answers by Q: and A:. See **question mark** for example.

NOT IN TEXTS: Quotation marks are not required in full texts, condensed texts or textual excerpts. See **ellipsis**.

COMPOSITION TITLES: See **composition titles** for guidelines on the use of quotation marks in book titles, movie titles, etc.

NICKNAMES: See **nicknames**.

IRONY: Put quotation marks around a word or words used in an ironical sense: *The "debate" turned into a free-for-all.*

UNFAMILIAR TERMS: A word or words being introduced to readers may be placed in quotation marks on first reference:

Broadcast frequencies are measured in "kilohertz."

Do not put subsequent references to *kilohertz* in quotation marks.

See **foreign words**.

AVOID UNNECESSARY FRAGMENTS: Do not use quotation marks to report a few ordinary words that a speaker or writer has used:

Wrong: *The senator said he would "go home to Michigan" if he lost the election.*

Right: *The senator said he would go home to Michigan if he lost the election.*

PARTIAL QUOTES: When a partial quote is used, do not put quotation marks around words that the speaker could not have used.

Suppose the individual said, *"I am horrified at your slovenly manners."*

Wrong: *She said she "was horrified at their slovenly manners."*

Right: *She said she was horrified at*

their "slovenly manners."

Better when practical: Use the full quote.

QUOTES WITHIN QUOTES: Alternate between double quotation marks ("or") and single marks ('or'):

She said, "I quote from his letter, 'I agree with Kipling that "the female of the species is more deadly than the male," but the phenomenon is not an unchangeable law of nature,' a remark he did not explain."

Use three marks together if two quoted elements end at the same time: *She said, "He told me, 'I love you.'"*

PLACEMENT WITH OTHER PUNCTUATION: Follow these long-established printers' rules:

— The period and the comma always go within the quotation marks.
— The dash, the semicolon, the colon, the question mark and the exclamation point go within the quotation marks when they apply to the quoted matter only. They go outside when they apply to the whole sentence.

See **comma**.

semicolon (;) In general, use the semicolon to indicate a greater separation of thought and information than a comma can convey but less than the separation that a period implies.

The basic guidelines:

TO CLARIFY A SERIES: Use semicolons to separate elements of a series when the items in the series are long or when individual segments contain material that also must be set off by commas:

He is survived by a son, John Smith, of Chicago; three daughters, Jane Smith, of Wichita, Kansas, Mary Smith, of Denver, and Susan, of Boston; and a sister, Martha, of Omaha, Nebraska.

Note that the semicolon is used before the final *and* in such a series.

Another application of this principle may be seen in the cross-references at the end of entries in this book. Because some entries themselves have a comma, a semicolon is used to separate references to multiple entries, as in: *See the* **felony, misdemeanor** *entry*; **pardon, parole, probation**; *and* **prison, jail**.

See **dash** for a different type of connection that uses dashes to avoid multiple commas.

TO LINK INDEPENDENT CLAUSES: Use semicolon when a coordinating conjunction such as *and, but* or *for* is not present: *The package was due last week; it arrived today.*

If a coordinating conjunction is present, use a semicolon before it only if extensive punctuation also is required in one or more of the individual clauses: *They pulled their boats from the water, sandbagged the retaining walls, and boarded up the windows; but even with these precautions, the island was hard-hit by the hurricane.*

Unless a particular literary effect is desired, however, the better approach in these circumstances is to break the independent clauses into separate sentences.

PLACEMENT WITH QUOTES: Place semicolons outside quotation marks.

Business

Our market is the individual consumer of business news. We must write in a lively, clear and accessible style that provides explanation and content for people who may not have a deep knowledge of business and finance. We must avoid insider jargon and present complex issues in an understandable, straightforward manner. No story is too small or routine to meet this standard: Each has meaning for readers and viewers. They may own a stock we are writing about, live in a community where a company is based, use a product or service or have some other connection to the news we are providing. We must keep in mind that we are writing on a global scale and make sure that our reporting reflects that and think about creative ways to tell stories.

AP business journalists must be careful with numbers; quickly grasp what those numbers mean and turn those numbers into real stories, not just about companies or profits but about people's lives.

When stories break, or when you set out to break a story yourself, you need experts or insiders who can help. And you need to know where you can find all the facts you need: in SEC filings, court documents, lists of shareholders and creditors, company histories, etc.

COVERING CORPORATE EARNINGS REPORTS

U.S. federal law requires corporations whose stock is publicly traded to report revenue and profit or losses every three months. This is what business is all about, whether a corporation made money or lost it, and why. These statements are usually released on the major public relations wire services during earnings season, a three- or four-week period that begins roughly two weeks after the end of each quarter.

Before each quarterly reporting period begins, AP business editors and reporters determine which companies will receive expanded coverage based on reader interest, corporate developments, legal or regulatory issues, and influence on financial markets and consumers. When these companies report earnings, AP typically will publish a several-hundred word report and, in some cases, additional elements such as video and graphics.

The AP automates the writing of thousands of quarterly earnings stories using software. These stories average about 200 words and provide customers with the basics: the net income and revenue that the company reported for the quarter — and year — when applicable. An algorithm that creates the stories also is designed to report if the company beat the expectations of Wall Street analysts that cover the company and to include forward-looking guidance when that information is available. The standard style for slugs is BC-US--Earns-Company Name.

While AP is automating many earnings reports, there are times when reporters can and should write original earnings stories or add to automated earnings reports. The decision to add original reporting depends on many factors including the stock activity following an earnings announcement.

Many of the following principles should be followed whether a reporter writes an earnings story from the beginning or adds to one that was automatically generated.

— We should tell the reader what the company does and give the increase or decline of net income either in percentage or absolute terms, along with the reason. Net income is synonymous with profit or earnings. The story should also include the company's revenue, which is sometimes called sales. In AP copy, however, this should always be referred to as revenue.

— Comparisons of profits or losses and revenues/sales should be made with the same period a year earlier, expressed both as a total and as earnings-per-share, which is simply the profit divided by the number of shares of stock outstanding. Company statements sometimes express this figure as fully diluted. Many company statements also include basic earnings-per-share, but AP uses fully diluted as a more meaningful figure.

— Use active verbs — rose, fell and the like — not passive constructions like were up/down. And to calculate the percentage change in profit, use the year-over-year change in net income, not the earnings-per-share numbers. The number of shares outstanding can, and often does, change year to year, which doesn't make it a clear apples-to-apples comparison.

— Include comments on the corporation's performance from the chief executive or outside analysts, and any background that puts the performance in perspective.

— Be alert to announcements of job cuts, executive resignations, acquisitions, changes in strategy, data about key products, warnings of a reduction of future earnings or upward revisions of earnings forecasts.

Why net income is important

Net income truly is the bottom line and the benchmark for companies' performance over time. It's what they are required to report to the SEC in accordance with generally accepted accounting principles, and it gives us a standard reporting format that brings a consistency to our news report.

In the rare cases where companies don't provide the net income number in their news release, we need to press their representatives for those numbers. And if they are not immediately available, we need to be as transparent as possible in explaining to readers why we are providing pro forma or some other adjusted or non-GAAP representation of the company's results instead of the net income figures, which were not disclosed.

Wall Street analysts have been much more concerned in recent years with operating earnings per share, which are calculated by excluding one-time *extraordinary* gains or charges, and revenue totals. Operating earnings may exclude the costs of a big reorganization, such as severance payments to laid-off workers or penalties for breaking leases on factories that are closed. If a company has no extraordinary events, operating earnings and net earnings can be identical.

In the days and weeks before earnings reports, analysts issue EPS predictions, and these predictions are compiled into a consensus figure by research companies such as FactSet and Zacks Investment Research.

On the day of the report, investors compare the consensus prediction for operating earnings per share with the actual number and the stock price often moves up or down based on whether the company falls short of, meets or exceeds expectations. When AP says in a story "Company X's performance beat Wall Street analysts' predictions," this is the number we're referring to. In most stories we explain how the adjusted number was calculated and immediately compare the adjusted earnings per share to the consensus, or average, analyst forecast.

It's worth noting that the analysts' forecast for earnings and revenue in a quarter often reflects the guidance provided by companies about what they expect their earnings and sales will be. That's why it's important to not only review what the analysts' consensus forecast is, but to determine whether a company has made a public forecast. When earnings or revenue disappoint, it's a much more powerful statement for us to say the company's earnings fell short of its own forecast, as well as analysts' expectations — assuming those facts are obtainable.

Operating earnings is sometimes confused with *earnings from continuing operations*. Continuing operations is a subset of operations. It refers to business units that existed in the past and will exist in the future. It excludes *discontinued operations* which represent businesses that have been sold or shut down in the past year. Companies often downplay earnings of these operations since they are no longer relevant to future profits.

Importance of the conference call

Stocks often move within seconds of an unexpected pronouncement by the CEO or CFO on the analyst conference call after the earnings are released. It could come from their response to a question about a big contract, the reason for a revised sales or earnings forecast, or any number of other reasons. That's information we obviously will want in a quick writethru of the story. But even if there are no dramatic announcements, it's important to listen to the call to gain a more complete understanding of how the company is positioning itself going forward. And it may provide a colorful key quote from a top company executive.

Make the company come to life

Earnings are the report cards for top corporate executives. The results, more often than not, are a consequence of decisions they made — acquisitions they engineered, factories they convinced their boards of directors to build or shutter, advertising campaigns they approved. Including detail about the decisions corporate executives have made helps us show that companies are made up of people who win or lose based on the decisions they make.

How to assemble a wrap story

When two or more companies in the same industry report earnings on the same day, we often want an earnings wrap story after the separate earnings stories are out and updated with details from the conference calls. These should read like a seamless narrative with one or more thematic elements holding them together. And in almost every case, a wrap should have a forward-looking element that gives readers a sense of whether the good or bad earnings are likely to get better or worse in future quarters, and why.

The basis for the thematic element may come from one or more of the conference calls that company executives hold after releasing earnings. Or there may be cases where your reporting will take you in a different direction in identifying the unifying theme. Talk to money managers who own the stock, competitors and others who you think can provide insight into what is going on. There also may be cases where the earnings are so divergent that the theme could be that the industry appears to be in disarray. But in all cases, our aim should be to convey to readers who is winning, who is losing and why. That often means that the wrap story may have a more complete explanation of how specific decisions made by executives impacted the earnings.

It also isn't necessary to repeat in the wrap version every number that is in the separate earnings stories. Instead, you should use a common sense approach that asks the question: Is this number necessary to convey the main points we are trying to make? They don't have to be lengthy expositions; if you can tell the tale in 400 or 500 words, all the better.

INTERNATIONAL BUREAUS

Currency Conversions

Currency conversions are necessary in stories that use foreign currency to make clear for readers how a number translates into dollars. But conversions should be used sparingly and preferably not in the lead unless it's a significant part of a story. A conversion is generally needed only the first time a currency is mentioned. The reader can make the necessary conversions after that.

Do not convert amounts that are not current because exchange rates change over time. If necessary for clarity in the story, specify that the conversion is at current exchange rates.

When conversions are needed, use the $ sign to report U.S. dollar amounts and write euros in the form *100 euros*. Do not use the euro symbol (€). Examples:

AMSTERDAM (AP) — Anheuser-Busch InBev, the world's largest brewer, says its third-quarter profits rose as the takeover of new brands and higher selling prices offset the impact of lower sales volumes.

The company, based in Leuven, Belgium, said Thursday that net profit was up 31 percent to $2.37 billion (1.73 billion euros), from $1.81 billion in the same period a year earlier.

The gain largely reflects the company's $20 billion purchase in June of the 50 percent of Mexico's Grupo Modelo it didn't already own.

PARIS (AP) — French cosmetics giant L'Oreal says sales of its Maybelline makeup, Garnier shampoo and other beauty aids helped lift earnings to a new record in 2013.

The company behind Lancome cosmetics and the Body Shop retail chain reported net profit of 2.96 billion euros ($4 billion) last year, up 3.2 percent from 2.87 billion in 2012.

For all other currencies, following the amount, spell out the name of the currency followed in parentheses by the equivalent in U.S. dollars. *Japan approved* *a 1.8 trillion yen ($18 billion) extra budget to partially finance an economic stimulus package.*

When dealing with a dollar currency of a country other than the United States, use the following abbreviations before the amount on second and subsequent references:

AU$ Australian dollars
CA$ Canadian dollars
SG$ Singapore dollars
NZ$ New Zealand dollars
HK$ Hong Kong dollars
NT$ New Taiwan dollars
ZW$ Zimbabwe dollars

Treasurer Wayne Swan approved a 16 billion Australian dollar ($10.74 billion) deal. Swan said AU$8 billion would be reserved for capital expenditure.

Different Accounting Rules

In some countries, companies don't report every quarter. The reports may come out every six months or even annually. Many foreign companies don't report *net income* or *earnings per share*. Some report *earnings before taxes*. If that's all they report, call them to see if they will give you net income. If they won't, use whatever number seems closest.

For the companies that report only half-year and full-year results, add a line saying, "The company did not break out quarterly results," so it's clear why we're not using them. Similarly, when reporting sales results for French companies, note that they often report sales a week or two before profit.

Foreign companies that sell shares in the United States (called American depositary receipts) often issue a separate earnings statement using American accounting standards. Use this when you can.

BANKRUPTCY

Bankruptcy categories — personal and business

Federal courts have exclusive jurisdiction over bankruptcy cases, and each of the 94 federal judicial districts handles bankruptcy matters. The primary purposes of the federal bankruptcy laws are to give an honest debtor a "fresh start" in life by relieving the debtor of most debts, and to repay creditors in an orderly manner to the extent that the debtor has property available for payment. Bankruptcies can also be **voluntary** or **involuntary**.

Chapter 7 of the Bankruptcy Code is available to both individual and business debtors. Its purpose is to achieve a fair distribution to creditors of the debtor's available non-exempt property. It provides a fresh financial start for individuals, although not all debt is wiped away; debts for certain taxes, fraudulently incurred credit card debt, family support obligations — including child support and alimony — and most student loans must still be repaid. And the new bankruptcy law that took effect in October 2005 limits Chapter 7 as an option for many Americans: Those deemed by a **"means test"** to have at least $100 a month left over after paying certain debts and expenses will have to file a 5-year repayment plan under the more restrictive Chapter 13 instead. **When a company files for Chapter 7, it usually leads to liquidation.** But a company in Chapter 7 proceedings can continue to operate under the direction of a court trustee until the matter is settled, and if it can settle with creditors in the interim, it may not have to be liquidated.

Chapter 11 of the Bankruptcy Code is available for both business and consumer debtors. Its purpose is to rehabilitate a business as a going concern or reorganize an individual's finances through a **court-approved reorganization plan**. When we refer to such a filing, we should say the company is **seeking Chapter 11 protection**. This action frees a company from the threat of creditors' lawsuits while it reorganizes its finances. The debtor's reorganization plan must be accepted by a majority of its creditors. Unless the court rules otherwise, the debtor remains in control of the business and its assets.

Chapter 12 of the Bankruptcy Code is designed to give special debt relief to a family farmer with regular income from farming.

Chapter 13 of the Bankruptcy Code is likely to be required for an increasing percentage of individuals seeking to wipe the slate clean. As mentioned above, those deemed by a "means test" to have at least $100 a month left over after paying certain debts and expenses will have to file a 5-year repayment plan under Chapter 13 that allows **unsecured creditors to recover part or all of what they are owed**. Supporters believe the changes will help rein in consumers who pile up credit card debt only to wipe it out with a Chapter 7 filing. Opponents say the law will hurt those who incur debt unexpectedly such as with health problems or lost jobs.

Chapter 15 of the Bankruptcy Code is a new section added in the 2005 reforms that deals with foreign bankruptcies. It is a way for companies with U.S. assets that are organized or nominally headquartered overseas to file bankruptcy in that foreign jurisdiction and in the U.S. as well, and have the U.S. court recognize the foreign bankruptcy as the primary one. The chapter is based on a model law developed by the United Nations in 1997. It has thus far been relatively uncommon, but **may be used more in the future, particularly by hedge funds that are organized overseas but operate in the U.S.**

How to prepare if a big corporate bankruptcy filing seems imminent

Burdensome debt and the refusal of lenders to extend new loans are the common denominators for most companies seeking bankruptcy court protection. Those tend not to crop up suddenly, which means you should be able to judge the likelihood that one of your companies may be filing. That's why we encourage all reporters to set up **SEC filing alerts** for key companies using their own user name and password on the Morningstar Document Research service. Bankruptcy should be one of the keywords you choose because outside auditors often force companies to tip their hands by flagging to investors the possibility of a bankruptcy filing. One expression you'll want to add to your company alert setup is **"going concern."** That's the term companies use when they note that their outside auditors are questioning their ability to remain in business.

Beyond that, you need to have a good understanding of the **balance sheet** and the **income statement** of the major companies you cover to answer these questions: How much debt do they have and how much of it must be repaid or refinanced in this quarter or the quarters to come? Have they demonstrated an inability to raise fresh cash through the sale of stock or debt financing? Has cash flow gone negative?

After a company seeks Chapter 11 protection, **holders of the company's debt** are often the best source of information about the status of bankruptcy negotiations since they often stand to gain control of the company in the reorganization process.

Few companies will be chatty about bankruptcy filings ahead of time, but it's still a good idea to plant the seed with company spokesmen that you want to be alerted as soon as a filing is made, that you want to know in which court it will come (more and more of the big ones seem to be ending up in the Southern District of New York in Manhattan), and that you would like a full set of documents if possible.

Another question to ask is: What will happen to the company's employees? When a company seeks bankruptcy protection, it often pushes for job cuts, pay cuts and reductions in benefits. If any workers are represented by unions, those unions will likely fight those cuts. A company seeking Chapter 11 protection will sometimes try to use bankruptcy court to achieve concessions if it can't reach an agreement on its own with unions. So stay in contact with union representatives to keep up with out-of-court negotiations, and check docket reports on Pacer for requests for permission to impose wage concessions, to reject union contracts or anything similar.

Also, companies seeking bankruptcy protection often turn over their pension plans to the Pension Benefit Guaranty Corporation, the federal pension insurance agency (http://www.pbgc.gov). But eliminating pension plans altogether is also common — United Airlines, US Airways, TWA and Pan Am, among others, all canceled their pension plans in bankruptcy.

And a reminder on tracking a company's stock after it files for bankruptcy: Companies are usually **delisted** by the New York Stock Exchange and the Nasdaq stock market after they seek bankruptcy court protection. That means they usually begin trading on the over-the-counter market known as the **Pink Sheets**. The **letter Q** at the end of a ticker signifies that the company is operating under bankruptcy protection and **PK** means it trades on the Pink Sheets. (Example: Delphi Corp. went from DPH on the New York Stock Exchange to DPHIQ.PK — four letters required in the ticker symbol for bankrupt companies — on the Pink Sheets.)

Is it a reorganization or a liquidation?

Knowing the answer to this question is key to how we describe the filing in our story. If it's a Chapter 11 filing and the company hopes to stay in business, don't say "Company XX filed for bankruptcy on DATE TK ..." Instead, we should say "Company XX **sought bankruptcy court protection** on DATE TK ..."

If a company closes its doors, says it's unable to raise new cash and is **going out of business** via a Chapter 7 filing, spell that out in the lead.

Secured and unsecured creditors

When you borrow money to buy a car, the lender is a **secured creditor**; they get to reclaim the car if you stop making payments. Similarly, companies usually have to pledge some kind of **collateral** when they sell bonds or otherwise borrow money. There can be several levels or rankings of security pledged for various categories of a company's debt. For our purposes, we need to know which creditor stands first, second and so on in line for repayment if a company files for bankruptcy because their claims and desires often conflict with what management wants to happen.

In a bankruptcy reorganization, secured lenders and debt holders obviously want to be repaid 100 cents on the dollar. Management often is against that idea, because they need whatever money they still have to continue operating the company. What often happens is that after extensive negotiations (and big lawyer bills) secured debt holders agree to **exchange their securities for new shares of stock** (i.e., equity) in the post-bankruptcy company, which emerges as a consequence with a much-reduced debt load.

So what happens to **existing shareholders**? In most cases, **their shares become worthless**. But every so often, secured debt holders' claims can be satisfied in a way that leaves some residual equity value in the company. But even then, existing shareholders' ownership stake in the company is often **severely diluted** by the issuance of new shares to former debt holders. That's why the stocks of companies seeking bankruptcy protection often continue to trade at a few dollars a share. It's mostly a fool's game, but something we need to be able to explain as part of our reporting and writing.

Prepackaged bankruptcies and DIP financing

Companies heading toward bankruptcy sometimes start negotiations with major secured creditors on what is known as a **prepackaged bankruptcy** filing. If a company can reach agreement on key details before the bankruptcy court supervision begins, it can speed its eventual reorganization and exit from bankruptcy. Known as an out-of-court restructuring plan, it is filed simultaneously with a Chapter 11 petition. But such plans require the approval of at least two-thirds in amount and more than one-half in the number of allowed claims held by creditors.

One study makes the case that the prepackaged bankruptcy approach is taken most often by companies that had a higher ratio of operating income to total debt in the years before financial stress set in, and when long-term debt represents a larger percentage of total debt (which makes sense because there typically would be fewer debt holders to negotiate with).

These prepackaged plans, as well as regular Chapter 11 reorganizations, often are accompanied by what is known as **debtor-in-possession financing**. This is a term for new money extended by a lender in Chapter 11 cases. Investopedia.com describes DIP financing as being unique from other financing methods in that it usually has priority over existing debt, equity and other claims.

Why should we care about DIP financing? It's a profitable line of business for banks. And companies' ability to obtain it often is a critical factor in whether they continue to operate or have to shut down.

Emerging from bankruptcy

When the reorganization is completed and a company emerges from bankruptcy, we should be able to spell out how much of the company's debt has been wiped away. If debt holders swap their holdings for shares of the reorganized company, spell that out and explain what role they will play. Also include whether the company attracted new equity holders as part of the reorganization.

MERGERS AND ACQUISITIONS

Is it a merger or a takeover?

Few business combinations are truly a merger of equals, so we need to be precise and sparing in the use of the word "merger." It is **not a synonym for an acquisition or takeover**, which should be the preferred descriptive used in most of our stories. But how do we first decide whether or not it's a merger, and if the answer is not, what are the rules that should guide us in concluding who's buying whom?

The AP M&A Checklist:

1. Is one of the companies' stock being used as the currency? If the answer is yes, that's usually a good sign that company is the acquirer and it is not a merger.

2. What is the message from the exchange ratio in stock transactions? Typically when shareholders of Company A are offered new shares in a combined company at a 1-for-1 ratio, and Company B shares are exchanged at something less or more (i.e., each Company B share will be exchanged for 0.47 percent of a share of the new company), it's an indication that Company A's stock is being used as the basis for the transaction. But it also could be a sign that the companies' boards have agreed to a merger that uses a formula to compensate for the differing market value (total number of shares multiplied by the closing stock price the day before the announcement) of the two companies to come up with an exchange ratio for stock in the new company.

3. What is the message from the stock movements after the announcement? Shares of companies being acquired typically rise and shares of the acquirer often fall after the announcement. Not always, of course, but that's usually the case because most bidders **pay a premium**, or an above-market price, for the shares of the company being acquired, and investors often are worried about the amount of debt the acquirer is taking on to complete the transaction.

4. Whose cash is being used to fund the cash portion of a transaction? If the announcement says Company A's cash will be used or that its existing lines of credit will be tapped to pay for Company B's shares, that's a pretty strong indication that Company A is the acquirer.

5. Which company's executives are filling most of the top management roles?

The key distinction usually is who gets the CEO slot. But if one of the two CEOs is named to head the company for a limited period (say two years or less) before his fellow CEO takes over, that's a good sign of a political compromise to paper over the fact that the second CEO's company is going to be in charge long-term.

6. Which company will end up with the majority of the seats on the new board of directors? This is often a key tiebreaker. It's a good indication of which outfit is going to be in charge if one ends up with 60 percent of the board and the other gets 40 percent. Also, make sure to get not only the short-term makeup of the board of the combined company, but also whether there were any deals cut for some members to retire in short order.

7. Whose name will be on the big sign outside the headquarters? Usually an obvious tell, but not always. First Union clearly was the acquirer of Wachovia, but the board members decided for their own reasons to use the Wachovia name when the two North Carolina banks combined operations. It may have been a deal killer for some Wachovia board members if their name didn't survive, or it may have simply been a marketing decision by First Union's brass that the name Wachovia had a better chance of standing out in the crowded banking space. Wachovia, incidentally, was acquired by Wells Fargo in 2008.

8. Where will the company be headquartered? Since CEOs typically do the negotiating and they typically aren't anxious to move, this can be an informative tell.

How to value the transaction

Our basic rule is to **exclude the debt** of the acquired company when calculating the value of a takeover. If Company A has agreed to pay $50 a share in cash for all of the stock of Company B, you would multiply $50 times the fully diluted number of shares outstanding of Company B to come up with transaction's total value. Companies often include the debt in their news release, which places a higher total value on the transaction. In cases like that, if they spell out the debt total, back it out and fashion a lead something like this:

Company A, the world's largest TK, agreed Monday to pay $XX million to acquire Company B, whose product line XXX will do XXXX. The transaction, valued at $50 per share, or a X.X premium to Friday's closing price, includes the assumption of $XXX million of Company B's debt.

Unfortunately, news releases sometimes only provide the per-share number for the transaction. So in addition to calling the company to get the key numbers we need to value the transaction, we should backstop by reviewing the latest 10-Q filing of the acquired company to get the number of fully diluted shares outstanding so we can do the math ourselves. In some cases, companies only give the per-share number because they don't want to call attention to the fact that there are an enormous number of options of the acquired company that can be exercised as part of transaction.

When stock is the currency used in the transaction, or is part of a stock and cash offer, the valuation equation changes. If Company A offers 1 share of its stock for each share of Company B, for the NewsNow you would multiply the previous day's closing price of Company A by the number of fully diluted shares outstanding of Company B. When there is a cash component per share, or if the exchange ratio is greater or lesser than 1-for-1, the math gets a little more complicated, but it's also straightforward. First calculate the value of the stock portion (If Company A is offering 0.47 of a share of its stock that was trading at $50 yesterday, the stock portion is worth 50 x .47, or $23.50.) Then add whatever will be paid in cash per share (say $10) to give a total value of $33.50 per Company B share and multiply that times the total number of shares of Company B outstanding.

Any time stock of the acquirer is used as a currency in a takeover, the value of the transaction obviously can change throughout the day based on the stock movement of the acquirer. But for our purposes, on the day the takeover is announced, we should stay with our initial valuation (based on the closing price of the acquirer a day earlier) until the markets close.

Then we should redo the math based on that day's closing value of the acquirer's stock — and make it clear to readers why the total has changed from what they have been reading throughout the day.

What needs to be in the APNewsNow

Lead with the **full name of the buyer** and include a descriptive size and scope, **explain the terms** and **value of the deal** as simply as possible (all cash? cash and stock? all stock?) while adding the name of the company to be acquired, and **provide a reason why** the deal is happening — or, if the release is mum on that point, a description of what the combined company will look like or the capabilities it will have (making it the world's biggest maker of fish tacos).

If there are **job cuts** or other major corporate developments, including a warning that future earnings will be lower because of **earnings dilution**, aim to get those in the NewsNow. Dilution occurs when a stock-based transaction increases the number of shares of the acquirer without a near-term corresponding increase in earnings per share.

Specify where the two companies are **headquartered**. Also include **stock price history** and **premarket trading**, if it is available, for both the acquirer and the acquiree. And if it is easily obtainable, specify what the **premium** that the acquiring company is offering and whether it is a **hostile bid**.

As the urgent series continues, include any pertinent details about potential antitrust issues, contingencies like the need for board approval, government approval, shareholder approval, court approval, break-up fees, **due diligence** (the review by the acquirer of a target company's internal books and operations), and **nondisclosure/confidentiality agreements**.

Also specify the **stage of the transaction** — letter of intent, definitive agreement, closing, etc. And if not added already, provide details about how the acquirer will finance the takeover, what the seller's plans are for the proceeds it will be receiving, the projected effect on future sales/earnings, other details on how the companies will change as a result of the deal (layoffs, management changes, etc.), and when the deal is expected to close.

Add historical perspective. A news story showed a good example: In early 2003, Overture bought Altavista from CMGI for $140 million in cash and stock. That didn't look like much of a deal until they added the needed perspective that

CMGI bought Altavista from Compaq only four years earlier for $2.3 billion.

What is the stock reaction telling us?

If Company A offers $50 in cash for Company B and the share price of Company B rises to $55 or $60, that's a pretty strong indication that some investors are betting at least one **competing bid** will emerge. Alternatively, if Company B's shares trade way below $50, we need to find out why investors are skittish about the deal closing.

It also should be standard practice to keep track of the stock prices of both the acquirer and the target in the days and weeks after the initial announcement. Depending on how they perform, you may want to write additional stories about whether investors are betting the deal is on track or in trouble. And when stock is used as part or all of the currency for a proposed takeover, it's a good idea to build the formula into a spreadsheet and track it daily to see whether the spread between the market price is narrowing or widening from the offer's valuation.

Some investors make and lose millions on these bets, so be careful when you interview them about these deals — and make sure to explain what they have at stake if we quote them either speaking in support of or objecting to the transaction.

Assessing the deal's chances for success

Besides the market implications about whether a deal will close or not, we should also from the first day be sharpening our analysis about whether the proposal makes business sense. There are several ways to approach this. Are the promised cost cuts doable, and what will they cost in human terms (jobs lost) and the effects on local economies? Will it deliver the higher profits the acquirer is promising? Will it position the acquirer's stock for future market gains? We should be asking these questions as part of our first-day coverage and come back as often as needed for deals both pending and completed.

Data journalism

Why this section

Data journalism has become a staple of reporting across beats and platforms. The ability to analyze quantitative information and present conclusions in an engaging and accurate way is no longer the domain of specialists alone. Government agencies, businesses and other organizations alike all communicate in the language of data and statistics. To cover them, journalists must become conversant in that language as well.

Acquiring data

Data can come from a variety of public and private sources, each presenting its own benefits and challenges. Some data sets might be downloadable from public websites, while some might depend on negotiation with government officials or other sources. Journalists should evaluate data sources as critically as they would any other source of information.

Requesting government data

SOURCES OF GOVERNMENT DATA: All government agencies collect data that can be useful to reporters. The Briefing on Media Law section includes a useful introduction to the Freedom of Information Act, which can be used to request data from agencies in the executive branch of the U.S. federal government. The National Freedom of Information Coalition maintains a list of resources about similar laws that cover state and local governments: http://www.nfoic.org/state-foi.

DATA FORMAT REQUEST: In a records request for data, be sure to ask for data in an "electronic, machine-readable" format that can be interpreted by standard spreadsheet or database software. The alternative, which is the default for many agencies, is to provide records in paper form or as scans of paper pages, which present an obstacle to analysis. Public records laws vary significantly from federal to state and local governments; some state governments do not require records to be provided in searchable form, for example. In some cases paper records may be the only option.

Whenever possible, ask to speak with technical experts who manage the data as well as "domain experts" who can provide insight about idiosyncrasies of a data set, its place within a regulatory framework, and other important background information.

Scraping data from websites

Sometimes, a data provider's website allows users to browse or search a data set but fails to provide direct download of the data. In this situation it may be possible to use software to step through the pages of the site and extract the data in a process known as web scraping.

Some website operators sanction this practice, and others oppose it. A website with policies limiting or prohibiting scraping often will include them in its terms of service or in a "robots.txt" file, and reporters should take these into account when considering whether to scrape.

Scraping a website can cause its servers to work unusually hard, and in extreme cases, scraping can cause a website to stop working altogether and treat the attempt as a hostile attack. Therefore, follow these precautions:

— Scraping should be seen as a last resort. First try to acquire the desired data by requesting it directly.
— Limit the rate at which the scraper software requests pages in order to avoid causing undue strain on the website's servers.
— Wherever feasible, identify yourself to the site's maintainers by adding your contact information to the scraper's requests via the HTTP headers.

Legal and ethical considerations of leaked or hacked data

Reporters may come into possession of data that was not intended to be released to the public. Such data may have been leaked by a person within the company or agency that collected it, or it might have been released by a third party who hacked into the company or agency.

Treat data sets obtained in this manner with skepticism and extreme caution. Leaked and hacked data sets can contain private information of people who individually might not be relevant to the story. The data files themselves may contain malicious programs that can compromise computer networks. And the authenticity and accuracy of any hacked or leaked data sets should be confirmed before their use. If the subject of a leak has refused to confirm its authenticity, provide appropriate caveats. See the Briefing on Media Law section for other relevant legal considerations, and seek legal advice before using such data or publishing findings based on it.

Evaluating data sources

Data sources, much like human sources, should be evaluated for reliability, currency, scope and bias. Before working with a data set, take time to background it:

— If the data collectors used a data entry form, ask to see a copy of the form and any directions they received about how to enter the data.
— Request a record layout (also known as a data dictionary) for any data used. This document should describe the fields, the types of data they contain and details such as the meaning of any codes in the data and how missing data is indicated.
— Determine whether the data set is up to date, how frequently it is normally updated and when it will be updated next.
— Look for any anomalies in the data that would invalidate the analysis, such as outliers, blank values, placeholder values or different types of data appearing in the same field.
— As with any other release of information, consider the source. Did the data come from a government agency or from an advocacy group? Examine the methodology used for data collection. The purpose and methods of the original data collection will determine what is included and excluded from a

DATA JOURNALISM

data set. These decisions can affect the usefulness of the data.
— If possible, compare the data against another source of similar information. Does the data for a parallel industry, organization or region look similar? If not, what could explain the discrepancy? It might also be possible to verify the consistency of summary statistics included with the data, such as sums and percentages; consider calculating a few of them by hand to check whether they agree with the values provided.

Reproducible analysis and transparency

As a general rule, all assertions in a story based on data analysis should be reproducible. The methodology description in the story or accompanying materials should provide a road map to replicate the analysis. Such a road map provides visibility into the analysis for editors, story subjects and the public. It also allows the reporter or others to more easily update and expand upon the work in the future.

If at all possible, an editor or another reporter should attempt to reproduce the results of the analysis and confirm all findings before publication. This crucial step can help avoid significant errors and is made much easier by maintaining a log of all steps in the analysis.

At a minimum, maintain a data log including:
— Details on data source(s), such as URLs to download the data or copy of a formal records request for the data. Note: Keep original copies of all data used in analysis, and annotate/transform data only in copies of the originals.
— Copies of the data dictionary and any other documentation that accompanied the original data set.
— Description of all steps required to transform the data and perform the analysis.

Sharing data and methodology

PRE-PUBLICATION SHARING: When applicable, key results of an analysis, along with the code or a description of the methodology, should be shared with data providers or subjects of a story before publication, so they can answer questions based on the findings and offer a response. Share the results only, not the full story.

METHODOLOGY STATEMENT: If the methodology behind an analysis can be explained in one or two sentences, include the full explanation in the story. If the methodology is more complex, provide a separate text box or story that accompanies the main piece. A similar explanation should accompany any interactive graphics based on a data analysis.

Guidelines for publishing data

Where possible, provide the source data for download along with the story or visualization. When distributing data consider the following guidelines:
— The data should be distributed in a machine-readable, widely useable format, such as a spreadsheet.
— The data should be accompanied by thorough documentation that explains data provenance, transformations and alterations, any caveats with the data analysis and a data dictionary.

Reporting on data

When performing data analysis and conveying conclusions, strive for accuracy and simplicity. Do not obfuscate analysis with technical terms or overstate conclusions.

Compared to what?

A number alone does not signify much. It must be compared against something (a previous year's figure, measures from other places, a benchmark or goal, etc.). Make sure your comparison is weighing two similar types of values and that units of measurement and means of collecting the data are similar. When reporting numbers, provide the comparison for context: About 40 percent of male students passed the test compared to 55 percent of female students.

— Per capita and related calculations allow you to compare values among groups of different sizes. Per capita values are calculated by dividing the value of interest by the population of interest. For larger populations, calculating the rate per 10,000 may be more instructive.
— Rankings should include raw numbers to provide a sense of relative importance.
— When comparing dollar amounts across time, be sure to adjust for inflation or seasonal adjustment
— Data should reflect the appropriate population for the topic: For example, use voting-age population as a base for stories on demographic voting patterns.

Conveying measures of change

— Actual change: When measuring actual change over time, subtract the older number from the newer number. However, this raw measure of difference may not be the best way to convey change to the reader. For example, if a town's budget went up $200 million from one year to the next, that may not tell much.
— Percent change: Percent change describes the relative change of the new number from the old number. To calculate percent change, take the actual change, divide by the old number and multiply by 100. If that same town had a budget last year of $1.5 billion, an increase of $200 million would represent around a 13 percent change. This number can then be compared to other towns or other years.
— Percentage point change: Do not confuse percent change and percentage point change. A change from 10 percent to 13 percent is a rise of 3 percentage points. This is not equal to a 3 percent change.
— Avoid percentage and percent change comparisons from a small base. Use the raw numbers in these cases.

Understanding averages

— Measures of central tendency: Calculating an average or measure of central tendency is an attempt to represent a set of numbers using a value that best describes the group as a whole. There are three common ways to measure a typical or central value for a set of numbers. One measure may be more appropriate for a given data set:
    — Mean: The most common measure of central tendency is the mean,

commonly called the average. To calculate the mean of a group of numbers, add them together and divide the sum by the quantity of numbers in the group. The mean of 20, 6 and 4 would be (20+6+4)/3 or 10. The mean is very sensitive to outliers. If the data set contains some values that are much larger or much smaller than the bulk of the values, use the median as a representative value for the set.
— Median: The median is the middle value of a set of numbers when arranged from smallest to largest. The median of 20, 6 and 4 is 6. The median is more resistant to outlier values than the mean and so often better represents the center point of the set.
— Mode: Another common measure used to indicate a typical value is the mode, which simply means the most frequent value. In a histogram or bar chart, it is the value that is represented by the highest bar.
— When communicating average values, indicate if you are using the median or mode as opposed to the mean. For example, if you are reporting the median, use a median income of $35,000 instead of an average income of $35,000.
— Do not average averages. Be aware that taking the mean of a set of mean values is not appropriate. If the groups represented are of different sizes, adding their means and dividing by the number of groups will not provide an accurate overall mean.

Correlation and causation

When exploring the relationship between two variables in a data set, be careful to distinguish correlation from causation.
— Correlation indicates that two variables are related to each other: When one changes, the other appears to change, as well.
— Causation implies that a change in one variable caused the change in the other.
Many variables have a connection, but which variable causes a change in the other can be inconclusive or unknown. The common change in both variables may be caused by a third factor or even by random chance. When reporting on correlations, look for an explanatory basis of the causal relationship and consider lurking factors that may better explain the relationship.

Writing with numbers

— When possible, round numbers to avoid overemphasizing precision in reporting. Supplying the full number may signal to the reader that each digit is important, when that is not the case.
— Avoid overloading a sentence or paragraph with numbers. While there is no absolute maximum, a good rule of thumb is to use no more than eight or 10 digits in a single paragraph.
— Use fractions, ratios, and percentages to make numbers understandable: Reformulating numbers in these ways helps to limit the number of digits per paragraph: 75 percent can be written as three of four, ¾, etc. (See fractions, ratios, percent.)
— Add appropriate cautions or caveats to numbers. Providing this information can make stories more credible and reduce the need to publish updates when new data become available.
— Include measures of uncertainty. Often, calculations are based on

measurements that include some level of uncertainty. Uncertainty can be communicated using confidence intervals or a margin of error. (See polls and surveys.)
— Mention sample sizes of surveys, particularly if small. (See polls and surveys.)

Data visualization

Data visualization should be both compelling and nondeceptive. Published visuals must serve a concrete narrative purpose and present data in a straightforward and clear fashion. Visuals used for analysis must be checked carefully to make sure they accurately represent the underlying data.
— A visual experience should require as little external explanation or background knowledge as possible. Avoid creating both low-information graphics and graphics that are so complex that they require detailed explanation.
— Bar charts should set the baseline of the y-axis at zero. The y-axis of a line chart should fall within the normal expectations. For example, gas prices tend to range between $1.50 and $4 per gallon. A line chart visualizing these prices could have a y-axis stretching from $1 to $4 in increments of $1. In all cases, clearly indicate the scale of both axes.
— Remove outliers from the visualization only with extremely good justification (e.g. a known data entry error).
— Circles and other 2D shapes used in visualization should be scaled using their area, rather than the radius or side length.
— Don't involve 3D elements unnecessarily. Perspective can distort the visualization.

Clarity in design
— Use as few fonts as possible. Use either bold or italic to differentiate but not both.
— Use color to convey or highlight information, not as decoration.
— Use as few elements as possible to keep visuals clean and crisp. Complexity should be added only when it conveys additional information.

Mapping

Maps are useful visualizations for an analysis in which geography is critical. If geography is not central to the story, consider alternative ways to present the information. Beware of using maps to compare frequency by place, as such maps often reflect the population distribution rather than a meaningful rate.

Polls and surveys

Reporting on public opinion research requires rigorous inspection of a poll's methodology, provenance and results. The mere existence of a poll is not enough to make it news. Do not feel obligated to report on a poll or survey simply because it meets AP's standards.

Poll results that seek to preview the outcome of an election must never be the lead, headline or single subject of any story. Pre-election horse race polling can and should inform reporting on political campaigns, but no matter how good the poll or how wide a candidate's margin, results of pre-election polls always reflect voter opinion before ballots are cast. Voter opinions can change before Election Day, and they often do.

When evaluating a poll or survey, be it a campaign poll or a survey on a topic unrelated to politics, the key question to answer is: Are its results likely to accurately reflect the opinion of the group being surveyed?

Generally, for the answer to be yes, a poll must:
— Disclose the questions asked, the results of the survey and the method in which it was conducted.
— Come from a source without a stake in the outcome of its results.
— Scientifically survey a random sample of a population, in which every member of that population has a known probability of inclusion.
— Report the results in a timely manner.

Polls that pass these tests are suitable for publication.

Do not report on surveys in which the pollster or sponsor of research refuses to provide the information needed to answer these questions.

Always include a short description of how a poll meets the standards, allowing readers and viewers to evaluate the results for themselves: *The AP-NORC poll surveyed 1,020 adults from Dec. 7-11 using a sample drawn from NORC's probability-based AmeriSpeak Panel, which is designed to be representative of the U.S. population.*

Some other key points:
— Comparisons between polls are often newsworthy, especially those that show a change in public opinion over time. But take care when comparing results from different polling organizations, as difference in poll methods and question wording — and not a change in public opinion — may be the cause of differing results. Only infer that a difference between two polls is caused by a change in public opinion when those polls use the same survey methodology and question wording.
— Some organizations publish poll averages or aggregates that attempt to combine the results of multiple polls into a single estimate in an effort to capture the overall state of public opinion about a campaign or issue. Averaging poll results does not eliminate error or preclude the need to

examine the underlying polls and assess their suitability for publication. In campaign polling, survey averages can provide a general sense of the state of a race. However, only those polls that meet these standards should be included in averages intended for publication, and it is often preferable to include the individual results of multiple recent surveys to show where a race stands.

— Some pollsters release survey results to the first decimal place, which implies a greater degree of precision than is possible from scientific sampling. Poll results should always be rounded to whole numbers. Margins of sampling error can be reported to the first decimal place.

— Take care to use accurate language when describing poll results. For example, only groups comprising more than 50 percent of the population can be said to be the majority. If the largest group includes less than 50 percent of the surveyed population, it is a plurality. See **majority, plurality**.

— In most cases, *poll* and *survey* may be used interchangeably.

Polls are not perfect

When writing or producing stories that cite survey results, take care not to overstate the accuracy of the poll. Even a perfectly executed poll does not guarantee perfectly accurate results.

It is possible to calculate the potential error of a poll of a random sample of a population, and that detail must be included in a story about a poll's results: *The margin of sampling error for all respondents is plus or minus 3.7 percentage points.* See **Margin of error** later in this entry.

Sampling error is not the only source of survey error, merely the only one that can be quantified using established and accepted statistical methods. Among other potential sources of error: the wording and order of questions, interviewer skill and refusal to participate by respondents randomly selected for a sample. As a result, total error in a survey may exceed the reported margin of error more often than would be predicted based on simple statistical calculations.

Be careful when reporting on the opinions of a poll's subgroup — women under the age of 30, for example, in a poll of all adults. Find out and consider the sample size and margin of error for that subgroup; the sampling error may be so large as to render any reported difference meaningless. Results from subgroups totaling less than 100 people should not be reported.

Very large sample sizes do not preclude the need to rigorously assess a poll's methodology, as they may be an indicator of an unscientific and unreliable survey. Often, polls with several thousand respondents are conducted via mass text message campaigns or website widgets and are not representative of the general population.

There is no single established method of estimating error for surveys conducted online among people who volunteer to take part in surveys. While they may not report a margin of error, these surveys are still subject to error, uncertainty and bias.

Margin of error

A poll conducted via a scientific survey of a random sample of a population will have a margin of sampling error. This margin is expressed in terms of *percentage points*, not *percent*.

For example, consider a poll with a margin of error of 5 percentage points. Under ideal circumstances, its results should reflect the true opinion of the population being surveyed, within plus or minus 5 percentage points, 95 of every 100 times that poll is conducted.

Sampling error is not the only source of error in a poll, but it is one that can be quantified. See the first section of this entry.

The margin of error varies inversely to the poll's sample size: The fewer people interviewed, the larger the margin of error. Surveys with 500 respondents or more are preferable.

Evaluating the margin of error is crucial when describing the results of a poll. Remember that the survey's margin of error applies to every candidate or poll response. Nominal differences between two percentages in a survey may not always be meaningful.

Use these rules to avoid exaggerating the meaning of poll results and deciding when to report that a poll finds one candidate is leading another, or that one group is larger than another.
— If the difference between two response options is more than twice the margin of error, then the poll shows one candidate is leading or one group is larger than another.
— If the difference is at least equal to the margin of error, but no more than twice the margin of error, then one candidate can be said to be *apparently leading* or *slightly ahead*, or one group can be said to be *slightly larger* than another.
— If the difference is less than the margin of error, the poll says a race *is close* or *about even*, or that two groups *are of similar size*.
— Do not use the term *statistical dead heat*, which is inaccurate if there is any difference between the candidates. If the poll finds the candidates are exactly tied, say *they are tied*. For very close races that aren't exact ties, the phrase *essentially tied* is acceptable, or use the phrases above.

There is no single established method of estimating error for surveys conducted online among people who volunteer to take part in surveys. These surveys are still subject to error, uncertainty and bias.

Evaluating polls and surveys

When evaluating whether public opinion research is suitable for publication, consider the answers to the following questions.

— Has the poll sponsor fully disclosed the questions asked, the results of the survey and the method in which it was conducted?

Reputable poll sponsors and public opinion researchers will disclose the methodology used to conduct the survey, including the questions asked and the results to each, so that their survey may be subject to independent examination and analysis by others. Do not report on surveys in which the pollster or sponsor of research refuses to provide such information.

Some public opinion researchers agree to publicly disclose their methodology as part of the American Association for Public Opinion Research's transparency initiative. Participation does not mean polls from these researchers are automatically suitable for publication, only that they are likely to meet the test for disclosure. A list of transparency initiative members can be found on the association's website at: http://www.aapor.org/Standards-Ethics/Transparency-Initiative/Current-Members.aspx

— Does the poll come from a source without a stake in the outcome of its results?

Any poll suitable for publication must disclose who conducted and paid for the research. Find out the polling firm, media outlet or other organization that conducted the poll. Include this information in all poll stories, so readers and viewers can be aware of any potential bias: *The survey was conducted for Inside Higher Ed by Gallup.*

Polls paid for by candidates or interest groups may be designed to produce results that are beneficial to that candidate or group, and they may be released selectively as a campaign tactic or publicity ploy. These polls should be carefully evaluated and usually avoided.

— How are people selected to take part in the poll? Does the poll rely on a random sample of a population, in which every member of that population has a known probability of inclusion?

These are known as *probability-based polls*, and they are the best method of ensuring the results of a survey reflect the true opinion of the group being surveyed.

Those conducted by telephone must include people interviewed on their cellphones. Those that only include landline interviews have no chance of reaching the more than half of American adults who have only a mobile phone.

Avoid polls in which computers conduct telephone interviews, sometimes referred to as IVR (for *interactive voice response*), *automated* or *robopolls*. These surveys cannot legally dial cellphones, and while they sometimes are supplemented with online interviews to reach cellphone users, such supplements are usually of dubious quality. These surveys also cannot randomly select respondents within a household, which can lead to underrepresentation of some demographic groups such as younger adults.

Polls conducted online are valid if the poll is of a panel of respondents recruited randomly from the entire population, with internet access or the option to take surveys over the phone provided to those who don't have internet access.

Many online polls are conducted using opt-in panels, which are composed of people who volunteer to take part, often in response to web advertisements. As of 2018, research into such surveys finds that traditional demographic weighting is often insufficient to make such opt-in panels representative of the population as a whole. Results among demographic groups such as African-Americans and Hispanics can be especially inaccurate, and biases within these groups are especially difficult to correct. These surveys lack representation of people without internet access, a population that differs in key ways from those who do have internet access.

However, opt-in surveys that use additional variables as part of their weighting schemes have shown more promising results, particularly those that use a probability-based sample that is supplemented and/or combined with other sample sources. Because of the difficulty in assessing such approaches and ongoing research into how well they work to reduce bias, the results from such polls should be published only after careful consideration of the techniques used to ensure the results are truly representative. The sample selection and weighting process must be disclosed in detail before they can be considered for publication.

Do not accept assurances from pollsters that "proprietary" sampling and weighting methods that are not made available for review and scrutiny are able to produce representative results.

Balloting of visitors to a website, of a company's email list or polls conducted by Twitter users rely on self-selected samples that should always be avoided. They are both unrepresentative of a broader population and subject to manipulation.

For surveys conducted by mail and sent to a random selection of addresses, pay especially close attention to how long it took to field these polls, especially if they include topics in the news or pertaining to elections. Before publishing results of polls by mail, carefully consider whether the results of time-sensitive questions may be outdated.

Outside of the United States, many polls are conducted using in-person interviews of people at randomly selected locations. Many are of high quality. Pay close attention to how the pollsters tried to include rural and other hard-to-reach places in the survey sample.

Many political polls are based on interviews with registered voters, since registration is usually required for voting. Polls may be based on likely voters closer to an election; if so, ask the pollster how that group was identified. Polls that screen for likely voters at the sample level by only attempting to interview those who have a history of voting may include fewer nonvoters, but may also exclude some potential new voters.

— Are the results being reported in a timely manner?

Public opinion can change quickly, especially in response to events. Make every effort to report results from a poll as close to the period when the survey was conducted as possible.

Be careful when considering results from polls fielded immediately after major events, such as political debates, that often sway public opinion in ways that may only be temporary. Similarly, if events directly related to a poll's questions have taken place since they were asked, the results may no longer reflect the opinion of the populations being surveyed. That does not mean they are no longer valid, but must be placed into the proper context. Often, such results are valuable in describing how public opinion has changed — or remained consistent — in the wake of such events.

In all cases, consider whether it is useful to inform readers and viewers directly when the poll was conducted: *The poll was taken three days after the president proposed new tax cuts. The poll was conducted the week before Congress passed the new health care legislation.*

The timeliness of results is especially crucial in reporting on pre-election polls. Voter opinions often change during the course of a political campaign, and results from questions asked several weeks or in some cases days prior likely no longer provide an accurate picture of the state of a race.

When describing voter opinions about candidates for political office, it's best to summarize results from several recent polls, or the trend in polls over time, rather than cite the results of a single survey in isolation.

Methods statement

When publishing poll or survey results, as an additional effort in transparency, consider also publishing a stand-alone statement about the survey and its methods:

The Associated Press-NORC Center for Public Affairs Research poll on the nation's priorities was conducted by NORC at the University of Chicago from Nov. 30 to Dec. 4. It is based on online and telephone interviews of 1,444 adults who are members of NORC's nationally representative AmeriSpeak Panel.

The original sample was drawn from respondents selected randomly from NORC's national frame based on address-based sampling and recruited by mail, email, telephone and face-to-face interviews.

NORC interviews participants over the phone if they don't have internet access. With a probability basis and coverage of people who can't access the internet, surveys using AmeriSpeak are nationally representative.

Interviews were conducted in English.

As is done routinely in surveys, results were weighted, or adjusted, to ensure that responses accurately reflect the population's makeup by factors such as age, sex, race, education, region and phone use.

No more than 1 time in 20 should chance variations in the sample cause the results to vary by more than plus or minus 3.7 percentage points from the answers that would be obtained if all adults in the U.S. were polled.

There are other sources of potential error in polls, including the wording and order of questions.

The questions and results are available at http://www.apnorc.org/

AP social media guidelines

Why this section?

Journalists everywhere have looked to The Associated Press Stylebook for advice about how to gather and disseminate news since the guide was first published in 1953. During that time, methods of newsgathering and delivery have changed drastically.

Social networks have changed that even more quickly. As daily life plays out all over the world, social networks give us access to the content that hundreds of millions of people choose to share.

Study after study finds that the vast majority of the world's internet users are active on social networks and that people are increasingly turning to social networks as their primary source of news.

This section will show ways social media can enhance beat reporting, simplify finding sources for stories and give journalists a direct connection with people who care about the news they cover. Fluency in social media takes time and effort, and challenges journalists to use the networks in a way that doesn't undermine their credibility.

While the popularity of individual networks may ebb and flow, this guide hopes to present a foundation that is relevant today but can similarly apply to tomorrow's digital landscape.

The fundamentals of our news cooperative — accuracy, speed and honesty — are set down in AP's **News Values and Principles**. These goals have remained paramount for more than 170 years.

This section extends from those principles, urging journalists to apply the same standards to their use of social networks, while addressing the challenges and opportunities that are specific to these platforms.

What does the term social media mean?

The term refers to tools that allow the sharing of information and content and the formation of communities through online and mobile networks of people.

What are some examples of social media?

There are many manifestations of social media — and new ones are being developed all the time. Some of the most common types:
— Social networks like Facebook and LinkedIn form communities around common interests and share content.
— Blogs, which are generally written by a single person or specified group of

people, but where comment fields and the ability to follow bloggers and see their updates often allow for a broader discussion among readers.

— Microblogging sites, like Twitter and China's Sina Weibo, where a user can send short bits of information, visuals and links to longer content, which are then seen by those who choose to follow that user and can be found by the service's broader community.

— Livestreaming services, like Periscope and Facebook Live, where anyone can broadcast video in real time and interact with viewers.

— Wikis, where content is collectively created by those who choose to participate in the process.

— Content-sharing services, like Flickr, Instagram and YouTube, where anyone can upload content for easy sharing and discussion with others on the Web.

— Messaging apps like Snapchat, WhatsApp Messenger and WeChat, where users share short messages privately with individuals or with specified groups of fellow users.

— Online forums, where participants can share ideas, debate topics and get help.

— Check-in services, like Swarm, where users form communities and find out when fellow users have checked themselves into certain locations, events or activities. (Many general-purpose social networks offer check-in functions as well.)

— All sorts of other sites, from dating services to electronic pinboards to collaborative essay-writing projects.

How do journalists use social media in their work?

— To track down sources — in particular, people who witnessed a news event or who have a direct stake in a reporting topic.

— To gather user-generated content, like photos or videos, that a news provider may want to acquire and distribute/publish as part of its news report.

— To look for news tips or discussion trends that might lead to or form a story.

— To produce and distribute original content that's tailored to a given platform, such as a blog post, live broadcast, GIF or visual quote card.

— To find new sources and keep up with existing ones.

— To interact with news consumers directly to inform their reporting and to promote their work.

— To share links that provide an additional entry point to existing journalism.

— To get a preliminary sense of how members of the public — or at least social media users — are reacting to an event.

How, as a journalist, should I balance my public, professional presence with my personal privacy?

There are no one-size-fits-all answers to how journalists should manage their social media accounts with respect to their personal privacy. But journalists should consider various factors, including their newsroom's conduct and ethics policy, and approach social networks with clarity regarding their personal feelings and professional needs. At the AP, our social policies are built atop the foundation of our **News Values and Principles**. Some things to consider:

— Not all social networks allow users to create more than one profile.

— Posts or messages that are intended to be personal can easily be shared, just like emails can be forwarded and conversations recorded. Journalists should never violate their newsroom's conduct or ethics policy under the assumption that their posts are personal, not professional. Social networks bring into clear focus that journalists are considered journalists by the public 24/7.

— Those reluctant to share at all on social media should think about whether they share parts of themselves outside of social media — and when and how. Are you comfortable enough with a source to share small talk about last night's baseball game or some new music? Perhaps sharing some of that during social media interactions with others won't stray too far from what you're comfortable with. There may be subjects that are off-limits for you — that's OK, too.

— Social credibility: When approaching sources on the street, journalists often gains credibility by presenting a business card or identifying themselves. On social networks, credibility is gained through consistency and by building connections through interaction and sharing.

How, in all formats, do you vet sources found through social media?

In general, you should apply the same principles used in vetting a source found any other way. But there can be additional challenges, since it can be difficult to verify the identity of sources found online.

Most importantly, never simply lift quotes, photos or video from social networking sites and attribute them to the name on the profile or feed you found them under. Most social media sites offer a way to send a message to a user . Use this to establish direct contact, over email or phone, so you can explain what you're working on and get more detailed information about the source.

If a source claims to be an official from a company, organization or government agency, call the place of business to confirm identity, just as you would if a source called on the phone. And if the source provides factual information that's central to a story, always pursue at least one additional source for confirmation.

If you come across photos, videos or other content that you would like to use in your news report, you'll need to verify the authenticity of the piece of content. You'll also need to determine who controls the copyright of the material and get permission from that person/organization to use it.

Use particular caution if you find a social networking page or feed that appears to belong to a person who is central to a story, especially if you can't get confirmation from that person. Phony accounts are rampant, so examine the details to determine whether the page could have just as easily been created by somebody else.

How should social media not be used?

Social networks should never be used as a reporting shortcut when another method, like picking up a phone or knocking on a door, would yield more reliable or comprehensive information. For example, if a key question in a story is only partly or indirectly answered by a tweet sent by a government official, don't settle for that — reach out to the official to find out more. (Though the tweet might also be reported.)

SOCIAL MEDIA

THE BASICS

Each social network has unique characteristics, but a few basic rules generally apply:

HANDLE/USERNAME: When deciding on a username, choose something clear-cut and easy to remember. First name, last name is always a good option. AP may be used for its staffers, though it is not required.

PHOTO: Upload a professional-looking photo of yourself and use it on all networks. People won't take you seriously without one.

BIO: Write a bio that accurately describes who you are. Feel free to include a personal tidbit or two, but remember that you are always representing the AP. You may want to include your email address so people can easily get in touch with you privately.

GOALS: Define some goals about how often you post or tweet and strike a balance among personal and professional posts, responses, links to stories, retweets or shares.

BUILD CREDIBILITY: It comes through posting regularly. Show you're active, engaged and committed to the tool. You can't parachute in and expect to have people's trust instantly.

CONNECT AND INTERACT: Seek out people who have the same interests as you and pay attention when they post.

BE YOURSELF: No one wants to interact with a robot. You can control how much of you to share, but you need to make it clear that you're human. Use colorful, persuasive language, insert some personality and use humor. Entice users to click your links.

SHARE WHAT YOU SEE: Journalists have a front row seat to history. Use that vantage point to engage with people. If you witness a major news development, report it to the relevant AP desk first; otherwise, you're welcome to share general observations of what's going on around you.

USING LISTS TO STAY ORGANIZED AND PROTECT YOUR PRIVACY

Twitter

Twitter lists are a powerful, convenient way to organize and find new people. When you view a list you've created, you'll only see updates from the users you chose for that list. If you're using a third-party program like TweetDeck or Hootsuite, you can organize lists into different columns, so you don't have to search through one long feed to find certain types of tweets. This can make things much easier if you're organizing information from lots of users. Lists can be public or private, allowing you to track users discreetly without directly following them or even share feeds of entire groups of people with the Twitterverse.

For reporters, private lists are an easy way to see tweets by newsmakers, regardless of whether you actually follow them. You may want to start organizing a private list by adding sources you already know. For a legislative reporter, that could include lawmakers and their staffs, party officials, legislative research staffers, the top elected officials and their key staffers, lobbyists, other reporters and bloggers. For a crime reporter, prosecuting and defense attorneys, court staff (clerks, bailiffs, court administrators), other reporters or incarcerated criminals. If you are sharing a list with colleagues you should come back to it regularly to ensure it is always up-to-date. Browsing through lists others have created is a smart way to find other people who might be relevant to you.

Twitter's help section is a great resource for managing your account, finding and following people and creating lists.

Facebook

Facebook has discontinued its Interest Lists feature for organizing the pages you follow. But you can still keep your personal and work contacts separate by creating Friend Lists. Facebook's help section offers detailed instructions on managing your privacy settings.

See **Social Media Guidelines for AP Employees**.

SEARCH FOR PEOPLE – AND THEIR PHOTOS AND VIDEOS

Regardless of where and when news develops, it will likely be shared using social networks. Journalists should be able to quickly use social media tools to find people, photos and video related to news. Even routine stories can benefit from sources found through social media.

Quick, smart reaction to breaking news can be key to finding people or securing exclusive photos and video. It can also help save time and resources. And often, it's the only way to reach people.

To get strong results from a social network search, be thoughtful about your search terms and refine them as you gauge your results. People who aren't journalists don't always think like journalists, so simplify your language and try to think of what they might say.

For example, if you're seeking user-generated content from passengers trapped on a cruise ship, try to think of what tourists, their friends and families might say. You might try different combinations of words: "Carnival," "Splendor" "cruise," "stuck," "vacation," "port," "aboard," "sick" or "miserable." Also consider the expletives that someone might be inclined to utter when trapped in an uncomfortable situation.

The **Facebook** search field near the top of the page makes it easy to type in what you're looking for and then refine the search by type of result (people, pages, posts, etc.). When you find someone, message them privately or comment on the post that you're contacting them about (while logged in), identify yourself and give the person a way to reach you through phone or email.

Note that Facebook messages sent to strangers will generate "message requests," which recipients may or may not notice among their notifications. You can also try to find other ways to contact users — maybe they have a link to a blog or an email address, or perhaps you can find the same person on Twitter or

LinkedIn. Or a public records search might turn up a phone number.

You can do people and keyword searches on **Twitter** and save them. When you find someone, hit "Reply" (while logged into Twitter) and write something like:

Compose new Tweet ✕

@(username) I'm with Associated Press. Would like to talk to you about XXXXX. Pls call (number) or email (staffer/bureau@ap.org). Thx.

Add photo   Location disabled   6   ✓ Tweet

You may also follow people and ask them to follow you, so they can direct message you and make contact privately. Stakes in each situation will vary, but feel free to err on the side of private direct messages if the topic or your discovery seems competitive. Don't forget: Other media outlets can follow your tweets for tips and clues to what you're pursuing and can find what you write when you reply to someone.

Most days, it's pretty easy to find a reporter on a social network post something like: *"Are you or do you know anyone who's affected by Event X? If so, please msg me; I may want to talk with you for my story."*

That method can sometimes yield results, especially if a reporter has a specialized, tuned-in audience of people willing to either share the request or offer themselves up as sources without hesitation. But it's somewhat limiting.

Think about it: If you were on assignment doing a story about voters on Election Day (and were prohibited from using social media), would you simply walk outside your office and shout: "Hey, has anyone voted today?" Probably not. More likely, you'd head to a local polling place, watch voters walk in and out and try to speak with them there.

Finding people through social media requires the same detective-like mentality reporters use when they're wielding nothing more than a notepad and pencil.

Advanced searches allow you to narrow results by location, weed out posts by people simply passing along news links of a story you're working on, and quickly pinpoint relevant, real-world people with the ability to give firsthand contributions to your story.

The **Twitter Advanced Search** (https://twitter.com/search-advanced), in particular, is simple but powerful. Try different combinations of keywords to find what you're looking for. Search results can be sorted to show most recent first, or filtered to limit the tweets to photos or videos.

General tips:

— Put keywords and hashtags (the number # symbol followed by a keyword, which is used to convey the subject a user is addressing) in the top boxes. You can use "and" and "or" in the searches and also choose among several languages.

— Under "None of these words" put "http" to eliminate people who are passing along story links — but note that this will also eliminate many tweets that contain photos and video, since sharing such content often involves a link. You can also focus your search here. Considering the cruise ship example, if you're searching for a Carnival ship you might put "church" in this box to eliminate tweets about church carnivals.

— The "People" search area lets you look for tweets from or to specific user accounts.
— Under "Places," put the city, ZIP code or landmark. The default area is 15 miles, but you can change that after the results are returned by changing the 15 to another number in the gray search box. Not all tweets are tagged with a location, so try omitting the location if you don't get any results.
— Under "Dates," you can specify a date range for when the tweets were originally sent. The Advanced Search page can access tweets back to Twitter's launch in 2006.
— There's also a save option on top of the search results page.

Video Searches

Besides Twitter, Facebook and other networks, there are some good sites to specifically search for video.

On **YouTube**, conduct a search using the search box and click "Filter" when the results are returned. You can then narrow the results by time frame or change

Upload date	Type	Duration	Features	Sort by
Last hour	Video	Short (< 4 minutes)	HD	Relevance
Today	Channel	Long (> 20 minutes)	Subtitles/CC	Upload date
This week	Playlist		Creative Commons	View count
This month	Movie		3D	Rating
This year	Show		Live	
			Purchased	

SOCIAL MEDIA

how they are displayed.

Display your results by upload date and refresh the page frequently to see new postings. Track down the earliest example of a video to make sure you are chasing original content. Consider the words someone uploading video may use, as well as the city and specific streets or landmarks they may refer to.

To contact the person who posted the video, click on his or her username and go to their "About" page. Then you'll find a button for sending a message.

On **Vimeo** (http://vimeo.com), put in your search terms and click enter. On the page that comes up, click "Advanced Filters" on the right to limit the results to the last 24 hours, last week or beyond.

On **Periscope** (http://periscope.tv), you can search for keywords that appear in a video's title using the search bar on the website. Since Periscope videos are tagged to a particular location, however, it is usually preferable to search for the place you are looking for. To find live and recent streams in a particular location, use the mobile app instead of the website. Click on the globe icon, then browse the map or search for the place name. You can enter a broad region or a specific street address or landmark.

Find **Facebook Live** videos as they are streamed by browsing the map (http://facebook.com/livemap). Live videos disappear from the map as soon as they end, so take note of the URL of the video if you want to be able to find it again easily after the broadcast."

Photo Searches

Several sites are available to search for photos posted to social networks. Photos shared through Facebook or Twitter can be search using those networks' own search functions, which allow you to narrow results to zero in on images. Some other sites worth searching for photos:

— **Flickr** (http://www.flickr.com) has a wealth of visual content. You can search it without logging in, but you'll need a Yahoo account to reach out to users to ask about using their content.
— **Google Plus** (https://plus.google.com) also draws a lot of user-generated content.
— **Instagram** (https://www.instagram.com) allows you to search for photos and videos by hashtag, user or geographic location.

USER-GENERATED CONTENT

User-generated content, or UGC, is the term commonly used in the news industry for content with news or editorial value that has been produced by anyone who isn't working as a professional journalist. Sometimes this is also referred to as citizen journalism, when members of the public capture news events on their own devices either by chance or by pursuing a story. User-generated content may be found via social networks or given to a reporter on the scene of a news event. It is essential to hold UGC to the same standards as all other information taken in and reported by the AP.

Journalists handling UGC face a number of challenges, most notably verification. Do we know exactly what we are seeing, and how we have determined this? We should seek to tell the story surrounding each piece of video and audio and every photo we acquire with the level of accuracy people expect from the AP. This means tapping into our considerable knowledge base, drawing on the expertise of AP staff around the world.

Securing access to content can often be a challenge, especially in a breaking news situation when video or photos have been posted to social networks. You must always strive to seek the original source of the media you are seeking to acquire. Once that content owner has been identified, ask for permission to use the material, following all the established protocols the AP has in place. Also ask tough questions about when they captured material, why there were there, and anything else that can help you determine the authenticity of the content.

When publishing UGC, make every effort to give due credit to the person who has created that content. Use the person's name if he or she is happy for you to do so, or a username (from a social network or platform) if it is applicable or the preference of the individual.

It can sometimes be useful for AP or individual journalists to put out tweets or posts asking the public to come forward with UGC related to a particular story. When doing so, emphasize that members of the public should not put themselves in danger gathering content for AP. The same caution should be taken when directly communicating with these content owners privately.

Referencing user-generated content

When using or referencing UGC in the AP report, we must be consistent about how we refer to the content. Here is some recommended language for use in various formats. The material in parentheses will need to be adjusted based on individual circumstances.

Video or photos references in text

The video (or photo) was supplied to The Associated Press by (local activists, a local videographer, etc.). It has been authenticated, based on (the AP's examination of the evidence) and was consistent with (AP's own reporting on the incident, human rights officials' accounts of the event, etc.).

Photo captions

This photo, which AP obtained from (an activist group / the activist group xxxxx / a local photographer on the scene / etc.), has been authenticated based on its contents and other AP reporting.

This photo, which AP obtained from (an activist group / the activist group xxxxx / a local photographer on the scene / etc.), has been authenticated based on details in it. (For situations where we don't have other AP reporting)

Video scripts and shotlists

Use whichever of the following apply in the form of caveats or worked into a storyline:
— Video and audio translated and content checked by regional experts against known locations and events.

— Video is consistent with independent AP reporting.

— Video cleared for use by all AP clients by content creator (or via third-party permission — insert as appropriate).

To be read in voiced video reports

An amateur videographer/activists (as appropriate — and name the group when possible) says/say this video shows (whatever it may be). It has been authenticated based on its contents and other AP reporting.

DIGITAL SECURITY FOR JOURNALISTS

It's impossible to be a productive journalist without extensive use of digital communication and production tools. But journalists are not always aware of how to keep their online accounts and private material secure.

Strong security is a combination of good technology and meticulous habits. It might sound attractive to employ the best possible security on all files and every communication channel, but this isn't practical because security always has a cost in terms of time, money or inconvenience. But you can secure your data against some types of unauthorized access.

Here are some basic techniques that will make your data more secure and help you to understand what is not protected. Probably, many of them will already be familiar to you. They may seem simplistic, but most security compromises are the result of lapses in good habits, not high-tech hacking.

1. Use secure passwords. If your passwords are easy to break, nothing else matters.

It is possible to log into an astonishing number of systems with the passwords "123456," "password" and "qwerty." Needless to say, these are terrible choices. But words in the dictionary are also no good because automated password crackers can make thousands of guesses per second. Passwords with letters replaced by numbers (such as zero for "o," three for "e" and one for "l") are also easily guessed by computer. The best passwords are actually passphrases, short sentences that are personally relevant and therefore memorable. If that's too long to type, you can make an acronym from the first letter of each word in your passphrase. Ideally, every password should contain at least one capital letter, lowercase letter, number and symbol.

Particularly protect your email password. Most online services will email you a new password in case you forget yours, so if someone has control of your email, they pretty much have control of all of your accounts. Make sure your email password is well chosen and different from all other passwords. Change it immediately if you suspect someone has compromised your account. In fact you should change your important passwords several times a year to put a time limit on the damage that a stolen password can do.

Social networking and instant messenger passwords are also frequently compromised. Be sure to use a different password for each account. Otherwise, an attacker could gain control of all of your accounts simultaneously – and then change all the passwords, leaving you with few public channels to contest the identity theft!

Ideally, each place you log in should use a different password. No one can remember dozens of different passwords, but you can use a program like 1Password to securely store a completely random and un-guessable password for each service. The downside is that you must have your personal password database with you at all times, your master password exposes everything at once if it is compromised, and if you lose your master password you lose all of your access simultaneously.

Never share your password with anyone over email. If you need to share your password with someone you trust — such as a tech support staffer or a colleague with whom you co-manage a social account — do so verbally.

2. Some computers and networks are more secure than others.

Sending an email at the office to a colleague is very secure if your organization runs its own mail servers (rather than using cloud-based email), because the message only travels across the internal network, not the internet. But an email sent over Wi-Fi at a coffee shop can be intercepted by anyone nearby, if they have the right software on their laptop.

In general, different networks have different levels of security. A computer attached directly to the public internet is quite vulnerable, whereas a computer on an internal network, talking only to other internal servers, is insulated from the outside world.

VPN software creates a "virtual private network" that connects a remote computer to an internal network over an encrypted channel. It is quite secure — as long as you trust the computer you are running it on and don't forget to log out.

Other people's computers might have viruses, key-logging software or other malware installed. Avoid doing sensitive work on machines you can't vouch for. Especially try to avoid typing your passwords on a public computer or other system that might have key-logging software installed. If you must log in from an untrusted machine, change your password later from a secure computer.

3. Be suspicious of people sending you links with generic descriptions, and always read the URL before you log in.

"Phishing" is the practice of tricking someone into revealing their password, and it's the most common method of gaining unauthorized access. There are many different ways to phish, but all of them are based on sending you a message with a link in it.

The original phishing scams involved an email or other message asking you to re-enter your password for "security purposes" that contained a link to a fake login screen that looks like a legitimate bank or social networking site. It's very easy to create a copy of a website at a fake address, and most people won't notice that the URL is wrong before happily typing in their passwords. For example, if the login screen looks like Twitter, the URL displayed in your browser must start with "twitter.com." Other addresses such as "itwitter.com" are scams. Be very wary of messages with links that take you to a login screen of any sort, and get into the habit of reading the URL before typing in your password.

SOCIAL MEDIA

Other phishing schemes are even more insidious because they exploit security flaws to steal passwords stored in your browser without ever asking you to log in. These attacks still come in the form of links, usually accompanied by very generic messages such as "check out this picture of you" or "did you see this site?" Be very suspicious of such generic links even if they come from a trusted source — your friends' accounts may have been compromised, and if you click the bad link, your account may be compromised too. Also, keep your web browser up to date, including automatically downloaded updates to minimize your vulnerability to these types of attacks.

There have been hundreds of phishing scams, and there are sure to be more variants in the future. The only protection is to understand how these scams operate, read URLs before logging in and be wary of generic links delivered by email, Twitter, Facebook or any other messaging system.

4. Different communications tools have different levels of security.

Email has the weakest security of any communication method. It's transmitted unencrypted, so it's no more secure than sending a post card. Emails can be intercepted by any network operator between the source and destination, viewed by the administrators of the mail servers at either end or snooped by someone on the same public wireless network. Instant messages are often vulnerable in the same way.

All web traffic is similarly transmitted without encryption, except for sites that can be accessed using "https" instead of "http," which is normally indicated by a little "lock" icon in the browser. When a website offers both, a URL starting with https is greatly preferable because https connections are encrypted, which makes it harder for eavesdroppers to record your password or other sensitive information. Standard mobile phones are difficult to intercept over the air, but of course the telecommunications company has full access to the connection, as well as your location (even when no calls are made). This may or may not be a problem depending on who wants to listen.

Skype connections are encrypted so that they cannot be intercepted en route by telecommunications companies or anyone else. Skype can be more secure than regular telephone calls in many situations, but it depends on who wants to eavesdrop and that person's relationship to Skype. Skype could still decrypt recorded conversations if it wants to — or if it is compromised or compelled by a third party. Other digital-telephony services have similar security profiles.

Email encrypted using the popular encryption program PGP can be very secure, but PGP is quite difficult to set up and use correctly — and can be compromised after the fact if a private key leaks.

The best solution for truly private communication is the OTR ("off the record") instant messaging system. OTR is built into many IM programs, including the popular Adium application. It is quite secure, even against state-level attackers and about as simple as secure communication gets. But it still demands good habits.

OTR will not hide whom you are communicating with, only what you are saying. Similarly, it's easy to pretend to be someone else over IM. The first time you connect, use another channel simultaneously (such as the phone) to ensure that the person on the other end is really who you think it is. Finally, no amount of communication security will help if someone later reads the chat logs stored on your computer. With Microsoft Office Communicator, chat logs are in the "Conversation History" folder in Outlook. You need to find where such logs are for OTR or other instant messaging programs.

5. Think about what data is stored and where. Caution on cloud computing.

How many copies of that sensitive chat log, photograph or private message are floating around on your laptop? Are there any on other computers? Did you give a copy to someone who might store it insecurely? Are there any copies in the cloud?

Many communications programs make automatic copies. There could be a sensitive email in a saved folder, or an online service might be saving your chat logs (as gchat does by default). Your organization may already have data retention policies or guidance on best practices. If your organization doesn't, consult with your own attorney about types of data to keep while reporting.

It's also important to know where your information is stored. Cloud computing can solve many problems, but whenever you store sensitive information on others' computers you are depending on them to keep it safe. In essence, you are betting on their competence and will to resist your attackers. Even if a cloud computing provider is honest and smart, do you know what they will do when served with a subpoena? It's best to consult with an attorney before placing sensitive material in the cloud.

This applies especially to email and social networking service providers, most of whom routinely turn their users' data over to law enforcement agencies if asked. In many circumstances, this happens without any sort of warrant or other judicial oversight, or even notification to the user that their privacy has been compromised. This includes major vendors, such as Facebook, Google and Yahoo, and applies in many countries including the United States.

Further, many governments operate massive internet surveillance operations, so anything transmitted unencrypted must be assumed to be in the hands of one state agency or another.

6. Consider what might happen if your equipment falls into the wrong hands.

Communication security is important, but many people neglect physical security. A laptop can be lost or stolen, or someone might wander into the office while you are at lunch or even sneak into your hotel room. Computers and other electronics are also routinely seized by authorities of all stripes, including law enforcement and international customs. Encrypt your hard drive if you have sensitive material on your computer, and be careful to track all copies of critical files, including those on thumb drives or other media. The same precautions apply to camera memory cards, phones containing images or video, etc.

7. If a security breach might cause serious harm, you need expert advice.

Tools such as OTR instant messaging and the Tor anonymity network can be enormously powerful and offer the possibility of truly secure communication, but they require considerable thought and care to use them correctly. Encryption systems come in many flavors, but even the most sophisticated software is useless if you forget to log out at the right time. And digital security is just one part of operational security — it takes more than technology to keep secrets.

This little guide is no substitute for specialized training, technology and procedures. If the stakes are high, you need to consult an expert.

SOCIAL MEDIA GUIDELINES FOR AP EMPLOYEES

REVISED MAY 2013

AP's Social Media Guidelines are based on our Statement of News Values and Principles. The guidelines below apply these long-tested principles to the social media space. The Social Media Guidelines are designed to advance the AP's brand and staffers' personal brands on social networks. They encourage staffers to be active participants in social networks while upholding our fundamental value that staffers should not express personal opinions on controversial issues of the day.

Any exceptions to the guidelines below must be approved by a senior AP manager. Nothing in this policy is intended to abridge any rights provided by the National Labor Relations Act.

Accounts

All AP journalists are encouraged to have accounts on social networks. They have become an essential tool for AP reporters to gather news and share links to our published work. We recommend having one account per network that you use both personally and professionally.

Many AP journalists have had great success with this strategy.

Employees must identify themselves as being from AP if they are using their accounts for work in any way. You don't have to include AP in your Twitter or other usernames, and you should use a personal image (not an AP logo) for the profile photo. But you should identify yourself in your profile as an AP staffer.

Posting AP proprietary or confidential material is prohibited.

Employees may not include political affiliations in their profiles and should not make any postings that express political views.

Opinion

AP staffers must be aware that opinions they express may damage the AP's reputation as an unbiased source of news. AP employees must refrain from declaring their views on contentious public issues in any public forum and must not take part in organized action in support of causes or movements.

Sometimes AP staffers ask if they're free to comment in social media on matters like sports and entertainment. The answer is yes, but there are some important things to keep in mind:

First, trash-talking about anyone (including a team, company or celebrity) reflects badly on staffers and the AP. Assume your tweet will be seen by the target of your comment. The person or organization you're deriding may be one that an AP colleague is trying to develop as a source.

Second, if you or your department covers a subject — or you supervise people who do — you have a special obligation to be even-handed in your tweets. Whenever possible, link to AP copy, where we have the space to represent all points of view.

Posts and tweets aimed at gathering opinions for a story must make clear that we are looking for voices on all sides of an issue.

Privacy

Employees should be mindful that any opinions or personal information they disclose about themselves or colleagues may be linked to the AP's name. That's true even if staffers restrict their pages to viewing only by friends.

We recommend customizing your privacy settings on Facebook to determine what you share and with whom.

However, as multitudes of people have learned all too well, virtually nothing is truly private on the internet. It's all too easy for someone to copy material out of restricted pages and redirect it elsewhere for wider viewing.

Friending/following

It is acceptable to extend and accept Facebook friend requests from sources, politicians and newsmakers if necessary for reporting purposes, and to follow them on Twitter.

However, friending and "liking" political candidates or causes may create a perception among people unfamiliar with the protocol of social networks that AP staffers are advocates. Therefore, staffers should try to make this kind of contact with figures on both sides of controversial issues.

We should avoid interacting with newsmakers on their public pages – for instance, commenting on their posts.

AP managers should not issue friend requests to subordinates. It's fine if employees want to initiate the friend process with their bosses or other managers.

Publishing

AP staff are encouraged to link to AP content in all formats. They can also link to content from other media organizations, except if the material spreads rumors or is otherwise inappropriate. Staffers should always refrain from spreading unconfirmed rumors online, regardless of whether other journalists or news outlets have shared the reports; because of staffers' affiliation with AP, doing so could lend credence to reports that may well be incorrect.

Be mindful of competitive and corporate issues as you post links. And while we compete vigorously with other news organizations, you should think twice before you tweet or post anything that disparages them. This may affect perceptions of your objectivity.

Staffers should link to content that has been published online, rather than directly uploading or copying and pasting the material.

AP journalists have live-tweeted news events on several occasions with great success. Here are some guidelines on live-tweeting:

— News events (press conferences, sports events, etc.) that are being broadcast live: AP staffers are welcome to live-tweet these events. However, when

SOCIAL MEDIA

major news breaks, a staffer's first obligation is to provide full details to the appropriate news desk for use in AP services if the desk isn't tuned in already. After providing this information and handling any other immediate AP work, the staffer is then free to tweet or post information about the news development.

— Exclusive material: AP news services must have the opportunity to publish exclusive text, photo and video material before it appears on social networks. Once that material has been published, staffers are welcome to tweet and post a link to it on AP or subscriber platforms.

— Incremental reporting threads: AP staffers should never share on social networks incremental information that, if closely held, could lead to important, exclusive content.

— Other content: Other material you have gathered may be shared on social networks. This includes material we commonly refer to as "cutting room floor" content — material that is not needed for a specific AP product.

A note about the safety of AP staff: Staffers must not post on social networks any information that could jeopardize the safety of AP staff — for example, the exact location of staffers reporting from a place where journalists may be kidnapped or attacked. This also applies to reports of the arrest or disappearance of staffers. In some cases, publicity may in fact help a staffer, but this determination must be made by AP managers handling the situation.

Retweeting

Retweets, like tweets, should not be written in a way that looks like you're expressing a personal opinion on the issues of the day. A retweet with no comment of your own can easily be seen as a sign of approval of what you're relaying.

Examples of retweets that can cause problems:

1. RT @jonescampaign: Smith's policies would destroy our schools
2. RT @dailyeuropean: At last, a euro plan that works

These kinds of unadorned retweets must be avoided.

However, we can judiciously retweet opinionated material if we make clear we're simply reporting it, much as we would quote it in a story. Introductory words help make the distinction.

Examples:

1. Jones campaign now denouncing Smith on education. RT @jonescampaign: Smith's policies would destroy our schools
2. Big European paper praises euro plan. RT @dailyeuropean: At last, a euro plan that works

These cautions apply even if you say on your Twitter profile that retweets do not constitute endorsements. Many people who see your tweets and retweets will never look at your Twitter bio.

Staffers should steer clear of retweeting rumors and hearsay. They can, however, feel free to reply to such tweets in order to seek further information, as long as they're careful to avoid repeating the questionable reports.

When a newsmaker breaks significant news on a social network, a staffer who sees this should report it to the appropriate AP news desk and do any related reporting work asked of him or her. The staffer can then feel free to retweet or share the original tweet or post, if the newsmaker account is judged to be authentic. Policies and best practices on verifying accounts are outlined in more detail below.

Showcasing AP work on personal sites, blogs and social networks

AP staffers may wish to share their work on their personal websites and blogs. Staffers may post a sampling of their text stories, photos, videos or interactives once they have been published by AP. The material must be clearly identified as AP content.

When highlighting their work on social networks or other sites and services that are focused on the sharing of content among users, staffers must link to the content rather than uploading it directly.

Non-AP content created by AP staffers, such as personal photos, videos and writings, can be shared on personal websites, blogs and social networks. All postings must be consistent with the rules in the AP News Values and Principles and Social Media Guidelines, including those on expressing opinions on contentious public issues. Staffers working in a hostile or otherwise sensitive environment should be mindful of security issues, as well as the impact on AP's ability to gather the news, when deciding what personal content to share online.

Sourcing

It can be difficult to verify the identity of sources found on social networks. Sources discovered there should be vetted in the same way as those found by any other means. If a source you encounter on a social network claims to be an official from a company, organization or government agency, call the place of business to confirm the identity, just as you would if a source called on the phone.

You must never simply lift quotes, photos or video from social networking sites and attribute them to the name on the profile or feed where you found the material. Most social media sites offer a way to send a message to a user; use this to establish direct contact, over email or by phone, so you can get more detailed information about the source.

Use particular caution if you find a social networking account that appears to belong to a person who is central to a story, especially if you can't get confirmation from that person. Fake accounts are rampant in the social media world and can appear online within minutes of a new name appearing in the news. Examine the details to determine whether the page could have just as easily been created by somebody else.

Many athletes, celebrities and politicians have verified Twitter accounts, identified by a white-on-blue check mark on the profile page, which means Twitter has determined that the account really does belong to that person. However, Twitter's verification process has been fooled, meaning we should still do our own checking with the newsmaker. The same goes for verified Google Plus pages, which have a check mark — we need to verify the page through our own reporting.

Also, before you quote from newsmaker's tweets or posts, confirm who is managing the account. Is it the famous person? His or her handlers? A combination? Knowing the source of the information will help you determine just how newsworthy the tweet or post is and how to characterize it.

To include photos, videos or other multimedia content from social networks in our news report, we must determine who controls the copyright to the material and get permission from that person or organization to use it. Any exceptions must be discussed with the Nerve Center and Legal. The authenticity of the content also needs to be verified to AP's standards.

Staffers should take a sensitive and thoughtful approach when using social networks to pursue information or user-generated content from people in dangerous situations or from those who have suffered a significant personal loss. They should never ask members of the public to put themselves in danger, and in fact should remind them to stay safe when conditions are hazardous. Staffers should use their journalistic instincts to determine whether inquiring through social media is appropriate at all given the source's difficult circumstances, and should consult with a manager in making this decision. For more details on how to handle this situation, see the broader memo that was distributed to AP staff.

Interacting with users

AP is strongly in favor of engaging with those who consume our content. Staffers should feel free to ask their followers on social networks for their opinions on news stories, or to put out a call for witnesses and other sources, including people who have captured photos or video that AP might want to authenticate and use. They're also encouraged to answer questions about their areas of coverage that are directed their way on social media, as long as they answer in a way that's consistent with AP's News Values and Principles and Social Media Guidelines.

Most feedback we receive is constructive, and any substantive criticism of our content should be taken seriously, however it may be phrased.

AP's News Values and Principles say, "Staffers must notify supervisory editors as soon as possible of errors or potential errors, whether in their work or that of a colleague." Beyond that, responses to our audience can largely be guided by the nature of the comments that come in.

A thoughtful note from a reader or viewer that leads to a correction by us deserves an email or tweet of thanks (try to avoid repeating the original error). If someone offers a businesslike criticism of a story or image but has the facts wrong, it's good to reply, time permitting, to clarify the facts.

However, it's best to avoid protracted back-and-forth exchanges with angry people that become less constructive with each new round. Abusive, bigoted, obscene and/or racist comments should be flagged to the Nerve Center immediately and, if appropriate, to AP Global Security (contact dspriggs@ap.org).

Other things to keep in mind:

1. Any response we make to a reader or viewer could go public. Email, Facebook messages and Twitter direct messages may feel like private communications, but may easily find their way to blogs and political pressure groups, attorneys and others. In the case of a story or image that stirs significant controversy, the editor is likely the best person to reply, rather than the person who created the content. The Standards Center can also reply.

2. Any incoming message that raises the possibility of legal action should be

reviewed by an AP attorney before a response is made

Interacting with AP accounts

Staff are welcome to retweet and share material posted by official AP-branded accounts on social networking sites (e.g. @AP or an AP Facebook or Google Plus page). We ask that AP staff refrain from liking or commenting on official AP-branded Facebook or Google Plus posts and chats. These accounts are official, public-facing channels of communication, and we want to reserve the comments and interactions for the public, not for journalists talking among themselves in a public-facing spot. It can be off-putting for an average Facebook user to click on a post and see conversations between colleagues or virtual insider pats on the back.

Deleting tweets

Twitter.com allows us to delete tweets we've sent. Deletion, however, removes the tweet only from Twitter.com and perhaps some other Twitter clients. Tweets of ours that have been retweeted or reposted elsewhere will still remain publicly visible. If you believe a tweet should be deleted, contact a Nerve Center manager to discuss the situation.

Corrections

Erroneous tweets or other social media posts need to be corrected as quickly and transparently as errors in any other AP service. This applies to AP-related tweets or posts on personal accounts as well.

The thing to do is to tweet or post that we made a mistake and explain exactly what was wrong.

Example:

Correction: U.S. Embassy in Nigeria says bombings could happen this week at luxury hotels in Abuja (previously we incorrectly said Lagos): apne.ws/uxr9ph

Serious errors need to be brought to the attention of a Nerve Center manager and the appropriate regional or vertical desk.

SOCIAL MEDIA

Religion

a

abaya Robe-like outer garment worn by Muslim women.

Advent Period including the four Sundays preceding Christmas.

Adventist See **Seventh-day Adventist Church**.

agnostic, atheist An *agnostic* is a person who believes it is impossible to know whether there is a God.

An *atheist* is a person who believes there is no God.

Al-Aqsa Mosque The mosque completed in the eighth century atop the Haram al-Sharif, or *Noble Sanctuary*, in the Old City of Jerusalem; Arabs also use *Al-Aqsa* to refer to the whole area, which houses the Dome of the Rock shrine, too. To Jews the area is known as the *Temple Mount*, the site of the ancient Jewish temples.

Allah The Arabic word for God. The word *God* should be used, unless the Arabic name is used in a quote written or spoken in English.

Allahu akbar The Arabic phrase for *God is great*.

altar, alter An *altar* is a tablelike platform used in a religious service.

To alter is to change.

Anglican Communion The name for the worldwide association of national Anglican churches.

Each national church is independent. A special position of honor is accorded to the archbishop of Canterbury, as the pre-eminent officer in the original Anglican body, the Church of England.

The test of membership in the Anglican Communion traditionally has been whether a church has been in communion with the See of Canterbury. No legislative or juridical ties exist, however.

BELIEFS: Anglicans believe in the Trinity, the humanity and divinity of Christ, the virginity of Mary, salvation through Christ, and everlasting heaven and hell.

A principal difference between Roman Catholics and Anglicans is still the dispute that led to the formation of the Church of England — refusal to acknowledge that the pope, as bishop of Rome, has ruling authority over other bishops. See **catholic, catholicism**.

ANGLICAN CHURCHES: Members of the Anglican Communion, in addition to the Church of England, include the Scottish Episcopal Church, the Anglican Church of Canada, and, in the United States, the Episcopal Church.

See **Episcopal Church**.

Antichrist, anti-Christ *Antichrist* is the proper name for the individual the Bible says will challenge Christ.

The adjective *anti-Christ* would be applied to someone or something opposed to Christ.

Antiochian Orthodox Christian Archdiocese of North America

Formed in 1975 by the merger of the Antiochian Orthodox Christian Archdiocese of New York and All North America and the Archdiocese of Toledo, Ohio, and Dependencies in North America. It is under the jurisdiction of the patriarch of Antioch.

See **Eastern Orthodox churches**.

apostolic delegate, papal nuncio

An *apostolic delegate* is a Roman Catholic diplomat chosen by the pope to be his envoy to the church in a nation that does not have formal diplomatic relations with the Vatican.

A *papal nuncio* is the pope's envoy to a nation with which the Vatican has diplomatic relations.

archbishop See **Episcopal Church**; **Roman Catholic Church**; and **religious titles**.

archbishop of Canterbury In

general, lowercase *archbishop* unless it is used before the name of the individual who holds the office.

Capitalize *Archbishop of Canterbury* standing alone only when it is used in a story that also refers to members of Britain's nobility. See **nobility** in the A-Z section for the relevant guidelines.

archdiocese Capitalize as part of

a proper name: *the Archdiocese of Chicago, the Chicago Archdiocese.* Lowercase when it stands alone.

See the entry for the particular denomination in question.

Armenian Church of America The

term encompasses two independent dioceses that cooperate in some activities. The Eastern Diocese of the Armenian Church of America serves much of the U.S., while the Western Diocese of the Armenian Church of America serves California, Washington, Nevada, New Mexico, Utah and Arizona.

Ashoura The Shiite Muslim

commemoration marking the death of Hussein, the grandson of the Prophet Muhammad, at the Battle of Karbala in present-day Iraq in the seventh century.

Ash Wednesday The first day of

Lent, 46 days before Easter.
See **Easter** and **Lent**.

b

Baha'i A monotheistic religion

founded in the 1860s by Baha'u'llah, a Persian nobleman considered a prophet by the Baha'is. Baha'u'llah taught that all religions represent progressive stages in the revelation of God's will, leading to the unity of all people and faiths. The Baha'is have no clergy; they are governed by local, national and international elected councils. The international governing body, the Universal House of Justice, is based in Haifa, Israel. Its U.S. offices are in Evanston, Illinois.

baptism See **sacraments**.

Baptist churches It is incorrect to

apply the term church to any Baptist unit except the local church.

There are a wide range of Baptist bodies in the U.S. with varied beliefs

RELIGION

and practices.

The largest is the Southern Baptist Convention; most of its members are in the South, although it has churches nationwide. The largest predominantly Northern body is American Baptist Churches in the U.S.A.

Three other large Baptist bodies are predominantly African-American: the National Baptist Convention of America, the National Baptist Convention U.S.A. Inc., and the Progressive National Baptist Convention Inc.

Other Baptist groups include the Cooperative Baptist Fellowship, formed in the 1990s by Southern Baptists who disagreed with the denomination's conservative direction, and the Baptist World Alliance, an international voluntary association for Baptists located in the Washington, D.C. area.

CLERGY: All members of the Baptist clergy may be referred to as *ministers*. *Pastor* applies if a minister leads a congregation.

On first reference, use *the Rev.* before the name of a man or woman. On second reference, use only the last name.

See **religious titles**.

See **religious movements** for definitions of some descriptive terms that often apply to Baptists but are not limited to them.

bar mitzvah The Jewish rite of passage and family celebration that marks a boy's 13th birthday. A similar ceremony for girls is held at age 12 or 13 and called the *bat mitzvah* or *bas mitzvah*. Many, but not all, branches of Judaism, hold the ceremony for girls. Judaism regards the age as a benchmark of religious maturity. Bar mitzvah translates

as "one who is responsible for the Commandments."

Bible Capitalize, without quotation marks, when referring to the Scriptures in the Old Testament or the New Testament. Capitalize also related terms such as the *Gospels, Gospel of St. Mark, the Scriptures, the Holy Scriptures.*

Lowercase *biblical* in all uses.

Lowercase *bible* as a nonreligious term: *My dictionary is my bible.*

Do not abbreviate individual books of the Bible.

Old Testament is a Christian designation; Hebrew Bible or Jewish Bible is the appropriate term for stories dealing with Judaism alone.

The standard names and order of Old Testament books as they appear in Protestant Bibles are: Genesis, Exodus, Leviticus, Numbers, Deuteronomy, Joshua, Judges, Ruth, 1 Samuel, 2 Samuel, 1 Kings, 2 Kings, 1 Chronicles, 2 Chronicles, Ezra, Nehemiah, Esther, Job, Psalms, Proverbs, Ecclesiastes, Song of Solomon, Isaiah, Jeremiah, Lamentations, Ezekiel, Daniel, Hosea, Joel, Amos, Obadiah, Jonah, Micah, Nahum, Habakkuk, Zephaniah, Haggai, Zechariah, Malachi.

Jewish Bibles contain the same 39 books, in different order. Roman Catholic Bibles follow a different order, usually use some different names and include the seven Deuterocanonical books (called the Apocrypha by Protestants): Tobit, Judith, 1 Maccabees, 2 Maccabees, Wisdom, Sirach, Baruch.

The books of the New Testament, in order: Matthew, Mark, Luke, John, Acts, Romans, 1 Corinthians, 2 Corinthians, Galatians, Ephesians, Philippians, Colossians, 1

Thessalonians, 2 Thessalonians, 1 Timothy, 2 Timothy, Titus, Philemon, Hebrews, James, 1 Peter, 2 Peter, 1 John, 2 John, 3 John, Jude, Revelation.

Citation listing the number of chapter and verse(s) use this form: *Matthew 3:16, Luke 21:1-13, 1 Peter 2:1.*

Bible-believing Do not use the term to distinguish one faction from another, because all Christians believe in the Bible. The differences are over interpretations.

Bible Belt Those sections of the United States, especially in the South and Middle West, where strictly conservative Christian beliefs prevail. The term was believed to be coined by H.L. Mencken as a derisive commentary on fundamentalism. The term should be used with care, because in certain contexts it can give offense.

bishop See **religious titles** and the entry for the denomination in question.

Blessed Sacrament, Blessed Virgin

B'nai B'rith See **fraternal organizations and service clubs** in the A-Z section.

Brahman, Brahmin *Brahman* applies to the priestly Hindu caste and a breed of cattle.

Brahmin applies to aristocracy in general: *Boston Brahmin.*

See **Hindu, Hinduism**.

Buddha, Buddhism The religion founded in India around 500 B.C. based on the teachings of Siddhartha Gautama, who was called Buddha, or enlightened one, by his followers.

Buddhism is considered the world's fourth-largest religious tradition. The overwhelming majority of Buddhists live in the Asia-Pacific region. About half live in China.

Countries with Buddhist majorities include Thailand, Cambodia and Myanmar. Small communities of Buddhists can be found in North America and Europe.

Buddhists believe that right, or virtuous, thinking and behavior can liberate people from suffering. Nirvana is the state of ultimate enlightenment and peace. Until nirvana is reached, believers cannot be freed from the cycle of death and rebirth.

There are many variants of Buddhist practice and teaching, but scholars generally categorize the streams as:
— Mahayana Buddhism. Prevalent in China, Japan, South Korea and Vietnam. Stresses enlightenment is possible for all.
— Theravada Buddhism. Found in countries such as Thailand, Myanmar and Sri Lanka. Stresses monastic discipline and meditation.
— Vajrayana Buddhism. Concentrated in Tibet, Nepal and Mongolia. Sometimes called Tibetan Buddhism.

C

canonization The process of declaring a person a saint in the Roman Catholic Church. It involves a church investigation of whether, after the person dies, miracles can be attributed to his or her intercession from heaven. When the church

RELIGION

confirms a first miracle, the person is *beatified*, then is *canonized* after confirmation of a second miracle. The process can take years, but can be shortened by the pope.

cantor See **Jewish congregations**.

cardinal See **Roman Catholic Church**.

Catholic, Catholicism Use *Roman Catholic Church, Roman Catholic* or *Roman Catholicism* in the first references to those who believe that the pope, as bishop of Rome, has the ultimate authority in administering an earthly organization founded by Jesus Christ.

Most subsequent references may be condensed to *Catholic Church, Catholic* or *Catholicism. Roman Catholic* should continue to be used, however, if the context requires a distinction between Roman Catholics and members of other denominations who often describe themselves as Catholic. They include some high church Episcopalians (who often call themselves *Anglo-Catholics*), members of Eastern Orthodox churches, and members of some national Catholic churches that have broken with Rome. Included in this last category is the Polish National Catholic Church.

Lowercase *catholic* where used in its generic sense of general or universal, meanings derived from a similar word in Greek.

Those who use *Catholic* in a religious sense are indicating their belief that they are members of a universal church that Jesus Christ left on Earth.

See **Roman Catholic Church**.

celebrant, celebrator Reserve *celebrant* for someone who conducts a religious rite: *He was the celebrant of the Mass.*

Use *celebrator* for someone having a good time: *The celebrators kept the party going until 3 a.m.*

Central Conference of American Rabbis See **Jewish congregations**.

charismatic groups See **religious movements**.

Christian Church (Disciples of Christ) The parentheses and the words they surround are part of the formal name.

The body owes its origins to an early-19th-century frontier movement to unify Christians.

The Disciples, led by Alexander Campbell in western Pennsylvania, and the Christians, led by Barton W. Stone in Kentucky, merged in 1832.

The local church is the basic organizational unit.

National policies are developed by the General Assembly, made up of representatives chosen by local churches and regional organizations.

All members of the clergy may be referred to as *ministers. Pastor* applies if a minister leads a congregation.

On first reference, use *the Rev.* before the name of a man or woman. On second reference, use only the last name.

Christian Science Church See **Church of Christ, Scientist**.

Christmas, Christmas Day Dec. 25. The federal legal holiday is observed on Friday if Dec. 25 falls on a Saturday, on Monday if it falls on a Sunday.

Never abbreviate *Christmas* to *Xmas* or any other form.

Christmastime One word.

Christmas tree Lowercase *tree* and other seasonal terms with *Christmas*: *card, wreath, carol,* etc. Exception: *National Christmas Tree.*

church Capitalize as part of the formal name of a building, a congregation or a denomination; lowercase in other uses: *St. Mary's Church, the Roman Catholic Church, the Catholic and Episcopal churches, a Roman Catholic church, a church.*

Lowercase in phrases where the church is used in an institutional sense: *She believes in the separation of church and state. The pope said the church opposes abortion.*

See **religious titles** and the entry for the denomination in question.

Churches of Christ Thousands of independent U.S. congregations cooperate under this name. Each local church is autonomous and operates under a governing board of elders. The minister is an *evangelist,* addressed by members as *Brother.* The ministers do not use clergy titles. Do not precede their names by a title.

The churches do not regard themselves as a denomination. Rather, they stress a nondenominational effort to preach what they consider basic Bible teachings and they restrict worship activities to those they've identified in the New Testament. For this reason, they generally exclude instrumental music from worship. The churches also teach that baptism by immersion is essential for salvation.

Within the U.S., the churches are concentrated in the South and Southwest. But many of the churches are located overseas, in countries such as India.

See **religious movements**.

churchgoer

Church of Christ, Scientist This denomination was founded in 1879 by Mary Baker Eddy. Her teachings are contained in "Science and Health with Key to the Scriptures," which, along with the Bible, she ordained as the "dual and impersonal pastor" of the church.

The Mother Church in Boston is the international headquarters. Its government provides for a board of directors, which transacts the business of the Mother Church.

A branch church, governed by its own democratically chosen board, is named First Church of Christ, Scientist, or Second Church, etc., according to the order of its establishment in a community.

The terms *Christian Science Church* or *Churches of Christ, Scientist,* are acceptable in all references to the denomination.

The word *Christian* is used because its teachings are based on the word and works of Jesus Christ. The word *Science* is used to reflect the concept that the laws of God are replicable and can be proved in healing sickness and sin.

The church is composed entirely of lay members and does not have clergy in the usual sense. Both men and women may serve as *readers, practitioners,* or *lecturers.*

The preferred form for these titles is to use a construction that sets them off from a name with commas. Capitalize them only when used as a formal title immediately before a name. Do not continue use of the title in subsequent references.

RELIGION

The terms *reverend* and *minister* are not applicable. Do not use *the Rev.* in any references.

See **religious titles**.

Church of England See **Anglican Communion**.

Church of Jesus Christ of Latter-day Saints, The Note the
capitalization and punctuation of *Latter-day*. *Mormon church*, *LDS church* or the *Latter-day Saints* can be used, but the official name is preferred in first reference in a story dealing primarily with church activities.

Members are referred to as *Latter-day Saints* or *Mormons*, the latter based on the church's sacred Book of Mormon.

The church is based on revelations that Joseph Smith said were brought to him in the 1820s by heavenly messengers.

The headquarters is in Salt Lake City, but millions of its members live outside the U.S.

Church hierarchy is composed of men known as general authorities. Among them, the policymaking body is the First Presidency, made up of a president and two or more counselors. It has final authority in all church matters.

CLERGY: All worthy young men over the age of 12 are members of the priesthood. They can be ordained elders after age 18, usually after graduating from high school and before serving as missionaries. They may later become high priests, or bishops.

The only formal titles are *president* (for members of the First Presidency), *bishop* (for members of the Presiding Bishopric and for local bishops) and *elder* (for other general authorities and church missionaries). Capitalize these formal titles before a name on first reference; use only the last name on second reference.

The terms *minister* or *the Rev.* are not used.

See **religious titles**.

SPLINTER GROUPS: The term Mormon is not properly applied to the other Latter Day Saints churches that resulted from the split after Smith's death.

This includes polygamous groups. The LDS church renounced polygamy in 1890.

One splinter group is the Community of Christ, headquartered in Independence, Missouri. From 1860 to 2001, it was called the Reorganized Church of Jesus Christ of Latter Day Saints (note the lack of a hyphen and the capitalized Day).

College of Cardinals See **Roman Catholic Church**.

conclave A private or secret meeting. In the Roman Catholic Church it describes the private meeting of cardinals to elect a pope.

confirmation See **sacraments**.

Conservative Judaism See **Jewish congregations**.

Coptic Christian The Coptic
Orthodox Church traces its origins to the Apostle Mark in first-century Alexandria. The word Copt is derived from the Greek word for Egypt. Coptic Christians generally share the beliefs of other Orthodox churches, but have some distinct teachings, mainly concerning Christology, or the nature of Christ. There are no definitive statistics for

the Coptic Christian population, but they are considered to be the largest Christian community in the Mideast. Scholars estimate that Copts comprise 10 percent of the Egyptian population, or 8.5 million people. Significant diaspora Coptic Christian communities can be found in the United States, Canada and Australia.

curate See **religious titles**.

Curia See **Roman Catholic Church**.

d

dalai lama The traditional high priest of Tibetan Buddhism. *Dalai lama* is a title rather than a name, but it is all that is used when referring to the man. Capitalize *Dalai Lama* in references to the holder of the title, in keeping with the principles outlined in the **nobility** entry. The title is lowercase in generic references to the religion and history.

deacon See the entry for the individual's denomination.

deity Lowercase. See **gods** and **religious references**.

devil But capitalize *Satan*.

diocese Capitalize as part of a proper name: *the Diocese of Rochester, the Rochester Diocese, the diocese.*
See **Episcopal Church** and **Roman Catholic Church**.

Druze A tradition that developed from a medieval sect of Shiite Islam. The religion draws from Christian, Muslim and Jewish beliefs and was influenced by gnosticism, with believers divided into two main classes: the "initiated" who have studied the faith's sacred writings and serve as authorities, and the "uninitiated" who comprise the majority of Druze.

The Druze call themselves the "People of Unity." The exact number of Druze is not known, but they are concentrated in Syria, Lebanon and Israel, with diaspora populations in Europe, North America, Australia and elsewhere.

e

Easter Christian holy day commemorating the resurrection of Jesus Christ. Christians believe Jesus was raised from the dead three days after his crucifixion.

Western Christian churches and most Orthodox Christian churches follow different calendars and observe Easter on different dates.

Eastern Orthodox churches The term applies to a group of churches that have roots in the earliest days of Christianity and do not recognize papal authority over their activities.

Churches in this tradition were part of the undivided Christendom that existed until the Great Schism of 1054. At that time, many of the churches in the western half of the old Roman Empire accorded the bishop of Rome supremacy over other bishops. The result was a split between eastern and western churches.

The autonomous churches that constitute Eastern Orthodoxy are organized along mostly national lines. They recognize the patriarch

RELIGION

RELIGION

of Constantinople (modern-day Istanbul) as their leader. He convenes councils, but his authority is otherwise that of a "first among equals."

Eastern orthodox churches include the Greek Orthodox Church and the Russian Orthodox Church.

In the United States, organizational lines are rooted in the national backgrounds of various ethnic groups, such as the Greek Orthodox Archdiocese of America, and the Orthodox Church in America, which includes people of Bulgarian, Romanian, Russian and Syrian descent.

The churches have their own disciplines on matters such as married clergy — a married man may be ordained, but a priest may not marry after ordination.

Some of these churches call the archbishop who leads them a *metropolitan*; others use the term *patriarch*. He normally heads the principal archdiocese within a nation. Working with him are other archbishops, bishops, priests and deacons.

Archbishops and bishops frequently follow a monastic tradition in which they are known only by a first name. When no last name is used, repeat the title before the sole name in subsequent references.

Some forms: *Metropolitan Tikhon, archbishop of Washington and metropolitan of America and Canada.* On second reference: *Metropolitan Tikhon. Archbishop* may be replaced by *the Most Rev.* on first reference. *Bishop* may be replaced by *the Rt. Rev.* on first reference.

Use *the Rev.* before the name of a priest on first reference.

See **religious titles**.

Eastern Rite churches The term applies to a group of Catholic churches that had been organized along ethnic lines traceable to the churches established during the earliest days of Christianity.

These churches accept the authority of the pope, but they have considerable autonomy in ritual and questions of discipline such as married clergy — a married man may be ordained, but marriage is not permitted after ordination.

Among the churches of the Eastern Rite are the Antiochean-Maronite, Armenian Catholic, Byzantine-Byelorussian, Byzantine-Russian, Byzantine-Ruthenian, Byzantine-Ukrainian and Chaldean Catholic.

Eid al-Adha Meaning "Feast of Sacrifice," this most important Islamic holiday marks the willingness of the Prophet Ibrahim (Abraham to Christians and Jews) to sacrifice his son. During the holiday, which in most places lasts four days, Muslims slaughter sheep or cattle, distribute part of the meat to the poor and eat the rest. The holiday begins on the 10th day of the Islamic lunar month of Dhul-Hijja, during the annual hajj pilgrimage to Mecca.

Eid al-Fitr A three-day holiday marking the end of Ramadan, Islam's holy month of fasting.

elder For its use in religious contexts, see the entry for an individual's denomination.

encyclical A high-level papal teaching document on faith and morals. Always lowercase "e" except when starting a sentence.

Episcopal Church Acceptable in all references for *the Episcopal Church*, the U.S. national church that is a member of the Anglican Communion.

The church is governed nationally by two bodies — the permanent Executive Council and the General Convention, which meets every three years.

After the council, the principal organizational units are, in descending order of size, provinces, dioceses or missionary districts, local parishes and local missions.

The Executive Council is composed of bishops, priests, laymen and laywomen. One bishop is designated leader of the church and holds the formal title of presiding bishop.

The General Convention has final authority in matters of policy and doctrine. All acts must pass both of its houses — the House of Bishops and the House of Deputies. The latter is composed of an equal number of clergy and lay delegates from each diocese.

A province is composed of several dioceses. Each has a provincial synod made up of a house of bishops and a house of deputies. The synod's primary duty is to coordinate the work of the church in its area.

Within a diocese, a bishop is the principal official. He is helped by the Diocesan Convention, which consists of all the clergy in the diocese and lay representatives from each parish.

The parish or local church is governed by a vestry, composed of the pastor and lay members elected by the congregation.

The clergy consists of bishops, priests, deacons and brothers. A priest who heads a parish is described as a *rector* rather than a pastor.

For first reference to bishops, use *Bishop* before the individual's name: *Bishop Rob Wright*. An acceptable alternative in referring to U.S. bishops is *the Rt. Rev.* The designation *the Most Rev.* is used before the names of the archbishops of Canterbury and York.

For first references, use *the Rev.* before the name of a priest, *Deacon* before the name of a deacon.

See **Anglican Communion** and **religious titles**.

Episcopal, Episcopalian *Episcopal* is the adjective form; use *Episcopalian* only as a noun referring to a member of the Episcopal Church: *She is an Episcopalian.* But: *She is an Episcopal priest.*

Capitalize *Episcopal* when referring to the Episcopal Church. Use lowercase when the reference is simply to a body governed by bishops.

evangelical See **religious movements**.

Evangelical Friends Alliance See **Quakers**.

evangelism See **religious movements**.

evangelist Capitalize only in reference to the men credited with writing the Gospels: *The four Evangelists were Matthew, Mark, Luke and John.*

In lowercase, it means a preacher who makes a profession of seeking conversions. Often confused with the term *evangelical*. See **evangelical**.

exorcise, exorcism

RELIGION

f

father Use *the Rev.* in first reference before the names of Episcopal, Orthodox and Roman Catholic priests. Use *Father* before a name only in direct quotations.

See **religious titles**.

fundamentalist See **religious movements**.

g

gentile Generally, any person not Jewish; often, specifically a Christian.

gods and goddesses Capitalize *God* in references to the deity of all monotheistic religions. Capitalize all noun references to the deity: *God the Father, Holy Ghost, Holy Spirit, Allah,* etc. Lowercase personal pronouns: *he, him, thee, thou.*

Lowercase *gods* and *goddesses* in references to the deities of polytheistic religions.

Lowercase *god, gods* and *goddesses* in references to false gods: *He made money his god.*

See **religious references**.

Good Friday The Friday before Easter.

Gospel(s), gospel Capitalize when referring to any or all of the first four books of the New Testament: *the Gospel of St. John, the Gospels.*

Lowercase in other references: *She is a famous gospel singer.*

Greek Orthodox Church See **Eastern Orthodox churches**.

gurdwara A house of worship in the Sikh religion where the faith's scriptures are stored.

h

Hades But lowercase *hell*.

hajj The pilgrimage to Mecca required once in a lifetime of every Muslim who can afford it and is physically able to make it. Some Muslims make the journey more than once. The hajj occurs once a year during the Islamic lunar month of Dhul-Hijja, the 12th and final month of the Islamic calendar year. The person making the *hajj* is a *hajji*.

halal Arabic for *permitted* or *lawful*. The word is used to describe foods allowed under Islamic dietary laws. Always lowercase.

hallelujah Lowercase the biblical praise to God, but capitalize in composition titles: Handel's "Hallelujah" chorus.

Hanukkah The Jewish Festival of Lights, an eight-day commemoration of rededication of the Temple by the Maccabees after their victory over the Syrians.

Usually occurs in December but sometimes falls in late November.

Haram al-Sharif Arabic for *Noble Sanctuary*, the Muslim name for the walled, elevated area in Jerusalem's Old City that was the site of the ancient Jewish temples. Better known as the *Temple Mount*, the area now houses the centuries-old Dome of the Rock shrine and Al-Aqsa mosque. Muslims believe Prophet Muhammad made his night journey to heaven from the site.

heaven

hell But capitalize *Hades*.

Hindu, Hinduism The dominant religion of India and the world's third-largest religion, after Christianity and Islam.

Nearly all the world's 1.1 billion Hindus live in India, Nepal, Bangladesh, Indonesia, Malaysia and the United States. They are a majority in India, Nepal and Mauritius. The original Hindu scriptures are called the Vedas.

Hindus believe the soul never dies, but is reborn — in either human or animal form — each time the body dies. Under the Hindu rule of karma, a person's every action and thought will affect how the soul is reborn. The cycle of death and rebirth continues until a soul reaches spiritual perfection, and can then be united in total enlightenment and peace, known as nirvana, with the supreme being, ending the cycle.

Hindus believe in one supreme being who is represented in different gods and goddesses. The primary gods are Brahma, the creator; Vishnu, the preserver; and Siva, the destroyer. Vishnu has had important human incarnations such as Krishna and Rama.

The primary goddess is Devi, who has several manifestations including Durga, Kali, Sarasvati and Lakshmi. She represents in her forms either motherhood and good fortune or destruction. There are thousands of other deities and saints that also may receive prayers and offerings.

Hindus also believe that animals have souls and many are worshipped as manifestations of god.

There are thousands of sects. There is no formal clergy.

holidays and holy days Capitalize them: *New Year's Eve, New Year's Day, Groundhog Day, Easter, Hanukkah*, etc.

The federal legal holidays are New Year's, Martin Luther King Jr. Day, Washington's Birthday, Memorial Day, Independence Day, Labor Day, Columbus Day, Veterans Day, Thanksgiving and Christmas. See individual entries for the official dates and when they are observed if they fall on a weekend.

The designation of a day as a federal legal holiday means that federal employees receive the day off or are paid overtime if they must work. Other requirements that may apply to holidays generally are left to the states. Many follow the federal lead in designating a holiday, but they are not required to do so.

Holy Communion See **sacraments**.

Holy Father The preferred form is to use *the pope* or *the pontiff*, or to give the individual's name.

Use *Holy Father* in direct quotations or special contexts where a particular literary effect is desired.

Holy Land Capitalize the biblical region.

holy orders See **sacraments**.

Holy See The headquarters of the Roman Catholic Church in Vatican City.

Holy Spirit Preferred over *Holy Ghost* in most usage.

RELIGION

i

iftar The breaking of the daily fast during the holy Islamic month of Ramadan.

imam Lowercase when describing the leader of a prayer in a Muslim mosque. Capitalize before a name when used as the formal title for a Muslim leader or ruler.
See **religious titles**.

Inner Light See **Quakers**.

Islam Followers are called Muslims. Their holy book is the Quran, which according to Islamic belief was revealed by Allah (God) to the Prophet Muhammad in the seventh century in Mecca and Medina. The place of worship is a mosque. The weekly holy day is Friday.

It is the religion of more than 1 billion people in the world, making it the world's second-largest faith, after Christianity. Although Arabic is the language of the Quran and Muslim prayers, not all Arabs are Muslims and not all Muslims are Arabs. Most of the world's Muslims live in a wide belt that stretches halfway around the world: across West Africa and North Africa, through the Arab countries of the Middle East and on to Turkey, Iran, Afghanistan, Pakistan and other Asian countries, parts of the former Soviet Union and western China, to Indonesia and the southern Philippines.

There are two major divisions in Islam:
— *Sunni* The biggest single sect in Islam, comprising about 85 percent of all Muslims. Nations with Sunni majorities include Egypt, Saudi Arabia and most other Arab nations, as well as non-Arab Turkey and Afghanistan. Most Palestinian Muslims and most West African Muslims are Sunnis.

The Saudis sometimes are referred to as Wahhabi Muslims. This is a subgroup within the Sunni branch of Islam.
— *Shiite* The second-largest sect. Iran is the only nation with an overwhelming Shiite majority. Iraq, Lebanon and Bahrain have large Shiite communities, in proportion to their overall populations.

(The schism between Sunni and Shiite stems from the early days of Islam and arguments over Muhammad's successors as caliph, the spiritual and temporal leader of Muslims during that period. The Shiites wanted the caliphate to descend through Ali, Muhammad's son-in-law. Ali eventually became the fourth caliph, but he was murdered; Ali's son al-Hussein was massacred with his fighters at Karbala, in what is now Iraq. Shiites considered the later caliphs to be usurpers. The Sunnis no longer have a caliph.)

Titles for the clergy vary from sect to sect and from country to country, but these are the most common:
Grand Mufti — The highest authority in Quranic law and interpretation, a title used mostly by Sunnis.
Sheikh — Used by most clergymen in the same manner that the Rev. is used as a Christian clerical title, especially common among Sunnis. (Not all sheikhs are clergymen. *Sheikh* can also be a secular title of respect or nobility.)
Ayatollah — Used by Shiites, especially in Iran, to denote senior clergymen, such as *Ayatollah Ruhollah Khomeini*.

Hojatoleslam — A rank below ayatollah.

Mullah — Lower-level clergy.

Imam — Used by some sects as a title for the prayer leader at a mosque. Among the Shiites, it usually has a more exalted connotation.

The adjective is *Islamic. Islamist* is an advocate of political Islam, the philosophy that the Quran should rule all aspects of life — religious, political and personal. *Islamic fundamentalist* should not be used as a synonym for *Islamic militant* or *radical*.

Islamic holy days See **Ashoura**, **Eid al-Adha**, **Eid al-Fitr** and **Ramadan**. Because the Muslim faith operates on the lunar calendar, these commemorations fall on different days each year on the Western calendar.

Islamist An advocate or supporter of a political movement that favors reordering government and society in accordance with laws prescribed by Islam. Do not use as a synonym for *Islamic fighters*, *militants*, *extremists* or *radicals*, who may or may not be Islamists. Where possible, be specific and use the name of militant affiliations: *al-Qaida-linked, Hezbollah, Taliban,* etc. Those who view the Quran as a political model encompass a wide range of Muslims, from mainstream politicians to militants known as jihadis.

j

Jehovah's Witnesses The denomination was founded in Pittsburgh in 1872 by Charles Taze Russell, a former Congregationalist layman.

Witnesses do most of their work through three legal corporations: the Watch Tower Bible and Tract Society of Pennsylvania, the Watchtower Bible and Tract Society of New York Inc., and, in England, the International Bible Students Association. A governing body consisting largely of the principal officers of the corporations oversees the denomination.

Jehovah's Witnesses believe that they adhere to the oldest religion on Earth, the worship of Almighty God revealed in the Bible as Jehovah.

They regard civil authority as necessary and obey it "as long as its laws do not contradict God's law." Witnesses refuse to bear arms, salute the flag or participate in secular government.

They refuse blood transfusions as being against the Bible, citing the section of Leviticus that reads: "Whatsoever man ... eats any manner of blood, I will cut him off from among his people."

There are no formal titles, but there are three levels of ministry: *publishers* (baptized members who do evangelistic work), *regular pioneers*, who devote greater time to activities, and *special pioneers* (full-time workers).

Jesus The central figure of Christianity, he also may be called *Jesus Christ* or *Christ*.

Personal pronouns referring to him are lowercase as is *savior*.

Jewish congregations A Jewish congregation is autonomous. No synods, assemblies or hierarchies control the activities of an individual

RELIGION

synagogue.

Among the major expressions of Judaism in North America are:

1. Orthodox Judaism. The Orthodox Union is the umbrella organization for modern or centrist Orthodox congregations whose rabbis are represented by the Rabbinical Council of America. Many additional Orthodox congregations and rabbis in North America are part of strictly observant ultra-Orthodox communities.

2. Reform Judaism. Congregations are represented by the Union for Reform Judaism, and clergy by the Central Conference of American Rabbis.

3. Conservative Judaism. Congregations are represented by the United Synagogue of Conservative Judaism, and clergy are represented by the Rabbinical Assembly.

Reform is the largest organized movement in Judaism, while Orthodoxy is the fastest-growing.

Jews generally believe that a divine kingdom will be established on Earth, opening a messianic era that will be marked by peace and bliss. They also believe that they have a mandate from God to work toward this kingdom.

The spiritual leader of congregation is called a *rabbi*, while the individual who leads the congregation in song is called a *cantor*. Capitalize these titles before an individual's full name on first reference. On second reference, use only the last name.

See **religious titles** and **Zionism**.

Jewish holy days See separate listings for **Hanukkah**, **Passover**, **Purim**, **Rosh Hashana**, **Shavuot**, **Sukkot** and **Yom Kippur**.

The High Holy Days are Rosh Hashana and Yom Kippur. All Jewish holy days and the Jewish Sabbath start at sunset before the day marked on most calendars.

jihad Arabic noun used to refer to the Islamic concept of the struggle to do good. In particular situations, that can include holy war, the meaning extremist Muslims commonly use. Use *jihadi* and *jihadis*. Do not use *jihadist*.

k

Koran Use *Quran* in all references except when preferred by an organization or in a specific title or name. See **Quran**.

Kwanzaa A seven-day celebration, based on African festivals, from Dec. 26 through Jan. 1.

l

Last Supper

Latin Rite See **Roman Catholic Church**.

Latter Day Saints, Latter-day Saints See **Church of Jesus Christ of Latter-day Saints**.

lecturer A formal title in the Christian Science Church. An occupational description in other uses.

Lent The period from Ash Wednesday through Holy Saturday, the day before Easter. The 40-day Lenten period for penance, suggested by Christ's 40 days in the desert, does not include the six Sundays between Ash Wednesday and Easter.

Lord's Supper See **sacraments**.

Lutheran churches The basic unit of government in Lutheran practice is the congregation. It normally is administered by a council, headed either by the senior pastor or a lay person elected from the membership of the council. The council customarily consists of a congregation's clergy and elected lay people.

The Evangelical Lutheran Church in America is the largest Lutheran group in the U.S.

The Lutheran Church-Missouri Synod, founded in 1847, is a separate and distinct body.

Lutheran teachings go back to Martin Luther, a 16th-century Roman Catholic priest whose objections to elements of Roman Catholic practice began the movement known as the Protestant Reformation.

Members of the clergy are known as *ministers*. *Pastor* applies if a minister leads a congregation.

On first reference, use *the Rev.* before the name of a man or woman. On second reference, use only the last name.

See **religious titles**.

m

Magi Wise men who brought gifts to the infant Jesus at Epiphany, celebrated Jan. 6.

Mass It is *celebrated*, not *said*. Always capitalize when referring to the ceremony, but lowercase any preceding adjectives: *high Mass, low Mass, requiem Mass*.

In Eastern Orthodox churches the correct term is *Divine Liturgy*.

See **Roman Catholic Church**.

matrimony See **sacraments**.

megachurch Generally used to describe a Protestant church with an average of 2,000 or more attendees at weekly worship services.

Melkite Church See **Eastern Rite churches**.

menorah The seven-branch candelabrum from the ancient temple in Jerusalem. Also the popular term for the nine-branch candelabrum, or hanukkiah, used on the Jewish holiday of Hanukkah.

messiah Capitalize in religious uses, such as references to the promised deliverer of the Jews or to Jesus in Christianity. Lowercase when referring to the liberator of a people or country.

Methodist churches The term *Methodist* originated as a nickname applied to a group of 18th-century Oxford University students known for their methodical application to Scripture study and prayer.

The principal Methodist body in the United States is the United Methodist Church, which also has member conferences in other countries.

The General Conference, which meets every four years, has final authority in all matters.

A Methodist bishop presides over a "church area," which may embrace one or more annual conferences. Bishops have extensive administrative powers, including

RELIGION

the authority to place, transfer and remove local church pastors, usually in consultation with district superintendents.

Districts in each conference are responsible for promotion of mission work, support of colleges, hospitals and publications, and examination of candidates for the ministry.

Methodism in the United States also includes three major black denominations: the African Methodist Episcopal Church, the African Methodist Episcopal Zion Church and the Christian Methodist Episcopal Church.

Methodists believe in the Trinity and the humanity and divinity of Christ. There are two sacraments, baptism and the Lord's Supper.

Ordained individuals are known as *bishops* and *ministers*. *Pastor* applies if a minister leads a congregation.

For first references to bishops use the word: *Bishop W. Kenneth Goodson* of Richmond, Virginia.

For first reference to ministers, use *the Rev.* before the name of a man or woman. On second reference, use only the last name.

See **religious titles**.

minister It is not a formal title in most religions, with exceptions such as the Nation of Islam, and is not capitalized. Where it is a formal title, it should be capitalized before the name: *Minister John Jones*.

See **religious titles** and the entry for an individual's denomination.

monsignor See **Roman Catholic Church**.

Mormon church Acceptable in references to *The Church of Jesus Christ of Latter-day Saints*, but the official name is preferred in first reference in a story dealing primarily with church activities.

See **Church of Jesus Christ of Latter-day Saints, The**.

Muhammad The chief prophet and central figure of the Islamic religion, *Prophet Muhammad*. Use other spellings only if preferred by a specific person for his own name or in a title or the name of an organization.

mullah An Islamic leader or teacher, often a general title of respect for a learned man.

Muslims The preferred term to describe adherents of Islam. The term *Black Muslim* has been used in the past to describe members of predominantly African-American Islamic sects that originated in the United States. However, the term is considered derogatory.

n

National Baptist Convention of America See **Baptist churches**.

National Baptist Convention U.S.A. Inc. See **Baptist churches**.

National Council of the Churches of Christ in the U.S.A. This interdenominational, cooperative body includes most major Protestant and Eastern Orthodox denominations in the United States.

The shortened form *National Council of Churches* is acceptable in all references.

Headquarters is in Washington. See **World Council of Churches**.

Nation of Islam The nationalist religious movement traces its origins in 1930 to W.D. Fard, also known as Wali Fard, who called for racial separation. Elijah Muhammad took over the leadership in 1934, holding the post until his death in 1975. A son, Warith (Wallace) Dean Muhammad, succeeded to the leadership and pointed the movement toward integration and traditional Islam. Louis Farrakhan led a militant faction into a separatist movement in 1976.

The Nation of Islam does not release membership figures.

Use the title *minister* on first reference to clergymen: *Minister Louis Farrakhan.*

Nativity scene Only the first word is capitalized.

New Testament See **Bible**.

nondenominational Term used by Protestants to describe churches or ministries that are not affiliated with a specific denomination. *Independent* is also acceptable. Always lowercase.

O

Old Testament See **Bible**.

orthodox Capitalize when referring to membership in or the activities of an Eastern Orthodox church. See **Eastern Orthodox Churches**.

Capitalize also in phrases such as *Orthodox Judaism* or *Orthodox Jew.* See **Jewish congregations**.

Do not describe a member of an Eastern Orthodox church as a *Protestant.* Use a phrase such as *Orthodox Christian* instead.

Lowercase *orthodox* in nonreligious uses: *an orthodox procedure.*

Orthodox Church in America See **Eastern Orthodox churches**.

P

papal nuncio Do not confuse with an *apostolic delegate.* See **apostolic delegate, papal nuncio**.

parish Capitalize as part of the formal name for a church congregation or a governmental jurisdiction: *St. John's Parish, Jefferson Parish.*

Lowercase standing alone or in plural combinations: *the parish, St. John's and St. Mary's parishes, Jefferson and Plaquemines parishes.*

parishioner Note this spelling for the member of a parish, an administrative district of various churches, particularly Roman Catholic and Anglican. Do not use for Judaism or non-hierarchal Protestant denominations.

Passover The weeklong Jewish commemoration of the deliverance of the ancient Hebrews from slavery in Egypt. Occurs in March or April.

Capitalize *Seder* in references to the *Passover* feast commemorating the exodus.

pastor See **religious titles** and the entry for the individual's denomination.

patriarch Lowercase when describing someone of great age and dignity.

Capitalize as a formal title before a name in some religious uses. See

RELIGION

Eastern Orthodox churches; **religious titles**; and **Roman Catholic Church**.

Pentecost The seventh Sunday after Easter.

Pentecostalism See **religious movements**.

pontiff Not a formal title. Always lowercase.

pope Capitalize when used as a formal title before a name; lowercase in all other uses: *Pope Francis spoke to the crowd. At the close of his address, the pope gave his blessing. Pope Emeritus Benedict XVI* or *Benedict XVI, the pope emeritus. Benedict* alone on second reference.

Use *St. John Paul II* and *St. John XXIII* on first reference for the canonized popes. On second reference *John Paul* and *John*. Make clear in the body of a story they were popes.

See **Roman Catholic Church** and **religious titles**.

practitioner See **Church of Christ, Scientist**.

preacher A job description, not a formal religious title. Do not capitalize.

See **titles** and **religious titles**.

Presbyterian churches Presbyterian churches in the U.S. have roots in Calvinism and in churches in Scotland and England, and are distinguished in part by how they govern their church. They typically have four levels of authority — individual congregations, presbyteries, synods and a general assembly.

Congregations are led by a pastor and a session composed of ruling elders who represent congregants on matters of government and discipline.

Presbyteries, composed of a district's ministers and ruling elders, form a synod, which generally meets once a year to decide matters not related to doctrine or the church constitution.

A general assembly, composed of delegations of pastors and ruling elders from each presbytery, meets every two years to decide issues of doctrine and discipline.

The northern and southern branches of Presbyterianism merged in 1983 to become the Presbyterian Church (U.S.A.).

There are also several distinctly conservative Presbyterian denominations, such as the Presbyterian Church in America. Be careful to specify the denomination being written about.

Presbyterians believe in the Trinity and the humanity and divinity of Christ. Baptism, which may be administered to children, and the Lord's Supper are the only sacraments.

All Presbyterian clergymen may be described as *ministers*. Pastor applies if a minister leads a congregation.

On first reference, use *the Rev.* before the name of a man or woman. On second reference, use only the last name.

See **religious titles**.

priest A vocational description, not a formal title. Do not capitalize.

See **religious titles** and the entries for the **Roman Catholic Church** and **Episcopal Church**.

prophet Capitalize when used before the name of a person considered by a religious group to be divinely inspired: *Prophet Elijah*, *Prophet Muhammad*.

Protestant Episcopal Church See Episcopal Church.

Protestant, Protestantism

Capitalize these words when they refer either to denominations formed as a result of the break from the Roman Catholic Church in the 16th century or to the members of these denominations.

Church groups covered by the term include Anglican, Baptist, Congregational, Methodist, Lutheran, Presbyterian and Quaker denominations. See separate entries for each.

Protestant is not applied to Christian Scientists, Jehovah's Witnesses or Mormons.

Do not use *Protestant* to describe a member of an Eastern Orthodox church. Use a phrase such as *Orthodox Christian* instead.

See **religious movements**.

Purim The Jewish Feast of Lots, commemorating Esther's deliverance of the Jews in Persia from a massacre plotted by Haman. Occurs in February or March.

q

Quakers This informal name may be used in all references to members of the *Religious Society of Friends*, but always include the full name in a story dealing primarily with Quaker activities.

The denomination originated with George Fox, an Englishman who objected to Anglican emphasis on ceremony. In the 1640s, he said he heard a voice that opened the way for him to develop a personal relationship with Christ, described as the Inner Light, a term based on the Gospel description of Christ as the "true light."

Brought to court for opposing the established church, Fox tangled with a judge who derided him as a "quaker" in reference to his agitation over religious matters.

The basic unit of Quaker organization is the weekly meeting, which corresponds to the congregation in other churches. Quaker practices and beliefs vary from a more Bible-centered Christianity with pastors as worship leaders to a more liberal approach with less structured worship and a wide range of teachings.

Quaker associations include the Friends United Meeting, which has a global membership focused on evangelism, communications and other projects; Evangelical Friends Church International and the more liberal Friends General Conference.

Fox taught that the Inner Light emancipates a person from adherence to any creed, ecclesiastical authority or ritual forms.

There is no recognized ranking of clergy over lay people. However, there are meeting officers, called *elders* or *ministers*. Quaker ministers sometimes use *the Rev.* before their names and describe themselves as *pastors*.

Capitalize *elder*, *minister* or *pastor* when used as a formal title before a name. Use *the Rev.* before a name on first reference if it is a minister's practice. On second reference, use only the last name.

See **religious titles**.

RELIGION

Quran The preferred spelling for the Muslim holy book. Use the spelling *Koran* only if preferred by a specific organization or in a specific title or name.

r

rabbi See **Jewish congregations**.

Rabbinical Assembly See **Jewish congregations**.

Rabbinical Council of America See **Jewish congregations**.

Ramadan The Muslim holy month, marked by daily fasting from dawn to sunset, ending with the Islamic holiday of Eid al-Fitr. Avoid using *holiday* on second reference.

rector See **religious titles**.

Reform Judaism See **Jewish congregations**.

religious affiliations Capitalize the names and the related terms applied to members of the orders: *He is a member of the Society of Jesus. He is a Jesuit.*

religious movements The terms that follow have been grouped under a single entry because they are interrelated and frequently cross denominational lines.

  evangelical Historically, *evangelical* was used as an adjective describing Protestant dedication to conveying the message of Christ. Today it also is used as a noun, referring to a category of doctrinally conservative Protestants. They emphasize the need for a definite, adult commitment or conversion to faith in Christ and the duty of all believers to persuade others to accept Christ.

  Evangelicals make up some conservative denominations and are numerous in broader denominations. Evangelicals stress both doctrinal absolutes and vigorous efforts to win others to belief.

  The National Association of Evangelicals is an interdenominational, cooperative body of relatively small, conservative Protestant denominations.

  evangelism The word refers to activity directed outside the church fold to influence others to commit themselves to faith in Christ, to his work of serving others and to infuse his principles into society's conduct.

  Styles of evangelism vary from direct preaching appeals at large public meetings to practical deeds of carrying the name of Christ, indirectly conveying the same call to allegiance to him.

  The word *evangelism* is derived from the Greek *evangelion*, which means the gospel or good news of Christ's saving action on behalf of humanity.

  fundamentalist The word gained usage in an early-20th century fundamentalist-modernist controversy within Protestantism. In recent years, however, *fundamentalist* has to a large extent taken on pejorative connotations except when applied to groups that stress strict, literal interpretations of Scripture and separation from other Christians.

  In general, do not use *fundamentalist* unless a group applies the word to itself.

  neo-Pentecostal, charismatic These terms apply to a movement that has developed within mainline

Protestant and Roman Catholic denominations since the mid-20th century. It is distinguished by its emotional expressiveness, spontaneity in worship, speaking or praying in "unknown tongues" and healing. Participants often characterize themselves as "spirit-filled" Christians.

Unlike the earlier Pentecostal movement, which led to separate denominations, this movement has swelled within major churches.

Pentecostalism A movement that arose in the early 20th century and separated from historic Protestant denominations. It is distinguished by the belief in tangible manifestations of the Holy Spirit, often in demonstrative, emotional ways such as speaking in "unknown tongues" and healing.

Pentecostal denominations include the Assemblies of God, the Pentecostal Holiness Church, the United Pentecostal Church Inc. and the International Church of the Foursquare Gospel founded by Aimee Semple McPherson.

religious references The basic guidelines:

DEITIES: Capitalize the proper names of monotheistic deities: *God, Allah, the Father, the Son, Jesus Christ, the Son of God, the Redeemer, the Holy Spirit*, etc.

Lowercase pronouns referring to the deity: *he, him, his, thee, thou, who, whose, thy*, etc.

Lowercase *gods* in referring to the deities of polytheistic religions.

Capitalize the proper names of pagan and mythological gods and goddesses: *Neptune, Thor, Venus*, etc.

Lowercase such words as *god-awful, goddamn, godlike, godliness, godsend*.

LIFE OF CHRIST: Capitalize the names of major events in the life of Jesus Christ in references that do not use his name: *The doctrines of the Last Supper, the Crucifixion, the Resurrection and the Ascension are central to Christian belief.*

But use lowercase when the words are used with his name: *The ascension of Jesus into heaven took place 40 days after his resurrection from the dead.*

Apply the principle also to events in the life of his mother: *He cited the doctrines of the Immaculate Conception and the Assumption.* But: *She referred to the assumption of Mary into heaven.*

RITES: Capitalize proper names for rites that commemorate the Last Supper or signify a belief in Christ's presence: *the Lord's Supper, Holy Communion, Holy Eucharist.*

Lowercase the names of other sacraments. See **sacraments**.

Capitalize *Benediction* and *Mass.* But: *a high Mass, a low Mass, a requiem Mass.*

HOLY DAYS: Capitalize the names of holy days. See **holidays and holy days** and separate entries for major Christian, Jewish and Muslim feasts.

OTHER WORDS: Lowercase *heaven, hell, devil, angel, cherub, an apostle, a priest*, etc.

Capitalize *Hades* and *Satan.*

For additional details, see **Bible**, entries for frequently used religious terms, the entries for major denominations, **religious movements** and **religious titles**.

Religious Society of Friends See **Quakers**.

religious titles The first reference to a clergyman or clergywoman normally should include a capitalized title before the individual's name.

In many cases, *the Rev.* is the

RELIGION

designation that applies before a name on first reference. Use *the Rev. Dr.* only if the individual has an earned doctoral degree (doctor of divinity degrees frequently are honorary) and reference to the degree is relevant.

On second reference to members of the clergy, use only a last name: *the Rev. Billy Graham* on first reference, *Graham* on second. If known only by a religious name, repeat the title: *Pope John XXIII* on first reference, *John, the pope* or *the pontiff* on second; *Pope Emeritus Benedict XVI* or *Benedict XVI, the pope emeritus. Benedict* alone on second reference. *Metropolitan Herman* on first reference, *Metropolitan Herman* or *the metropolitan* on second.

Detailed guidance on specific titles and descriptive words such as *priest* and *minister* is provided in the entries for major denominations. In general, however:

CARDINALS, ARCHBISHOPS, BISHOPS: The preferred form for first reference is to use *Cardinal, Archbishop* or *Bishop* before the individual's name: *Cardinal Daniel DiNardo, archbishop of Galveston-Houston.* On second reference: *DiNardo* or *the cardinal*.

Substitute *the Most Rev.* if applicable and appropriate in the context: *He spoke to the Most Rev. Jose Gomez, archbishop of Los Angeles.* On second reference: *Gomez* or *the archbishop*.

Entries for individual denominations tell when *the Most Rev., the Very Rev.,* etc., are applicable.

MINISTERS AND PRIESTS: Use *the Rev.* before a name on first reference.

Substitute *Monsignor* before the name of a Roman Catholic priest who has received this honor.

Do not routinely use *curate, father, pastor* and similar words before an individual's name. If they appear before a name in a quotation, capitalize them.

RABBIS: Use *Rabbi* before a name on first reference. On second reference, use only the last name.

NUNS: Always use *Sister,* or *Mother* if applicable, before a name: *Sister Agnes Rita* in all references if the nun uses only a religious name; *Sister Mary Ann Walsh* on first reference if she uses a surname. *Walsh* on subsequent references.

OFFICEHOLDERS: The preferred first-reference form for those who hold church office but are not ordained clergy in the usual sense is to use a construction that sets the title apart from the name by commas. Capitalize the formal title of an office, however, if it is used directly before an individual's name.

Reorganized Church of Jesus Christ of Latter Day Saints Now called *the Community of Christ*. Not properly described as a *Mormon church*. See the explanation under **Church of Jesus Christ of Latter-day Saints**.

Rev. When this description is used before an individual's name, precede it with the word *the* because, unlike the case with *Mr.* and *Mrs.*, the abbreviation *Rev.* does not stand for a noun.

If an individual also has a secular title such as *Rep.*, use whichever is appropriate to the context.

See **religious titles**.

Roman Catholic Church The church teaches that its bishops have been established as the successors of the apostles through generations of ceremonies in which authority was passed down by a laying-on of hands.

Responsibility for teaching the faithful and administering the church rests with the bishops. However, the church holds that the pope has final authority over their actions because he is the bishop of Rome, the office it teaches was held by the Apostle Peter at his death.

The Curia serves as a form of governmental cabinet. Its members, appointed by the pope, handle both administrative and judicial functions.

The pope also chooses members of the College of Cardinals, who serve as his principal counselors. When a new pope must be chosen, they meet in a conclave to select a new pope by majority vote. In practice, cardinals are mostly bishops, but there is no requirement that a cardinal be a bishop.

In the United States, the church's principal organizational units are archdioceses and dioceses. They are headed, respectively, by archbishops and bishops, who have final responsibility for many activities within their jurisdictions and report directly to Rome.

The church counts more than 1 billion members worldwide. In the United States it has more than 66 million members, making it the largest single body of Christians in the nation.

Roman Catholics believe in the Trinity — that there is one God who exists as three divine persons — the Father, the Son and the Holy Spirit. They believe that the Son became man as Jesus Christ.

In addition to the Holy Eucharist, there are six other sacraments — baptism, confirmation, penance (often called the sacrament of reconciliation), matrimony, holy orders, and the sacrament of the sick (formerly extreme unction).

The clergy below pope are, in descending order, cardinal, archbishop, bishop, monsignor, priest and deacon. In religious orders, some men who are not priests have the title *brother*.

Capitalize *pope* when used as a title before a name: *Pope John XXIII*, *Pope Francis*. Lowercase in all other uses. See **religious titles**.

The first-reference forms for other titles follow. Use only last names on second reference.

CARDINALS: *Cardinal Daniel DiNardo*. The usage *Daniel Cardinal DiNardo*, a practice traceable to the nobility's custom of identifications such as *William, Duke of Norfolk*, is still used in formal documents but otherwise is considered archaic.

ARCHBISHOPS: *Archbishop Gregory Aymond*, or *the Most Rev. Gregory Aymond, archbishop of New Orleans*.

Bishops: *Bishop Thomas Paprocki*, or *the Most Rev. Thomas Paprocki, bishop of Springfield, Illinois*.

MONSIGNORS: *Monsignor Martin Krebs*. Do not use the abbreviation *Msgr*. Do not use *the Rt. Rev.* or *the Very Rev.* — this distinction between types of monsignors no longer is made.

Priests: *the Rev. James Martin*. See **religious titles**.

rosary It is *recited* or *said*, never *read*. Always lowercase.

Rosh Hashana The Jewish new year. Occurs in September or October.

Russian Orthodox Church See **Eastern Orthodox churches**.

RELIGION

S

Sabbath Capitalize in religious references.

sacraments Capitalize the proper names used for a sacramental rite that commemorates the life of Jesus Christ or signifies a belief in his presence: *the Lord's Supper, Holy Communion, Holy Eucharist.*

Lowercase the names of other sacraments: *baptism, confirmation, penance* (now often called the *sacrament of reconciliation*), *matrimony, holy orders,* and *the sacrament of anointing the sick* (formerly *extreme unction*).

See entries for the major religious denominations and **religious references**.

sacrilegious

Satan But lowercase *devil* and *satanic.*

savior Use this spelling for all senses, rather than the alternate form, *saviour.*

Seventh-day Adventist Church The denomination, with headquarters in Silver Spring, Maryland, has its roots in the preaching of William Miller of New Hampton, New York, a Baptist layman who said his study of the Book of Daniel indicated the end of the world would come in the mid-1840s.

When Christ did not return as predicted, the Millerites split into smaller groups. One, influenced by the visions of Ellen Harmon, later the wife of James White, is the precursor of the Seventh-day Adventist practice today.

The term *adventist* reflects the belief that a second coming of Christ is near. *Seventh-day* reflects the church teaching that the Bible requires observing the Sabbath on the seventh day of the week.

Baptism, by immersion, is reserved for those old enough to understand its meaning. Baptism and the Lord's Supper are the only sacraments.

The head of the General Conference, the top church administrative authority, is the *president*. Ministers are *pastor* or *elder*. Capitalize immediately before a name on first reference. On second reference, use only the last name.

The designation *the Rev.* is not used.

See **religious titles**.

Shariah Islamic law.

Shavuot The Jewish Feast of Weeks, commemorating the receiving of the Ten Commandments. Occurs in May or June.

Shiite The spelling for this branch of Islam. Plural is *Shiites*. The alternate spelling *Shia* is acceptable in quotes. See **Islam**.

sister Capitalize in all references before the names of nuns.

If no surname is given, the name is the same in all references: *Sister Agnes Rita.*

If a surname is used in first reference, drop the given name and sister on second reference: *Sister Mary Ann Walsh* on first reference, *Walsh* in subsequent references.

Use *Mother* the same way when referring to a woman who heads a group of nuns.

See **religious titles**.

Society of Friends See **Quakers**.

Sukkot The Jewish Feast of Tabernacles, celebrating the fall harvest and commemorating the desert wandering of the Jews during the Exodus. Occurs in September or October.

synagogue Capitalize only when part of a formal name.

synod A council of churches or church officials. See the entry for the denomination in question.

t

Talmud The collection of writings that constitute the Jewish civil and religious law.

Temple Mount The walled, elevated area in Jerusalem's Old City that was the site of the ancient Jewish temples. It now houses the centuries-old Dome of the Rock shrine and Al-Aqsa Mosque and is known to Muslims as the *Haram al-Sharif*, or *Noble Sanctuary*. Muslims believe the Prophet Muhammad made his night journey to heaven from the site.

Ten Commandments Do not abbreviate or use figures.

Twelve Apostles The disciples of Jesus. An exception to the normal practice of using figures for 10 and above.

u

Ukrainian Catholic Church See **Eastern Rite churches**.

United Church of Christ The Evangelical and Reformed Church merged with the Congregational Christian Churches in 1957 to form the United Church of Christ.

The word *church* is correctly applied only to an individual local church. Each such church is responsible for the doctrine, ministry and ritual of its congregation.

A small body of churches that did not enter the United Church of Christ is known as the National Association of Congregational Churches.

Jesus is regarded as man's savior, but no subscription to a set creed is required for membership.

Members of the clergy are known as *ministers*. *Pastor* applies if a minister leads a congregation.

On first reference, use *the Rev.* before the name of a man or woman. On second reference, use only the last name.

See **religious titles**.

United Methodist Church See **Methodist churches**.

United States Conference of Catholic Bishops Formerly the National Conference of Catholic Bishops, it is the national organization of Roman Catholic bishops.

United Synagogue of Conservative Judaism Not *synagogues*. See **Jewish congregations**.

v

Vatican City Stands alone in datelines.

RELIGION

Very Rev. See **Episcopal Church**; **religious titles**; and **Roman Catholic Church**.

Voodoo Capitalize when referring specifically to the religion, practiced primarily in Haiti and parts of Africa, and note in the story that the religion is known in Haiti as *Vodou*. Lowercase in other uses, especially when ascribing magical solutions to problems, as in *voodoo economics*.

W

Wahhabi Follower of a strict Muslim sect that adheres closely to the Quran; it's most powerful in Saudi Arabia.

Western Wall The last remaining part of the second Biblical temple and the holiest site where Jews can pray. *The Western Wall* is located in Jerusalem's Old City, on the edge of the site known as the *Temple Mount* to Jews and *Haram al-Sharif (the Noble Sanctuary)* to Muslims. Some non-Jews refer to the site as the *Wailing Wall*.

Wicca Religion shaped by pagan beliefs and practices. The term encompasses a wide range of traditions generally organized around seasonal festivals, and can include ritual magic, a belief in both female and male deities, and the formation of covens led by priestesses and priests. *Wiccan* is both an adjective and a noun. Uppercase in all uses.

World Council of Churches An international, interdenominational cooperative body of Anglican, Eastern Orthodox, Protestant and old or national Catholic churches.

The Roman Catholic Church is not a member but cooperates with the council in various programs. Headquarters is in Geneva.

worship, worshipped, worshipper

y

Yom Kippur The Jewish Day of Atonement. Occurs in September or October.

Z

Zionism The effort of Jews to regain and retain their biblical homeland. It is based on the promise of God in the Book of Genesis that Israel would forever belong to Abraham and his descendants as a nation.

The term is named for Mount Zion, the site of the ancient temple in Jerusalem.

Sports

SPORTS IDENTIFICATION CODES

ARC — Archery
ATH — Athletics (Track & Field)
BAD — Badminton
BBA — Baseball-American League
BBC — Baseball-College
BBM — Baseball-Minor Leagues
BBN — Baseball-National League
BBO — Baseball-Other
BBH — Baseball-High School
BBI — Baseball-International
BBW — Baseball-Women's
BBY — Baseball-Youth
BIA — Biathlon
BKC — Basketball-College
BKH — Basketball-High School
BKL — Basketball-Women's Pro (WNBA)
BKN — Basketball-NBA
BKO — Basketball-Other
BKW — Basketball-Women's College
BOB — Bobsled
BOX — Boxing
BVL — Beach Volleyball
CAN — Canoeing
CAR — Auto Racing
CRI — Cricket
CUR — Curling
CYC — Cycling
DIV — Diving
EQU — Equestrian
FEN — Fencing
FIG — Figure Skating
FHK — Field Hockey
FBC — (American) Football-College
FBH — (American) Football-High School
FBN — (American) Football-NFL
FBO — (American) Football-Other
FRE — Freestyle skiing
GLF — Golf
GYM — Gymnastics

HNB — Handball
HKC — (Ice) Hockey-College
HKN — (Ice) Hockey-NHL
HKO — (Ice) Hockey-Other
HKW — (Ice) Hockey-Women's
JUD — Judo
JUM — Ski Jumping
LAC — Lacrosse
LUG — Luge
MMA — Mixed Martial Arts
NOR — Nordic combined
PEN — Modern Pentathlon
MOT — Motorcycling
OLY — Olympics (with a specific sport code added where applicable)
RAC — (Horse) Racing
ROW — Rowing
RGL — Rugby League
RGU — Rugby Union
SAI — Sailing
SHO — Shooting
SKE — Skeleton
SKI — Alpine Skiing
SPD — Speedskating and Short Track Speedskating
SBD — Snowboarding
SOC — Soccer
SOF — Softball
SQA — Squash
SUM — Sumo Wrestling
SWM — Swimming
TAE — Taekwondo
TEN — Tennis
TRI — Triathlon
TTN — Table Tennis
VOL — Volleyball
WPO — Water Polo
WEI — Weightlifting
WRE — Wrestling
XXC — Cross-Country Skiing

SPORTS

a

abbreviations It is not necessary to spell out the most common abbreviations on first reference: *NFL, AFC, NFC, NBA, NHL, NCAA, PGA, LPGA, USGA, NASCAR, MLB, AL, NL, FIFA.*

Achilles tendon No apostrophe for the tendon connecting the back of the heel to the calf muscles. But it's *Achilles' heel*, with an apostrophe, for a vulnerable spot.

ACL When describing injuries, acceptable in all references to the *anterior cruciate ligament.*

-added Follow this form in sports stories: *The $500,000-added sweepstakes.*

agate See **basic summary** and **match summary**.

All-America, All-American The Associated Press recognizes only one All-America football and basketball team each year. In football, only Walter Camp's selections through 1924, and the AP selections after that, are recognized. Do not call anyone not listed on either the Camp or AP roster an *All-America* selection.

Similarly do not call anyone who was not an AP selection an *All-America basketball player*. The first All-America men's basketball team was chosen in 1948.

Use *All-American* when referring specifically to an individual: *All-American Breanna Stewart*, or *She is an All-American.*

Use *All-America* when referring to the team: *All-America team*, or *All-America*

selection.

all-star, All-Star, All-Star Game Use uppercase All-Star only when referring to players who have been officially named All-Stars in a sport that refers to its best players each season as All-Stars. The term does not apply in pro football, where players selected to The Associated Press NFL All-Pro team should be referred to as *All-Pro*, while those selected to the Pro Bowl should be referred to as *Pro Bowl players* or *Pro Bowlers*. Use lowercase all-star sparingly to refer informally to performances or players in casual constructions. Use All-Star Game in references where it is the official title of the game.

Alpine skiing In Olympics, slalom, giant slalom, super-G, downhill, Alpine combined

apostrophe See the **possessives** entry in main section and the **apostrophe** entry in the Punctuation Guide, including its descriptive phrases section. Use only in constructions where warranted: *Patriots quarterback Tom Brady* doesn't get an apostrophe as a descriptive but *Tom Brady, the Patriots' starting quarterback*, gets an apostrophe as a possessive.

archery At the Summer Olympics, individual and team events for men and women. Use a **basic summary**.

AstroTurf A trademark for a type of artificial grass.

athlete's foot, athlete's heart

athletic club Abbreviate as *AC* with the name of a club, but only in sports summaries: *Illinois AC*. See **match**

SPORTS

summary for an example of such a summary.

athletic director Use the singular *athletic* unless otherwise in a formal title.

athletic teams Capitalize teams, associations and recognized nicknames: *Red Sox, the Big Ten, the A's, the Colts*.

athletic trainers Health care professionals who are licensed or otherwise regulated to work with athletes and physically active people to prevent, diagnose and treat injuries and other emergency, acute and chronic medical conditions including cardiac abnormalities and heat stroke. Specify where necessary to distinguish from personal trainers, who focus primarily on fitness.

auto racing Common terms include *victory lane, pit road*.
Follow the forms below for all major auto races:

NASCAR
LINEUP
NASCAR-Sprint Cup-Daytona 500 Lineup
By The Associated Press
After Thursday qualifying; race Sunday
At Daytona International Speedway
Daytona Beach, Fla.
Lap length: 2.5 miles
(Car number in parentheses)
1. (99) Carl Edwards, Ford, 194.738.
2. (16) Greg Biffle, Ford, 194.087.
3. (14) Tony Stewart, Chevrolet, 193.607.

RESULTS
NASCAR Sprint Cup-Daytona 500 Results
By The Associated Press
Monday
At Daytona International Speedway
Daytona Beach, Fla.
Lap length: 2.5 miles
(Start position in parentheses)

1. (4) Matt Kenseth, Ford, 202 laps, 100.9 rating, 47 points, $1,589,387.
2. (5) Dale Earnhardt Jr., Chevrolet, 202, 99.5, 42, $1,102,175.
3. (2) Greg Biffle, Ford, 202, 126.2, 42, $804,163.

For cars not finishing the race, include reason:
41. (17) Robby Gordon, Dodge, engine, 25, 30.5, 3, $268,150.
42. (8) Jimmie Johnson, Chevrolet, accident, 1, 28.3, 2, $327,149.
43. (25) David Ragan, Ford, accident, 1, 25.9, 1, $267,637.

After the final driver, add:
Race Statistics
Average Speed of Race Winner: 140.256 mph.
Time of Race: 3 hours, 36 minutes, 2 seconds.
Margin of Victory: 0.210 seconds.
Caution Flags: 10 for 42 laps.
Lead Changes: 25 among 13 drivers.
Lap Leaders: G.Biffle 1-9; R.Smith 10-11; G.Biffle 12-14; P.Menard 15-16; D.Hamlin 17-40; J.Burton 41-57; J.Gordon 58; T.Stewart 59-60; J.Burton 61-67; G.Biffle 68-76; M.Truex Jr. 77-81; G.Biffle 82; T.Labonte 83-85; G.Biffle 86-99; M.Truex Jr. 100-101; D.Hamlin 102-129; G.Biffle 130; M.Martin 131-132; G.Biffle 133-138; D.Hamlin 139-143; J.Logano 144-145; M.Kenseth 146-157; G.Biffle 158; D.Blaney 159-164; M.Kenseth 165-202.
Leaders Summary (Driver, Times Led, Laps Led): D.Hamlin, 3 times for 57 laps; M.Kenseth, 2 times for 50 laps; G.Biffle, 8 times for 44 laps; J.Burton, 2 times for 24 laps; M.Truex Jr., 2 times for 7 laps; D.Blaney, 1 time for 6 laps; T.Labonte, 1 time for 3 laps; P.Menard, 1 time for 2 laps; J.Logano, 1 time for 2 laps; M.Martin, 1 time for 2 laps; T.Stewart, 1 time for 2 laps; R.Smith, 1 time for 2 laps; J.Gordon, 1 time for 1 lap.
Top 12 in Points: 1. M.Kenseth, 47; 2. D.Earnhardt Jr., 42; 3. G.Biffle, 42; 4. D.Hamlin, 42; 5. J.Burton, 40; 6. P.Menard, 39; 7. K.Harvick, 37; 8. C.Edwards, 36; 9. J.Logano, 36; 10. M.Martin, 35; 11. C.Bowyer, 33; 12. M.Truex Jr., 33.

Formula One-Abu Dhabi Grand Prix Results
By The Associated Press
Sunday
At Yas Marina circuit
Abu Dhabi, United Arab Emirates
Lap length: 3.45 miles
1. Kimi Raikkonen, Finland, Lotus, 55 laps, 1:45:58.667, 107.421 mph.
2. Fernando Alonso, Spain, Ferrari, 55, 1:45:59.519.

Constructors Standings
1. Red Bull, 460 points.
2. Ferrari, 400.

IndyCar-MAVTV 500 Results
By The Associated Press
Saturday

At Auto Club Speedway
Fontana, Calif.
Lap length: 2 miles
(Starting position in parentheses)
1. (5) Ed Carpenter, Dallara-Chevrolet, 250, Running.
2. (9) Dario Franchitti, Dallara-Honda, 250, Running.
24. (13) Will Power, Dallara-Chevrolet, 66, Contact.
25. (11) E.J. Viso, Dallara-Chevrolet, 65, Mechanical.

___
Race Statistics
Winners average speed: 168.939.
Time of Race: 2:57:34.7433.
Margin of Victory: Under Caution.
Cautions: 7 for 43 laps.
Lead Changes: 29 among 12 drivers.
Lap Leaders: Kanaan 1, Andretti 2-4, Hildebrand 5-35, Briscoe 36-37, Sato 38-39, Newgarden 40, Hildebrand 41-65, Carpenter 66-75, Jakes 76-85, Carpenter 86-109, Dixon 110, Carpenter 111-122, Dixon 123-133, Kanaan 134-147, Castroneves 148-149, Sato 150-152, Kanaan 153-184, Dixon 185-195, Carpenter 196, Dixon 197-198, Carpenter 199-203, Tagliani 204-217, Carpenter 218, Tagliani 219-223, Franchitti 224-225, Tagliani 226-227, Sato 228, Carpenter 229-236, Franchitti 237-249, Carpenter 250.
Points: Hunter-Reay 468, Power 465, Dixon 435, Castroneves 431, Pagenaud 387, Briscoe 370, Franchitti 363, Hinchcliffe 358, Kanaan 351, Rahal 333.

NHRA Results
By The Associated Press
Sunday
At Firebird International Raceway
Chandler, Ariz.
Final Results
Top Fuel_Tony Schumacher, 4.606 seconds, 213.20 mph def. Morgan Lucas, 4.652 seconds, 258.67 mph.
Funny Car_Ron Capps, Dodge Charger, 4.064, 314.90 def. Matt Hagan, Charger, 4.158, 300.33.
Pro Stock_Erica Enders-Stevens, Chevy Cobalt, 6.538, 211.99 def. Mike Edwards, Chevy Camaro, 6.520, 213.74.

b

backboard, backcourt, backfield, backhand, backspin, backstop, backstretch, backstroke Some are exceptions to Webster's New World, made for consistency in handling sports stories.

badminton Games are won by the first player to score 21 points, unless it is necessary to continue until one player has a two-point spread. Most matches go to the first winner of two games.
Use a **match summary**.

ball carrier

ballclub, ballgame, ballpark, ballplayer

baseball The spellings for some frequently used words and phrases, some of which are exceptions to Webster's New World College Dictionary:

backstop
baseline
bullpen
center field (n., adj.)
center fielder
designated hitter
doubleheader
double play
fair ball
fastball
first baseman
foul ball line
foul tip
ground-rule double
home plate
home run
left field (n., adj)
line drive
line up (v.)
lineup (n.)
major league(s) (n.)
major league (adj.)
major leaguer (n.)
outfielder
passed ball

pinch hit
pinch hitter (n.)
pitchout
put out (v.) putout (n.)
RBI (s.), RBIs (pl.)
right field (n., adj.)
rundown (n.)
sacrifice
sacrifice fly
sacrifice hit
shortstop
shut out (v.)
shutout (n., adj.)
slugger
squeeze play
strike
strike zone
Texas leaguer
third base coach
triple play
twinight doubleheader
walk-off
wild pitch

NUMBERS: Some sample uses of numbers: *first inning, seventh-inning stretch, 10th inning, first base, second base, third base, first home run, 10th home run, first place, one RBI, 10 RBIs. The pitcher's record is now 6-5. The*

SPORTS

final score was 1-0.

LEAGUES: Use *American League, National League, American League West, National League East,* or *AL West* and *AL East,* etc. On second reference: *the league, the pennant in the West, the league's West Division,* etc.

Note: No hyphen in *major league, minor league, big league* (n. or adj.)

PLAYOFFS: Use *American League Championship Series,* or *ALCS* on second reference; *National League Championship Series,* or *NLCS; AL Division Series,* or *ALDS;* and *NL Division Series,* or *NLDS.* In the early rounds, use *series* lowercase. Use uppercase *Series* only to refer to the World Series.

ERA Acceptable in all references for earned run average.

Green Monster Acceptable in all references to the left field wall at Fenway Park, home of the Boston Red Sox.

BOX SCORES: A sample follows.

The visiting team always is listed on the left, the home team on the right.

Only one position, the first he played in the game, is listed for any player.

BC-BBN--BOX-Atl-SD

BRAVES 8, PADRES 3

ATLANTA					**SAN DIEGO**			
	ab	r	h	bi		ab	r	h	bi
Ogllen ss	5	1	1	1	QVeras 2b	4	1	0	0
Lckhrt 2b	5	2	2	0	SFinley cf	4	0	1	0
ChJnes 3b	4	2	2	1	Gwynn rf	4	1	1	1
Glrrga 1b	2	1	1	4	Cminiti 3b	3	0	1	0
Klesko lf	4	0	1	1	Leyritz 1b	3	1	2	2
Rocker p	0	0	0	0	Joyner 1b	1	0	1	0
Perez p	0	0	0	0	CHrndz c	4	0	1	0
Seanez p	0	0	0	0	RRivra lf	3	0	1	0
Lgtnbr p	0	0	0	0	MaSwy ph	1	0	0	0
JLopez c	4	1	1	1	Gomez ss	3	0	0	0

AJones cf	4	1	2	0	Miceli p	0	0	0	0
Tucker rf	2	0	1	0	Bhrngr p	0	0	0	0
GerWm rf	2	0	1	0	Lngstn p	0	0	0	0
Neagle p	2	0	0	0	GMyrs ph	0	0	0	0
DeMrtz p	0	0	0	0	JHmtn p	2	0	0	0
Clbrnn ph	1	0	0	0	RayMys p	0	0	0	0
DBtsta lf	1	0	0	0	Sheets ss	1	0	0	0
VnWal ph	1	0	0	0					
Totals	**36**	**8**	**12**	**8**		**34**	**3**	**8**	**3**

Atlanta   000 101 600 - 8
San Diego   000 200 000 - 2

DP_Atlanta 1, San Diego 2. LOB_Atlanta 4, San Diego 7. 2B_ChJones (1), Gwynn (1), RRivera (2). 3B_Lockhart (1). HR_Galarraga (1), JLopez (1), Leyritz (1).

	IP	H	R	ER	BB	SO
Atlanta						
Neagle	5 2-3	7	3	3	1	7
DeMrtz W, 1-0	1-3	0	0	0	0	0
Rocker	1 1-3	0	0	0	0	3
Perez	0	1	0	0	1	0
Seanez	2-3	0	0	0	0	0
Ligtenberg	1	0	0	0	1	2
San Diego						
JHamilton L, 0-1	6	7	4	4	2	5
RaMyers	2-3	2	3	3	1	0
Miceli	1-3	1	1	1	0	1
Boehringer	1	2	0	0	0	0
Langston	1	0	0	0	0	0

Perez pitched to 2 batters in the 8th, JHamilton pitched to 2 batters in the 7th.

Umpires_Home, Bonin; First, Davis; Second, Rippley; Third, Tata; Left, Poncino; Right, Hallion.

T_2:58. A_65,042 (59,772).

Example of an expanded box score:

BC-BBA--EXP-BOX-Ana-Tex

Rangers 3, Angels 2

Anaheim	AB	R	H	BI	BB	SO	Avg.
Erstad cf	4	0	3	2	0	0	.750
Gil ss	3	0	0	0	0	0	.000
a-OPalmeiro ph	1	0	0	0	0	0	.000
Nieves ss	0	0	0	0	0	0	.000
Salmon rf	4	0	1	0	0	1	.250
Glaus 3b	4	0	1	0	0	1	.250
GAnderson lf	3	0	1	0	1	0	.333
GHill dh	4	0	0	0	0	1	.000
BMolina c	4	1	1	0	0	0	.250
Spiezio 1b	3	1	1	0	0	1	.333
Eckstein 2b	3	0	1	0	0	0	.333
Totals	**33**	**2**	**9**	**2**	**1**	**5**	

Texas	AB	R	H	BI	BB	SO	Avg.
Greer lf	3	0	0	1	0	1	.143
Velarde 2b	4	0	1	0	0	1	.250
ARodriguez ss	4	0	1	0	0	3	.375
RPalmeiro 1b	2	0	0	0	2	0	.167
IRodriguez c	4	1	2	0	0	0	.250
Galarraga dh	3	1	1	1	0	0	.167

SPORTS

Caminiti 3b	2	0	1	0	1	0	.500
Curtis cf	2	1	1	0	0	0	.500
Mateo rf	3	0	1	0	1	0	.429
^Totals	27	3	8	2	3	6	

Anaheim 001 000 010_2 9 2
Texas 020 000 10X_3 8 0

a-grounded into double play for Gil in the 8th.

LOB_Anaheim 5, Texas 5. 2B_Erstad 2 (2), Glaus (1), BMolina (1), Spiezio (1), Velarde (1), IRodriguez (1), Galarraga (1). RBIs_Erstad 2 (2), Greer (1), Galarraga (1). SB_ARodriguez (1). SF_Greer. GIDP_OPalmeiro, GHill 2, IRodriguez, Curtis, Mateo.

Runners left in scoring position_Anaheim 4 (Salmon, Glaus, BMolina 2); Texas 3 (Greer, RPalmeiro, Caminiti). RISP_L.A. Angels 2 for 12; Texas 2 for 9.

Runners moved up_Gil 2, Eckstein.

DP_Anaheim 3 (Gil, Eckstein and Spiezio), (Gil, Eckstein and Spiezio), (Eckstein, Gil and Spiezio); Texas 3 (ARodriguez, Velarde and RPalmeiro), (Velarde, ARodriguez and RPalmeiro), (Caminiti, IRodriguez and RPalmeiro).

	IP	H	R	ER	BB	SO	NP	ERA
Anaheim								
Schoeneweis L, 0-1	7	8	3	3	3	5	108	3.86
Weber	1	0	0	0	0	1	13	0.00
Texas								
Rogers W, 1-0	7 1-3	7	2	2	0	5	96	2.45
JRZimmermn H, 4	2-3	0	0	0	0	0	2	0.00
Crabtree S, 1	1	2	0	0	1	0	12	0.00

Inherited runners-scored_JRZimmermn 2-0.

IBB_off Crabtree (GAnderson) 1. HBP_by Schoeneweis (Curtis).

Umpires_Home, Rippley; First, Winters; Second, Barrett, Ted; Third, Marquez.

T_2:31. A_49,512 (49,115).

LINESCORE: When a bare linescore summary is required, use this form:

Philadelphia	010 200 000 - 3 4 1
San Diego	000 200 000 - 2 9 1

K. Gross, Tekulve (8) and Virgil; Dravecky, Lefferts (3) and Kennedy. W - KGross, 4-6. LDravecky, 4-3. Sv - Tekulve (3). HRs - Philadelphia, Virgil 2 (8).

LEAGUE STANDINGS:

The form:
All Times EDT
NATIONAL LEAGUE

		EAST		
	W	L	Pct.	GB
Pittsburgh	92	69	.571	-
Philadelphia	85	75	.531	61/2
		WEST		
	W	L	Pct.	GB
Cincinnati	108	54	.667	-
Los Angeles	88	74	.543	20

Monday's Results
Chicago 7, St. Louis 5

Atlanta at New York, ppd., rain
Tuesday's Games
Cincinnati (Gullett 14-2 and Nolan 4-4) at New York (Seaver 12-3 and Matlack 6-1) 2, 6 p.m.
Wednesday's Games
Cincinnati at New York, 7:05 p.m.
Chicago at St.Louis, 8:05 p.m.
Only games scheduled.

In subheads for results and future games, spell out day of the week as: *Tuesday's Games*, instead of *Today's Games*.

BASE jumping Acceptable on first reference for the extreme sport, but explain later in the story. *BASE* is an acronym for *building, antenna, span* (such as a bridge) and *earth* (such as a cliff).

basic summary This format for summarizing sports events lists winners in the order of their finish. The figure showing the place finish is followed by an athlete's full name, his affiliation or hometown, and his time, distance, points or whatever performance factor is applicable to the sport.

If a contest involves several types of events, the paragraph begins with the name of the event.

A typical example:
60-yard dash – 1, Steve Williams, Florida TC, 6.0. 2, Hasley Crawford, Philadelphia Pioneer, 6.1. 3, Mike McFarland, Chicago TC, 6.2. 4

100 – 1, Steve Williams, Florida TC, 10.1. 2, ...

Most basic summaries are a single paragraph per event, as shown. In some competitions with large fields, however, the basic summary is supplied under a dateline with each winner listed in a single paragraph. See the **auto racing** and **bowling** entries for examples.

Other examples:
Archery
(After 3 of 4 Distances)
1. Darrell Pace, Cincinnati, 914 points.
2. Richard McKinney, Muncie, Ind. 880.

Bobsled, Women

SPORTS

1. Kaillie Humphries and Jennifer Ciochetti, Canada, 3 minutes, 48.57 seconds (57.10- 57.07-57.22-57.18).

2. Sandra Kiriasis and Petra Lammert, Germany, 3:48.90 (57.30-57.28-57.21-57.11).

3. Elana Meyers and Katie Eberling, United States, 3:49.57 (57.22-57.45-57.41-57.49).

—

Canoeing, Men

Kayak Singles, 500 meters

Heat 1 – 1, Rudiger Helm, Germany, 1:56.06. 2, Zoltan Sztanity, Hungary, 1:57.12. Also: 6, Henry Krawczyk, New York, 2 04.64. First Repechage – 1, Ladislay Soucek, Czech Republic, 1:53.20. 2, Hans Eich, Germany, 1:54.23.

—

Gymnastics:

Parallel Bars – 1, Joe Smith, Houston, 9.675 points. 2, Ed Jones, Albany, N.Y., 9.54. 3, Andy Brown, Los Angeles, 9.4.

—

ATHENS, Greece (AP) – Final results Saturday of the weightlifting event from the Summer Olympics:

Men's 85kg

1. Juan Jose Madrigal, Costa Rica, 472.5 kg.

2. Rampa Mosweu, Botswana, 470.0.

Additional examples are provided in the entries for several of the sports that are reported in this format.

For international events in which U.S. competitors are not among the leaders, add them in a separate paragraph as follows:

Also: 14, Dick Green, New York, 6.8.

In events where points, rather than time or distance, are recorded as performances, mention the word points on the first usage only:

1. Jim Benson, Springfield, N.J., 150 points. 2. Jerry Green, Canada, 149.

basketball

The spellings of some frequently used words and phrases:

air ball	half-court pass
alley-oop	hook shot
backboard	jump ball
foul line	jump shot
foul shot	layup
free throw	man-to-man
free-throw line	pivotman
frontcourt	tip off (v.)
full-court press	tipoff (n., adj.)
goaltending	

NUMBERS: Some sample uses of numbers: *in the first quarter, a second-quarter lead, nine field goals, a 3-pointer, 3-point play, 10 field goals, the 6-foot-5 forward, the 6-10 center. He is 6 feet 10 inches tall.*

LEAGUE: *National Basketball Association* or *NBA.*

For subdivisions: *the Atlantic Division of the Eastern Conference, the Pacific Division of the Western Conference,* etc. On second reference: *the NBA East, the division, the conference,* etc.

PLAYOFFS: In the NBA, *Eastern Conference first round, Western Conference semifinals, Eastern Conference finals, Western Conference finals, NBA Finals.*

NCAA Tournament It is acceptable to refer to the regional semifinals as the *Sweet 16,* the regional finals as the *Elite Eight* and the national semifinals as the *Final Four.* For early-round games, use *round of 64* or *round of 32* if needed, though it is easier in many cases to say a team's first or second game if they begin in the round of 64: *California won its opening game of the NCAA Tournament. First Four* is acceptable to refer to the NCAA Tournament games played to reach the round of 64.

BOX SCORE: A sample follows. The visiting team always is listed first.

In listing the players, begin with the five starters — two forwards, center, two guards — and follow with all substitutes who played.

Figures after each player's last name denote field goals made and attempted, free throws made and attempted and total points.

EXAMPLE:

Hornets-Bulls, Box

NEW ORLEANS (95)

Ariza 7-12 0-0 16, Ayon 2-6 1-2 5, Kaman 7-18 3-4 17, Vasquez 4-10 4-4 12, Belinelli 3-7 0-0 6, Jones 4-10 2-2 10,

SPORTS

Aminu 0-4 2-2 2, Jack 4-9 0-0 10, Henry 3-10 6-7 12, Thomas 2-3 1-1 5. Totals 36-89 19-22 95.

CHICAGO (99)

Deng 6-16 1-2 14, Boozer 7-14 0-0 14, Noah 7-12 1-3 15, Rose 11-24 9-11 32, Hamilton 2-5 1-1 5, Brewer 3-6 0-0 6, Gibson 2-4 1-2 5, Watson 0-2 0-0 0, Korver 2-6 0-0 5, Asik 1-1 1-1 3. Totals 41-90 14-20 99.

New Orleans 26•24•20•25_95

Chicago 30•17•29•23_99

3-Point Goals_New Orleans 4-9 (Jack 2-2, Ariza 2-2, Henry 0-1, Vasquez 0-1, Belinelli 0-3), Chicago 3-18 (Korver 1-5, Deng 1-5, Rose 1-5, Brewer 0-1, Hamilton 0-1, Watson 0-1). Fouled Out_None. Rebounds_New Orleans 55 (Kaman 11), Chicago 56 (Noah 16). Assists_New Orleans 22 (Kaman 5), Chicago 25 (Rose 9). Total Fouls_New Orleans 18, Chicago 16. Technicals_Boozer, Noah. A_21,919 (20,917).

An expanded box example:

BC-BKN--Lakers-Nuggets, Long Box

NUGGETS 119, LAKERS 108

L.A. LAKERS	Min	FG M-A	FT M-A	Reb O-T	A	PF	PTS
World Peace	30:53	6-11	1-2	2-2	0	3	15
Clark	22:40	4-9	0-2	0-1	0	2	8
Howard	38:20	6-8	3-14	4-14	1	2	15
Nash	34:03	6-8	4-5	0-3	5	3	16
Bryant	38:44	12-23	5-6	0-6	9	3	29
Jamison	24:15	5-12	1-2	0-3	1	0	14
Meeks	31:34	3-5	0-0	2-5	1	3	8
Blake	19:31	1-2	0-0	0-2	4	1	3
Totals	240:00	43-78	14-31	8-36	21	17	108

Percentages: FG .551, FT .452.

3-Point Goals: 8-19, .421 (Jamison 3-4, Meeks 2-4, World Peace 2-5, Blake 1-2, Bryant 0-1, Nash 0-1, Clark 0-2).

Team Rebounds: 13. Team Turnovers: 15 (22 PTS).

Blocked Shots: 5 (Howard 4, Clark).

Turnovers: 15 (Nash 6, Bryant 4, World Peace 2, Blake, Howard, Meeks).

Steals: 6 (World Peace 3, Clark, Jamison, Meeks).

Technical Fouls: World Peace, 11:37 first; Defensive three second, 10:02 first; Bryant, 12:00 third.

DENVER	Min	FG M-A	FT M-A	Reb O-T	A	PF	PTS
Chandler	25:24	10-18	0-0	2-4	1	3	23
Faried	31:48	6-10	0-0	4-10	0	5	12
Koufos	14:24	3-4	2-4	3-5	0	5	8
Lawson	40:30	8-19	5-7	0-4	8	3	22
Iguodala	36:45	6-9	2-5	0-4	12	0	14
Brewer	25:40	6-15	3-5	0-2	3	3	16
McGee	23:19	3-4	1-2	2-7	0	3	7
AMiller	27:41	3-4	3-4	0-3	5	0	9
Randolph	6:18	3-3	0-0	2-4	0	1	6
Hamilton	4:15	0-1	0-0	0-1	1	0	0
Mozgov	3:56	1-1	0-0	0-0	0	2	2
Totals	240:00	49-88	16-27	13-44	30	25	119

Percentages: FG .557, FT .593.

3-Point Goals: 5-18, .278 (Chandler 3-5, Brewer 1-5, Lawson 1-6, Iguodala 0-1, A.Miller 0-1).

Team Rebounds: 9. Team Turnovers: 10 (16 PTS).

Blocked Shots: 7 (McGee 4, Faried 2, Iguodala).

Turnovers: 9 (Lawson 4, Iguodala 2, Brewer, Faried, McGee).

Steals: 13 (Faried 3, McGee 2, A.Miller 2, Brewer, Chandler, Iguodala, Koufos, Lawson, Randolph).

Technical Fouls: Coach Karl, 7:27 first; Defensive three second, 3:56 second; Defensive three second, 4:17 third.

L.A. Lakers 29 25 29 25_108

Denver 35 32 28 24_119

A_19,155 (19,155). T_2:14.

Officials_Joe Crawford, David Guthrie, Josh Tiven.

STANDINGS: The format for professional standings:

Eastern Conference

Atlantic Division

	W	L	Pct.	GB
Boston	43	22	.662	–
Philadelphia	40	30	.571	5 1/2

In college boxes, the score by periods is omitted because the games are divided only into halves.

No. 19 CONNECTICUT 74, No. 8 SYRACUSE 66

CONNECTICUT (15-5)

Villanueva 9-13 3-7 21, Boone 2-4 3-5 7, Brown 0-2 5-6 5, Williams 3-11 1-2 9, Gay 6-13 4-4 18, Armstrong 2-2 2-2 6, Kellogg 0-0 0-0 0, Anderson 1-4 2-3 4, Nelson 1-1 2-3 4. Totals 24-50 22-32 74.

SYRACUSE (21-3)

Warrick 6-13 4-7 16, Pace 7-9 0-0 14, Forth 0-1 0-0 0, McNamara 4-18 0-0 9, McCroskey 2-5 0-0 4, Watkins 2-2 0-0 4, Edelin 3-8 1-2 7, Roberts 4-10 4-5 12. Totals 28-66 9-14 66.

Halftime_Connecticut 37-36. 3-Point Goals_Connecticut 4-14 (Gay 2-5, Williams 2-5, Brown 0-2, Anderson 0-2), Syracuse 1-9 (McNamara 1-9). Fouled Out_Roberts. Rebounds_Connecticut 36 (Villanueva 10), Syracuse 34 (Warrick 7). Assists_Connecticut 14 (Williams 6), Syracuse 17 (Edelin, McNamara 6). Total Fouls_Connecticut 15, Syracuse 24. A_27,651.

The format for college conference standings:

	Conference			All Games		
	W	L	Pct.	W	L	Pct.
Missouri	12	2	.857	24	4	.857

betting odds Use figures and a hyphen: *The odds were 5-4, he won despite 3-2 odds against him.*

The word *to* seldom is necessary, but when it appears it should be hyphenated in all constructions: *3-to-2 odds, odds of 3-to-2, the odds were 3-to-2.*

bettor A person who bets.

billiards Use a **match summary**.

SPORTS

bobsledding, luge Scoring is in minutes, seconds and tenths of a second. Extend to hundredths if available.

Identify events as *two-man, four-man, men's luge, women's luge*. In Olympics, *women's bob, two-man bob, four-man bob, men's luge, women's luge*.

Use a **basic summary**. Example:

Women

1. Kaillie Humphries and Jennifer Ciochetti, Canada, 3 minutes, 48.57 seconds (57.10- 57.07-57.22-57.18).

2. Sandra Kiriasis and Petra Lammert, Germany, 3:48.90 (57.30-57.28-57.21-57.11).

3. Elana Meyers and Katie Eberling, United States, 3:49.57 (57.22-57.45-57.41-57.49).

bowl games Capitalize them: *Cotton Bowl, Orange Bowl, Rose Bowl*, etc.

bowling Scoring systems use both total points and won-lost records.

Use the **basic summary** format in paragraph form. Note that a comma is used in giving pinfalls of more than 999.

EXAMPLES:

ST. LOUIS (AP) — Second-round leaders and their total pinfalls in the $100,000 Professional Bowlers Association tournament:

1. Bill Spigner, Hamden, Conn., 2,820.

2. Gary Dickinson, Fort Worth, Texas, 2,759.

ALAMEDA, Calif. (AP) — The 24 match play finalists with their won-lost records and total pinfall Thursday night after four rounds — 26 games — of the $65,000 Alameda Open bowling tournament:

1. Jay Robinson, Los Angeles, 5-3, 5,937.

2. Butch Soper, Huntington Beach, Calif., 3-5, 5,932.

boxing The four major sanctioning bodies for professional boxing are the World Boxing Association, the World Boxing Council, the World Boxing Organization and the International Boxing Federation.

Weight classes and titles by organization:

105 pounds — Mini Flyweight, WBF, IBF, WBO; Strawweight, WBC

108 pounds — Light Flyweight, WBA, WBC; Junior Flyweight, IBF, WBO

112 pounds — Flyweight, WBA, WBC, IBF, WBO

115 pounds — Super Flyweight, WBA, WBC; Junior Bantamweight, IBF, WBO

118 pounds — Bantamweight, WBA, WBC, IBF, WBO

122 pounds — Super Bantamweight, WBA, WBC; Junior Featherweight, IBF, WBO

126 pounds — Featherweight, WBA, WBC, IBF, WBO

130 pounds — Super Featherweight, WBA, WBC; Junior Lightweight, IBF, WBO

135 pounds — Lightweight, WBA, WBC, IBF, WBO

140 pounds — Super Lightweight, WBA, WBC; Junior Welterweight, IBF, WBO

147 pounds — Welterweight, WBA, WBC, WBO, IBF

154 pounds — Super Welterweight, WBA, WBC; Junior Middleweight, IBF, WBO

160 pounds — Middleweight, WBA, WBC, IBF, WBO

168 pounds — Super Middleweight, WBA, WBC, IBF, WBO

175 pounds — Light Heavyweight, WBA, WBC, IBF, WBO

190 pounds — Cruiserweight, WBA, WBC, IBF, WBO

More than 200 pounds — Heavyweight, WBA, WBC, IBF, WBO

Some other terms:

kidney punch A punch to an opponent's kidney when the puncher has only one hand free. It is illegal. If the puncher has both hands free, it is legal.

knockout (n. and adj.) **knock out** (v.) A fighter is knocked out if he takes a 10-count.

If a match ends early because one fighter is unable to continue, say that the winner stopped the loser. In most boxing jurisdictions there is no such thing as a technical knockout.

outpointed Not *outdecisioned*.

rabbit punch A punch behind an opponent's neck. It is illegal.

box office (n.) **box-office** (adj.)

bullfight, bullfighter, bullfighting

C

canoeing Scoring is in minutes, seconds and tenths of a second. Extend to hundredths if available.

In Olympics, slalom and sprint events for both men and women. See **basic summary**.

chronic traumatic encephalopathy A degenerative brain disease that researchers have linked to concussions or repeated blows to the head. It is most closely associated with football but also has been diagnosed in some athletes from other contact sports and military combat veterans. It can be identified only posthumously through an examination of the brain. *CTE* is acceptable on second reference, and in headlines if essential.

cliches A team losing a game is not a "disaster." *Home runs* are *homers*, not "dingers," "jacks" or "bombs." A player scored 10 *straight points*, not 10 "unanswered" points. If a football team scores two touchdowns and the opponent doesn't come back, say it "never trailed" rather than "never looked back." In short, avoid hackneyed words and phrases, redundancies and exaggerations.

coach See **titles** entry in sports guidelines.

collective nouns Nouns that denote a unit take singular verbs and pronouns: *class, committee, crowd, family, group, herd, jury, orchestra, team.*

However, team names such as *the Jazz, the Magic, the Avalanche* and *the Thunder* take plural verbs.

Many singular names take singular verbs: *Boston is favored in the playoffs. Stanford is in the NCAA Tournament.*

College Football Playoff Use *the playoff* or *the national championship* as applicable on second reference. The abbreviation *CFP* is acceptable only when referring directly to rankings, whether or not the term has been spelled out earlier in a story. In game stories, reflect the committee's ranking when referring to a team's record: *Alabama (7-1, 4-1, No. 3 CFP)*. Do not use the abbreviation in other forms in stories or in headlines. The AP Top 25 ranking should be used in headlines and at the top of stories, and can be used without distinction: *No. 1 Alabama, top-ranked Alabama.* While deferring to AP ranking, stories should later make note of where a team stands in the College Football Playoff rankings because the measurement matters for playoff and bowl placement, and fans will be aware of both rankings. When writing about the committee that determines the College Football Playoff, use *the committee, the selection committee* or *playoff selection committee*.

conferences Major college basketball and football conferences are listed

SPORTS

Major College Basketball Conferences

AMERICA EAST CONFERENCE – Albany (N.Y.); Binghamton; Hartford; Maine; Mass.-Lowell; New Hampshire; Stony Brook; UMBC (Maryland-Baltimore County); Vermont.

AMERICAN ATHLETIC CONFERENCE – Cincinnati; ECU (East Carolina); Houston; Memphis; SMU; South Florida; Temple; Tulane; UCF (Central Florida); UConn; Tulsa.

ATLANTIC 10 CONFERENCE – Davidson; Dayton; Duquesne; George Mason; Fordham; George Washington; LaSalle; Richmond; St. Bonaventure; Saint Joseph's; Saint Louis; Rhode Island; UMass; VCU (Virginia Commonwealth).

ATLANTIC COAST CONFERENCE – Boston College; Clemson; Duke; Florida State; Georgia Tech; Louisville; Miami; North Carolina; North Carolina State; Notre Dame; Pittsburgh; Syracuse; Virginia; Virginia Tech; Wake Forest.

ATLANTIC SUN CONFERENCE – Florida Gulf Coast; Jacksonville; Kennesaw St.; Lipscomb; North Florida; Northern Kentucky; S.C. Upstate; Stetson.

BIG 12 CONFERENCE – Baylor; Iowa State; Kansas; Kansas State; Oklahoma; Oklahoma State; Texas; TCU; Texas Tech; West Virginia.

BIG EAST CONFERENCE – Butler; Creighton; DePaul; Georgetown; Marquette; Providence; St. John's; Seton Hall; Villanova; Xavier.

BIG SKY CONFERENCE – Eastern Washington; Idaho; Idaho State; Montana; Montana State; North Dakota; Northern Arizona; Northern Colorado; Portland State; Sacramento State; Southern Utah; Weber State.

BIG SOUTH CONFERENCE – North Division: Campbell; High Point; Liberty; Longwood; Radford. South Division: Charleston Southern; Coastal Carolina; Gardner-Webb; Presbyterian; UNC-Asheville; Winthrop.

BIG TEN CONFERENCE – Illinois; Indiana; Iowa; Maryland; Michigan; Michigan State; Minnesota; Nebraska; Northwestern; Ohio State; Penn State; Purdue; Rutgers; Wisconsin.

BIG WEST CONFERENCE – Cal Poly; Cal State Fullerton; CS Northridge; Hawaii; Long Beach State; UC Davis; UC Irvine; UC Riverside; UC Santa Barbara.

COLONIAL ATHLETIC ASSOCIATION – College of Charleston; Delaware; Drexel; Elon; Hofstra; James Madison; Northeastern; Towson; UNC-Wilmington; William & Mary.

CONFERENCE USA – Charlotte; East Carolina; FAU (Florida Atlantic); FIU (Florida International); Louisiana Tech; Marshall; Middle Tennessee; North Texas; Old Dominion; Rice; Southern Mississippi; Tulane; Tulsa; UAB (Alabama-Birmingham); UTEP; UTSA (Texas-San Antonio); Western Kentucky.

HORIZON LEAGUE – Cleveland State; Detroit; Green Bay; Illinois-Chicago; Milwaukee; Oakland; Valparaiso; Wright State; Youngstown State.

IVY LEAGUE – Brown; Columbia; Cornell; Dartmouth; Harvard; Pennsylvania; Princeton; Yale.

METRO ATLANTIC ATHLETIC CONFERENCE – Canisius; Fairfield; Iona; Manhattan; Marist; Monmouth (N.J.); Niagara; Quinnipiac; Rider; St. Peter's; Siena.

MID-AMERICAN CONFERENCE – East Division: Akron; Bowling Green; Buffalo; Kent State; Miami (Ohio); Ohio. West Division: Ball State; Central Michigan; Eastern Michigan; Northern Illinois; Toledo; Western Michigan.

MID-EASTERN ATHLETIC CONFERENCE – Bethune-Cookman; Coppin State; Delaware State; Florida A&M; Hampton; Howard; Maryland-Eastern Shore; Morgan State; Norfolk State; N.C. A&T; N.C. Central; Savannah State; S.C. State.

MISSOURI VALLEY CONFERENCE – Bradley; Drake; Evansville; Illinois State; Indiana State; Loyola of Chicago; Missouri State; Northern Iowa; Southern Illinois; Wichita State.

MOUNTAIN WEST CONFERENCE – Air Force; Boise State; Colorado State; Fresno State; Nevada; New Mexico; San Diego State; San Jose State; UNLV; Utah State; Wyoming.

NORTHEAST CONFERENCE – Bryant; CCSU (Central Connecticut State); Fairleigh Dickinson; LIU Brooklyn; Mount St. Mary's (Md.); Robert Morris; Sacred Heart; St. Francis (NY); St. Francis (Pa.); Wagner.

OHIO VALLEY CONFERENCE – East Division: Belmont; Eastern Kentucky; Jacksonville State; Morehead State; Tennessee State; Tennessee Tech. West Divsion: Austin Peay; Eastern Illinois; Murray State; SIU-Edwardsville; Southeast Missouri State; UT-Martin.

PACIFIC-12 CONFERENCE – Arizona; Arizona State; California; Colorado; Oregon; Oregon State; Southern California; Stanford; UCLA; Utah; Washington; Washington State.

PATRIOT LEAGUE – American U.; Army; Boston U.; Bucknell; Colgate; Holy Cross; Lafayette; Lehigh; Loyola (Md.); Navy.

SOUTHEASTERN CONFERENCE – Alabama; Arkansas; Auburn; Florida; Georgia; Kentucky; LSU; Mississippi; Mississippi State; Missouri; South Carolina; Tennessee; Texas A&M; Vanderbilt.

SOUTHERN CONFERENCE – Chattanooga; ETSU (Eastern Tennessee State); Furman; Mercer; Samford; UNC Greensboro; Western Carolina; The Citadel; VMI; Wofford.

SOUTHLAND CONFERENCE – Abilene Christian; Central Arkansas; Houston Baptist; Incarnate Word; Lamar; McNeese State; New Orleans; Nicholls State; Northwestern State; Oral Roberts; Sam Houston State; Southeastern Louisiana; Stephen F. Austin; Texas A&M-Corpus Christi.

SOUTHWESTERN ATHLETIC CONFERENCE – Alabama A&M; Alabama State; Alcorn State; Arkansas-Pine Bluff; Grambling State; Jackson State; MVSU (Mississippi Valley State); Prairie View; Southern U.; Texas Southern.

SUMMIT LEAGUE – Denver; IPFW (Indiana-Purdue-Fort Wayne); IUPUI (Indiana-Purdue-Indianapolis); Nebraska-Omaha; North Dakota State; Oral Roberts; South Dakota; South Dakota State; Western Illinois.

SUN BELT CONFERENCE – Appalachian State; Arkansas State; Georgia State; Georgia Southern; Louisiana-Lafayette; Louisiana-Monroe; South Alabama; Texas-Arlington; Texas State; Troy; UALR (Arkansas-Little Rock).

WEST COAST CONFERENCE – BYU; Gonzaga; Loyola Marymount; Pacific; Pepperdine; Portland; Saint Mary's (Calif.); San Diego; San Francisco; Santa Clara.

WESTERN ATHLETIC CONFERENCE – CS Bakersfield; Chicago State; Grand Canyon; New Mexico State; Seattle; Texas-Pan American; UMKC (Missouri-Kansas City); Utah Valley.

INDEPENDENTS – NJIT.

Major College Football Conferences

AMERICAN ATHLETIC CONFERENCE – Cincinnati; East Carolina; Houston; Memphis; South Florida; SMU; Temple; Tulane; Tulsa; UCF (Central Florida); UConn.

ATLANTIC COAST CONFERENCE – Atlantic Division: Boston College; Clemson; Florida State; Louisville; NC State; Syracuse; Wake Forest. Coastal Division: Duke; Georgia Tech; Miami; North Carolina; Pittsburgh; Virginia; Virginia Tech.

BIG 12 CONFERENCE – Baylor; Iowa State; Kansas; Kansas State; Oklahoma; Oklahoma State; Texas; TCU; Texas Tech; West Virginia.

BIG TEN CONFERENCE – East Division: Indiana; Maryland; Michigan; Michigan State; Ohio State; Penn State; Rutgers. West Division: Illinois; Iowa; Minnesota; Nebraska; Northwestern; Purdue; Wisconsin.

CONFERENCE USA – East Division: Florida Atlantic; Florida International; Marshall; Middle Tennessee; Old Dominion (FCS); Western Kentucky. West Division: Louisiana Tech; North Texas; Rice; Southern Mississippi; UTEP; UTSA.

MID-AMERICAN CONFERENCE – East Division: Akron; Bowling Green; Buffalo; Kent State; Massachusetts; Miami (Ohio); Ohio. West Division: Ball State; Central Michigan; Eastern Michigan; Northern Illinois; Toledo; Western Michigan.

MOUNTAIN WEST CONFERENCE – Mountain Division: Air Force; Boise State; Colorado State; New Mexico; Utah State; Wyoming. West Division: Fresno State; Hawaii; Nevada; San Diego State; San Jose State; UNLV.

PACIFIC-12 CONFERENCE – North Division: California; Oregon; Oregon State; Stanford; Washington; Washington State. South Division: Arizona; Arizona State; Colorado; Southern California; UCLA; Utah.

SOUTHEASTERN CONFERENCE – East Division: Florida; Georgia; Kentucky; Missouri; South Carolina; Tennessee; Vanderbilt. West Division: Alabama; Arkansas; Auburn; LSU; Mississippi; Mississippi State; Texas A&M.

SUN BELT CONFERENCE – Appalachian State; Arkansas State; Georgia Southern; Georgia State; Idaho; Louisiana-Lafayette; Louisiana-Monroe; New Mexico State; South Alabama; Texas State; Troy.

INDEPENDENTS – Army; BYU; Navy; Notre Dame.

Football Championship Subdivision

BIG SKY CONFERENCE – Cal Poly; Eastern Washington; Idaho State; Montana; Montana State; North Dakota; Northern Arizona; Northern Colorado; Portland State; Sacramento State; Southern Utah; UC Davis; Weber State.

BIG SOUTH CONFERENCE – Charleston Southern; Coastal Carolina; Gardner-Webb; Liberty; Monmouth (N.J.); Presbyterian.

COLONIAL ATHLETIC ASSOCIATION – Albany (N.Y.); Delaware; Elon; James Madison; Maine; New Hampshire; Rhode Island; Richmond; Stony Brook; Towson; Villanova; William & Mary.

IVY LEAGUE – Brown; Columbia; Cornell; Dartmouth; Harvard; Pennsylvania; Princeton; Yale.

MID-EASTERN ATHLETIC CONFERENCE – Bethune-Cookman; Delaware State; Florida A&M; Hampton; Howard; Morgan State; Norfolk State; North Carolina A&T; N.C. Central; Savannah State; South Carolina State.

MISSOURI VALLEY CONFERENCE – Illinois State; Indiana State; Missouri State; North Dakota State; Northern Iowa; South Dakota; South Dakota State; Southern Illinois; Western Illinois; Youngstown State.

NORTHEAST CONFERENCE – Bryant; CCSU (Central Connecticut State); Duquesne; Robert Morris; Sacred Heart; St. Francis (Pa.); Wagner.

OHIO VALLEY CONFERENCE – Austin Peay; Eastern Illinois; Eastern Kentucky; Jacksonville State; Murray State; Southeast Missouri State; Tennessee State; Tennessee Tech; UT-Martin.

PATRIOT LEAGUE – Bucknell; Colgate; Fordham; Georgetown; Holy Cross; Lafayette; Lehigh.

PIONEER LEAGUE – Butler; Campbell; Davidson; Dayton; Drake; Jacksonville; Marist; Morehead State; San Diego; Stetson; Valparaiso.

SOUTHERN CONFERENCE – Chattanooga; ETSU (East Tennessee State); Furman; Mercer; Samford; The Citadel; Western Carolina; Wofford; VMI.

SOUTHLAND CONFERENCE – Abilene Christian; Central Arkansas; Houston Baptist; Incarnate Word; Lamar; McNeese State; Nicholls State; Northwestern State; Sam Houston State; Southeastern Louisiana; Stephen F. Austin.

SOUTHWESTERN ATHLETIC CONFERENCE – East Division: Alabama A&M; Alabama State; Alcorn State; Jackson State; MVSU. West Division: Arkansas-Pine Bluff; Grambling State; Prairie View; Southern U.; Texas Southern.

INDEPENDENTS – Charlotte.

SPORTS

on the following pages.

cross-country Note hyphen, which is an exception to the practices of U.S. and international governing bodies for the sport.

Scoring for this track event is in minutes, seconds and tenths of a second. Extended to hundredths if available.

National AAU Championship
Cross-Country
Frank Shorter, Miami, 5:25.67; 2. Tom Coster, Los Angeles, 5:30.72

Adapt the **basic summary** to paragraph form under a dateline for a field of more than 10 competitors.

See **auto racing** and **bowling** for examples.

cross-country skiing Events include freestyle sprint, classical-style event; 10-kilometer race, also abbreviated 10km or 10K.

cycling Use the **basic summary** format.

d

day to day Hyphenate only as a compound modifier preceding a noun: *Aaron Rodgers will be evaluated on a day-to-day basis.* Otherwise, no hyphen: *Candace Parker was day to day with an injured right ankle.*

decathlon Summaries include time or distance performance, points earned in that event and the cumulative total of points earned in previous events.

Contestants are listed in the order of their overall point totals. First name and hometown (or nation) are included only on the first and last events on the first day of competition; on the last day, first names are included only in the first event and in the summary denoting final placings.

Use the **basic summary** format. Include all entrants in summaries of each of the 10 events.

An example for individual events:

Decathlon
(Group A)
100 – 1, Fred Dixon, Los Angeles, 10.8 seconds, 854 points. 2, Bruce Jenner, San Jose State, 11.09, 783.
Long jump – 1, Dixon 14-7 (7.34m), 889, 1,743. 2, Jenner, 23-6 (7.17m), 855, 1,638.
Decathlon final – Bruce Jenner, San Jose State, 8,524 points. 2, Fred Dixon, Los Angeles, 8,277.

discus The disc thrown in track and field events.

diving Use a **basic summary**.

e

esports Acceptable in all references to competitive multiplayer video gaming. Use alternate forms like *eSports* or *e-sports* only if part of a formal name, like an organization or arena. Capitalize at the start of sentences. Like other collective nouns that are plural in form, *esports* takes singular form when the group or quantity is regarded as a unit. *Some gamers are finding esports is a viable profession; nine esports were added to the competition.* It is also acceptable to refer to individual esports events as *games* or *events*.

event names See **sports sponsorship**.

f

fast break

FBS Abbreviation for *Football Bowl*

SPORTS

Subdivision. The higher level of NCAA Division I football. Formerly known as the I-A Division. *FBS* is used on second reference.

FBS (Football Bowl Subdivision) conferences: Atlantic Coast, Big 12, Big East, Big Ten, Conference USA, Mid-American, Mountain West, Pacific-12, Southeastern, Sun Belt, Western Athletic, Independents (Army, Navy, Notre Dame)

FCS Abbreviation for *Football Championship Subdivision.* The lower level of NCAA Division I football. Formerly known as the I-AA Division. *FCS* is used on second reference.

FCS (Football Championship Subdivision) conferences: Big Sky, Big South, Colonial Athletic Association, Great West, Ivy League, Mid-Eastern Athletic, Missouri Valley, Northeast, Ohio Valley, Patriot League, Pioneer League, Southern, Southland, Southwestern Athletic, Independents (North Carolina Central, Old Dominion, Savannah St.)

field goal

fencing Identify epee, foil and saber classes as: *men's individual foil, women's team foil,* etc.

Use **match summary** for early rounds of major events, for lesser dual meets and for tournaments.

Use **basic summary** for final results of major championships.

For major events, where competitors meet in a round-robin and are divided into pools, use this form:

Epee, first round (four qualify for semi-finals) Pool 1 – Joe Smith, Springfield, Mass., 4-1. Enrique Lopez, Chile, 3-2.

figure skating All jumps, spins and other moves are lowercase even if

named after someone: *double axel, triple flip-triple toe loop, triple lutz, triple salchow, sit spin, camel spin, death spiral.* Use a **basic summary**.

football The spellings of some frequently used words and phrases:

blitz (n., v.)	*out-of-bounds (adj.)*
cornerback	*pick six (n.) pick-six*
end line	*(adj)*
end zone	*pitchout (n.)*
fair catch	*place kick*
fourth-and-1 (adj.)	*place-kicker*
fullback	*play off (v.)*
goal line	*playoff (n., adj.)*
goal-line stand	*quarterback*
halfback	*runback (n.)*
handoff	*running back*
kick off (v.)	*split end*
kickoff (n., adj.)	*tailback*
left guard	*tight end*
linebacker	*touchback*
lineman	*touchdown*
line of scrimmage	*wideout*
nickel back	*wide receiver*
onside kick	*X's and O's*
out of bounds (adv.)	

NUMBERS: Use figures for yardage: *The 5-yard line, the 10-yard line, a 5-yard pass play, he plunged in from the 2, he ran 6 yards, a 7-yard gain; a fourth-and-2 play.*

Some other uses of numbers: *The final score was 21-14. The team won its fourth game in 10 starts. The team record is 4-5-1.*

PLAYOFFS: *wild-card round, wild card, divisional round, NFC championship game, AFC championship game.*

SUPER BOWL: Refer to the Super Bowl by the year of the game, not by Roman numeral. If a counter is needed, use cardinal numbers: *2017 Super Bowl* preferred over *Super Bowl 51;* do not use *Super Bowl LI.*

LEAGUE: *National Football League,*

SPORTS

or *NFL*.

TD Acceptable in all references to touchdown.

O-line, D-line Acceptable abbreviations for offensive line, defensive line.

STATISTICS: All football games, whether using the one- or two-point conversion, use the same summary style.

The visiting team always is listed first.

Field goals are measured from the point where the ball was kicked — not the line of scrimmage. The goal posts are 10 yards behind the goal lines. Include that distance.

Abbreviate team names to four letters or fewer on the scoring and statistical lines as illustrated.

The passing line shows, in order: completions-attempts-interceptions.

A sample agate package:

Jets-Giants Stats

N.Y. Jets	7	10	7	0_24
N.Y. Giants	0	7	14	14_35

First Quarter

NYJ_Rhodes 11 fumble return (Nugent kick), 8:36.

Second Quarter

NYG_Ward 8 run (Tynes kick), 10:54.

NYJ_B.Smith 16 pass from Pennington (Nugent kick), :33.

NYJ_FG Nugent 47, :00.

Third Quarter

NYG_Jacobs 19 run (Tynes kick), 11:17.

NYJ_L.Washington 98 kickoff return (Nugent kick), 11:03.

NYG_Shockey 13 pass from Manning (Tynes kick), :33.

Fourth Quarter

NYG_Burress 53 pass from Manning (Tynes kick), 7:52.

NYG_Ross 43 interception return (Tynes kick), 3:15.

A_78,809

	NYJ	NYG
First downs	16	21
Total Net Yards	277	374
Rushes-yards	22-55	39-188
Passing	222	186
Punt Returns	2-20	2-16
Kickoff Returns	5-200	3-62
Interceptions Ret.	1-1	3-68
Comp-Att-Int	21-36-3	13-25-1
Sacked-Yards Lost	1-7	0-0
Punts	4-45.3	5-46.8
Fumbles-Lost	0-0	1-1
Penalties-Yards	6-40	3-37

Time of Possession	26:15	33:45

INDIVIDUAL STATISTICS

RUSHING_N.Y. Jets, T.Jones 13-36, L.Washington 9-13, Pennington 2-6, B.Smith 1-0. N.Y. Giants, Jacobs 20-100, Ward 13-56, Manning 4-17, Droughns 2-15.

PASSING_N.Y. Jets, Pennington 21-36-3-229. N.Y. Giants, Manning 13-25-1-186.

RECEIVING_N.Y. Jets, Coles 8-89, Cotchery 4-31, Baker 3-52, B.Smith 3-44, T.Jones 2-14, L.Washington 1-(minus 1). N.Y. Giants, Burress 5-124, Ward 3-8, Shockey 2-33, Moss 1-10, Matthews 1-6, Hedgecock 1-5.

MISSED FIELD GOAL_N.Y. Jets, Nugent 42 (WL).

The rushing and receiving paragraph for individual leaders shows attempts and yardage gained. The passing paragraph shows completions, attempts, interceptions and total yards gained.

STANDINGS: The form for **professional standings**:

American Conference
East

	W	L	T	Pct.	PF	PA
y-New England	12	3	0	.800	464	321
N.Y. Jets	8	7	0	.533	360	344
Buffalo	6	9	0	.400	351	385

y-clinched division

The form for college **conference standings**:

Atlantic Coast Conference
Atlantic Division

	Conference			All games		
	W	L	PF	PA	W	L	PF	PA
Wake Forest	6	2	175	145	11	2	289	191
Boston College	5	3	189	133	9	3	313	180

In college conference standings, limit team names to nine letters or fewer. Abbreviate as necessary.

fractions In general, follow **fractions** entry in the Stylebook's main section, writing fractions with two numerals separated by a forward slash: *1/2, 2/3* or *3/4.* Do not use single fractional characters, which do not appear properly for some computer systems. For mixed numbers, separate the whole integer from the fraction with a space: *J.J. Watt had 2 1/2 sacks, Matt Cain pitched*

7 2/3 innings. In baseball, avoid using fractions to describe outings of less than an inning. Simply write: *Craig Kimbrel got the last two outs for the save.*

free agent, free agent signing

freestyle skiing
Events are *halfpipe, moguls, aerials.*

g

game day
Two words rather than one. *The commissioner said he expects a strong game day atmosphere in Mexico City.* Use one word only if part of a formal title or other name.

game plan

golf
Some frequently used terms and some definitions:
birdie, birdies, birdied One stroke under par.
bogey, bogeys One stroke over par. The past tense is *bogeyed.*
caddie
eagle, eagled Two strokes under par.
fairway
green fee A fee paid to play on a golf course. Not *greens fee. Green* refers to all parts of a golf course, not just the putting green.
hole-in-one
Masters, Masters Tournament No possessive. Use *the Masters* on second reference.
tee, tee off

NUMBERS: Some sample uses of numbers:
Use figures for handicaps: *He has a 3 handicap; a 3-handicap golfer, a handicap of 3 strokes; a 3-stroke*

handicap.
Use figures for par listings: *He had a par 5 to finish 2-up for the round, a par-4 hole; a 7-under-par 64, the par-3 seventh hole.*
Use figures for club ratings: *a 5-iron, a 7-iron shot, a 4-wood, 3-hybrid.*
Miscellaneous: *the first hole, a nine-hole course, the 10th hole, the back nine, the final 18, the third round. He won 3 and 2.*

ASSOCIATIONS: *Professional Golfers' Association of America* (note the apostrophe) or *PGA.* Headquarters is in Palm Beach Gardens, Florida. Members teach golf at golf shops and teaching facilities across the country.
The *PGA Tour* is a separate organization made up of competing professional golfers. Use *tour* (lowercase) on second reference.
The PGA conducts the PGA Championship, the Senior PGA Championship, and the Ryder Cup as well as other golf championships not associated with the PGA Tour.
The *United States Golf Association* or *USGA* is headquartered in Far Hills, New Jersey. It conducts the United States' national championships. These include the U.S. Open, the U.S. Women's Open, the U.S. Senior Open, 10 national amateur championships and the State Team Championships.
SUMMARIES — Stroke (Medal) Play: List scores in ascending order. Ties are listed in the order in which they were played. Use a dash before the final figure, hyphens between others.
On the first day, use the player's score for the first nine holes, a hyphen, the player's score for the second nine holes, a dash and the player's total for the day:
First round:

SPORTS

Lorena Ochoa	35-34 – 69
Se Ri Pak	36-33 – 69

On subsequent days, give the player's scores for each day, then the total for all rounds completed:

Second round:

Rory McIlroy	66-69 – 135
Tiger Woods	65-71 – 136

Final round, professional tournaments, including prize money:

Final Round:

(FedExCup points in parentheses)

J.B. Holmes (4,500), $1,080,000 68-65-66-70 – 269

Phil Mickelson (2,700), $648,000 68-68-67-67 – 270

Use hometowns only on national championship amateur tournaments. For tournaments including both amateurs and professionals, indicate amateurs with an "a-" before the name:

a-Stacey Lewis, The Woodlands, Texas 70-69 – 139

The form for cards:

Par out	444 343 544-35
Watson out	454 333 435-34
Nicklaus out	434 243 544-33
Par in	434 443 454-35 – 70
Watson in	434 342 443-31 – 65
Nicklaus in	433 443 453-33 – 66

SUMMARIES — Match Play: In the first example that follows, "and 2" means that the 17th and 18th hole were skipped because Rose had a three-hole lead with two to play. In the second, the match went 18 holes. In the third, a 19th and 20th hole were played because the golfers were tied after 18.

Justin Rose def. Charles Howell III, 3 and 2.

Paul Casey def. Shaun Micheel, 2 up.

Nick O'Hern def. Tiger Woods, 20 holes.

Grey Cup The Canadian Football League's championship game.

Group of Five Spell out the number when referring to the group of NCAA conferences that are not among the Power Five but play at the highest level of college football. The group includes the American Athletic Conference, Conference USA, the Mid-American Conference, the Mountain West and the Sun Belt Conference.

Gulfstream Park The racetrack.

gymnastics Scoring is by points. Identify events by name: Men: *floor exercise, vault, pommel horse, still rings, horizontal bar* (or *high bar*), *parallel bars.* Women: *floor exercise, vault, balance beam, uneven bars.*

Use a **basic summary**. Example:

Parallel Bars – 1, Joe Smith, Houston, 9.675 points. 2, Ed Jones, Albany, N.Y., 9.54. 3, Andy Brown, Los Angeles, 9.4.

h

halftime

handball Use a **match summary**.

heatstroke

hit-and-run (n. and adj.) **hit and run** (v.) *The coach told him to hit and run. He scored on a hit-and-run.*

hockey The spellings of some frequently used words:

blue line	*penalty box*
crease	*power play*
face off (v.)	*power-play goal*
faceoff (n., adj.)	*red line*
goalie	*short-handed*
goal line	*slap shot*
goal post	*two-on-one break*

hat trick Three goals in one game. *Natural hat trick* means three goals scored consecutively by one player in a game or period. *Gordie Howe hat trick* refers to a goal, an assist and a fight by one player. Use sparingly and with explanation.

Stanley Cup The trophy awarded

to the NHL champion, the Cup on second reference. It is a traveling trophy awarded to the league champion for one year and then passed to the next winner. Accordingly, it should never be plural: *Mark Messier won six Stanley Cup titles.*

LEAGUE: *National Hockey League* or *NHL.*

For NHL subdivisions: *the Central Division of the Western Conference, the division, the conference,* etc.

SCORING: A player's points total is equal to the sum of his goals and assists. The format G-A--P may be used on second reference and in notes. *Anze Kopitar led the Kings in scoring (29-41--70) en route to the team's 2014 Stanley Cup championship.*

RECORDS: In the NHL, a team's record is expressed in the Win-Loss-Overtime Loss format in which a win is worth 2 points, an overtime loss is worth 1 point and a loss is zero. In college and international play, records are written in the Win-Loss-Tie format. Unless there is a likelihood of confusion, no further explanation is necessary. *The Bruins went 54-19-9 last season to finish with 117 points, the most in the league. Rick DiPietro had an 18-5-5 record in college before going 130-138-28 with eight ties in his NHL career.*

PLAYOFFS: *Stanley Cup* or *NHL playoffs* until the final round, then *Stanley Cup Final.* Note singular *Final.* But *final* or *finals,* lowercase, when used alone.

SUMMARIES: The visiting team always is listed first in the score by periods.

Note that each goal is numbered

according to its sequence in the game.

The figure after the name of a scoring player shows his total goals for the season.

Names in parentheses are players credited with an assist on a goal.

The final figure in the listing of each goal is the number of minutes elapsed in the period when the goal was scored.

Senators-Flyers, Sums

Ottawa		1 1 1_3
Philadelphia		3 1 1_5

First Period_1, Ottawa, Neil 8 (Simpson, Havlat), 4:07. 2, Philadelphia, Lapointe 4 (Somik, Slaney), 10:41. 3, Philadelphia, Recchi 25 (LeClair, Handzus), 11:11. 4, Philadelphia, Markov 6 (Handzus, LeClair), 16:10. Penalty_Amonte, Phi (ob.-holding), 5:17.

Second Period_5, Philadelphia, Johnsson 9 (Zhamnov, Slaney), 5:22 (pp). 6, Ottawa, Chara 15 (Spezza, Schaefer), 14:32 (pp). Penalties_Fisher, Ott (tripping), 3:57; Simpson, Ott (holding), 6:06; Somik, Phi (slashing), 13:08; Fisher, Ott (high-sticking), 17:07.

Third Period_7, Philadelphia, Zhamnov 10 (Gagne, Amonte), 6:54. 8, Ottawa, Bondra 23 (Alfredsson, Schaefer), 19:47 (pp). Penalties_Alfredsson, Ott (rough) 9:03; Zhamnov, Phi (roughing), 9:03; Smolinski, Ott (roughing), 12:18; Sharp, Phi (roughing), 12:18; Simpson, Ott (slashing), 14:21; Philadelphia bench, served by Sharp (too many men), 15:57; Van Allen, Ott, major-double game misconduct (fighting), 18:15; Ray, Ott, major (fighting), 18:15; Lalime, Ott, minor-major-game misconduct (leaving the crease, fighting), 18:15; Simpson, Ott, major-game misconduct (fighting), 18:15 Brashear, Phi, double minor-double major-misconduct-game misconduct; (instigator, roughing, fighting), 18:15; Radivojevic, Phi, major-double game misconduct (fighting), 18:15; Esche, Phi, minor-major-double game misconduct (leaving the crease, fighting), 18:15; Markov, Phi, major-game misconduct (fighting), 18:15; Chara, Ott, minor-major-misconduct-game misconduct (instigator, fighting), 18:18; Neil, Ott, major (fighting), 18:18; Somik, Phi, major (fighting) 18:18; Timander, Phi, major (fighting), 18:18.

Shots on goal_Ottawa 7-9-10_26. Philadelphia 13-11-6_30.

Power-play Opportunities_Ottawa 2 of 6; Philadelphia 1 of 4.

Goalies_Ottawa, Lalime 22-19-7 (30 shots-25 saves), Prusek (18:15 third, 0-0). Philadelphia, Esche 18-7-5 (22-20), Burke (18:15 third, 4-3).

A_19,539 (19,519). T_2:39.

Referees_Marc Joannette, Dan Marouelli. Linesmen_Jonny Murray, Tim Nowak.

STANDINGS: The form:

Eastern Conference

Atlantic Division

	GP	W	L	OT	Pts.	GF	GA
Philadelphia	71	47	10	14	108	314	184

SPORTS

NY Islanders 71 45 17 9   99 310 192

home field (n.) **home-field** (adj.)

horse races Capitalize their formal names: *Kentucky Derby, Preakness, Belmont Stakes*, etc.

horse racing Some frequently used terms and their definitions:

across the board A bet on a horse to win, place and show. If the horse wins, the player collects three ways; if second, two ways; if third, one way.

also-ran Fails to finish in the money: first, second or third.

backstretch Straight portion of the far side of the racing surface between the turns.

Belmont Stakes First run in 1867, the Belmont is three weeks after the Preakness at Belmont Park on Long Island. The distance is 1 1/2 miles on a dirt track.

broodmare A female horse used for breeding.

bug boy An apprentice jockey, so-called because of the asterisk beside the individual's name in a program. It means that the jockey's mount gets a weight allowance.

colt A male thoroughbred horse 4 years old and under, or a standardbred 3 years of age.

daily double Wager calling for the selection of winners of two consecutive races, usually the first and second.

entry Two or more horses owned by same owner running as a single betting interest. In some states two or more horses trained by same person but having different owners also are coupled in betting.

exacta Wager in which the first two finishers in a race, in exact order of finish, must be picked.

filly A female horse under the age of 5.

furlong One-eighth of a mile. Race distances are given in furlongs up through seven furlongs (spell out the number), after that in miles, as in *one-mile, 1/1-16 miles.*

gelding A castrated male horse.

graded stakes A thoroughbred race that derives its name from the stake, or entry fee, that owners must pay. There are three levels, assigned by the American Graded Stakes Committee. *Grade 1* is the highest level, the most prestigious, based partly on purse but also on such considerations as previous winners and race history. The other levels are *Grade 2* and *Grade 3*. Do not use Roman numerals. *Grade 2*, not *Grade II*.

half-mile pole The pole on a racetrack that marks one-half mile from the finish. All distances are measured from the finish line, meaning that when a horse reaches the quarter pole, he is one-quarter mile from the finish.

horse A male horse over 4 years old.

Kentucky Derby Dating from 1875, the "Run for the Roses" is held on the first Saturday in May at Churchill Downs. The race distance is 1 1/4 miles on a dirt track.

length A measurement approximating the length of a horse, used to denote distance between horses in a race.

long shot (two words)

maiden A horse that has not won a race.

mare A female horse 5 years and older.

margin of victory Expressed in lengths of a horse, or other part of the horse's anatomy at the finish line: by a nose, by a neck, or in a photo finish: *Seattle Slew won by three lengths.*

SPORTS

mutuel field Not *mutual field*. Two or more horses, long shots, that have different owners and trainers. They are coupled as a single betting interest to give the field not more than 12 wagering interests. There cannot be more than 12 betting interests in a race. The bettor wins if either horse finishes in the money.

odds-on For a strong favorite to win, odds of less than even money: *Overanalyze was sent off as the 4-5 favorite.*

Preakness Stakes First run in 1873, the Preakness is two weeks after the Derby at Pimlico Race Course in Maryland. The distance is 1 3/16 miles on a dirt track.

race distances Under a mile expressed in furlongs: six furlongs (3/4ths of a mile); more than a mile in figures: 1 1/4 miles, 1 3/16 miles.

stallion A male horse used for breeding.

trifecta A wager picking the first three finishers in exact order.

Triple Crown Annual series of races for 3-year-old horses: the Kentucky Derby, the Preakness Stakes and Belmont Stakes.

winning times Expressed In minutes, seconds and hundredths of a second: *I'll Have Another's winning time in the Derby was 2:01.83.*

wire-to-wire A horse leading a race from start to finish.

horses' names Capitalize. See **animals** in main section.

i

IAAF Acceptable in first reference for the *International Association of Athletics Federations*. The full name of the organization, which is world track's governing body, should be given in full later in the story.

IC4A Abbreviation for *Intercollegiate Association of Amateur Athletes of America*. In general, spell out on first reference. A phrase such as *IC4A tournament* may be used on first reference, however, to avoid a cumbersome lead. If this is done, provide the full name later in the story.

indoor (adj.) **indoors** (adv.) *He plays indoor tennis. He went indoors.*

injuries Be precise in describing injuries. Instead of knee injury describe how a player hurt his or her left knee, right knee or both knees. Avoid medical jargon as much as possible and try to define injuries as simply as information allows without just parroting team or league language if vague.

j

judo Use the **basic summary** format by weight divisions for major tournaments; use the **match summary** for dual and lesser meets.

k

Kentucky Derby *The Derby* on second reference. An exception to normal second-reference practice. Plural is *Derbys* — an exception to Webster's New World College Dictionary.

See **capitalization** in main section.

knuckleball One word is an exception to Webster's New World College

SPORTS

Dictionary.

l

lacrosse Scoring in goals, worth one point each.

The playing field is 110 yards long. The goals are 80 yards apart, with 15 yards of playing area behind each goal.

A match consists of four 15-minute periods. Overtimes of varying lengths may be played to break a tie.

Adapt the summary format in **hockey**.

Ladies Professional Golf Association No apostrophe after *Ladies*. Use *LPGA Tour* in all references.

left hand (n.) **left-handed** (adj.) **left-hander** (n.)

m

marathon Use the formats illustrated in the **cross-country** and **track and field** entries.

match summary This format for summarizing sports events applies to individual contests such as tennis, match play golf, etc.

Give a competitor's name, followed either by a hometown or by a college or club affiliation. For competitors from outside the United States, a country name alone is sufficient in summaries sent for U.S. domestic use.

Rafael Nadal, Spain, def. Jarkko Nieminen, Finland, 7-5, 6-3, 6-1.

Serena Williams, United States, def. Nicole Vaidisova, Czech Republic, 6-3, 6-4.

Some other examples:

Billiards

Minnesota Fats, St. Paul, Minn., def. Pool Hall Duke, 150-141.

Handball

Bob Richards, Yale, def. Paul Johnson, Dartmouth, 21-18, 21-19.

Tom Brenna, Massachusetts, def. Bill Stevens, Michigan, 21-19, 17-21, 21-20.

MCL When describing injuries, acceptable in all references to the *medial cruciate ligament.*

midcourt, midfield

minicamp

mixed martial arts *MMA* acceptable in all references.

motor sports Two words unless different in the official name of an event.

motorboat racing Scoring may be posted in miles per hour, points or laps, depending on the competition.

In general, use the **basic summary** format. For some major events, adapt the basic summary to paragraph form under a dateline. See **auto racing** for an example.

motorcycle racing Follow the formats shown under **auto racing**.

MVP Acceptable in all references for most valuable player.

n

NASCAR Acceptable in all references for *National Association for Stock Car Auto Racing.*

NCAA Acceptable in all references for *National Collegiate Athletic Association.*

New Year's Six Spell out the number when referring to the group of college football bowl games that rotate the College Football Playoff semifinal games. The games include the Orange Bowl, the Fiesta Bowl, the Peach Bowl, the Cotton Bowl, the Rose Bowl and the Sugar Bowl and are typically played on or around New Year's Eve or New Year's Day.

nonconference No hyphen.

numerals In general, follow numerals entry in main section, spelling out one through nine in most uses and using figures for 10 or above. Use figures whenever preceding a unit of measure or points, as well as for team records or game numbers. Some sample uses of numbers: *first place; second quarter; 10th inning; a 3-pointer with 0.2 seconds left; 3-of-8 shooting; he made 3 of 4; the 6-foot-5 player; the 6-5 tight end; the 5-yard line; Game 6; The final score was 21-14. The team won its fourth game in 10 days. The team's record is 4-5-1. Johnson had seven catches for 188 yards. Stafford was 8 for 18 for 200 yards and two touchdowns.* See entries for individual sports for specialized uses, as well as entries for **fractions** and **time**.

O

offseason No hyphen.

Olympics, Olympic, Olympic Games, Olympian Always capitalized: Winter Olympics and Summer Olympics. Each is staged every four years, but two years apart. The next Winter Games are in 2018 in Pyeongchang, South Korea. Capitalize *Games* when attached to the host city or year: the *Pyeongchang Games* and the *2018 Games*. When standing alone, spell games lowercase: *The games open Feb. 9, 2018.* Note that AP style for Pyeongchang includes a lowercase C, not uppercase as sometimes used by organizers.

Names and acronyms:

IOC International Olympic Committee. Either is OK on first reference, but use full title in the story. IOC President Thomas Bach; the title is capitalized.

International sports federations. All Olympic sports are run by international federations. Avoid abbreviation IF; use international federation or governing body.

National Olympic committee. In news stories, avoid NOC and use national Olympic committees or national bodies. Abbreviations for U.S. Olympic Committee (USOC) and British Olympic Association (BOA) acceptable on second reference.

Sports in the 2018 Winter Olympics in Pyeongchang, South Korea, Feb. 9-25: biathlon, bobsled, curling, hockey, luge, figure skating, speedskating, short track speedskating, Alpine skiing, cross-country skiing, Nordic combined, freestyle skiing, ski jumping,skeleton, snowboarding.

Sports in the 2020 Summer Olympics in Tokyo, July 24-Aug. 9: archery, badminton, basketball, beach volleyball, boxing, canoe/ kayak, cycling, diving, equestrian, fencing, golf, gymnastics, handball, hockey, judo, pentathlon, rowing, rugby, sailing, shooting, soccer, swimming, synchronized swimming, table tennis, taekwondo, tennis, trampoline, triathlon, volleyball

SPORTS

(indoor), water polo, weightlifting, wrestling.

overtime, double overtime, triple overtime

over/under Use a slash, not a hyphen, for the gambling phrase that describes wagers on a total set by oddsmakers, such as total points in a game or total wins in a season. *Bettors drove the over/under down to 51 points for the Alabama-Clemson national title game after Nevada casinos initially set the total higher.*

p

pari-mutuel

performance-enhancing drugs Avoid using abbreviations *PEDs, PED* in stories and headlines unless in direct quotes. Whenever possible, be more specific in describing drugs considered performance-enhancing, including anabolic steroids, stimulants and human growth hormone.

play Use names for set plays or packages but do not automatically capitalize. Instead use standard AP style for the descriptive word: *wildcat package, West Coast offense, triangle offense.*

playoff (n.) play off (v.)

possessives See **apostrophes** in Punctuation Guide.

postgame, pregame

postseason, preseason No hyphen.

Power Five Spell out the number when referring to the group of conferences that generate the most athletic revenue in the NCAA and have some autonomy to create rules. The group includes the Big Ten, Big 12, Atlantic Coast Conference, Southeastern Conference and Pac-12.

r

racket Not *racquet*, for the light bat used in tennis and badminton.

racquetball Amateur games are played to 15 points in a best-of-three match. Professional matches are played to 11 points, unless it is necessary to continue until one player has a two-point spread. Most matches go to the winner of three of five games.
Use a **match summary**.

record Avoid the redundant *new record*.

right hand (n.) **right-hander** (n.) **right-handed** (adj.)

rodeo Use the **basic summary** format by classes, listing points.

rowing Scoring is in minutes, seconds and tenths of a second. Extend to hundredths if available.
Use a **basic summary**. An example, for a major event where qualifying heats are required:
Single Sculls Heats (first two in each heat qualify for Monday's quarterfinals, losers go to repechage Friday): Heat 1 — 1, Peter Smith, Australia, 4:24.7. 2. Etc. Heat 2 — 1, John Jones, Canada, 4:26.3. 72

runner-up, runners-up

S

school names A list of university names as used for sports is under **Major College Basketball Conferences, Major College Football Conferences and Football Championship Subdivision**. Use abbreviations on first reference only for well-known schools with unique acronyms that can easily stand alone without being mistaken for other universities. Abbreviations for other schools on second reference are permissible when the shorthand is commonly used and clear.

scores Use figures exclusively, placing a hyphen between the totals of the winning and losing teams: *The Reds defeated the Red Sox 4-3, the Giants scored a 12-6 football victory over the Cardinals, the golfer had a 5 on the first hole but finished with a 2-under-par score.*

Use a comma in this format: *Boston 6, Baltimore 5.*

See individual listings for each sport for further details.

series Best-of-seven series, best of seven. Hyphenate when used as a modifier with the number spelled out: *best-of-seven matchup.* On its own, no hyphens in the term: *The Red Sox and Phillies meet in a best of seven.*

shoestring catch

short-course swimming
Use *short-course* on second reference.

short-handed

skiing Identify events as: *men's downhill, women's slalom,* cross-country (note hyphen), etc. In ski jumping, note style where two jumps and points are posted.

Use a **basic summary**. Example:
90-meter special jumping – 1, Karl Schnabel, Austria, 320 and 318 feet, 234.8 points. 2, Toni Innauer, Austria, 377-299, 232.9. 3, Etc. Also; 27, Bob Smith, Hanover, N.H., 312-280, 201. 29

ski, skis, skier, skied, skiing Also: *ski jump, ski jumping.*

soccer Soccer is the preferred term in the United States, but around the world the sport is referred to as football.

The spellings of some frequently used words and phrases:

AFC Asian Football Confederation.

backpass A pass that a player makes back toward his own goal, to the goalkeeper on his team. The goalkeeper is unable to pick up the ball if the pass comes from the player's foot.

Bundesliga German League first division.

CAF Confederation Africaine de Football. Refer to it as the governing body of African soccer rather than spelling out French acronym.

Champions League

coach Also known as *manager* on British teams and *technical director* on some Latin American teams.

CONCACAF The Confederation of North, Central American and Caribbean Association Football.

Conference National Fifth-highest division of English soccer.

Conference North, Conference South Sixth-highest division of English soccer.

CONMEBOL Confederacion Sudamerica de Futbol. Refer to it as South America's governing body rather than spelling out Spanish acronym.

Copa America South American national team championship. Use the Spanish name, not *America Cup*.

Copa Libertadores South American club championship. Use the Spanish name, not *Liberators Cup*.

corner A kick taken from the corner of the field by an attacking player. Awarded when the ball has passed over the goal line after last touching a defensive player. The shot is taken from the corner nearest to where the ball went out.

defender Do not use *defenseman*.

Eredivisie Netherlands first division.

FA Cup Acceptable on first reference for The Football Association Cup.

false nine A forward player who appears to be playing as a team's main attacker but who drops back, closer to the midfield. It leaves the defense of the opposing team with no one to mark.

FIFA Federation Internationale de Football Association. *FIFA* acceptable on first reference. Refer to it as the international soccer governing body rather than spelling out French acronym.

forward or **striker**

4-2-3-1 formation The typical lineup of a modern-day soccer team, with four defenders, two deep midfielders, three attacking midfielders and a lone forward.

free kick A kick awarded to a team if its player is fouled by an opponent anywhere on the field except for the two penalty areas near the goals. The kick can either be direct (able to shoot straight into the net) or indirect (cannot shoot into the net).

friendly An exhibition game.

goalkeeper *Goalie* is acceptable. Do not use *goaltender*.

hand ball A foul awarded when a player deliberately touches the ball with his hand or any part of his arm.

La Liga Spanish first division.

League Championship Second-highest division of English soccer.

League Cup The No. 2 cup competition in England. Do not refer to as *Carling Cup*.

League One Third-highest division of English soccer.

League Two Fourth-highest division of English soccer.

Ligue 1 French first division.

midfielder

MLS Major League Soccer. *MLS* acceptable on first reference.

OFC Oceania Football Confederation.

offside Offside occurs when a player is nearer to his opponent's goal line than the second-to-last opponent when a ball is passed to him by a teammate. It does not apply if the player is in his half of the field. A free kick is awarded to the opposing team at the place where the offside happened.

one-two When a player passes the ball to a teammate, who then returns it to the same player with his first touch. A move usually done on the run, making it hard to defend against.

parking the bus A phrase used to describe how a team packs its defense to protect a lead or a draw.

penalty A refereeing decision awarded if a player from the defensive team fouls a player from the attacking team inside the penalty area. The attacking team chooses a player to have a free shot at goal from the penalty spot, 12 yards from the goal line.

penalty area Sometimes referred to as *penalty box*. Do not refer to solely as *box* on U.S. wires.

Premier League Top league in England. Also the name of the top league in Scotland. Note that

England, Scotland, Wales and Northern Ireland have separate national teams. Do not refer to *Premiership* or *Barclay's Premier League*.

red card Issued to a player who commits a serious foul or who has been issued with two yellow cards in the same game. The player must leave the field and cannot be replaced.

Serie A Italian League first division.

sideline *Touchline* for international wires.

throw-in When a player restarts play by throwing the ball back onto the pitch from its perimeter. The player must keep both feet on the ground and have both hands behind his head as he throws the ball.

"tiki-taka" A system of intricate, one-touch and rapid passing artistry developed by Spanish club Barcelona and eventually adopted by Spain's national soccer team.

total football The label given to a tactical theory, pioneered in international soccer by the Netherlands in the 1974 World Cup, in which any outfield player can take over the role of any of his teammates.

UEFA Union of European Football Associations.

wall A line of defensive players that protects the team's goalkeeper at a free kick.

World Cup Not *World Cup Finals*.

zonal marking A system of defending at corners where players from the defensive team mark areas rather than opposition players. An alternative to man-to-man marking.

In summaries and key lines for international wires, the home team is listed first; on U.S. wires, the visiting team is listed first.

SUMMARY:
At Saint-Denis, France
Italy 0 2 – 2
France 2 0 – 2
(France won 4-3 on penalty kicks)
First half – 1, France, Zidane 4 (Djorkaeff), 12th minute. 2, France, Deschamps (penalty kick), 45th minute.
Second half – 3, Italy, own goal, 88th minute. 4, Italy, R. Baggio 6 (D. Baggio), 90th minute.
First overtime – None.
Second overtime – None.
Penalty kicks – France 4 (Zidane G, Lizarazu NG, Trezeguet G, Henry G, Blanc G); Italy 3 (Baggio G, Albertini NG, Costacurta G, Vieri G, Di Biagio NG).
Yellow Cards – Italy, Del Piero, 26th minute; Bergomi, 28th; Rostacurta, 113th. France, Guivarc'h, 53rd minute; Deschamps, 63rd.
Referee – Dallas (Scotland). Linesmen – Grigorescu (Romania),
Warren (England).
A –77,000
Lineups
Italy – Gianluca Pagliuca; Giuseppe Bergomi, Fabio Cannavaro, Alessandro Costacurta, Paolo Maldini; Francesco Moriero, Dino Baggio (Demetrio Albertini, 52nd), Luigi Di Biagio, Gianluca Pessotto (Angelo Di Livio, 90th); Christian Vieri, Alessandro Del Piero (Roberto Baggio, 67th).
France – Fabien Barthez; Lilian Thuram, Laurent Blanc, Marcel Desailly, Bixente Lizarazu; Didier Deschamps, Emmanuel Petit, Zinedine Zidane, Christian Karembeu (Thierry Henry, 65th); Stephane Guivarc'h (David Trezeguet, 65th), Youri Djorkaeff.

Lineup order is goalkeepers, defenders, midfielders, forwards.

Separate the different positions with semicolons and the players within a position with commas.

STANDINGS:

Scores and standings move in separate files.

Schedule on world wires has times GMT instead of EST or EDT.

Schedule lists home teams first.
Sunday, Jan. 31
Bari vs. Lazio of Rome, 0130
Cagliari vs. Juventus of Turin, 0130
Fiorentina vs. Vicenza, 0130

Standings for international leagues have a different style: *GP* (games played), *W* (wins), *D* (draws), *L* (losses), *GF* (goals for),

GA (goals against) and *Pts* (points). Standings for Major League Soccer follow the same style as National Football League: *W* (wins), *L* (losses), *T* (ties), *Pts* (points), *GF* (goals for) and *GA* (goals against).

Spanish Soccer At A Glance

By The Associated Press

La Liga

Team	GP	W	D	L	GF	GA	Pts
Real Madrid	25	8	2	5	54	21	56
Barcelona	25	16	6	3	49	17	54
Villarreal	25	14	4	7	43	35	46

Major League Soccer

By The Associated Press

EASTERN CONFERENCE

	W	L	T	Pts	GF	GA
D.C. United	16	7	7	55	56	34
New England	14	8	8	50	51	43
New York	12	11	7	43	47	45

speedskating Scoring is in minutes, seconds and tenths of a second. Extend to hundredths if available. Use a **basic summary**.

sports editor Capitalize as a formal title before a name. See **titles** in main section.

sports sponsorship If the sponsor's name is part of the event name, such as Buick Open, use the name in the title. If there is a previously established name commonly accepted for the event — *Orange Bowl, Sugar Bowl* — use that name even if there currently is a corporate sponsor. *Orange Bowl*, not *Discover Orange Bowl*. However, mention the sponsor somewhere in the story or in a self-contained paragraph after a 3-em dash at the bottom of the story.

sports writer Two words. An exception to Webster's New World College Dictionary.

stadium, stadiums Capitalize only when part of a proper name: *Yankee Stadium.*

swimming Scoring is in minutes, if appropriate, seconds and tenths of a second. Extend to hundredths if available.

Most events are measured in metric units.

Identify events as *men's 4x100 relay, women's 100 backstroke,* etc.

See **track and field** for the style on relay teams and events where a record is broken

Use a **basic summary**. Examples, where qualifying heats are required:

100 Butterfly

Final

1, Michael Phelps, United States, 50.77. 2, Ian Crocker, United States, 50.82. 3, Albert Subirats, Venezuela, 51.82.

t

table tennis Do not use the synonym *pingpong* to refer to the sport. The trademark name is *Ping-Pong*.

tennis Some commonly used terms: *double-fault, double-faulted. Love, 15, 30, 40, deuce, advantage, tiebreaker*. Report set scores thusly: *Serena Williams defeated Madison Keys 7-6 (5), 6-2*. Indicate tiebreakers in parentheses after the set score, using only the loser's total points in the tiebreaker.

time Follow advice in **time sequences** and **times** entries in Stylebook's main section. Use common descriptions for time frames in sports events unless the exact time is truly relevant: *Midway through the second quarter rather than 6:28 into the second quarter*. Precise times down to the second are usually reserved for the final minute or two minutes of each period, depending on the sport.

titles Capitalize or use lowercase according to guidelines in **titles** in Stylebook's main section. Job descriptions, field positions and informal titles are lowercase: *coach John Calipari; forward Alex Morgan; general manager John Elway*. Some other informal titles commonly used in sports include *general manager, trainer, team doctor, manager, captain*.

Tommy John surgery Acceptable when referring to *ulnar collateral ligament reconstruction surgery* in the elbow, more commonly referred to as *surgery to repair a torn ligament in the elbow*.

track and field Scoring is in distance, time or height, depending on the event.

Most events are measured in metric units. For those meets that include feet, make sure the measurement is clearly stated, as in *men's 100-meter, women's 880-yard run*, etc.

For time events, spell out *minutes* and *seconds* on first reference, as in *3 minutes, 26.1 seconds*. Subsequent times in stories and all times in agate require a colon and decimal point: *3:26.1*. For a marathon, it would be *2 hours, 11 minutes, 5.01 seconds* on first reference then the form *2:11:5.01* for later listings.

In running events, the first event should be spelled out, as in *men's 100-meter*. Later references can be condensed to phrases such as *the 200, the 400*, etc.

For hurdle and relay events, the progression can be: *100-meter hurdles, 400 hurdles*, etc.

For field events — those that do not involve running — use these forms: *26 1/2* for *26 feet, one-half inch; 25-10 1/2* for *25 feet, 10 1/2 inches*, etc.

In general, use a **basic summary**. For the style when a record is broken, note the mile event in the example below. For the style in listing relay teams, note 4x400 meter relay.

60-yard dash – 1, Steve Williams, Florida TC, 6.0. 2, Hasley Crawford, Philadelphia Pioneer, 6.2. 3, Mike McFarland, Chicago TC, 6.23.

100 – 1, Steve Williams, Florida TC, 10.1. 2.

Mile – 1, Filbert Bayi, Tanzania, 3:55.1, meet record, old record 3:59, Jim Beatty, Los Angeles TC, Feb. 27, 1963. 2, Paul Cummings, Beverly Hills TC, 3:56.1.

Women's 880 – 1, Johanna Forman, Falmouth TC, 2:07.9.

4x400 relay – 1, St. John's (John Kennedy, Doug Johnson, Gary Gordon, Ordner Emanuel), 3:21.9. 2, Brown, 3:23.5. 3, Fordham, 3:24.1.

Team scoring – Chicago TC 32, Philadelphia Pioneer 29.

Where qualifying heats are required:

Men's 100-meter heats (first two in each heat qualify for Friday's semifinals): Heat 1 – 1, Steve Williams, Florida TC, 10.1.

U

Ultimate Fighting Championship *UFC* is acceptable in all references to the company that promotes mixed martial arts fights. Do not use *UFC* to refer to MMA fights held by other promoters. See **mixed martial arts**.

untracked Do not use this term for an athlete or team now performing well after a slow period. Use clearer expressions such as *back on track*.

up-tempo

USGA Acceptable in all references for the *United States Golf Association*.

V

versus Follow guidance under **versus** in the main section, spelling out the word in ordinary speech and writing, as well as in quotes: *Belichick's unconventional passing game versus Seattle's secondary.* It is permissible to abbreviate as *vs.* in short expressions: *Clippers vs. Warriors.*

volleyball In all indoor international, U.S. college and USA Volleyball games, each of the first four sets is won by the first team to score 25 points. If the match is tied in sets after the first four sets, a deciding fifth set will be played to 15 points. In all five sets, teams must win by two points without a cap on points.
   Use a **match summary**. Example:
U.S.-Women def. Korea 21-25, 25-16, 29-27, 16-25, 15-12.

volley, volleys

W

warmup (n.) **warm up** (v.)

water polo Scoring is by goals. List team scores. Example:
World Water Polo Championship
First Round
   United States 7, Canada 1
   Britain 5, France 3

water skiing Scoring is in points. Use a **basic summary**. Example:
World Water Skiing Championships
Men
   Overall – 1, George Jones, Canada, 1,987 points. 2, Phil Brown, Britain, 1,756.
   Slalom – 1, George Jones, Canada, 73 buoys (two rounds).

water sports

weight In agate listings, use abbreviations for some sports,

such as *lbs.* for pounds and *kg.* for kilograms.

weightlifting Use a **basic summary**. Example:
   ATHENS, Greece (AP) – Final results Saturday of the weightlifting event from the Summer Olympics:
   Men's 85kg
   1. Juan Jose Madrigal, Costa Rica, 472.5 kg.
   2. Rampa Mosweu, Botswana, 470.0.

wild card (n.) **wild-card** (adj.)

World Series Or *the Series* on second reference. A rare exception to the general principles under **capitalization**.

wrestling Identify events by weight division.

y

yachting Use a **basic summary**, identifying events by classes.

yard Equal to 3 feet.
   The metric equivalent is approximately 0.91 meter.
   To convert to meters, multiply by 0.91 (5 yards x 0.91 = 4.55 meters).
   See **foot**; **meter**; and **distances**.

yard lines Use figures to indicate the dividing lines on a football field and distance traveled: *40-yard line, he plunged in from the 2, he ran 6 yards, a 7-yard gain.*

yearling An animal 1 year old or in its second year. The birthdays of all horses arbitrarily are set at Jan. 1. On that date, any foal born in the preceding year is considered 1 year old.

Z

zone, zone defense

Food

Common Culinary Conversions
1 tablespoon = 3 teaspoons
2 tablespoons = 1 fluid ounce
1 cup = 16 tablespoons = 8 fluid ounces
1 pint = 2 cups = 16 fluid ounces
1 quart = 4 cups = 32 fluid ounces
1 pound = 16 ounces
1 stick butter = 1/2 cup = 8 tablespoons = 4 ounces

AP Recipe Style
Recipe guidelines. Always use figures. See **fractions**.

Break out recipes in list and instruction format. Do not write as regular text. Use figures for all quantities in recipes. Do not use abbreviations. Spell out *teaspoon, tablespoon*, etc.

Following is the format for recipes:
— The title of the recipe is capitalized.
— Start to finish time goes below the title, noting estimate for active time in parentheses if hands-off cooking time is significantly longer than active prep time.
— Savory recipes that call for measured amounts of salt should always refer to kosher salt, *1 1/2 teaspoons kosher salt*. Recipes for baked goods should call for table salt, *2 teaspoons salt*, as table salt is the preferred ingredient for baking. Recipes that do not specify volume can simply call for salt, *salt and ground black pepper*.
— The number of servings appears next.
— List ingredients in the order used and spell out all measurements. When appropriate, unusual ingredients can be clarified within the list, *ghee (clarified butter)*.
— Use numerals for all measurements, times and oven settings. Exception: When two numbers follow one another, write out the first for clarity, *two 12-ounce cans*.
— Instructions for making the recipe follow, and should be written in short, easy-to-digest paragraphs.
— When an oven is used, *Heat the oven to 350 F*, should be the first line of the method (unless the oven is not used until more than 30 minutes after the start of the recipe).
— Begin sentences with equipment and technique, rather than ingredients. *In a medium saucepan over low heat, whisk together the butter and sugar.*
— Nutrition information, if available, follows the method.
— If the recipe source is not the bylined writer of the story, the source should

appear at the bottom in parentheses:

(Recipe from John Smith's "Book of Recipes," Recipe Publishers, 2007.)
(Recipe from January 2007 issue of Gourmet.)
(Recipe from epicurious.com.)
(Recipe from the January issue of Gourmet, as listed at epicurious.com.)
(Recipe from AP Food Editor J.M. Hirsch)
(Recipe adapted from John Smith's "Book of Recipes," Recipe Publishers, 2007)

PIZZA WITH RAINBOW CHARD, GOAT CHEESE AND EGG
Start to finish: 30 minutes
Servings: 4
1 tablespoon olive oil
1 bunch rainbow chard, chopped
1 medium yellow onion, diced
1/4 teaspoon red pepper flakes
2 cloves garlic, minced
20-ounce ball prepared pizza dough, room temperature
4 ounces (about 8 slices) prosciutto, finely chopped
8-ounce log chevre (fresh goat cheese)
4 large eggs
Heat the oven to 400 F. Lightly spritz 2 baking sheets with cooking spray.

In a large skillet over medium-high, heat the oil. Add the chard, onion, red pepper flakes and garlic. Saute until the chard is wilted, about 8 minutes. Set aside.

Divide the dough into 4 pieces. On a lightly floured surface, roll out each to the size of a dinner plate. Place 2 rounds of dough on each baking sheet. Top each piece of dough with a quarter of the chard mixture, spreading it evenly.

Top with the prosciutto, then crumble goat cheese over each pizza.

Bake for 12 minutes, or until the crust is lightly puffed, but not browned. Crack an egg into the center of each pizza, then bake for another 12 minutes, or until the whites are cooked but the yolks are still runny. Serve immediately.

Nutrition information per serving: 650 calories; 240 calories from fat (37 percent of total calories); 27 g fat (11 g saturated; 0 g trans fats); 265 mg cholesterol; 2,260 mg sodium; 66 g carbohydrate; 4 g fiber; 2 g sugar; 33 g protein.

(Recipe from AP Food Editor J.M. Hirsch)

See the **food** entry in the main section for guidelines on when to capitalize the names of foods.

FOOD

a

absinthe A bitter green liqueur made from wormwood.

adobo sauce A spicy red sauce made from chilies, herbs and vinegar that is common to Mexican cooking.

agave A honeylike syrup made from succulent plants.

ahi Hawaiian term for several varieties of tuna, especially *yellowfin* and *bigeye*. The terms *ahi*, *ahi tuna*, *yellowfin tuna* and *bigeye tuna* are acceptable. Bigeye tuna are generally caught in deeper water than yellowfin and typically have a higher fat content.

aioli A garlic mayonnaise, an emulsification of olive oil, egg yolks and lemon juice.

a la carte A restaurant menu in which each item is individually priced.

a la mode In the U.S., a dessert served with ice cream, often pies or cakes.

al dente Italian for *to the tooth*, refers to pasta cooked until tender, but slightly firm.

Alfredo A creamy Italian sauce made with butter and Parmesan cheese; *fettuccine Alfredo*.

alfresco A meal eaten outside.

all-purpose flour Preferred term for *white wheat flour*.

amaretti An Italian macaroon made with almonds rather than coconut.

amaretto Almond liqueur.

amaro Italian herbal liqueur usually drunk as an after-dinner drink to aid digestion. Amari (the plural) include Campari, Fernet-Branca and Aperol and other liqueurs.

amuse-bouche French, a bite-sized dish served at restaurants before the meal, usually free.

andouille sausage

angel food cake

angel hair pasta A thin pasta resembling spaghetti.

angostura bitters A cocktail flavoring made from the bark of a South American tree.

Angus Angus cattle comprises two breeds of hornless cattle from the original Scottish Aberdeen stock, Black Angus and Red Angus. Black is the predominant color. Black Angus is the most popular breed for beef in the U.S.

antipasto Italian for *hors d'oeuvre* or *appetizer*.

apples Most varieties are capitalized, including *Cortland, Golden Delicious, Granny Smith, Honeycrisp* and *McIntosh*.

applesauce

arborio rice A short-grain, starchy Italian variety of white rice, used in risotto.

arctic char A trout, native to Alaska and northern Canada.

artisanal Foods and drinks produced in small batches often using traditional techniques and local ingredients.

Asiago cheese A sharp, aged cow's milk cheese from Italy's Veneto region.

avocado toast Toast spread with mashed avocado.

b

baba ghanoush A Middle Eastern dish of pureed roasted eggplant with tahini, lemon juice and garlic.

baby back ribs

Baileys A brand name cream-based liqueur.

baked Alaska A cake topped with ice cream and meringue that is briefly baked.

baker's dozen 13, not 12.

baking sheet Preferred to *cookie sheet*.

baklava A Middle Eastern pastry of layered phyllo dough, honey and chopped nuts.

bananas Foster A dessert of sauteed bananas served with rum and vanilla ice cream. Created during the 1950s at Brennan's Restaurant in New Orleans. Named for a customer.

banh mi Both Vietnamese bread and, in the U.S., a Vietnamese-style sandwich.

barbecue The verb refers to the cooking of foods (usually meat) over flame or hot coals. As a noun, can be both the meat cooked in this manner or the fire pit (grill). Not *barbeque, Bar-B-Q* or *BBQ*.

basmati rice A long-grain aromatic rice.

bearnaise sauce A French sauce made from reduced wine, vinegar, tarragon, shallots, egg yolks and butter.

Beaujolais A fruity wine from France. *Beaujolais Nouveau* is a young version.

bechamel French milk-based savory sauce.

beef stroganoff

beef Wellington A fillet of beef wrapped and roasted in pastry.

Belgian waffle A waffle with deep indentations made in a special waffle maker.

Bellini A cocktail made from sparkling wine and peach juice.

Benedictine French liqueur made with herbs and spices.

beurre blanc A creamy sauce, often for seafood, made from butter, shallots and lemon juice.

bialy, bialys A Jewish-American yeast roll that is large, round and chewy, topped with onions.

bibb lettuce A variety of butter lettuce.

Bing cherries A variety of sweet cherries.

FOOD

bisque A rich, thick soup often made from seafood and cream.

black-eyed pea A small beige bean with a black dot.

Black Forest cake A German layered chocolate cake with cherries and whipped cream.

blackstrap molasses

blanch To briefly cook by submerging in boiling water, then cooling in cold water.

bloody mary A cocktail of tomato juice, vodka, Worcestershire sauce and hot sauce.

BLT Acceptable on first reference for a *bacon, lettuce and tomato sandwich.*

blue cheese Not *bleu.*

boilermaker Cocktail of whiskey in beer, or whiskey with a beer chaser.

bok choy A leafy vegetable, also called *pak choi* or *Chinese white cabbage.*

bologna The lunch meat.

Bolognese A thick Italian meat sauce made from beef or veal and vegetables, often served over pasta, also called *ragu.*

bonbon A filled chocolate candy.

bone broth stock made with roasted bones.

Bordeaux Red or white wines made in France's Bordeaux region.

borscht A Russian or Polish soup made from beets.

Boston brown bread A steamed bread made from rye and wheat flours, cornmeal and molasses.

Boston cream pie Not a pie, two layers of spongecake with custard filling, usually dusted with powdered sugar or chocolate glaze.

Boston lettuce

bouillabaisse French seafood stew.

bourbon An American whiskey named for Kentucky's Bourbon County.

bow tie pasta Also called *farfalle.*

brandy A spirit distilled from wine or fermented fruit.

Brazil nut

bread-and-butter pickles

breadbox

breadcrumb

breadstick

brie A soft, mold-ripened cow's milk cheese.

brioche A rich French yeast bread made with butter and eggs.

broccoli

broccoli raab

Broccolini A trademark for a broccoli hybrid.

Brussels sprouts

Buffalo wings Also: *Buffalo sauce.*

FOOD

bulgur wheat A wheat that has been steamed, dried and crushed.

bulkie roll Bulkie roll, also called kaiser roll, Vienna roll or a hard roll, is popular in the United States and Canada. Often used as a bun for sandwiches. *Bulkie roll* is used in New England.

Bundt pan A trademark for a fluted cake pan, also called a *tube pan*.

Burgundy Red or white wines, typically dry, produce in France's Burgundy region.

burrito, burritos A Mexican dish in which a flour tortilla is wrapped around meat, vegetables, cheese or a combination of ingredients, then heated.

busboy

buttercream A variety of frosting.

butterfat The fatty part of milk, from which butter is made.

C

cabernet sauvignon A grape variety used to produce many of the top red wines in California and Bordeaux. The wines tend to be full-bodied, fruity and boldly flavored.

cactus pear A pear-shaped fruit of a cactus, also *prickly pear*.

Caesar salad A salad of greens, cheese, croutons and anchovies.

caipirinha A Brazilian cocktail.

calamari Italian for *squid*.

California roll An American variety of rolled sushi (called *maki*), now popular worldwide. Generally contains avocado, crab and vegetables.

Calvados A French brandy made from apple cider.

Camembert A soft, creamy, partly ripened cheese.

Campari A bitter Italian liqueur.

Canadian bacon A lean smoked pork, called *back bacon* in Canada.

canape, canapes Hors d'oeuvres made from small pieces of bread or crackers topped with cheese, meat or vegetables.

cannellini A white bean common in Italian dishes.

cannelloni A large tubular pasta, often stuffed and baked.

cannoli A tube-shaped Italian pastry fried and filled with sweetened ricotta cheese and other fillings.

cantaloupe

cappuccino An espresso topped with the foam from steamed milk.

carnaroli rice An Italian variety of rice similar to arborio, often used in risotto.

cast-iron (adj.) **cast iron** (n.) A *cast-iron pot*, but the pot is made from *cast iron*.

catfish

FOOD

cava A Spanish sparkling wine.

ceviche Seafood marinated in an acidic liquid.

Chablis Dry white wine named for Chablis, France.

challah Jewish braided bread.

Champagne A sparkling wine from the Champagne region of France. If made elsewhere, call it *sparkling wine*.

chardonnay A grape variety used in white wines such as Champagne and white Burgundy. Chardonnays tend to be dry with buttery, creamy notes.

cheddar

cheesecloth

cheesemaker

chevre A soft goat cheese.

Chianti A bold, dry red wine made in the Chianti region of Italy.

chicken cordon bleu

chicken-fried steak

chicken Kiev A dish in which boneless, flattened chicken breasts are rolled, breaded and fried.

chicken Marsala Chicken cooked with mushrooms and Marsala wine.

chickpea Preferred to *garbanzo bean*.

chiffonade To slice vegetables very thinly.

chili, chiles Any of a variety of spicy peppers or the sauces or gravies derived from them. The meat- and/or bean-based dish is chili.

chimichurri Sauce typically containing parsley, garlic, vinegar, olive oil and chili pepper.

china The tableware.

chipotle A dried, smoked jalapeno pepper, often packed in adobo sauce.

chocolate Bittersweet, dark, milk, semisweet, white.

chopsticks

chorizo A type of pork sausage that can be spicy or sweet.

churros Fried pastries covered in cinnamon sugar and sometimes dipped in chocolate sauce. Popular in Latin America.

ciabatta A long, wide loaf of Italian bread.

Cobb salad Made famous by Hollywood's Brown Derby Restaurant in the 1920s. It typically consists of finely chopped chicken or turkey, bacon, hard-cooked eggs, tomatoes, avocado, scallions, watercress, cheddar cheese and lettuce tossed with a vinaigrette dressing and topped with a large portion of crumbled Roquefort or other blue cheese.

Coca-Cola, Coke, Coca-Cola Co.

coffeecake

cognac A variety of French brandy.

Cointreau A sweet, orange-flavored

liqueur.

colander *Strainer* is preferred.

colby cheese A cow's milk cheese similar to cheddar.

Collins glass

confit Salt-cured meat, usually duck and goose.

cooking spray Use for nonstick cooking spray.

corkscrew

corn dog

corn flour

Cornish hen

corn on the cob

cornbread

cornflakes

cornmeal

cornstarch

couscous A North African dish made from crushed semolina.

cow's milk cheese

crabcake

crabmeat

cracklings The crisped skin from cooked pork.

craft brewery A small, independent beer producer. Preferred term for *microbrewery*.

crawfish Not *crayfish*. An exception to Webster's New World College Dictionary based on the dominant spelling in Louisiana, where it is a popular delicacy.

creme brulee A custard served topped with a crust of caramelized sugar.

creme fraiche A thickened cream similar in texture to Greek yogurt.

Crisco A trademark for a brand of vegetable shortening.

Crock-Pot A brand name, not to be used unless referencing that brand, otherwise *slow cooker*.

cupful, cupfuls

d

Danish pastry A flaky pastry, usually filled with fruit or cheese.

deep-dish pizza.

deep-fry, deep-fried *Deep-fried pickles.*

demi-glace A rich, beef stock-based sauce seasoned with Madeira or sherry.

Dijon mustard

dimensions Pan dimensions are expressed as: *a 9-by-12-inch pan.*

dolmades Stuffed grape leaves.

double boiler A pair of saucepans, one filled with water and heated, the other set above it for gentle cooking.

FOOD

doughnut

draft beer Not draught.

Drambuie A trademark for a brand of Scottish liqueur.

dredge A cooking technique in which food is lightly coated with flour or another ingredient before frying.

dressing, stuffing *Dressing* is cooked outside of the bird; *stuffing* is cooked inside. Use of the terms also varies regionally in the U.S., with one preferred over the other in some places regardless of how it's prepared.

drive-thru

Dr Pepper No period after *Dr*

dry-roasted

dulce de leche A blend of cooked milk and sugar resembling caramel.

Dungeness crab A Pacific coast crab found from Alaska to Mexico.

Dutch oven A large, lidded heavy pot.

e

edamame Soybeans, often served steamed in the pod.

egg foo young Chinese-American dish of bean sprouts, eggs and sometimes meat or seafood, fried into large patties.

eggnog Thick holiday drink made from eggs, milk, cream and sometimes liquor.

egg rolls Chinese-American dish in which fillings are rolled in a wonton or other wrapper, then fried or sometimes steamed or baked.

eggs Benedict A poached egg served with ham over an English muffin with hollandaise sauce. In eggs Florentine, spinach is substituted for the ham.

eggshell

Emmenthal Also *Emmenthaler*. A mild, hard Swiss cheese.

enchilada, enchiladas A Mexican dish in which a soft corn tortilla is wrapped around meat or other fillings. Served hot and topped with salsa and cheese.

endive A bitter green. Two most common varieties are Belgian, which resembles small, oval cabbages, and curly, which has frilly, loose leaves.

English muffin

entree

escargot French for *snail*. Generally refers to the dish of cooked snails served with melted butter.

escarole A variety of endive with a mild flavor.

espresso The coffee is *espresso*, not *expresso*.

extra-virgin olive oil

f

fair trade

FOOD

fajita, fajitas A Mexican dish in which warm flour tortillas are wrapped around strips of marinated and grilled meat.

falafel A Middle Eastern fritter made from ground chickpeas.

farmers market No apostrophe.

farmstead Generally used to describe a cheese produced solely from the milk of one farm.

farm-to-table A popular restaurant trend in which ingredients are sourced locally.

fettuccine A wide, flat pasta. Often confused with *linguine*, which is narrower.

filet mignon An extremely tender boneless cut of beef from the tenderloin. Usually cut 1 to 2 inches thick and cooked by searing briefly on the stove and finished in the oven cr under a broiler.

Filet-O-Fish The fish sandwich served at McDonald's.

fillet As a noun, a boneless cut of fish or meat. As a verb, to cut or prepare as a fillet.

five-spice powder A Chinese spice blend.

flatbread

flat iron steak

flaxseed

Fluffernutter A trademarked name for a sandwich made with peanut butter and Marshmallow Fluff.

focaccia A flat Italian yeast bread drizzled with olive oil and salt, sometimes rosemary.

foie gras The fatty liver of a force-fed goose or duck, often made into pate.

foil Use for *tin foil* or *aluminum foil*.

fontina cheese Also called fontina Val d'Aosta after the Italian valley from which it originated. It is a semi-firm and creamy cow's milk cheese. It has a mild, nutty flavor.

foodie Slang for a person with a strong interest in good food.

foodways Refers to a set of food traditions.

fra diavolo An Italian dish with a spicy tomato sauce.

frankfurter

free-range (adj.)

french To trim the meat from the end of a bone, or to cut thin strips (often string beans).

French bread

French dressing

french fries Lowercase *french* because it refers to the style of cut, not the nation.

French toast

frisee A small, bitter salad green.

frittata Italian dish similar to an omelet, typically made with eggs, vegetables, cheese and/or meat.

FOOD

fruitcake

g

ganache A rich filling or icing made from chocolate and heavy cream.

garam masala Indian spice blend.

garbanzo bean The preferred term is *chickpea*.

gazpacho Chilled vegetable soup.

gelato An Italian ice cream made from whole milk. Generally denser than American ice cream.

General Tso's chicken

ghee A clarified butter used in Indian cooking.

ginger Distinguish ground (dry) or fresh (usually grated or minced).

gingerbread

gluten-free Describes foods without wheat, barley or rye grain, the three groups of whole grains that naturally contain the protein *gluten*. Usage: *He ordered gluten-free pizza; the pizza is gluten free.*

GMO Genetically modified organism. *GMO* is acceptable on second reference. Refers to food grown from seeds that are genetically engineered in a laboratory.

gnocchi Italian dumpling, often made with potatoes.

gochujang Fermented Korean chili paste.

Gorgonzola cheese An Italian blue cheese.

Gouda A Dutch cow's milk cheese.

gourmand, gourmet A *gourmand* is a person who likes good food and tends to eat to excess; a *glutton*. A *gourmet* is a person who likes fine food and is an excellent judge of food and drink.

graham crackers Crackers made from a finely ground whole-wheat flour named for Sylvester Graham, a U.S. dietary reformer.

grain bowl An all-in-one meal made in a bowl. Includes rice, quinoa, barley, couscous, farro or other grains as a base. Other ingredients can include protein, raw or cooked vegetables, legumes, and a sauce.

grand cru wines Wines produced from a specialized group of high-end French vineyards.

Grand Marnier An orange liqueur.

Grape-Nuts

grapeseed oil

Greek salad A cold salad typically made with tomatoes, cucumbers, onion, feta cheese and olives.

grits Ground hominy, eaten as a porridge. The word normally takes plural verbs and pronouns.

Gruyere cheese A rich Swiss cheese.

h

half-and-half A blend of equal parts cream and milk.

hard-boil (v.) **hard-boiled** (adj.)

harissa North African red pepper sauce.

Hass avocado Dominant avocado sold in the U.S.

havarti cheese A semisoft Danish cheese.

hazelnut Preferred to *filbert*.

heatproof

herbes de Provence An herb blend from southern France.

Hereford A breed of hardy red-coated beef cattle of English origin with white faces and markings. Also raised in North and South America, Australia and New Zealand.

hibachi

hoisin sauce A dark, savory Chinese sauce.

hollandaise A creamy sauce made from butter, egg yolks and lemon juice.

horchata Spanish and Mexican drink made by steeping nuts, seeds and grains, and served cool.

hors d'oeuvre, hors d'oeuvres

horseradish

hot dog

hot plate

hot sauce A generic term for hot pepper-based sauces, such as *Tabasco*.

huitlacoche Also called *corn smut*. A fungus that grows on corn. Considered a delicacy of Mexican cuisine, it has a smoky-sweet flavor.

hummus

i

icebox pie Pie with a filling that is chilled or frozen, rather than baked.

icing Use to describe sugar decorations applied to cookies; use *frosting* for cupcakes and cakes. Both cookies and cakes can be *glazed* (drizzled with a thin sugar mixture).

IHOP Restaurants franchised and run by International House of Pancakes LLC and its affiliates. International House of Pancakes LLC is a subsidiary of DineEquity Inc.

India pale ale A hoppy beer style within the broader category of pale ale. *IPA* is acceptable on second reference.

Instant Pot Brand name for a combined pressure cooker and slow cooker. Users often refer to it as an *InstaPot*.

Irish coffee A coffee blended with Irish whiskey and topped with whipped cream.

FOOD

j

Jamaican jerk chicken Chicken seasoned with a blend of chilies and spices, then grilled.

Jamaica rum Not *Jamaican rum*.

Jarlsberg cheese A buttery cheese from Norway.

jasmine rice An aromatic rice from Thailand, similar to basmati.

Jell-O

jellyroll

jigger Also called a shot or shot glass, about 1 ½ fluid ounces.

k

kaiser roll A large round roll with a hard crust.

Kalamata olive A black Greek olive.

kamut Considered an "ancient grain," *kamut* is an older, high-protein variety of wheat.

kebabs

ketchup Not catchup or catsup.

Key lime

kielbasa A smoked Polish sausage.

kimchi Korean pickled vegetables.

Kobe beef Kobe, a city, is the capital of Japan's Hyogo prefecture. Only beef from cattle raised in Hyogo prefecture can be called Kobe.

kombucha A fermented, slightly effervescent tea beverage. Kombucha can contain trace amounts of alcohol.

Kool-Aid

kosher food Food that has been produced or prepared according to Jewish dietary laws.

kosher salt A coarse, additive-free salt. 1 1/4 teaspoons kosher salt = 1 teaspoon table salt.

l

ladyfinger A finger-shaped cookie. Can be spongy or crisp.

lager A beer aged at a low temperature after brewing.

latke Fried pancake, often made of potatoes.

latte An espresso mixed with steamed milk.

leavener An ingredient, such as baking powder, that causes baked goods to rise or have a lighter texture.

lemon grass A Thai herb.

Limburger cheese

liqueur A sweetened, flavored spirit.

liquor An alcoholic drink, usually distilled.

locavore The preferred term for a person who strives to eat locally produced foods. Also, *locavorism*: a movement that embraces food grown nearby, offering the promise of better nutrition and being less burdensome to the environment.

London broil A boneless beef steak that is marinated, broiled, then served thinly sliced.

low-fat

m

M&M's

macaron A French, often brightly colored sandwich cookie made from egg whites, sugar and almond powder, typically filled with jam or ganache.

macaroon A soft, chewy cookie typically made from coconut, egg whites and sugar, often confused with the *macaron*.

Madeira A fortified wine.

madeleine A small, shell-shaped French cake.

mai tai Rum and juice cocktail.

manchego cheese A Spanish sheep's milk cheese.

mandarin orange

mandoline A vegetable slicer.

Manhattan cocktail A classic cocktail made from rye whiskey or bourbon.

Manhattan clam chowder A tomato-based soup of clams.

maraschino cherries

Marsala An Italian fortified wine.

Marshmallow Fluff A trademark. Use *marshmallow spread* unless specifically referring to the *Marshmallow Fluff* brand.

mascarpone cheese A thick spreadable cream from Italy, similar to clotted cream.

Mason jar Glass jar used to preserve food. Named for John Mason, who patented a system of jars and self-sealing zinc lids in 1858. *Canning jar* is preferred.

matcha Japanese-style powder of specially grown and processed green tea leaves.

matzo Unleavened Jewish bread.

McDonald's Corp.

meatball

meatloaf

medium-rare

medjool dates A large, soft variety of date fruit.

melon baller

meringue A dessert made from egg whites and sugar beaten until stiff, then usually baked.

merlot A grape variety and a wine. The wines are similar to cabernet sauvignon, but milder.

mesclun A popular salad greens mix.

Meyer lemon

FOOD

mezcal Clear liquor from Mexico made from a variety of agave plants.

meze Middle Eastern appetizers.

microgreens

milkshake

mise en place A French term for having ingredients prepared before making a recipe.

mixologist A person who specializes in making high-end cocktails.

mole Mexican sauce.

molecular gastronomy An often deconstructive approach to cooking in which science and laboratory approaches and equipment are used in the kitchen. Also known as *modernist cuisine*.

Monterey Jack cheese A mild semisoft cheese, also called jack cheese.

Mornay sauce A *bechamel* to which cheese has been added.

MSG Acceptable on first reference for *monosodium glutamate*.

Muenster cheese A mild semisoft cheese.

multicooker An electric kitchen appliance with a timer that typically simmers, boils, fries, roasts, stews, steams and browns food.

mushrooms Generally not capitalized, as in *button, chanterelle, cremini, morel, porcini, portobello* and *shiitake*.

mustard Use for the condiment. Use *dry mustard* for powdered form.

n

naan An Indian flatbread.

napa cabbage

napoleon A dessert made with crisp layers of puff pastry spread with pastry creme and either glazed with a thin icing or dusted with powdered sugar.

navel orange A seedless orange so named because it has a small depression, like a navel.

Negroni Cocktail of gin, Campari and sweet vermouth.

Neufchatel cheese A soft cow's milk cheese, similar to cream cheese.

New England clam chowder A dairy-based soup of clams.

non-GMO Non-genetically modified organisms.

nonstick

o

omelet

onions *Spanish onion*, also called *yellow onion*; *red onion*, also called *Italian onion*; *Vidalia onion*.

open-faced sandwich

orecchiette A small pasta shaped like a disk.

Oreo A trademark for a brand of chocolate sandwich cookie held together by a white filling.

ovenproof Also *oven-safe*.

p

pad thai A Thai noodle dish.

paella Spanish rice dish.

palate, palette A *palate* refers to the roof of the mouth and the sense of taste (*to have a sophisticated palate*); *palette* is the term for an artist's paint board.

paleo Short for Paleolithic diet. A diet composed of grass-fed meat, fish and seafood, eggs, nuts, fresh vegetables and fruit, healthy oils, and nuts and seeds. Those who follow a paleo diet avoid legumes, potatoes, processed foods, dairy, refined sugar, cereal grains, refined vegetable oils and salt.

pan-fry

panko Coarse Japanese-style breadcrumbs.

parboil To partially cook in boiling water.

parkerhouse roll

Parmesan A hard, sharp cow's milk cheese style after Italy's Parmigiano-Reggiano.

Parmigiano-Reggiano An Italian Parmesan cheese, only used with cheese made in specific regions of Italy.

parsley Common varieties are *flat-leaf* (Italian) and *curly-leaf*.

passion fruit

pasteurize

PB&J Peanut butter and jelly sandwich.

pears In general, capitalize most varieties, including *Anjou*, *Asian* (also called *apple pear*), *Bosc* and *Bartlett*.

pecorino An Italian sheep's milk cheese.

peperonata An Italian blend of sweet peppers and vegetables.

pepitas Hulled pumpkin seeds popular in Mexican cuisine.

Peppadew A brand name for jarred red pepper from South Africa.

pepper jack cheese

Pepsi, Pepsi-Cola, PepsiCo Inc.

petit four, petits fours Bite-sized cakes.

Philly cheesesteak Also called *Philadelphia cheesesteak* or *cheesesteak*.

phyllo A paper-thin pastry dough common to Mediterranean cooking.

piccata A classic Italian dish using very thin, flattened slices of meat, such as veal or chicken, sauteed and served in a sauce of pan drippings, lemon, butter and white wine. Capers, chopped Italian parsley, shallots and garlic are common additions.

FOOD

Pilsner A pale lager.

pimento A tree and berry.

pimiento A sweet, mild pepper.

pine nut Term is preferred to *pignoli*.

pinot grigio A light, dry white wine that originated in Italy.

pinot noir A grape and wine. The wines tend to be spicy and complex.

pitmaster

Pizza Hut

po'boy No space, classic New Orleans sandwich.

poke Hawaiian raw fish salad of cubed fish marinated in soy sauce and sesame oil.

pomegranate

Popsicle A trademark for a brand of flavored ice on a stick. Use *ice pop* or *frozen pop* as the generic.

port A sweet, fortified Portuguese wine.

porterhouse A beef steak cut from the loin.

pot sticker A small Asian-style dumpling.

potatoes Varieties are written *fingerling, new, red bliss, russet, Yukon Gold*.

potluck

potpie

pound cake

powdered sugar Not *confectioner's sugar*.

pozole A thick pork soup from Mexico.

precooked

preheat Avoid use of the term: *Preheat the oven to 350 F.* Use instead: *Heat the oven to 350 F.*

prix fixe A menu for which a set price is charged for all courses of the meal.

profiterole Small cream puff.

prosciutto A salt-cured Italian ham, served thinly sliced.

prosecco An Italian sparkling wine.

provolone A tangy cow's milk cheese, originally from Italy.

puff pastry Flaky pastry made from numerous thin layers.

puree (v.) To grind until smooth (n.) food reduced to a smooth liquid or paste.

Pyrex A trademark for a brand of oven-safe glassware.

q

quinoa A high-protein seed originally from the Andes. It is cooked similar to rice and resembles couscous. It has a nutty flavor and a lightly crunchy texture.

r

ramen Refers to either a type of wheat noodle or a noodle soup dish popular in Japan and elsewhere typically composed of wheat noodles and broth. Can include other ingredients such as pork, egg, vegetables, tofu and seaweed.

ranch dressing A creamy salad dressing containing buttermilk.

ratatouille A popular vegetable dish from France's Provence region.

recipe titles Recipe titles that appear in stories or regular text are not capitalized (unless the recipe title includes proper nouns). Recipe titles at the top of actual recipes are written in all caps.

refried beans

restaurateur

Reuben sandwich The classic corned beef sandwich.

rib-eye steak

Rice Krispies The cereal. Also: *Rice Krispies Treats*.

rickey Usually a cocktail with lime juice, soda water and liquor. Also a nonalcoholic drink, often made of seltzer water, lime juice and flavored syrups.

riesling A white wine that can range from quite sweet to dry.

rocky road ice cream

romaine lettuce

Romano Sharp, hard Italian cheese.

Roquefort cheese A strong blue cheese from France.

root beer

roux (singular and plural) A cooked blend of fat and flour, usually used to thicken sauces.

ruby red grapefruit

rugelach Jewish filled pastry.

Russian dressing A mayonnaise- and chili sauce-based dressing.

s

salade nicoise

Salisbury steak

salmon Types are *king*, *coho* and *sockeye*.

saltine cracker

sandwich

sashimi A Japanese dish of thinly sliced raw seafood.

saute, sauteed, sauteing To cook with fat on the stovetop.

saute pan A wide, shallow pan with straight sides.

sauvignon blanc A grape and a wine. Wines are white and tend to be dry.

savoy cabbage

scallions The preferred term for *green*

FOOD

onions.

scotch Capitalize *Scotch* and use the spelling *whisky* only when the two words are used together.

scotch barley, scotch broth, scotch salmon, scotch sour

Scotch whisky A type of whiskey distilled in Scotland from malted barley. The malt is dried over a peat fire.

seasonings In recipes, note whether herbs are fresh or dried: *1 teaspoon fresh oregano* or *1/2 teaspoon dried thyme.* For spices and other seasonings, when appropriate note whether ground or whole: *1 teaspoon ground black pepper* or *1 teaspoon whole cardamom pods.*

seltzer water Carbonated water. Differs from *soda water* (also called *club soda*), which contains sodium bicarbonate.

serrano chili A small, hot chili.

serrano ham Dry-cured Spanish ham.

7-Eleven Trademark for stores operated and licensed by 7-Eleven Inc., a subsidiary of Seven-Eleven Japan Co. Ltd.

7UP Trademark for a brand of soft drink.

shawarma Middle Eastern sandwich of slow-roasted meat topped with hummus and served in flatbread.

shepherd's pie A baked dish that consists of layers of ground meat and mashed potatoes.

sherbet A frozen dessert similar to ice cream but made from sweetened fruit juice and water.

sherry A Spanish fortified wine.

shiraz A grape and a red wine, known as *syrah* in France. The wine tends to be bold and spicy.

Sichuan The preferred spelling; *Sichuan peppercorns* (not *Szechwan*).

skillet A long-handled shallow pan with gently sloping sides. Also called a *frying pan*, though *skillet* is preferred.

sloppy Joes

slow cooker

Smithfield Ham A trademark for a ham dry-cured, smoked and aged in Smithfield, Virginia.

s'more A campfire dessert of toasted marshmallow and chocolate between graham crackers.

soba Thin noodles made from buckwheat flour or buckwheat and wheat flours. *Soba noodles* is redundant.

soft serve ice cream

soft-shell crab A crab that has recently molted, often served battered and fried.

soppressata A variety of cured Italian salami.

sous vide A method of cooking in which food is vacuum sealed in plastic bags, then slowly cooked in water at low temperatures.

Spam

spareribs

spongecake

springform pan A baking pan with removable sides.

Sriracha sauce A Thai hot chili sauce.

stand mixer The preferred term for a stationary kitchen mixer. Use *electric mixer* for a hand-held mixer.

steakhouse

Stilton An English blue cheese.

stir-fry (n. and v.) The plural is *stir-fries*.

stockpot

sun-dried tomatoes

sugar Common varieties include *brown*, *granulated* (*white*), *powdered* (preferred to *confectioners'*), *superfine* and *turbinado* (a raw sugar). In recipes, if only granulated sugar is called for, *sugar* can be used alone.

sugarplums

superfoods Foods thought to be nutritionally dense. Mostly plant-based, they also include some fish and dairy. Foods that have been labeled as *superfood* include salmon, blueberries and acai.

sushi A Japanese dish of cooked, seasoned and cooled rice served topped with or wrapped around seafood, vegetables or egg.

sweet-and-sour sauce

Swiss chard

Swiss cheese

t

Tabasco A trademark for a brand of hot pepper sauce.

tabbouleh A Middle Eastern salad made from bulgur, vegetables, herbs, olive oil and lemon juice.

tacos

tahini

takeout

tamale, tamales A Mexican dish, usually wrapped and cooked in corn husks.

tapas The small plates of food usually served in bars in Spain.

tapenade A spread of black olives, capers and anchovies from France's Provence region.

taproom

Tater Tots

T-bone steak

temperatures In recipes written as *450 F* or *232 C*.

Tex-Mex Characterized by elements of Texas and Mexico, such as *Tex-Mex cooking*.

Thai chilies, Thai chili sauce

Thai red curry paste

FOOD

thermos

Thousand Island dressing

Tiki bar

tiramisu Dessert composed of ladyfingers, coffee, eggs, sugar, mascarpone and cocoa.

Toll House cookie

tomatoes Varieties are capitalized, as in *Brandywine*.

tonic water A carbonated water flavored with sugar and quinine.

triple sec A generic name for a clear orange liqueur.

tsimmes Jewish sweet stew often made from carrots and dried fruit.

turducken A deboned chicken stuffed inside a deboned duck stuffed inside a deboned turkey.

tureen A large, deep serving dish with a lid, usually used for soups and stews. *Terrine* refers to a pate, as well as the dish it is made in.

Turkish delight A soft, gelatinous candy popular in the Middle East.

tzatziki A Greek yogurt sauce.

U

udon Thick noodles made from wheat flour. *Udon noodles* is redundant.

umami A Japanese term roughly translated as *savory*, the suspected fifth taste (in addition to sweet,

salty, sour and bitter).

upside-down cake

V

vegan A person who abstains from eating animal products, such as meat, dairy, eggs and seafood. Some also avoid honey. Can also be used as an adjective in a food-related context: *vegan menu*, *vegan cookbook*.

vegetarian Generally understood as a person who abstains from eating meat but does eat dairy. There are many variations of vegetarian, including some who eat seafood or poultry.

vinaigrette A blend of oil and vinegar, usually used as salad dressing.

vitamin Lowercase *vitamin C*.

W

wagyu The term refers to several breeds of cattle that are genetically bred to produce intense marbling. It is also known as *Kobe-style beef*.

Waldorf salad

waxed paper

wheat germ

wheatgrass

whisky, whiskey Class of liquor distilled from grains. Includes bourbon, rye and Irish whiskey. Use spelling *whisky* only in conjunction

with *Scotch whisky, Canadian whisky*
and *Japanese whisky*.

whole wheat (n.) **whole-wheat**
(adj.) *Whole-wheat bread.*

whole-grain (adj.) *Whole-grain bread,
whole-grain mustard.*

whoopie pie

wineglass

winemaker

wines Wine names for grape varietals,
such as *chardonnay* and *shiraz*, are
not capitalized. Wines named for
regions, such as *Champagne* or
Chianti, are capitalized.

Wonder bread

wonton

Worcestershire sauce A condiment
originally made by the English in
India.

y

yam Botanically, yams and sweet
potatoes are not related, although
several varieties of moist-fleshed
sweet potatoes are popularly called
yams in some parts of the United
States.

yogurt Also, *Greek yogurt.*

York peppermint patties

z

za'atar A blend of herbs that typically
includes ground dried thyme,
oregano, marjoram, toasted sesame
seeds and salt. Sometimes contains
sumac.

zest As a noun, the thin, colorful outer
skin of citrus, not the white pith
beneath it. As a verb, to remove the
thin outer skin of citrus, usually with
a grater or zester.

zip-close bag Not *Ziploc* (a brand
name).

FOOD

Fashion

a

A-line Skirt that is narrow at the waist, then flares out along a straight line to the hem like a triangle or an A.

anorak Hooded jacket, often a pullover silhouette.

applique Decoration fastened to a larger piece of material.

argyle Geometric pattern on knitted garments of colored diamonds on plain background.

Armani, Giorgio (1934–) Italian-born designer who started his label in 1975, making his mark with tailored suits. He also forged an early relationship with Hollywood, both on screen and on red carpets.

atelier A designer's workshop or studio.

b

babydoll

back-to-school clothing

Balenciaga, Cristobal (1895–1972) Spanish-born designer moved to Paris during the Spanish Civil War, where he solidified his reputation as a fine couturier.

ballgown

Barneys New York New York-based department store. No apostrophe.

batik Method of making colored designs on textiles using wax to resist the dye. Originated in Indonesia.

bespoke Custom-made item.

bias cut Fabric cut on an approximately 45-degree angle to create a clingy, draped effect. French designer Madeleine Vionnet introduced it in the 1920s.

Blahnik, Manolo (1942–) Spanish high-end shoe designer often mentioned by Carrie Bradshaw on the television series "Sex and the City."

Bloomingdale's Upscale U.S. department stores, owned by Macy's Inc. Flagship store is at 59th Street and Lexington Avenue in Manhattan.

boatneck, bateau Neckline named for its similarity in shape to a skimmer boat. It has a narrow opening that extends almost shoulder to shoulder.

bodice The part of a dress that's above the waist

bodysuit

boho Style that draws on bohemian influences.

boucle Curly yarn that gives fabric a tufted or knotted texture.

bra Acceptable in all references for *brassiere*.

brogue Lace-up shoe with perforations in the leather.

brooch

buffalo check Checkered pattern with bold, well-defined squares.

Burch, Tory (1966–) American fashion designer who serves as chairman, CEO and designer of Tory Burch LLC.

bustier Formfitting, corset-style garment shaped around the bustline and bodice that cinches the waist. Originally worn as an underpinning, it has been adapted to street clothes and, particularly, eveningwear.

button-down

C

camisole, cami Thin-strapped, sleeveless top for women.

capelet Short cape.

chambray Lightweight fabric woven with colored and white yarns.

Chanel Gabrielle Bonheur "Coco" Chanel (1883–1971) French designer, one of most famous names in modern fashion. Her skirt suits, with collarless jackets and braided chain hardware, are often imitated. German designer Karl Lagerfeld has been at the helm of the company since 1983.

Chelsea boots An elastic-sided, ankle-high boot.

cloche Close-fitting hat. Takes its name from French for bell.

closed-toe shoes

collections

colorblocking Garments with geometric chunks of bright colors, fashion staples since French designer Yves Saint Laurent's 1965 collection inspired by Dutch painter Piet Mondrian.

compliment, complement *Complement* is a noun and a verb denoting completeness or the process of supplementing something: *The ship has a complement of 200 sailors and 20 officers. The tie complements his suit.*
   Compliment is a noun or a verb that denotes praise or the expression of courtesy: *The captain complimented the sailors. She was flattered by the compliments on her project.*

couture, couturier *Couture* refers to the design and manufacture of fashionable clothing, usually custom made. *Couturier* is someone who makes and sells couture clothes. See **haute couture**.

cowl Draped, loose neckline with a cascading effect; also used as back of dress.

crinoline Stiff cloth used as a lining for stiffening garments.

culottes

d

Dacron A trademark for a brand of polyester fiber.

de la Renta, Oscar (1932–2014) Dominican-born fashion designer. After stints in Europe with the houses of Balenciaga and Lanvin, he opened his own label in New York in 1965. His specialties were elaborate eveningwear and dressed-up daywear with a refined uptown aesthetic. The label continues after de la Renta's death with Peter Copping as its executive director.

decolletage, decollete A low neckline on a dress or top.

deconstructed Look implies edginess with exposed seams, fraying fabric edges and distressed finishes.

Dior, Christian (1905–1957) French designer who dominated post-World War II fashion with his hourglass-shaped New Look, which debuted in 1947. Pierre Cardin and Yves Saint Laurent both served as his assistants before starting their own houses.

dirndl Dress style that features a tightly fitted bodice, a low neck and a gathered skirt. Also used to describe full skirts with tightly fitted waistbands.

Dolce & Gabbana Italian fashion house started by designers Domenico Dolce (1958–) and Stefano Gabbana (1962–). Note ampersand in name.

dolman sleeve Sleeve that is wide at the armhole and narrows toward the wrist, often creates the effect of a dropped shoulder.

d'Orsay Shoe style resembling pumps, but with high vamp on the front of the foot and cutout sides, exposing arch of foot.

double-breasted

double-faced

duchesse Soft, heavy type of satin.

dyeing Refers to changing colors.

e

Elizabethan Characteristic of the time when Queen Elizabeth I ruled England in the 16th century. Her ornate neck ruffs, cloaks and jewels helped shape the royal look.

embellishment Decoration on articles of clothing and accessories.

empire waist Waistline hits above the natural waist, sometimes right under the bust. Popular for babydoll tops, evening gowns and maternity clothes.

epaulet Fabric tab that sits on the shoulder, often found on military uniforms and military-inspired fashion.

espadrille Shoe with a rope sole, often with laces that tie around the ankles.

f

faille Soft fabric with ribbed texture.

Fair Isle sweater Multicolored geometric design in woolen sweaters, originating in the Shetland Islands, off Scotland.

fascinator Headpiece often anchored by a flower or feather, often called a *cocktail hat.*

fashion-forward label

fashion week Capitalize in an official name, such as *New York Fashion Week* or *London Fashion Week.*

fast fashion (n.)**, fast-fashion** (adj.) An approach to the design, creation and marketing of clothing fashions that emphasizes making fashion trends quickly and cheaply available to consumers.

Ferragamo, Salvatore (1898–1960) Italian shoe designer. Family-owned company, which now includes larger collections of clothing and accessories, continues to operate under his name.

fishnet Fabric often used in lingerie or hosiery, with an open-mesh weave resembling a fishing net.

flair, flare *Flair* is conspicuous talent or style. *Flare* is a curving or spreading outward, as in a skirt.

flannel Soft, brushed-finish fabric, typically made of cotton or wool.

Ford, Tom (1961–) American fashion designer. Former Gucci and Yves Saint Laurent creative director who launched his own fashion, beauty and accessories line in 2006. Also directed the 2006 film "A Single Man."

formfitting

froufrou Fussy or showy dress or ornamentations.

g

Galliano, John (1960–) Gibraltar-born British-Spanish fashion designer who was head designer for Givenchy, Christian Dior and his own label. He now is creative director for Maison Margiela. In 2011, he was fired from Dior and found guilty of expressing anti-Semitic ideas by a French court.

Gaultier, Jean Paul (1952–) French fashion designer and former creative director of Hermes who created costumes for singer Madonna.

gazar Silk organza.

girlie Connotes young, feminine, flirty.

Givenchy French fashion, beauty and accessories label founded in 1952 and owned by LVMH Moet Hennessy Louis Vuitton SA.

Goth A dark, medieval-inspired style that also borrows elements from Victoriana, mourning clothes and the punk music scene.

gray

Gres, Madame Germaine Emilie Krebs (1903–1993) Parisian couturier who used the name *Madame Gres.* She was considered master of the bias cut and credited with adapting the modern goddess gown. Gres was based on an anagram of her artist husband's first name, Serge. He signed his work Gres.

guayabera Lightweight sport shirt,

FASHION

usually short-sleeved, designed to be worn untucked.

Gucci Italian fashion and leather goods company founded by Guccio Gucci in 1921.

h

Halston Roy Halston Frowick (1932–1990) American designer who started as a milliner, famously designing the pillbox hat Jacqueline Kennedy wore on Inauguration Day in 1961. Halston's clothing, though, is more closely associated with the disco era, especially his jersey dresses.

haute couture French term refers to one-of-a-kind clothing produced by design houses that meet criteria established by French Ministry of Industry. A protected appellation. Used informally to mean fancy, expensive fashion.

headscarf, headscarves

henley Pullover shirt that is collarless, split with a short row of vertical buttons.

Herrera, Carolina (1939–) Venezuelan fashion designer known for dressing celebrities and first ladies, including Laura Bush, Michelle Obama and Jacqueline Kennedy Onassis.

high-waisted

Hilfiger, Tommy (1951–) American designer who founded the Tommy Hilfiger Corp. in 1985.

hoodie Short for hooded sweatshirt.

houndstooth Large dog-tooth pattern.

i

indigo Blue dye originally derived from plants in the pea family, often used to color denim. Used to describe deep blue colors with purple overtones.

inverted pleats Pleats are folds of fabric. This style is a stacked box pleat on the inside of a garment so it lies flatter.

j

Jacobs, Marc (1963–) New York-born designer has his own collections and was creative director for French fashion house Louis Vuitton. He is considered an industry showman, staging elaborate runway productions.

Jacquard Fabric with woven pattern, sometimes an elaborate one. In 1801, Joseph Marie Jacquard invented the loom that could control the pattern sequence using punch cards.

k

Karan, Donna (1948–) New York-born designer who first served as head designer of Anne Klein before launching her own label in 1984. She routinely cites working women and her hometown as her inspirations.

Kawakubo, Rei (1942–) Japanese

FASHION

fashion designer and founder of Comme des Garcons

keyhole Peek-a-boo opening used on neckline, front or back of garment. Oblong shape like a keyhole.

kimono Japanese wrap-style robe with wide sleeves and tied with a wide sash, or *obi*.

Klein, Calvin (1942–) New York-born designer who made as much of a splash with his provocative advertising as his sexy, minimal styles. In 2003, he gave up his role in the company he co-founded in 1968 after a corporate sale to Phillips-Van Heusen Corp.

knife pleat Fold in fabric that creates a fanlike effect. Knife pleats are basic pleating technique.

Kors, Michael (1959–) American designer. Honorary chairman and chief creative officer for Michael Kors Holdings Ltd., which sells men's and women's clothing and accessories, shoes and fragrances.

l

Lagerfeld, Karl (1933–) German-born designer who moved to Paris in his teens. He is best known as the longtime creative director at Chanel but also designs for Fendi and under his own name. Also a photographer, he often shoots his own ad campaigns.

Lauren, Ralph (1939–) New York-born designer known for polo pony logo and elegant sportswear. He has created a huge public company

that has expanded to categories that range from home goods to uniforms for the U.S. Olympic teams.

Louboutin, Christian (1963–) French footwear designer whose trademark is shiny red-lacquered soles.

luxe Luxury.

LVMH Moet Hennessy Louis Vuitton SA. Leading luxury goods conglomerate based in Paris. Parent company of fashion houses Louis Vuitton, Celine, Donna Karan, Givenchy, Marc Jacobs, Fendi and Christian Dior.

Lycra Unless referring to the trademark fiber or fabric, use a generic term such as *spandex* or *elastic* or *stretch fabric*.

m

Macy's Inc. The largest department store chain in the United States, with about 860 stores under the Macy's, Bloomingdale's and other store names. Macy's flagship store in Manhattan's Herald Square is one of the world's largest. The Macy's Thanksgiving Day Parade began in 1924. Formerly Federated Department Stores.

madras Lightweight cotton cloth, usually striped or plaid, originating in India.

maillot One-piece swimming suit or bodysuit.

makeup

mannequin

McQueen, Alexander (1969–2010) British designer who was considered one of the industry's most creative and skillful designers. After his 2010 suicide, his label was taken over by assistant Sarah Burton.

menswear Not men's wear.

messenger bag Bag with a large zippered central compartment or compartments and a fold-over flap at the front.

Met Gala Annual fundraiser for the Costume Institute at the Metropolitan Museum of Art in New York. Held in May, the Met Gala attracts major celebrities and is themed to an exhibit at the museum.

miniskirt

monokini Topless swimsuit introduced by Austrian designer Rudi Gernreich in 1964. Term has evolved to describe one-piece swimsuits with deep cutouts.

mousseline Semi-opaque fabric.

n

negligee Light, filmy dressing gown.

Neiman Marcus Inc. Dallas-based high-fashion retail stores.

neoprene A synthetic rubber, originally used for gloves and wetsuits, incorporated into figure-hugging apparel.

New Look 1947 silhouette by French designer Christian Dior, with a nipped waist and full skirt that ushered in a different post-World War II style.

normcore A fashion trend that combines "normal" and "hardcore" and is characterized by unpretentious, unisex, average dressing.

notched lapel Flap on front of a jacket that is common to business suits and tuxedos.

nude Avoid as a description of a color. Use more specific terms, such as *champagne* and *sand*.

nylon Not a trademark.

O

ombre Effect created by dip dyeing fabric with various gradations. Sometimes called *degrade*. Color appears lighter in some spots and darker in others. It can be done with more than one color, but shading a single color is more common.

opera gloves Over-the-elbow gloves, known in French as *mousquetaire gloves*, inspired by the gauntlets worn by musketeers in the 19th century.

organza Sheer and delicate, yet stiff, fabric.

Orlon Trademark for a form of acrylic fiber, similar to nylon.

overlay Outer layer of a garment.

Oxford shoes A type of lace-up shoe.

p

paillette Flat sequin.

palette Color range.

pantsuit

passe

peacoat Double-breasted, hip-length coat with slash pockets and notched lapels, often made of heavy wool.

peplum Flounce of fabric that juts out just above the hips, typically on a fitted fabric or dress.

plait Braiding of hair.

pleat Fold in fabric.

plus-size clothing But *plus size* when used alone.

polka dot (n.) **polka-dot** (adj.)

pompom Ornamental ball or tuft on clothing; also crepe paper ball waved by cheerleaders.

pouf, poufy, pouffed Any part of a garment with excess, gathered fabric.

Prada, Miuccia (1949–) Italian designer whose usually minimalist designs largely set broader fashion trends. Prada, the brand, was founded in 1913 by her grandfather, Mario, as a leather company.

Proenza Schouler American designers Jack McCollough and Lazaro Hernandez founded their company — named after their mothers' maiden names — in 2002, after selling their final project for Parsons School of Design to Barneys New York.

pret-a-porter line Designer clothing sold ready-to-wear.

q

queens *Elizabethan* and *Victorian* refer to Britain's Queen Elizabeth I, who ruled in the 16th century, and Queen Victoria, 19th-century ruler. Elizabeth's ornate neck ruffs, cloaks and jewels helped shape the royal look. Queen Victoria moved from oversized crinoline-cage garments with high collars to a sleeker, elongated shape with a lower neckline.

quilting Sewing technique, initially used for bedding, now part of popular fashion. Quilted garments have three layers, two pieces of fabric as well as insular batting, sewn together with visible, often artful, stitching.

r

rayon Not a trademark.

riding pants Pants with roomy hips and tight-fitting legs started for equestrians. Modern fashion has interpreted them with an exaggerated shape. Also *jodhpurs*.

Rodarte California-based clothing company founded by sisters Kate and Laura Mulleavy.

ruching Detail of gathered fabric, often at a seam and, in particular, on the sides of the bodice.

FASHION

S

Saint Laurent, Yves (1936–2008) Algerian-born designer who popularized many silhouettes that have since become fashion classics, including menswear for women, trapeze dresses, safari jackets and peasant skirts. He opened his own house in Paris in 1962 after years as Christian Dior's assistant and then hand-picked successor. When Hedi Slimane took over as creative director in 2012, the name for collections and garments changed to Saint Laurent Paris.

Saks Fifth Avenue Inc. Upscale retail store owned by Hudson's Bay Co. Flagship store is on Fifth Avenue in Manhattan. No apostrophe.

Savile Row Shopping street in London known for its bespoke tailoring.

serape Shawl or blanket worn as a cloak in Latin America.

shapewear Undergarments that mold the body's appearance; the 2000s brought a surge in popularity with improved shaping fabrics.

sheath Dress silhouette that is long and lean with a nipped waist, usually without a waistband, to create an hourglass shape.

shirtdress

shirt sleeve, shirt sleeves (n.) **shirt-sleeve** (adj.)

sizes Use figures: *a size 8 dress, size 40 long, 10 1/2B shoes, a 34 1/2 sleeve.*

sleeve (n.) That part of a garment that covers an arm or part of an arm.

sleeved (adj.) Fitted with sleeves, often in hyphenated compounds: *short-sleeved.*

soigne Elegant, well-groomed.

soiree Party or gathering in the evening.

spandex See **Lycra**.

spectator Style of two-tone shoes. Men's are typically wing-tips and women's are pumps with wing tip-style perforation and details.

super-skinny

supermodel

sweatpants, sweatshirt, sweatsuit

t

tie-dye

Tiffany & Co. New York-based jewelry stores. No apostrophe.

trapeze Short dress style with narrow shoulders and a bodice that flares out in a trapezoid shape.

trenchcoat

T-shirt Acceptable to use *tee* on subsequent references.

tulip skirt Skirt shape that mimics an upside-down tulip; waist and hemline are similar widths.

tulle Fine net material used to make veils and dresses.

FASHION

twin set Pairing of cardigan and crew neck sweaters.

U

underlay Underneath layer of a garment, often under a sheer fabric.

Uniqlo A Japanese retailer of casual wear.

unitard Tight-fitting body stocking covering legs, torso and usually arms.

utilitarian Inspired by practical clothing. Cargo pants, ripstop nylon and hoodies have become fashionable details.

V

valise Small travel case with handles.

Velcro A trademark for a brand of fabric fastening products that can be pressed together or pulled apart. Use a generic term such as *fabric fastener*.

Versace Fashion house based in Milan, Italy, known for super sexy styles. Founded in 1978 by Gianni Versace; his younger sister Donatella took over as creative director when he was murdered in 1997.

Victorian Characteristic of the reign of England's Queen Victoria from 1837 to 1901. Victoria moved from oversized crinoline-cage garments with high collars to a sleeker, elongated shape with a lower neckline.

Victoria's Secret American retailer of lingerie founded in 1977.

vintage Term to describe clothes from another era. Antique clothes need to be more than 100 years old; vintage clothes are generally assumed to be newer but older than the most recent decade.

V-neck (n. and adj.)

von Furstenberg, Diane (1946–) Belgian-born American fashion designer known for the wrap dress.

Vuitton, Louis French fashion house founded in 1854, known for its monogrammed products that include shoes, leather goods, clothing and trunks. Owned by LVMH Moet Hennessy Louis Vuitton SA.

W

wash and wear Clothes that can be cleaned with soap and water, dried and worn without ironing.

-wear *Activewear, daywear, eveningwear, eyewear, headwear, menswear, outerwear, sportswear, swimwear, womenswear.*

windbreaker

Wintour, Anna (1949–) British-born editor-in-chief of American Vogue magazine since 1988 and artistic director for Conde Nast since 2013. Widely considered the most powerful person in fashion, making or breaking trends and careers.

womenswear Not *women's wear.*

FASHION

wool

y

yoke Line across the shoulders or hips that creates a more fitted shape.

z

zebra print Print that mimics the black-and-white stripes of a zebra. Zebra, cheetah and leopard prints became trends in the 1960s and are now considered classics.

zigzag

Briefing on media law

INTRODUCTION

The courts significantly changed the legal standards governing the work of reporters and editors during the era of the civil rights movement and the Vietnam War, applying the First Amendment's protection of speech and press with new force and meaning.

In *New York Times v. Sullivan* (1964), the Supreme Court held for the first time that the First Amendment limits the ability of states to impose damages for the publication of a statement even when it is false, in some circumstances. Sixteen years later, in *Richmond Newspapers v. Virginia* (1980), the court reached the equally unprecedented conclusion that the First Amendment establishes an affirmative right of the press and public to compel access to certain information concerning the exercise of government power. The fallout from these two watershed cases has reshaped a great deal of the law that governs the publication of the news and the way it is gathered.

This chapter addresses some of the key legal issues facing journalists. With respect to newsgathering *activity*, it explores three topics of direct significance:

Access to government information, including the rules governing reporter access to the courts and to government information generally;

Confidential sources, including the law relating to promises of confidentiality and the reporter's privilege; and

Newsgathering conduct, including common law and statutory rules that may create liability for actions taken while a reporter is seeking out the news.

With respect to news *content*, this chapter addresses the legal principles in three branches of the law that govern liability for the publication of information:

Defamation, including the elements of a claim arising from the publication of a *false* statement, and the common law and constitutional defenses to liability;

Privacy, including claims for the disclosure of private facts, misappropriation and "false light," which can arise when the facts reported are *true*; and

Copyright infringement, including the elements of a copyright claim and the "fair use" defense.

While the law can vary in significant ways from one state to another, particularly in its details, the broad principles affecting newsgathering and reporting in the United States are largely consistent, due in part to the federal constitutional principles protecting speech and the press that overlay state law. Reporters and editors naturally will become familiar over time with the particulars of media law in the places where they work, and this chapter is intended only as a general primer on some basic principles that are likely to apply across a range of situations. It should not be construed as legal advice and should not substitute for obtaining legal guidance when you are in doubt.

LEGAL PRINCIPLES OF NEWSGATHERING

Several legal rules have special importance to the way the news is gathered. This chapter takes up three of them: the affirmative rights that can be invoked to compel access to government *proceedings* and the release of government documents; the legal protections that often allow reporters to obtain information through a promise of confidentiality; and the "laws of general applicability," such as intrusion, trespass, and misrepresentation, that reporters must usually follow, even when they inhibit the ability to seek out the news.

Access to government information

Public access to information about the actions of government is essential in a democracy. James Madison made just this point in 1832:

"A Popular Government, without popular information, or the means of acquiring it, is but a Prologue to a Farce or a Tragedy; or perhaps both. Knowledge will forever govern ignorance: And a people who mean to be their own Governors, must arm themselves with the power which knowledge gives."

The press and public have affirmative rights, both constitutional and statutory, to compel access to the type of government information that is essential to the functioning of our democracy. A right of access extends to official *proceedings*, including court trials, hearings, and the meetings of some legislative bodies and administrative agencies. Access rights also extend to the inspection of *documents* held by the government, with only specific exceptions. Given the independence of the three branches of government, the scope of access to judicial proceedings and court records is largely governed by constitutional and common law principles articulated by judges, while access to information in the executive and legislative branches is largely governed by statutes and administrative regulations.

These access rights are not absolute; they can be abridged in a number of situations. Nonetheless, clear legal standards define the scope of these rights and the procedures available to reporters to enforce them.

– Recognition of a First Amendment right of access

The articulation by the Supreme Court in 1980 of a constitutional *right* to certain information about the exercise of government power, and the delineation of the proper scope and application of that right over the ensuing years, would provide a fascinating case study of the meaning of a "living constitution." In *Richmond Newspapers v. Virginia*, the Supreme Court ruled for the first time that the First Amendment encompasses an affirmative, enforceable right of public access to criminal trials. As the court later explained the rationale for this new constitutional right, "a major purpose" of the First Amendment's protection of free speech, a free press and the right to petition the government is the public's need to know what the government is up to, if democracy is to function. Just as other provisions of the Bill of Rights have been read to imply the right to travel, a right to privacy, and the right to be presumed innocent, the court concluded that the First Amendment implies a right of the public to certain information concerning the direct exercise of government power.

In a series of rulings following *Richmond Newspapers*, the Supreme Court reaffirmed the existence of this constitutional right of access and defined its scope. In *Globe Newspaper Co. v. Superior Court* (1982), the court said that the right to attend a criminal trial applies even during the testimony of a minor victim of a sex crime. The court in that case struck down as unconstitutional a Massachusetts statute mandating closed proceedings during all such testimony, saying that the First Amendment right of access requires a judge to determine on a case-by-case basis whether the privacy concerns of a particular victim outweigh the public's right to attend and observe the proceedings. In 1984, the Supreme Court held that the right of public access extends to the proceedings to select a jury in a criminal case, *Press-Enterprise Co. v. Superior Ct. I*, and two years later said the right extends to preliminary hearings in a criminal prosecution. *Press-Enterprise Co. v Superior Ct. II.* The First Amendment protects the public's right to attend such judicial proceedings unless specific findings are made, on the record, demonstrating that a closed proceeding is essential in order to "preserve higher values," and any limitation imposed on public access must be narrowly tailored to serve that interest. In 2010, in *Presley v. Georgia*, the court held a trial judge must ensure that these standards are satisfied before a courtroom is closed to the public, even if no one objects to the closure.

While the Supreme Court has not substantively revisited the right of access in detail since 1986, lower federal and state courts have considered and applied the right to a wide variety of judicial and administrative proceedings over the intervening years. Courts have recognized a constitutional right to attend a given type of proceeding if public access will generally play a positive role in the performance of the proceeding (encouraging diligent attention by officials, ensuring that proper procedures are followed, preventing perjury or other misconduct, facilitating public understanding of decisions made), and if it is the type of proceeding that historically has been open to the public. This right has been held also to apply to administrative proceedings conducted like trials, such as deportation hearings and agency adjudications.

The constitutional right is generally recognized to apply to all aspects of a criminal prosecution, except to matters involving a grand jury. Grand jury investigations historically have been completely secret, and this secrecy itself advances the important public policy of protecting innocent people in those cases where an investigation does not result in any criminal charge being filed. The right of access has been held to extend to civil trials and proceedings, although in some states there are important exceptions. Family Court proceedings, for example, raise significant privacy concerns, as do juvenile delinquency matters, and these are often closed to the public.

— Limits on constitutional access

As noted, the constitutional right to attend government proceedings is not absolute. That a First Amendment right protects public access to a type of proceeding does not mean that such a proceeding can never be closed to the press and public. The Supreme Court has identified four factors that must each be satisfied before the right of access may be restricted:

1. Those who want to close a proceeding must prove that holding a public proceeding would directly threaten some compelling interest, such as a defendant's right to a fair trial or the right of privacy, that outweighs the public interest in openness.

2. There must be no alternative short of closing the proceeding that could protect the threatened interest.

3. Any limitation on access must be as narrow as possible.

4. The limitation imposed must be effective in protecting the threatened interest or else closure may not be ordered.

Applying these factors, courts have required journalists and the public to be excluded from proceedings in a number of situations, such as during the testimony of a sexual assault victim whose identity has not previously been disclosed to the public, or during testimony by an undercover police officer whose effectiveness or safety would be jeopardized by public identification.

Sidebar conferences between the attorneys and the judge generally involve discussions intended to be kept confidential from the jury, but these discussions should usually be available to the press. A transcript is generally kept of such sidebar discussions and should be available for inspection as part of the record of the proceeding. To withhold the transcript of such a sidebar conference held during an open proceeding, the same four-part test would need to be met.

One recurring but unsettled issue concerns reporters' access to information identifying jurors, and their right to speak to jurors after a verdict. The Supreme Court has said specifically that the First Amendment right of access extends to jury selection proceedings, where names and other identifying information are normally disclosed. Some lower courts have concluded that this principle also requires disclosures of written juror questionnaires when they are used. Nonetheless, in some high profile cases such as the prosecutions of Martha Stewart, Michael Jackson, Illinois Gov. Rod Blagojevich, and baseball slugger Barry Bonds, courts have sought to keep the identities of jurors private during the trial or to minimize press contact with jurors following a verdict. Sometimes a judge will conduct jury selection by reference only to juror numbers, to prevent public disclosure of juror names or addresses before a trial is over. The U.S. Court of Appeals in Philadelphia concluded in *United States v. Wecht* (2008) that the public access right requires juror names to be disclosed before the start of a trial, but this position is not universally embraced. In other cases, courts have barred reporters from speaking with jurors long after a verdict is returned. Limitations on disclosure of juror identities before a verdict is returned are sometimes permitted, but restrictions after a verdict is returned can rarely be squared with the First Amendment right of access.

Reporters confronted with such court orders should seek legal advice on the validity of the restriction imposed.

— What to say if a hearing is about to be closed without prior notice

Because a constitutional right is at stake, the press has a right to be heard before a proceeding is closed to the public. The following statement should be read in court when confronted with an attempt to close a hearing without advance notice. It allows a reporter, when permitted to address the court, to state the basic concerns and to seek time for counsel to appear to make the legal argument. Any parts of the statement that are not applicable to a specific case can be changed or omitted:

May it please the Court, I am (name) of The Associated Press (or other news organization). I respectfully request the opportunity to register on the record an objection to closing this proceeding to the public. The Associated Press (or other organization) requests a hearing at which its counsel may present to the Court legal authority and arguments showing why any closure in this proceeding would be improper.

The press and the public have a constitutional right to attend judicial proceedings, and may not be excluded unless the Court makes findings, on the record, that: (1) closure is required to preserve a compelling constitutional interest, (2) no adequate alternatives to closure exist, and (3) the closure ordered is narrowly tailored to protect the threatened interest effectively.

The Associated Press (or other news organization) submits that these findings cannot be made here, especially given the public interest in this proceeding. The public has a right to be informed of what transpires in this case, the positions being argued by the parties, and the factual basis for rulings made by the Court. The Court should avoid any impression that justice is being carried on in secret. The Associated Press (or other news organization) objects to any closure order and respectfully requests a hearing at which it can present full legal arguments and authority in support of this position. Thank you.

If the court will not allow a reporter to be heard, a brief written statement — handwritten is fine — should be delivered to the courtroom clerk, making these same points.

— A word about gag orders

The tension between the right of a free press and the right of a fair trial is nothing new. Finding an impartial jury for the treason trial of Aaron Burr in 1807 was difficult, the Supreme Court has noted, because few people in Virginia "had not formed some opinions concerning Mr. Burr or his case, from newspaper accounts." Nonetheless, an apparently increasing number of cases involving celebrity defendants or notorious crimes generating intense publicity have led to an increased number of orders preventing lawyers, parties to a case, and sometimes even witnesses, from discussing the case outside of the courtroom.

The Supreme Court has said that speech by attorneys, as officers of the court, may be regulated to protect the integrity of the judicial system. Orders more broadly barring the speech of other trial participants, including the parties and witnesses, are permitted only when absolutely necessary to ensure an accused's right to a fair trial. Such orders have been entered in cases involving extraordinary press coverage that threatens the ability to select an impartial jury, when other measures are not likely to mitigate the effects of unrestrained pretrial publicity.

A typical gag order does not prevent a reporter from asking questions, but it does bar trial participants and court officers from answering them. Because a gag order restricts access to news, most courts acknowledge that a reporter has legal standing to challenge an order, and may be successful if a gag order was entered without adequate factual findings to justify the need for the specific restraint on speech imposed by the court, or if the order is overbroad in the categories of individuals restrained or the range of topics they are prohibited from discussing.

— Media protocols in high-profile cases

Over the years "decorum orders" have been entered by some courts to regulate the conduct of reporters covering high profile trials. Sometimes requested by the parties and sometimes imposed unilaterally by the court, these orders may restrict the use of cameras and recording devices at specific locations in and around the courthouse, direct that witnesses or jurors not be photographed as they come and go from court, restrict the use of cellphones, or impose other restrictions to protect the decorum of a trial and operations at the courthouse. In the aborted Kobe Bryant prosecution, for example, a Colorado state judge imposed a decorum order specifying such details as where cameras could be positioned outside the courthouse, limiting the times when reporters could enter or leave the courtroom, and specifying where reporters could sit, where they could park their cars and how they could enter the courthouse.

Restrictions on the actions of journalists that directly affect their ability to gather news must be narrowly tailored to protect a compelling governmental interest. Decorum orders that become necessary in high-profile cases to ensure safety, protect physical access to the courts by the public, or prevent interference with the integrity of the proceedings in the courtroom, are likely to be allowed as long as their terms are reasonable, content-neutral and limited to clearly defined restrictions on conduct within the courthouse and its immediate environs. A decorum order likely goes too far, however, if it also controls the content of a news report rather than just the conduct of a reporter. For example, for privacy reasons a court might restrict the taking of photographs of jurors as they enter or leave the courthouse, but could not properly bar the press from ever publishing the image of a juror, even if it were obtained through other sources. One restriction is limited to conduct at the courthouse; the other is aimed at the content of a news report.

— The right to attend other types of proceedings

In some instances, the constitutional right of access has been held to extend to proceedings beyond court hearings. For example, the U.S. Court of Appeals in Cincinnati has held that the public had a constitutional right to attend deportation proceedings conducted by the Immigration and Naturalization Service. (*Detroit Free Press v. Ashcroft*, 2002.) The U.S. Court of Appeals in New York has held that the right of access applies in transit agency tribunals to assess fines. (*New York Civ. Lib. Union v. N.Y.C. Transit Authority*, (2011)). The First Amendment right of access similarly has been found to extend to military courts-martial, proceedings of judicial review boards and hearings of the Federal Mine Safety and Health Administration.

Most states and the federal government also have statutes known as "open meetings laws" or "government in the sunshine" acts that protect the right of the public and the press to attend meetings of public authorities. These laws essentially provide that every meeting where a public board or public authority convenes to conduct business must be open to the public, with only limited exception. The federal law, for example, allows a meeting to be closed only if one of 10 identified categories of information is to be discussed, such as personnel and salary decisions. Even when a portion of a meeting is closed, a transcript or minutes must be prepared, and must be disclosed to the extent that disclosure would not reveal the exempt information.

These access laws typically apply to executive agencies, but not to the legislative bodies, in most cases. Most state constitutions separately require open legislative sessions, although each house is usually free to make its own rules about access to committee meetings.

— The right of access applies to court records

The right of access generally includes the right to inspect transcripts of open proceedings, evidence introduced at a trial and most motion papers, orders and other records of open court proceedings. Some courts have concluded that this right to inspect judicial records is implicit in the First Amendment right of access, holding that the right covers any documents relating to a proceeding that is itself subject to the First Amendment right of access.

Other courts analyze the right of access to documents filed with the court as a common law right that may be more easily restricted, sometimes with unfortunate results. For example, in the famous case of *McConnell v. Federal Election Commission* (2003), a challenge to the constitutionality of the McCain-Feingold campaign finance reform act was decided by the courts entirely on the basis of written submissions, without any public evidentiary hearing. A massive record of some 100,000 pages was presented to the court, apparently detailing the types of campaign abuses that Congress found to justify restrictions on election speech. Despite the public interest in knowing the factual basis for the competing arguments being made, the District of Columbia court concluded that the public had only a common law right to inspect the documents presented to the court, and that this right extended only to information "relied upon" by the court in reaching its decision. The court therefore rejected an application by several news organizations to inspect the evidence filed with the court, saying the public was only entitled to inspect specific pages of the record actually cited in the court's opinions. Other courts have rejected this limitation and have found a constitutional right of access to records submitted to courts in support of requests for judicial action, regardless of whether the court ultimately relies on the record, an approach embraced by the U.S. Court of Appeals in New York (*Lugosh v. Pyramid Corp.*).

Whether the right to inspect court records is a constitutional right or a common law right is not fully settled in some areas of the country. Whatever the scope of the right to inspect court records, however, it does not generally extend to pretrial discovery documents and other litigation records that are not filed with the courts. While compelled public access to discovery has been afforded on rare occasions, involving highly newsworthy disputes, reporters generally have no right to require parties to a lawsuit to allow inspection of litigation material that is never filed with the court.

— Access to other government records

The federal Freedom of Information Act (FOIA), originally passed by Congress in 1966, creates a presumptive right of access to all documents held in the executive branch, other than documents in the possession of the president and his immediate staff. It does not cover Congress or the courts. All Cabinet agencies, independent agencies, regulatory commissions and government-owned

MEDIA LAW

corporations are covered.

Records made available for inspection under the act include virtually anything recorded in a physical medium that can be reproduced. This includes all documents, papers, reports, and letters in the government's possession, as well as films, photographs, sound recordings, databases, computer disks and tapes. A 1996 law expanded FOIA to require federal agencies, whenever possible, to share data in a specific format, such as on computer diskette or CD-ROM. The 1996 amendments also broadened citizen access to government by placing more information directly online.

The act contains nine exemptions that permit — but do not require — agencies to withhold information. Those exemptions are: (1) national security; (2) internal agency personnel rules; (3) information specifically exempt from disclosure by another law; (4) trade secrets; (5) internal agency memorandums and policy deliberations; (6) personal privacy; (7); law enforcement investigations; (8) federally regulated bank information; and (9) oil and gas well data.

Different agencies apply these exemptions in different ways even when issues ostensibly have already been settled in court. If you want something, ask for it. Let the government decide whether it has any grounds or willingness to deny your request. The statutory exemptions allow information to be withheld, but do not require it. Even an exempt document can be released at the government's discretion.

Because of the various exemptions, documents are often produced with large sections blacked out as "exempt." And, because of a lack of manpower assigned to implement the act, there are often long delays in getting documents at all. Under the law, information is supposed to be produced within 20 days, but there is no effective enforcement mechanism when an agency misses this deadline, short of going to court.

— Making a request under FOIA

There is no set format for making a FOIA request for documents. Although most agencies have adopted regulations describing specific steps to follow, any reasonably precise identification of the information sought, submitted to the proper person, will trigger an obligation for an agency to respond. Here are a few elementary steps to consider in making a FOIA request that may help avoid problems:

— Call the public information office of the agency you believe has the records before filing your request, to make sure you have the right agency and the right address for filing it. Ask if the information you are seeking could be released without a written FOIA request.
— Be as specific as possible about what you want. Give dates, titles, and authors for documents if you know them. In your letter, provide your telephone number, email address, and offer to supply any other information that might help narrow the search.
— Even if you are using the letterhead stationery of a news organization, state specifically that you are a reporter for that organization and plan to use the material in news stories. The act does not require you to state your purpose, but disclosures in the public interest are eligible for fee waivers, exemption waivers and in some cases expedited handling.

— Request a waiver of search and copying fees. To avoid delays if the waiver is denied, also state a limit you are prepared to pay, such as $100, without the agency's need to obtain your prior, specific consent.
— If you want field office files checked as well as those at headquarters, be sure to request that specifically. Some agencies, such as the FBI, will not check beyond the office where the request is submitted, unless asked. It is good practice to send a separate request directly to the FOI officer at the field office of an agency in any event, if you think relevant documents exist there.
— Ask the agency to cite specific exemptions for each item it withholds in the event that any part of the request is denied.
— Request that redacted copies of documents be provided if only a specific portion of a document is subject to an exemption.
— If your initial request is denied, file an administrative appeal. Some agencies take a very different view on appeal. The denial letter will specify to whom the appeal must be sent and the deadline for making an appeal. If you do not first pursue an administrative appeal, you cannot go to court to compel release of the information.
— An appeal can be made through a simple letter that explains why the public will benefit from disclosure and asks for a review of the grounds on which the request was denied. Several exemptions require a balancing of private and public interests, and reviewers on an administrative appeal may be more likely to exercise their right to waive an exemption if a good case for disclosure is made.

You may want to consult FOIA experts or manuals before proceeding with a request. A FOI Service Center is maintained by the Reporters Committee for Freedom of the Press. The committee publishes a pamphlet with sample FOIA letters and appeal forms as well as analyses of the act. (Available on the web at: http://www.rcfp.org/foiact/index.html.) The committee maintains a toll-free hot line (800-336-4243), 24 hours a day, seven days a week, with attorneys available to provide FOIA advice to journalists.

On the web, the U.S. Department of Justice publishes a "Guide to the Freedom of Information Act," which gives the current government understanding of what is covered and not covered by each exemption, http://www.justice.gov/oip/foia-guide.html. Also on the web, the U.S. Department of Justice publishes a collection of "FOIA Resources," which includes up-to-date copies of relevant statutes and recent court decisions, http://www.justice.gov/oip/foia-resources.

It is advisable to check on specific state freedom of information laws. Each individual state has its own freedom of information laws that apply to state and local government agencies.

Issues concerning sources

For better or worse, some sources who possess important information of great public significance will speak to a journalist only if they are promised confidentiality. This has been true from the earliest history of an independent press in America. John Peter Zenger, whose New York trial in 1735 is best remembered for establishing the principle that truth is a defense to a claim for libel, was also the first American newspaperman to establish the tradition that journalists will protect their sources to the point of imprisonment. Zenger refused to divulge to British authorities the identities of those who made the statements that authorities considered libelous.

The use of confidential sources remains an important means for reporters to uncover the news. Such sources make available to the public more than the sanitized "spin" of government and corporate press releases. Yale professor Alexander Bickel noted:

"Indispensable information comes in confidence from officeholders fearful of superiors, from businessmen fearful of competitors, from informers operating at the edge of the law who are in danger of reprisal from criminal associates, from people afraid of the law and government — sometimes rightly afraid, but as often from an excess of caution — and from men in all fields anxious not to incur censure for unorthodox or unpopular views." ("The Morality of Consent," 1975.)

In one study of some 10,000 news reports conducted in 2005, 13 percent of the front-page newspaper articles reviewed were based, at least in part, on anonymous sources.

Promising confidentiality to a source always raises a number of issues, legal and journalistic. If a reporter refuses to identify a source, there is always the potential that a publisher may be hauled into court or a reporter thrown into jail. If a publisher is sued for libel, having a story based on sources that were promised confidentiality creates an entirely separate set of concerns: it is hard to prove the "truth" of a statement if the source of the information cannot be revealed. In one case, a Massachusetts court entered a default judgment against the Boston Globe for refusing to reveal its confidential source for a story that became the subject of a libel claim. A jury subsequently awarded the plaintiff $2.1 million — a hefty price to pay to uphold a promise to a source.

— A promise to a source creates an enforceable agreement

A reporter who reveals the name or identity of someone who was promised confidentiality can be held liable for breach of the agreement.

The Supreme Court decided just this issue in *Cohen v. Cowles* (1991), a case involving "dirt" on one political candidate that was provided to a newspaper reporter on the eve of the election by a political consultant for the candidate's opponent. The reporter promised the consultant confidentiality. His editors, however, considered the identification of the source necessary for the public to weigh the significance of the new disclosures, and overruled the reporter. As a result, the no-longer confidential source lost his job, and sued. A jury verdict of $200,000 in favor of the spurned source was upheld by the Supreme Court, which found the First Amendment no defense to a claim for the damages caused by breaking a promise freely made.

The same result was reached by a New York court in a case involving a promise to mask someone's identity in a photograph. A journalist promised a man receiving treatment in an AIDS clinic that he would not be "identifiable" if he allowed his photograph to be taken. The journalist used a rear-angle setup and retouching techniques to obscure his identity, but the man's friends still recognized him when the photograph was published. The New York court held that the burden of carrying out the promise to disguise rested with the journalist who made the promise, and upheld the jury's award of damages to the patient.

Reporters can unwittingly create problems for themselves in making agreements with sources to protect confidentiality, or in failing to clarify with the source the meaning of an agreement. A few common-sense steps can minimize the risk that problems with sources will develop:

— Before making any promise, consider whether it is worth doing: How important is the information that the source is going to provide? Can the information be obtained or confirmed from any "on-the-record" source?

— If a promise of some protection is to be made, express it in terms of the steps that will be taken to protect the source rather than the result to be achieved. For example, promise a source to not use the name, or agree on how the source will be identified in the story (a "high-ranking military officer," or a "knowledgeable Defense Department official"), rather than promising "no one will know you gave me this information." If a photograph or videotape is involved, the key is still to promise a specific action ("I will photograph you only from behind") rather than promising a result ("no one will recognize you").

— Make sure the source has the same understanding of the scope of the promise made as you do. Avoid using ambiguous terms as a shorthand for an agreement, such as "this will be off the record," or this is "confidential." Instead, be specific about the terms of the agreement and how far the promise extends. Must confidentiality be maintained if litigation results? If a court order requires disclosure? Or, will the source allow disclosure in certain situations?

— Follow through with any agreement, making sure to inform editors and others who need to know to carry out the promise. The broader the promise, the more the effort needed to make sure that it is upheld.

The bottom line is this: promises of confidentiality or anonymity should be made cautiously, and only after a determination that the risk of such promises is outweighed by the need for the information. When a promise is made, make sure it is as precise as possible, and then make sure it is carried out.

— Reporter's privilege

Given the importance of confidential sources, reporters have long asserted a right to protect the identity of those to whom confidentiality was promised. All states except Wyoming have provided some level of protection for reporters who are called to testify about their sources. Thirty-nine states and the District of Columbia have enacted "shield laws" that provide legal protection against the disclosure of sources; Hawaii's statute expired under a sunset provision and it has not as of this writing been re-enacted; nine additional states have recognized some form of a "reporter's privilege" through judicial decisions. About half of the state shield laws provide reporters with an absolute privilege not to disclose confidential sources, while the remainder establish a high standard that must be met before a reporter's promise of confidentiality can be pierced.

The existence and scope of the reporter's privilege is more confused in federal courts. Although significant efforts have been made in recent years, there is no federal shield law, and the Supreme Court has addressed the "reporter's privilege" only once — in a ruling that is far from clear.

In *Branzburg v. Hayes* (1972), the Supreme Court considered claims of privilege asserted by three journalists who had been subpoenaed to reveal confidential information and sources before grand juries investigating possible criminal activity. The reporters had written stories describing the synthesizing of hashish, conversations with admitted drug users, and eyewitness accounts of events at Black Panther headquarters at a time of civil unrest in the surrounding neighborhood. In each instance, the journalist claimed a privilege under the First Amendment not to answer questions concerning confidential information and sources.

A closely divided Supreme Court held in a 5-4 ruling that it did not violate the First Amendment to require these journalists to testify in the grand jury investigations, conducted in good faith, concerning the identities of persons allegedly engaged in criminal conduct. The court, however, did not reject altogether the notion of a First Amendment privilege. To the contrary, the majority opinion expressed the view that its narrow focus should not apply to "the vast bulk of confidential relationships between reporters and their sources," and emphasized that even grand juries "must operate within the limits of the First Amendment as well as the Fifth."

Justice Lewis Powell cast the decisive fifth vote and wrote separately to underscore further the "limited nature" of the court's holding. He explained that reporters would still have access to the courts, and could move to quash a subpoena if confidential source information were being sought "without a legitimate need of law enforcement."

Court decisions over the ensuing decades have embraced a qualified reporter's privilege that accommodates the interests of the press and those who seek to obtain information through judicial process. The United States Courts of Appeals in 10 of the 12 federal circuits have specifically applied the First Amendment reporter's privilege in civil lawsuits.

Courts, however, have read *Branzburg* more restrictively in the criminal context, sometimes declining to recognize a privilege at all, or allowing only a very limited balancing of interests. Three different federal appellate courts affirmed contempt citations requiring reporters to be jailed for refusing to reveal confidential sources sought in criminal investigations. In 2001, freelance writer Vanessa Leggett served nearly six months in a Texas prison for declining to reveal sources of information related to a notorious murder, almost four times longer than any prison term previously imposed on any reporter by any federal court. In 2004, James Taricani, a reporter for WJAR-TV in Rhode Island, completed a four-month sentence of home confinement for declining to reveal who leaked a videotape capturing alleged corruption by public officials in Providence. And, in 2005 The New York Times reporter Judith Miller was jailed in Virginia for several months for refusing to disclose her confidential source for a story she never wrote about CIA operative Valerie Plame.

Most recently, the U.S. Court of Appeals for the Fourth Circuit rejected any First Amendment-based or common law reporter's privilege in a criminal proceeding in which the subpoenaed journalist, James Risen, was an "eyewitness" to a crime. In this case, a confidential source allegedly leaked classified information to Risen and Risen was then subpoenaed to testify whether the criminal defendant was, in fact, his source. (*U.S. v. Sterling*). The U.S. Court of Appeals in Richmond held that Risen had no privilege whatsoever to refuse to testify in this context, and the Supreme Court refused to review the holding. When the case against the source went to trial, however, Attorney General Eric Holder decided that Risen's testimony was not needed, and Risen was not forced to testify. The CIA officer accused of being the source was convicted without compelling the reporter to testify or go to jail.

The aggressive court actions in criminal investigations have encouraged private litigants and federal courts adjudicating their civil cases also to demand confidential information from reporters. In one civil suit, five reporters (including two Pulitzer Prize winners) were held in contempt and subjected to fines of $500 per day each for declining to reveal their confidential sources of information about Dr. Wen Ho Lee, who claimed information about him was provided to reporters by government agents in violation of the Privacy Act.

Because the scope of a reporter's privilege in the federal courts is unsettled, reporters have been aided in federal investigations by Department of Justice guidelines that severely limit the circumstances under which U.S. attorneys may attempt to subpoena or search members of the news media. These guidelines were first enacted in 1970, but were most recently revised in 2014 and 2015 after public uproar over revelations that the department had secretly subpoenaed the telephone records of the AP in connection with a national security leak investigation and had obtained a search warrant for the email of a Fox News reporter in another leak investigation.

The guidelines currently in effect apply to subpoenas and similar compulsory process, court orders issued pursuant to 18 U.S.C. § 2703(d) or 18 U.S.C. § 3123, and warrants intended either "to obtain information from members of the news media" or to procure "communications records" or "business records" of members of the news media that are held by third parties. A notable limitation is that the guidelines protect only information related to "newsgathering activity," a term which is left undefined.

Where the guidelines apply, they generally require that all members of the department obtain the approval of the attorney general or relevant assistant attorney general before issuing a subpoena or requesting a court order seeking documents or information covered by the guidelines. They make clear that steps to seek information from a member of the news media are considered "extraordinary measures, not standard investigatory practices."

In deciding whether to authorize such a subpoena or seek a court order, the attorney general considers (a) in criminal matters, whether there are reasonable grounds to believe that a crime has occurred, and whether the information sought is essential to a successful investigation or prosecution; (b) in civil matters, whether there are reasonable grounds to believe that the information is essential to the successful completion of the investigation or litigation in a case of substantial importance; and (c) in all matters, whether the government has made all reasonable attempts to obtain the information from alternative, non-media sources. The government is also generally required to give reasonable notice to the journalists implicated before seeking a subpoena or court order, and to negotiate with them. The attorney general will generally limit any authorization to seeking evidence needed to verify the accuracy of published information and the circumstances surrounding such information, and requires all requests for information from the news media to be "narrowly drawn" to avoid imposing an undue burden.

These regulations provide the same types of protection contained in some state shield laws, and the Department of Justice has demonstrated a serious desire to enforce these regulations strictly. Any time a subpoena is received by a reporter from a U.S. attorney, the first question to ask the attorney is: Did you comply with the media guidelines at 28 C.F.R. 50.10 before issuing this subpoena? Not infrequently, just asking the question results in the subpoena being withdrawn.

— Liability for newsgathering conduct

A reporter for Mother Jones won a national award in 1984 for posing as a job applicant at a chemical factory and covertly taking photographs documenting illegal pesticides being manufactured for the export market. That conduct today would more likely win a lawsuit.

In holding that a reporter's promise of confidentiality is legally binding, the Supreme Court in *Cohen v. Cowles* (1991) announced that "generally applicable" laws having only "incidental effects" on the ability of the press to gather the news do not offend the First Amendment. Ever since, a flow of lawsuits have been filed against reporters asserting claims for such "generally applicable" torts as intrusion, trespass, and fraud, and more recently, asserting claims for accessing password-protected computers or voicemail. From the muzzling effect of the tobacco industry's threat of "tortious interference" liability against CBS for an expose based on a confidential source who was party to a standard confidentiality agreement as an employee of a tobacco company, through *Food Lion's* claim of trespass, fraud and breach of duty leveled against ABC and a spate of other hidden camera lawsuits, reporters since *Cohen v. Cowles* have faced an increased number of claims alleging misconduct in the gathering of the news.

This section highlights briefly some of the legal theories that can create problems for the unwary reporter.

— Intrusion upon seclusion

A claim for intrusion exists in most states if someone intentionally commits a "highly offensive" intrusion upon another's solitude or seclusion, invading either a physical space or the private affairs of the plaintiff, such as reviewing private financial statements or personal email without permission. Intrusion claims against the press most commonly arise in three contexts: (1) surreptitious surveillance; (2) trespass of private property, and (3) instances where consent to enter a private setting for one purpose has been exceeded (as where a reporter gains access to information under false pretenses).

Intrusion is a branch of the law of privacy. Where the potentially offending conduct occurs is therefore important. For example, in the United States a person generally has no legitimate basis to complain if a picture is taken in a public place, but if the picture is taken in or around the person's home, a claim for intrusion may exist if the person had a "reasonable expectation" of privacy where the photograph was taken.

In one noted lawsuit a few years back, the family of an officer of a large health care corporation successfully obtained an injunction against the elaborate efforts of a news organization that was seeking information about the family. The organization's camera crew followed the children to school, and sat in a boat outside the family's Florida home with a camera equipped with a high-powered telescopic lens. In issuing an injunction, the court concluded that "a persistent course of hounding, harassment and unreasonable surveillance, even if conducted in a public or semi-public place," could support a claim for intrusion upon seclusion.

A claim for intrusion generally requires (1) an intentional intrusion, (2) that impinges upon the solitude or seclusion of another, or his private affairs, and (3) that would be highly offensive to a reasonable person. The term "highly offensive" is ill-defined, but can include harassing behavior, surreptitious surveillance, or the use of high-power lenses and listening devices to invade typically private places.

The tort of intrusion is based on wrongful conduct rather than on the publication of any information, so a claim may exist even when the news story being pursued is never published. For this reason, in many states it is no defense to an intrusion claim to assert the newsworthiness of the information that was being sought. The issue is whether a reasonable person would view the conduct as highly offensive under all the circumstances.

Some examples where courts have upheld claims for intrusion illustrate the nature of the tort:

—Two journalists in California, without discussing who they were, gained access to the home of a disabled veteran who purported to provide healing aids in the form of clay, minerals and herbs. While there, they surreptitiously photographed and tape-recorded the veteran, for use in a magazine report. The court allowed a claim for intrusion even though the reporters were invited into the home by the veteran. While a person takes the risk that someone allowed into their home is not what he seems, and even though a visitor is free to repeat anything he sees or hears, the court held that the homeowner's risk does not extend to the risk that secret photographs and recordings will be transmitted to the world at large.

—The unauthorized recording of an unplanned interview conducted when the plaintiff answered his own front door has similarly been held to constitute an actionable "intrusion," while secretly recording an interview of a person who stepped from their home onto a public sidewalk was held not to be an intrusion.

—Televising an image of a person's home is not an intrusion if the broadcast shows no more than what can be seen from the street, and secretly recording a conversation in a place of business was held not to be an intrusion if the reporter was invited into the office and the state wiretap law permitted the secret recording.

— Trespass

A person commits a trespass by entering property that is in the possession of another, without authorization or consent. To avoid a claim, permission must be obtained by an owner, a tenant or someone acting on their behalf. Like intrusion, a trespass claim arises from conduct in gathering news, not from the content of any report that may subsequently be published.

Permission to be on private property can be implied by custom or by the nature of the premises. For example, someone has implied permission to enter a store or restaurant during business hours, even though it may be located on private property. There is similarly an implied right to approach someone's house on a driveway or sidewalk to see if they are home. Permission, whether express or implied, can also be revoked. If a posted sign says "Do Not Enter," or if the owner came to the door and said to leave, remaining on the property likely would be a trespass.

Trespass is also a strict liability tort. Entering on someone's property without permission, even by accident or mistake, will constitute a trespass. On the other hand, trespass protects only against a physical invasion of property; it does not limit the collection or use of information gathered while on the property. The law of trespass does not restrict a reporter on a public sidewalk from using what can be seen or heard on the adjacent private property.

The impact of trespass on newsgathering is also tempered by the nature of the damages that may be recovered through a claim for trespass. The trespass tort is intended to protect property, not privacy or reputation. A trespasser therefore can be held responsible only for physical harm done while on the land and other injury that is a "natural consequence" of the trespass. Courts generally will not recognize injury to reputation or emotional distress caused by the later publication of a photograph obtained during a trespass to be a "natural consequence" of the trespass itself.

A vivid example of a trespass claim involved a television camera crew that was preparing a report on credit card fraud. The United States Secret Service obtained a warrant to search an apartment for evidence of credit card fraud, and a news magazine camera crew followed the Secret Service into the apartment. Part of the search was taped, including a sequence of a mother and child cowering on the couch asking not be photographed. In refusing to dismiss a lawsuit asserting claims for trespass and a constitutional tort (for improperly accompanying federal agents in executing a search warrant), an outraged court said the reporters "had no greater right than that of a common thief to be in the apartment." Like intrusion, the trespass was complete once the invasion of private property occurred. The trespass claim could be asserted even though the news report being pursued was never broadcast.

In situations rife with the potential for trespass, common sense can once again minimize the risk of litigation:
— Whenever possible, ask the property owner or those who appear to be in charge for permission to enter, or seek their approval to remain. In situations where police or fire officials have taken control of a crime or disaster scene, they may stand in for the owner and grant or deny access. Their presence does not defeat the owner's rights, however, and the owner can still require a reporter to leave private property.
— Always identify yourself — verbally, by displaying a press credential, and through insignias on clothing and cameras — so that those present know you are a reporter and will not assume you are part of any police or emergency response team. If not asked to leave, the fact that your status as a reporter was disclosed may be sufficient to establish an implied consent to remain.
— If asked to leave, retire to the sidewalk, street, or other position on public property.
— Consent obtained through fraud or misrepresentation will not be considered

valid consent and will not defeat a claim for trespass.

— Consent obtained from minors or others who are not legally capable of giving consent (mentally incapacitated people, for example) will not defeat a claim for trespass.

— Electronic eavesdropping

Both state and federal law regulate the electronic recording of conversations, including telephone conversations.

Under the federal law, a conversation may not be recorded without the consent of at least one of the participants. That means reporters are not prohibited by federal law from recording any conversation in which they participate, whether or not they disclose that the conversation is being recorded. But, leaving a hidden tape recorder in a room to record a conversation between others, secretly listening in on an extension phone and recording the conversation, or recording a telephone call picked up on a scanner or listening device, is a violation of federal law if done without permission of one of the parties.

The law in most states is similar to the federal law, allowing a conversation to be recorded so long as one party to the conversation consents. The laws in a minority of states are more strict, and prohibit recording any conversation unless permission is given by all the parties to the conversation. This requirement of consent extends only to conversations where there is some expectation of privacy, and does not prohibit tape-recording at speeches, press conferences and similar public events.

— Misrepresentation and similar forms of wrongdoing

Laws of general applicability govern the actions of reporters, yet conduct that might sometimes be deemed "deceit," "misrepresentation" or "fraud" can be useful in ferreting out the news. Reporters are often less than candid in dealing with those from whom they want information. Recognizing this reality, some courts have held that claims such as fraud and misrepresentation cannot be pursued against journalists unless the wrong is "particularly egregious," or part of a broader pattern of wrongdoing. For example, courts have rejected claims for fraud based on a false message left on a telephone answering machine to induce the disclosure of information, and for falsely promising that no "ambush" techniques would be used if an interview were granted.

Other courts have been less willing to weigh the public interest in a news report against the allegedly wrongful conduct. In one instance, a judge allowed claims for fraud and breach of contract to proceed against Business Week after a reporter gained access to records of a credit reporting agency by misrepresenting that a subscription to the credit service was being sought in order to conduct background checks on potential Business Week employees. In reality, information was sought for an exposé on the credit-reporting industry, and the reporter promptly obtained the credit history of then-Vice President Dan Quayle without his consent. The court held that such "wanton misconduct" can result in liability, and allowed a recovery of the costs incurred by the credit agency as a result of the misrepresentation.

Remember, the basic rule is that reporters must obey rules and regulations when they are gathering the news. While there are some exceptions, the First

Amendment will not generally provide a defense to a reporter who violates the law while gathering the news.

— Special Considerations When Dealing with National Security Issues

The Espionage Act (of 1917) makes it a federal crime to publish classified information that either (a) reveals the communications intelligence activities of the United States or any foreign country, or (b) discloses classified information obtained from a foreign government or military force through the "processes of communications intelligence." The Espionage Act also broadly makes it a crime for any unauthorized person either to communicate to another, or to retain possession of "information relating to national defense" if there is "reason to believe" the information could harm the U.S. or help a foreign nation or military force.

In the decades since the statute was enacted, there has never been a prosecution of a news organization for violating the Espionage Act, but there has been saber-rattling from time to time. In December 2010, for example, Sen. Joseph Lieberman publicly called upon the Justice Department to investigate whether The New York Times had violated the Espionage Act by publishing confidential U.S. diplomatic cables it had obtained from WikiLeaks. And, in June 2013, Rep. Peter King, chairman of the House Subcommittee on Counterterrorism, repeatedly called for the prosecution of journalists who "severely compromise national security," singling out Glenn Greenwald, then a journalist for The Guardian, for publishing news reports based on the documents leaked by Edward Snowden. The application of the Espionage Act to a news organization would raise significant First Amendment issues and might well run afoul of the doctrine barring application of criminal sanctions against the press for publishing truthful information on matters of public concern. It would also raise a number of significant issues, including the propriety of the classification of the information at issue; the vagueness and breadth of the statute when applied to the press; and the lack of the meaning of "harm" to our national security and the burden of proving it.

Given the continuing uncertainty surrounding the Espionage Act, special care should be taken before accepting or communicating information known to be classified, and legal guidance sought where appropriate. Because the act is not literally limited to "classified" information, special care should be taken with any nonpublic information concerning official intelligence activities or communications with foreign governments.

In order to avoid exposure for possible conspiracy and "aiding and abetting" liability or both, it is also important to maintain a traditional source-news organization relationship with those individuals who may provide you with national security information, although this is no guarantee of immunity from prosecution.

In 2011, as part of a national security leak investigation, the Justice Department obtained a search warrant for the email of a Fox News reporter who allegedly obtained classified information from a State Department source. In applying for the warrant, the department told the court that the reporter had asked the source to disclose newsworthy information he knew to be classified, and asserted that in doing so the reporter was aiding and abetting a violation of the Espionage Act.

When the search warrant application was made public months later, a firestorm erupted over the assertion that a reporter had committed a crime simply by asking for information. Attorney General Holder subsequently acknowledged that the department had never intended to prosecute the reporter and had over-stepped its bounds in making the allegation of criminality. Holder vowed that no reporter would go to jail for "engaging in journalism" so long as he was attorney general. Holder then revised the departmental guidelines to prevent a search warrant from being sought for a reporter's records unless the reporter is indeed the target of an active criminal investigation. Holder's successor, Loretta Lynch, indicated that she would stand by his policy of not jailing journalists for doing their jobs. The Trump administration's position in this regard is uncertain, though Attorney General Jeff Sessions has declined to "make a blanket commitment" endorsing the prior approach.

LEGAL PRINCIPLES OF PUBLICATION

When a news report is published, the nature of its content poses three principal legal risks to a journalist: that the report contains incorrect information that harms someone's reputation, contains correct information that invades someone's privacy, or contains material that is subject to someone else's copyright. This section provides an overview of the law of defamation, privacy and copyright infringement, by examining what a plaintiff is required to prove against news organizations to succeed on such claims and the defenses that are available.

Defamation

In 1967, shortly after *New York Times v. Sullivan* was handed down, Associate Justice John Harlan remarked that "the law of libel has changed substantially since the early days of the Republic." Unfortunately, the news stories that still generate the most claims of injury to reputation — the basis of libel — are still the run-of-the-mill.

Perhaps 95 of 100 libel suits result from the routine publication of charges of crime, immorality, incompetence or inefficiency. A Harvard Nieman report makes the point: "The gee-whiz, slam-bang stories usually aren't the ones that generate libel, but the innocent-appearing, potentially treacherous minor yarns from police courts and traffic cases, from routine meetings and from business reports."

Most lawsuits based on relatively minor stories result from factual error or inexact language — for example, getting the plea wrong or inaccurately making it appear that all defendants in a case face identical charges. Libel even lurks in such innocent-appearing stories as birth notices and wedding announcements. Turner Catledge, former managing editor of The New York Times, noted in his autobiography, "My Life and the Times," that people sometimes would "call in the engagement of two people who hate each other, as a practical joke." The fact that some New York newspapers have had to defend suits for such announcements illustrates the care and concern required in every editorial department.

In publishing, no matter what level of constitutional protection, there is just no substitute for accuracy.

— *What is libel?*

Libel is one side of the coin called "defamation," slander being the flip side. At its most basic, defamation means injury to reputation. Libel is generally distinguished from slander, in that a libel is written, or otherwise printed, whereas a slander is spoken. While defamation published in a newspaper universally is regarded as libel, it is perhaps not so self-evident that, in many states, defamation broadcast by television or radio also is considered libel, rather than slander: Because broadcast defamation is often recorded on tape and carried to a wide audience, it is viewed as more dangerous to reputation than a fleeting, unrecorded conversation, and so is classed with printed defamation. In any case, the term defamation generally includes both libel and slander. Words, pictures, cartoons, photo captions and headlines can all give rise to a claim for defamation.

The various states define libel somewhat differently, but largely to the same effect. In Illinois, for example, libel is defined by the courts as "the publication of anything injurious to the good name or reputation of another, or which tends to bring him into disrepute." In New York, a libelous statement is one that tends to expose a person to hatred, contempt or aversion or to induce an evil or unsavory opinion of the person in the minds of a substantial number of people in the community.

In Texas, libel is defined by statute as anything that "tends to injure a living person's reputation and thereby expose the person to public hatred, contempt or ridicule, or financial injury or to impeach any person's honesty, integrity, virtue, or reputation or to publish the natural defects of anyone and thereby expose the person to public hatred, ridicule, or financial injury."

— *Liability for republication: the 'conduit' fallacy*

A common misconception is that one who directly quotes a statement containing libelous allegations is immune from suit so long as the quoted statement was actually made, accurately transcribed and clearly attributed to the original speaker. This is not so. In fact, the common law principle is just the opposite — a republisher of a libel is generally considered just as responsible for the libel as the original speaker. That you were simply an accurate conduit for the statement of another is no defense to a libel claim.

In many circumstances, therefore, a newspaper can be called to task for republishing a libelous statement made by someone quoted in a story. This rule can lead to harsh results and therefore exceptions exist. For example, reporting the fact that a plaintiff has filed a libel suit against a defendant could, in certain circumstances, lead to a claim against a newspaper for repeating the libel alleged in the complaint. In most states, a "fair report privilege" shields the publisher of an accurate and impartial report of the contents of legal papers filed in court to avoid this result.

Many states also recognize that newspapers under the pressure of daily deadlines often rely on the research of other reputable news organizations in republishing news items originally appearing elsewhere. In such cases, reliance on a reputable newspaper or news agency often is recognized as a defense to a libel claim. Of course, this so-called "wire service defense" may not be available if the republisher had or should have had substantial reason to question the accuracy or good faith of the original story.

The fair report privilege and the wire service defense are exceptions to the basic rule. When the press reports that X has leveled accusations against Y, the press may be held to account not only for the truth of the fact that the accusations were made, but also for the steps taken to verify the truth of the accusations. Therefore, when accusations are made against a person, it generally is prudent to investigate their truth as well as to obtain balancing comment with some relation to the original charges. Irrelevant countercharges can lead to problems with the person who made the first accusation.

In short, always bear in mind that a newspaper can be held responsible in defamation for republishing the libelous statement made by another, even when the quote is correct.

— The five things a successful libel plaintiff must prove

Although the terminology may differ from state to state, a libel plaintiff suing a reporter or a news organization will have to prove five things in order to prevail on a claim for defamation:

1. A defamatory statement was made.
2. The defamatory statement is a matter of fact, not opinion.
3. The defamatory statement is false.
4. The defamatory statement is about ("of and concerning") the plaintiff.
5. The defamatory statement was published with the requisite degree of "fault."

By developing an understanding of the legal elements of a claim for libel, reporters and editors can fashion guideposts that will assist them in practicing their craft in a way that avoids wrongfully injuring the reputation of the subjects of their stories — and thereby reducing the legal risk to the publications for which they write.

1. A defamatory statement was made

It may seem self-evident that a libel claim cannot exist unless a defamatory statement was made, but subjects of news stories (and their lawyers) often bring claims for libel without being able to demonstrate that what was written about them is capable of conveying a defamatory meaning. Put differently, not every negative news report is defamatory.

Generally, statements accusing someone of being a criminal, an adulterer, insane or infected with a loathsome disease are considered automatically "capable of defamatory meaning," as are statements that injure someone's professional reputation (such as that they are corrupt or incompetent). However, to determine whether any particular statement is susceptible of defamatory meaning, reference must be made, first, to the definition of libel adopted in the relevant state, and second, to the full context in which the challenged statement appeared when it was published.

For example, a New York court found that a statement identifying an attorney as a "flashy entertainment lawyer" was not, without more, defamatory, although a statement that a lawyer was an "ambulance chaser" with an interest only in "slam dunk" cases would be. The reasoning is that the first statement would not necessarily damage a lawyer's reputation, while the latter would. Likewise, in New York, allegations of drunkenness, use of "political clout" to gain governmental benefit, membership in the "Mafia," communist affiliation or that someone has cancer may or may not be defamatory, depending on the circumstances of the case.

In Illinois, courts make determinations about defamatory meaning on a case-by-case basis, though in Illinois, most statements will not be considered defamatory unless they charge a person with commission of a crime, adultery/fornication, or incompetence or lack of integrity in their business or profession. Under this approach, the statement that plaintiff left his children home at night and lost his job because of drinking was held to be defamatory as an accusation of child neglect and inability to discharge the duties of his job due to alcoholism. Similarly, reporting that an alderman had disclosed confidential information was held to be defamatory as indicating that the official lacked the integrity to properly discharge the duties of his office.

In Texas, a statement may be false, abusive and unpleasant without being defamatory. For example, a Texas court held that describing someone as resembling a "hard boiled egg," referring to baldness and pudginess, was not defamatory. Likewise, describing a political candidate as a "radical," "backed and financed by big-shot labor bosses" was not considered defamatory in Texas. On the other hand, an insinuation that a person is connected with gambling and prostitution was found to be defamatory. The assertion that a person who had made an allegation against another of child molestation had fabricated and since recanted the allegation was defamatory when no recantation had, in fact, been made.

While each potentially defamatory statement must be assessed in its own context, particular caution is in order where the statement involves allegations of crime or similar wrongdoing, incompetence or unprofessionalism, or infidelity.

2. The defamatory statement is a matter of fact, not opinion

To be actionable as libel, a defamatory statement must be provably false (or carry a provably false implication). Stated differently, only factual statements that are capable of being proven true or false can form the basis of a libel claim. "Opinions" that do not include or imply provably false facts cannot be the basis of a libel claim. Similarly, epithets, satire, parody and hyperbole that are incapable of being proven true or false are protected forms of expression.

The Supreme Court, in *Gertz v. Robert Welch Inc.* (1974), recognized a constitutional dimension to the prohibition of libel claims based on opinion, stating that "there is no such thing as a false idea." In a later case, *Milkovich v. Lorain Journal Co.* (1990), the Supreme Court denied that there is a distinct constitutional "opinion privilege," but held that any claim for libel must be based on a statement of fact that is provably false, thus shielding purely subjective opinions from liability. Under this approach, a statement is not protected "opinion" merely because it contains qualifying language such as "I think" or "I believe," if what follows contains an assertion of fact that can be proven true or false (e.g., "I believe he murdered his wife.").

Some examples of actual cases can provide a better sense of the distinction between an actionable false fact and a protected opinion:

In Virginia, "pure expressions of opinion" cannot be the basis of a claim for defamation. Under this standard, the statement "I wouldn't trust him as far as I could throw him" and the caption "Director of Butt-Licking" were held to be nonactionable opinion. The Virginia Supreme Court has found words charging that an architect lacked experience and charged excessive fees, or accusing a charitable foundation with failing to spend a "reasonable portion" of its income on program services, also to be protected opinions rather than to be verifiable facts.

In New York, the test for distinguishing a fact from an opinion asks whether: (1) the statement has a precise core of meaning on which a consensus of understanding exists; (2) the statement is verifiable; (3) the textual context of the statement would cause an average reader to infer a factual meaning; and (4) the broader social context signals usage as either fact or opinion. The first two factors focus on the meaning of the words used, the latter two factors consider whether the content, tone and apparent purpose of the statement should signal to the reader that the statement reflects the author's opinion.

Under these principles, calling a doctor a "rotten apple," for example, is incapable of being proved true or false and is therefore protected as an expression of opinion. Similarly, a statement that someone lacked "talent, ambition, initiative" is a nonactionable expression of opinion, since there is no provable, common understanding of what quantum of talent or ambition constitutes a "lack." In one New York case, a letter to the editor published in a scientific journal submitted by the International Primate Protection League and which warned that a multinational corporation's plans for establishing facilities to conduct hepatitis research using chimpanzees could spread hepatitis to the rest of the chimpanzee population was, given its overall context, protected as opinion.

Even when a fact is implicit in an opinion, the common law often protects the statement from liability. In many states, a statement of opinion based on true facts that are themselves accurately set forth is not actionable. Where the facts underlying the opinion are reported inaccurately, however, and would adversely affect the conclusion drawn by the average reader concerning the opinion expressed, the publication may give rise to a claim for libel. For example, the statement, "I believe he murdered his wife because he was found with a bottle of the same kind of poison that killed her," likely would not be actionable even if the plaintiff could prove he did not murder his wife *if* it is true that he was found with a bottle of the same kind of poison that killed her. The true facts on which the (erroneous) opinion was based were disclosed to the readers. If there was no bottle of poison, however, the suggestion that he was a murderer would certainly be actionable. If an opinion suggests or appears to rely on an undisclosed fact, however, a libel claim may still be brought upon the unstated, implied facts if they are both false and defamatory.

The statement that a sports commentator was a "liar" without reference to specific facts, under this approach, was considered to be protected opinion. Taken in the total context of an article, the statement that the plaintiff was a "neo-Nazi" was protected as opinion. Likewise, a statement calling a plaintiff a "commie," suggesting that he does not understand the subject he teaches and that he is "not traveling with a full set of luggage," was also protected as opinion. Statements accusing doctors of being "cancer con-artists," of practicing "medical quackery," and of promoting "snake oil remedies," were also protected. A newspaper column and editorial characterizing a nudist pageant as "pornography" and as "immoral" were also protected.

One federal appeals court has held that three questions should be considered to distinguish opinion from fact: (1) does the statement use figurative or hyperbolic language that would negate the impression that the statement is serious? (2) does the general tenor of the statement negate the impression that the statement is serious? (3) can the statement be proved true or false?

Under this test, a commentator's statement that a product "didn't work" was not an opinion because, despite the humorous tenor of the comment, it did not use figurative or hyperbolic language, it could reasonably be understood as asserting an objective fact and the fact could be proven true or false. Likewise, a statement made in a newspaper interview that plaintiff was an "extortionist" was not protected as opinion.

The common thread to these variations is that opinions offered in a context presenting the facts on which they are based will generally not be actionable. On the other hand, opinions that imply the existence of undisclosed, defamatory facts (i.e., if you knew what I know) are more likely to be actionable. In addition, a statement that is capable of being proven true or false, regardless of whether it is expressed as an opinion, an exaggeration or hyperbole, may be actionable.

3. The defamatory statement is false

In almost all libel cases involving news organizations, the plaintiff has the burden of proving that the defamatory statement is false. (The states are divided on whether a purely private individual has to prove falsity when the defamatory statement does not involve a matter of public concern.) Nonetheless, as a practical matter, a libel defendant's best defense is often to prove that the statement is true. While this may sound like six-of-one-half-dozen-of-the-other, there is considerable significance to placing on the plaintiff the legal burden of proving falsity: Where a jury feels it cannot decide whether a statement is true or false because the evidence is mixed, it is required to rule against the plaintiff — ties go to the defendant.

In almost all states, the question is not whether the challenged statement is literally and absolutely true, in every jot and tittle, but whether the statement as published is "substantially true." That is, a court will consider whether the gist or sting of the defamatory statement is accurate, or whether the published statement would produce a different effect in the mind of a reader than would the absolutely true version.

For example, most courts will dismiss a libel claim brought by a person charged with second degree burglary, if a newspaper mistakenly reported that he had been charged with first-degree burglary: The gist of the story (that the man is an accused burglar) is true, and most readers would not form a better opinion of the man had they been correctly informed that it was only second degree burglary with which he had been charged. But, where a newspaper mistakenly reports that the accused burglar has been charged with murder (or that a person thus far only accused of murder has been convicted of it), a court might well conclude that the "sting" of the statement is not substantially accurate, and that readers would think less of the person based on the false statement than they would have had the published report been accurate.

4. The defamatory statement is about the plaintiff

Since the law of libel protects the reputation of an individual or a business entity, only the individual or entity whose reputation has been injured is entitled to complain. Thus, a libel plaintiff must prove that the defamatory statement was "of and concerning" the plaintiff. It often is obvious whether a statement is about a particular person (for example, because it gives his or her full name, place of residence and age). But even where no name is used, a libel claim may be brought if some readers would reasonably understand the statement to be about the plaintiff. For example, the statement referring to "the woman who cooks lunch at the diner," when there is only one woman who cooks at that diner, will be considered "of and concerning" the female cook.

In a recent Illinois case, a news report on the commencement of a murder trial referred to the defendant as "suburban car dealer John Doe." While "John Doe" was indeed on trial for murder, he was not a suburban car dealer. His brother, "Joe Doe," was a suburban car dealer, but was not on trial for murder. The court concluded that reasonable readers could have understood the report to be about Joe (despite the fact that Joe's name was never mentioned, while John's was correctly used), and that Joe therefore would have the opportunity to show the statement was understood to be "of and concerning" him.

A few words about "group libel." Where a statement impugns a group of persons, but no individual is specifically identified, no member of the group may sue for libel if the group is large. For example, the statement, in a large city, that "all cab drivers cheat their customers out of money," does not allow any cab driver to sue for libel as a result, no matter how many fares the plaintiff cab driver may have lost because of the published statement. But, beware of publishing the same statement in a newspaper in a town with only a handful of cab drivers, where a court might well conclude the readers would reasonably think the statement was specifically referring to each of the town's four cab drivers, despite the absence of their names in the statement. Some courts have questioned whether the First Amendment permits claims for group libel under any circumstances, because the Supreme Court has said that the requirement that the statement be "of and concerning" the plaintiff is constitutionally required.

In this regard, it is worth noting, most courts have held that a statement about a company is not, without more, "of and concerning" its officers, directors or employees (provided it is not a sole proprietorship). By the same token, a statement about a CEO or other corporate official is not, without more, "of and concerning" the company itself.

Finally, a word about the dead: It is mostly correct that you cannot defame the dead. Again, because libel protects personal reputation, and one has no practical need for a good personal reputation in this world after one has departed it, most states do not permit a person's survivors to bring a claim for statements made after the person's death.

5. The defamatory statement was published with the requisite degree of fault

For almost 200 years, libel in this country was a tort of strict liability. It did not matter whether the defendant was at fault or had acted in some improper way. The mere fact that a libel was printed was sufficient to establish liability

New York Times v. Sullivan changed everything. In that case the Supreme Court first recognized the constitutional requirement that a public official must demonstrate not only that an error was made, but also a high degree of fault by the publisher in order to prevail on a libel claim. Somewhat confusingly referred to as "actual malice," what such a plaintiff is required to prove is that the defendant published a "calculated falsehood" — that is, that the defendant knew the statement was false when published, or published the statement despite having a high degree of awareness that it probably was false (the latter is sometimes called "reckless disregard" for the truth). This additional burden was required under the First Amendment, the court said, in order to provide the "breathing room" for the exercise of free speech that is essential to public discussion by citizens on matters concerning their self-government.

The court considered the *Sullivan* case "against the background of a profound national commitment to the principle that debate on public issues should be uninhibited, robust and wide-open, and that it may well include vehement, caustic and sometimes unpleasantly sharp attacks on government and public officials."

The ruling in *Sullivan* with respect to libel claims by public officials was extended three years later to libel claims by public figures, in *The Associated Press v. Walker*. The court reversed a $500,000 libel judgment won by former Maj. Gen. Edwin A. Walker in a Texas state court against the AP, after it had reported that Walker "assumed command" of rioters at the University of Mississippi and "led a charge of students against federal marshals" when James H. Meredith was admitted to the university in September 1962. Walker alleged those statements to be false.

In ruling for the AP, the Supreme Court found: "Under any reasoning, Gen. Walker was a public man in whose public conduct society and the press had a legitimate and substantial interest." It therefore held that Walker, too, was required to prove higher fault by the publisher even though he was not a public official.

The rulings in the *Sullivan* and *Walker* cases were landmark decisions for freedom of the press and speech. They established safeguards not previously defined, but they did not provide news organizations with absolute immunity against libel suits by officials who are criticized. Rather, they stand for the principle that, to encourage public debate on matters of public concern, when a newspaper publishes information about a public official or public figure and publishes it without "actual malice," it should be spared a damage suit even if some of the information turns out to be wrong.

The *Walker* decision made an additional important distinction concerning the context in which an article is prepared. In a companion case consolidated before the Supreme Court, Wallace Butts, former athletic director of the University of Georgia, had obtained a libel verdict against Curtis Publishing Co. His suit was based on an article in the Saturday Evening Post accusing Butts of giving his football team's strategy secrets to an opposing coach prior to a game between the two schools.

The Supreme Court found that Butts was a public figure, but said there was a substantial difference between the two cases. Unlike the AP report on the actions of Walker, "the Butts story was in no sense 'hot news' and the editors of the magazine recognized the need for a thorough investigation of the serious charges. Elementary precautions were, nevertheless, ignored."

Chief Justice Earl Warren, in a concurring opinion, referred to "slipshod and sketchy investigatory techniques employed to check the veracity of the source" in the Butts case. He said the evidence disclosed "reckless disregard for the truth."

The differing outcomes against The Associated Press and the Saturday Evening Post should be noted carefully. Although both involved public figures who were required to establish "actual malice," the evidence sufficient to make this showing differed in the context of a "hot news" report from investigative reporting.

By 1974, in *Gertz v. Robert Welch, Inc.*, the Supreme Court had extended the requirement that a libel plaintiff show some fault on the part of the defendant to include all defamation claims against news organizations, although not all types of plaintiffs must show the highest degree of fault. The level of "fault" that a plaintiff must prove will vary depending on who the plaintiff is.

— Fault required for public officials and public figures

If the plaintiff is a public official or public figure, the plaintiff must establish by clear and convincing evidence that the publication was made with "actual malice," which, as noted, is an unfortunate choice of phrase by the Supreme Court for a concept that might better have been called "constitutional fault," since the standard has little to do with whether a reporter harbored spite or ill will against the plaintiff.

The first type of actual malice, "knowing falsity," is easy to understand. "Reckless disregard" has required further elaboration by the courts, the best description of which perhaps is publication of a statement "with a high degree of awareness of its probable falsity." Put differently, a reporter may act with reckless disregard for truth if he or she publishes despite holding serious doubts about the truth of the published statement.

The test for actual malice thus looks to the subjective state of mind of the reporter/publisher at the time of publication. It inquires into whether the reporter or publisher believed the statement was false or whether he/she proceeded to publish despite recognizing that there was a good chance that the statement was false. Because most reporters and publishers are not in the business of publishing news reports unless they have good grounds to believe them to be true, generally speaking, it is difficult for a plaintiff to show that a newspaper published a story with actual malice.

As one Illinois court phrased it, actual malice is shown only when a reporter's investigation "has revealed either insufficient information to support the allegations in good faith or information which creates substantial doubt as to the truth of published allegations."

Thus, as interpreted by most states, "actual malice" cannot be proven simply by showing that a reporter made mistakes (either by getting facts wrong or by failing to talk to one or more key sources), or that the reporter disliked the plaintiff, or that the newspaper frequently published items critical of the plaintiff. Rather, the test focuses on whether the reporter in fact disbelieved, or strongly doubted the truth of, the published statement. In some cases, plaintiffs may establish actual malice if they can show that a reporter willfully turned a blind eye to the truth and, if acting in good faith, would have known that the statement was false.

— *Fault required for private individuals*

Under the First Amendment, even private individuals must show some degree of fault before they can recover for a libel by a news organization in a report on a matter of public concern. States are free to set the standard of care that must be met in reporting on private individuals, so long as they require at least a showing of negligence.

A number of states have decided to adopt the minimum standard and require a private libel plaintiff to show only that a reporter was negligent. That means the plaintiff must show that the reporter's conduct was less careful than one would expect of a reasonable journalist in similar circumstances. In Texas and California, for example, the question in a private figure libel case is whether the defendant should have known, through the exercise of reasonable care, that a statement was false.

The courts have looked at a number of factors to evaluate whether "negligence" exists. The considerations include:
— Did the reporter follow the standards of investigation and reporting ordinarily adhered to by responsible publishers? In many libel cases plaintiffs will use "expert" witnesses to testify about what are the "acceptable journalistic practices."
— Did the reporter follow his or her own normal procedures? Any time that you do something differently from what you usually do in reporting a story — particularly if the change involves exercising less care, rather than more care — you had better have a good explanation for why that was done.
— Did the reporter have any reason to doubt the accuracy of a source, or any advance warning that the story might not be right? Was it possible to find out the truth? This — like many of the factors the courts consider — is a matter of common sense. If you have received information that just does not ring true to you, and it is something that is easily checked, check it out before you run with the story!
— How *much* did the reporter do to check out the facts? Did the reporter take steps to confirm the information received, or simply run with the story without verifying the facts?
— Who are your sources of information? Are they reliable, and objective — or known "flakes" or people with a clear ax to grind? Are they anonymous sources? How many independent sources do you have (and how do they know the information they are giving you)?

Some courts set different fault levels for private figures depending on whether the publication at issue involved a matter of "public concern" or of "private concern." New York, for example, has held that if the plaintiff is a private individual involved in a matter of legitimate public concern, the plaintiff must establish by a preponderance of the evidence that the publication was made in a "grossly irresponsible" manner without due regard for the standards of information gathering and dissemination ordinarily followed by responsible parties involving similar matters. In cases involving matters of private concern,

New York, too, applies a negligence standard, although New York courts typically defer to the press in determining what constitutes a matter of "public concern" (and thus the vast majority of New York private figure cases apply the "gross irresponsibility" standard).

— Who is who?

Needless to say, being able to determine whether the subject of a news story is a public official or figure or a private figure bears directly on the amount of legal risk posed by the story.

While it is clear that not every government employee will be considered a public official for purposes of what they must prove in a libel case, the Supreme Court has yet to lay down definitive standards. Thus, the definition varies somewhat from state to state.

In New York, public officials are those who are elected or appointed to office and who appear to have substantial responsibility for control over public and governmental affairs. Judges, police officers, state troopers and corrections officers have all been held to be public officials under this standard. Similarly, a public official is defined in California to be someone who has, or appears to the public to have, substantial responsibility for or control over the conduct of governmental affairs. In California, people found to be public officials have included a police officer, an assistant public defender and an assistant district attorney.

Texas, in contrast, looks to the following criteria as relevant to determine whether a libel plaintiff is a public official: (1) the public interest in the public position held by the plaintiff; (2) the authority possessed by the plaintiff to act on behalf of a government entity; (3) the amount of governmental funds controlled by the plaintiff; (4) the number of employees the official supervises; (5) the amount of contact between the plaintiff and the public, and (6) the extent to which the plaintiff acts in a representative capacity for the governmental entity or has any direct dealings with the government.

Under this standard, (1) a county sheriff; (2) a Child Protective Services specialist with authority to investigate charges of child abuse, remove children from their homes and place them in foster care; (3) an undercover narcotics agent employed by the state's law enforcement agency; (4) a ranking officer in charge of a narcotics squad of four men; (5) an individual who was a high school athletic director, head football coach and teacher; (6) an assistant regional administrator of a branch office of the Securities and Exchange Commission, and (7) a part-time city attorney have all been found to be public officials.

But under the same Texas test, the following people were found not to be public officials: (1) a high school teacher; (2) a prominent member of two private organizations affiliated with a state university; (3) a former special counsel for a court of inquiry into county fund management; (4) a court reporter, and (5) an appointed justice of the peace (where the article appeared in a city where plaintiff was not justice of the peace and did not refer to plaintiff's official capacity).

While, at least at higher ranks, it is relatively easy to identify public officials, both reporters and the courts have confronted substantial difficulty in the area of public figures, particularly in separating those who are merely socially or professionally prominent from those who, because of their influence over public matters, are properly considered public figures for libel purposes.

For example, the 1976 case of *Time v. Firestone* stemmed from Time magazine's account of the divorce of Russell and Mary Alice Firestone. The magazine said she had been divorced on grounds of "extreme cruelty and adultery." The court made no finding of adultery. She sued. The former Mrs. Firestone was a prominent social figure in Palm Beach, Florida, and held press conferences in the course of the divorce proceedings. Yet, the Supreme Court said she was not a public figure because "she did not assume any role of special prominence in the affairs of society, other than perhaps Palm Beach society, and she did not thrust herself to the forefront of any particular public controversy in order to influence resolution of the issues involved in it."

Similarly, Sen. William Proxmire of Wisconsin was sued for $8 million by Ronald Hutchinson, a research scientist who had received several public grants, including one for $50,000. Proxmire gave Hutchinson a "Golden Fleece" award, saying Hutchinson "has made a fortune from his monkeys and in the process made a monkey of the American taxpayer." The Supreme Court held in 1979 that, despite the receipt of substantial public funds, Hutchinson was not a public figure because he held no particular sway over the resolution of matters of public concern.

Note also the case of Ilya Wolston, who pleaded guilty in 1957 to criminal contempt for failing to appear before a grand jury investigating espionage. A book published in 1974 referred to these events. Wolston alleged that he had been libeled. In ruling on *Wolston v. Reader's Digest*, the Supreme Court said that he was not a public figure. The court said people convicted of crimes do not automatically become public figures. Wolston, the court said, was thrust into the public spotlight unwillingly, long after the events of public concern had ended.

At bottom, although the Supreme Court has yet to definitively resolve the issue, the point appears to be that public figures are those who seek the limelight, who inject themselves into public debate, and who seek to influence public opinion. A person who has widespread influence over public opinion on many matters may be deemed a "general purpose public figure" and required to prove actual malice no matter the subject of a particular allegedly defamatory statement. Oprah Winfrey is an example of someone who likely would be deemed a general purpose public figure.

A person who seeks to influence public opinion in only one area (such as, for example, by leading a campaign to enact animal rights legislation), however, may be deemed a "limited purpose public figure" and required to prove actual malice only with respect to allegedly defamatory statements about his or her animal rights activities. Limited purpose public figures have included: a prominent attorney; religious groups; a belly dancer; and a "stripper for God," among others.

Texas courts generally ask three questions in order to determine whether someone is a limited purpose public figure: (1) is the controversy truly a public controversy? (i.e., (a) are people talking about the controversy and (b) are people other than those immediately involved in the controversy likely to feel the impact of its resolution?); (2) does the plaintiff have more than a trivial or tangential role in the controversy?; (3) is the alleged defamation relevant to the plaintiff's participation in the controversy? Under this standard, an abortion protester on a public street in the vicinity of an abortion clinic was considered a limited purpose public figure, as was a zoologist who appeared on television shows and gave interviews on his controversial work.

On the other hand, a public school teacher whose participation in public controversy did not exceed that which she was required to do by school district regulations (except that she responded to media inquiries), was not a public figure in California. Similarly, a corporation which conducted a closeout sale for a landmark department store was not a public figure simply because it was doing business with a party to a controversy.

A note on corporations: In many states, the same standards that determine whether an individual is a public figure apply to corporations. Some states, however, conclude that corporations are always public figures, while others apply a narrower standard. For example, a British corporation that did not deal in consumer goods and had not received significant past publicity was a private figure for the purposes of a Texas libel claim.

In addition, a few lower courts have embraced the concept of an "involuntary public figure," in which an otherwise private person becomes a public figure by virtue of his or her having become drawn into a significant public controversy.

While this area of the law is freighted with subtleties to which lawyers and judges devote considerable energy, the practical bottom line is that, while public officials and public figures always bear a high burden of proof in making out a libel claim, where a news story concerns a private individual, whether involved in a matter of public concern or not, his or her burden is likely to be lower, perhaps much lower, if the story is wrong. Accordingly, there are more legal risks to publishing reports about private individuals (especially where the matter is not of legitimate public concern).

— Defenses commonly available to news organizations

Where a news story is written in such a way that a plaintiff might be able to prove all five of the elements of a libel, the law nevertheless affords defenses to news organizations in certain circumstances. Among the most prominent are the "fair comment privilege," the "fair and accurate report privilege," and the "neutral report privilege." They are referred to as privileges because, where properly invoked, a news organization is "privileged" to print what otherwise would be an actionable libel.

1. Fair comment

The fair comment (sometimes, "fair criticism") privilege long predates the opinion doctrine and continues, in most states, to exist as an independent matter of state law. The right of fair comment has been summarized as follows: "Everyone has a right to comment on matters of public interest and concern, provided they do so fairly and with an honest purpose. Such comments or criticism are not libelous, however severe in their terms, unless they are written maliciously. Thus it has been held that books, prints, pictures and statuary publicly exhibited, and the architecture of public buildings, and actors and exhibitors are all the legitimate subjects of newspapers' criticism, and such criticism fairly and honestly made is not libelous, however strong the terms of censure may be." (*Hoeppner v. Dunkirk Pr. Co.*, 1930.)

Some states, such as Texas, have recognized the fair comment privilege as a matter of statutory law. The Texas statute protects reasonable and fair comment or criticism of the official acts of public officials and of other matters of public concern when published for general information.

Not all states recognize this privilege, and the specifics of its application vary among the states that do recognize it. But where an otherwise potentially libelous story is important to the public interest, careful consideration of whether this privilege might protect publication of the report may be appropriate.

2. Fair and accurate report

Under this privilege, a fair and accurate report of a public proceeding (such as a city council hearing) or document (such as a pleading filed in court) generally cannot be the basis of a libel suit.

Pursuant to the Texas fair report statute, for example, the privilege applies to "a fair, true and impartial account" of: (a) judicial proceedings; (b) an official proceeding to administer the law; (c) all executive and legislative proceedings; and (d) the proceedings of public meetings dealing with public purposes. New York and several other states likewise have created the privilege by statute along similar lines; in some states, the privilege is a product of judge-made law.

In order to qualify for the privilege in the states that recognize it, the account must be both substantially accurate and fair. This does not mean the newspaper is required to publish a verbatim account of an official proceeding or the full text of a government document, but any abridgement or synopsis must be substantially accurate and fairly portrayed. Where it applies, the privilege relieves a news organization of responsibility for determining the underlying truth of the statements made by the participants in these contexts, precisely because the very fact that the comments were made in an official proceeding is newsworthy regardless of whether the statements are actually true.

Some jurisdictions require that, to be privileged, the report expressly identify the official proceeding or document being reported upon.

It bears emphasis that the privilege is limited to statements made in the contexts defined under state law, and it behooves reporters to learn the particulars of the privilege in the states in which they practice journalism.

Statements made by government officials outside of official proceedings (e.g., statements by police or a prosecutor or an attorney on the courthouse steps), or in documents that have not been officially made part of the government record (e.g., a draft pleading provided by a lawyer that has not yet been filed with the court) may or may not qualify as privileged, depending on what state you are in and on the circumstances in which the statements are made. Some states only extend the privilege to such out of court statements if made by specified top officials. At least one New York trial court, however, has applied this fair report privilege to a news report based on information provided "off the record" by police sources.

In New York and some other states, court rules provide that the papers filed in matrimonial actions are sealed and thus not open to inspection by the general public. It is not clear whether the fair report privilege will attach to publication of the contents of such papers, which by court rule, or order of the judge, are to be kept confidential.

In one case where this very situation arose, the vice president of a company filed a libel suit in New York alleging that he was fired because a newspaper published his wife's charges of infidelity set forth in divorce proceedings. The newspaper responded that its report was a true and fair account of court proceedings. The New York Court of Appeals rejected that argument on grounds that the law makes details of marital cases secret because spatting spouses frequently make unfounded charges.

The lesson of this case is that information gleaned from "confidential" court documents might not be covered under the fair report privilege. In such a case, the paper will be put to the test of proving that it made a reasonable effort to determine the truth of the allegations before publishing them.

Similarly, not all U.S. states recognize a privilege for reporting the contents of foreign government proceedings or documents, at least in part because, according to some courts, it is not clear that the records of foreign governmental entities are as reliable as the records of American governmental units.

There are other "traps" to be aware of when relying on this privilege. For example, statements made on the floor of convention sessions or from speakers' platforms organized by private organizations may not be privileged under the fair report privilege. Strictly speaking, conventions of private organizations are not "public and official proceedings" even though they may be forums for discussions of public questions.

Similarly, while statements made by a governor in the course of executive proceedings have absolute privilege for the speaker (even if false or defamatory), the press' privilege to report all such statements is not always absolute. For example, after a civil rights march, George Wallace, then governor of Alabama, appeared on a television show and said some of the marchers were members of communist and communist-front organizations. He gave some names, which newspapers carried. Some libel suits resulted.

3. Neutral reportage

Once viewed as a promising development in the law likely to spread across most states, the advancement of the neutral report privilege has not proceeded as once anticipated. Many states have declined to consider whether the privilege should exist, while others have rejected it outright (including in Pennsylvania in 2004). Where recognized, the neutral report privilege protects a fair, true and impartial account of newsworthy statements, regardless of whether the reporter knows or believes those statements to be true, if the statements have been made by prominent and typically responsible persons or organizations. The rationale is that some statements are newsworthy, and should receive public attention just because of who has made them.

Thus, for example, a news report concerning a statement by Michael Jordan concerning corruption in basketball, or by the NAACP regarding discrimination committed by a business, likely would be privileged as a neutral report, even if it should later turn out that Jordan or the NAACP were mistaken, since the mere leveling of charges by such prominent sources typically is of public concern.

Significantly, the privilege, where it exists, does not apply when the author of an article goes beyond reporting the fact the statements were made and espouses or adopts the charges as the author's own.

California is one of the few states to recognize the neutral report privilege.

There, the privilege is available when the plaintiff is a public figure, the defamatory statement is made by one who is a party to a public controversy and the publication is accurate and neutral. One California court applying the privilege found that a newspaper's account of an accusation that a police officer had improperly obtained a false confession to a crime from a person later released as innocent was not actionable where the newspaper also printed the officer's denial of the charge.

In some states, courts appear to have applied the principle without naming the privilege as such. In one 1997 case in Texas, for example, the court held that a story that accurately reported that parents of school children had accused a school teacher of physically threatening and verbally abusing their children was substantially true regardless of whether the parents' allegations themselves were accurate. More recently, in 2013, the Texas Supreme Court initially cast doubt on this line of cases, but then later clarified that it was not completely "foreclosing" the possibility that a news report, the sole purpose of which was to report allegations, could be tested for truth by examining whether it had accurately conveyed the allegations. Similarly, in Illinois, a federal appeals court in 2004 held that several stories that accurately reported that a charitable organization was the target of a federal investigation into terrorism funding were not actionable because the fact that the organization was under investigation was true, regardless of whether it was actually guilty of funding terrorism.

New York state courts do not recognize a privilege for neutral reportage, though a federal court in New York has actually found a neutral reportage privilege grounded in the U.S. Constitution. As the federal court described the neutral report privilege in that case, "when a responsible, prominent organization … makes serious charges against a public figure, the First Amendment protects the accurate and disinterested reporting of those charges, regardless of the reporter's private views regarding their validity." (*Edwards v. National Audubon Society*, 1977.)

— *Summary of practical points*

Although every AP story is expected to be accurate and fair, stories that involve negative reports about individuals or companies warrant particular attention. When evaluating such a story, it usually is prudent to ask these questions:

1. Are any statements in the story capable of defamatory meaning? In this regard pay close attention to the use of certain "red flag" words that may sound more negative (and thereby more defamatory) than if a different, but similar, word had been chosen. Words such as "fraud," "crony," "linked," "suspicious" and "contaminated" may suggest or imply bad conduct or have criminal connotations (like: "connected" to the Mafia or organized crime). Careful editing can ensure that the facts get reported without the use of "buzz words" that may trigger a libel claim.

— Remember that the fact that police are questioning someone about a crime does not necessarily justify the label suspect. Witnesses are obviously also questioned about a crime.

2. Are those statements ones of fact (capable of being proven true or false), or protected as opinion, or simply rhetorical hyperbole that no reasonable reader would understand as a statement of fact?

3. Could someone reading the report reasonably understand it to be about a specific person, whether or not the person is actually named? Could readers understand it to be about more than one person – the person we intend, but also someone else?

— Remember to be careful of descriptive phrases that may give rise to cases of mistaken identity. A report that "an elderly janitor for a local school" was arrested could lead to suits from every elderly janitor in the school district.

4. Could you prove that the statements in question are true (and do so without violating promises to any confidential sources)?

5. If it turns out that you have the facts wrong, would a jury think you failed to do something that any reasonable journalist would have done to get it right?

6. Assuming there is some possibility that the first five questions could be answered in the plaintiff's favor, is there a privilege that nevertheless justifies proceeding to publish? For example, is the report a fair and accurate report of an official government proceeding or document?

— If a privilege applies, remember that the privilege does not remove the need for careful reporting and the use of editorial judgment. In many cases, courts have held that it is up to the jury to decide whether a particular publication was a fair and accurate report or whether there was "actual malice."

Headlines, photos and captions must be as accurate and objective as news stories. Remember that each of these elements of a story can also give rise to claims of libel.

— Document preservation and discovery

A 1979 Supreme Court ruling, *Herbert v. Lando*, has had a significant impact on what materials a libel plaintiff can compel a news organization to disclose. The case ruled that retired Army Lt. Col. Anthony Herbert, a Vietnam veteran, had the right to inquire into the editing process of a CBS "60 Minutes" segment, produced by Barry Lando, which provoked his suit. Herbert had claimed the right to do this so that he could establish actual malice.

The decision formalized and called attention to something that was at least implicit in *New York Times v. Sullivan*: that a plaintiff had the right to try to prove the press was reckless or even knew that what it was printing was a lie. How else could this be done except through inquiry about a reporter's or editor's state of mind?

Despite an admonition in *Herbert v. Lando* that lower courts should carefully monitor (and, if necessary, rein in) discovery in libel cases, reporters and publications involved in libel suits are often forced to expend significant time and resources on discovery concerning their newsgathering, writing and editing activities.

Different reporters follow different practices about retaining their notes. There are potential litigation advantages and disadvantages from following a policy of either keeping notes for a number of years or disposing of notes as soon as they are no longer needed for reporting. The best practice is the one that best advances a reporter's journalistic goals. Whatever practice you follow, however, should be followed uniformly. A difficult issue is presented in litigation if a reporter generally keeps notes, but just doesn't happen to have the notes for a disputed story. Similarly, a reporter who never keeps notes, but happens to save them for a story that ends in litigation, can send a message that the story posed some unique concerns. Adopt a policy and follow it consistently.

Of course, once a lawsuit arrives, no documents (including electronic files, notes, email messages and the like) should be destroyed or deleted, regardless of your usual practice. At that point any notes and drafts are potential evidence and their destruction, with knowledge of the lawsuit, may be illegal.

— Motions practice

If litigation arises, lawyers for a reporter will often seek to dispose of the claims without the necessity of a trial. A number of issues, such as whether a story is "of and concerning" the plaintiff or conveys the defamatory meaning alleged, can often be decided by a judge as a matter of law before any litigation discovery begins.

Courts also can impose "summary judgment" dismissing a case at any point when the evidence developed by the parties demonstrates that the plaintiff's claims are legally defective. A judge may not enter summary judgment if it rests on any facts in dispute. Only the jury may decide disputed issues of fact.

In a 1986 decision, *Anderson v. Liberty Lobby*, the Supreme Court held that summary judgment should be granted in libel actions against public officials and public figures unless the plaintiff can prove actual malice with "convincing clarity" or by "clear and convincing evidence." This rule further facilitates the dismissal of unmeritorious claims without the expense and burden of proceeding to trial.

Over the past twenty years, some states have gone one step further, enacting so-called anti-SLAPP statutes to bring to an end more expeditiously libel lawsuits involving issues of public concern that lack significant merit. The concept initially was to prevent baseless claims asserted by plaintiffs who did not hope to win the lawsuit, but who used litigation to intimidate and censor others. Prime examples were unscrupulous real estate developers seeking to silence opponents of a zoning variance, and others engaged in "strategic litigation against public participation." Anti-SLAPP statutes typically require a defamation plaintiff at the outset of a case to convince the court that reasonable grounds exist to believe a valid defamation claim exists, and they provide for an award of attorneys' fees to the defendant if the claim is found to be meritless. California has one of the broadest statutes, which applies its rules and procedures to any lawsuit challenging defendants for exercising their right of free speech "in connection with a public issue." The California law can be invoked in certain situations to strike lawsuits challenging news reports on public issues, and in recent years some other jurisdictions have adopted similar broad press protections.

— Trials and damages

The huge jury verdicts that sometimes occur in libel cases have caused much concern among legal commentators and the press. A number of remedies have been proposed, including statutory caps on both compensatory and punitive damages. A 1996 non-press Supreme Court case, holding that some excessive damage verdicts might violate the Constitution, holds out some possible promise of relief.

The Supreme Court addressed libel damages in *Gertz v. Robert Welch, Inc.*

(1974), and held that in private figure cases, where "actual malice" has not been proven, any award of damages must be supported by competent evidence, represent compensation only for actual damages, must not be "presumed," and must not be punitive. "Actual damages," however, may include compensation for injury to reputation and standing in the community, personal humiliation, and mental anguish and suffering — all items to which a jury assigns a dollar value. In cases where a plaintiff has proved "actual malice," he or she may also recover "presumed" and "punitive" damages.

While the First Amendment imposes severe restrictions on libel claims, and court rules encourage the dismissal of meritless cases at the earliest point, litigation can be a long, expensive, and disruptive process. The key to avoiding the distraction of litigation is always to remember AP's credo: Get it fast, but get it right.

— *Invasion of privacy*

The roots of the right of privacy are often traced to an article titled "The Right to Privacy" that appeared in the Harvard Law Review in 1890, and was co-authored by Louis D. Brandeis, who later became a Supreme Court justice. The article asserted that the press of the day was "overstepping in every direction the obvious bounds of propriety and decency," and urged courts to recognize a distinct cause of action that would protect the individual's "right of privacy." As a Supreme Court justice, Brandeis later wrote:

"The makers of our Constitution recognized the significance of man's spiritual nature, of his feelings and of his intellect. They knew that only a part of the pain, pleasure and satisfactions of life are to be found in material things. They sought to protect Americans in their beliefs, their thoughts, their emotions and their sensations. They conferred, as against the government, the right to be let alone — the most comprehensive of rights and the right most valued by civilized men." (*Olmstead v. United States*, Brandeis, J. dissenting.)

Over the following decades, legal commentators have vigorously debated the scope and nature of a cause of action for privacy, and identified four distinct forms of the "right of privacy:" (1) misappropriation of someone's name or likeness for a commercial purpose; (2) public disclosure of private facts; (3) unreasonable intrusion upon seclusion, and (4) false light in the public eye. In recent times, these causes of action have taken on significance to the press as plaintiffs have attempted to avoid the heavy burdens of proof placed on the libel plaintiff by alleging an invasion of a form of the right of privacy, instead.

The four distinct "branches" of the privacy tort each seek to protect a different aspect of an individual's privacy. The "intrusion" tort, which is discussed in more detail above, primarily seeks to protect against physical intrusions into a person's solitude or private affairs. The tort does not require publication of information for recovery, and it therefore is referred to as a "newsgathering tort." The other three branches of privacy all require publication of some information in order for the plaintiff to have a claim.

States vary widely both in terms of their acceptance of any of these right to privacy claims and in terms of the rules governing any such claims. Of the four forms of the "privacy" cause of action, New York only recognizes the claim for misappropriation of name or likeness for commercial purposes. Texas recognizes claims for intrusion upon seclusion, public disclosure of private facts and misappropriation of name or likeness for commercial purposes. The California state constitution expressly incorporates a right of privacy and California courts recognize all four forms of the right of privacy cause of action. Illinois courts also recognize all four privacy torts.

The right of privacy creates liability for the publication of facts that are true, and thus raises particular concerns under the First Amendment. In a number of contexts the Supreme Court has struck down rulings imposing liability for reporting information that was both true and newsworthy, but it has consistently declined to hold that the First Amendment always bars such liability altogether.

It can generally be said that when people become involved in a news event, voluntarily or involuntarily, they forfeit aspects of the right to privacy. A person somehow involved in a matter of legitimate public interest, even if not a bona fide spot news event, normally can be written about with safety. However, the same cannot be said about a story or picture that dredges up the sordid details of a person's past and has no current newsworthiness.

Paul P. Ashley, then president of the Washington State Bar Association, summarized the privacy concern for reporters at a meeting of the Associated Press Managing Editors association:

"The essence of the wrong will be found in crudity, in ruthless exploitation of the woes or other personal affairs of private individuals who have done nothing noteworthy and have not by design or misadventure been involved in an event which tosses them into an arena subject to public gaze."

— Publication of private facts

When most people speak of an "invasion of privacy," they have in mind the public disclosure of highly embarrassing private facts. In those states where such a claim is recognized, the elements of a cause of action generally include: (1) "publicity" given to private information, (2) that a reasonable person would find highly offensive, and (3) which is not of any legitimate public interest.

In some states the lack of "legitimate public interest" or lack of "newsworthiness" is an element of the tort, meaning it is a plaintiff's burden to prove. In others, this element is an affirmative defense and the defendant must show how the information was indeed a matter of legitimate public concern. In all cases, newsworthiness is a complete defense to the tort. The First Amendment bars a claim for the true and accurate disclosure of a private fact so long as the information is newsworthy.

The first element of the tort requires "publicity" given to private information. This requires some element of widespread disclosure to the general public, not simply a communication to a single person or small group of people. Conversely, facts that are already known to the general public cannot be the basis of a public disclosure claim, while facts known only to a small group can be.

For example, a California court allowed a privacy claim to be based upon the publication of a photograph of a Little League team in a national magazine to illustrate a story about the team's coach who had sexually abused some of the athletes. Although the photograph had been given to all the members of the team, the identities of the minors shown in the photograph were not known to a broader national audience. The court said their identities could therefore be considered "private" in the context of the story about sex abuse. Some courts have similarly ruled that a person who is recognizable in a picture of a crowd in a public place is not entitled to the right of privacy, but if the camera singled him out for no news-connected reason, then his privacy might be invaded.

The second element of the tort requires that the disclosure be "highly offensive" to a reasonable person. This factor goes to the embarrassing nature of the information itself. Reporting someone's age, for example, would not be highly offensive to a reasonable person, even if that information were not widely known. Reporting, over their objection, that someone was a victim of sexual abuse or suffered from an incurable disease might be.

Finally, no claim will lie if the information is newsworthy, or of legitimate public concern. Courts generally will defer to reporters and editors to determine what is "newsworthy," but the line is not always clear. Even in the context of a report on a plainly newsworthy topic, the disclosure of a highly embarrassing private fact may give rise to a claim for invasion of privacy if the facts are not logically related to the matter of public concern. For example, disclosure of the intimate sexual practices of a celebrity might support a claim for invasion of privacy if it were unrelated to any newsworthy report and amounted to prying into someone's life for its own sake.

Some examples can help to demonstrate the nature of this branch of the privacy tort:

— In a case against a Chicago newspaper, an Illinois trial court held that a mother had stated a cause of action for invasion of privacy when she alleged that she told the newspaper reporter that she did not want to make any public statement about her son's death and where the reporter nevertheless remained in the private hospital room with the mother, recorded her grief-stricken last words to her son and subsequently published a picture of the son's dead body and the mother's "last words" to her son.

— The unsavory incidents of the past of a former prostitute, who had been tried for murder, acquitted, married and lived a respectable life, were featured in a motion picture. She sued for invasion of privacy by public disclosure of private facts. The court ruled that the use of her name in the picture and the statement in advertisements that the story was taken from true incidents in her life violated her right to pursue and obtain happiness.

— Another example of spot news interest: A child was injured in an auto accident in Alabama. A newspaper took a picture of the scene before the child was removed and ran it. That was spot news. Twenty months later a magazine used the picture to illustrate an article. The magazine was sued for public disclosure of private facts and lost the case, the court ruling that 20 months after the accident the child was no longer "in the news."

— In another case, a newspaper photographer in search of a picture to illustrate a hot weather story took a picture of a woman sitting on her front porch. She wore a house dress, her hair in curlers, her feet in thong sandals. The picture was taken from a car parked across the street from the woman's home. She sued, charging invasion of privacy by intrusion upon seclusion and public disclosure of private facts. A court, denying the newspaper's motion for dismissal of the suit, said the scene photographed "was not a particularly newsworthy incident," and the limits of decency were exceeded by "surreptitious" taking and publishing of pictures "in an embarrassing pose."

— False light invasion of privacy

A claim for false light basically complains about publicity that places the plaintiff in a false light in the public eye. In those states that recognize this tort, the publicity must be of a kind that would be highly offensive to a reasonable person, and the defendant generally must have acted with the same level of fault that would be required if the plaintiff had filed a libel claim.

One form in which a claim for false light occasionally arises occurs when an opinion or utterance is falsely attributed to the plaintiff. In another version of the claim, the plaintiff's picture is used to illustrate an article to which he has no reasonable connection, as where the picture of an honest taxi driver is used to illustrate an article about the cheating propensities of cab drivers.

The Supreme Court of the United States ruled in 1967 that the constitutional guarantees of freedom of the press are applicable to claims for invasion-of-privacy by false light involving reports of newsworthy matters. *Time Inc. v. Hill* (1967). The ruling arose out of a reversal by the Supreme Court of a decision of a New York court that an article with photos in Life magazine reviewing a play, "The Desperate Hours," violated the privacy of a couple who had been held hostage in a real-life incident. In illustrating the article, Life posed the actors in the house where the real family had been held captive.

The family alleged violation of privacy by false light in the public eye, saying the article gave readers the false impression that the play was a true account of their experiences. Life said the article was "basically truthful."

The court said:

"We create grave risk of serious impairment of the indispensable service of a free press in a free society if we saddle the press with the impossible burden of verifying to a certainty the facts associated in a news article with a person's name, picture or portrait, particularly as related to non-defamatory matter."

The court added, however, that these constitutional guarantees do not extend to "knowing or reckless falsehood." A newspaper still may be liable for invasion of privacy if the facts of a story are changed deliberately or recklessly, or "fictionalized." As with The New York Times and The Associated Press decisions in the field of libel, "The Desperate Hours" case does not confer a license for defamatory statements or for reckless disregard of the truth.

An Illinois court allowed a "false light" claim to proceed where a news report allegedly broadcast the plaintiff's comments (which were covertly recorded) out of context. In a more famous case, a federal appeals court concluded that Gennifer Flowers could maintain a false light claim against James Carville for publishing facts suggesting she had lied about the nature of her relationship with President Bill Clinton. The court said the false light claim could compensate for emotional injury that would not be covered by a claim for defamation.

— Misappropriation

The final of the three "publication"-related forms of invasion of privacy recognized by the courts is misappropriation of the name or likeness of a living person for purposes of trade or advertising without that person's consent. In recent years, some states have included voice as well as name or likeness. This tort is intended to allow people to control the commercial use and exploitation of their own identities. The First Amendment provides for at least some exceptions to such a right — as where a candidate for public office includes his opponent's name and likeness in campaign advertisements.

The misappropriation tort is not generally a concern to reporters because it applies to the *commercial* exploitation of a person's name and likeness. It does not bar editorial uses and provides no remedy when a person's name or image (questions of copyright aside) is used in a news report. This branch of privacy is of little concern outside of the advertising department of a news organization.

— *Publishing on the internet and social media*

Content published on the internet in blogs, chat rooms, discussion groups, social media sites and the like is generally subject to the same rules and standards for libel, privacy and other legal actions as any print publication.

AP has adopted Social Media Guidelines that are intended to be followed by its employees. Those Guidelines require, among other things, that AP employees always "identify themselves as being from the AP if they are using [social networking site] accounts for work in any way." And, "if you or your department covers a subject . . . you have a special obligation to be even-handed in your tweets." The Guidelines also restrict AP employees from "declaring their views on contentious public issues in any public forum and must not take part in organized action in support of causes or movements."

The Guidelines say that it is acceptable to extend and accept Facebook friend requests from sources, politicians and newsmakers if necessary for reporting purposes, and to follow them on Twitter. "However, friending and 'liking' political candidates or causes may create a perception among people unfamiliar with the protocol of social networks that AP staffers are advocates. Therefore, staffers should try to make this kind of contact with figures on both sides of controversial issues. We should avoid interacting with newsmakers on their public pages — for instance, commenting on their posts."

AP employees are also cautioned to avoid retweeting in a way that makes it look like they are expressing a personal opinion on the issues of the day. "A retweet with no comment of your own can easily be seen as sign of approval of what you're relaying."

Because of the difficulty in verifying the authenticity of material posted on social media sites, it is important not simply to lift quotes, photos or video from social networking sites and attribute them to the domain or feed where the information was found. Before photos, videos or other online content is used, it is important to both verify its authenticity and ensure that any necessary rights for the reuse are obtained. (See discussion of Copyright, below).

Copyright infringement

Copyright is the right of an author to control the reproduction and use of any creative expression that has been fixed in tangible form, such as on paper or computer disk. The right of Congress to pass laws protecting copyright is itself protected in the Constitution, and the First Amendment is generally not a defense to a valid claim for copyright infringement under the Copyright Act.

The types of creative expression eligible for copyright protection include literary, graphic, photographic, audiovisual, electronic and musical works. In this context, "tangible forms" range from film to videotape to material posted on the internet. Personal letters or diaries may be protected by copyright even though they may not have been published and may not contain a copyright notice. Probably of greatest concern to reporters and editors are the copyrights in photographs and videos used to illustrate a news report.

A copyright comes into existence the moment an original work of expression is captured in a tangible form. No government approval or filing is required for a work to be protected by copyright. Upon creation of the work, ownership of the copyright in that work is vested in the "author" of a work — the person to whom the work owes its origin.

The owner will generally be the author of the work, or the photographer in the case of an image. Under certain circumstances, however, someone other than the person who actually created the work may be deemed to be the work's "author" and thereby own the copyright. Under the work made for hire doctrine, copyright ownership of a particular work vests with the employer of the author when the work is created by an employee who is acting within the scope of his or her employment.

The owner of a copyright is given the exclusive right to reproduce, distribute, display and prepare "derivative works" of the copyright material. These rights exist for the life of the author plus 70 years. In the case of a "work for hire" owned by a corporation, the right exists for 95 years from the first publication or 120 years from creation, whichever is shorter.

— Limitations on copyright

Not all uses of copyright material constitute infringement. The most important limitation on the reach of copyright law for journalists is that ideas and facts are never protected by a copyright. What is protected by the copyright law is the manner of expression. The copyright pertains only to the literary, musical, graphic or artistic form in which an author expresses intellectual concepts.

For example, an author's analysis or interpretation of events, the way the material is structured and the specific facts marshaled, the choice of particular words and the emphasis given to specific developments, may all be protected by copyright. The essence of a claim for copyright infringement lies not in taking a general theme or in covering specific events, but in appropriating particular expression through similarities of treatment, details, scenes, events and characterizations.

This printed page illustrates the distinction between protected expression and nonprotected ideas and facts. Despite the copyright protecting this page, a subsequent author is free to report any of the facts it contains. The subsequent author may not, however, employ the same or essentially the same combination of words, structure, and tone, which constitute the expression of those facts.

A second limitation on the reach of copyright is the doctrine of "fair use." This doctrine permits, in certain circumstances, the use of copyright material without its author's permission. Courts will invoke "fair use" when a rigid application of the copyright law would stifle the very creativity the law is designed to foster.

To determine whether a particular use is "fair" and hence permitted, courts are required to evaluate and balance such factors as: (1) the purpose of the use; (2) the nature of the copyrighted work that is being used; (3) the amount and substantiality of the portion used in relation to the copyrighted work as a whole; and (4) the effect of the use upon the potential value of the copyrighted work. Courts generally consider how "transformative" the use is. Uses that can be said to have transformed portions of the original work into something entirely new by "altering the first [work] with new expression, meaning or message" would factor in to a fair use finding. (See *Campbell v. Acuff-Rose Music Inc.*) Uses that merely supplant the work by presenting it essentially as it was in the original version tend not to be fair.

News reporting, criticism and comment are favored purposes under the fair-use doctrine, but "scooping" a copyright holder's first use of previously unpublished material is not. Note, though, that "purpose" is only one of the fair-use factors. Thus, a use for a proper purpose may nevertheless constitute an infringement if other factors weigh against that use being fair.

Here are some general guidelines to keep in mind when dealing with material written by others:

— Content created by the federal government is not protected by copyright, but content created by state and local governments may be. Works created for any level of government by a private contractor may be protected by copyright.
— The greater the amount of the copyrighted work used, the less likely that a court will characterize the use as fair. The amount of use alone, however, is not necessarily decisive; courts have found uses not to be fair when the portion used was small but so important that it went to the heart of the copyrighted work.
— Uses that decrease any potential market for the copyrighted work weigh against a finding of fairness. For instance, if a literary critic reproduces all five lines of a five-line poem, the potential market for the poem will be diminished because any reader of the critic's piece can also obtain a copy of the poem for free.

Reporters and editors having questions about whether their use in a news story or column of copyrighted material is a fair use should review these factors. No mathematical formula can yield the answer. Where there is a question as to whether a particular use is fair, consideration may be given to seeking permission (or a license) from the copyright owner.

If a use is not "fair" within the meaning of copyright law, it will be no defense to claim the use of the copyrighted material was newsworthy and therefore protected by the First Amendment. Moreover, proper attribution alone cannot transform an infringing use into a fair one.

In using copyrighted material in a news story or column, writers should make sure that no more of a copyrighted work than is necessary for a proper purpose is used, and that the work is not used in a way that impairs its value.

In this regard, many people who post material to the internet (photographs, descriptions of events they have witnessed, or other creative works) intend for people to copy and pass them along. It is important to remember, however, that, absent express permission, copying or distributing those works will constitute infringement of copyright unless the fair use doctrine applies. (It also may constitute breach of contract, since the terms of use of many social media sites contain restrictions on use that may be made of material posted there.) And it is often particularly difficult to determine who is the actual owner of the copyright in material posted on the internet, precisely because it is so often reproduced (or re-posted) by others. For these reasons, special care is required when considering the use of material posted by others to the web or on social media platforms.

The Associated Press statement of news values and principles

For more than 170 years, the people of The Associated Press have had the privilege of bringing news and information to the world. We have gone to great lengths, overcome great obstacles – and, too often, made great sacrifices – to ensure that the news was reported quickly, accurately and honestly, in a balanced and impartial way. Our efforts have been rewarded with trust: More than half the world's population sees AP news content on any given day.

In the 21st century, that news is transmitted in more ways than ever before – online and mobile, in print and on the air, in words, video, photographs, interactives, graphics, data and audio. No matter the platform, we insist on the highest standards of integrity and ethical behavior as we gather and deliver the news.

We abhor inaccuracies, carelessness, bias or distortions. We will not knowingly introduce rumor or false information into material intended for publication or broadcast; nor will we distort visual content. Quotations must be accurate and precise. We preserve the appropriate professional distance from those we cover.

We always strive to identify all the sources of our information. We shield them with anonymity only when they insist upon it for a valid reason and when they provide vital information — not opinion or speculation; when there is no other way to obtain that information; and when we are confident the source is reliable and in a position to know. We don't plagiarize, and we respect copyright.

We avoid behavior or activities that could be perceived as a conflict of interest, that compromise our ability to report the news fairly and accurately, uninfluenced by any person or action.

We clearly identify advertising on our platforms, and keep AP commercial activities separate from our newsroom.

We don't misidentify or misrepresent ourselves to get a story. When we seek an interview, we identify ourselves as AP journalists. We balance the newsworthiness of a story with respect for people's privacy, and do not engage in paparazzi-style pursuit of images.

We don't pay newsmakers for interviews, to take their photographs or to film or record them. We do not provide full lists of questions in advance or allow interview subjects to approve our text or images before publication.

We must be fair. Whenever we portray someone in a negative light, we must make a real effort to obtain a response from that person.

When mistakes are made, they must be corrected – fully, quickly, transparently and ungrudgingly.

Automatically produced content must be thoroughly checked and transparent, and the sources of data clearly identified.

It is the responsibility of every one of us to ensure that these standards are upheld. Any time a question is raised about any aspect of our work, it should be taken seriously.

* * *

The policies set forth in these pages are central to the AP's mission. Any failure to abide by them could result in disciplinary action, up to and including dismissal, depending on the gravity of the infraction.

ANONYMOUS SOURCES

Transparency is critical to our credibility with the public and our subscribers. Whenever possible, we pursue information on the record. When a newsmaker insists on background or off-the-record ground rules, we must adhere to a strict set of guidelines, enforced by AP news managers.

Under AP's rules, material from anonymous sources may be used only if:

1. The material is information and not opinion or speculation, and is vital to the report.

2. The information is not available except under the conditions of anonymity imposed by the source.

3. The source is reliable, and in a position to have direct knowledge of the information.

Reporters who intend to use material from anonymous sources must get approval from their news manager before sending the story to the desk. The manager is responsible for vetting the material and making sure it meets AP guidelines. The manager must know the identity of the source, and is obligated, like the reporter, to keep the source's identity confidential. Only after they are assured that the source material has been vetted by a manager should editors and producers allow it to be used.

Reporters should proceed with interviews on the assumption they are on the record. If the source wants to set conditions, these should be negotiated at the start of the interview. At the end of the interview, the reporter should try once again to move onto the record some or all of the information that was given on a background basis.

The AP routinely seeks and requires more than one source when sourcing is anonymous. Stories should be held while attempts are made to reach additional sources for confirmation or elaboration. In rare cases, one source will be sufficient – when material comes from an authoritative figure who provides information so detailed that there is no question of its accuracy.

We must explain in the story why the source requested anonymity. And, when it's relevant, we must describe the source's motive for disclosing the information. If the story hinges on documents, as opposed to interviews, the reporter must describe how the documents were obtained, at least to the extent possible.

The story also must provide attribution that establishes the source's credibility; simply quoting "a source" is not allowed. We should be as descriptive as possible: "according to top White House aides" or "a senior official in the British Foreign Office." The description of a source must never be altered without consulting the reporter.

We must not say that a person declined comment when that person is already quoted anonymously. And we should not attribute information to anonymous sources when it is obvious or well known. We should just state the information as fact.

Stories that use anonymous sources must carry a reporter's byline. If a reporter other than the bylined staffer contributes anonymous material to a story, that reporter should be given credit as a contributor to the story.

All complaints and questions about the authenticity or veracity of anonymous material – from inside or outside the AP – must be promptly brought to the news manager's attention.

Not everyone understands "off the record" or "on background" to mean the same things. Before any interview in which any degree of anonymity is expected, there should be a discussion in which the ground rules are set explicitly.These are the AP's definitions:

On the record. The information can be used with no caveats, quoting the source by name.

Off the record. The information cannot be used for publication.

Background. The information can be published but only under conditions negotiated with the source. Generally, the sources do not want their names published but will agree to a description of their position. AP reporters should object vigorously when a source wants to brief a group of reporters on background and try to persuade the source to put the briefing on the record.

Deep background. The information can be used but without attribution. The source does not want to be identified in any way, even on condition of anonymity. In general, information obtained under any of these circumstances can be pursued with other sources to be placed on the record.

ANONYMOUS SOURCES IN MATERIAL FROM OTHER NEWS SOURCES

Reports from other news organizations based on anonymous sources require the most careful scrutiny when we consider them for our report.

AP's basic rules for anonymous source material apply to material from other news outlets just as they do in our own reporting: The material must be factual and obtainable no other way. The story must be truly significant and newsworthy. Use of anonymous material must be authorized by a manager. The story we produce must be balanced, and comment must be sought.

Further, before picking up such a story we must make a bona fide effort to get it on the record, or, at a minimum, confirm it through our own reporting. We shouldn't hesitate to hold the story if we have any doubts. If another outlet's anonymous material is ultimately used, it must be attributed to the originating news organization and note its description of the source.

ATTRIBUTION

Anything in the AP news report that could reasonably be disputed should be attributed. We should give the full name of a source and as much information as needed to identify the source and explain why the person is credible. Where appropriate, include a source's age; title; name of company, organization or

NEWS VALUES

government department; and hometown.

If we quote someone from a written document — a report, email or news release — we should say so. Information taken from the internet must be vetted according to our standards of accuracy and attributed to the original source. File, library or archive photos, audio or videos must be identified as such.

For lengthy stories, attribution can be contained in an extended editor's note detailing interviews, research and methodology.

AUDIO

AP's audio content always must be accurate. We do not alter or manipulate newsmaker actuality in any way, except as provided below:

With the permission of a manager, overly long pauses by news subjects may be shortened.

To make sound clearer, the AP does permit the use of subtle, standard audio processing methods: normalization of levels, general volume adjustments, equalization and reduction of extraneous sounds such as telephone line noise. AP permits fading in and out of the start and end of sound bites. However, the use of these methods must not conceal, obscure, remove or otherwise alter the content of the audio.

Bleeping is allowed, with a manager's permission, to cover obscenities when there is no option but to use a piece of audio containing an obscenity. An employee with questions about the use of such methods or the AP's requirements and limitations on audio editing should contact the desk supervisor prior to the transmission of any audio.

We don't use sound effects or substitute video or audio from one event to another. We do not "cheat" sound by adding audio to embellish or fabricate an event. A senior editor must be consulted prior to the introduction of any neutral sound (ambient sound that does not affect the editorial meaning but corrects a technical fault).

Voice reports by AP correspondents may be edited to remove pauses or stumbles.

BYLINES AND DATELINES

A dateline tells the reader where we obtained the basic information for a story. A byline tells the reader who wrote the story.

On short, unbylined stories (routine speeches, game stories, announcements, etc.), the dateline generally should reflect where the story took place. However, when a story is longer, contains multiple elements, has analytical material or occurs at a place that is difficult for reporters to access, the dateline should be where the staffer covering the story is located.

When a datelined story contains supplementary information obtained in another location — say, when an official in Washington comments on a disaster elsewhere — we should note it in the story. The dateline for video, photos or audio must be the location where the events depicted actually occurred. For voice work, the dateline must be the location from which the reporter is speaking; if that is not possible, the reporter should not use a dateline. If a reporter covers a story in one location but does a live report from another location, the dateline is the filing point.

For text stories with datelines, bylines may be used only if the journalist was in the datelined location. If a reporter in the field works with another staffer and both deserve bylines, the name of the staffer in the field normally goes first and a tag line gives each staffer's location. We give bylines in text stories to photographers, broadcast reporters and video journalists who provide information without which there would be no story.

For stories without datelines, the byline goes to the writer, with credit in a tag line o the reporters who contributed substantial information.

For staffers who do voice or on-camera work, we do not use pseudonyms or "air names." Any exceptions – for instance, if a staffer has been known professionally by an air name for some time – must be approved by a manager.

CONFLICTS OF INTEREST

The AP respects and encourages the rights of its employees to participate actively in civic, charitable, religious, public, social or neighborhood organizations.

However, AP employees must avoid behavior or activities that could create a conflict of interest or compromise our ability to report the news fairly and accurately, uninfluenced by any person or action.

Nothing in this policy is intended to abridge any rights provided by the National Labor Relations Act.

Here is a sampler of AP practices on questions involving possible conflict of interest. It is not all-inclusive; if you are unsure whether an activity may constitute a conflict or the appearance of a conflict, consult your manager at the onset.

Expressions of opinion

Those who work for the AP must be mindful that opinions they express may damage the AP's reputation as an unbiased source of news. They must refrain from declaring their views on contentious public issues in any public forum, whether through blogs, social networks, comments pages, petitions, bumper stickers or lapel buttons. They must not take part in demonstrations in support of causes or movements- or contribute to them in any way.

Favors

Employees must not ask news sources or others they meet in a professional capacity to extend jobs or other benefits to anyone. They also must not offer jobs, internships or any benefits of being an AP employee to news sources.

Financial interests

To avoid any conflict of interest or the appearance of any such conflict, AP employees must abide by the following rules and guidelines when making personal investment and financial decisions.

Inside information

All employees may not act upon, or inform any other person of, information gained in the course of AP employment, unless and until that information becomes known to the general public. Employees must comply with federal and local laws concerning securities and financial transactions, including those prohibiting actions based upon inside information.

Family investments

Employees are expected to make every effort to ensure that no spouse or other member of their household has investment or business interests that could pose a conflict of interest. The appearance of such a conflict may make it inappropriate for the employee to accept certain assignments. Employees must consult with their managers before accepting any such assignment.

Divestiture

Employees might be asked to divest or to suspend any activity involving their holdings. They will have one year from the date of request to do so.

For business reporters and editors

Employees who regularly write or edit business news must not own stock or have any personal financial investment or involvement with any company, enterprise or industry that they regularly cover for the AP. A technology writer, for example, must not own any technology equities.

New staff members should immediately disclose such holdings to their manager or to HR. Staff members who are temporarily assigned to such coverage must immediately notify a manager of possible conflicts to determine whether the assignment is appropriate.

Writers and editors who cover the stock markets may not own stock in any individual company. They may invest in publicly available diversified mutual funds.

Business news employees must avoid speculative, short-term investment activities such as day-trading individual stocks or commodities.

Freelance work:

Individuals who seek to engage in non-AP work are subject to the following restrictions:

— A manager must be advised in advance of all freelance work.
— Freelance work must not represent a conflict of interest for either the employee or the AP.
— Such activities may not interfere with the employees' job responsibilities, including availability for newsgathering.
— Such activities may not exploit the name of The Associated Press or the employee's position with the AP without permission of the AP.
— Employees who wish to use material they accumulated in their AP work - notes, stories (either written or broadcast), images, videotape, graphics - for other-than-AP uses must seek written AP approval, copyright clearance and a license to syndicate. This approval must be received prior to submission to any outside publisher, purchaser, organization broadcaster, or to posting on websites or social networks.

Under no circumstances should the AP incur expenses for research material that is not used for AP purposes.

Free tickets

We do not accept free tickets to sports, entertainment or other events for anything other than coverage purposes. If we obtain tickets for a member or subscriber as a courtesy, they must be paid for, and the member or subscriber should reimburse the AP.

Gifts

Associated Press offices and staffers often are sent or offered gifts by sources, public relations agencies, corporations and others. Sometimes these are designed to encourage or influence AP news coverage or business; sometimes they are gift bags handed out routinely to journalists covering a particular event.

Whatever the intent, we cannot accept such items; an exception is made for trinkets like caps or mugs that have nominal value, approximately $25 or less. Otherwise, gifts should be politely refused and returned, or if that is impracticable, they should be given to charity.

Books, DVDs and other items received for review may be kept for a staff member's professional reference or donated to charities, but may not be sold or raffled off for personal gain. In cases where restrictions forbid transfer to third parties, these items should be discarded. Items of more than nominal value that are provided for testing, such as electronics, must be returned.

AP staff should pay their expenses at meals with news sources. When several journalists are invited to an event with news value, such as a dinner with a senior official, staff may accept so long as an effort is made to reciprocate with the official or a staff member.

AP and its employees may accept discounts from companies only if those discounts are standard and offered to other customers.

We do not accept unsolicited contest awards from non-journalistic organizations or any organization that has a policy or financial interest in our coverage; nor do we enter such contests.

The aim in all matters involving contests should be to underscore the AP's reputation for objectivity.

Official scorers

Employees may not serve as official scorers at sports events.

Outside appearances

Employees frequently appear on radio and TV news programs as panelists asking questions of newsmakers; such appearances are encouraged.

However, there is potential for conflict if staffers are asked to give their opinions on issues or personalities of the day. Advance discussion and clearance from a staffer's supervisor are required.

Employees may speak or teach at the invitation of news industry groups and educational institutions. The AP accepts reimbursement of expenses for such appearances if the event is one that AP would not routinely participate in. AP staffers may accept honoraria, with a supervisor's approval, for appearances and teaching that require substantial preparation. We do not normally accept honoraria for routine speeches and panel discussions. We avoid addressing, or accepting fees or expenses from, governmental bodies; trade, lobbying or special interest groups; businesses, or labor groups; or any group that would pose a conflict of interest.

Political activities

Editorial employees are expected to be scrupulous in avoiding any political activity, whether they cover politics regularly or not. They may not run for political office or accept political appointment; nor may they perform public relations work for politicians or their groups. Under no circumstances should they donate money to political organizations or political campaigns. They should use great discretion in joining or making contributions to other organizations that may take political stands.

Non-editorial employees must refrain from political activity and contributions unless they obtain approval from a manager.A supervisor must be informed when a spouse or other members of an employee's household have any ongoing involvement in political causes, either professionally or personally.

Trips

If a reporting trip is organized, and we think the trip is newsworthy, we go and pay our way. If we have a chance to interview a newsmaker on a charter or private jet, we reimburse the news source for the reasonable rate of the costs incurred - for example, standard airfare. There may be exceptional circumstances, such as a military trip, where it is difficult to make other travel arrangements or calculate the costs. Consult a manager for exceptions.

CORRECTIONS

Staffers must notify supervisory editors as soon as possible of serious errors or potential errors, whether in their work or that of a colleague. Every effort should be made to contact the staffer and supervisor before a correction is sent.

When we're wrong, we must say so as soon as possible. When we make a correction, we point it out both to subscriber editors (e.g. in Editor's notes, metadata, advisories to TV newsrooms) and in ways that news consumers can see it (bottom-of-story corrections, correction notes on graphics, photo captions, etc.)

A correction must always be labeled a correction. We do not use euphemisms such as "recasts," "fixes," "clarifies," "minor edits" or "changes" when correcting a factual error.

When we correct an error from a previous day, we ask subscribers that used the erroneous information to carry the correction as well.

For live broadcasts, we correct errors in the same newscast if at all possible. If not, we make a correction in the next appropriate live segment. Audio correspondent reports that contain factual errors are eliminated and, when possible, replaced with corrected reports.

DATA

Data for stories and visual presentations must be vetted for integrity and validity. Data should be assessed in terms of the methodology behind it, sample sizes, when it was collected and the availability of other data to confirm or challenge it.Combining more than one dataset into a presentation should be done carefully and transparently. Avoid percentage and percent change comparisons from a small base, including raw numbers when appropriate for perspective.

We must distinguish carefully between correlations and causal relationships.

FABRICATIONS

Nothing in our news report – words, photos, graphics, sound or video – may be fabricated. We don't use pseudonyms (except for established literary names or noms de guerre, which should be identified as such), composite characters or fictional names, ages, places or dates.

We don't stage or re-enact events for the camera or microphone.

Virtual reality presentations must consist of real, unmanipulated imagery and sound.

GRAPHICS AND INTERACTIVES

We use only authoritative sources. We do not project, surmise or estimate in a graphic. We create work only from what we know. Except as authorized by a manager, we do not use graphics provided by others for which we lack the underlying data.

We create charts at visually proper perspectives to give an accurate representation of data. The information must be clear and concise. We do not skew or alter data to fit a visual need.

We credit our sources on every interactive and graphic, including graphics for which AP journalists have created the database.

IMAGES

AP images must always be accurate. We do not alter or digitally manipulate the content of a photo or video except as stated below.

We avoid the use of generic photos or video that could be mistaken for imagery photographed for the specific story at hand, or that could unfairly link people in the images to illicit activity.

Photos

No element should be digitally altered except as described below.

Minor adjustments to photos are acceptable. These include cropping, dodging and burning, conversion into grayscale, elimination of dust on camera sensors and scratches on scanned negatives or scanned prints and normal toning and color adjustments. These should be limited to those minimally necessary for clear and accurate reproduction and that restore the authentic nature of the photograph. Changes in density, contrast, color and saturation levels that substantially alter the original scene are not acceptable. Backgrounds should not be digitally blurred or eliminated by burning down or by aggressive toning. The removal of "red eye" from photographs is not permissible.

Employees with questions about the use of such methods or the AP's requirements and limitations on photo editing should contact a senior photo editor prior to the transmission of any image.

Photo-based graphics, including those for television, often involve combining various photographic elements, which may mean altering portions of each photograph. The background of a photograph, for example, may be removed to leave the headshot of the newsmaker. This may then be combined with a logo representing the person's company or industry, and the two elements may be layered over a neutral background.

Such compositions must not misrepresent the facts and must not result in an image that looks like a photograph – it must clearly be a graphic. Similarly, when we alter photos to use as graphics online, we retain the integrity of the image, limiting the changes to cropping, masking and adding elements like logos.

It is permissible to display photos online using techniques such as 360-degree panoramas or dissolves as long as they do not alter the original images.

Video

For video, the AP permits the use of subtle, standard methods of improving technical quality, such as adjusting video and audio levels, color correcting due to white balance, eliminating buzzing, hums, clicks, pops, or overly long pauses or other technical faults, and equalization of audio to make the sound clearer _ provided the use of these methods does not conceal, obscure, remove or otherwise alter the content of the image.

Video can produced with titles and logos, the images toned and the audio quality improved.

When editing audio within a video, generally the specific audio associated with each video shot must be used without alteration. However in cases where music is the principal ambient sound – e.g. when the video portrays a marching band or an orchestra playing - audio may be laid unbroken and video images edited over the top, provided the video was shot contemporaneously and the meaning of the scene is not altered.

Obscuring identities

We should not use mosaics or blurring to grant anonymity in any AP-created images. Instead we should shoot the subject in silhouette or use other photo or video techniques - such as using the person's shadow naturally cast on a wall or ground – to achieve the goal of anonymity. Exceptions may be granted rarely, when other anonymity techniques have failed, with permission of a senior manager. Images may be treated so that end-users of our content cannot readjust the levels to bring a shadowed face into view. In cases in which anonymity is deemed essential for the safety of the interviewee, the voices of silhouetted persons being interviewed may be digitally distorted with a manager's permission strictly for purposes of hiding identity. However any such alteration will be noted and disclosed in the accompanying script or shot-list.

When approved by a manager, the AP allows the use of material from third parties, such as government authorities, where faces are digitally obscured. In such cases, it must be stated in the shot-list, or caption and special instructions, who is responsible for the obscuring of a face. Similarly, the caption or shot-list must clearly disclose any other manipulation of imagery by a source that otherwise would not be allowed under AP guidelines.

Posing and re-enactments

We do not stage, pose or re-enact events except in the circumstances described here. When we shoot B-roll "walking shot" video, "environmental" portraits of subjects at work, home, etc., or photograph subjects in a studio, care should be taken to avoid misleading viewers to believe that the moment was spontaneously captured in the course of gathering the news. The precise circumstances of such portraiture must be revealed in the shot-list or caption and special instructions box so it can't be mistaken as an attempt to deceive.

User-generated and internet content

When obtaining imagery from the internet or any other source, we must be certain it is accurate, un-manipulated, shows what it is said to show and that we have the right to use it. When acquiring user-generated content, we must give priority to the safety of providers and caution them against taking risks. We should credit them appropriately.

Offensive and gory content

AP does not seek to sanitize news events; sometimes a gory or disturbing image is essential to cover a story. However, such imagery must be appropriate and newsworthy, not gratuitous. Care must be taken with images that could be offensive toward religions, nationalities or ethnic groups. In some cases, we may decide not to send such material to consumer-facing platforms, but to distribute it to subscribers — with appropriate warnings — for them to decide on its usage.

Special warnings to consumers about disturbing content may be needed for online and virtual reality content. In the rare case that an obscene image is necessary to tell the story, we may blur the portion of the image considered offensive. This must be approved by a manager.

MUSIC

Music added to AP productions must not have an editorial effect, such as evoking sympathy, suspicion or ridicule. We must have rights to use the material.

OBSCENITIES, PROFANITIES, VULGARITIES, HATE AND PROPAGANDA

AP resists being used as a conduit for speech or images that espouse hate or spread propaganda. When hate speech or images are the basis of a news story, it is often sufficient to briefly refer to the speech or images in a text story rather than carry the speech or propaganda at length or redistribute the images. A senior manager must vet any material showing hostages or conveying kidnappers' statements or demands. Quoting from such materials should be kept to the minimum necessary to convey the story and must note that the hostage is speaking under duress.

We do not use obscenities, racial epithets or other offensive slurs in stories unless they are part of direct quotations and there is a compelling reason for them. We do not run imagery of such slurs; a manager must be consulted regarding any exceptions.

If a story cannot be told without reference to slurs, we must first try to find a way to give the reader a sense of what was said without using the specific word or phrase. If a profanity, obscenity or vulgarity is used, the content must be flagged at the top, advising editors of what the offensive material is.

Recognizing that standards differ around the world and from platform to platform, we tailor our advisories and selection of video and audio according to customer needs.

We do not refer readers to websites that are obscene, racist or otherwise offensive, and we must not directly link from stories to such sites.

We link our text content to the least offensive image necessary to tell the story. For photo galleries and interactive presentations we alert readers to the nature of the material in the link and on the opening page of the gallery or interactive.

PRIVACY OF VICTIMS

We generally do not identify, in text or images, those who say they have been sexually assaulted or subjected to extreme abuse. We may identify victims of sexual assault or extreme abuse when victims publicly identify themselves.

We generally do not identify minors who are accused of crimes or who are witnesses to them. Identification of such minors must be approved by a manager; it may depend on the severity of the alleged crime; whether police have formally released the juvenile's name; and whether the juvenile has been formally charged as an adult. Other considerations might include public safety, such as when the youth is the subject of a manhunt; or widespread publication of the juvenile suspect's name, making the identity de facto public knowledge.

QUOTATIONS

Quotes must not be taken out of context. We do not alter quotations, even to correct grammatical errors or word usage. If a quotation is flawed because of grammar or lack of clarity, it may be paraphrased in a way that is completely true to the original quote. If a quote's meaning is too murky to be paraphrased accurately, it should not be used. Ellipses should be used rarely and must not alter the speaker's meaning.

When relevant, stories should provide information about the setting in which a quotation was obtained – for example, a press conference, phone interview or hallway conversation with the reporter. The source's affect and body language – perhaps a smile or deprecatory gesture – is sometimes as important as the quotation itself.

Use of regional dialects with nonstandard spellings should generally be limited to a writer's effort to convey a special tone or sense of place. In this case, as in interviews with a people not speaking their native language, it is especially important that their ideas be accurately conveyed. Always, we must be careful not to mock the people we quote.

Quotes from one language to another must be translated faithfully. If appropriate, we should note the language spoken.

Internal editing of audio soundbites of newsmakers is not permitted. Shortened soundbites by cutaway or other video transition are permitted as long as the speaker's meaning is not altered or misconstrued.

RESPONSES

We must make significant efforts to reach anyone who may be portrayed in a negative way in our content, and we must give them a reasonable amount of time to get back to us before we send our reports. What is "reasonable" may depend on the urgency and competitiveness of the story. If we don't reach the parties involved, we must explain in the story what efforts were made to do so.

SOCIAL NETWORKS

The use of social media by AP's journalists is held to the same high standards as reporting, communication and distribution over any other medium. Those standards include, but are not limited to:

— Avoiding expressions of opinion on contentious issues, even in supposedly password-protected conversations.
— Getting explicit permission when seeking to distribute copyrighted material; any breaking news exceptions should be cleared by a senior manager.
— Not disseminating rumors and unconfirmed reports, and attributing information.
— Carefully verifying information and content before it is distributed.
— Transparently correcting errors on all platforms on which the erroneous material was distributed.

AP journalists are encouraged to maintain accounts on social networks, and must identify themselves in their profiles as being with AP if they use the accounts for work in any way. We must not share AP proprietary or confidential information or include political affiliations or preferences. If we retweet or otherwise share opinionated material by others, we should add language that makes it clear that we're simply reporting someone else's opinions.

In social posts related to sports and entertainment, we must steer clear of both trash-talking and over-the-top, fawning praise directed at teams, athletes and celebrities. In international competitions, AP staffers should not cheer for any national team.

Staffers are encouraged to share AP content in all formats to social platforms. We should do so by using the "share" buttons on apps, browsers and sites that cause an item to be posted, or by posting a link to the content. We should not manually upload or copy and paste published photos, videos or the full text of published stories into social accounts. Staffers should not upload directly to social networks images they captured that closely resemble those the AP is publishing.

Staffers may share content from other news organizations, but we should be mindful of potential competitive issues and refrain from sharing unconfirmed material. We should also keep in mind that denouncing fellow users, newsmakers or anyone else can reflect badly on AP and may one day harm a colleague's ability to get important information from a source.

AP journalists who have confirmed urgent breaking news should not share that information over social accounts until they have provided it to the appropriate AP desk and done any immediate reporting work that is asked of them. Exclusive material and important tips should not be shared online before the related story has been published.

We may follow or friend sources or newsmakers, but when doing so with politicians or political causes, we should try to connect with accounts on both sides of a given issue or campaign. AP managers should not issue friend requests to subordinates; otherwise, friend requests among AP employees are fine.

Employees must not post any information that might endanger a colleague, and shouldn't post about a missing or detained AP staffer without clearance from senior AP managers.

Posts and tweets aimed at gathering opinions for a story must make clear that we are looking for voices on all sides of an issue.

If an AP tweet or social media posting contains an error of fact, emphasis or tone, the tweet or posting promptly should be removed from the platform where it occurred, followed by a note acknowledging the deletion and a substitute corrected tweet or posting issued where appropriate.

USE OF OTHERS' MATERIAL

An AP staffer who reports and writes a story must use original content, language and phrasing. We do not plagiarize, meaning that we do not take the work of others and pass it off as our own. When we match a report that news outlet was first with due to significant reporting effort, we should mention that the other outlet first reported it.

At the same time, it is common for AP staffers to include in their work passages from previous AP stories by other writers – generally background, or boilerplate. This is acceptable if the passages are short. Regardless, the reporter writing the story is responsible for the factual and contextual accuracy of the material.

Also, the AP often has the right to use material from its members and subscribers; as with material from other news media, we credit it.

Unless we are clearly retransmitting in full a story by a member outlet, we do not transmit stories in their original form; we rewrite them, so that the approach, content, structure and length meet our requirements and reflect the broader audience we serve.

Under no circumstances can news releases be published in their original form; we can use information, quotes and properly cleared images from releases, but we must judge the material's credibility, augment it with information from other sources, and then prepare our own stories, with the release material duly credited.

For video, if another broadcaster's material is required and distributed, we advise the name of that broadcaster on the accompanying shot list.

Pickups of audio and of television graphics are credited in billboards/captions when the source requests it.

Broadcast

"Donald Trump has been elected president of the United States."
"Osama bin Laden is dead."
"The Dow Jones industrial average has reached 20,000."

These sentences illustrate AP's broadcast news writing style. They are easily understood, but intelligent; conversational, but not stiff. Many broadcast stories can be effectively told using such straightforward writing and this simple structure:

Lead –> Backup –> Details –> Background

For example:

A huge wildfire in eastern Arizona is expected to spread to New Mexico. Both wind and dry lightning are forecast over the next two days.
Arizona fire officials say more than 1,000 firefighters are working the blaze. There have been no serious injuries, but hundreds of people have been evacuated, and 11 buildings have been destroyed.
The fire has burned more than 350 square miles. It's the third-largest wildfire in Arizona's history.

Lead. The first sentence in this story reports the essential facts that are the news:
A huge wildfire [*the subject of the story*] in eastern Arizona [*location*] is expected to spread to New Mexico [*the story's latest development*].
Backup. The second sentence "backs up" the lead:
Both wind and dry lightning are forecast over the next two days [*answers the implied question "Why is the fire expected to spread?"*].
Details. These next sentences report additional important facts — mainly, the extent to which people are injured or at risk.
Arizona fire officials [*the story's sources*] say more than 1,000 firefighters are working the blaze [*these lives are potentially at risk*]. There have been no serious injuries, but hundreds of people have been evacuated [*impact of the fire on people*], and 11 buildings have been destroyed [*impact on property*].
Background. The story ends by putting the fire into current and historical perspective:
The fire has burned more than 350 square miles. It's the third-largest wildfire in Arizona's history.

The fire story follows principles used by AP's broadcast writers:

1. Lead with the news. The story first reports its latest newsworthy development. If the latest development had been evacuations, the lead would have been: "Hundreds of people are being evacuated because of a huge wildfire in eastern Arizona."

2. In leads, use forms of the present or future verb tenses. "The fire is expected to spread," not "The fire was expected to spread today." But don't write in the simple present tense "headline" style: "Twelve buildings are destroyed in a wildfire." Present perfect tense sounds more natural: "A wildfire has destroyed 12 buildings."

3. Keep leads short and to the point. It's easy for listeners and viewers to miss details. Use the lead to introduce a story, and save details for subsequent sentences.

4. Favor the active voice. "Firefighters are working the blaze," not "the blaze is being worked by firefighters."

5. Attribute at the beginning of sentences. "Fire officials say...," not "...said fire officials."

6. Identify newsmakers before naming them. Write: "Fire information officer Ed Toby," not "Ed Toby, the fire information officer, says..."

7. Omit needless words. "It's the third-largest fire in Arizona's history," not "This particular blaze is the third-largest in the history of the state of Arizona."

8. Prefer the simple to the complex. "Fire" or "blaze" but not "conflagration."

9. Don't strain for synonyms. "Arizona," not "the state." Someone who hears "... in the state's history" might not have heard the rest of the story.

10. Use direct quotes only when a paraphrase doesn't work better. In most cases, it does. "There have been no serious injuries," not, "Toby says, 'Two people reported bruises and five others pulled muscles carrying heavy suitcases while being evacuated, but otherwise no one was hurt.'"

11. Simplify numbers. "More than 350 square miles," not "352.67 square miles."

12. Use a variety of sentence lengths, but keep most of them short. The sentences in the fire story are 8, 9, 12, 13, 13 and 19 words long – and that's counting every word, including "a."

A radio story on the fire could include recorded sound of a newsmaker talking:

(*Reporter*) A huge wildfire in eastern Arizona is expected to spread to New Mexico. Both wind and dry lightning are forecast over the next two days.

Arizona fire officials say more than 1,000 firefighters are working the blaze. Fire information officer Ed Toby says still more may be needed:

(*Newsmaker*) *"We already have firefighters from New York, Colorado and Texas helping us. We might bring some more in from California."*

(*Reporter*) There have been no serious injuries, but hundreds of people have been evacuated, and 11 buildings have been destroyed.

The fire has burned more than 350 square miles. It's the third-largest wildfire in Arizona's history.

Always identify newsmakers before their voices are heard. Give a general sense of the subject of the upcoming sound bite, but don't "parrot." Write: "Toby says still more may be needed," not "Toby says firefighters from New York, Colorado and Texas are already helping."

A television story might incorporate not only sound and video, but also locator maps and graphics:

(*Reporter reading over animated map showing fire's location*) A huge wildfire in eastern Arizona is expected to spread to New Mexico. (*Over video of fire*) Both wind and dry lightning are forecast over the next two days.

(*Over video of firefighters working*) Arizona fire officials say more than 1,000 firefighters are working the blaze. Still more may be needed:

(*On-screen identification, seen over shot of newsmaker talking*)
Ed Toby
Fire Information Officer

"We already have firefighters from New York, Colorado and Texas helping us. We might bring some more in from California."

(*Reporter reading over shots of people evacuating; then shots of destroyed buildings*) There have been no serious injuries, but hundreds of people have been evacuated, and 11 buildings have been destroyed.

(*Reporter on-camera, with fire burning in distance*) The fire has burned more than 350 square miles. It's the third-largest wildfire in Arizona's history.

A grasp of these basic concepts will help you go on to create more complicated stories, whether for wires, radio, TV or new media.

BROADCAST

Corrections, correctives, clarifications

Factual errors in AP video stories need to be immediately repaired with either a CORRECTION if the story is in that six-hour news cycle, or a CORRECTIVE if the time from the error having occurred to setting the record straight extends beyond six hours.

Both a CORRECTION and a CORRECTIVE must begin with an Editor's Note citing the date of the story's original publication, the original story keyword (or slug) and the specifics of the error. If the error being corrected is of a serious enough nature to materially change the original item, a story KILL should be immediately sent stating: Please KILL the story filed from Switzerland on World Peace on January 31, 2017, titled SWIWORLDPEACE20173101. A replacement item, correcting a material error, will run shortly.

In a CORRECTION, write a brief description of what has gone wrong and how it has been changed. For example: Editor's Note: Please replace the shotlist and storyline in SYRIA FIGHTING first transmitted today Jan. 31 at 1038GMT and slugged SYR FIGHTING 20170131. This version corrects that the fighting took place in a southern suburb of Idlib and not in the heart of the city as was initially reported.

In a CORRECTIVE where the error is being fixed in a subsequent news cycle — beyond six hours — a similar approach should be taken but a more detailed explanation may be needed depending on the nature of the mistake. For example: Editor's Note: On Jan. 31, 2017, The Associated Press published a story from Switzerland titled SWI WORLD PEACE 20170131 which incorrectly named Fred Smith as chairman of the Committee for World Peace and described the comments he made as the official view of the organization. Smith in fact held no formal office within the organization, having resigned his position at an earlier meeting. He was participating in the gathering in support of the organization's ideals, but his comments were his personal view and not made formally as a spokesman of, or office bearer on, the committee.

In the case of a CORRECTION, it shall be at the discretion of the senior manager in charge of video production whether the video itself needs to be retransmitted to customers. Updating the script and shotlist may be sufficient. In the case of a CORRECTIVE where changes were necessary to the video or the script/shotlist, all stories must be retransmitted.

In circumstances where a clarification is required but no inaccuracy needs correcting, issue an Editor's Note slugged with the term CLARIFICATION. A rewritten script and shot list should be sent specifying what is clarified in the updated version. So, for example, we might say: "This version clarifies the people seen in shot 7 were villagers heading from the conflict who were given food by an aid agency rather than locals who lived near the aid agency feeding station, as originally stated based on initial information."

Correctives, corrections and clarifications need to be published and posted.

actuality In radio, the sound of a newsmaker talking. Generally, an actuality should be 10 to 20 seconds long. Don't use an actuality just to have newsmaker sound in a story. Use an actuality only if it makes sense, can be clearly understood and contributes something of substance to the story, such as the newsmaker's point of view or the unique way the newsmaker said something. If you, as a reporter or an anchor, can say something more effectively than the newsmaker, write the story without actuality.

b-roll In a video story, the supporting shots and scenes used to provide context and continuity for the main story. B-roll can be file or stock tape containing background or historical information. It is sometimes provided by sources outside the news organization, as when newsmakers provide personal videos.

cut In radio, a piece of audio, whether the sound of a newsmaker talking, a reporter's narrative or natural sound.

fade In radio, a gradual increase (fade-up) or decrease (fade-down) in sound. In video, a gradual increase (fade-in) or decrease (fade-out) in the appearance of video and, usually, in the volume of accompanying sound.

fast file Video segment with in and out points, but no additional edited-in content.

first person In a video piece, a newsmaker's description of a news event or subject matter, presented as one long sound bite.

incue, inq, in-point The first two or three seconds of sound signaling the start of a segment of audio or video. An incue can consist of any man-made or natural sound, including words, music or ambient noise.

live shot Broadcast report delivered in real time from the scene of a news event or a studio or newsroom.

lockout Words used by a reporter to end a radio story. A common format is name and location: *Sagar Meghani, Washington*. See **sigout**.

LSR Live Special Report. Short or long-form live program covering breaking news or a special event. Reports may be anchored from a studio or an outside location.

MOS Man on the street. Sound of randomly chosen people, traditionally walking on a city sidewalk, commenting on a news event. Also known as *vox pops*, shortened form of *vox populi* or *voice of the people*.

natural sound or **NATS** Nonverbal sound of a news event. Natural sound can include ambient sound, such as trucks rumbling or background cheers. It can also be the dominant sound of a news event, such as a band playing or a chainsaw cutting up debris from a storm. For AP Radio, a piece of natural sound should run 30 to 40 seconds, with fades at the beginning and end. Generally, the fade-up is fast (about four seconds) and the fade-down is slow (about eight seconds). If you're writing natural sound into a story for AP, begin with sound up and let it play long enough for the audience to recognize it, then fade down low enough to talk over it.

nonlinear editing Digital video and audio systems that allow editors to swiftly copy video sequences and sound bites in any order onto a new timeline, without altering the original file (recording).

outcue, outq, out-point The final two or three seconds of sound signaling the end of a segment of audio or video. An outcue can consist of any man-made or natural sound, including words, music and/ or ambient noise.

package For video, an umbrella term for fully edited stories with sound, fonts and possibly on-camera appearances by reporters. For audio, an umbrella term for fully edited stories with a reporter's voice and possibly newsmaker actuality. An audio package often includes a wrap or voicer and several individual sound bites. See **wrap** and **voicer**.

Q-and-A In radio, a sound bite of a correspondent taken from a question-and-answer session with another colleague. Q-and-A cuts run from 10 to 20 seconds and provide the reporter with a format in which a brief aspect of the story is reported. The rules of balance, objectivity and attribution all apply. A reporter should never express views or draw conclusions. There is no lockout. Reporters and their locations are identified in the anchors' lead-ins. In AP's online video products, Q-and-A pieces show a reporter or newsmaker answering questions posed in writing displayed on a graphic.

raw edit or **rough cut** Video and sound loosely edited together

without voice track, reporter presence or font. This allows broadcast customers to have their own newspeople narrate a video package and gives them editing flexibility.

rough cut See **raw edit**.

scener In radio, a report from the actual scene of an event, with the sound of the event in the background. Whether live or taped, a scener must be done while the sounds in the background actually are taking place. The idea is to use words and background sound to create a picture of what's happening in the listener's mind. If you play back tape of an event behind your voice in a studio, that is not a scener — it's a voicer. AP Radio sceners run 35 seconds maximum.

sigout Words used to end a video story. A common format is name and location: *Haven Daley, San Francisco*. See **lockout**.

sound bite Snippet of sound of someone talking.

standup A portion of a video story in which a reporter faces the camera and addresses the audience directly. When a standup appears at the end of a story, it contains a sigout. When a standup appears between two pieces of video in the same story, it is referred to as a bridge. A hand-held standup is when a reporter holds a camera at arm's length and focuses on his or her own face. This allows the reporter to react to and narrate from the scene of a breaking news story.

UGC User-generated content.

Information in the form of text, photos, video or audio supplied by users of a product which then becomes part of that product. Websites and, increasingly, TV news broadcasts, often contain UGC.

voice-over or **VO** Sound of a reporter's voice narrating a story as videotape plays. In radio, reporters may also speak over a music or natural sound track.

voice track or **track** Narration of an audio or video piece. In video, it may occur along with a voice-over or standup.

voicer Self-contained radio correspondent report. All the listener hears from beginning to end is the sound of a reporter talking. AP Radio voicers run no more than 35 seconds and end in a lockout: *Sagar Meghani, Washington.* Many voicers are done in-studio. Compare to scener, which has no lockout and must be created at the scene of a news event, with natural sound in the background. See **scener**.

vox pops See **MOS**.

wall-to-wall coverage Continuous broadcast reporting, with few or no interruptions, of a single news story. Generally reserved for transcendent stories, such as the 9/11 terrorist attacks, the outbreak of war or the results of a U.S. presidential election.

wrap A radio voice report that includes both the correspondent and a newsmaker actuality. AP Radio wrap runs no more than 40 seconds and ends in a lockout: *Jerry Bodlander, Capitol Hill.* The newsmaker actuality generally

should be no shorter than 10 seconds and no longer than 15 seconds.

BROADCAST

Editing marks

HONG KONG (AP) — The organization | indent for paragraph

said Thursday. It was the first and last | paragraph

attempts. | no paragraph

With this the president tried

the Jones Smith company is not | transpose

over a period of sixty or more years | use figures

there were 5 in the group. | spell it out

former Governor Rothwell attended | abbreviate

The Ga. man was the guest of | don't abbreviate

prince edward said it was his | uppercase

as a result This will be | lowercase

the ac cuser pointed to them | remove space

In these times it is necessary | insert space

The order for the later devices STET | retain

The ruling a fine example is | insert word

according to the this source | delete

By DONALD AMES | boldface, center

J.P. Slavens | flush right

J.P. Slavens | flush left

insert comma

insert apostrophe

insert quotation marks

insert period

hyphen

dash

Bibliography

The following are standard references for the AP Stylebook and for material not covered by the Stylebook.

First reference for spelling, style, usage and foreign geographic names:
Webster's New World College Dictionary, Fifth Edition, Houghton Mifflin Harcourt, Boston and New York, 2016.

Other references for spelling, style, usage and foreign geographic names:
The American Heritage Dictionary of the English Language, Fifth Edition, Houghton Mifflin Harcourt, Boston and New York, 2011.
http://www.ahdictionary.com/
Concise Oxford English Dictionary, Twelfth Edition, Oxford University Press, Oxford, 2011.
Webster's Third New International Dictionary of the English Language, unabridged, Merriam-Webster, Springfield, Mass., 1993.
National Geographic Atlas of the World, 10th Edition, 2014. National Geographic Society, Washington, D.C.
http://maps.nationalgeographic.com/maps

For aircraft names:
IHS Jane's All the World's Aircraft, IHS, Englewood, Colorado.

For military ships:
IHS Jane's Fighting Ships, IHS, Englewood, Colorado.

For nonmilitary ships:
Lloyd's Register of Ships, IHS, Englewood, Colorado.

For railroads:
Official Railway Guide — Freight Service Edition; JOC Group Inc., Newark, New Jersey.

For federal government questions:
Congressional Directory; U.S. Government Printing Office, Washington.
This link allows searching of the directory for the 104th Congress (1995–1996) through the 114th Congress (2015-2016).
http://www.gpo.gov/fdsys/browse/collection.action?collectionCode=CDIR
For the current Congress: https://www.congress.gov

For non-U.S. government questions:
Political Handbook of the World, 2015; CQ Press, an imprint of SAGE Publications, Washington, D.C.

CIA World Factbook online: https://www.cia.gov/library/publications/the-world-factbook/

For a company's formal name:
Consult the national stock exchanges: the New York Stock Exchange, http://www.nyse.com, or Nasdaq, http://www.nasdaq.com. Also consult Stylebook entry for individual company name, and the entry "company names," as AP usage may differ.

For religion questions:
Handbook of Denominations in the United States, 13th Edition, 2010; Abingdon Press, Nashville, Tennessee, and New York.
World Christian Encyclopedia; Second Edition, 2001; Oxford University Press, New York. http://worldchristiandatabase.org
Yearbook of American and Canadian Churches, 2012; National Council of Churches of Christ in the U.S.A., New York. http://yearbookofchurches.org/

For medical questions:
Centers for Disease Control and Prevention: http://www.cdc.gov/
The Merck Manuals Online Medical Library: http://www.merck.com/mmpe/index.html
U.S. National Library of Medicine and the National Institutes of Health, MedlinePlus: http://www.nlm.nih.gov/medlineplus/

Addictions and drugs:
Office of National Drug Control Policy: http://bit.ly/2mQLSwy
International Society of Addiction Journal Editors: http://www.parint.org/isajewebsite/terminology.htm
AMA Task Force to Reduce Opioid Abuse: http://www.asam.org/magazine/read/article/2015/12/15/patients-with-a-substance-use-disorder-need-treatment---not-stigma
Synthetic cannabis: https://www.drugabuse.gov/publications/drugfacts/synthetic-cannabinoids

Other references and writing guides consulted in the preparation of the AP Stylebook:
The American Heritage Guide to Contemporary Usage and Style, Houghton Mifflin Co., Boston - New York, 2005
Bernstein, Theodore M. *The Careful Writer: A Modern Guide to English Usage.* Free Press, Second Edition, 1995.
Cappon, Rene J. *The Word.* The Associated Press, 1982; Second Edition, 1991.
Follett, Wilson. *Modern American Usage: A Guide.* lst rev. ed. Revised by Erik Wensberg. New York: Hill and Wang, 1998.
Fowler, H.W. and R.W. Burchfield. *Fowler's Modern English Usage*, Rev. Third Edition. Oxford University Press, 2004.
The Chicago Manual of Style, 17th Edition. University of Chicago Press, 2017.
Newton, Harry with Steven Schoen; *Newton's Telecom Dictionary, 30th Updated, Expanded Anniversary Edition.* Telecom Publishing, Feb. 2016

Shaw, Harry. *Dictionary of Problem Words & Expressions*. McGraw-Hill Book Co., 1975; Revised Edition, 1987.

Strunk, William Jr. and White, E.B. *The Elements of Style*, Second Edition. The Macmillan Co., 1972. New Edition: 4th Edition. Longman 1999.

Index

Index entries with figures and symbols are alphabetized as if spelled out.

Entries with no page numbers refer to terms that are provided for spelling purposes only; no additional information is given in the text.

Cross-references (*See* and *See also*) refer to entries in the index itself. For convenience, cross-references to a single entry also include the page number for that entry.

Cross-references in most indexes lead from general terms (e.g., "states") to narrower terms (e.g., "Alabama"). However, in this index, such references often lead to an entry that contains general information about treatment of the particular kind of word or phrase, e.g., "colonel. *See* military titles."

Some complex entries contain indented subheadings. References to these individual sections are indicated by the form "*x in y*," e.g., "overseas territories *in* datelines" refers to the section titled "overseas territories" within the main entry "datelines."

Some terms or phrases are designated as "derogatory." They represent insulting or offensive usage and should not be used except in extremely rare circumstances.

A page number after a heading that also includes subheadings refers to the specific entry for the heading term itself.

The following chapters have been indexed at the section level only: Briefing on media law, Broadcast guidelines, Business guidelines. All others have been indexed in detail.

a

at large, 25
ATM (automated teller machine), 25
ATM machine (improper). *See* ATM, 25
Atomic Age. *See* historical periods and events, 138
attache, 25
attempted suicide. *See* suicide, 272
attorney at law. *See* attorney, lawyer; lawyer
attorney general, attorneys general, 25. *See also* titles, 285–286
attorney in fact. *See* attorney, lawyer, 25
attorney, lawyer, 25–26. *See also* lawyer, 166
attribution, 26
  in broadcast writing, 524
  commas before, 323–324
  dashes with, 324
  in headlines, 134
  standards and practices on, 511–512
ATV. *See* all-terrain vehicle, 13
audio, standards and practices on, 512
augmented reality. *See* virtual reality, augmented reality, 300
augur, 26
"Auld Lang Syne," 26
Australia. *See* Down Under, 89
author, 26
autism spectrum disorder, 26. *See also* Asperger's syndrome, 23–24
automaker, automakers. *See also* Big Three automakers, 33
automated teller machine. *See* ATM, 25
automatic (weapon), 304
autonomous vehicles, 26
Autopilot, 26
auto racing, 404–405
Auto Train, 26
autoworker, autoworkers, 26
autumn. *See* seasons, 257
avatar, 27
avenue, 27. *See also* addresses, 6
average, mean, median, norm, 27
average of, 27
averages, in data, 346–347
averse. *See* adverse, averse, 7
Avianca, 27
avian influenza (nonpreferred). *See* bird flu, 33
avocado, Hass, 443
avocado toast, 435
avowed. *See* out, outing, 215

awards and decorations, 27. *See also* Nobel Prize; Pulitzer Prizes
awhile, a while, 27
AWOL (absent without leave), 27
ax, 27
Axis, 27
Ayatollah. *See* Islam, 155, 386
Aymara (people/language), 27
Azerbaijan. *See* Commonwealth of Independent States, 58

b

baba ghanoush, 435
baby back ribs
baby boom, baby boomer, 28. *See also* Generation X; millennials
baby bump (nonpreferred), 28
babydoll
baby-sit, baby-sitting, baby-sat, baby sitter
baccalaureate
Bachelor of Arts, Bachelor of Science, 28. *See also* academic degrees, 3
bachelor's, bachelor's degree. *See* academic degrees; Bachelor of Arts, Bachelor of Science
back bacon. *See* Canadian bacon, 437
backboard
backcourt
backfield
backfire (in wildfire management), 28
background (news writing), 511, 523
backhand
backpass, 425
backspin
backstage, 28
backstop
backstretch, 420
backstroke
back-to-school clothing
backup (news writing), 523
backup, back up, 28
backward, 28
backyard, 28
bacon, Canadian, 437
bacon, lettuce and tomato sandwich. *See* BLT, 436
bad, badly, 28. *See also* good, well, 126
Badlands (South Dakota). *See* capitalization, 43

Belarus. *See* Commonwealth of
   Independent States, 58
Belgian waffle, 435
Bellini, 435
bellwether
Belmont Stakes, 420
Benedictine, 435
benefit, benefited, benefiting
Ben-Gurion International Airport, 31.
   See also airport, 11
Berkshire Hathaway Inc., 31–32
Berlin, 32
Berlin Wall
Bermuda collar, Bermuda grass,
   Bermuda shorts
beside, besides, 32
bespoke, 454
best-seller, 32
betting. *See* gambling, 120
betting odds, 32, 409. *See also* numerals,
   207
bettor, 32, 409
between. *See* among, between, 17
beurre blanc, 435
bi- (prefix), 32
bialy, bialys, 435
biannual, biennial, 32. *See also*
   semiannual, 258
bias cut, 454
bibb lettuce, 435
Bible, 32, 376–377
Bible-believing, 377
Bible Belt, 377
biblical. *See* Bible, 32, 376–377
bibliography, 531–533
biennial. *See* biannual, biennial;
   semiannual
Big Board, 32
big brother, Big Brother, 33–34
Big Brothers Big Sisters of America Inc.
   See big brother, 34
Big Dipper. *See* heavenly bodies, 135
Big Three automakers (nonpreferred),
   33
bill. *See* act, amendment, bill, law,
   measure, ordinance, resolution,
   rule, statute, 4
billiards, 409. *See also* match summary,
   422
billion, 33. *See also* millions, billions,
   trillions
Bill of Rights, 33
bimonthly, 33

bin (in Arabic names). *See* Arabic
   names, 21
binary digit (bit). *See* bit, 33
Bing (internet search engine), 33
Bing cherries, 435
bin Laden, Osama, 33. *See also* al-Qaida,
   13
bioterrorism
bipolar disorder. *See* mental illness, 182
biracial, multiracial, 33
bird flu (avian influenza), 33
birdie, birdies, birdied. *See* golf, 417
birth control pill. *See* pill, 222
birthday, 33
bishop. *See* religious titles; Roman
   Catholic Church; *specific
   denominations*
bisque, 436
bit (binary digit), 33
bitcoin, 33
biweekly, 34
bizarre, 34
black, 34. *See also* African-American;
   nationalities and races; race
Black Angus (beef). *See* Angus, 434
BlackBerry, BlackBerrys, 34
black-eyed pea, 436
Black Forest cake, 436
Black Muslim (derogatory). *See*
   Muslims, 390
blackout, brownout, 34
blackstrap molasses
Blahnik, Manolo, 454
blanch, 436
blastoff, blast off, 34
bleed. *See* hemorrhage, 136
Blessed Sacrament, Blessed Virgin
bleu cheese (improper). *See* blue
   cheese, 436
blind. *See* disabled, handicapped, 85–86
blizzard, 306
bloc, block, 34
blog, 34
blog entry (blog post). *See* blog, 34
blond, blonde, 34
blood alcohol content, 34
bloodbath, 34
bloody mary, 436
Bloomberg LP, 34
Bloomingdale's, 454
BLT (bacon, lettuce and tomato
   sandwich), 436
blue cheese, 436

cant, 42. *See also* dialect, 84
cantaloupe
Canton. *See* Guangzhou, 130
cantor. *See* Jewish congregations, 388
Canuck (sometimes derogatory), 42
canvas, canvass, 42
cape, 42
Cape Canaveral, Florida (formerly Cape Kennedy). *See* John F. Kennedy Space Center, 158
capelet, 455
capital, 42. *See also* Capitol, 44
capital gain, capital loss, 42
capitalization, 42–44
    of abbreviations, 2
    of animal names in Chinese lunar calendar (*See* Chinese names, 49)
    of awards and decorations, 27
    of brand names, 37
    of company names, 59
    of composition titles, 63–64
    of geographic names, 124
    See also academic titles; courtesy titles; legislative titles; magazine names; military titles; newspaper names; nobility; religious titles; titles; *individual entries*
Capitol, 44. *See also* capital, 42
cappuccino, 437
captain, 44. *See also* military titles, 188–190
carat, caret, karat, 44
carbine (rifle), 304
cardholder, credit card holder
cardiac arrest. *See* heart attack, heart failure, cardiac arrest, 135
Cardin, Pierre. *See* Dior, Christian, 456
cardinal (religious title). *See* religious titles; Roman Catholic Church
cardinal numbers, 209. *See also* amendments to the Constitution; channel; court names; decades; election returns; fleet; formula, formulas; latitude and longitude; mile; parallels (geographic); proportions; serial numbers; telephone numbers; weights
cardiopulmonary resuscitation. *See* CPR, 72

CARE, 44
caret. *See* carat, caret, karat, 44
Caribbean, 312
Carioca, 44
carmaker, carmakers
carnaroli rice, 437
Carnival, 44. *See also* Mardi Gras, 178
car pool, carpool, 44
carry-on
carry-over, 44
cartridge. *See* bullet, 304
car wash
cash or collect on delivery (nonpreferred), 44. *See also* c.o.d., 55
caster, castor, 44
cast-iron, cast iron, 437
catalog, cataloged, cataloger, cataloging, catalogist
catchup. *See* ketchup, 444
categories
    for bankruptcies, 335–336
    for earthquakes, 93–94
    for hurricanes, 307–308
Caterpillar, 44–45
catfish
Cathay Pacific Airways Ltd., 45
catholic. *See* Catholic, Catholicism, 45, 378
Catholic, Catholicism, 45, 378. *See also* Roman Catholic Church, 250–251, 396–397
cat litter. *See* Kitty Litter, 162
cats. *See* animals, 18
CAT scan. *See* CT scan, 72-73
catsup. *See* ketchup, 444
cattle. *See* animals, 18
Caucasian
Caucasus Mountains
causation and correlation, 347
cava, 438
cave-in, cave in, 45
CB (citizens band radio), 45
CBC. *See* Canadian Broadcasting Corp., 41
CBOE. *See* Chicago Board Options Exchange, 48
CBS, 45
CD. *See* compact disc, 58
CDC. *See* Centers for Disease Control and Prevention, 46
CD-ROM (compact disc, read-only memory), 45

548

INDEX

city editor, 51. *See also* titles, 285–286
city hall, 51
city names, commas with, 324. See also
    names of individual cities
citywide
civil cases, criminal cases, 51
civil lawsuit (redundant). *See* lawsuit,
    166
Civil War. *See* historical periods and
    events, 138
claim, 51
classical music, titles of. *See*
    composition titles, 64
classical Rome. *See* historical periods
    and events, 138
claustrophobia. *See* phobia, 222
cleanup, clean up, 51
clear-cut, 51
cleft lip. *See* harelip, 133
clergy. *See* religious titles; *specific
    religions and denominations*
clerical titles. *See* religious titles, 246–
    247, 395–396
C-level. *See* CEO, CFO, COO, 47
Cleveland, 51
cliches (in sports), 411
cliches, jargon, 51–53
click-thrus, 53
clientele
climate change. *See* global warming,
    125–126
clinically dead, clinical death, 53–54. *See
    also* brain-dead, brain death, 37
Clinton, Hillary, 54
clip (for ammunition), 304. *See also*
    magazine, 305
cloak-and-dagger
cloche, 455
clock time. *See* time of day, 282
Clorox, 54
closed shop, 54. *See also* right-to-work,
    249
closed-toe shoes
closely held corporation, 54
close-up, 54
closure. *See* cloture, 54
cloture, 54
cloud (remote servers), 54
    security of, 367
club soda (soda water). *See* seltzer
    water, 450
cm (centimeter). *See* metric system,
    186

CME Group Inc., 54
CNN (Cable News Network), 54
Co. *See* company, companies, 58
co- (prefix), 54–55
coach. *See* titles, in sports, 429
coach, in soccer, 425. *See also* titles
    (sports), 429
co-anchor
coast, 55
coastal waters, 306
Coast Guard, 55
    military titles for, 189
    See also military academies, 188
Coast Guardsman, 55. *See also* military
    titles, 188–190
coastline
coattails
Cobb salad, 438
Coca-Cola, Coke, Coca-Cola Co.
cocaine, 90
co-chair. *See* chairman, chairwoman, 47
cocktail (drug mixture), 55
cocktail hat. *See* fascinator, 457
c.o.d., 55. *See also* cash or collect on
    delivery, 44
coffeecake
cognac, 438
Cointreau, 438–439
Coke (Coca-Cola)
coke (slang). *See* cocaine, 90
colander (nonpreferred), 439
colby cheese, 439
Cold War, 55
collateral, 55, 172, 338
collateralized debt obligations, 55
collectibles
collections (fashion)
collective nouns, 55–56
    in sports, 411
collectors' item
college, 56. *See also* organizations and
    institutions, 214
College Football Playoff (CFP), 411
College of Cardinals. *See* Roman
    Catholic Church, 250, 397
college sports
    conference standings (football), 416
    football championship subdivision,
        413 (*See also* FCS, 415)
    major college basketball
        conferences, 412–413
    major college football conferences,
        413

Collins glass
colloquialisms, 56. *See also* dialect, 84
colon (punctuation), 322
colonel. *See* military titles, 188–190
colonial, 56
colonies, 56
Colorado, 56. *See also* state names,
  268–269
colorblind
colorblocking, 455
colored (nonpreferred). *See* black
colt, 420
Colt (weapon), 304
Columbus Day, 56. *See also* Indigenous
  Peoples Day, 149
coma, 56–57. *See also* minimally
  conscious state; vegetative
  state
combat, combated, combating
Combat Zone (Boston). *See*
  capitalization, 43
combustible
Comcast Corp., 57
comets. *See* heavenly bodies, 135
comma, 322–324
  with academic degrees, 3
  in company names, 58–59
  See also colon; dates; essential
    clauses, nonessential
    clauses; essential phrases,
    nonessential phrases;
    semicolon; *specific entries
    such as "dash" and "scores"*
commander. *See* military titles, 188–190
commander in chief, 57. *See also* titles,
  285–286
commercial paper, 57
commissioned officers. *See* military
  titles, 188–190
commissioner, 57. *See also* titles,
  285–286
commitment
commit suicide. *See* suicide, 272
committee, 57. *See also* subcommittee,
  271
commodities futures contract, 57
commodities markets, major U.S. *See*
  futures, 118–119
commodity, 57
Commons. *See* House of Commons,
  House of Lords, 141
common stock, preferred stock, 57
commonwealth, 57. *See also* state, 268

Commonwealth of Independent States,
  57–58
  in datelines, 78
Commonwealth, the (formerly British
  Commonwealth), 58
communication, security of, 366–367
Communications Workers of America
  (CWA), 58
communism, communist. *See* political
  parties and philosophies,
  225–226
Communist China. *See* China, 49
communities, cliches about. *See* cliches,
  jargon, 52
Community of Christ. *See* Church
  of Jesus Christ of Latter-day
  Saints, The, 380
commutation, 58. *See also* pardon,
  parole, probations, 218
compact disc (CD), 58
compact disc (acting as) read-only
  memory. *See* CD-ROM, 45
companion. *See* mistress, 192
company, companies, 58
company (military), 58
company names, 58–63
  financial institutions, major U.S.-
    based, 111
  major non-U.S. companies, 61–63
  major U.S. companies, 59–61
  See also *names of individual
    companies*
compared to, compared with, 63
compass directions. *See* addresses;
  directions and regions
compatible
competitive multiplayer video gaming.
  See esports, 414
complacent, complaisant, 63
complement, compliment, 63
complementary, complimentary, 63
compliment, complement, 63, 455
compose, comprise, constitute, 63
composition titles, 63–64
  capitalization of, 43–44
compound modifiers, hyphens with,
  4326
compound proper nouns and
  adjectives, hyphen with, 326
compound subjects. *See* either...or,
  neither...nor, 96
compound words
  plurals of, 224

document preservation and discovery, in libel, 499–500
DOD (Department of Defense, Pentagon). *See* department, 82
DOE (Department of Energy). *See* department, 82
dogs. *See* animals, 18
dog walker, 88
DOJ (Department of Justice). *See* department, 82
Dolce, Domenico. *See* Dolce & Gabbana, 456
Dolce & Gabbana, 456
dollars, 88. *See also* cents, 46
dollar sign. *See* dollars, 88
dolmades, 439
dolman sleeve, 456
domain names, 88
Domain Name System. *See* DNS; internet
domestic datelines. *See* datelines, 77
domestic geographic names. *See* geographic names, 123
domino, dominoes
"don't ask, don't tell," 88
door to door, door-to-door, 88
d'Orsay, 456
do's and don'ts
DOT (Department of Transportation). *See* department, 82
dot-com, 89
double boiler, 439
double-breasted
double bylines. *See* bylines, 40
double-click
doubled prefixes. *See* prefixes, 230
double-faced
double overtime
double possessive, 228–229, 321
doughnut
the Dow. *See* Dow Jones industrial average, 89
Dow Jones & Co., 89
Dow Jones industrial average, 89
-down (suffix), 89
down- (prefix), 89
Down East, 89
downlink. *See* satellite communications, 255
down payment
downside risk, 89
downstage
downstate, 89

Down syndrome, 89
Down Under, 89
dpa (Deutsche Presse-Agentur GmbH), 89
Dr. *See* doctor, 87–88
draft beer, 440
drag performer, drag queen, drag king, 88. *See also* gender
drama. *See* composition titles, 63–64
Dramamine, 89
Drambuie, 440
draught beer (improper term). *See* draft beer, 440
DREAM Act, "Dreamers," 145
dredge, 440
dreidel, 89
dressing, stuffing, 440
dressing room
drive. *See* addresses, 6
drive-by, 90
drive-in, 90
Drive Pilot. *See* Autopilot, 26
driverless vehicles. *See* autonomous vehicles, 26
driver's license(s)
drive-thru, 90
driving under the influence, driving while intoxicated. *See* DUI, DWI, 91
drop-down, 90
dropout, drop out, 90
drought
drowned, was drowned, 90
Dr Pepper, 440
Drug Enforcement Administration (DEA), 90
drugmaker
drugs, 90–91. See also *names of specific drugs*
drugstore
drunk, drunken, 91. *See also* addiction, 5–6
drunkenness
drunks (nonpreferred). *See* alcoholic, 12
Druze, 381
dry measures
  bushel, 40
  ounce (dry), 215
  peck, 220
  pint (dry), 222
  quart (dry), 239
  See also metric system, 185–186
dry mustard. *See* mustard, 446

f

FEMA. *See* Federal Emergency
Management Agency, 109
female, 110. *See also* woman, women,
315
female impersonator. *See* drag
performer, drag queen, drag
king, 89
fencing, 415. *See also* basic summary;
match summary
fentanyl, 90
Fenway Park. *See* Green Monster, 406
FERC. *See* Federal Energy Regulatory
Commission, 109
Ferragamo, Salvatore, 457
Ferris wheel
ferryboat
fertility rate, 110
Festival of Lights. *See* Hanukkah, 133,
384
fettuccine, 441
fetus. *See* embryo, fetus, unborn baby,
unborn child, 98
fewer, less, 110–111
Fez, 111
FFA. *See* National FFA Organization,
197
FHA. *See* Federal Housing
Administration, 109
fiance, fiancee, 111
Fiberglas, 111
field goal
field house
FIFA (Federation International de
Football Association), 426
figuratively, literally, 111
figure(s) (number(s)), 111
in addresses, 6
in baseball, 405–406
in betting odds, 32
for boats and ships, 35
in clothing sizes, 462
for congressional districts, 65
in court decisions, 71
in dimensions, 84
in election returns, 97
in football, 415
large, commas with, 324
for percentages, 221
plurals of (*See* plurals, 224)
for political divisions, 225
for room numbers, 250
for route numbers, 252
for schools, 256

in serial numbers, 259
in spacecraft designations, 265
in speeds, 266
See also numerals 206–207
figure skating, 415. *See also* basic
summary, 407–408
figures of speech, numbers in. *See*
numerals, 208
filbert (nonpreferred). *See* hazelnut,
443
file formats
GIF (Graphics Interchange Format),
124–125
JPEG, JPG, 158
MP3, 194
file server. *See* server, 259
filet mignon, 441
Filet-O-Fish, 441
filibuster, 111
Filipina. *See* Filipinos, 111
Filipinos, 111. *See also* Philippines, 221
fillet, 441
filly, 420
filmgoer
filmmaker
film noir
film ratings. *See* movie ratings, 194
Financial Accounting Standards Board.
See FASB, 108
financial editor, 111. *See also* titles,
285–286
financial institutions, 111
financial interests, standards and
practices on, 513
fingerling potatoes
Finland, 111
firearms. *See* weapons, 303–306
fire department, 111. *See also*
governmental bodies; military
titles; titles
firefight
firefighter, fireman, 111–112
firefighters, titles for. *See* military titles,
190
fire names, 112. *See also* storm names
fires, numbers of alarms for
(nonpreferred). *See* alarms, 12
firewall, 112
firm (business partnership), 112
first aid, first-aid, 112
First Amendment right of access,
466–467

INDEX

freeze-dry, freeze-dried, freeze-drying
freezing drizzle, freezing rain, 307. *See also* ice storm, freezing drizzle, freezing rain, 308
freight carriers. *See* railroads, 243
french, 441
French bread
French Canadian, 117–118
French dressing
French Foreign Legion, 118
french fries, 441
French toast
frequency modulation. *See* FM, 114
frequent flyer
frequently asked questions. *See* FAQ, 107
freshman, freshmen, 118
friend. *See* mistress, 192
friend, follow, like, 118
friending/following, for AP employees, 369
friendly (soccer), 426
Friends General Conference. *See* Quakers, 393
Friends United Meeting. *See* Quakers, 393
Frigidaire, 118
Frisbee, 118
frisee, 441
frittata, 441
Frontier Airlines, 118
front line, front-line, 118
frontman
frontpage, front-page, 118
front-runner
frost, 307
froufrou, 457
Frowick , Roy Halston (Halston), 458
frozen pop. *See* Popsicle, 448
fruitcake
F-scale rating, for tornadoes, 310–311
FTC. *See* Federal Trade Commission, 110
fulfill, fulfilled, fulfilling
full- (prefix), 118
full-body scanner
full faith and credit bond, 172
full HD resolution. *See* television sets, 277
full house (poker), 118
full name
　of governmental bodies, 127
　of presidents, 231

full time, full-time, 118
full vs. partial quotes. *See* quotations in the news, 239–240
fully automatic (weapon), 304
fulsome, 118
fundamentalist, 394
fundraising, fundraiser, 118
funnel cloud, 307
furlong, 420
furlough
further. *See* farthur, further, 108
fuselage
fusillade
Future Farmers of America. *See* National FFA Organization, 197
future planning (redundant). *See* planning, 223
futures (contracts), 118–119
future titles. *See* titles, 286
F-word. *See* obscenities, profanities, vulgarities, 210

g

G (general audiences). *See* movie ratings, 194
g (gram). *See* metric system, 186
GAAP (generally accepted accounting principles), 120
Gabbana, Stefano. *See* Dolce & Gabbana, 456
gage, gauge, 120
gag orders, 469
gaiety
gale, 307
Galliano, John, 457
gallon, 120
　of oil, conversion from tonnage, 211
　See also imperial gallon; liter; metric system
Gallup Poll, 120
gambling, 120
game day, 417
game plan
games (Olympics). *See* Olympics, Olympic, Olympic Games, Olympian, 423–424
gaming (nonpreferred). *See* gambling, 120
gamut, gantlet, gauntlet, 120
ganache, 442

United States; supreme courts
of the states
government information, access to,
466–467
constitutional access, limits on,
467–468
court records, right of access to, 471
First Amendment right of access,
466–467
Freedom of Information Act
requests, 472–473
gag orders and, 469
government records, right of access
to, 471–473
hearings closed without prior
notice, 468–469
high-profile cases, media protocols
in, 470
proceedings, right to attend, 470–
471
government, junta, regime,
administration, 128
Government National Mortgage
Association. See Ginnie Mae,
125
government officials. See titles; titles in
department
government records, right of access to,
471–473
governor, 128. See also titles, 285–286
governor general, governors general,
128
GPA (grade-point average), 128
GPS (Global Positioning System), 128
grade, grader, 128
graded stakes, 420
grade-point average. See GPA, 128
grades (in schools), figures in. See
numerals, 207
graduate (verb), 128
graham crackers, 442
Graham Holdings Co., 129
grain (weight), 129. See also ounce
(weight); pound
grain bowl, 442
gram, 129. See also metric system,
185–186
Grammy Awards (Grammys), 129
grandad, granddaughter, 129. See also
family names, 107
grand cru wines, 442
grand jury, 129
Grand Marnier, 442

Grand Mufti. See Islam, 155, 386
Grand Old Party (Republican Party).
See GOP, 127
grant-in-aid, grants-in-aid
granulated (white) sugar. See sugar, 451
Grape-Nuts
grapeseed oil
graphics, standards and practices on,
517
Graphics Interchange Format. See GIF,
124–125
gray (color), 129
gray (Gy, radiation measure), 206
great- (prefix), 129
Great Britain (Britain), 129. See also
Britain; United Kingdom
Great Depression. See depression, 82-83
greater, 129
great-grandfather, great grandfather.
See great-, 129
Great Lakes, 129
Great Plains (the Plains), 129
Great Recession, 129
Greece, ancient. See historical periods
and events, 138
Greek Orthodox Archdiocese of
America. See Eastern Orthodox
churches, 94–95, 381–382
Greek Orthodox Church. See Eastern
Orthodox churches, 94–95,
381–382
Greek salad, 442
Greek yogurt
Green Berets (U.S. Army Special
Forces). See special forces, 266
green fee. See golf, 417
Green Monster (at Fenway Park), 406
green onions (nonpreferred). See
scallions, 449–450
Greenwich Mean Time (Coordinated
Universal Time, UTC). See
GMT, 126
Gres, Madame (Germaine Emilie
Krebs), 457
grey. See gray, 129
Grey Cup, 418
greyhound. See gray, 129
gringo (derogatory), 130. See also
nationalities and races, 197
grisly, grizzly, 130
grits, 442
grizzly. See grisly, grizzly, 130
gross domestic product (GDP), 130

holy days, 246, 385, 395. *See also* holidays and holy days; Islamic holy days; Jewish holy days; religion guidelines; *specific holy days*; *specific religions*
Holy Father, 385. *See also* pope, 226, 392
Holy Ghost (nonpreferred). *See* Holy Spirit, 385
Holy Land, 139, 385
holy orders. *See* sacraments, 398
Holy See, 139, 385
Holy Spirit, 385
Holy Week, 139
HomeAway. *See* vacation rental websites, 298
homebuilder
homebuyer, homeowner
Home Depot Inc., 139
home equity line of credit (HELOC), 139
home field, home-field, 420
homefront
homemade
homeowner
homeowner's equity. *See* equity, 100
home page, 139
home schooling, home-schooler, home-school, home-schooled, 139
home-sharing sites (nonpreferred). *See* vacation rental websites, 298
hometown, 139
    commas with, 324
    See also state names; within stories in datelines
homicide, murder, manslaughter, 140. *See also* assassin, killer, murderer; execute
homophobia, homophobic, 140. *See also* gay; phobia
homosexual. *See* gay, 120–121
Hong Kong, 140
Honolulu, 140. *See also* Hawaii, 134
Honorable, The. *See* nobility, 202–203
honorary degrees, 140
honorary titles. *See* nobility, 202–203
hoodie, 458
hoof-and-mouth disease (improper), 140. *See also* foot-and-mouth disease, 115
hooky
hopefully, 140
horchata, 443
hors d'oeuvre, hors d'oeuvres

horse, 420
horse meat
horsepower, 140. *See also* watt, 303
horse races, 140, 420
horse racing, 420–421
horseradish
horses, names for, 140–141, 421. *See also* animals, 18
hot dog
hotel, 141
hotline, 141
hot plate
hot sauce, 443
hot spot, 141
houndstooth, 458
hourlong, hourslong
household, housing unit, 141
House of Commons, House of Lords, 141
House of Representatives, 141. *See also* organizations and institutions, 214
housing unit. *See* household, housing unit, 141
Houston, 141
howitzer, 305
HP. *See* HP Inc., 141
HP Inc., 141
HPV (human papillomavirus), 141
HTML (HyperText Markup Language), 142
HTTP (Hypertext Transfer Protocol), 142
HUD (Department of Housing and Urban Development). *See* department, 82
HuffPost, 142
huitlacoche (corn smut), 443
human, human being, 142
Humane Society of the United States, 142
human immunodeficiency virus (HIV). *See* AIDS, 9-10
human papillomavirus. *See* HPV, 141
Hummer. *See* Humvee, 142
hummus
Humvee, 142
hung. *See* hang, hanged, hung, 133
hurricane, 142
    hurricane categories, 307–308
    hurricane eye, 308
    hurricane or typhoon, 308
    hurricane season, 308

mental illness, 181–183
MERS, 184
Parkinson's disease, 218
polio, 225
illusion. *See* allusion, illusion, 13–14
ILO. *See* International Labor
      Organization, 151
IM (instant message), 145
images, standards and practices on,
      517–518
imam, 386. *See also* Arabic names;
      Islam; religious titles
Imax Corp., 145
IMF. *See* International Monetary Fund,
      151
immigrate. *See* emigrate, immigrate,
      99, 146
immigration, 145–146
impassable, impassible, impassive,
      146–147
impeachment, 147
impel, impelled, impelling
imperative sentences, periods with, 327
imperial gallon, 147. *See also* liter,
      171–172
imperial quart, 147
implausible
imply, infer, 147
impostor
impressionism (art movement). *See*
      artworks, 23
impromptu, 147
improvement. *See* reform, 245
improvised explosive device (IED), 147.
      See also IED, 144
in, into, 147
-in (suffix), 147
in- (prefix), 147
"in," 147
inanimate objects, possessives of, 229,
      321
inasmuch as
Inauguration Day, 147
inbox
Inc. *See* incorporated, 148
inch, 147. *See also* centimeter;
      dimensions; foot
incident, 147–148
include, 148. *See also* compose,
      comprise, constitute, 63
income. *See* profit terminology, 234–235
income before taxes, 235

incorporated, 148. *See also* company
      names, 58–63
incorporator, 148. *See also* titles, 285–
      286
incredible, incredulous, 148
incue, inq, in-point, 527
incur, incurred, incurring
Independence Day, 148. *See also* Fourth
      of July, July Fourth, 116
independent (nondenominational). *See*
      nondenominational, 391
independent clauses, semicolons with,
      330
independent film. *See* indie, 149
index, indexes
Index of Leading Economic Indicators,
      148
India, 148
Indiana, 148. *See also* state names,
      268–269
Indianapolis, 148
Indian Ocean. *See* ocean, 210
Indians, 148. *See also* nationalities and
      races; Native American; race;
      tribe, tribal
India pale ale, 443
indict, 148–149. *See also* accused; allege;
      arrest
indie (independent film, recorded
      music), 149
indigenous, 149. *See also* nationalities
      and races; race
Indigenous Peoples Day, 149
indigo, 458
indirect questions
   periods with, 327
indiscreet, indiscrete, 149
indiscriminate, indiscriminately
indispensable
individual possession, joint possession.
      See possessives, 228, 320–321
individual retirement account (IRA),
      149
indo- (prefix), 149
Indonesia, 149
indoor, indoors, 149, 421
IndyCar races, reporting on, 404–405
infant, 149
infantile paralysis (nonpreferred), 149.
      See also polio, 225
infer. *See* imply, infer, 147
inflation, 149
information technology. *See* IT, 156

Interpol, 153. *See also* International
Criminal Police Organization,
151
interpolated questions, question marks
with, 328
intersex. *See* gender, 121–122
intifada, 153
into. *See* in, into, 147
intra- (prefix), 153
intranet, 153
intrauterine device. *See* IUD, 156
intravenous. *See* IV, 156
introductory clauses and phrases,
commas with, 323
intrusion on seclusion, 478–479
Inuit. *See* Eskimo, 101
invasion of privacy, 501–502
inverted pleats, 458
in vitro fertilization (IVF), 153
IOC (International Olympic
Committee), 423
iOS, 153
IOU, IOUs
Iowa, 153. *See also* state names, 268–269
IPA. *See* India pale ale, 443
iPad, 153
IP address (Internet Protocol address),
153. *See also* domain names, 88
iPhone, 153
IPO. *See* initial public offering, 149
iPod, 153
IQ (intelligence quotient), 153
IRA. *See* individual retirement account,
149
Iran, 153
Iranians. *See* Iran, 153
Iran's Revolutionary Guard, 153–154
Iraq, 154
Ireland, 154
Irish coffee, 443
Irish Republic. *See* Ireland, 154
Irish Republican Army (Provisional
IRA), 154
irony, quotation marks with, 329
irregardless (incorrect), 154
IRS (Internal Revenue Service), 154. *See
also* Internal Revenue Service,
150
IS. *See* Islamic State group, 155
Islam, 154–155, 386–387. *See also*
Ashoura; Eid al-Adha; Eid al-
Fitr; Muslims; Nation of Islam;
Ramadan

Islamabad, 155
Islamic fundamentalist. *See* Islam, 155,
387
Islamic holy days, 387. *See also* Ashoura;
Eid al-Adha; Eid al-Fitr;
Ramadan
Islamic Republic of Iran. *See* Iran, 153
Islamic Resistance Movement. *See*
Hamas, 133
Islamic Revolution. *See* Iran, 153
Islamic State group (IS), 155
Islamist, 155, 387
Islamophobia. *See* phobia, 222
island, 155–156. *See also* island nations
and territories *in* datelines, 78
ISM. *See* Institute for Supply
Management, 150
ISP. *See* internet service provider, 153
Istanbul, 156
IT (information technology), 156
Italian (red) onion
Italian (flat-leaf) parsley. *See* parsley,
447
italics, 156
ITAR-Tass. *See* Tass, 275
it's, its, 156
ITSO. *See* International
Telecommunications Satellite
Organization, 151
IUD (intrauterine device), 156
IV (intravenous), 156
IVF. *See* in vitro fertilization, 153
Ivy League, 156

J

jack-o'-lantern
Jacobs, Marc, 458
Jacquard, 458
Jacquard, Joseph Marie. *See* Jacquard,
458
Jacuzzi, 157
jail, 157. *See also* prison, jail, 232–233
JAL. *See* Japan Airlines Corp., 157
Jamaican jerk chicken, 444
Jamaica rum, 444
Jane's Fighting Ships. *See* IHS Jane's All
the World's Aircraft, IHS Jane's
Fighting Ships, 144
Japan Airlines Corp. (JAL). *See* Japan
Airlines Corp., 157

Japan Current, 157

jargon, 157. *See also* cliches, jargon; dialect

Jarlsberg cheese, 444

jasmine rice, 444

Java (programming language), 157

Jaws of Life, 157

Jaycees, 157. *See also* fraternal organizations and service clubs; Junior Chamber of Commerce

Jay-Z

J.C. Penney Co., 157

jeep, Jeep, 157

Jehovah's Witnesses, 387

Jell-O

jellyroll

Jemaah Islamiyah, 157

jerry-built, 157. *See also* jury-rig, 160

Jerusalem, 157

    Old City of, 212

    See also Al-Quds, 14

Jesus (Jesus Christ, Christ), 157, 387. *See also* life of Christ, 246, 395

JetBlue Airways Corp., 157

jet, jetliner, jet plane. *See* aircraft terms, 10

Jet Ski, 157

Jewish Bibles, books of. *See* Bible, 32, 376

Jewish congregations, 387–388. *See also* religious titles; Zionism

Jewish holy days, 388. *See also* Hanukkah; Passover; Purim; Rosh Hashana; Shavuot; Sukkot; Yom Kippur

jibe. *See* gibe, jibe, 124

Jiddah, Saudi Arabia

jigger, 444

jihad, 158, 388

jihadist (nonpreferred). *See* jihad, 158, 388

job descriptions, 158. *See also* titles, 285–286

jodhpurs. *See* riding pants, 461

Johannesburg, 158

John F. Kennedy Space Center, 158. *See also* Lyndon B. Johnson Space Center, 175

Johns Hopkins University, 158

Johnson & Johnson, 158

Johnson Space Center. *See* Lyndon B. Johnson Space Center, 175

Joint Photographic Experts Group. *See* JPEG, JPG, 158

joint possession, individual possession, 228, 320–321

Joints Chiefs of Staff, 158

journalists, digital security for, 364–368

JPEG, JPG (Joint Photographic Experts Group), 158

JPMorgan Chase & Co., 158

Jr. *See* junior, senior, 159

Judaism. See *entries beginning "Jewish"*

judge, 158

    administrative law judge, 6–7

    bankruptcy judges (*See* judicial branch, 159)

    chief justice, 48

    judge advocate, 159

    magistrate, 174

    of U.S. District Court (*See* federal, 108)

    See also court names; judicial branch; justice; magistrate; titles

judge advocate, 159

judgment

judicial branch, 159

Judicial Conference of the United States, 159

judo, 421. *See also* basic summary; match summary

jukebox

July Fourth. *See* Fourth of July, July Fourth; Independence Day

jumbo jet, 159

jumbo loan, 159

Junior Chamber of Commerce, 159. *See also* Jaycees, 157

Junior Girl Scouts. *See* Girl Scouts, 125

junior, senior, 159. *See also* names, 196

junk bonds, 159–160. *See also* bond ratings, 35–36

junta. *See* government, junta, regime, administration, 128

Jupiter. *See* planets, 223

jury, 160. *See also* grand jury, 129

jury-rig, 160. *See also* jerry-built, 157

justice, 160. *See also* judge; Supreme Court of the United States; titles

justice of the peace, 160. *See also* titles, 285–286

justify, 160

m

Minnesota, 191. *See also* state names, 268–269

minority leader, 191. *See also* legislative titles, 168–169

minuscule, 191

minus sign, 192

mirroring (online copying), 192. *See also* scraping, 256

MIRV, MIRVs (multiple independently targetable re-entry vehicle(s)), 192

misappropriation, invasion of privacy by, 504–505

misdemeanor. *See* felony, misdemeanor, 110

mise en place, 446

mishap, 192

misrepresentation, reporting and, 481–482

Miss. *See* courtesy titles, 71

missile names, 192. *See also* ABM; ICBM; MIRV; SAM

Mississippi, 192. *See also* state names, 268–269

Missouri, 192. *See also* state names, 268–269

mistakes. *See* corrections/correctives

mistress, 192

mixed martial arts (MMA), 422

mixed numbers (with fractions). *See* fractions, 117

mixed-race (nonpreferred). *See* biracial, multiracial, 33

mixologist, 446

mix-up, mix up, 192

mL (milliliter). *See* metric system, 186

MLS (Major League Soccer), 426

mm (millimeter). *See* metric system, 186

MMA. *See* mixed martial arts, 422

mock-up, 192

mode (central tendency measure), 347

model numbers. *See* serial numbers, 259

modem, 192

modernism (art movement). *See* artworks, 23

modernist cuisine. *See* molecular gastronomy, 446

moguls. *See* freestyle skiing, 417

Moldova. *See* Commonwealth of Independent States; Trans-Dniester

mole, 446

molecular gastronomy (modernist cuisine), 446

molly. *See* ecstasy, molly, MDMA in drugs, 90

mom. *See* family names, 107

moment magnitude (for earthquakes). *See* earthquakes, 93

Monaco, 192

M1, M16 (rifles), 305

monetary. *See* fiscal, monetary, 112

monetary units. *See* cents; dollars; numerals; pound (monetary)

money. *See* currencies; currency conversions

moneymaker

monokini, 460

monosodium glutamate. *See* MSG, 446

monsignor. *See* Roman Catholic Church, 251, 397

monsoon, 309

Montana, 192. *See also* state names, 268–269

Monterey Jack cheese, 446

Montessori method, 192–193

monthlong, monthslong, 193

months, 193. *See also* dates; years

Montreal, 193

monuments, 193

Moody's Investors Service. *See* bond ratings, 35

moon, 193. *See also* heavenly bodies, 135

mop-up, mop up, 193

moral obligation bond, 173

more equal (improper). *See* equal, 100

morel mushrooms

more than, over, 193. *See also* over, 216

Morgan Stanley, 193

Mormon church, 193, 390. *See also* Church of Jesus Christ of Latter-day Saints, The, 380

Mornay sauce, 446

mortar (weapon), 305

mortgage, 193. *See also* adjustable-rate mortgage; balloon mortgage

mortgage-backed security, 193

MOS (man on the street), 527

Moscow, 193

mosquito, mosquitoes

most valuable player. *See* MVP, 422

Mother (nun). *See* sister, 398

Mother's Day, 193

mother-in-law, mothers-in-law

Mother Nature

n

news conference. *See* press conference, 231

News Corp., 200

newsgathering, legal principles of, 466–483
government information, access to, 466–467
sources, issues concerning, 473–483

newsgathering conduct, liability for, 478

News Media Alliance, 200

News Media Guild. *See* Newspaper Guild-Communications Workers of America, The, 200

news organizations, libel defenses commonly available to, 495–498

Newspaper Association of America. *See* News Media Alliance, 200

Newspaper Guild-Communications Workers of America, The, 200

newspaper names, 200–201

newsstand

news values and principles, statement of, 509–522

New Testament. *See* Bible, 32, 376–377

New World, 201

New Year's, New Year's Day, New Year's Eve, Happy New Year, 201. *See also* happy holidays, merry Christmas..., 133

New Year's Six, 423

New York, 201. *See also* state names, 268–269

New York City, 201

New York Fasion Week

New York Stock Exchange (NYSE), 201. *See also* Big Board, 32

The New York Times Co., 201

New Zealand. *See* Down Under, 89

NGO (nongovernmental organization), 201

NHL. *See* league *in* hockey, 419

NHRA races, reporting on, 405

nicknames. *See* pseudonyms, nicknames, 237

nightclub

nighttime

9/11 (terrorist attacks), 201

911 (emergency number), 201

niqab, 201. *See also* burqa; chador; hijab

nitpicking

nitty-gritty

NKorea. *See* Korea, 163

NLRB. *See* National Labor Relations Board, 197

NNA. *See* National Newspaper Association, 198

No., 201–202. *See also* numerals, 206–209

Nobel Memorial Prize in Economic Sciences. *See* Nobel Prize, Nobel Prizes, 202

Nobel Prize, Nobel Prizes, 202

nobility, 202–203. *See also* courtesy titles; titles

Noble Sanctuary. *See* Al-Aqsa; Haram al-Sharif

NOC (National Olympic committee, nonpreferred). *See* National Olympic committee, 423–424

no contest, no-contest plea. *See* nolo contendere, 203–205

noisome, noisy, 203

Nokia Corp., 203

nolo contendere, 203–204

no man's land

non- (prefix), 204

Non-Aligned Movement. *See* nonaligned nations, 204

nonaligned nations, 204

noncombat, noncombatant

nonconference, 423

nondenominational, 391

none, 204

nonessential clauses. *See* essential clauses, nonessential clauses, 101–102

nonessential clauses, commas with, 323

nonessential phrases. *See* essential phrases, nonessential phrases, 102

nonessential phrases, commas with, 323

non-GMO, 446

nongovernmental organization. *See* NGO, 201

non-Hodgkin lymphoma. *See* Hodgkin lymphoma, 138

nonlinear editing, 528

nonprofit

nonrestrictive clauses. *See* essential clauses, nonessential clauses, 101–102

nonrestrictive phrases. *See* essential phrases, nonessential phrases, 102

N-word (derogatory term), 209. *See also* obscenities, profanities, vulgarities; race

nylon, 209, 460

NYSE. *See* New York Stock Exchange, 201

O

OAO Gazprom. *See* Gazprom, 121

OAS. *See* Organization of American States, 214

oasis, oases

"Obamacare." *See* Affordable Care Act, 8

OB-GYN, 210

obscenities, profanities, vulgarities, 210
    standards and practices on, 519–520
    See also nationalities and races

obscuring identities, standards and practices on, 518

obsessive-compulsive disorder (OCD). *See* mental illness, 182

obstetrics and gynecology. *See* OB-GYN, 210

Occupational Safety and Health Administration (OSHA), 210

occupational titles, 210. *See also* titles, 285–286

occur, occurred, occurring

occurrence

OCD (obsessive-compulsive disorder). *See* mental illness, 182

ocean, 210
    coastal waters, 306
    nearshore waters, 309
    offshore waters, 309
    See also Seven Seas, 260

oceangoing

Oceania Football Confederation. *See* OFC, 426

o'clock. *See* times, 282

odd- (prefix), 210. *See also* betting odds, 32

odds, figures in. *See* numerals, 207

oddsmaker

odds-on, 421

OEM. *See* original equipment manufacturer, 214

OFC (soccer league), 426

off-Broadway, off-off-Broadway. *See* Broadway, off-Broadway, off-off-Broadway, 38

offensive content, 519

offensive language. *See* obscenities, profanities, vulgarities, 210

offensive line (O-line), 416

offering (financial), 211

office, 211. *See also* Oval Office, 215

officeholder

officeholder (religious). *See* religious titles, 246–247, 395–396

Office of Thrift Supervision (OTS), 211

official scorers, standards and practices on, 515

offline, 211

off of, 211

off-, -off (prefix, suffix), 211

off-off-Broadway. *See* Broadway, off-Broadway, off-off-Broadway, 38

offseason, 423

offshore waters, 309

offside (soccer), 426

off-site, 211

off the record, 511

Ohio, 211. *See also* state names, 268–269

oil, 211. *See also* barrel, 30

oil field

OK, OK'd, OK'ing, OKs, 211

Oklahoma, 211. *See also* state names, 268–269

Oklahoma City, 211

Old City of Jerusalem, 212

Old South, 212

Old Testament. *See* Bible, 32, 376–377

Old West, 212

Old World, 212. *See also* Eastern Hemisphere, 94

OLED television. *See* television sets, 276

O-line (offensive line), 416

Olympic Airways, 212

Olympics, 212

Olympics, Olympic, Olympic Games, Olympian, 423–424

ombre (degrade), 460

omelet

on, 212

onboard, 212

one- (prefix), 212. *See also* fractions, 117

one another. *See* each other, one another, 93

partially deaf. *See* disabled, handicapped, 85–86

partially self-driving vehicles. *See* autonomous vehicles, 26

partial quotes, 240, 329. *See also* quotations; quotations in the news

particles. *See* foreign names, 115

partner. *See* husband, wife, 142

partnerships. *See* firm, 112

part time, part-time, 219

party. *See* political parties and philosophies, 225–226

party affiliation, 219. *See also* legislative titles, 168–169

pass. *See* act, amendment, bill, law, measure, ordinance, resolution, rule, statute, 4–5

passe

passed away. *See* death, die, 80

passenger mile, 219

passer-by, passers-by

passion fruit

Passover, 391

passwords, standards and practices on, 364–365

past and future titles. *See* titles, 285–286

pasteurize

past history (redundant phrase). *See* history, 138

pastor. *See* religious titles, 246-247, 395-396; *specific denominations*

past titles, 286

pat-down, 220

Patient Protection and Affordable Care Act. *See* Affordable Care Act, 8

patriarch, 391–392. *See also* Eastern Orthodox churches; religious titles; Roman Catholic Church

patrolman, patrolwoman, 220. *See also* titles, 285–286

patrol, patrolled, patrolling

patrol torpedo boat. *See* PT boat, 237

payload

PB&J, 447

PBS. *See* Public Broadcasting Service, 237

PCP (phencyclidine), 91

PDF (Portable Document Format), 220

PDT (Pacific Daylight Timer). *See* time zones, 282–285

peacekeeping

peacemaker, peacemaking

peace offering

peacetime

peacoat, 461

peacock, 220

peafowl. *See* peacock, 220

peahen. *See* peacock, 220

pears, 447

peasant (derogatory term), 220

peck, 220. *See also* liter, 171–172

pecorino, 447

pedal, peddle, 220

peddler

PEDs, PED (nonpreferred). *See* performance-enhancing drugs, 424

pellet gun. *See* airsoft gun, 11

penalty (soccer), 426

penalty area (penalty box, soccer), 426

peninsula, 220

penitentiary. *See* prison, jail, 232–233

Pennsylvania, 220. *See also* state names, 268–269

Pennsylvania Dutch, 220

penny-wise. *See* -wise, 315

Pentagon (Department of Defense, DOD). *See* department, 82

Pentecost, 392

Pentecostalism, 395

People of Unity. *See* Druze, 381

people, persons, 220

people's, 220

people, searching for, on social media, 359–361

People's Republic of China. *See* China, 49

peperonata, 447

pepitas, 447

peplum, 461

Peppadew, 447

pepper jack cheese

Pepsi, Pepsi-Cola, PepsiCo Inc.

PepsiCo Inc., 220

percent, 221. *See also* numerals, 207

percentage point change, of data, 346

percent change, of data, 346

performance-enhancing drugs, 424

periods, 327
  in abbreviations and acronyms, 2
  See also ellipsis; quotation marks

Periscope, video searches on, 362

perk (perquisite), 221

permissible

Portable Document Format. *See* PDF, 220
Porteno, 227
porterhouse, 448
portobello mushrooms
Portuguese names, 227
posing and re-enactments, standards and practices on, 518–519
possessives, 227–229, 320–321
  with "corporation," 69
possum. *See* opossum, 213
post- (prefix), 229
postal codes
  state abbreviations (*See* state names, 269)
Postal Service. *See* U.S. Postal Service, 296
Postal Workers union. *See* American Postal Workers Union, 16-17
post bail. *See* bail, 28–29
postgame
Post-it, 229
post office, 229
postseason, preseason, 424
post-traumatic stress disorder (PTSD), 229. *See also* mental illness, 182
pot. *See* marijuana, medical marijuana, 90, 178–179
potatoes, 448
pothole
potluck
potpie
pot sticker, 448
pouf, poufy, pouffed, 461
pound (monetary), 229
pound (weight), 229. *See also* gram; kilogram
pound cake
pour. *See* pore, pour, 227
poverty level, 229
powdered sugar, 448. *See also* sugar, 451
Power Five, 424
power of attorney. *See* attorney, lawyer, 25-26
power plants. *See* watt, 303
POW(s). *See* prisoner(s) of war, 233
pozole, 448
practical points of defamation, summary of, 498–499
practitioner. *See* Church of Christ, Scientist, 379–380
Prada, Miuccia, 461
Prague, 229

pre- (prefix), 229–230
preacher, 392. *See also* religious titles; titles
Preakness Stakes, 421
precincts. *See* political divisions, 225
precooked
pre-election polls. *See* polls and surveys, 349–354
preferred stock, 230. *See also* common stock, preferred stock, 57
prefixes, 230
  hyphens with, 326
  See also *entries for individual prefixes*
pregame
preheat (nonpreferred), 448
pre-K. *See* kindergarten, kindergartners, 162
premiere, 230
Premier League, 426–427
premier, prime minister, 230. *See also* Commonwealth; titles
prepackaged bankruptcy, 338
prepositions, with "arrive." *See* arrive, 23
Presbyterian Church (U.S.A). *See* Presbyterian churches, 392
Presbyterian churches, 392. *See also* religious titles, 246–247, 395–396
preseason. *See* postseason, preseason, 424
presently, 230
presidency, 230
president, 230–231. *See also* titles
presidential, 231
Presidential Medal of Freedom, 231. *See also* Medal of Freedom, 180
Presidents Day, 231. *See also* Washington's Birthday, 303
presiding officer, 231
press conference (nonpreferred), 231
Presse Canadienne, La. *See* Canadian Press, The, 41–42
press secretary, 231. *See also* titles
pret-a-porter line, 461
pretax
pretense, pretext, 231
preventive
price-earnings ratio, 231. *See also* profit terminology, 234–235
price indexes
  chained consumer price index, 67
  consumer price index, 67

q

r

S

sauvignon blanc, 449

Savile Row, 462

savings and loan associations, 256

savior, 398. *See also* Jesus, 157, 387

savoy cabbage

scallions (green onions), 449–450

scene numbers, 256. *See also* sequential
  designations in numerals,
  207–208

scener (radio), 528

scheme, 256

Schengen Area, 256. *See also* European
  Union, 103

schizophrenia. *See* mental illness, 182

Scholastic Aptitude Test, Scholastic
  Assessment Test. *See* SAT, 255

school, 256

school grades, figures in. *See* numerals,
  207

school names, in sports, 425. *See
  also* Football Championship
  Subdivision; major college
  basketball conferences; major
  college football conferences

scissors, 256

scores (sports), 425. *See also* numerals,
  208

scoring, in hockey, 419

scotch, 450

scotch barley

scotch broth

scotch salmon

scotch sour

Scotch tape, 256

Scotch whisky, 450

Scotland, 256. *See also* spelling and
  choice of names *in* datelines;
  United Kingdom

Scot, Scots, Scottish, 256

scraping, 256, 343–344. *See also*
  mirroring, 192

Screen Actors Guild-American
  Federation of Television and
  Radio Artists, 256

screen saver

E.W. Scripps Co., 256

Scripps Networks Interactive Inc., 256

Scripture, Scriptures, 256–257. *See also*
  Bible, 32, 376–377

scuba (self-contained underwater
  breathing apparatus), 257

Scud missile

sculptures, titles of. *See* artworks, 23

scurrilous

Sea Islands, 257

SEAL(s), 257. *See also* special forces,
  266

seaman. *See* military titles, 188–190

search engine optimization (SEO), 257

Sears Holdings Corp., 257

seasonings, 450

seasons, 257

season's greetings. *See* happy holidays,
  merry Christmas..., 133

seat belt, 257. *See also* safety belt, 254

Seattle, 257

SEC. *See* Securities and Exchange
  Commission, 258

seclusion, intrusion on, 478–479

second guess, second-guess, second-
  guesser, 257

second hand, secondhand, 257

second-rate, 257

second reference, 257–258. *See also*
  abbreviations and acronyms;
  capitalization; courtesy titles;
  titles

secretary, 258. *See also* titles, 285–286

secretary-general, 258. *See also* titles,
  285–286

secretary of state, 258. *See also* titles,
  285–286

secretary-treasurer, 258. *See also* titles,
  285–286

Secret Service, 258

section, 258

secured creditor, 338

Securities and Exchange Commission
  (SEC), 258

Securities Exchange Act. *See* Securities
  and Exchange Commission, 258

securitization, 258

security
  of communications tools, 366–367
  of computers and networks, 365

Security Council (U.N.), 258. *See also*
  United Nations, 293

Seder. *See* Passover, 391

See also web

Seeing Eye dog, 258

seesaw

SEIU. *See* Service Employees
  International Union, 259–260

self- (prefix), 258

self-contained underwater breathing
  apparatus. *See* scuba, 257

S.O.S. *See* SOS, 264

sound barrier, 264. *See also* Mach number, 176

sound bite, 528

sounds, in pronouncers. *See* pronouncers, 235–236

soundstage

source (nonpreferred), 264. *See also* anonymous sources, 18–19, 510–511

source code, 264

sources, 473–483

anonymous sources, 18–19, 510–511

for data, evaluating, 344–345

electronic eavesdropping and, 481

misrepresentation and, 481–482

national security issues and, 482–483

newsgathering conduct, liability for, 478

overview, 473–474

promises as enforceable agreements with, 474–475

reporter's privilege and, 475–478

seclusion, intrusion upon, 478–479

on social media, 371–372

trespass and, 479–481

sous vide, 450

South, 264. *See also* Midwest region; Northeast region; West

South America, 312

South Atlantic states. *See* South, 264

South Carolina, 265. *See also* state names, 268–269

South Dakota, 265. *See also* state names, 268–269

Southeast Asia, 265. *See also* Asian subcontinent; Far East

Southern Baptist Convention. *See* Baptist churches, 376

Southern California. *See* directions and regions, 85

South Korea (Republic of Korea). *See* Korea, 163

South Korean place names. *See* Korean names, 163

South Side (Chicago). *See* capitalization; cities and towns

south, southern, southeast, southwest. *See* directions and regions, 85

South Sudan. *See* Sudan, 272

south tower. *See* twin towers, 290

Southwest Airlines Co., 265

Soviet Union (USSR). *See* Commonwealth of Independent States, 58

Space Age, 265

space agency. *See* National Aeronautics and Space Administration, 197

space centers. *See* John F. Kennedy Space Center; Lyndon B. Johnson Space Center

spacecraft designations, 265

figures in (*See* numerals, 206)

sequence of (*See* aircraft names, 10)

spaces

after periods, 327

with dashes, 324

spaceship

space shuttle, 265

spacewalk

spam, Spam, 265

spandex. *See* Lycra, 174–175, 459

Spanish-American War

Spanish names, 265–266

Spanish (yellow) onion

spareribs

sparkling wine. *See* Champagne, 438

SPCA. *See* Society for the Prevention of Cruelty to Animals, 264

speaker, 266. *See also* titles, 285–286

speaking privately. *See* anonymous sources, 18–19, 510–511

special agent. *See* agent, 9

special contexts, 266

special effects, using ellipses, 325

special expressions, possessives of, 320

special forces, 266

special operations forces. *See* special forces, 266

Special Weapons and Tactics. *See* SWAT, 274

species, 266. *See also* genus, species, 123

spectator (shoes), 462

speeches, 266. *See also* composition titles, 63–64

speech impaired. *See* mute in disabled, handicapped, 86

speechmaker, speechmaking

speed of sound. *See* Mach number, 176

speeds, 266. *See also* numerals, 208

speedskating, 428. *See also* basic summary, 407–408

speedup, speed up, 266

spelling, 266

in datelines, 78

tapenade, 451
taproom
taps (bugle call), 275
Target Corp., 275
Taser, 275
Tass, 275
tastes, types of. *See* umami, 452
Tater Tots
tattletale
tax-free, 275
TB. *See* tuberculosis, 289
TB (terabyte). *See* byte, 40
T-bone steak
TCU. *See* Transportation
        Communications International
        Union, 288
TD (touchdown), 416
teachers college, 276
team, 276. *See also* collective nouns,
        55–56
teammate
teamster, 276
Teamsters union, 276. *See also*
        International Brotherhood
        of Teamsters, Chauffeurs,
        Warehousemen and Helpers of
        America, 150
tea party, tea partyers, 275–276
tear gas, 276. *See also* Chemical Mace,
        48
teaspoon, 276. *See also* liter, 171–172
teaspoonful, teaspoonfuls, 276. *See also*
        recipes, 244
technical director (soccer). *See* coach *in*
        soccer, 425
tee. *See* T-shirt, 462
tee, tee off
teen, teenager, teenage, 276
teenage prostitute (nonpreferred). *See*
        prostitute, 236
Teflon, 276
Tegna Inc. *See* Gannett Co., 120
telecast, televise, 276
telephone numbers, 276
teleprompter, 276
televise. *See* telecast, televise, 276
television
    abbreviation for (*See* TV, 290)
    program titles, 276–277
    See also composition titles, 63–64
television sets, 277
television station, 277

television stories. *See* broadcast
        guidelines, 523–526
telltale
temblor. *See* earthquake, 94
temperatures, 277–278
    below zero (*See* minus sign, 192)
    Fahrenheit-Celsius conversions of,
        107
    figures in (*See* numerals, 208)
    in recipes, 451
    See also Celsius; Fahrenheit; weather
        terms
Temple Mount, 278, 399. *See also* Al-
        Aqsa, 12, 374
Ten Commandments, 399
tenfold
Ten Most Wanted Fugitives, 278
Tennessee, 278. *See also* state names,
        268–269
Tennes*See* Valley Authority (TVA), 278
tennis, 428
tera- (prefix), 278. *See also* metric
        system, 185–186
terabyte (TB). *See* byte, 40
terrace (in addresses), 278. *See also*
        addresses, 6
terrine. *See* tureen, 462
territories, Canadian. *See* Canada, 41
test-tube babies. *See* in vitro
        fertilization, 153
Tet. *See* Lunar New Year, 174
tetrahydrocannabinol (THC). *See*
        marijuana, medical marijuana,
        178
Texas, 278. *See also* state names,
        268–269
Texas Hold 'em, 278
Tex-Mex, 451
text, texting, texted, 278
text messaging
    quotations from, 240–241
    See also SMS, 263
texts, transcripts, 278–279. *See also*
        ellipsis, 324–325
Thai, 279
Thai Airways International PLC, 279
Thai chilies, Thai chili sauce
Thai red curry paste
Thanksgiving, Thanksgiving Day, 279
than, then, 279
that (conjunction), 279

U

W

washed-up, 302
Washington, 302. *See also* state names, 268–269
Washington Monument. *See* monuments, 193
The Washington Post, 302
Washington's Birthday, 303
wastebasket
water features. See *name of specific feature, e.g., bay, ocean*
water polo, 430
water skiing, 430. *See also* basic summary, 407–408
water sports
waterspout, 311
watt, 303
watt-hour. *See* watt, 303
waxed paper
weapons, 303–306. *See also* military ranks, used as titles with names, military terms and weapons *in* numerals, 207
weapons of mass destruction. *See* WMD, 315
-wear (suffix), 463
weather-beaten
weather forecaster. *See* weatherman, 306
weatherman (nonpreferred), 306
weather service. *See* National Weather Service, 198
weather terms, 306–311
weather vane
web (the web, World Wide Web), 311. *See also* internet, 151–152
web address
web browser, 311
webcam
webcast
webfeed
webmaster
webpage
web server. *See* server, 259
website. *See also* composition titles, 63–64
Webster's New World College Dictionary. *See* dictionaries, 84
weeklong, weekslong, 311
weight classes (boxing), 410
weightlifting, 430. *See also* basic summary, 407–408
weight(s) (mass), 311
  grain, 129

metric conversion chart for, 185
ounce, 215
pound, 229
in sports, 430
See also metric system, 185–186
well, 312. *See also* good, well; hyphen
well-being
well-informed
Wells Fargo & Co., 312
well-to-do
well-wishers
West, Western, west, western, 312. *See also* directions and regions, 85
West Bank. *See* Palestine, 217
Western Europe. *See* Eastern Europe, 94
Western Hemisphere, 312–313
Western Wall, 313, 400
West Germany. *See* Germany, 124
West Indies, 312–313
West North Central region. *See* Midwest region, 187
West Point, 313. *See also* military academies, 188
West South Central states. *See* South, 264
West Texas. *See* directions and regions, 85
West Virginia, 313. *See also* state names, 268–269
Weyerhaeuser Co., 313
Wh (watt-hour). *See* watt, 303
WhatsApp, 313
wheat, 313
wheat germ
wheatgrass
wheelchair-bound (nonpreferred). *See* disabled, handicapped, 86
wheelchair user. *See* disabled, handicapped, 86
whereabouts, 313
wherever
which. *See* essential clauses, nonessential clauses; that, which; who, whom
whip (political position), 313. *See also* legislative titles; titles
whirlpool bath/spa. *See* Jacuzzi, 157
whisky, whiskey, 452–453
whistleblower
white-collar, 313
White House. *See* Executive Mansion, 104

world court. *See* International Court of
Justice, 150-151
World Cup, 427
World Health Organization, 315. *See
also* WHO, 313–314
World Series, 315, 430
World Trade Center, 315–316. *See also*
One World Trade Center; twin
towers
World War I, World War II
worldwide
World Wide Web. *See* web, 311
worm (computers). *See* virus, worm,
300
worn-out, 316
worship, worshipped, worshipper
worthwhile
would. *See* should, would, 261
wrack. *See* rack, wrack, 242
wracked, 316
wrap (radio), 529. *See also* actuality, 527
wrap stories, for corporate earnings
reports, 333–334
wrestling, 430
write-down, write down, 316
write-in, write in, 316
written. *See* oral, verbal, written, 214
wrongdoing
Wyoming, 316. *See also* state names,
268–269

X

xe. *See* they, them, their, 280
xenophobia. *See* phobia, 222
Xerox, 317
Xinhua News Agency, 317
Xmas (nonpreferred), 317. *See also*
Christmas, Christmas Day, 49
XML (Extensible Markup Language),
317
X-ray, 317

y

the Y. *See* Young Men's Christian
Association, 317–318
yachting, 430. *See also* basic summary,
407–408

Yahoo, 17
yam, 453
yard (measure), 317, 430. *See also*
distances; foot; meter
yard lines, 430
year-end, 317
yearling, 430
yearlong, yearslong, 317
year-round, 317
years, 317
figures in (*See* numerals, 207)
See also A.D.; B.C.; century; historical
periods and events; months
yellow (Spanish) onion
Yellow Pages, 317
yesterday, 317
yesteryear
YMCA. *See* Young Men's Christian
Association, 317-318
yogurt, 453
yoke, 464
Yom Kippur, 317, 400
York peppermint patties
Young Men's Christian Association
(the Y, YMCA), 317–318
Young Women's Christian Association
(YWCA), 318
youth, 318. *See also* boy, girl; names
YouTube, 318
video searches on, 361–362
Yukon, 318. *See also* Canada, 41
Yukon Gold potatoes
Yule, Yuletide, 318
Yum Brands Inc., 318
YWCA. *See* Young Women's Christian
Association, 318

Z

za'atar, 453
ze. *See* they, them, their, 280
zebra print, 464
zero, in decimal units, 80
zero, zeros
zest, 453
Zika, 318
Zionism, 400
zip-close bag, 453
ZIP code, 318
zip line

Choose the right tool to keep you in style

The Associated Press Stylebook, the definitive guide to journalistic writing, is available in a variety of formats and tools. Whichever you choose, you will always be in style. Learn more about all of these products at **store.stylebooks.com.**

THE SPIRAL-BOUND AP STYLEBOOK

We update our spiral-bound Stylebook annually, adding new listings and updating existing ones. The comprehensive index and functional spiral binding make it easy to find the entry you need and flip open to that page. Sign up to receive a copy of the new version automatically when it launches each spring and you will save 20 percent every year.

AP STYLEBOOK ONLINE

This web-based, searchable and customizable version of the AP Stylebook includes online-only bonus features and a responsive design for your desktop, laptop, smartphone and tablet. Get email alerts as AP updates its style throughout the year, submit questions via Ask the Editor and use Topical Guides to help you cover events in the news.

AP STYLEBOOK & WEBSTER'S NEW WORLD ONLINE

AP and Houghton Mifflin Harcourt offer this combined online resource for your writing and editing needs. The Stylebook's authoritative guidance is supported by about 185,000 definitions from Webster's New World College Dictionary, AP Stylebook's first reference for spelling, style, usage and foreign geographic names for decades.

AP STYLE QUIZZES

Test your knowledge of AP style with dozens of quick, informative online quizzes you can take as many times as you like. Automatic scoring won't just tell you which of your answers were right or wrong, it will also provide an explanation of the relevant style rule so you'll understand why the right answer is correct.

AP STYLEGUARD

AP StyleGuard provides automatic checking for AP style in Microsoft Word and Outlook using defined structure and rules similar to Word's spelling and grammar checking. StyleGuard includes the latest AP Stylebook guidance, with rules updated throughout the year. It works on both the PC and Mac versions of Word, and with Outlook for PC.

AP LINGOFY

AP Lingofy proofs content you create in web browsers, helping find errors in spelling, usage and AP style as you post to WordPress, Blogger, Twitter, Tumblr, Facebook and more. Lingofy is a browser plug-in that provides style checking directly in Mozilla Firefox, Apple's Safari and Google Chrome. AP Lingofy now includes a plug-in especially for Google Docs, too.

AP STYLEBOOK E-BOOK

If you want portable AP Stylebook guidance that's accessible even when you don't have connectivity, the e-book version is for you. Get searchable style guidance on the go with a comprehensive, dynamic index to help you quickly find the words, definitions and rules you need. Our e-book is offered exclusively on Amazon.

STYLEBOOK OFFERS 24/7 SUPPORT

Whether you have a question about when you can get the next edition of the spiral-bound Stylebook, how to reset your Stylebook Online password or how to pay for an order by check, AP Stylebook can help. We have answers to many of the most common questions listed on our self-service help center: **apstylebook.com/help.**

You can browse by topic to find what you need or search the help center to get an answer. If you don't find the answer to your question, we offer a toll-free number to call and a form to request help via email, so you can get a personal response 24/7.

We value your business. We want to make it easy for you to get answers any time of day or night.